Theatre Histories

This thoroughly revised and updated third edition of the innovative and widely acclaimed *Theatre Histories: An Introduction* offers a critical overview of global theatre and drama, spanning a broad wealth of world cultures and periods. Bringing together a group of scholars from a diverse range of backgrounds to add fresh perspectives on the history of global theatre, the book illustrates historiographical theories with case studies demonstrating various methods and interpretive approaches.

Subtly restructured sections place the chapters within new thematic contexts to offer a clear overview of each period, while a revised chapter structure offers accessibility for students and instructors. Further new features and key updates to this third edition include:

- A dedicated chapter on historiography
- New, up-to-date, case studies
- Enhanced and reworked historical, cultural, and political timelines, helping students to place each chapter within the historical context of the section
- Pronunciation guidance, both in the text and as an online audio guide, to aid the reader in accessing and internalizing unfamiliar terminology
- A new and updated companion website with further insights, activities and resources to enable students to further their knowledge and understanding of the theatre.

Tobin Nellhaus is an independent scholar and former Librarian for Performing Arts, Media and Philosophy at Yale University. He writes mainly on the relationship between theatre and communication practices, and on critical realism in theatre historiography.

Bruce McConachie is Chair of Theatre Arts at the University of Pittsburgh, where he also directs and performs. He has published widely in American theatre history, theatre historiography, and performance and cognitive studies, and is a former President of the American Society for Theatre Research.

Carol Fisher Sorgenfrei is Professor Emerita of Theatre and Performance Studies and former Vice Chair for Graduate Programs at UCLA and former Research Fellow in the Institute for Theatre Studies at Berlin's Free University. She is a scholar, translator, playwright, and director focusing on Japanese and cross-cultural theatre.

Tamara Underiner is Associate Dean for Research for the Herberger Institute for Design and the Arts at Arizona State University, and director of the Ph.D. program in Theatre and Performance of the Americas.

Theatre Histories: An Introduction

Third Edition

General Editor: Tobin Nellhaus

Bruce McConachie, Tobin Nellhaus,
Carol Fisher Sorgenfrei and
Tamara Underiner

Routledge
Taylor & Francis Group

LONDON AND NEW YORK

Third edition published 2016
by Routledge
2 Park Square, Milton Park, Abingdon, Oxon OX14 4RN

and by Routledge
711 Third Avenue, New York, NY 10017

Routledge is an imprint of the Taylor & Francis Group, an informa business

First edition published by Routledge 2006

Second edition published by Routledge 2010

British Library Cataloguing-in-Publication Data
A catalogue record for this book is available from the British Library

Library of Congress Cataloging-in-Publication Data
Theatre histories: an introduction / general editor: Tobin Nellhaus;
    Bruce McConachie, Tobin Nellhaus, Carol Fisher Sorgenfrei and
    Tamara Underiner. — Third edition.
    pages cm
    Includes bibliographical references and index.
    1. Theater—History. 2. Performing arts—History. I. Nellhaus,
    Tobin, editor.
    PN2101.T48 2016
    792.09—dc23
    2015026618

ISBN: 978-0-415-83797-2 (hbk)
ISBN: 978-0-415-83796-5 (pbk)
ISBN: 978-0-203-78871-4 (ebk)

Typeset in Bembo and Frutiger
by Florence Production Ltd, Stoodleigh, Devon, UK

Printed and bound in Great Britain by Ashford Colour Press Ltd.

Contents

Figures

About the authors

Bruce McConachie is Professor and Director of Graduate Students at the University of Pittsburgh, where he also directs and performs. He has published widely in U.S. theatre history, theatre historiography, and performance and cognitive studies. Some of his major books include *Interpreting the Theatrical Past*, with Thomas Postlewait (University of Iowa Press, 1989); *Melodramatic Formations: American Theatre and Society, 1820–1870* (University of Iowa Press, 1992, awarded the Barnard Hewitt Prize in Theatre History); *American Theater in the Culture of the Cold War* (University of Iowa Press, 2003); *Performance and Cognition*, with F. Elizabeth Hart (Routledge, 2006); *Engaging Audiences: A Cognitive Approach to Spectating in the Theatre* (Palgrave Macmillan, 2011); and *Evolution, Cognition, and Performance* (Cambridge University Press, 2015). Professor McConachie is also a co-editor of the Cognitive Studies in Literature and Performance series for Palgrave Macmillan and a former President of the American Society for Theatre Research.

Tobin Nellhaus is an independent scholar and former Librarian for Performing Arts, Media and Philosophy at Yale University. He has published mainly on the relationship between theatre and communication practices, and on critical realism in theatre historiography. He is the author of *Theater, Communication, Critical Realism* (Palgrave Macmillan, 2010) and co-editor (with Susan Haedicke) of *Performing Democracy: International Perspectives on Urban Community-Based Performance* (University of Michigan Press, 2001). His articles have appeared in *Theatre Journal, Journal of Dramatic Theory and Criticism, Journal of Critical Realism, Journal for the Theory of Social Behaviour*, the collections *Performance and Cognition* (ed. Bruce McConachie and F. Elizabeth Hart, Routledge, 2006) and *Staging Philosophy: Intersections of Theater, Performance, and Philosophy* (ed. David Krasner and David Z. Saltz, University of Michigan Press, 2006), and elsewhere. He was a Fulbright fellow at the University of Helsinki, and received a fellowship from the American Council of Learned Societies.

Carol Fisher Sorgenfrei is Professor Emerita of Theatre at UCLA and was recently a Fellow at the Institute for Theatre Studies' International Research Center on Interweaving Performance Cultures at Berlin's Freie Universität. In 2014, she was honored by the Association for Asian Performance as one of the Founding Mothers of Asian Theatre Studies. She is the author of *Unspeakable Acts: The Avant-Garde Theatre of Terayama Shūji and Postwar Japan* (University of Hawaii Press, 2005), translations from Japanese, and many articles and essays on Japanese and intercultural performance. Her sixteen original plays include the award-winning *Medea: A Noh Cycle Based on the Greek Myth*, the kabuki-flamenco *Blood Wine, Blood Wedding*, and (with director Zvika Serper) the Japanese-Israeli fusion *The Dybbuk: Between Two Worlds*. Her newest play *Ghost Light: The Haunting* (with director Penny Bergman) fuses the kabuki *Yotsuya Kaidan* and *Macbeth*. She is Associate Editor of *Asian Theatre Journal* and Editor of the *Newsletter of the Association for Asian Performance*.

Tamara Underiner is Associate Dean for Research for the Herberger Institute for Design and the Arts at Arizona State University, and Associate Professor in the School of Film, Dance and Theatre, where she directs the Ph.D. program in Theatre and Performance of the Americas. She is the author of *Contemporary Theatre in Mayan Mexico: Death-Defying Acts* (University of Texas Press, 2004), and has published on indigenous and Latina/o theatre and critical pedagogy in *Theatre Journal*, *Signs*, *Baylor Journal of Theatre and Performance*, *TDR*, and critical anthologies from academic presses in the U.S., Mexico, and Canada. She is active in the American Society for Theatre Research, the Association for Theatre in Higher Education, and the Hemispheric Institute for Performance and Politics.

Preface to the third edition

The third edition of *Theatre Histories* constitutes a major revision. Our overarching aims for the book are the same, including global coverage, case studies on particular developments or issues in theatre history, discussions of historiographical approaches, and a focus on communication practices. For this edition, however, we sought four particular goals that proved transformative: to address the connections between communication and theatre more sharply; to reexamine the narratives or themes of each chapter; to rebalance the amount of discussion on some topics; and to keep the book at roughly the same length to control costs.

As a result, material has been extensively reorganized and re-thought. The chapters of this edition seldom match those of the second – most of them differ in their chronological coverage and sometimes their themes. The material in the second edition's lengthy Part introductions has moved into regular chapters, and each Part now has a brief introduction which establishes overall contexts and keynotes. Similarly, we decided that instead of a chapter on popular entertainment, we would distribute those topics among other chapters. The second edition's Preface, which addressed some of the functions of a book introduction, has been replaced with a fuller General Introduction that explains several central issues in historiography and orients students to the book's goals, focus, and structure. To accommodate expanded discussion of some topics, material that we felt was useful but no longer central was transferred to the website, to keep it available to instructors. The substantial percentage of the book that was absorbed by bibliographies has been much reduced, to allow more space for the chapters: we include the media resources and the works actually cited within the book, and we list other consulted works on the *Theatre Histories* website.

We reshaped Part I of *Theatre Histories* most substantially. Topics that were in three different chapters now appear in one, and coverage of ritual has been greatly reduced. There were several reasons for these changes. We wanted to move to discussions of theatre sooner, and in the process, sharpen the focus on how theatre is affected by changes in communication. In addition, although the material on ritual was meant to illuminate the sorts of performance appearing in oral cultures, due to its quantity it seemed to offer inadvertent support for the now much-doubted theory that ritual (or alternatively, religion) is theatre's origin. However, instructors who want to address ritual and the development of language in more detail will find those discussions on the website.

The apparent quieting of the "theory wars" within theatre studies and our desire to give instructors more flexibility when addressing topics in theatre history led us to loosen the relationship between case studies and theoretical approaches. In this edition, some case studies introduce a specific approach, but others do not. Likewise, some of what we previously called "Interpretive approaches" are now independent of a case study; but between expanding the range of topics that the "Interpretive approaches" sections could encompass, and realizing that the phrase "interpretive approaches" could be misconstrued as meaning the analysis of theatre history consists merely of opinions, we decided to rename those segments "Thinking through theatre histories." They now discuss not only historiographical methods and perspectives, but also narrative strategies and particular historiographical problems. Readers may notice that there is no section explicitly on feminist approaches (of which, of course, there are many). However, women's activities and gender issues (including feminist and queer theory) are addressed throughout the text and in some of the case studies.

The third edition provides several new case studies; we moved others to the website (corrected as needed) so instructors who want to use them can do so. In several instances, the new edition has a condensed version of a case study and we have put the full version on the website. In the course of *Theatre Histories'* revisions and online resource development, we aim to build a repertory of case studies and other materials which instructors can select in order to shape their courses in a manner that is both flexible yet consistent with the overall approach taken in this book.

Readers of *Theatre Histories'* first and second editions will notice a different roster of authors for the third. Such turnover was intended from the book's beginnings. Gary Jay Williams and Phillip B. Zarrilli took the opportunity to step down; Tobin Nellhaus and Tamara Underiner came on board. The new team adopted two connected goals for our revision process: more collaboration and greater coordination. Toward the former, we took numerous steps. All of the authors had a voice in major content and organizational decisions. Rather than have a single author take sole responsibility for one of the book's Parts, each author was assigned chapters in at least two Parts. Nearly every chapter became the product of combined authorship, bringing new perspectives throughout. The contributors are shown in each chapter's byline. And once all of the chapters were near their final form, we all read and commented on each other's work. To provide unity within this extensive collaboration, we established the role of General Editor.

In the midst of our collaboration, however, we of course have our individual outlooks. We agree on the main principles of theatre historiography, but we have differing views on how to weigh the many factors that shape theatre at any particular time, and we have our own interests within theatre history. We believe that these differences in themselves help this book achieve its goals. Thus the plural in "theatre histories" refers to several things: the multiplicity of performance practices in the world, both geographically and chronologically; the diversity of theories, facets, emphases, and goals in theatre historiography; and the mix of perspectives and personalities that contributed to the making of *Theatre Histories'* third edition.

All of us, however, owe a deep debt of gratitude to the authors who are no longer involved in the book. Specifically, Phillip B. Zarrilli's contributions are embedded in Chapters 1–4 and

12, and work by Gary Jay Williams appears in Chapters 6–9 and 12–15. In addition, both of them wrote materials in the previous editions that are now available on the website. Readers will continue to hear their voices in this new edition of *Theatre Histories*.

Bruce McConachie
Tobin Nellhaus
Carol Fisher Sorgenfrei
Tamara Underiner

Acknowledgments

The authors want to express again our gratitude to Routledge's Talia Rodgers, Publisher, for her belief in and long support of this project, from conception through this third edition. Talia's support of this new approach to creating a theatre history text has been an act of faith. We also want to thank Suzanne Richardson, Development Editor, who assisted us through the numerous complexities of producing this new edition, and the rest of Routledge's textbook production staff.

A history of this scope is possible in great part, of course, because of the specialized works of many dedicated scholars. We are indebted to them; we have drawn on them often and happily. Their works are cited in this text and in the extended bibliographies on our website.

Many of our colleagues have been especially supportive. We especially wish to thank for their advice and encouragement Jay Ball, Daniel Banks, Jason Bush, Claire Conceison, Dave Escoffery, Faye C. Fei, Lance Gharavi, Richard Hornby, David Jortner, Margaret Knapp, Marianne McDonald, David Mayer, Paul Murphy, Stuart Sillars, Julia Walker, Andrew Weintraub, E.J. Westlake, Gary Jay Williams, S.E. Wilmer, W.B. Worthen, and Jiayun Zhuang. Simon Williams was initially involved in this project and provided valuable contributions at an early stage. We have listened to and benefited from the external reviewers of our work, including our critics; they have helped us serve our readers better. We look forward to future conversations with our readers.

We are grateful to our students, who have been there at every stage of the journey, helping to shape what we think is a necessary new step for thinking about theatre and performance history. We have each benefited also from the long-term research support of our universities: the University of Exeter, the University of Wisconsin – Madison, the University of Pittsburgh, the Catholic University of America – Washington, DC, the University of California – Los Angeles, and Arizona State University.

We have also had the strong, enduring support of families and partners. Their considerable sacrifices made it possible for the work to get done, and we express our heartfelt thanks to all of them, including Gerry Magallan, Stephanie McConachie, and Richard Hornby.

Routledge would like to thank all those archives and individuals who have given permission to reproduce images in this textbook. In a few rare cases, we were unable, despite the utmost efforts, to locate owners of materials. For this we apologize and will make any corrections in the next reprint if contacted.

Bruce McConachie
Tobin Nellhaus
Carol Fisher Sorgenfrei
Tamara Underiner

General introduction

Tobin Nellhaus

Theatre Histories aims to introduce the history – or as we will explain, histories – of theatre, drama, and performance. The meaning of that sentence may seem obvious: the book presents information about people, plays, and performance practices such as acting, costumes, and staging. But we also have two other goals. One is to consider theatre's relationships with some of its many social contexts. The other is to raise questions about the meaning of evidence and events, and discuss different ways of interpreting them. Raising such questions often entails "unpacking" facts and statements because they contain more (or perhaps less!) than meets the eye.

For example, as the first sentence of this introduction shows, we will often use two or three terms, sometimes in combination, to describe our focus: "theatre," "drama," and "performance." The three terms overlap each other, but one can distinguish them reasonably clearly.

"Drama" is generally used to describe plays, collectively or in the singular. Occasionally it's used more broadly in order to refer to *what* is performed (fictional characters and actions, even if based on historical people and events), as distinct from *how* it is performed; the drama might not be a script at all, just ideas and character types in the performers' minds. For some people, "drama" carries the narrower sense of plays as literary works, printed texts to be read as "dramatic literature," apart from performance; however, for the authors of this book, the connection to performance is essential.

By "theatre" we usually mean live performances by skilled artists for live audiences, usually of drama or something drama-like. Such performances engage the spectators' imagination, emotion, intellect, and cultural perspectives, at varying levels. They may or may not take place in buildings built specifically for theatrical performance. Sometimes the audience members are also the performers. In theatre, everyone involved is aware that the performance presents a fiction. True, occasionally people use "theatre" to describe performances which attempt to lead observers into thinking that what they are watching is not fictional, or situations in which spectators observe other people as though (unbeknownst to them) they are fictional characters; but for the purposes of this book, these cases apply the term "theatre" metaphorically.

The term "performance" generally refers to embodied presentation on stage (or with surrogates for the body, such as puppets). However, the term has a special meaning today in the field of performance studies to include *all* the ways in which humans represent themselves in embodied ways. Scholars apply that sense of "performance" not only to the staging of plays but also to religious rituals, state ceremonies, carnivals, political demonstrations, athletic contests, the customs of a family dinner table, the ways people portray themselves in social media, and many other activities. In that sense, theatre is but one of many kinds of performance.

Occasionally *Theatre Histories* employs this broader sense of "performance." We think it is natural and enlightening to make connections between theatre and other types of performance. For that reason, even though *Theatre Histories* is not a performance studies textbook, we consider a wide range of performances – from Japanese puppetry to productions of plays by Samuel Beckett, from the dance-dramas of India to early twentieth-century high-fashion musical revues, and from ancient Greek drama to the Hip Hop plays created globally. We believe the juxtapositions among these will attune the reader to appreciate better the wide spectrum of theatre and performance in many cultures.

The scope of "theatre history" in *Theatre Histories* must also be unpacked. Knowing about theatre globally is vital today. For example, it is not unusual for playwrights, directors, and designers to be inspired by the theatre of other cultures (possibly ancient ones), and sometimes actors are expected to know or quickly absorb foreign acting methods. In addition, cultures today are constantly crossing national borders and influencing each other, such as the importation of K-Pop music and Bollywood movies into Western countries, or the performance of Arthur Miller's *Death of a Salesman* in China and the adoption of rap music across the planet. For those reasons we strive to provide an understanding of theatrical performance around the world, throughout its known existence. We also believe that isolating the study of Western from non-Western theatre does not serve students well. For that reason, most chapters in *Theatre Histories* include theatre from various parts of the world, with a few exceptions where thematic or other reasons made it unfeasible.

In our view, the history of theatre involves more than actors, performance spaces, plays, and staging. Theatrical performances occur within society. Thus *Theatre Histories* often discusses political, cultural, economic, and other social issues, and how they affected theatre, drama, and performance. The relationships among these various social dynamics, and between them and theatre, are extremely complex. However, *Theatre Histories* will pay one element special attention: a society's communication practices (its uses of speech, handwriting, printing, and electronics). We discuss this focus in more detail below.

Writing theatre history involves more than accumulating facts. Historians have to make decisions about what information is most important, and develop an understanding of how events are related. In other words, the process of writing about history – historiography – always involves interpretations of the past. One of the goals of *Theatre Histories* is to provide not just information about theatre, and not just our own interpretations of that information, but also an understanding of how interpretations come into being – how history is written – in order to enable students to evaluate historical writing. The remainder of this introduction surveys some of the core issues in historiography, the approach adopted by the authors, and its influence on our discussions and even the organization of the book.

Historiography: Thinking about history

If historiography involves interpreting the past, then we need to consider what it means to "interpret." One view frequently encountered today is that any claim that "X is true" is really "just an interpretation" – a complete matter of opinion. According to this perspective, there is no way to choose between them: all opinions are equally valid, and whatever is "true for me" is inherently unassailable.

As a general theory, this notion doesn't stand up to analysis, since it is logically self-defeating (the idea that every claim is merely an opinion must itself be merely an opinion), and it cannot account for actual practice. Nobody has ever actually stopped gravity by not believing in it; Western science hasn't explained (in its own terms) how the Asian medical technique of acupuncture works, but it has generally accepted that acupuncture can successfully treat pain and nausea. Beliefs about these things do not alter their efficacy. In addition, although many of those professing this theory intend well by trying not to impose their views on others, they open the door wide for arguments that are incorrect, misinforming, and/or malignant. The denial that during the Second World War the Nazi's extermination programs murdered 11 million people – Jews and non-Jews – is not an "equally valid opinion," it is a falsehood.

Nevertheless, the notion that every claim is "just an opinion" does sound a useful cautionary note for historiography, because interpretation is a necessary part of it. Determining exactly what, how, and why things happened is often extraordinarily difficult or even impossible; frequently evidence is fragmentary and ambiguous; and innumerable events are always happening simultaneously. One cannot perform experiments on history, and it is difficult to perceive one's own mistaken assumptions about the meaning of historical evidence. Although history is often imagined (and occasionally taught) as a simple, plodding path of dry facts, people experience history as a realm of fierce argument. We know what happened in history, until we realize we don't or we discover that someone else knows it differently. Even at the personal level, when talking with someone about a shared event, we all encounter moments when we say: "I don't remember it that way!" There clearly are facts, but even if we agree on them, we can fit them together in different ways, bringing out different perspectives, illuminating different connections, or formulating different explanations. To give one example of the role of perspective in historiography, the U.S. view of the American Revolutionary War is often that the British government was increasingly imposing itself on local governance, and demanded oppressive taxes to pay for the French and Indian War (1756–63, also called the Seven Years' War) in which many colonists had lost their lives; in contrast, to the British Parliament the Americans were ingrates refusing to pay their fair share for a war that had secured the colonies' very existence, and the Parliament's deliberations on managing the rebellion were based on assumptions drawn from prior (but inapplicable) experience, leading to serious miscalculations. Interpretation is intrinsic to historiography, and our understanding of history is necessarily always open to revision.

Social context and cultural relativity

A theatre historian could try to evade the problem of interpretation by writing a history that simply looks at what happens within theatrical practice: the eighteenth-century *kabuki* stage had such-and-such shape and size, during the late sixteenth century Isabella Andreini was an important *commedia dell'arte* actor in Italy and Christopher Marlowe was a major English playwright, the philosophy espoused by Auguste Comte shaped nineteenth-century realist theatre in Europe, and so forth. A theatre history like that would present no particular reason for theatre's changes or for the direction of change, such as why X was influential instead of Y. What happens in the society at large (such as economic transformations, religious conflicts, new ideas, and political rivalries) might be mentioned as the "larger context," but the larger context has little real bearing on theatre practices – it explains little and stays "outside the building."

Few theatre scholars today would accept such an approach to theatre history. In fact it could never achieve its goal, because the idea that theatre can be divorced from its social context is itself an interpretation. *Theatre Histories* is particularly emphatic that what happens inside the theatre is deeply connected to what happens outside, not just as a matter of the topics playwrights present on stage, but also how plays are performed, who performs them, who attends them, and what social developments produced changes in cultural ideas that were manifested in stylistic shifts. For instance, approaches to acting can be rooted in scientific developments; the sorts of characters one sees in a play can be connected to the way people use the printing press; whether plays are written at all (rather than improvised or orally transmitted) may be the result of the society's political and economic configuration. The theatre's doors are always open to the world, and the world always enters. In fact the world is already part of theatre itself.

Just as theatre is thoroughly embedded in society, perspectives on history and society are often connected to particular cultures and their values. We can see how ideas can be relative to a specific society in an example drawn from theatre history. In Europe during the Middle Ages and well into the Renaissance, people believed there was a hierarchy among all things in the world, starting with rocks at the bottom and rising through plants, animals, humans, angels, and ultimately God. Humans themselves were ranked from the lowliest beggars, up through serfs, knights, earls, dukes, and finally the king. (Actors, incidentally, were lumped with prostitutes.) All told, this vertical understanding of the world was called the Great Chain of Being, and people acted on that understanding by (for instance) passing laws regarding what clothes people could wear. But in the late seventeenth century another view began to emerge, which slowly consolidated into a more horizontal concept of society expressed in statements such as "All men are created equal," and people acted on that belief (at least to some extent) by establishing nations with democracies.

Such vertical and horizontal concepts are evident in theatre architecture. In the early 1600s, theatre buildings in Europe usually allowed only one person, such as the king or duke, to have a perfect view of the perspective scenery; everyone else's view was fragmented and distorted. In the late 1800s a new building design gave everyone a more equal view of the stage. Is either the vertical or the horizontal concept of society "true"? Most historians today would answer that each view is "valid" – acceptable – within some societies, but neither one is valid for all societies: their validity is culturally relative.

The point is important because historians can unwittingly project their own perceptions, assumptions, and beliefs (which may seem like common sense in their own culture) on to earlier and foreign societies, leading to severe misunderstandings. For instance, scholars may believe that religion involves the same type of concepts in other cultures as it does in their own, not realizing that there can be significant differences. There is also a long, unpleasant history of historians projecting their ideas and values in a way that implies (or states outright) that their own society is superior to others. We will discuss examples of this practice at several points in *Theatre Histories*.

For certain purposes, however, historians apply their perspective intentionally and for good reasons, particularly when they pursue questions such as "Who gains?" and "Who is harmed?" These concerns frequently arise in analyses of economics, gender, race, and politics. Capitalism is one such topic often discussed in terms of gain and harm. Some people argue that capitalism is good because competition and the search for profit have led to innumerable innovations that have benefited people around the globe, and allow individuals to improve their economic standing. Others hold that capitalism is bad because it makes working people dependent on companies and corporations that prioritize profit over people's needs, and because the system suffers drastic cycles which can suddenly throw millions of people into poverty. Still others believe that capitalism doesn't exist: there are only free markets in which employers and employees are on a level playing field and meet to conduct a fair exchange of labor for payment, so the entire question is moot. Each perspective leads to different ways of writing history, as does an approach that seeks to "balance" the pros and cons rather than say that one side outweighs the other. (Notice that one can ask not only whether these claims are true, but also who benefits or is harmed by the claim itself!) Questions of gain and harm also arise in theatre history: for instance, as we will see, in the past many cultures allowed only men to perform in plays, which historians deemed insignificant until some argued that the practice was misogynistic, and others that it was homoerotic. (Its treatment as insignificant is itself often considered misogynistic.) Further interpretations emerged in response. Such debates force scholars to reexamine evidence and their own attitudes, and they have deepened our insight into theatre's complexity.

Clearly, however, there is tension between the desire to avoid projecting our own society's views on to others, and the desire to criticize inequality. There may be no completely satisfactory solution to that tension. In *Theatre Histories* our goal is to introduce both, since both bring much of value (and important values) to theatre history. We present some examples of historical critique. At the same time we also strive to consider what performances meant to their original audience; we recognize, however, that we can seldom be certain that we've succeeded – the people of third-century India, for instance, aren't around to tell us whether we got things right, and their judgments would be colored by their own perspectives.

Evidence–theory connections

Evidence, then, is often subject to interpretation due to the historian's assumptions, values, and informational contexts. A historian's social position, need to justify one side's actions, and sometimes even wishful thinking can also surreptitiously slip into historiography. One topic where historians' projections have strongly influenced their interpretations is the question of theatre's origins, especially in ancient Greece. In the early 1900s, Gilbert Murray and other classical anthropologists contended that Greek tragedy evolved from religious rituals. The hypothesis was surrounded by just enough apparent evidence to be taken as proved.

By the late 1920s, however, classicists showed that the logic behind Murray's theory was flawed, much of the evidence it presented was misconstrued, and contrary evidence had not been considered. The problems with Murray's thesis are so acute that the classical scholar Gerald Else asserted that Murray had not accumulated evidence which he then realized could be explained by the "ritual origins" theory, but instead was driven by "the determination at all costs to find the origin of tragedy in religion, and therefore in ritual" (1965: 4) – in other words, that Murray selected and interpreted his evidence in order to fit the theory he already had in mind.

Although ancient Greek theatre may have had some sort of relationship to ritual, it was not the evolutionary one that Murray proposed. But the "religious ritual origins" theory captured many people's imagination, and still appears in one form or another to this day, including among some classicists. (Some writers dub refuted yet tenacious theories "zombie ideas.") One reason it persists is that some theatre practitioners and scholars feel that the theory offers an inspiration for vitality in performance and a way to comprehend that vitality. Inspiration is always "true" in the sense that a lived experience cannot be falsified (if you feel excited, I can't demonstrate that you're actually bored), and in a sense, the inspiration is more valid if one believes that the theory of "religious ritual origins" is correct. In other words, if an inspiration is true then its source must be as well. For these practitioners and scholars, theatre's factual origin is not the most important truth: its "origin" as a belief or subjective experience is. (Note, however, that rejecting ritual as the *origin* of theatre does not exclude other possible relationships between them.)

In this example we see that there can be different perspectives on "what actually happened," but these different perspectives are not equally valid, nor are they impervious to criticism. We can also see that for some people there are different "kinds" of truth (a position that itself can be interpreted in various ways), and that not everyone thinks the different kinds have the same level of importance; for others, there is only one kind of truth. We will return to the question of theatre's origins in Chapter 1.

In contrast, a historian may make an argument based on both strong argument and solid evidence . . . and then the evidence changes. In one case of "facts" changing, the first known theatre building – the Theatre of Dionysus, in Athens, Greece – was long thought to seat 15,000–17,000 people; but in light of recent archaeological evidence, classical scholars now believe the theatre's initial capacity was closer to 3,700–6,000 spectators, and the larger figure refers to a later expansion (Roselli 2011: 64–5). As a result of this change in the evidence, an excellent theory about the role of theatre in ancient Athens based on the previous estimate might need to be revised or even rejected. People may discover that a piece of evidence about theatre is more recent than was thought, or that the evidence believed to demonstrate something true everywhere actually pertains only to one city, or that evidence was misinterpreted, or that other pieces of evidence must be considered, or that a facet of theatre (say, the significance of the actors' gender) was left out of the picture entirely, or that the source isn't reliable.

Although historians usually strive to avoid forcing evidence into a predetermined theory, or at least to be aware that there may be contrary evidence, historical evidence is always sought, chosen, and interpreted. Evidence doesn't "speak for itself," the historian makes it speak to us. Because historians must select and interpret, they can misunderstand or misrepresent historical events; but by the same token, new interpretations can reveal aspects of history that weren't recognized before – "historical discoveries" may arise by understanding preexisting evidence in innovative ways. In either case, whether one thinks the selection and description of evidence is a problem or an advantage, it is a necessary part of historiography, and the condition under which writing history must occur.

Intelligibility, plausibility, and narrative

Historians do more than select and interpret evidence: they also organize the evidence in order to create an intelligible (and, they hope, persuasive) narrative. Chronological order is generally part of making history plausible, especially when the causes of change are central, although in practice much historical writing must go back and forth in time in order to pick up various threads of a complex story. Historians also make events understandable by casting them in a particular light or giving their narrative a particular tone. For example, a historian might highlight historical ironies, such as the way President George W. Bush once criticized "nation building," in which the U.S. rebuilds a country's economic and political structure when its government fails; but later, as a consequence of launching a war in Iraq, Bush had to attempt exactly that. Historians can also romanticize events, as did those who described John F. Kennedy's term as President as "Camelot," alluding to a Broadway musical about the gallant King Arthur and the Knights of the Round Table. Similarly, one historian may view a certain chain of events as improvement, while another may perceive it as a decline. These are just a few of the ways historians may make narrative sense of history.

Of course, although historians strive to present a plausible narrative, "plausible" is not a synonym for "true." To take just one of the many complexities, discussions about historical causes can run into a logical problem that's often hard to detect. Imagine that the President of the United States made a speech about the stock market, and later that day the stock market indexes fell. It's easy to infer that the President's speech worried stock traders and led to the sell-off. But even though that interpretation is very plausible, it might not be correct: the traders might have actually been reacting to bad news coming from abroad. One would need additional evidence to show what really caused the market decline. (This error, in which one thinks that one event must have caused another event because it preceded the second, is called a *post hoc* argument, short for the Latin *post hoc, ergo propter hoc,* translated as "after this, therefore because of this.") To avoid such mistakes, historians have to think carefully about what evidence is required to support their analysis – and sometimes no further evidence is available, or at least known to the historian. Plausibility may be the best we can get. This is yet another reason why history is often subject to debate.

Causes of historical change

Narrative is intrinsic to any discussion of how and why societies change. True, to some observers societies don't fundamentally change at all: "the more things change, the more they stay the same." A less cynical and more truly historiographical view is that social changes operate in regular cycles such as rise and fall. A related idea is that social change consists of swings of a pendulum (say, between permissiveness and conformism). In contrast, sometimes history is depicted as consistent progress toward some definite goal, at times perhaps delayed but ultimately inexorable – the "march of reason," for instance.

A problem facing all of these views is that they don't provide any reason why there would be cycles, pendulum swings, or progress, or why they should apply to the particular matter of interest: these things just happen on their own, guided by an invisible hand. One answer to this question is that there is no "why," or even things like cycles and progress. Instead, history is a matter of happenstance, contingency, and accident, without any particular direction or pattern: the only agent of change lies in personal interactions. And certainly at the micro level, little more than chance may explain why one person became a historical figure rather than another. But this view misses the "big picture" of historical developments. For instance, it is striking that during roughly 1550–1650, there were substantial changes in theatrical practices throughout Europe, not always in synchrony but in the same basic direction. Performance spaces increasingly moved indoors and used more realistic scenery; characters became more psychologically driven. What drove this "change in taste"? Why had large numbers of people come to prefer it? How and why had the concept of "realistic" changed? Surely more than coincidence or personal influence was involved.

Those questions raise others. If there were large forces behind cultural changes, one must ask what those forces were, or which of many forces was the most important. Various answers have been proposed, most of them boiling down to three kinds. One kind points to material activities, for example the production and exchange of goods and services (economics), relationships between and among women and men (the sex/gender system), technological developments, or the methods of communication. Another answer focuses on institutions, such as political systems, religious organizations, or family structures. The third view assigns primacy to ideas – theology, philosophy, science, or other sorts of worldview. One can of course also see the three factors as interacting, although in the end, usually one has the greatest weight. Earlier we explained how the Great Chain of Being was supplanted by a more horizontal concept of the world, an example of idea-driven history; but a historian might then ask what caused that change in ideas, and point to some material activity. Historians' views of the main type of force that drives society, as well as the specific force they consider, lead to very different historical narratives.

Theories of society

A key element of historians' interpretations and narratives is their general concept of how individuals and society are related. Their concept may be difficult to detect, since it is seldom explicit (even to the historian) and sometimes several different concepts seem to be invoked. As we will see, a particular concept of society directly shaped *Theatre Histories*. Understanding these different theories helps explain some of this book's organization and themes.

Sociologist Margaret S. Archer (1995) identifies four basic concepts of the relationship between individuals and society. One is that society boils down to individuals. Nothing happens in a society unless individuals do things; further, on this view the most important things about individuals – their personal traits, abilities, experiences, and achievements – are independent of any social context. According to this view, known as "methodological individualism," talk about social groups, institutions, power relationships, and society as a whole is problematic or erroneous because such things cannot be perceived: all that can be perceived are individuals' behaviors. "Social relationships" are simply interactions between individuals – family ties, buying and selling, being someone's boss, and the like. But racism, economic systems, and political power are abstractions about things that individuals do, nothing more. History is essentially about individuals: "great men (and a few great women)."

Methodological individualism breaks down when one realizes that much of what describes individuals is determined by society, such as economic class, race, age group ("generation"), citizenship, language, and so forth, and these things regulate what people do (or may do). One example is that laws, institutions and/or customs establish whether two people are married, unmarried, or not permitted to marry. Even personal interactions involve social frameworks: to understand, say, what happens between a store clerk and a customer, you need to know what "shopping," "store clerks," "customers," and "money" are, all of which require a concept of society as a whole.

The second theory of society acknowledges this by focusing on the rules and systems that govern social activities, continue a society's existence, and keep it functioning as smoothly as possible (and so one version of this theory is called "functionalism"). The rules and systems are embodied in systems such as a society's larger political and economic structures, and people just follow their roles within them. People don't have to be conscious that they're maintaining social structures: it happens by default, in the same way that speaking English keeps the English language alive. Individuals and their activities are determined by their position within the social systems that they're part of.

The first theory suggests that individuals live in virtually unfettered freedom and are wholly responsible for their personal fates, as if larger social conditions don't exist or have no power to limit or eliminate choices; the second theory describes people as having practically no control over the world in which they live, to the point where they may be simply "cogs in the machine" or "victims of society." A third position proposes that the difficulty behind these extreme positions lies in seeing individuals and society as wholly different things. But rules and resources don't exist independently – they depend on the existence of people and their ideas about what they are doing. Equally, what individuals do is always within the context of a society. At every moment, individuals are constructing society, and society is constructing individuals. The two are inextricable. Thus, like the sides of one coin, if you look at an activity from one perspective, you'll see individuals going about their daily lives; look at it another way, you'll see rules and resources comprising social structures. The two are conjoined in a single, active process, and once a moment in history has passed, what remains are but the traces it leaves in memory. Society operates the same way as language does: speaking English draws on one's knowledge of the rules that make up the English language, and simultaneously continues the language's existence; but the language only exists when we speak, read or write it. Thus society exists only through individuals' acts of repeating the rules, in the present. However, individuals can introduce small changes, which can accumulate. All told, institutions, ideas, and individuals always have a social nature, and they have a fluid, ever-changing quality. One version of this theory is termed "social constructionism."

The final view agrees that individuals and society mutually shape each other, but it maintains that the two remain different things, not flip sides of one thing. Individuals and society each have features that are largely independent of the other, such as physical bodies for the one and economic systems for the other. But because they're different things, they aren't in sync, and society doesn't exist only in the present. Time and the causes of social change snap into focus as aspects of society's existence. People can't wake up one day with new ideas about social roles and resources, and instantly transform the society they live in; conversely, social rules may alter, yet some individuals will behave just as they did before (e.g., some people discriminate even after it becomes illegal). People can change society, but only within the preexisting circumstances that society has placed upon their actions. We live in(side) the past: society depends on people's activities for its existence, but principally on the activities of people who lived previously. Some of their legacy has been swept away, some of it remains but has been reshaped, some of it continues largely unaltered. (For instance, the latest hit song in Western countries probably uses the notes of the twelve-tone scale that began taking shape in ancient Greece 2,500 years ago, rather than a pentatonic scale like those of Asia and Africa.) Thus one historical era may begin long before the previous one has come to a close, and incremental adjustments can suddenly spark radical upheavals. Likewise, a world phenomenon like globalization may seem to bulldoze everything in its path, yet its impact on different countries varies drastically. In short, under this theory (which has been called a "transformational" model of social activity), history is messy.

Although the authors of *Theatre Histories* have somewhat varying positions, on the whole we take the last view. Theatre history's messiness is reflected in every chapter, because cultures don't change at the same rate or in the same manner, and their genres of theatrical performance vary widely. We make one aspect of theatre history's untidiness particularly conspicuous through our periodization. Chapters always overlap chronologically, sometimes in complicated ways: for instance, Chapter 4 covers roughly 1250–1650, Chapter 5 addresses 1550–1650, and Chapter 6 examines 1600–1770, which overlaps even Chapter 4. Many different factors came into play regarding our decisions about where to draw the dividing lines (which are necessarily a bit arbitrary), and we often had to wrestle with questions about where to place certain topics. In fact among historians generally, periodization is often disputed. Was there a Renaissance in Europe, and if so, when, where and for whom? It depends on what countries and social groups one has in mind, what activities one thinks distinguish that period, and whether one thinks "Renaissance" is even a valid description. Similarly, how does one periodize when developments in (say) East Asia and Western Europe follow different paths? Sometimes themes tell us more than chronology.

History as the construction of truth

The need to focus on particular aspects of historical events, the collection and interpretation of evidence, the development of a narrative, and the historian's perspective and concept of society can be summarized by the sentence "History is constructed." We piece it together and build an argument. However, even though any understanding of history is a construct, and a range of interpretations may be supported by evidence and logic, neither the notion that all perspectives are equally true nor the idea that they are all merely opinions (lacking a distinctive validity) holds up to scrutiny. In short, interpreting the past is not a free-for-all. It possesses objective as well as subjective facets. Not all interpretations are valid, historians can make mistakes, and some theories are flat-out wrong, no matter how insistently they might be espoused. We may never know with *absolute* certainty that certain claims are correct. But absolute certainty isn't required in order for us to be confident that a statement is true: truth is more like "certainty beyond a reasonable doubt."

Theatre and the history of communication

The interpretation of history adopted in *Theatre Histories* appears in the way we perceive an interplay between individuals and society; it is also manifested through how we handle social structures. Society has numerous structures, including the economic system, political power relations, sex/gender relationships, race and ethnicity, religion, education, transportation, agriculture, health care, international relations, and so on. Changes in one structure often affect the others, and several may be involved in a single historical change. The relative importance or weight one should give to a particular structure depends partly on what one is discussing, and the perspective one brings to it. To take one example, the history of American popular music might pay special attention to the role of race. Theatre, we believe, was most deeply affected historically by communication practices, by which we mean the way a society develops and uses one or more means of communication, such as speech, handwriting, printing, and electric/electronic media.

Why communication? The principal reason is "the primacy of practice," a theory about the formation of knowledge, which holds that many of our ideas and thought processes arise through ordinary practical activities rather than abstract reasoning; at a larger level, it also means that testing ideas in the real world provides better evidence for truth claims than logic alone – as the saying goes, "the proof of the pudding is in the eating." The "primacy of practice" theory has a long pedigree in such fields as philosophy and child development. Lately it has received additional support from cognitive science and linguistics, which have shown that much of human thought is structured by metaphors derived from experiences interacting with the world. For instance, by putting objects into a container and taking them out again, we form the conceptual models or "schemas" of inside/outside and container/contained. These schemas become the basis for metaphors that help us interpret the world we live in, through expressions like "Andy felt *out* of place," "Lucinda ran *in* a marathon on Saturday," and "They're *within* their rights to insist on a refund." Similarly, crawling on a floor as an infant teaches us the schema source–path–goal, which is expressed in statements like "Carol is *headed for* trouble," "Dana and Drew have been *going out* together for months," and "Marcus *started* working as a systems analyst." All sorts of objects, conditions, and activities can be the source of metaphors: "He's *hot* but he's got a *cold* heart" (temperature is attractiveness), "She's in it for the *long haul*" (commitment is lengthy travel), "I think Professor Merrimack has a *screw loose*" (the mind is a machine), and so forth. We use most of these metaphors without being aware of them.

If our everyday interactions with the world provide metaphors for understanding it, then some of those metaphors must come from our communication practices. *How* we communicate – through speech, handwritten notes, text messages, etc. – is clearly different from *what* we communicate. But how we communicate is also more than the means of communication themselves, because as we will see, it involves the ways in which people in a particular society actually use the means of communication. Communication practices provide ways of understanding the world that help define a culture. The point is extremely important for the study of theatre, because in its most commonplace, paradigmatic form, theatre involves the *oral* performance of a *written* script, thus combining the two fundamental modes of communication. That blend forges a strong bond between theatrical performance and communication practices.

Even though one can't separate the means of communication from its social usage, the historical development of communication technology is still important. One can periodize the history of communication in various ways. The most obvious approach is to distinguish between oral cultures, manuscript cultures, print cultures, and electric and electronic cultures. But there are other possibilities. For example, one could argue that there are really only two major eras: first, oral cultures, which have no form of writing whatsoever; then, the era of literate cultures, which has numerous sub-periods. But this simple dividing line turns out to be not quite so simple. On the one hand, there have been cultures which had writing but gave it a minor role culturally, so in a technical sense they may have been literate, but for most practical purposes, they remained oral; on the other hand, oral communication is hugely important in even the most technologically sophisticated society with nearly universal literacy. Another approach to periodizing communication history might hold that there is a significant shift between the electronic culture of the television, radio, and telephone, vs. the socially networked culture of the computer, the internet, and especially mobile devices; in other words, one could break down the history of communication into shorter periods.

For *Theatre Histories*, we are using four periods, which are represented in the four parts of the book. Our focus, however, is on the connection between changes in a society's communication practices, and the shifts and commonalities in performance and in the culture at large. For that reason, the book's parts don't match the technological changes. First, after considering performance in oral culture, we examine theatre in various types of early literate and then manuscript cultures, when all writing had to be done by hand; but in all of these cultures, to a greater or lesser extent the spoken word still played a major cultural role. The next period hinges on the introduction of the printing press, which radically transformed the way books were produced and disseminated, and made writing culturally dominant throughout Europe. Our third period arises from a change that occurred not in communication technology, but in the way an existing technology was used: publishing on a recurrent, periodical basis became logistically viable, leading to the creation of newspapers, magazines, and journals of various sorts. Finally, we address the rise of electric and electronic modes of communication, which have undergone numerous technological transformations that have not ended to this day. Although there's reason to think that electronic communication is not yet dominant in the sense of structuring thought and there are numerous explorations in how to use it (some successful, some not), that seems to be the direction world culture is taking.

But it's vital to remember that the dominance of any mode of communication is always relative to other modes of communication, and specific to particular societies. What emerges in North America, Europe, Japan, Australia, and similarly developed parts of the world can't be extrapolated elsewhere. The reality is that in 2015, about 15 percent of the world's population had no access to electricity, let alone computers; roughly 55 percent had no access to the internet. Although mobile technologies are making rapid inroads, the digital divide between the connected and unconnected will be extremely difficult to overcome, and might never be eliminated. As for the developed world, assuming online communication becomes dominant, the older means of communication – speech, handwriting, and printing – will nevertheless continue to be used in one form or another. Their techniques and functions may change, as they have for handwriting: it used to serve all purposes, but today the only activity that requires it is writing signatures (and increasingly, not even that); signatures were once written on parchment, which was replaced by paper, and now paper is being replaced by an electronic pad and stylus. However, whatever else changes in the face of electronic communication, the older communication media will not vanish.

The continuing role of older modes of communication touches on questions of how quickly and completely changes occur. There is a tendency to view or at least present changes in communication as revolutionary and total – a sudden, radical shift from an oral culture to a literate culture, thoroughly dominated by writing; a quick, wholesale change from a print culture to an electronic culture. This idea suffers many problems, one of which is how one should define "literate." Historically, many people have been able to read but unable to write: is that an acceptable definition of literacy? Scholars don't all agree. Similarly, scholars who believe "literate" means "able to write" have varying opinions on whether the ability to write one's name but little else suffices for literacy. The problem in defining written literacy has its parallel in "computer literacy": for instance, even "digital natives" are often unable to code, are unfamiliar with the sophisticated tools available in their word processor, and have very poor online search skills. A further difficulty is determining the threshold at which a society is "literate": are there times when 1 percent is high enough because it includes the people in power, or 75 percent too low because it excludes too many people with little power? The problems in defining "literacy" and selecting a good threshold, together with the fact that there are long periods of overlap, make it attractive to reject "revolution" in favor of a slow "evolution." On the other hand, "slow" is vague: given that writing has existed for roughly 5,600 years, is 50 or even 100 years slow? To many historians, that's quite rapid. The position taken in *Theatre Histories* is that on the whole, change is evolutionary and uneven, but there are some periods that really can be described as revolutions in communication.

The key question, however, is how – or whether – changes in communication affect culture. There are three basic views. One is that communication technologies affect everything that pertains to communication and culture, and their impact is the same everywhere – they're the only factor one needs to consider. This view is called "technological determinism," and it is probably the most widespread. A contrasting argument is that actually, technologies have no particular effects or tendencies: instead, only social activities such as education have any role. *Theatre Histories* takes the view that both technological and social aspects are at play. Technologies present various possibilities, but they aren't infinitely malleable – they can only do a certain range of things, they are better suited for some purposes than for others, and they may serve or promote certain uses more than others (possibly inadvertently). Which specific possibilities become reality depends on things that people do in society at large. YouTube, for example, started as an online dating site, but within weeks its creators discovered that people were uploading all sorts of videos, and mere months later corporations were posting ads. Some people use YouTube as a sort of online radio with videos displaying a static image, but that's a weak usage of its capabilities. However, the technology behind YouTube renders it incapable of supplanting Skype.

What happened to YouTube is a good demonstration of the only indisputable law of history: the law of unintended consequences. People may believe that the intentions of great leaders and innovators are foremost in the "march of history," but at most that's only partly the case, and often not true at all. When the printing press was invented in Europe, nobody could have anticipated that it would facilitate a cultural renaissance, a scientific revolution, and the most savage religious schism the continent ever endured. Those effects and more had fundamental connections to the simple experience of using printed books, and the mental habits and metaphors that those experiences fostered. In the future too, history will have complex over-laps, multiple timelines, interweavings, lurches, and surprises. Theatre will trace a similarly unpredictable path as people absorb, respond to, act upon, and think within changing communication practices.

We will describe in more detail the specific ways in which communication shapes theatre and drama within each of *Theatre Histories*' four parts. Here, however, we need to observe that theatre not only has powerful ties to communication, it is also strongly affected by other social structures, such as economics, political structures, and the sex/gender system. The different factors influencing the stage interconnect in various ways and further complicate the history of theatre. To reflect that fact, within the larger context of communication that established this book's parts, the individual chapters often pay special attention to other social structures.

The structure of *Theatre Histories*

Theatre Histories has three primary types of material: the main text, boxes titled "Thinking through theatre histories," and case studies. There are also a few boxes concerning particular points or information that readers should be aware of, and we have a range of additional resources on the *Theatre Histories* website.

The main text describes the principal developments in theatre history, which broadly speaking we've organized chronologically. However, as we've observed, historical periods have no clear-cut boundaries, and so every chapter overlaps others. Within each chapter, we usually adopt either a geographic or a thematic approach. From continent to continent, theatre often develops independently, but within a continent, sometimes conditions are so similar or there is so much traffic – instructions on how to demonstrate religious devotion, touring theatre companies that display "how it's done," and other types of intercommunication – that a country-by-country approach would distract from the overall pattern. On the other hand, seeing the similarities and dissimilarities between theatre traditions during a single time frame can help readers think about performance comparatively.

But more often the chapter is organized thematically. The topics necessarily vary from chapter to chapter, but frequently the chapter begins with the historical context and the forces driving the events that shape theatrical performance. Chapter 4, for instance, observes that the growing cities in Europe and Asia were increasingly able to support theatre as a vocation. As a result, theatre was no longer tethered to festivals, aristocratic courtyards, and similar venues. Professional theatre troupes developed in China, Europe and Japan, dependent initially on touring, but in Europe and Japan they eventually resided in buildings built for play-going.

As noted above, we have grouped the chapters into four parts, characterized by the developments in communication practices.

- Part I briefly addresses performance in oral cultures, and then turns attention to theatre when writing could only be produced by hand, and the cultures in many respects remained oriented around orality. Several societies developed major theatre traditions during this period, among them Europe, India, Japan, and China; and everywhere, there were forms of celebratory and commemorative performance.
- Part II surveys theatre during the first 250 years or so of print culture in Europe, and contemporaneous developments in Asia. First, we consider the rise of professional theatre companies, which occurred in many parts of the world, mainly as the result of growing prosperity and urbanization. Our examination of the print revolution in Europe highlights the cultural changes and conflicts that arose out of it, and then the formation of highly centralized monarchies, which often utilized print as a way to shore up their power. These developments strongly influenced concepts of character and plot, and theatre professionals started seeking artistic realism in one sense or another.
- Part III concerns theatre in the next three centuries of print culture, distinguished by the development of the periodical press. This new use of print fostered new roles for theatre in European society, through which theatre contributed to and was influenced by the political structures that were emerging from capitalism, particularly nationalism. The trend toward globalization began, and the resulting intercultural contact had both innovative and oppressive effects. Realism became increasingly well-defined and established in Western theatre, and also spread to Japan. Toward the end of this era, entirely new media based mainly on electricity started to shatter print culture's modes of thought, promoting a new phenomenon: non-realistic, avant-garde theatre.

- Part IV picks up the thread as electric and then electronic communication played an increasingly prominent cultural role. On the one hand, various forms of realism dominated in mainstream theatre (except for musicals); on the other hand, avant-garde genres were constantly being invented. Avant-gardes challenged nearly every aspect of theatre, such as the importance of the dramatic text versus performance, what counted as a performance space and how it could be used, what performance consisted of, and who could be a performer. In addition, within both the mainstream and the avant-garde, some forms of theatre sought to challenge the political ideologies, institutions and forces of their society. Often electronic communication provided models or tools for these developments.

Each part opens with a short introduction that summarizes what that part will cover, and raises philosophical issues stemming from the broad developments in theatre's history.

The "Thinking through theatre histories" sections present subjects in historiography, such as theories and methodologies (for instance, queer theory, and the ideas of literary critic Mikhail Bakhtin); particularly topical questions (e.g., the notion of "origins," and theatre's connection to concepts of national identity); and the strategies historians use to obtain evidence, communicate their interpretations, or convince readers of their validity (such as how extreme examples can reveal larger trends). These sections aim to help the reader grasp the problems theatre historians face and the choices they make when studying historical events. Of course, these segments hardly exhaust the enormous variety of historiographical theories, questions, and strategies – they cover only the tip of the tip of the iceberg.

Finally, each chapter has one or two case studies, which look in depth at a performance genre, play, or dramatist, or some other aspect of theatre. Some case studies involve an explicit historiographical approach or issue, which is described in a "Thinking through theatre histories" box, enabling students to see how a theory or strategy might be applied in practice. In other instances we do not present any specific theory, allowing students to consider (on their own or with their instructor) what sorts of ideas and techniques guide the case study.

We close this introduction by returning to our starting point. We began by discussing some major terms: theatre, drama, and performance. There has been and continues to be enormous diversity in the theatrical performance practices of the world, both geographically and chronologically. Diverse forces have shaped theatre's development throughout its history. And there is a diversity of theories, facets, emphases, and goals in theatre historiography. In writing this book, our aim has been to introduce all of these dimensions of writing about theatre in history. That, then, is the meaning of the plural in the title, *Theatre Histories*.

A NOTE ON RESOURCES AND CONVENTIONS

Additional resources

We offer many resources beyond the text itself. At the end of the book's four parts, we list the books and articles that we cited in the text. That section also lists selected audiovisual resources, including recordings of performances, short documentaries, and websites, which

continued

are marked in the margin with a camera icon. Routledge's companion website for this book (www.theatrehistories.com) offers texts drawn from previous editions of this book, including case studies and short essays on various topics. These are indicated in the margin with a Companion Website icon. We include pronunciation guidance for many foreign terms within the text (in square brackets) and at the back of the book, with online recordings flagged with a headphone icon. Terms printed in blue are briefly defined in the Glossary toward the end of the book; other terms can be located by using the Index. The companion website lists further online resources, and the many books and articles that we used in writing *Theatre Histories* but didn't specifically cite in the text or that a reader wanting more information would find useful.

There is one caveat about online resources. The internet can be an astonishingly rich source of valuable information, thoughtful analysis, and videos of brilliant performance. On the other hand, anyone can put up a website with information and opinions that represent no special expertise, present outdated scholarship, or even intentionally misrepresent facts. It is best to use websites in conjunction with current scholarly books and articles, which have been vetted by experts and often represent new research and ideas not reflected in websites.

Diacritics, spellings, names, and capitalization

We have followed common scholarly usage in diacritical markings and Romanized spellings of terms from the many languages used in this text. Japanese and Chinese names place the family name first (e.g., Suzuki Tadashi), which we follow unless the person has adopted Western usage.

Scholarly practices for capitalization vary. To the extent possible, we capitalize the names of movements, reasonably identifiable groups, and geographical regions. Some examples are Romanticism, the Romantics, Realism (as an artistic movement), Symbolism, Asian, and Western. We leave in lower case the terms for ideas, theories, and styles, when they are not necessarily connected to a particular movement or group of people: for instance, positivism, positivists, realism (as a set of ideas and stylistic goals), and symbolism (the use of symbols in general). Occasionally this convention leads to seemingly odd combinations, such as when we discuss "realism and Naturalism," but the reason should be clear from the text.

Works cited

Other consulted resources and additional readings are listed on the **Theatre Histories** *website.*

Archer, M.S. (1995) *Realist Social Theory: The Morphogenetic Approach*, Cambridge: Cambridge University Press.

Else, G. (1965) *The Origin and Early Form of Greek Tragedy*, New York: W. W. Norton.

Lakoff, G. and Johnson M. (1999) *Philosophy in the Flesh: The Embodied Mind and its Challenge to Western Thought*, New York: Basic Books.

Nellhaus, T. (2010) *Theatre, Communication, Critical Realism*, New York: Palgrave Macmillan.

Roselli, D.K. (2011) *Theater of the People: Spectators and Society in Ancient Athens*, Austin: University of Texas Press.

Performance in oral and manuscript cultures

PART I TIMELINE

DATE	THEATRE and PERFORMANCE	CULTURE and COMMUNICATION	POLITICS and ECONOMICS
200,000–190,000 BCE			Beginnings of modern humans
100,000–60,000 BCE		Beginnings of language	
c.5500–c.4000 BCE			Ancient civilization in Sumer (southern Iraq)
c.3800 BCE			Ancient civilization in Crete
c.3200–1800 BCE			Earliest South American civilization (Peru)
c.3150–2686 BCE			First dynasty, Egypt
c.3000 BCE–[?]	Performance, festivals, Mesoamerica		
c.2700 BCE		Sumerian epic *Gilgamesh* Egyptian hieroglyphs	
c.2070–c.1600 BCE			Xia dynasty, China
c.2055 BCE–[?]	Abydos "Passion Play," Egypt		
c.2000–c.1000 BCE			Earliest Mayan civilization
c.1600–c.1046 BCE		Chinese writing	Shang dynasty, China
c.1180 BCE			Trojan War
c.1050 BCE		Phoenician script	
c.1000 BCE	Hopi performances, North America Celtic rituals, bardic festivals, Europe		
c.850 BCE		Greek alphabet	
c.800 BCE	Homer and bardic performance, Greece	Written Sanskrit	
776 BCE		Olympic games, Greece	
753 BCE			Founding of Rome
c.600 BCE		Writing in Mesoamerica	
c.563–483 BCE		Siddhartha Gautama (Buddha), India	
551–478 BCE		Confucius, China	
534 BCE	Early form of Greek tragedy performed by Thespis		
c.525–c.456 BCE	Aeschylus, playwright		
509–27 BCE			Roman Republic
499–479 BCE			Greco-Persian wars
c.497–c.405 BCE	Sophocles, playwright		
c.480–406 BCE	Euripides, playwright		
460–429 BCE			Periclean age, Athens
c.448–c.387 BCE	Aristophanes, playwright		
431–404 BCE			Peloponnesian War
c.400	*Mahabharata* and *Ramayana*, Sanskrit epics, India		

PART I TIMELINE

DATE	THEATRE and PERFORMANCE	CULTURE and COMMUNICATION	POLITICS and ECONOMICS
c.380 BCE		Plato, *The Republic*	
356–323 BCE			Alexander the Great, Europe and Asia
c.342–c.291 BCE	Menander, playwright		
c.330 BCE	Aristotle, *The Poetics*		
323 BCE–31 CE			Hellenistic period, Europe
c.254–184 BCE	Plautus, playwright		
206 BCE–220 CE			Han dynasty, China
204 BCE–65 CE	Roman drama		
200 BCE–200 CE	Bharata writes *Natyasastra*, India		
196 BCE		Rosetta stone	
c.190–c.159 BCE	Terence, playwright		
27 BCE–476 CE			Roman Empire
27 BCE–14 CE			Caesar Augustus, first emperor of Roman Empire
c.4 BCE–29 CE		Jesus of Nazareth, Middle East/Europe	
c.4 BCE–65 CE	Seneca, playwright		
50–150 CE		Buddhism enters China	
250–710 CE			Yamato period, Japan
250–900 CE			Mayan classical period, Yucatan peninsula
476 CE			Western Roman Empire falls; Eastern (Byzantine) Empire continues
533 CE	Last known theatre performance within the former Roman Empire		
570–632 CE		Mohammed, Middle East	
618–907 CE			Tang dynasty, China
790–1066 CE			Viking exploration
800–1100 CE			Trans-Sahara trade routes
c.900 CE	Chinese story recitation *Kutiyattam* temple theatre, India		
900–1550 CE			Mayan post Classic Period, Yucatan peninsula
c.925 CE	Catholic liturgical tropes		
c.1040 CE		Movable type, China	
1066 CE			Normans (Northern French) conquer England
1095–1099 CE		First Christian crusade against Muslims	
c.1100 CE	Development of carnival, Europe		

PART I TIMELINE

DATE	THEATRE and PERFORMANCE	CULTURE and COMMUNICATION	POLITICS and ECONOMICS
1254–1324 CE		Marco Polo, Italian merchant traveler	
1266–1337 CE		Giotto, artist	
1279–1368 CE			Yuan dynasty, China
1279–1654 CE	*Zaju*, China		
c.1300–c.1400 CE	*Ramlila*, India		
c.1300–c.1600 CE		Renaissance era begins in Italy; spreads throughout Europe in the sixteenth century	
1313–c.1600 CE	Passion plays, continental Europe		
1343–1400 CE		Geoffrey Chaucer, English writer	
c.1350–1569 CE	Cycle plays, England		
1363–1443 CE	Zeami, actor-playwright		
1368–1644 CE			Ming dynasty, China
1368–1644 CE	*Zaju* and *kunqu*, China		
c.1374 CE	*Nō*, Japan		
1428–1521 CE			Aztec Empire, Central America
c.1440 CE	*Rabinal Achi*, Mesoamerica	Movable type (printing press), Europe	
1452–1519 CE		Leonardo da Vinci, artist	
1453 CE			Ottomans capture Constantinople
1456 CE		First printed Bible	
1468–1834 CE			Spanish Inquisition
1475–1564 CE		Michelangelo, artist	
1492 CE			Spanish encounter with the Americas
1492–1898 CE			Spanish colonization of Western Hemisphere
c.1500 CE	Professional theatre companies begin to appear in various European countries		
c.1500–1600 CE	*Kathakali* dance drama, India		

Introduction: Speech, writing, and performance

Tobin Nellhaus

The focus of Part I is the transition from purely oral culture to literate culture. Its three chapters cover roughly 2,000 years of theatre history, from the fifth century BCE to the sixteenth century CE, in order to discuss performance in the context of oral culture and several different literate cultures. The importance and functions of writing varied across the world, and changed over time; as a result, its relationship with oral culture varied, as did its cultural impact. In most of the world, writing's usage and significance were quite limited. However, due to several unusual circumstances, in the fifth century BCE writing attained widespread importance in the city of Athens, Greece. The repercussions could not have been predicted, but they were vast.

Because of the importance of oral culture, we begin Chapter 1 by considering storytelling and ritual, two primary types of performance for over one hundred millennia before writing even existed. Writing first appeared some time around 3,500 BCE in a region of the Middle East. A few centuries later, hieroglyphic writing developed in Egypt. It was learned by portions of the society's upper echelons; the culture as a whole remained predominantly oral. As early as the nineteenth century BCE, a mass religious ceremony in Egypt may have had elements characteristic of theatre. Next we leap forward chronologically in order to discuss performance in

The Rosetta stone displays a decree of 196 BCE in three scripts: ancient Egyptian hieroglyphs, Demotic script, and ancient Greek.

Source: © AKG-images, London.

Central America and southern Mexico, where conditions of literacy were similar to those of ancient Egypt. Some time during the fifteenth century CE, the Mayan people created a performance which commemorated a historical event and appears to have been more like theatre as we know it. We then return to the ancient world to examine the rise of theatre in Athens, where literacy gained a far larger cultural role than ever before. Like Mayan performance, its topics drew from myths and known history, but (perhaps uniquely for the ancient world) it addressed these topics primarily as a way to focus on issues of civic life. In addition, Greek drama was strongly oriented around texts. When classical Greek plays became available in the West again 2,000 years later, they were highly influential, and they are performed even today.

Chapter 2 continues our study of early theatres. Rome in the second and first centuries BCE sought to imitate the culture of Greece, but its tragedies turned from civic commentary to sensationalism, and the comedies shifted from satires toward domestic issues. Eventually interest swung toward violent spectacles such as gladiatorial combat, presented to a mass audience in huge arenas. In classical India (roughly the first through the eleventh centuries CE), theatre was intended to be both popular entertainment and a source of good counsel, and the early plays often drew on two major epics for their narratives. Theatre practitioners in classical India paid exceptional attention to qualities of performance rather than the dramatic text. In the fourteenth century CE, a Japanese troupe offering variety performances came under aristocratic influence and developed a genre of serious drama, which spread across the country. In the course of this development, early Japanese theatre absorbed religious and philosophical ideas. As in India, theatre artists were keenly aware of performance.

The developments in these diverse parts of the world show the highly varied interactions and combinations of literary work and entertainment on the one hand, and elite and popular performance on the other. Those interactions were rooted in the complex interactions between oral culture and literate culture, which played out differently depending on the particular social circumstances.

In Chapter 3, our attention turns primarily to performance in the context of a significant change in literate culture: the rise of religions founded on a set of holy scriptures. Judaism was based on the Torah; Christianity used the Bible, comprising the Torah as the "Old Testament" and many later texts called the New Testament; and Islam's holy book was the Qur'an, a work which assumes knowledge of the Jewish and Christian biblical literature but is a separate set of texts. Unlike spiritual documents in other major religions, these books are considered holy in themselves – unalterable, doctrinal, and even thought to be dictated or revealed directly by God. As a result, these texts occupied extraordinary positions within their cultures and played a crucial role in the cultures' histories. That situation added to the complexity of the relationship between oral culture and literate culture in these societies.

Although the three religions all had a set of holy writings, both literacy and performance developed differently in each. Judaism and early Islam considered literacy part of religious practice, although in some contexts as a support to their oral traditions rather than an independent mode of communication. Jews were an oppressed minority within Europe who had limited opportunities to develop performance practices, but even so, evidence indicates that some Jews acted, and a play was based on a biblical text. Islam reversed its stand on education during the eleventh century and (to a greater or lesser extent) it condemned all representations of people, in theatre and elsewhere; but important types of performance arose nevertheless, such as puppetry. Unlike Judaism and Islam, medieval Christianity had no imperative toward widespread literacy. As in Islam, however, the Church long prohibited theatrical performance. But in the fourteenth century the Church began to find theatre useful, and allowed other types of performance as well. As a result, theatre developed furthest in Christian Europe. Many of the performances within all three religions commemorated events within each religion's sacred literature, honored major events in the religion's history, or enacted the religion's ideas and values. Within Europe there were also important types of wholly secular performance such as farce, and several occasions for boisterous public celebration, feasting, and release, sometimes involving masks and/or role-play.

The prohibition against theatre throughout the history of Islam, for over a millennium in Christianity, and occasionally in Judaism raises a puzzling question: why would a type of performance closely related to the rise of literacy be banned in cultures that depended on writing? The hostility toward theatre was occasionally venomous. For example, a few decades after the medieval Church began encouraging religious drama in England, an unknown author wrote an almost hysterical diatribe against it. It is as though theatre's adversaries found something fundamentally unnerving and disruptive about acting itself. Theatre was too deeply tied to the body and a notion of personal falsity, and so actors were eventually associated with licentious sex and considered similar to or the same as prostitutes. Such disapproval, which surrounded theatre for much of its existence, seems unfamiliar today.

But this **antitheatricality** is quite old. In Part I we consider the beginnings of theatre; however, when we speak of the birth of theatre, it's important to realize that in the Western world, theatre wasn't an only child: antitheatricality was its sibling. Despite its frequent association with religion, antitheatricality isn't strictly a matter of faiths and holy books: it arose soon after the creation of literary theatre itself, in a polytheistic culture without scriptures. In ancient Athens, the philosopher Plato (*c.*428–*c.*347 BCE), writing at a time when Greek drama was at its height, strongly condemned theatre, along with painting, sculpture, poetry, indeed anything that smelled of what he called *mimesis* (imitation). In fact, he decried writing as inferior to speech. Yet paradoxically, despite his distrust of writing, Plato wrote books, and stranger still, he wrote his books as dialogues – as near to drama as one can get without actual performance. Most ironically of all, according to classical scholar Eric Havelock (1963), Plato's antagonism toward theatre arose from the way literacy shaped his concept of rationality. And as Jonas Barish (1981) has shown, these are not the only peculiarities in Plato's antitheatrical arguments.

Plato's prosecution of theatre was based on the belief that true reality is to be found in abstractions, not in the embodied material world. From this assumption, Plato staged two fundamental attacks on the stage. On the one hand, philosophically, Plato construed theatre's fictions as lies, or at best, feeble imitations of the truth. Thus theatre trades in illusions and falsehoods, and the actor in particular violates personal identity by pretending to be someone else. On the other hand, moralistically, if truth resides in abstractions, then the mind as the seat of reason sharply contrasts with the body as the realm of unreason, passion, pleasures, and desires. Theatre, then, wrongly encourages audiences to enjoy unruly emotions and improper ideas instead of conducting rational thought.

Plato's antitheatrical ideas passed down through the centuries within Christianity, and they may also be the origin of antitheatricality in Islam. To a greater or lesser extent, mimesis was seen as an affront to God. The philosophical and moralistic strands did not always have the same importance – in fact the moralistic stance was usually expressed more vigorously – but they were always intertwined.

But why did Plato's antitheatrical prejudice arise in the first place, and why did later cultures accept it? Most likely several factors lay behind the sometimes panicky assaults on theatre in the Western world. According to Havelock, one reason for Plato's animosity is that when writing developed in ancient Greece, it created a break with oral culture and reshaped the reasoning process. Plato was creating an analytical, "objective" mode of thought based on literacy, and opposed to the more "subjective," participatory oral culture, and mimesis was intrinsic to orality's participatory nature (1963: 36–49). It appears that not only is there a connection between theatre and writing, there is also a connection between antitheatricality and writing.

Yet as we noted, in Plato's opinion speech is superior to writing and more closely aligned with truth and nature. At first glance, Plato seems to be contradicting himself, opposing oral culture on one hand but supporting it with the other. However, his opposition was not to all parts of oral culture, but to its embodied, performative element. In contrast, for Plato writing was intrinsically objectionable because the written word is secondary, an imitation (mimesis) of speech sounds – living speech bore truth. The philosopher Jacques Derrida uses the term "phonocentrism" to describe this view of writing as mimetic, and it has persisted even to the present. The logic of phonocentrism, Derrida observes, leads to antitheatricality, because it construes theatre as fundamentally mimetic as well. Thus both phonocentrism and anti-theatricality derived from the phonetic nature of alphabetic writing (1974: 304–7).

The embodiment necessary to communication in oral cultures seems to have long been distasteful or outright abhorrent to thinkers who believed that writing allowed the mind to become disembodied, creating a sharp body/mind division. However, this aversion arises not only when thinkers take a phonocentric position, but also when they prefer the written word. Some people have maintained that drama is best read as literature, unconnected with performance. The earliest instance is also from ancient Greece. Despite Plato, theatre remained popular there, and as a result it wasn't long before a more positive view of drama appeared in philosophy: Plato's former student Aristotle (384–322 BCE) argued that mimesis and the pleasure we take in it are vital to human learning, and based on this perspective he wrote the first dramatic theory in history. But notably, Aristotle preferred the dramatic text over its performance, reiterating a form of antitheatricality.

Today, when actors are among the greatest celebrities and can even become presidents, antitheatricality may seem utterly foreign and archaic. Closer examination shows otherwise. We saw in the General Introduction that both "drama" and "theatre" are sometimes applied metaphorically. Some of those uses are decidedly derogatory. For example, a person who behaves over-emotionally might be called a "drama queen." Public events or statements meant mainly to impress people are occasionally described as "theatre," such as in "The candidate's demand for a recount was just political theatre" or, deplorably, "*kabuki* theatre," insinuating that a Japanese genre is especially devious. The modern meanings of "hypocrite" and "histrionic" have antitheatrical roots as well. (The looser term "performance" generally has more positive associations.) The common view that drama should be studied strictly as literature, not in connection with performance, denigrates theatre as well.

Even in the history of Western theatre, key figures such as the seventeenth-century English dramatist Ben Jonson and the early twentieth-century French performer and writer Antonin Artaud have been sharply conflicted about theatricality. Performance art, a genre which emerged in the late twentieth century, has always spurned theatre. Strangely enough, antitheatricality can appear within theatricality itself.

Thus the history of theatre in the West is shadowed by an antitheatricality founded on the history of writing. In contrast, generally speaking, non-Western societies seem to have taken much more straightforward pleasure in performance. Although people in classical India, China, and Japan sometimes scorned actors and classed them with prostitutes just as in the West, they seem to have done so out of a fear of social disorder or class mixing, not a deep-seated suspicion of theatre as such. Why they didn't develop an antitheatrical prejudice is an open question. The absence of Plato's influence was undoubtedly one factor, but probably there were other reasons – perhaps a more fluid relationship between oral and literate culture. We do not yet know. But as we begin surveying theatre's histories, we should be aware that it has always been dense with complexities rooted in fundamental communication practices.

★

CHAPTER 1

From oral to literate performance

Tobin Nellhaus

Contributors: Phillip B. Zarrilli, Tamara Underiner, and Bruce McConachie

Nobody knows for certain how theatre began. Probably nobody ever will. But we do know some things about the earliest forms of theatre and about types of performance that preceded theatre. One increasingly evident element is that performance is shaped by communication practices. For tens or hundreds of millennia, the primary mode of communication – and the only one for language – was speech, usually accompanied by gesture. In oral cultures, the major forms of performance are ritual and storytelling. As we will see, characteristics of these performance genres are affected by the nature of live speech, which fosters certain strategies of thought. Writing first appeared around 3600–3400 BCE in Mesopotamia (a region within the Middle East), and slowly spread or was separately invented elsewhere. However, for thousands of years writing was so embedded within oral culture that it had few if any cognitive effects. Eventually new ways of thinking did arise, and with them a new form of performance: theatre.

But oral modes of performance are by no means "primitive" or solely part of the past: they are dynamic and adaptable practices that continue to shape people's personal and social identities, plus many other aspects of human thought and culture. Ritual and storytelling in particular remain important to this day. Likewise, the introduction of literate culture did not create a form of performance that was utterly separate from oral culture. The relationship between spoken and written communication is complex and varies depending on its social context, and it can be marked by a degree of tension, which sometimes is visible in performance itself, particularly during the transition from an oral to a literate culture. The presence of oral culture in literate culture is one of the primary reasons for discussing ritual and storytelling when examining the earliest forms of theatre.

In this chapter we will focus on how the introduction of writing affected performance, by considering four different communication contexts. First we will discuss ritual and storytelling in oral cultures. Then we will turn to a possibly theatrical ceremony in ancient Egypt, and a play-like performance in Mayan society (located in Central America and southern Mexico) –

two cultures which used writing but restricted it to a small number of people. Finally, we will look at theatre in ancient Greece, the earliest society where literacy was relatively widespread and figured in everyday life. Surveying these four contexts will suggest how the role and importance of writing varies from culture to culture, affecting numerous facets of performance. Even though we may not be able to identify theatre's origins, these social and cultural differences can help explain some of early theatre's known and likely characteristics.

THINKING THROUGH THEATRE HISTORIES

The problem of beginnings

Nothing in human society ever sprang from thin air, and so historians often want to learn how an activity began or what led to it. Starting in the 1870s, many people have asked that question about theatre, and in particular about Greek tragedy, for which we have more evidence than any other kind of ancient theatre. The question has three sides: identifying theatre's predecessor; explaining the process of change; and describing the relationship between theatre and its predecessor.

What *was* theatre's predecessor? There have been many answers, most of them anthropological. Probably the most popular answer has been religious ritual. One reason for this theory is that, as we will see, Greek tragedy had some sort of connection to the cult of the god Dionysus in the city of Athens (exactly what has been disputed). Other people have suggested that theatre originated in choral songs. But by the 1960s classical scholars had debunked the original forms of both of these theories because of major problems or gaps in their supporting evidence, the presence of contradicting evidence, and significant logical flaws. However, revised versions continue, and we will discuss a few ideas connected to them. Another answer has been hero worship, in which people honored dead heroes and kings by imitating events in their lives. This view has a somewhat stronger basis, but it doesn't have a firm grounding in our historical and archaeological knowledge about ancient Greece. A very different theory came from classical scholar Gerald Else, who argued that the major precedent for tragedy was a speech by Athens' leader Solon, in which he impersonated another man, a precedent that was developed further by others (Else 1965: 39–45). The evidence here is less speculative than in the other theories – but what makes Else's theory work well for Athens makes it less applicable to other places, which has limited its acceptance. Other theories have also been proposed.

The second side of any question about predecessors is the process of change and its possible implications. For example, if we accepted the popular (but dubious) "religious ritual" theory of theatre's inception, we should clarify how the one developed into the other. Did the development occur in a smooth or incremental progression of a more or less evolutionary nature? If so, then religious ritual and theatre probably existed (and perhaps still exist) along a continuum. In contrast, Else's view involves individuals taking distinct, innovative steps in order to accomplish something that couldn't be achieved with the existing forms of performance. Accordingly, religious ritual wouldn't be theatre's ancestor or origin, merely an antecedent. Theatre could be fundamentally different from ritual – a revolutionary cultural form. (Some scholars dismiss the process of change altogether, more or less saying "First there

continued

was religious ritual/choral songs/hero worship, then there was theatre, therefore there must be a connection even though we don't know how the former became the latter" – a version of the *post hoc* argument discussed in the General Introduction.)

Finally, one must consider the relationship between theatre and its predecessor. For example, what does it mean to say that X is the "origin" of theatre? Is that the same as saying it's the "earliest type" of theatre? One claim is that theatre's origin remains the essence of theatre itself (e.g., "theatre is fundamentally a religious ritual"). A converse view is that the origin was just the starting point: theatre was the goal or the final form of the previous activity ("ritual is fundamentally theatre"). A related position is that the origin of theatre is what caused it to develop. The validity of this idea depends on what the origin is thought to be: for example, if religious ritual is the origin of theatre, clearly it didn't drive theatre to become a more vigorous form of religion, so it probably didn't cause theatre to develop; a type of performance that strove for (say) social self-reflection would be more likely to generate what we now recognize as theatre. Theatre's predecessors could also be the "raw material" – the familiar activities – that people reworked when they created theatre. There are still further possibilities. Different ideas about the beginnings of theatre aren't mutually exclusive: much depends on what one is examining, and even on how one defines theatre. For instance, one can reject the ritual theory of theatre's origin yet believe that ritual and theatre exist on a continuum, so that each has qualities of the other. Likewise, one can hold that certain features are essential to all theatre, including the very earliest, but something else caused theatre to arise.

Theatre Histories focuses on the connections between the development of theatre and changes in communication. It seems likely that the activities involved in writing fostered methods of thinking that conflicted with oral culture's typical cognitive strategies, which appeared in cultural forms such as ritual and storytelling. In some societies the tension between the two modes of communication grew great enough to require new cultural forms, one of which was theatre – a fusion of oral performance and written text. But because some of oral culture's practices were adapted in order to create theatre, many of its features continued. Depending on how writing was used in a particular society, those elements of oral culture either remained more or less central to culture, or faded over several centuries until the spread of literacy made them unnecessary or possibly even undesirable. Although we cannot say that this theory has been definitively proven, understanding oral culture does help us understand several characteristics of early theatre. As we will see throughout this book, subsequent changes in communication practices similarly seem to have led to alterations in later forms of theatre.

Performance in oral cultures

For anyone silently reading this book (and for its authors too), it is difficult or impossible to completely grasp what oral culture is like because our own manner of thinking is already shaped by literacy. People unfamiliar with oral culture sometimes assume it is simply a relative of literate culture, or view it is a primitive form of thought devoid of abstraction and logical reasoning. However, studies conducted in Africa by cultural anthropologists, analyses of epic poetry from places ranging from ancient Greece to modern Serbia, and various other types of research have demonstrated that neither view is correct. Oral cultures can be sophisticated, but their methods of conceptualizing the world and people's relationships to it are very different from those common in highly literate societies. The research helps us to imagine what life and performance were like in cultures without writing and reading, and to see that some forms or features of oral culture exist in every culture today.

Many of oral culture's characteristics arise from practical aspects of speech. A living person has to be present to speak, and another there to listen. Words use tones and rhythms, they can create rhymes or assonance, they can be spoken softly or loudly. Speech uses not only the mouth, throat, and chest, but also facial expressions and usually gestures and other movements, potentially involving the whole body. One learns from others primarily by listening to them, so the sense of hearing has special importance. And crucially, speech only exists in the moment: after that, there is only memory. Consequently, in oral cultures, knowledge, historical legend, religious beliefs, mythology, and all other aspects of culture must be passed on by elders and by "cultural specialists" such as shamans and storytellers.

Memory aids in oral cultures

If knowledge in oral cultures can only be stored in memory and transmitted through speech, how is that done? Although people in wholly oral cultures relied on their memories more than people in literate cultures and excellent memory was often prized, it was unusual to need verbatim recollection. Sometimes verbatim memorization did occur; for an example, see the discussion of the Indian Vedas in the "Primary Orality" essay on the *Theatre Histories* website. But in most circumstances, such precision was unnecessary. The essential goal was to express ideas in a way that made them easily remembered and easily learned.

Various techniques can aid memory, as we can see from a scene from the ancient Greek epic poem *The Odyssey* (eighth century BCE), which was composed orally. *The Odyssey* recounts the warrior Odysseus's lengthy travel home from the Trojan War (which occurred between Greece and a part of modern Turkey probably during the thirteenth century BCE; *The Iliad* tells that story). In this scene, Odysseus's son Telemachos is travelling with the goddess Athena in search of his long-missing father. They arrive at the town of Pylos, and Athena advises Telemachos to ask Nestor (who knew Odysseus) if he has heard anything about his father's fate.

> Then the thoughtful Telemachos said to her in answer:
> "Mentor, how shall I go up to him, how close with him?
> I have no experience in close discourse. There is
> embarrassment for a young man who must question his elder."
> Then in turn the gray-eyed goddess Athena answered him:
> "Telemachos, some of it you yourself will see in your own heart,
> and some the divinity will put in your mind. I do not
> think you could have been born and reared without the gods' will."
> So spoke Pallas Athena, and she led the way swiftly,
> and the man followed behind her walking in the god's footsteps.
> They came to where the men of Pylos were gathered in session,
> where Nestor was sitting with his sons, and companions about him

were arranging the feast, and roasting the meat, and [skewering] more portions.
These men, when they sighted the strangers, all came down together
and gave them greeting with their hands and offered them places.
First Peisistratos, son of Nestor, came close up to him
and took them both by the hands, and seated them at the feasting
on soft rugs of fleece there on the sand of the seashore
next to his brother Thrasymedes and next to his father.

(Homer 1967: 51–2)

This single excerpt provides examples of many of the strategies that oral cultures use to preserve and transmit ideas:

- *Verbal patterns, such as rhyme, rhythm, and formulas.* Ancient Greek oral poetry did not use rhyme, but it did use rhythm, usually called "meter" (not replicated in the translation). Verbal patterns may also appear in everyday speech. Maxims, for instance, often use parallel phrases that can be memorized almost immediately (e.g., "Early to bed, early to rise"). By putting words to music, a bard or "singer of tales" patterns language further, which can increase the retention of cultural knowledge. Set phrases or "formulas" serve a similar role. In *The Odyssey* and *The Iliad*, for example, one finds recurrent formulas such as "said to her in answer," "the gray-eyed goddess Athena" and "rosy fingered dawn."
- *Stereotypical characters, scenes, and stories.* Epithets such as "thoughtful Telemachos" and "resourceful Odysseus" highlight the fact that characters in oral cultures tend to be character types: the wise, the evil, the innocent, the furious, and so forth. Character types do not have personalities in the modern sense: they are not "deep" or inwardly complex, they do not possess intricate private lives, nor do they mature with experience. They are "flat" because their nature is outward and publicly defined – which they must be, in order to communicate something memorable that can be passed down through the generations as a tale. Similarly, there are "type scenes": standard events such as holding a feast or receiving a guest (in this excerpt, both), which can be adapted as needed.
- *Strong, strange, and symbolic imagery.* Character stereotypes such as those indicated by epithets condense personal traits down to one or two strong qualities that are readily remembered. Even more memorable than character types are strange and unnatural images, such as the many-armed Hindu goddess Kali, and Greek mythology's multi-headed monster Scylla. Although the excerpt above does not involve strange images, many appear elsewhere in *The Odyssey*, including Scylla. Such images may possess symbolic aspects: for example, Scylla probably represented a geographical location, since she is associated with the Strait of Messina between Italy and Sicily; Kali's arms and what each hand holds all have religious meanings. Symbolic elements make it possible for an image to pack a vast amount of knowledge, which one can recall by decoding the image's parts.
- *Narrative development through episodes.* Typically, long oral narratives consist of many episodes strung together. One event follows another without a necessary causal or logical connection, just an (actual or implied) "and then." As a result, one could skip Telemachos's visit to Pylos or the Cyclops episode in *The Odyssey* without radically harming the overall story of Odysseus. A narrative constructed from independent modules is easier to work with than a plotline having a closely knit causal sequence where skipping a scene could

render the story incoherent. Episodes also allow storytellers to adapt tales to the occasion, the audience, and the time available. However, sometimes stories follow a standard structure – another example of patterning to simplify the work of memory and communicating thoughts. One of the most common narrative structures involves three steps, often distinguished by the major characters (such as the "Three Little Pigs"), personal interactions (lovers meet, separate, and rejoin), or objects (porridge that's too hot, too cold, and just right).

- *Codified gestures, actions, and bodily movements.* Customary physical actions can mark an event as memorable, identify relationships among people, and enact a culture's understanding of relationships among people or between people and the rest of the world; often they accomplish all of these things at once. Examples of customary behaviors range from a bow upon meeting or a handshake that seals an agreement, to the use of beads (such as a rosary) to repeat prayers a set number of times, to welcoming ceremonies, to ritual performances involving chants, dances, offerings to gods or ancestors, contests, and other sorts of activities. Inviting a stranger to a feast and giving them pride of place, as happens in the passage above, is a "type scene" laden with moral and religious values regarding the treatment of guests, teaching the audience the culture's mores. Our embodied interactions with the world also give us ways of understanding it. For instance, human bodies are symmetrical, providing the opposition between left and right, and our sense of balance, which we apply elsewhere. Other contrasts include night and day, male and female, hot and cold, and so forth. Thus in oral culture, ideas and expressions often involve pairing one thing against another.

The techniques described above are only some of the features of oral communication, but they show that in order to preserve ideas, the structure of thought in oral culture must be very different from its structure in literate culture. But the difference does not lie simply in how one phrases language or constructs a story. Oral techniques orient an understanding of the world itself. Characters, for example, are not simply flat or externally oriented because that's the easiest way to transmit them through history: people are actually understood as being psychologically flat or outward. In Europe, people only start to have psychological "depth" at the close of the Middle Ages and particularly during the Renaissance. We will recount that history in Chapter 5. (To read more about how oral cultures interpret the world, see the essay "Ritual" on the *Theatre Histories* website.) Yet despite these crucial differences, verse, three-step narratives, codified behaviors, and other features of oral culture continue to play a role in human culture to the present. This is one example of the way that cultural elements connected to one mode of communication may endure when a new mode of communication arises.

Oral cultures vary in all sorts of ways, because many different social structures play a role in cultural development: economic systems, gender relations, political structures, religions, and more. But all oral cultures develop two major types of performance: storytelling and ritual. Whether they are the "origins" of theatre or part of its "raw materials," storytelling and ritual are part of the background of oral culture that fed into the development of theatre.

Storytelling and ritual in oral cultures

Storytelling occurs in all cultures throughout history. Most tales are brief, but some can be quite lengthy. Many ancient cultures produced extended epics, such as *Gilgamesh* (Sumeria, eighteenth century BCE), *Mahabharata* (India, eighth or ninth century BCE), *Beowulf* (England, seventh century CE), *The Epic of King Gesar* (Tibet, twelfth century CE), and *Popol Vuh* (Central America/southern Mexico, date unknown). In an oral culture, everyone would be familiar with many of the stories that occurred in an epic and probably could link several together, but in some societies a few people learned numerous stories and made storytelling their vocation. Often these "cultural specialists" delivered their stories with musical accompaniment or in song. Storytellers could become highly skilled not only in recounting tales, but also in selecting episodes to suit the audience and occasion, improvising stories, and even commenting on current events. However, other societies did not develop the specialized role of storytellers; possibly their economy could not support even itinerant bards, or the shorter tales in their cultural repertory were sufficient for their needs.

An example of storytellers today is a notable group in western Africa (mainly in what is now Mali) known as griots (Figure 1.1). Griots could be male or female. The earliest reference to them was in 1352 CE, but they undoubtedly existed much earlier. "Storyteller" hardly begins to cover their numerous roles: sometimes described as bards or wordsmiths, they also served (and to some extent continue to serve) as historians, genealogists, praise-singers, advisors, spokespersons, diplomats, mediators, interpreters, musicians, composers, teachers, and other social functions. While any adult can perform most of a griot's general activities, professional griots are more skilled, knowledgeable, and engaging. They also tell lengthier stories, some

Figure 1.1

Mali: this Zoumana hunter is also a fetisher and griot.

Source: © Hemis/Alamy.

exceptionally long. The longest recorded has almost 8,000 lines of verse; for comparison, *Beowulf* has roughly 3,200 lines, and *The Odyssey* has about 12,000 lines. The griots' epics have features shared by epics around the world – the requirements of this genre are very consistent, following the techniques described above (Hale 1998: 18–58, 135, 137).

Notably, storytellers usually present characters' dialogues not by enacting the characters, as an actor plays roles, but via quoted speech. For instance, in the scene from *The Odyssey* that we excerpted above, there are the phrases "the thoughtful Telemachos said to her in answer" and "Then in turn the gray-eyed goddess Athena answered him." The storyteller quotes what the characters said, rather than speaking as them. Sometimes the quoted speech is lengthy, such as when Odysseus recounts his voyage. Within his story, Odysseus himself quotes others' speech in the same manner. Only occasionally do storytellers directly speak as a character. Since the 1970s theatre has occasionally used quoted speech, but normally actors speak as the character. This is a significant distinction between storytelling and theatre. However, theatre shares storytelling's focus on narrative.

Along with storytelling, a crucial form of oral culture is ritual. Ritual is a form of performance that draws participants' minds to ideas and feelings that have special social (often religious) importance. Rituals are essential for preserving a culture's memory of its identity, character, and beliefs. Both oral and literate cultures have rituals; literate societies can accomplish many of the same ends in other ways, but they still have rituals. Rituals can honor spiritual beings such as gods, spirits, or ancestors; conduct a rite of passage to mark an important life change such as puberty, marriage, or death; affirm or create a relationship toward someone (e.g., to a king or a guest) or a social commitment (an oath, an agreement); spiritually purify a space, object, or person; demonstrate power; confer political office; and serve many other purposes.

There are varying interpretations of ritual's primary social function, such as building cohesion within a society, hiding or justifying oppressive social relationships by giving them supernatural explanations and meanings, or creating opportunities to negotiate and sometimes transform social relationships. Whichever function(s) ritual serves, most societies require cultural specialists to lead them. At one end of the spectrum are shamans, who mediate between humans and the spirit world, heal people, and know most of the culture's mythology and history – but often live like everyone else in the village. (Occasionally most of the villagers can perform some shamanic duties, so the degree of specialization can be slight.) At the other end of the spectrum, a distinct priestly class arises with high entrance requirements demanding years of preparation through chants and other practices.

Ritual interests many people who study theatre because of its performative, "theatrical" character. In contrast to storytelling, rituals may involve the impersonation or embodiment of deities, which is similar to the enactment of character in theatre; however, unlike both storytelling and theatre, rituals usually present or refer to very brief narratives, such as a single incident from a lengthy story already known to the participants. Rituals usually involve a special set of symbolic objects, words, or sounds (such as drumming), which create an element of spectacle. Often there are well-established rules of procedure or behavior, but sometimes the rules are loose, and ritual events can even provide a license to playfulness and misbehavior. The case study on Yoruba ritual presents an interpretation of the *Egúngún* masquerade highlighting the importance of play. As we will see, *Egúngún* also incorporates many of the discursive techniques of oral culture.

CASE STUDY: Yoruba ritual as "play," and "contingency" in the ritual process

Phillip B. Zarrilli

> Aiyé l'ojà, òrun n'ilé.
> ("The world is a market, the otherworld is home.")
> (Drewal and Drewal 1983: 2)

If this world is a market, and one's permanent residence is the otherworld, then life in this world is contingent and transitory. For the Yoruba, life in this world is a constant process of

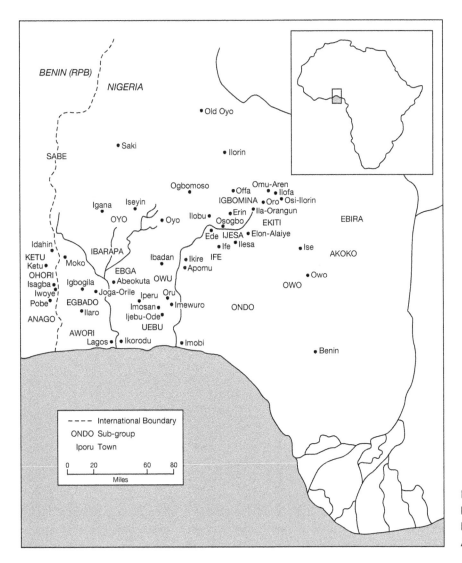

Figure 1.2

Map: The Yoruba of Nigeria and Benin, West Africa.

balancing or "playing" with and between opposing forces. The term "Yoruba" has been used only since the nineteenth century to identify a large, socially and culturally diverse set of subgroups speaking many dialects of Yoruba. The Yoruba peoples are spread across the coastal region of West Africa (Togo, Benin, and western Nigeria) (Figure 1.2). They are also in diasporic communities in Brazil, Cuba, and the United States.

Balance and symmetry (which, as we have noted, frequently appear in oral cultures) are central to Yoruba religion and are embedded in all aspects of Yoruba life – dance, speech, and ritual. Traditional Yoruba deities who have boundless energy and provoke action are classified as "hot," and must be counterbalanced by those who are "cool" – "whose strength is in the patience and gentleness they radiate" (Ajayi 1998: 38). Ésù, the capricious trickster god of the crossroads, and Orúnmìlà, the god of fate, are two opposites who complement one another, as reflected in the Yoruba's primordial creation myth. Dances of all types are informed by an aesthetic of balance and symmetry – in practice, a constant process of shifting between right and left. Indeed, Yoruba society does not expect rigid conformity, but "appreciates occasional lapses and personal idiosyncrasies" (Ajayi 1998: 29). This is also evidenced in the delight people take when engaging in both èdà-òrò (inverted discourse) and in the indirect handling of the "truths" of riddles and proverbs – a trait some Westerners ethnocentrically deride as "never straightforward" (Ajayi 1998: 31).

Some rituals are highly prescriptive in form, inviting absorption of ritual specialists in the intricacies of the repetition of highly codified scores. While all rituals have a structure, not all ritual structures possess a rigid score. Indeed, Yoruba ritual practices are founded on the transformative possibilities of ritual becoming a "journey" for its participants. Through ritual, deep learning may occur by "playing" in the moment.

The concept of Yoruba ritual (ètùtu) encompasses "annual festivals (odún), weekly rites (òsè), funerals (ìsìnkú), divinations (idáfá), and initiations and installations of all kinds" (Drewal 1992: 19). As Margaret Thompson Drewal explains, Yoruba say they go to "play" ritual, that is to say they spontaneously "improvise" dance steps or rhythmic patterns, and improvise through parody, elaboration, or invention. Some forms of improvisation are obvious, such as when the Yoruba incorporate in their Egúngún [EH-goon-goon] masquerade festival (described below) parodies of Western behavior or dress, using tuxedos or Second World War gas masks, for example.

Journey as a metaphor for this contingent life is embedded in all Yoruba ritual, as reflected in the final two lines of these verses by diviner Kolawole Ositola:

> We are going in search of knowledge, truth, and justice . . .
> We are searching for knowledge continuously.
> (Ajayi 1998: 33)

This is not a journey from predetermined point A to point Z, but rather a life-long processual journey of exploration and discovery through which consciousness is to be transformed.

Egúngún *masquerade spectacle*

The masquerade spectacle Egúngún, which honors the spirits of ancestors, is one of the many forms of Yoruba ritual. On publicly announced dates set by diviners, Egúngún festivals are organized by Egúngún societies and held in the open air in villages or towns annually,

THINKING THROUGH THEATRE HISTORIES

Theories of play and improvisation

In her study of Yoruba ritual, Margaret Thompson Drewal asserts that "playing is the power Yoruba actors exercise in transforming ritual itself, and indeed it may be more precise to say that ritual structures, or strategies, have no existence apart from the tactics, or play, of actors. It is in play that ritual's very efficacy resides" (Drewal 1992: 28). Here Drewal is counteracting many earlier anthropological accounts of ritual that overemphasize structure, convention, rigidity, and the role that "rules" play in the efficacy of ritual.

Drewal adopts an "actor-centered approach" focused on "the relationship between actors and the forms they operate on" (Drewal and Drewal 1983: xvi). She locates the "power" of ritual not in the structure, but in the active engagement of the individual "actor" within the experience of the structure as it is performed/practiced. Drewal emphasizes the way in which the Yoruba people situate the contingency of "playing" and improvisation as central to both their worldview and their engagement of ritual structures. Her analysis relates to the general theories of play as developed by sociologists Johan Huizinga (1970), Roger Callois (1979), and Brian Sutton-Smith (1997). Theories of play emphasize the enjoyment of engaging, stretching, and breaking rule-governed activities. Given its ephemeral mode of engagement "in the moment," this idea of "play" is usually lost in the writing of theatre histories. But the joy of "playing" or "attending to play" is central to the moment of both ritual and theatrical performance. An "actor-centered" approach to the study of performance histories necessarily will mean attempting to understand and interpret what cultural actors experience and how they engage in the moment of performance/practice.

biannually, or on the occasion of a funeral. Each occasion is unique, with great variation in the numbers and types of masked and unmasked performers that appear, in the order of performance, and in the type, range, and quality of audience engagement. During performances, the spectators' attention is drawn to what is happening in particular (often improvised) moments rather than to "repetition of a stock formal segment" (Drewal 1992: 93).

Egúngún begins at night in the center of the town when a spirit (Agan) "brings the festival into the world" (Drewal and Drewal 1983: 2). *Egúngún* society members invoke the elusive Agan into the world by using percussion instruments to simulate the "actual dynamic qualities" Agan possesses. He is likened to the "[small, quick, light, drizzling] . . . early night rain" (1983: 2–4). It is forbidden that anyone see Agan's entry into the world; therefore, all non-members must lock themselves in their houses as Agan is beckoned. The first rhythms played on the *bata* drum summoning ancestors or deities for this and other festivals are called *alùwási*, literally "drums come into the world."

Egúngún is an opportunity for the unseen ancestral spirits to visit. Performers are understood to possess *àse*, the "activating force or energy" (Drewal and Drewal 1983: 5), with "the power to bring things into existence" (Drewal 1992: 90). *Egúngún* performances weave together a series of equal, but quite different stylistic and thematic segments (modules), each of which has its own independent origin myth.

Figure 1.3

The masks worn in *Egúngún* are called *idan*, literally meaning "miracle." The "miracle" depicted here represents Gorilla, a character that figures significantly in *Egúngún* origin myths. Egbado area, town of Imasai, December 23, 1977.

Source: Margaret Drewal, *Yoruba Ritual*, p. 161, by kind permission of Indiana University Press.

These myths are available to the performance as source traditions, but each occasion of performance is a completely unique negotiation of that past with the present. Drewal witnessed the appearance of four maskers in a performance in the Nigerian town of Imasai, one of whom appeared as the Gorilla (*Inoki*), with "naturalistically carved wooden testicles and a penis painted red on the tip" (Drewal 1992: 93) (Figure 1.3). He represented a character that features significantly in the *Egúngún* origin myth in which a gorilla rapes Iya Mose, who thereby gives birth to a half-human, half-monkey child. The child eventually grows up to be "'One-Who-Brings-Sweetness' to the community" (Drewal 1992: 92). At this performance, Gorilla "sneaks up behind unsuspecting women in the performing space, raising his penis as if he is going to rape them" to the sound of the drums (*sabala-sabala-sa-o*) simulating the sounds of Gorilla's sexual movements. Because the attention of spectators was focused elsewhere, the Gorilla masker was able to catch out women in the audience, much to the amusement of the other spectators.

We can see the underlying creativity and sense of play informing Yoruba ritual in many other examples of improvisational intervention, especially when a segment of *Egúngún* is a competitive performance where individual skills and techniques are tested. So fluid is an *Egúngún* masquerade that master performers "continue to refine their skills," while "neophytes learn in plain sight of everyone" (Drewal 1992: 89). At the end of the festival, a spirit known as Aránta or Olodúngbódún "carries the spectacle back to the otherworld" (Drewal and Drewal 1983: 4). The playful improvisation at the heart of Yoruba practice points to an important dimension of many historical forms of ritual. It has allowed the Yoruba to creatively interact with and respond to neighboring peoples by creating items such as the mask of the Hausa Meat Seller, or to changing historical circumstances, such as the introduction of Islam and European colonialism. The modern play *Death and the King's Horseman* (1975) by Nigerian playwright and Nobel Laureate Wole Soyinka (discussed in Chapter 13) incorporates *Egúngún* as part of his critique of European colonialism.

To read more about ritual and shamanic performance, see the essay "Ritual Places and Performances" and the case study "Korean Shamanism and the Power of Speech" on the *Theatre Histories* website.

Key references

Ajayi, O.S. (1998) *Yoruba Dance*, Trenton, NJ: Africa World Press.

Apter, A. (1992) *Black Critics and Kings: The Hermeneutics of Power in Yoruba Society*, Chicago: University of Chicago Press.

Callois, R. (1979) *Man, Play, and Games*, New York: Schocken Books.

Drewal, M.J. and Drewal, M.T. (1983) *Gelede: Art and Female Power Among the Yoruba*, Bloomington: Indiana University Press.

Drewal, M.T. (1992) *Yoruba Ritual: Performers, Play, Agency*, Bloomington: Indiana University Press.

Huizinga, J. (1970) *Homo Ludens*, New York: Harper.

Sutton-Smith, B. (1997) *The Ambiguity of Play*, Cambridge, MA: Harvard University Press.

Performance in oral cultures with writing

Writing has a complex history and has taken a variety of forms. The basic systems are logograms, syllabaries, and alphabets. Logograms use a simple image or (frequently) an abstract symbol to represent a whole word, the way that ☼ means "sun" and the emoticon ;-) means "wink." Syllabaries utilize a character for each syllable, phonetically, such as *ba* and *ta*. And alphabets give each individual speech sound its own letter, like *t* and *u*. We will discuss a few of these below, and we offer a more detailed discussion of the history of language and the invention of writing in the essay "Human Speech and Early Writing" on the website.

In societies where writing developed, it stimulated economic and cultural growth. In many cases, eventually it also transformed people's thinking processes and their methods of preserving knowledge. The extent, character, and rapidity of that transformation differed according to the context. In some societies, writing fostered new forms of performance such as theatre or something similar to it, providing distinctive ways of encountering myths, epics, or narratives. This section examines performance in two ancient societies which used writing but kept it restricted to a small group of people (generally rulers, scribes, and priests), often for limited purposes. Important as those individuals often were, their literacy had little significant impact on people outside the courts and temples. Our first example of performance in such a culture is the "Passion Play" of Abydos, Egypt, which may or may not have been theatre. The second is the Maya's *Rabinal Achi*, which in many respects seems to be a play. At the end of the chapter we will discuss performance in a society where writing was relatively widespread and used for numerous purposes: classical Greece.

The sequence of our discussion (Egypt, the Mayan Empire, Greece) does not signal progress or evolution. For example, there is no evidence that ancient Greek theatre had once been similar to the Abydos "Passion Play": clearly it had a different path of invention. Instead, we are looking at forms of performance in connection with the relationship between literacy and orality in three societies. Both Egypt and Mesoamerica used forms of writing that were difficult to learn, and literacy extended only to a small elite. In Athens, however, because Greece used the more assimilable alphabetic script, literacy spread far more widely than was possible anywhere else at the time. The differences between these societies' uses of writing had consequences for their development of performance.

The ancient Egyptian and Mayan societies had the strongest commonalities. Public life was organized around elaborate annual religious festivals featuring commemorative celebrations, rituals, and other performances, held on specific dates in the sacred calendar. Some of these performances were highly choreographed and were believed necessary for maintaining social, civic, and cosmic cohesion. The idea that performances could have such power is related to the nature of religion in these early societies, which was less a matter of personal faith than the duties and actions which the gods or spirits required in order to receive their due and keep the universe in balance. To the religions of oral cultures, voice and gesture – especially in ritual – are themselves powerful, a view that could extend to other types of performance.

Many early forms of drama or quasi-dramatic activities were part of commemorative religious ceremonies that celebrated or re-enacted a fundamental mythological, cosmic, or historical event, or a source of power. Commemorative ceremonies sometimes provided dramatic means of encountering a religious power or a past event in the present, reminding a community of "its identity as represented by and told in a master narrative . . . making sense of [its] past as a kind of collective autobiography" (Connerton 1989: 70). Commemorative dramas may be enacted to honor appropriate deities; to pacify cosmic or natural forces; to enhance communication with the divine; or to commemorate mythic, quasi-historical, or historical moments in the society's history.

Although great artistry and imagination may be involved in the creation of commemorative ceremonies, artistic merit usually isn't the primary goal. Rather, these works are performed to enhance the relationship of the community or the individual to the divine, or to achieve a ritual purpose. Nevertheless, some early types of formalized performance are highly sophisticated works of art, combining enactment, music or song, and dance or movement. They employ non-realistic modes of representation in acting, staging, and costuming (including masking and makeup) in order to depict larger-than-life figures, such as epic heroes, gods, and ghosts, and the boundaries between spectating and participating may be blurred. We will see additional examples of commemorative performance in Chapter 3, most of them in cultures more affected by literacy; here we will consider two that arose in the context of highly restricted literacy.

Commemorative ritual "drama" in Abydos, Egypt

The religious background

By 3000 BCE, Egyptian civilization had evolved a highly complex set of religious practices and beliefs. For well over 3,000 years, Egyptian religious and cultural life exhibited a tolerant polytheistic openness to the worship of a spectacular array of many deities – gods and goddesses both old and new, local and foreign. Their myths and legends were often contradictory. Three distinct but interconnected accounts of creation existed, each focusing on a different group of deities and each considered equally valid.

As typical of oral cultures, dualities were fundamental to the Egyptian worldview, within which chaos was balanced by order. Life was associated with day and death with night. Their regular alternation demonstrated how the gods controlled the cosmos. The god Ra was both the lord of time and the sun-god who ruled the day. His counterpart was Osiris, ruler of death and the underworld. Death and life were not two different states, but two aspects of one state; therefore, life balanced death. The afterlife – an idealized version of Egyptian daily life – was an underworld (or in some versions, the sky) where the dead lived as eternally blessed spirits, transfigured both by their difficult journey to the afterworld and their final judgment by the great god, Osiris. The daily rebirth of the sun mirrored the constant rebirth of the dead in the afterlife. In the afterworld, Ra and Osiris became one. According to the *Egyptian Book of the Dead* (a text used for funerals) "Osiris is yesterday and Ra is tomorrow."

Arguably the most important Egyptian myth is that of Osiris and his sister and consort, Isis. Before human-time, when Osiris and Isis ruled the world, prosperity and peace reigned. But Osiris's brother, Set, became jealous. He killed Osiris by sealing him in a coffin and drowning him in the Nile at a location near Abydos, thereby bringing conflict to the world. When Isis recovered Osiris's body, Set took the body from her, dismembered it, and scattered it over the far expanses of Egypt. Isis and her sister Nephthys (protectors and restorers of the dead), taking bird form, scoured the kingdom in order to reassemble Osiris's body. After Isis located every piece, with the help of other deities and fanning him with her wings she revived him. From their union was born their son, Horus, raised to avenge his father's death. Osiris left to become ruler of the afterworld.

This legend was central to Egyptian belief in the rebirth of the dead into an afterlife. In the Egyptian view, Set represented chaos and Horus the divine nature of kingship, always to be reborn. Osiris, the god who died and was restored to life, was associated with the annual flooding of the Nile, agriculture, and fertility.

The commemorative ritual of Osiris at Abydos

Cosmic equilibrium could be maintained only through the cooperation of the gods and goddesses. Chaos was kept at bay by the earthly representative of the gods – the pharaoh. As the intermediary between divine and mortal worlds, the pharaoh (male or female) possessed the inherent dualities of the cosmos. Only the pharaoh was empowered to intercede on behalf of humankind; therefore, s/he was considered the main priest of every Egyptian temple. The pharaoh was at first regarded as a servant of the gods, but later was considered divinely conceived and equal to the gods. While alive, the pharaoh was considered an incarnation of Horus, son of Osiris. When a pharaoh died, s/he was then identified with Osiris.

The elaborate ritual life of Egyptian temples was based on making offerings that nourished the gods: food, libations, song, dance, incense, and annual festivals. Before conducting daily worship or public ceremonies, priests and priestesses purified themselves by bathing, chewing mineral salts, and removing body hair. Song and dance were especially central to worship of Hathor, the goddess of music, motherhood, and beauty. One hymn describes how even the king danced and sang before the goddess while wielding a sacred, golden rattle:

He comes to dance,
comes to sing,
Hathor, see his dancing,
see his skipping!
. . . O Golden One,
how fine is the song
like the song of Horus himself,
which Ra's son sings as the finest singer.
He is Horus, a musician!

(Fletcher 2002: 83)

Figure 1.4
The sacred barque of Amun-Ra in a relief from a temple of Seti I.

Source: Joann Fletcher, *The Egyptian Book of Living and Dying* (London: Duncan Baird Publishers, 2002), 103.

The Egyptian calendar featured numerous annual festivals, astrologically determined, during which statues of gods and goddesses were housed in sacred barques (boat-shaped shrines) (Figure 1.4). These barques usually were hidden from sight and were the subject of secret rituals inside temples. When they were taken in procession by land and water to visit other temples or burial tombs, the barques were carried out of the temple on the shoulders of priests and accompanied by dancers and musicians (Figure 1.5), making that deity's power present for the people.

Figure 1.5
Fragment from a relief from a tomb at Sakkara (c.1250 BCE) showing women and young girls playing tambourines and clapsticks and dancing at a festival procession (right), led by a baton-carrying official and other male officials, their arms raised in rejoicing.
© Cairo/Jurgen Liepe, Berlin.

The deity most honored with great public ceremonies was Osiris, especially at the main center of his worship in Abydos during the period of the Middle Kingdom (roughly 2055–1640 BCE). Middle Kingdom rulers lavished patronage on the cult. Osiris's statue was re-housed in a new "everlasting great barque," constructed of "gold, silver, lapis lazuli, bronze, and cedar." Annually, the barque containing Osiris processed from the temple to the desert site of his tomb and back again. At the center of this liturgy, lasting days if not weeks, was a commemorative re-enactment of dramatic moments of Osiris's story.

The way in which Egyptians understood their place within the world and cosmos was informed by two suppositions: the assumption that society was organized around "high centers," headed by divinely ordained monarchs, and the assumption that cosmology and history were indistinguishable. Both assumptions are evident in the commemorative ritual for Osiris at Abydos (Figure 1.6).

All that is known about the quasi-dramatic ritual often called the Abydos "Passion Play" is the information inscribed on a single stele (a flat stone), dating from the rule of Senusret III (1870–1831 BCE). It provides a description of the dual roles of the chief priest/organizer of the festival, Ikhernofert, who was both overseer of the ceremonies and a participant/actor playing the role of the "beloved son of Osiris." The stele reads:

> I arranged the expedition of Wepwawet when he went to the aid of his father. I beat back those who attacked the Barque of Neshmet. I overthrew the foes of Osiris. I arranged the Great Procession and escorted the god [Osiris] on his journey. I launched the god's ship . . . I decked the ship with gorgeous trappings so that it might sail to the region of Peker [near Abydos]. I conducted the god to his grave in Peker. I championed [avenged] Wenn-nefru [Osiris as the re-risen god] on the day of the Great Combat and overthrew all his adversaries beside the waters of Nedit. I caused him to sail in his ship. It was laden with his beauty. I caused the hearts of the Easterners to swell with joy, and I brought the gladness to the Westerners at the sight of the Barque of Neshmet.
>
> (Gaster 1950: 41–2)

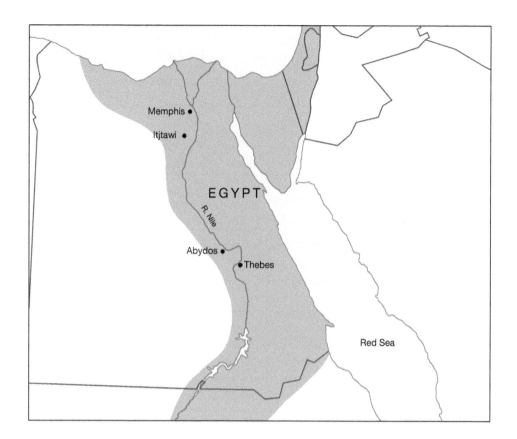

This text is thought not to have been a speech, but rather an outline of events that were performed over the course of eight days. Other major "roles" were taken by priests and priestesses, supported by a large group of "extras" who represented the warring factions of Set and Horus/Osiris. The "Great Combat" was a spectacular occasion, with thousands of participants on the two sides. The Greek historian Herodotus, writing fourteen centuries later, recorded that the massed armies at a similar event engaged in "a hard fight with staves . . . they break one another's heads, and I am of the opinion that many even die of the wounds they receive; the Egyptians however told me that no one died."

Hieroglyphic texts as mnemonic records

Egyptians borrowed the idea of writing (but not the system) from Sumer around 3400 BCE, before the establishment of the first dynasty of the pharaohs. They developed a mixed form of writing using hieroglyphs ("sacred carvings"), a system of logograms which possessed some phonetic elements. Writing was considered a sacred gift of the god Thoth, the healer, lord of wisdom, and scribe of the gods. Egyptians first used hieroglyphs for accountancy and then as a bureaucratic tool; eventually colorful hieroglyphic inscriptions decorated tombs and temples and were elaborated with special symbols and images of animals, birds, and humans to "activate" the scenes. There were thousands of hieroglyphs, and with less than 1 percent of the populace literate, scribes were a learned, specialist community. Learning was highly respected, and papyrus texts devoted to astrology, law, history, mathematics, medicine, geography and sacred liturgy were stored in great libraries attached to temples.

The reign of Senusret III during the Middle Kingdom "was a time when art, architecture, and religion reached new heights, but, above all, it was an age of confidence in writing" (Shah 2000: 183). Many literary forms flourished. Narratives such as *The Story of Sinuhe* and *The Shipwrecked Sailor* were composed. "Wisdom texts" recorded maxims on how to gain well-being in life, while "dream books" guided priests in their interpretation of dreams. Manuscripts such as *All Rituals Concerning the God Leaving His Temple in Procession on Festival Days* recorded sacred words and the correct performance of rites.

No specific manuscript has been located for the rites of Osiris at Abydos. If any manuscript had been used, most likely it would have recorded the sacred words used to animate and honor Osiris; there would have been no "dialogue" specially authored for the figures central to the re-enactment. The focus of the performance would have been on the processional spectacle and re-enactment manifesting the presence and power of Osiris in his annual going-forth, his conquering of death, and rebirth. Perhaps the contemporary focus on narrative in literary works of the Middle Kingdom helped create a climate within which dramatizing parts of the Osiris story was an obvious means of enhancing the efficacy of the annual commemoration.

The "drama" of Osiris was like many rituals, and may have incorporated impersonation of gods as some rituals did. Unlike most rituals, it probably also possessed the lengthy narrative we find in storytelling. However, there isn't adequate information to help us judge whether it was a type of theatre. Great caution is advisable when applying modern terminology to ancient forms of performance, especially when evidence is scarce, in order to avoid misinterpretation, anachronism, and perhaps ethnocentrism. Nevertheless it is clear that writing played a role in conceptualizing and organizing the Abydos "Passion Play."

Writing seems to have enabled a lengthening and standardization of ritual through a fusion with narrative, but still within the basic outlines of oral culture. Even though ancient Egyptian society possessed writing, and writing was crucial to the elite, ultimately writing was not the dominant mode of communication. Taken as a whole, it is better to describe ancient Egypt as an oral culture with writing, rather than a literate culture.

Mesoamerican performance

The early indigenous cultures of Mesoamerica – a region stretching from Central America up to southern Mexico (Figure 1.7) – provide not only another instance of performance in conditions of restricted literacy, but also powerful examples of the complexity of interpreting evidence noted in the General Introduction. The Maya and Mexica (Aztecs) ruled in parts of Mesoamerica until the late fifteenth and sixteenth centuries CE, when the Spanish invaded the Americas and conquered the indigenous peoples. The Mayan Empire reached its zenith during the Classic Period, 250–900 CE, and writing almost certainly contributed to its political control and economic growth.

Various writing systems were invented in Mesoamerica. The Mayan system, which most likely arose around 500 BCE, combined characteristics of logograms and syllabaries. But Mayan writing has only been partly translated, and we know little about its usage and the extent of reading and writing skills in Mesoamerica. The symbols changed over time and some had only local usage, but it seems that during any one place and time, scribes probably needed to know around 250 signs. As in most ancient societies, only the scribes could write with much

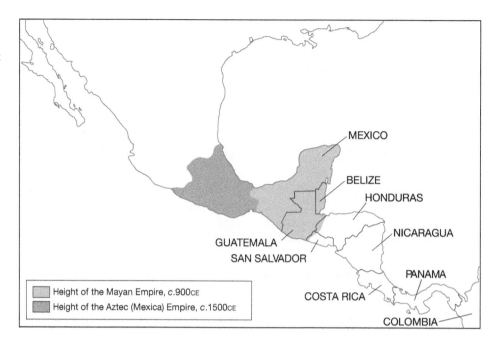

Figure 1.7
Map of the Mayan and Aztec Empires in Mesoamerica.

facility, although occasionally non-elites may have acquired some writing ability as well. Writing was read aloud, and most of Mayan culture and knowledge was transmitted orally. The scribes often sought to demonstrate their virtuosity, yet the pictographic aspect of Mayan writing may have made it interpretable (if unpronounceable) to a much larger population – highly advantageous in a multilingual region like Mesoamerica. In this manner Mayan writing may have unified a large region within a single political and administrative control.

Performance was integral to Mesoamerican societies. Evidence from pyramid walls and the few extant sacred books point to a vigorous Mesoamerican performance culture before the Maya had writing (Tedlock 1985: 151–2). Rigorous training in music and dance was normal for boys and girls from ages 12 to 15 and took place in "houses of song." Rulers performed "a 'princely dance' on special occasions," and priests "embodied god-figures" (Tedlock 1985: 358). Performances could involve thousands of highly skilled performers who "used elaborate and highly colorful costumes, masks, body make-up and, at times, puppets and stilts. The sets were lavishly adorned with arches, flowers, animals, and all sorts of natural and artfully designed elements" (Taylor 2004: 357). Performances were usually outdoors in public spaces (courtyards and temples), although some were in private patios.

The religious imperative for performance in Mesoamerica

Mesoamerican public celebrations always combined religious and theatrical elements. Performances in the festivals were set against the great architectural spaces of Mesoamerican cities, which included massive pyramids. These temples were regarded as the "navel of the world" and "the human-made equivalent of nature's mountains . . . forming a living link that conjoined the heavens above, the earth, and the underworlds below" (Tedlock 1985: 364). Public ceremonies were synchronized with the movement of heavenly bodies, making cosmic time palpable and elaborate calendar-keeping essential. The performances were not entertainment, but offerings to the gods. Mesoamerica's highly theatricalized ceremonies fulfilled a key purpose: to keep the lines of communication open between humans, their ancestors, and the gods they worshipped.

In many cultures the world over, an essential component of such communication has involved sacrifice, usually of animals. Among the Aztecs and occasionally among the Maya, these ceremonies could include human sacrifice. Recently scholars have begun to wrest an understanding of the meanings and purposes of this fact – human sacrifice – away from the perspective of the Spanish military and missionaries, and attempt to grasp what it might have meant to the peoples themselves. According to performance studies scholar Diana Taylor, human sacrifice

> reflected the belief that there was no firm division between life and death. . . . The sacrificial victims would be joining the gods, at times taking messages from those on earth, while the victims' energy and force would be transferred to others on earth through the donning of the skin. Notions of continuity and constantly recycling life forces, rather than cruelty or revenge, sustained these practices. The Mayas, for example, referred to certain forms of sacrifice as *ahil* (acts of creation).
>
> (Taylor 2004: 361–2)

Religious rites create a synergy between the divine and human realms. If the gods sacrificed themselves for humans as the world was formed, then the gods require similar sacrifices in return. Sacrificial rites performed by divinely ordained priests or kings maintained the social and cosmological orders mandated by the gods at the time of creation. Human sacrifice was therefore considered a necessity.

Taylor's reference to "the donning of the skin" suggests how some Mesoamerican peoples understood such theatrical concepts as "embodiment" and "representation" in ways that are both similar to and different from European understandings. When the Aztecs wanted to honor their creator-deity Quetzalcoátl (the feathered-serpent god who gave his own blood in order to usher in the current incarnation of the human race, and the inventor of books and the calendar), they purchased a slave, who for 40 days was fêted, feasted, and worshipped *as* the god. At the end of the 40 days, the slave/god would be sacrificed in a public ceremony, in which his heart would be cut out and his body rolled down the temple steps. The body would then be skinned and the flesh donned by various onlookers, who *became* Quetzalcoátl while in the skin of the slave/Quetzalcoátl. According to Adam Versényi, the ritual accomplished several things at once; first, it re-enacted the god's original sacrifice on behalf of humanity; second, it performed a real sacrifice of human blood in honor of the same god; and finally, it allowed the spectator/participants to be at once themselves, their fellow (sacrificed) man, and their god. As Versényi describes it, this rite and many others represented "a conflation of the entire matrix of actor/character/audience" (Versényi 1989: 219).

At the same time, as Taylor points out, "The massive performance festivals . . . made visible the very real economic and military power of a state that could afford to sacrifice hundreds – even thousands – of victims. . . . These spectacular synchronized acts were fundamental to maintaining power" (Taylor 2004: 364). Taylor's comments suggest that by describing sacrifices as "acts of creation," Mesoamerican rulers rationalized their use of violence, undoubtedly believing the rationalization themselves. In this example we see how evidence can have multiple meanings and reveal multiple social purposes.

THINKING THROUGH THEATRE HISTORIES

The multiple meanings of evidence

Mesoamerican performance and the complexities of writing its history provide rich examples of the ways a single piece of evidence is frequently embedded with multiple meanings and can serve as evidence about a variety of social practices and concerns. There is nothing unusual about the presence of multiple meanings, known as *polysemy*: in fact there are several ways in which evidence and activities can be polysemous.

The example we have just seen, in which the concept of *ahil* (acts of creation) simultaneously played a role in the Maya's religion and cosmology, but probably also helped Mayan rulers justify their use of violence and horror, illustrates one sort of polysemy. The function of ideas as part of a society's understanding of itself and its world, and also as an expression of power and self-justification, is scarcely limited to the Maya: in fact it is prevalent in most societies. It is common, for instance, in the expansion of national power through **imperialism**. The Spanish conquerors of South and Central America used the claim of Christianity's superiority over indigenous religions in just such a manner: they truly believed in Christianity and its preeminence, but they also saw it as a rationale for killing Mayan people, suppressing Mayan religious practices while imposing their own, and censoring Mayan culture, all of which secured the conquerors' power. The term **ideology** points to such connections between ideas and power. (Later chapters will discuss imperialism and its ideologies in more detail.)

Another type of polysemy involves ambiguity. One of the chief problems in understanding Mayan performance is the fact that much of our evidence comes from descriptions by the invading Spaniards, who were unfamiliar with the cultures of the people they conquered and described what they saw in terms of their own concepts and values. In addition, they generally weren't interested in learning about the indigenous people's culture – in fact the conquerors destroyed as much of Mayan culture as they could. Consequently the Spaniards' descriptions may be distorted and biased; they may tell us more about the Spanish than they do about the Maya. At the same time the descriptions cannot be written off. Some (possibly even all) parts may be substantially accurate, and they are almost all we have to guide us. As a result of these complexities, the documentary evidence about Mayan performance has uncertain meaning and value.

Activities can have multiple meanings in other ways. One of them is familiar to anyone who pays attention to politics. Proposed legislation (say, to cut taxes or to expand access to education) aims to address policy concerns – it strives to move the government and sometimes the entire society in a particular direction. At the same time it often seeks partisan goals, by advancing one political party's standing with the electorate, or placing its opposition in an awkward position. Sometimes, which of these goals is foremost is an open question. As a result, one cannot take the legislation at face value: there may be hidden agendas behind it. A variant of this type of polysemy can be seen in consumer culture. A car is a means of transportation – but one's choice of car (say, a Porsche versus a Volkswagen) can be partly a matter of obtaining a status or sex symbol. In short, an artifact or document may be polysemous because it can serve multiple practical and social functions.

continued

> Finally, every cultural object is the product of numerous processes. A book's text, for instance, can tell us many things about a culture's ideas and beliefs. In addition, however, its physical characteristics hint at the society's manufacturing capabilities, and its design may suggest what the society considers attractive (or whether it sees attractiveness as necessary for that object). Thus a piece of evidence can tell a historian a variety of things, or be used for a range of historical investigations.
>
> These are only some of the ways in which evidence often has manifold significance, and offers historians a wide variety of investigative opportunities, complexities, and interpretations.

Sung dance-drama: *Rabinal Achi*

While sacrificial rites performed by priests or kings maintained the social and cosmological orders mandated by the gods, more secular forms of performance were also common in Mesoamerica, entertaining the people and maintaining their collective memory. Farces ridiculed those who were ethnically different. In a "dramatic interlude" from central Mexico entitled "Song of the Little Women," several concubines debate the pros and cons of living a life devoted to satisfying male prerogatives. Sung dance-drama, which incorporated music, song, and dance, celebrated collective and individual histories and glories. One important Mayan song-dance-drama, *Rabinal Achi* [drah-vee-NAHL ah-CHEE], commemorated certain political and military events in the history of the town of Rabinal. The history of its performance is also an example of the suppression of indigenous systems of belief and cultural performances that came with Spain's conquest of the New World.

Rabinal Achi is a K'iche' (also spelled Quiché) language song-dance still performed today in the highlands of Guatemala. It is known both as *Rabinal Achi*, meaning "The Man of Rabinal," and *Xajoj Tun*, "Dance of the Trumpets" – a reference to the fact that during parts of the performance characters dance to the playing of trumpets. It is one of few extant plays with Mayan rather than Spanish dialogue. It relates the story of conflict between the noble warriors and leaders of two Mayan city-states, K'iche' and Rabinal, that reached a climax in the early fifteenth century, before the arrival of the Spanish.

The primary historical incident around which the performance score for *Rabinal Achi* evolved is the story of a famous king, Quicab – a member of the lineage of the house of Cawek of the Forest People. In the fourteenth and fifteenth centuries, Quicab ruled a confederation of the Rabinal, Cakchiquel, and Tzutuhil nations in what is now Guatemala. While Quicab was away on a military campaign expanding his kingdom, there was a revolt at home. One of those involved was his fifth son, who may have been the historical figure on whom the character Cawek in the drama is based.

In the play, the main characters are Lord Five Thunder, ruler of the mountaintop fortress of Rabinal; the Man of Rabinal (serving at his behest), who upholds the traditional order; and the renegade who disrupts that order, Cawek, the son of the Lord of K'iche'. All three wear distinctive helmet-masks and carry axes and shields, symbols of royal power (Figure 1.8).

Figure 1.8

Rabinal Achi, or the Man of Rabinal, a conjectural image similar to that of an eighth-century lord found in the Mayan Temple of the Inscriptions at Palenque (not depicted). He wears a feathered headdress, mask, short cape, and kilt, and he carries an upraised axe and a small round shield.

Drawing by Jamie Borowicz. © Dennis Tedlock.

Cawek's father was a noble who fought alongside the neighboring city-state of Rabinal. Rabinal's boundaries are guarded by Eagle and Jaguar, priests in the service of Lord Five Thunder, whose names are taken from the source of their spiritual power to protect. At Lord Five Thunder's court reside his wife and his unmarried daughter, "Mother of Quetzal Feathers." Cawek becomes a renegade warrior when he betrays the people of Rabinal, causing much suffering. As the drama opens, Cawek has already betrayed his father's former allies and been captured by Man of Rabinal. The drama presents the confrontation between Man of Rabinal and Cawek in the context of Cawek's trial. Cawek remains defiant toward his captors throughout, but accepts death by beheading at the end of the drama. Before dying, he is allowed to view aspects of the world he will leave. He is shown the lovely daughter of Lord Five Thunder and shown dances depicting the beauty of nature.

Everything we know about *Rabinal Achi* derives from evidence dating after the Spanish conquest of the Mayan Empire during the sixteenth century. Some of the evidence comes from accounts of performances seen through the Spanish colonizers' eyes. Most Spanish missionaries were wholly uninterested in the Maya's own views, but they recognized that the participation of the people in annual cycles of ceremonial performances (at which dramas like *Rabinal Achi* were performed) had great meaning for the Maya, and they attempted to suppress and/or alter the performances by a variety of means. They insisted that Christian hymns be substituted for Mayan songs, and as early as 1593 and as late as 1770, they issued bans against indigenous plays, "warning that representations of human sacrifices would lead to real ones" (Tedlock 2003: 5). The bans, however, were never wholly successful. The Spaniards also introduced Christian biblical theatre from medieval Europe, possibly affecting indigenous performance.

The Maya never used their own system of writing to record what performers spoke in their performances. It was only under the influence of Christian missionaries that the Maya wrote down "texts" like *Rabinal Achi* in their own language, using the Roman alphabet. The missionaries had created handwritten scripts for the European Bible and saint plays that they introduced, translating some speeches into local Mayan languages. These alphabetic texts contained details and content never included in the older Mayan hieroglyphic texts. Anthropologist Dennis Tedlock attributes these differences not to alphabetic writing per se, but to the fact that indigenous authors were responding to the missionary suppression of their performances and "the destruction of hieroglyphic texts." In order to save *Rabinal Achi* from complete censorship, the Mayan scribes separated the words of their play from its music, and removed "all but the main outlines of the original religious content from public view" (Tedlock 2003: 2). The Mayan scribes "sought to conserve the audible words of endangered performances for which those books provided prompts" (2003: 158).

Their "texts" of the sixteenth century were, then, written as records of oral performances and, according to Tedlock, are more like "a set of program notes than a libretto" (2003: 158). They are not single-author works but collectively created, mnemonic records of performance, which participants would have elaborated upon in the moment of performance.

The available evidence does not provide a fully accurate picture of pre-conquest Mayan performance, and we may never be able to apprehend the full scope, nature, and content of their drama. Nevertheless, the performances of *Rabinal Achi* in Guatemala today hint at what Mayan drama might have been like before the Spanish conquest. Today and probably historically, the theatrical conventions of *Rabinal Achi* are presentational – not representational or realistic. The audience is located on four sides of the playing space. "When the actors dance, they move around the perimeter of a square, and when they promenade they move in a circle. These pathways locate them all in one world" (Tedlock 2003: 14). The distinctive rhythms of the Mayan calendar are suggested in the counter-clockwise movements within a square, together with their temporal marking of the 260 days of the divinatory calendar during which Cawek says farewell to his homeland by moving "on all four edges/in all four corners." The overtly religious aspects of the performance today are the primary responsibility of the play's "Road Guide" – the native ritual specialist or priest-shaman whose prayers and offerings circumscribe and punctuate the performance. The actors deliver lengthy speeches as solos, similar to the renderings of ancient Mayan court songs. The main characters narrate more events from the past than they re-enact in the dramatic present. There is no fast-paced, realistic dialogue, and actors never attempt a conversational tone. When the Man of Rabinal captures Cawek with the rope he wears around his waist, he does not realistically lasso him, but rather, the two remain still and a stage assistant appears and ties the end of the rope carried by the Man of Rabinal around his prisoner.

Rabinal Achi never adopted the convention used in the later Spanish missionary plays, in which enemies are depicted in costumes indicating two different worlds – one "evil" and the other "good." Instead, the antagonists dress alike, and their arguments are shaped by a shared, rather than opposite set of values. One of the opponents may be misguided or wrong but he is not, as in the later dramas of the Christianizing missionaries, "evil" or living in "falsehood."

At the end of the drama, Cawek is executed, which is depicted in modern performances as a beheading. To show this, the captive kneels, and other characters dance around him. In a simple and unhurried manner, those with axes simply bring them toward but not to the prisoner's neck. Immediately following his "beheading," the performer stands, and joins the other dancers in a final collective dance. Shoulder to shoulder, they dance westward until they reach the foot of the steps leading to the door of the cemetery chapel. There the actors all kneel, and the Road Guide leads them in a prayer to their ancestors (Tedlock 2003: 19).

While contemporary performances of *Rabinal Achi* seem to bear strong traces of pre-conquest practices, there also is evidence that the drama has changed over time. For example, anthropologist Ruud van Akkeren (1999) has suggested that originally Cawek was likely put to death by arrows rather than by beheading. When and why it changed in performance is unclear.

Rabinal Achi seems to have different representational goals than the "drama" of human sacrifice described above. It commemorates a historic military conquest that resulted in a consolidation of power. In the Mayan Empire, such conquests featured ceremonial executions, which served as proof of their power. According to Tedlock, today's Mayan actors are speaking to and for their ancestors as much as to and for anyone else, including all those who ever acted in the play. Acting in this play, then, is not so much a matter of impersonating historical individuals – as if their lives could be relived in realistic detail – as it is a matter of impersonating their ghosts (Tedlock 2003: 14–15).

As a representation of Mayan royalty and culture, *Rabinal Achi* does reflect some pre-conquest local history. But its impulse is less toward full historical accuracy and more toward commemoration of the town of Rabinal's triumphal origins and ongoing cultural survival, as symbolized in its ability to withstand an internal threat to its cohesion. Instead of portraying an actual battle between ancient enemies, the enactment presents a montage of fragments of royal stories from across six different generations, gathered into the singular confrontation between the Man of Rabinal and the traitor Cawek. Generic character names allow the story and its examination of the power negotiations between rulers and city-states to remain open to interpretation.

Episodes from the history of royal lineages were the subject of many other pre-Spanish Mesoamerican dramas. In all such plays, the actors represented the main characters through costuming and dancing, while dialogue was sung or chanted by separate choruses (group performers) to musical accompaniment.

Rabinal Achi shares certain features with commemorative dramas elsewhere, of which we will present several more examples in Chapter 3. Like most commemorative dramas, *Rabinal Achi* tells a story that has been carefully preserved both orally and in written form; it celebrates a moment in the past that is of great contemporary importance for the audience in the present who witnesses it; and it is meant to be staged on a regular basis as an aid against the loss of that heritage in social memory. In addition, however, commemorative performances in Mesoamerica were understood not as representations but as doing something fundamental in the world. Whether Mesoamerican commemorative performances constitute theatre is, according to Taylor, a matter of dispute among Latin American specialists (Taylor 2004: 366), but clearly it shares many of theatre's features.

Although *Rabinal Achi* was heavily censored in the early days of the Spanish conquest by missionaries suspicious of its "pagan" content, it survived and is meant to be staged every year on January 25 (the feast day of the town of Rabinal's Catholic patron saint, Paul). Its importance beyond the Mayan world is evidenced in the fact that in 2005, UNESCO officially proclaimed it a "masterpiece of the oral and intangible heritage of humanity."

Performance in a literate culture: Theatre in the city-state of Athens

We have seen the divine god-kings of Egypt locate authority in a single person and produce festivals honoring gods like Osiris. In Mesoamerica, scattered kingdoms shared a culture and religion, and produced commemorative dramas such as *Rabinal Achi*, constituting something close to theatre, although (unlike Western theatre) addressing the gods and understood as an actual intervention in the universe. A very different way of negotiating the relationship between divine and civic authority, and between the cosmos and history, developed in Athens, Greece during the fifth century BCE, where distinctive forms of literary drama and theatre flourished. The forms of drama that developed in Athens may be said to have been "dialogic."

Figure 1.9
Map of the eastern Mediterranean during the fifth century BCE.

That is, they represent conflicts over cultural issues that would have invited social, political, and aesthetic debate.

We have far more information about theatre in classical Athens than any other early theatre: documents, the remains of buildings, pottery, engravings, and over 40 plays. One reason we have so much information is the spread of literacy itself: documents provide much of our evidence. Yet there are many tantalizing and frustrating gaps in our knowledge. For instance, we know who did something important for the development of theatre and the year in which they did it, but only vaguely what they did. We do know, however, that Greek theatre emerged during an era of major changes in political structures, economic systems, and communication methods.

Alphabetic writing and Athenian democracy

In the eighth and ninth centuries BCE, epic bards like Homer recited or sang their own versions of lengthy stories of the gods and epic heroes of bygone eras, such as *The Iliad* and *The Odyssey*. Their performances gave life to the deeds of a heroic aristocracy, populating a murky, distant, quasi-mythic, quasi-historical past. By the end of the fifth century BCE, however, the most important storytelling no longer appeared in solo oral epics or lyric poetry: instead it was composed in tragedies or comedies in which multiple actors performed characters and spoke dialogue, and the chorus, with choreographed dancing and singing, played a central but slowly diminishing role. How and why did this revolution occur? The nature of Greek alphabetic writing and the creation of an early form of democracy both played a part.

The alphabet started developing when, around 1200 BCE, the Phoenicians began to use a letter to indicate the initial consonant (somewhat like a syllabary) but let the appropriate vowel be inferred by context. This approach radically reduced the number of characters needed to represent speech to just a couple dozen, making the script almost alphabetic. Thus unlike logograms, with thousands of characters which could only be learned through long study (frequently by priests and scribes alone), or even syllabaries which commonly had two or three hundred (still requiring significant need as well as time), alphabets and proto-alphabets had few enough symbols to be quickly learned by anyone – a great advantage for a trading people like the Phoenicians. However, because vowels had to be inferred, Phoenician script sometimes created ambiguity, which was resolved by inserting an extra consonant symbol to indicate the correct vowel.

The Phoenicians traded throughout the Mediterranean, bringing their script with them. Probably around 850 BCE, the Greeks adopted Phoenician script. However, Greek has a large number of initial vowels, consonant clusters, and combined vowels (such as the *a*, *mn*, and *ia* in *amnesia*). Those weren't easily represented by the Phoenician script, even with its *ad hoc* approach to indicating vowels, so the Greeks introduced letters specifically for vowel sounds and used them systematically. That created the first full alphabet, which breaks speech into individual vowels and consonants. Although the script wasn't perfect, writing became more or less unambiguously phonetic.

However, many features of modern writing weren't invented for centuries. There was no spacing between words, no upper and lower cases, little or no punctuation, not even clear indications when the speaker in a play changed. Just as in other early cultures with writing, reading aloud – even in private – was both a cultural norm and a practical necessity.

The social contexts of the alphabet's development gave it advantages beyond clearly representing speech. The socio-political structures of ancient Greece were radically unlike those of its major neighbors (see Figure 1.9). The lands to the east belonged to the vast Persian Empire, Greece's adversary in many wars. To the south lay Egypt, by then ruled by the Persian Empire, but which still rang with its own history as a 3,000-year-old centralized empire. In contrast, Greece consisted of autonomous city-states, including Athens, Sparta, Thebes, and Corinth, that vied with one another for ascendancy and occasionally joined forces in alliances to face a common external threat, such as when they fought the Persians in 479 BCE.

The small-scale political structure and independence of the ancient Greek city-state (*polis* [POH-lis]) probably worked against the restriction of literacy to an educated bureaucracy; for instance, literacy seems to have been relatively high in Sparta, even though writing was disdained and relegated to just a few uses. Moreover, struggles for land redistribution had been endemic throughout Greece, during the seventh and sixth centuries BCE. In many cities, an autocrat (*tyrannos*) took control and implemented some of the demands. Athens, however, attempted to stave off autocracy by appointing Solon as a mediator during 594–591 BCE. Solon established a constitution that reduced aristocratic power, and he encouraged commerce and artisan manufacture – an approach that ultimately affected the prevalence of literacy in the *polis*. This history factored strongly in the development of theatre.

Despite Solon's work, beginning in the 560s a general named Pisistratus seized power. He was ousted several times, but in 546 BCE, he began an enduring rule. He strove to tilt power from the aristocracy to the state by helping the lower classes, supporting popular religion and festivals, and promoting mercantile activity.

Pisistratus was succeeded by one of his sons, who was deposed in a coup in 510 BCE. After further tumult, Cleisthenes gained leadership in 507 and led the *polis* down a unique path.

In order to distribute power and prevent autocracy from ever rising again, Cleisthenes abolished the hereditary tribes, replacing them with ten civic tribes based on place of residence. He also established legislative bodies and courts with members chosen by lottery. Athens became the first democracy.

Two aspects of Athenian society contributed to the rise of literacy there. Merchants and shopkeepers, although disparaged, were exceptionally important to Athens' economy, and they found the simplicity of the alphabet enormously useful. Even more important was the democratic structure. Citizenship in the new democracy was restricted to male Athenians, excluding slaves; at its founding, perhaps 20,000 citizens in all. But all citizens were called upon to fulfill civic obligations as soldiers or sailors, athletes, participants or spectators at annual religious festivals – and crucially, as legislators, debaters, judges, or jury members, which encouraged literacy.

Athenians grew increasingly interested in skillful public debate and oratory. At the same time, the legal and legislative need to consider issues from varying perspectives fostered diversity of ideas, which extended to all areas of thought – such as the view that the world is not governed by the whim of the gods but instead by natural, intelligible forces (although atheism *per se* was rare). Newly developing modes of education emphasized persuasive argument and eloquence, and some teachers, known as Sophists, expounded on their innovative and sometimes unconventional views. Instructors wrote manuals on persuasive oratory, called the art of rhetoric (*technē rhētorikē*, "speech art"). In this sense, writing in fifth-century Athens enhanced some forms of oral communication since speeches were given extemporaneously – no orator would ever speak from a prepared text, but by studying rhetorical techniques he could become a masterful speaker.

The interaction of speech and writing was so essential a part of the city's democratic life that in the fifth century BCE, boys were required to attend school, where they learned writing, music, and mathematics. By the fourth century BCE, writing had attained further cultural dominance. Aristotle's (384–322 BCE) *Art of Rhetoric* demonstrates how the invention of writing led to an organized, abstract analysis of speech itself.

Although in most of Greece probably no more than a few percent of the population was literate, in Athens it spread more broadly, possibly over 10 percent, and found many new applications. The cultural impact was profound, and according to classics and theatre scholar Jennifer Wise, by the fifth century BCE there was a literacy revolution in the city. "Everyday life was so overrun with books . . . that cheap editions of philosophy could be picked up from the bookstalls for a drachma" (Wise 1998: 21). The first literate culture was born. The circumstances in which that happened tell us much about the meaning of performance there.

The creation of democracy spurred not just literacy, but also theatre. As we will see, Greek drama drew from the same well of debate over civic matters as did the democracy. And as part of their civic duties, the wealthiest citizens were expected to undertake major responsibilities such as maintaining a warship, equipping a religious procession – or financing a chorus, which meant underwriting the production of a set of plays at the annual theatre festival honoring the god Dionysus.

The religious background

We mentioned that Pisistratus promoted popular religion in Athens. As in Egypt and Mesoamerica, ancient Greek religion was polytheistic. Within the Greek pantheon, a complex host of anthropomorphic gods and goddesses vied for power, prestige, and influence. The gods all had their own spheres of influence, and embodied a complex set of ways in which the Greeks understood their world. Greek gods behaved and misbehaved much like people, and they were often in conflict. However, each needed to be appropriately honored, propitiated, and worshipped to access their potential beneficence or prevent their wrath.

Panhellenic gods (such as Zeus and Apollo) were recognized throughout Greece, while other gods had narrower local significance. Most cities had patron gods, often panhellenic: in Athens' case it was Athena, goddess of wisdom, justice, military and heroic achievement, and art and artisanal skills. But another god figures prominently in the history of Athens and its theatre: Dionysus, the god of wine. He was said to have dwelled in Athens for a time, and the cult of Dionysus was highly popular there. As David Wiles puts it, Dionysus "is associated with darkness, with nocturnal drinking bouts, and the loss of mental clarity in moments of collective emotion, with the loss of boundaries around the self experienced in a crowd." Dionysus plays music on "the haunting double oboe which can whip up wild dances" (Wiles 2000: 7–8). He was strongly associated as well with freedom and intoxicated abandon – in fact the full name of the amphitheatre built in his honor is the Theatre of Dionysus Eleuthereus, "Dionysus the Liberator." Athens' democratic government officially sponsored the cult of Dionysus and established festivals in tribute. These festivals became occasions for theatrical performance.

Drama in the context of the Dionysian festivals in Athens

The theatrical performance of tragedy and comedy in ancient Athens also needs to be understood in the context of the civic/religious ceremonies and festivals of which theatre was a part. Fifth-century Greek theatre was woven into the fabric of civic/religious discourse. Greek festivals typically included processions, sacrifices, celebrations, feasting, and the performance of choral laments – group singing and dancing. Some also included competitions, particularly athletic contests; later, especially in Athens, there were also competitions in what we now call the arts (in classical Greece, the arts weren't separate from religion and other aspects of the culture as they are today).

Starting in 566–565 BCE under Pisistratus, every four years the Panathenaia festival honored Athena. Following a great procession, a new dress was presented to clothe the image of the goddess. Athletic contests were included, and a team event called the *pyrrhic* – a martial dance in which the dancers wore the full armor of the ancient Greek foot soldier and executed military movements. Additional competitions eventually included solo recitations of works by Homer, and musical contests.

There were four major Dionysian festivals annually: the Rural Dionysia, which was the oldest; the Lenaia; the Anthesteria; and the largest, the City (or Great) Dionysia, which was second only to the Panathenaia in importance.

The City Dionysia was crucial in the history of Greek drama. It has an uncertain history: it was long thought that Pisistratus established it to curry favor with the populace, that competitions in tragedy were instituted in 534 BCE, and that the first winner was Thespis, who is also said to be the first known actor. Now, however, many classical scholars believe that the City Dionysia and the cult's state sponsorship were established later, probably 503–501 BCE – *after* the Athenian democratic state was formed. According to this theory, the City Dionysia was part of a program to celebrate and strengthen the new democracy by taking advantage of Dionysus's association with liberation. If so, Thespis's performance in 534 BCE must have

THE CITY DIONYSIA IN FIFTH-CENTURY ATHENS: PROBABLE ORDER OF EVENTS

Day 1: Procession of the statue of Dionysus

Dionysus's arrival in Athens from the nearby town of Eleutherae was re-enacted. After a ritual sacrifice, Dionysus's statue was brought from a temple near Eleutherae in a procession to his temple in Athens, at the base of the Acropolis. The procession was probably conducted by a group of young men (*ephebes*) in the midst of their military training. They offered another sacrifice at the base of the Acropolis, within the sacred precinct of Dionysus's temple. Afterwards, the playwrights and their choruses who were competing in the tragic competition were introduced to the public and the subject of their plays announced.

Day 2: Dithyramb competitions

Dithyrambs [DIH-thih-ram] were performed – choral songs and dances in honor of Dionysus, first regularized in Corinth around 600 BCE. Dithyrambic competitions started in Athens in 509 BCE, before the establishment of the City Dionysia itself. Each of Athens' ten civic tribes sent performers with a poet who composed/choreographed the year's entry. These works were danced and sung by two choruses of 50 – one of younger boys, and a second of mature men. Although the verses were originally dedicated to Dionysus, the contest was eventually opened up to honor other deities.

Day 3: Comedy competition (added in 486 BCE)

Five different playwrights competed with comedies that offered keen satirical commentary on current socio-political matters, such as war, education, politics, the legal system, or even tragic poetry. The comedies of Aristophanes freely caricatured well-known individuals, including Socrates the philosopher, Cleon the politician, and even the greatest of the fifth-century writers of tragedy, Aeschylus, Sophocles, and Euripides. (We discuss all of these playwrights below.)

Days 4, 5, and 6: Tragedy and satyr play competition

Important civic-religious ceremonies were held before the assembled public on the day of the opening of the tragedy competition. These included the display of tributes by outlying cities under Athenian rule and the appearance of young men in full military dress, whose training was provided by Athens after their fathers had died in battle in service to the state. Citizens who had benefited the *polis* that year were honored as well.

The playwrights then presented their sets of four plays (three tragedies and a final satyr play, described below), probably one set by each playwright per day. Each set was an original interpretation of a Greek heroic narrative or historical event.

Probably on the last day, the judges announced the winners of the tragedy and comedy competitions and awarded prizes. At the end of the festival, officials held an open public assembly to receive any criticism of the proceedings, including complaints about the plays selected or the judging.

occurred elsewhere, possibly at a rural Dionysia (Connor 1989). In either case, the City Dionysia hosted the major drama competitions. Eventually all of the Dionysian festivals included dramatic performances.

The City Dionysia began with a raucous procession, celebrating the coming of the god Dionysus to Athens. This was followed by sacrificial rituals, civic ceremonies, and competitions in choral songs and dances, and competitions of tragedies and comedies. The procession, which began just outside the geographical boundary of the *polis*, incorporated the citizens of Athens as well as visitors. It opened with a complex series of events, civic and religious, and the theatrical performances are best understood within the fullness of this civic and religious context. The probable order of events is described in the box above.

The City Dionysia had not only religious significance, but tremendous economic, military, and political meaning as well. At its height in the fifth century, Athens was the leader of an alliance of cities, which turned into an empire. The member cities paid their tributes during the City Dionysia, and the Athenians made a show of their military prowess. For example, the second-year cadets put on a public demonstration in the theatre of their "hoplite military manoeuvres [combat exercises in battle dress] and close-order drill," while at least 36 of those in their first year were selected to perform as the chorus members in each of the three sets of tragedies (Goldhill 1990: 22–3). The philosopher Chameleon described choral dancing as "practically a manoeuvre in arms and a display not only of precision marching in general but more particularly of physical preparedness." It is these young "citizen soldiers in training" who are depicted on the famous Pronomos Vase (Figure 1.10) as members of the chorus in a satyr play.

The degree of direct civic participation as performers is staggering. Some 2,500–3,000 citizens took part in the processions, ceremonies, rites, or dramatic competitions constituting

Figure 1.10
This Greek vase for mixing wine, dating from the late fifth or early fourth century BCE, is famous for its theatrical figures, perhaps a company who performed a trilogy and satyr play. Called the "Pronomos Vase" after Pronomos, the *aulos* player seated at lower center, it shows (top center) the god of theatre, Dionysus, Ariadne (his wife), a muse, and to the sides, mature actors holding their masks – one costumed as a king, one as Herakles (with club), and the third as Silenus (leader of satyrs). Below left, is a playwright (with scroll) and a choral trainer (with lyre). The young beardless men (*ephebes*) are costumed as satyrs with erect phalluses.

Drawing by E.R. Malyon from the Pronomos Vase. © Museo Nazionale, Naples.

the festival. For the choral *dithyrambs* alone, each of ten tribes organized 50 boys under 18, and 50 men aged 20–30, totaling 1,000. The three days of tragedies utilized between 36 and 45 young men (at first 12 and later 15 in each chorus) and nine mature men to play the speaking roles (three for each playwright). These facts are in keeping with the view that the City Dionysia celebrated Athenian independence, democracy, and empire.

Space and performance in the Theatre of Dionysus

The civic, political, and religious importance of the City Dionysia is emphasized by where the plays were performed. Originally the performances were given in the marketplace at the foot of the Acropolis, the promontory at the center of Athens that served as both a stronghold and center of public life, on top of which stands the Parthenon. Later, the Theatre of Dionysus Eleuthereus – a large outdoor amphitheatre – was built at the base of the Acropolis on the downward slope near the temple of Dionysus (Figure 1.11).

During the fifth century, the *theatron* [THAY-ah-trohn] ("seeing place") was roughly divided into three sections, according to classics scholar David Kawalko Roselli (2011) (Figure 1.12). The *theatron* itself provided seating for 3,700–6,000 people. Each tribe's Council sat in a special section at the front, along with generals, foreign dignitaries, priests, and other honorees. In the rest of the *theatron*, spectators paid to sit on wooden benches behind them. But outside the official seating area, at least a thousand more people – including poor citizens, resident foreigners, and probably some slaves and women – found free seating on the hillside, in trees, and elsewhere. Many foreign visitors attended as well, increasing the festival's prestige.

Figure 1.11
Aerial photo of the Acropolis showing the Theatre of Dionysus (lower left) and the Parthenon (top).

Source: Simon Dawson/Bloomberg via Getty Images.

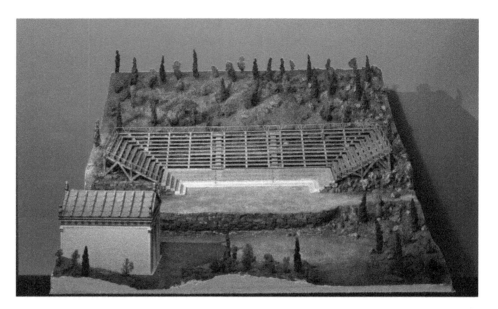

Figure 1.12

Model of the early classical Theatre of Dionysus at Athens.

Photograph after Hans R. Goette, in E. Pöhlmann, *Studien zur Buhnendichtung und zum Theaterbau der Antike: Studien zur Klassischen Philologie* 93, ed. M. V. Albrecht, 1995. Model: © Christian Schickel by order of the Deutsches Theatermuseum, München. Photograph: © Christine Sandt by order of the Deutsches Theatermuseum, München.

In 430 BCE, 40,000–60,000 men were citizens of Athens, during a period when the entire population was around 300,000. If one assumes somewhat conservatively that between the *theatron* and the hillside seating, 6,000 people attended each performance, then at least a tenth of Athens' citizens and about 2 percent of its residents attended the City Dionysia each day – not counting the performers. (A similar percentage would total around 165,000 residents of present-day New York or London.) The audience's size is another measure of the intense civic engagement in the festival.

The audiences responded vigorously to the quality of performance. Good shows received enthusiastic applause and accolades – but spectators in ancient Athens had no patience for poor performance or playwriting, and sometimes reacted with hissing, clucking, stomping, and prolonged noise-making. Occasionally actors and dramatists were driven off stage. Putting plays in a competition required audiences to judge the performances' artistic quality as well as their content. Unlike performance in a more ritual context, aesthetic merit most needed to please not the gods, but ordinary people.

But as theatre's popularity climbed, insufficient space created so many problems and even fistfights that in the fourth century BCE, the hillside was reshaped and benches were extended up the slope, allowing 14,000–17,000 people to attend (Figures 1.13 and 1.14). As classicist Rush Rehm notes, the *theatron* became "less a building than what we would call landscape architecture" (Rehm 2002: 37). However, because all seats now required payment, far fewer poor citizens and non-citizens could attend, until a fund was established to assist them.

Figure 1.13
Model of the
Theatre of
Dionysus after its
expansion in the
fourth century
BCE.

Photograph: Hans
R. Goette.

All performers in Greek theatre were male, including those playing female characters. The earliest form of tragedy, probably created by Thespis, consisted of a single actor before a chorus. It wasn't until some decades later that the playwright Aeschylus added a second actor, and possibly the third as well, each of whom would play several roles. Three actors became the maximum permitted.

The Pronomos Vase (Figure 1.10) shows several actors for a satyr play holding masks. Masks were an essential part of classical Greek theatre. None of the original masks from the classical era still exists, but vases, later masks, and other evidence suggest that tragic masks had formalized, expressionless faces. Comic masks, however, could present caricatures, grotesques, or even animal or bird heads. The mask in Figure 1.15, although later, is probably representative. Comic costuming was probably based on everyday wear, occasionally altered for amusing effect, and included a phallus. We have little information on tragic costumes, except that they included a tunic and sometimes a long or short cloak.

Figure 1.14
The Hellenistic theatre at Epidaurus (340–330 BCE), showing the *theatron*, *orchestra*, and *parodoi* (see double gates right and left at the ends of the *theatron*). At the top of the circular *orchestra*, archaeologists have laid out remaining fragments of the rectangular *skene*. The extant Greek stone theatres were built in the fourth century and after, although they likely derived some features from fifth-century theatres.

Photo © Gary Jay Williams.

Music was a constant part of all performances. Played on a double pipe called an *aulos* that sounded somewhat like an oboe, music was essential for dancing the choral odes and probably accompanied individual speeches. Other instruments, such as the harp shown on the Pronomos Vase, were occasionally played as well. Musical styles may have had specific emotional associations for ancient Greek audiences, deeply shaping their responses to performances.

The case study "Classical Greek Theatre: Space in *Oedipus the King*" on the *Theatre Histories* website offers more details on staging in fifth-century Athens.

Figure 1.15
Theatre mask dating from the fourth or third century BCE. On display in the Ancient Agora Museum in Athens, housed in the Stoa of Attalus. This mask was created after the death of the major Greek playwrights.

Source: AKG–images/John Hios.

The plays and playwrights

Only 44 plays survive from the classical era, written by Aeschylus (*c.*525–*c.*456 BCE), Sophocles (*c.*497–*c.*405 BCE), Euripides (*c.*480–406 BCE), and Aristophanes (*c.*448–*c.*387 BCE). They constitute a tiny fraction of the 2,100 or more plays performed between the establishment of Athenian democracy and Aristophanes's death; we have titles for about a quarter of them, but most are now unknown. A vast number of them were destroyed during a disastrous fire at the Great Library of Alexandria, Egypt, probably around 274 CE. The extant plays exist only as copies dating from the Middle Ages.

During the City Dionysia, on each of the three days designated for tragedy, a playwright presented three dramas (initially, complete trilogies; later, separate tragedies) followed by a satyr play; on the day for comedy, five playwrights competed with one play each. The playwrights staged their own dramas and thus had no need to write out separate stage directions or other directions for the performers. The actors probably learned their lines from the author reading the text aloud.

Greek tragedies weren't plays that end with a terrible event. Although they have a tragic situation at their heart, some close on an affirmative note. Many address the history and character of Athens itself. *The Oresteia* by Aeschylus – the only complete trilogy to survive – drew on one of the stories about the aftermath of the Trojan War, and culminated with a new (and chronologically impossible) mythology of how Athens replaced cycles of vengeance with a superior, democratic judicial system. In Sophocles's *Oedipus at Colonus* (probably the conclusion of another trilogy), Athens takes Oedipus under its protection as an act of mercy, and his death sanctifies a cave near the city. Euripides' *The Bacchae* shows Dionysus's terrifying power as he exacts vengeance on the king of Thebes for having disregarded him. Dionysus works his female followers into a frenzy in which they rip the king's body limb from limb. Although the play concludes with this horrific (off-stage) event and other punishments, its subtext points in another direction: according to one legend, originally Dionysus came to Athens from Thebes, so Euripides implicitly honored Athens' success at giving the god his due.

The Bacchae is unusual in one respect: it is about Dionysus. According to classical scholar Scott Scullion (2002), we have titles for about 500 Greek tragedies, but less than 4 percent concerned the wine god, and the extant plays seldom refer to him. Nearly all Greek tragedies, including the earliest ones, are about secular personages. When Dionysian ecstasy arises in the action or language, which occurs only occasionally, it is usually treated ironically, as premature or misguided joy. Sometimes Athenian audience members at the City Dionysia scoffed that the plays had "nothing to do with Dionysus," but evidently that was not a problem to most spectators or to the supervising authorities, otherwise more plays would have made him their subject.

There are considerable differences between the vision, structure, and poetic style of the plays of Aeschylus, written in the first half of the fifth century, and those of Euripides, written in the latter half. Aeschylus was clearly very religious, but not doctrinal, and he staunchly supported Athens' democratic institutions. His work is also clearly indebted to the Homeric epic tradition. Euripides was influenced by the development of Sophism, the philosophical movement that brought disciplined processes of critical thinking to Athens. Athenians associated Euripides with the philosopher Socrates, and the poet was a controversial figure. His tragedies critiqued traditional values and religion, no longer showing reverence for the heroes and gods of the myths. Yet his plays were highly popular, especially after his death.

The satyr plays were send-ups of incidents from the same narrative as the tragedies performed earlier in the day. These farcical, ribald pieces were named after the satyrs – the half-horse, half-human wine-drinking companions of Dionysus who constituted the chorus of these plays. Their costumes (see Figure 1.10) included a horse's tail, an erect phallus, and a head-mask with pointed/equine ears, snub-nose, and wild hair and beard. Only one satyr play survives: Euripides' *Cyclops*. The satyr plays were characterized by broad physical sight-gags and scatological humor.

Fifth-century Greek comedy was no less concerned with public affairs than tragedy was. The only extant comedies are by Aristophanes, but his plays seem to have been typical of the genre: highly satirical, and sometimes bawdy, obscene, fantastical, or absurd. The targets of its lampoons included politicians, militarists, "oracle mongers," and similar figures. Aristophanes caricatured Socrates in *The Clouds*, and in *The Frogs* he made fun not only of Euripides, but also of Dionysus himself.

Beyond Athens, an independent comic tradition also developed in Syracuse during the fifth century, but since none of the comedies have survived, it is impossible to characterize them with any accuracy. However, the city was a second major center of performance; for instance, Aeschylus premiered some of his plays there.

Despite the fact that only men could be citizens of Athens, the plays include many strong female characters. In the surviving tragedies, they range from Clytemnestra in Aeschylus's *The Oresteia* to the protagonists of Sophocles's *Antigone* and Euripides' *Medea*. The women in Aristophanes's comedy *Lysistrata* protest against war by refusing to sleep with their husbands. These memorable female characters are, as Helene Foley has observed, quite surprising in a patriarchal society in which women were largely restricted to the domestic sphere (Foley 1981: *passim*), although some scholars suspect an underlying misogyny because the characters were authored by men and played by male actors (Case 1985: *passim*).

Performances of Greek drama were not simple acts of affirmation of the values of an ideally homogeneous community. Rather, the dramatists frequently addressed issues of concern to the *polis*, often reworking myths and epic narratives to do so. As such, they often provoked debates about the *polis* of the playwrights' present. Aeschylus's *The Persians* (472 BCE), his prize-winning tragedy on the recent Battle of Salamis, could have been written either to praise the victorious Athenians or to express sympathy with the defeated Persians (Harrison 2000: 16–18). In one year, the playwright Phrynicus (who wrote between 511 and 475 BCE) was heavily fined for dealing with the painful subject of the Persians' destruction of Miletus, a city Athens had pledged to defend but did not. Its fall precipitated the Persian invasion of 492 BCE.

The ceremonies preceding the performances reinforced the connections between drama and the *polis*. The sons of fathers who died in battle processed in military dress into the same theatre where Sophocles's *Antigone* was played, with its central conflict between the rules of a state at war and the interests of the individual. Generals from each of the ten tribes offered ritual libations to Dionysus in the theatre where Euripides' *The Trojan Women* was played. In that tragedy, Euripides used the story of Greece's conquest of Troy to focus on the brutality of war and the suffering it brings to the innocent. Throughout the fifth century, there was almost no year without an Athenian military engagement, and the festival ceremonies would have prompted the citizens of Athens to reflect upon state decision-making (Winkler 1990: 21).

All of these examples show that Athenians expected their theatre to stage contemporary cultural issues in its dialogic process, stirring debate. The subjects of Greek drama ran the gamut: war, justice, politics, public life, fate, sanctity, and more. The theatre's roots in Athenian civic powers and responsibilities were ultimately more fundamental than whatever linkage it may have had to Dionysus. One might well call Greek drama political theatre – theatre of and for the *polis*.

Greek theatre after the fifth century BCE

Meanwhile, the Sophists were refining methods of argument, mathematics, and intellectual analysis. History, once the preserve of tales and epics, began to be written. Some thinkers (Euripides among them) cast doubt on traditional religious beliefs or even upon religion itself. Such views indicate that at least among a literate portion of classical Athenians, a profound change had occurred in their understanding of themselves and their agency in the world, specifically concerning the idea that gods played a direct role in their destinies. The philosopher Plato (*c.*428–*c.*347 BCE), on the other hand, vigorously opposed the Sophists and promoted older aristocratic values (including, paradoxically, scorn for writing); in *The Republic* (*c.*380 BCE) he imagined an ideal city where philosopher-kings ruled – and playwrights were expelled, launching a long history of antitheatrical prejudice in Europe.

At either the City Dionysia in 449 BCE or the Lenaia in 442 BCE, a competition among tragic actors was introduced, marking public recognition of the actor's art. An actor could win despite appearing in a losing tetralogy. Actors were celebrated or critiqued on the basis of their day-long performances. By the fourth century BCE when, instead of new plays, previously authored plays were re-staged and/or toured other cities, the emphasis shifted further toward celebrating actors rather than playwriting. Reportedly, the famous late fourth-century Greek actor Polos performed in the title role of Sophocles's *Electra*, and in the scene when Electra takes the ashes of her brother Orestes from his tomb, Polos used the ashes of his own recently deceased son in his performance. According to the story, he "filled the whole place, not with the appearance and imitation of sorrow, but with genuine grief and unfeigned lamentation" (Gellius 1927: II, 35–7).

Following Euripides' death in 406 BCE, Greek tragedy tended to use somewhat melodramatic plot devices. Only one play from this period survives. The satyr play seems to have declined, but comedy thrived. The satiric, smutty, and issue-oriented comedies of Aristophanes's time – Old Comedy – gradually gave way to comedies about private life, such as family, domestic slaves, prostitutes, and love. This more genial genre was called New Comedy; we will look at it more closely in Chapter 2.

Nearly a century after the peak achievements of Athenian theatre, Aristotle gave lectures that have come down to us as the *Poetics* (*c.*330 BCE). He focused on the formal attributes and proper aesthetic effects of tragedy. Drawing on plays that had won City Dionysia competitions, he discussed the kinds of plots, characters, and language appropriate to achieve the effects of a genre he considered a "natural" form. Sophocles's *Oedipus the King* often serves as Aristotle's prime example.

Probably Aristotle's most enduring idea is that mimesis – imitation or representation of action and characters – is the core of drama. Aristotle believed there were six constituent elements of tragedy: plot, characters, verbal expression, thought (the characters' analyses or debates), song, and visual elements such as masks and costumes – in descending order of importance. Plots should be structured in a linear manner in which one event plausibly or necessarily follows from another. The best plots, he claimed, involve *peripety* (a turning point, such as a reversal of circumstances or a dramatic irony) and/or the recognition of some hidden fact. Finally, plots should have *pathos*, a destructive or painful action. Bad fortune that befalls the protagonist should not be caused by wickedness but by a serious mistake (*hamartia*).

 One of tragedy's chief elements, Aristotle believed, was *catharsis* [kah-THAHR-sis], a term that has generated controversy due to its multiple meanings. Aristotle is frequently understood as saying that the audience is "purged" of fear, pity, or other emotions. But he might have meant that the events that caused the emotions were "clarified," or that the dramatic action "cleaned" the wrongdoing that caused the tragedy. His phrasing is too ambiguous for us to know for sure. In fact there are numerous difficulties in translating the *Poetics*; many misunderstandings and much debate have followed in its wake.

The *Poetics* is the first known work of literary analysis, and it is clearly the product of a literate culture – one in which writing is culturally dominant. Aristotle's focus is on plays as a genre of literature, not on theatrical performance (which he considered secondary or even unnecessary), still less on the plays' civic and religious contexts. Although he does take the audience into account and mentions performance, his attention is largely on literary structures such as plot and character. Nevertheless, the *Poetics* provides clues about the performance context and early history of Greek tragedy.

The *Poetics* was unknown in Europe until the late 1500s, but after that, Aristotle's ideas were highly influential, and are sometimes drawn upon even today. As we will see in Chapter 5, Renaissance scholars portrayed the *Poetics* as rigidly prescriptive rather than a description of what Aristotle believed made for effective drama, and it came to be used pervasively as a model for European dramatic writing and analysis. Objections to Aristotle's theories have also been frequent, beginning in the early 1700s, but increasingly from the end of that century on. Most of the criticism has been leveled against his views about plot structure and his indifference toward performance, but all of his ideas, including the role of mimesis, have come under fire at some point. Even so, because of its historical role the *Poetics* is usually the starting point for studying dramatic theory.

Between the appearance of early tragedy around 540 BCE and the *Poetics* two centuries later, Greek culture changed considerably. In particular, the rise of literacy shaped the development of tragedy, and of comedy as well. The chorus, which retained many characteristics of oral culture, slowly lost its dramatic function. Individual characters, in contrast, were given more "prose-like" and ordinary language as they increased in prominence. Instead of the episodic, modular narratives of epics, the drama focused on a single event, and plots were structured in a linear manner.

We can identify some key changes in narrative resulting from literate culture as it developed in Athens:

- Reduced dependence on verbal patterns. Versification remained; however, in the characters' speech (as distinct from the chorus's), language became increasingly colloquial and prose-like.
- Reduced dependence on formulaic phrases.
- Linear, causally oriented narrative structure focusing on a single event.

- A shift in the function of strange imagery to serve the plot rather than mnemonic needs, as seen for example in the monstrous bull that bursts from the sea to kill Hippolytus in Euripides' *Hippolytus*.

However, for decades clear elements of oral culture continued in tragedy, most notably in the choruses whose performances included dance and song.

Of conquerors and refugees

Classical Greece is often fetishized as the cradle of Western civilization. The facts, however, are more complicated, because Athens' massive cultural influence was not wholly of its own making.

Between 431 and 404 BCE, the Greek city-states of Athens and Sparta and their allies fought a series of devastating battles called the Peloponnesian War. The war occurred because Sparta (an oligarchy focused on military prowess) feared that Athens was growing too strong and imperialistic. Athens' defeat was hastened by poor military strategy and a disastrous plague. The city was never again the dominant power in ancient Greece.

In 338 BCE, King Philip II of Macedon (then part of northern Greece) subdued several of the Greek city-states, including Athens, placing them under his rule. His son Alexander the Great (356–323 BCE) – once Aristotle's pupil – widened his power over Greece, and then began a military campaign in which he conquered much of the Mediterranean region, as well as Egypt, Persia, and parts of India.

Seeking to make non-Greek lands more like Greece ("Hellenization"), Alexander introduced Athenian culture, including theatre, throughout the area. Actors became powerful, sometimes wealthy public figures, and some served as political negotiators or as ambassadors. At the end of the fourth century, a state official called the *agonothetes* – "arranger of contests" – oversaw the choruses and their budgets, ending the old Athenian tradition of wealthy citizens supporting theatre as a civic duty. Tragedy fossilized, but New Comedy grew highly popular.

After Alexander's death, his empire was divided and eventually weakened. During the Hellenistic era (317 BCE–27 CE), Rome arose as the major Mediterranean power. In 148–146 BCE, Rome formally annexed Greece. Roman authors sought to emulate the glory that was Macedonia, particularly its culture – that is, Athenian culture.

Eventually Romans lost interest in Greek literature, and after the city's fall in 476 CE, little of ancient Greek culture was known in the West until the twelfth century, when Aristotle commanded attention. However, it continued to be studied all across the Mediterranean, the Middle East, and Persia (today, Iran). It might have remained an "Eastern" subject – but when Constantinople (now Istanbul) was sacked in 1453, its scholars fled to Europe, bringing numerous manuscripts with them. Thus the culture of ancient Greece became part of the West's Renaissance construction of a classical heritage.

Ancient Athens had a long legacy, but one riddled with lengthy gaps and many losses, reinterpretations, and misunderstandings. And its legacy arose when it was no longer powerful. Classical Greek culture was spread by others, as conquerors' spoils of war, and the treasured belongings of refugees.

SUMMARY

For most of humankind's existence, the spoken word was the dominant mode of communication. When writing was invented, its significance and impact varied from society to society, and changed over time. In some cultures writing served for little more than bookkeeping and remained thoroughly subordinate to speech. Elsewhere, such as in Egypt and Mesoamerica, writing played a significant administrative and (to a greater or lesser extent) cultural role within the narrow elite of scribes, priests, and/or rulers, but it was seldom learned among people beyond that group. These were essentially oral cultures with restricted literacy. In Greece, the alphabet made it possible for a significant fraction of the population to learn how to read and write, vastly expanding the uses of literacy. In Athens, oral and literate communication practices vied for dominance, leading to numerous interactions, fusions, and juxtapositions as writing slowly gained the upper hand.

With these changes in communication practices came changes in performance. The capabilities of oral communication, including the strategies it requires to preserve knowledge, closely affected the features of oral culture's main types of performance: storytelling and ritual. Among the most notable contrasts between the oral and the literate strategies were the shifts from modularity to causality or probability for structuring narratives, and from verse and formulas to prose-like writing. Oral culture offered principally the collective performance of ritual, and the solitary performance of the storyteller before an audience; in ancient Athens, in the very earliest form of tragedy a single actor stood separate from a chorus (combining features of both ritual and storytelling), but then additional actors were added and the chorus slowly declined. The narrative structure and performer/audience distinction of storytelling were blended with ritual's enactment of personages.

But perhaps the most fundamental difference between ritual and theatre was that performance was no longer viewed as an offering to propitiate the gods or an act that preserved the balance of the universe: drama – even if it honored the gods or portrayed their influence in human life – primarily served as an intervention in human society. Plays approved or criticized human actions and sometimes challenged people's thought, even about the gods themselves. Although we have no information on how theatre arose outside of Greece, as we will see in Chapter 2, India, China, and Japan similarly made theatre a vehicle for human enjoyment and edification. As writing obtained an increasing social and cultural role, many characteristics of oral culture continued within theatre (and continue to this day), but new cultural genres emerged and orality's role in performance and in society itself irrevocably altered.

★

Pleasure, power, and aesthetics: Theatre in early literate societies, 500 BCE–1450 CE

Carol Fisher Sorgenfrei
Contributor: Phillip B. Zarrilli

As noted in the previous chapter, orality does not end with the development of written language. Rather, oral traditions not only continue alongside newer, written texts, but influence (or sometimes even determine) how these texts are performed. In this chapter, we will continue the discussion of how written theatre and aesthetic taste developed in relation to local politics, economics, and cultural imperatives such as gender and social status. We will look at major genres in a wide variety of cultures: the Roman Republic (509 BCE–27 BCE) and Roman Empire (27 BCE–476 CE), India (primarily *c*.200 BCE–*c*.200 CE), and fourteenth-and fifteenth-century Japan. We will see that, despite local differences, in each case the intended audience was not exclusive, and the values and tastes of disparate classes often mingle.

We begin by showing how some forms of Greek performance were adapted by Roman playwrights and how Roman comedy and spectacular entertainments catered to the desires of the masses. We will see how, as the political and economic situation changed, Roman tragedy and aesthetics, although intended for a more elite audience, retained the popular emphasis on spectacle and extreme violence.

We then turn to theatre in ancient India, looking at how significant cultural epics and the power of local political and religious leaders created several disparate genres. These culturally distinct genres mutually influenced each other, arriving at significant new forms. We will delve into the Indian aesthetic theory of *rasa* and *bhava*, which also has important similarities to contemporary understandings of audience reception and the actor's psychology.

The Hindu culture of ancient India gave birth to Buddhism, which spread rapidly throughout Asia. In Japan, the ruling samurai adopted a version of Chinese Buddhism, as well as the Chinese writing system and Chinese Confucian ideology. Theatre artists mingled these elements with native Shinto thought and with both local and imported performance practices, creating new genres that pleased both elite and non-elite audiences. For the samurai rulers, performance was used to mark their recent victories over other clan leaders as well as to help legitimate new political and economic realities (including those that shifted power away from women).

> ## THINKING THROUGH THEATRE HISTORIES
>
> ### Roadblocks, detours, and U-turns
>
> In reading any kind of history, most people would prefer a clear narrative with logical development – a fast lane taking us from point A to point B. However, as we will see throughout this book, the routes of theatre history are sometimes tangled, reversed, and not always logical. For example, it doesn't seem to make sense, as we shall see below, that the culture of ancient Rome became more barbaric and bloodthirsty as the centuries passed. Nor does it seem logical that the samurai culture of medieval Japan should prefer plays about tragic women to plays about heroic warriors, or that ancient India's aesthetic theories should so closely resonate with some of the West's most recent ideas. Similarly, a reader might well wonder why the theatres and cultures of ancient Rome, ancient India, and medieval Japan are included in a single chapter.
>
> The driving themes of this chapter are the similarities and differences in social, political, and economic structures of these intensely hierarchical, early-literate cultures. These forces are not stable, yet in their often twisting, bending, or forked ways, they – and other forces – influence the course of theatre's multiple histories. As we look around these corners, we will search for possible answers to questions such as how and why theatre develops in varied ways in different times and places, what forces cause these shifts to occur faster or more slowly, and why some cultures seem to stop or even go backwards in a "U-turn" rather than moving forward.

In all three of these cultures, the narration and/or enactment of performative events continued, whether members of the audience were literate or not.

Ancient Roman performance: From the Republic to the Empire

To understand Roman performance, we must consider its debt to the widespread influence of Greek civilization, even as the brilliance of Greek theatre declined. Rome, however, was a very different society. The Roman Republic was divided between two classes, the *patricians* (wealthy aristocrats) and the *plebeians* (ordinary, lower-class citizens). The classes were strictly segregated, and intermarriage was forbidden. Only males (eventually including freed slaves and even non-Romans under Roman jurisdiction) were citizens. The most powerful branch of the Republic was the Senate. Senators were almost always patricians who were skilled in the arts of rhetoric and verbal persuasion. Although plebeians gained political power in the late Republic, the patricians retained control – sometimes by using their wealth to buy influence and votes. By the time of the Empire, however, the political clout of the Senate and its patrician members had been diluted.

Every Roman institution operated as a sacred patriarchy, and each family was a state in miniature. The male head of each family (*pater familias*) legally held absolute power over members of his household. For example, in 340 BCE, Manlius Torquatus had his son executed for disobeying orders during the Great Latin War, even though his son's unauthorized attack resulted in military victory. Two types of behavior shaped and constrained Roman males during the Republican period: *pietas* and *gravitas*. *Pietas* is usually translated as "respect for elders," but also implies respect for authority, loyalty of wife to the husband, and devotion to the gods. *Gravitas* (a word related to "gravity") is usually translated as "dignity," and it implies seriousness.

Very few people in ancient Rome (perhaps as few as 10 percent) were able to read and write. Thus, the spoken word was a crucial element of performance. Romans remained deeply sensitive to the power of verbal language that the patrician orators had perfected. In describing the funeral of Julius Caesar, the Roman historian Plutarch gives an account of a speech which used rhetorical skill to subtly shift the audience's point of view. For an imagined version of this event, see Mark Antony's famous eulogy beginning "Friends, Romans, countrymen, lend me your ears. . ." in Shakespeare's *Julius Caesar* (Act III, sc. 2). All Roman playwrights (even those who wrote comedies) exhibit such skill with language. Similarly, actors were valued partly because of their skill in oral presentation.

Early Roman performance: Festivals, games, and mimes

The Romans adapted many aspects of Greek culture. For example, the Olympian gods were transformed into Roman gods, with Zeus becoming Jupiter, Aphrodite becoming Venus, and so on. One popular type of performance adapted from Greece was mime. Mime (not to be confused with wordless pantomime) was a verbal and physical form of theatre that originated in Syracuse, a town in Sicily. Mime was performed as early as the fourth century BCE in Athens. Unlike plays, which used only masked male actors (cross-dressed if depicting female characters), both males and female actors (without masks) performed mime. Some scholars suggest that because the face of the unmasked mime actor (Greek: *mimos*; Latin: *mimus*) was so expressive, mime fostered the development of a relatively more realistic acting style than a masked actor might use. Mimes used monologue, dialogue, dance, song, and skills such as acrobatics to elaborate on often sexually explicit scenes, political satire, everyday life, or farcical portrayals of incidents derived from mythology. While comedy and tragedy could rely on plot devices and the characterization of masked actors to sustain interest, the unmasked mime performer relied on his/her expressive physical abilities. In some ways, mime might be compared to the variety shows, striptease, and slapstick of vaudeville.

Public holidays in ancient Rome were of two kinds. Those called *feriae* were primarily religious and serious, while others were called *ludi* [LOO-dee] – "games," a term meaning both the holiday and the actual games, sports, and performances that were included along with religious observances.

Many *ludi* were held throughout the year. Some honored various deities while others were held for secular reasons (such as dignitaries' funerals or birthdays) or to celebrate military victories. The largest public *ludi*, the *Ludi Romani* ("Roman Games"), was held early in September to honor the god Jupiter. Although originally celebrated on a single day, after 220 BCE it expanded, until by 51 CE the *Ludi Romani* took place over a period of 14 days, supported primarily by public funds.

The *Ludi Romani* far surpassed the Greek *Panathenaea* in diversity of events. Chariot and horse racing, boxing, singing, and parades were joined by bloody spectacles that resulted in the deaths of the participants. These included gladiatorial combats, staged animal hunts, and even mock sea battles (*naumachia* [naw-MAH-khee-ah]) which are discussed below.

Dramatic performances (*ludi scaenici*, meaning "stage games") were first included in 240 BCE. These first Roman plays were written by Livius Andronicus (*c.*284–*c.*204 BCE), a former Greek slave. Although only fragments of his works survive, we know about his plays from descriptions written by other Romans. All of his comedies and tragedies were adaptations or translations of Greek plays, written in Latin (the language of ancient Rome).

Popular comedy in the Roman Republic

In the decades following Athens' defeat in the Peloponnesian War, the broad socio-political satire of Old Comedy, which had lampooned generals and politicians (exemplified by the plays of Aristophanes), was replaced by domestic comedies (New Comedy), such as those written by Menander (*c*.342–*c*.291 BCE). Of the more than 100 plays written by Menander, only two complete or nearly complete New Comedies survive – *The Bad-Tempered Man* (also translated as *The Grouch*) and *The Woman of Samos* – and fragments of others (Figure 2.1). Their plots focus on love affairs and family relationships, with somewhat generic characters defined by gender, age, or class. Rather than the pointed political messages of Old Comedy, Menander's plays reflected everyday events.

Greek New Comedy was reinvented in Rome as *fabula palliata* – "plays in Greek dress" and Greek locations. Two Roman playwrights of note adapted Greek New Comedies from the previous 200 years for their Roman audiences: Titus Maccius Plautus, known as Plautus (*c*.254–184 BCE) and Publius Terentius Afer, known as Terence (*c*.190–*c*.159 BCE).

Plautus transformed Greek New Comedy with his first production, *Stichus*, in 205 BCE. Plautus wrote about 130 plays. Of these, 21 are extant. His adaptations are characterized by a taste for fast-paced, pun-filled, bawdy, and almost slangy Latin. Parts of his plays are in a meter designed to be sung to music, making some contemporary scholars suggest they are actually an early form of musical comedy. Plautus's plays also use certain conventions of indigenous Italian performance, especially Atellan farce (*fabulae atellanae*) from southern Italy. Atellan farces

Figure 2.1
An image probably of the popular Menander, with three masks of Greek New Comedy: the mask of a young man (in his hand), and masks of a young woman and an older man or a comic slave. Marble relief sculpture of the first or second century BCE, after a third-century BCE work.

© 2004 The Trustees of Princeton Museum. Photo: Bruce M. White.

were improvised from simple core narratives, with easily recognizable stock characters weaving together jokes and comical stage business. For example, the audience would expect an old man to oppose his son's amorous adventures and a slave to cleverly thwart his old master. Both early Atellan farces and Plautus's dramas were performed on temporarily constructed wooden stages set up for each *ludi*. This simple playing space was not bound by a realistic depiction of locale or space; it could represent a harbor front or a street. A scene building backed the playing space, and the three openings in it serviced many different plots. Since none of these wooden structures has survived, we do not know if the scene building behind the *ludi* stage was temporary or permanent.

Because dramatic performances took place in the context of public games, Roman playwrights had to write plays that captured the attention of a popular audience. This is exemplified in the prologue to Plautus's *Poenulus*. An actor steps on the stage and directly addresses the raucous audience. In comical language, he orders them to be silent, to sit still, to stop eating, and to wake up. He forbids prostitutes from sitting on the stage, old men from clomping around, and everyone from blocking the audience's view of the actor. And because he wants to have a paying audience, he says:

> Keep slaves from occupying the seats, that there be room for free men, or let them pay money for their freedom. If they can't do that, let them go home and avoid a double misfortune − being raked with rods here, and with whips at home if their masters return and find they haven't done their work.

(Duckworth 1942: I, 727−8)

Figure 2.2
This Roman marble relief shows a performance of masked characters typical of Roman comedy, including the two older men at left and the young man at right with a scheming servant at his side. Between them, a musician plays the double-reed *aulos*, suggestive of the use of music and song in some of the comedies. Behind the actors is a door in the façade backing the stage and a small curtain (*siparia*), perhaps concealing a painted panel not relevant to this particular scene.

© Museo Nazionale, Naples.

This prologue reveals how the Roman state/religious festival context was in essence a "marketplace" where the increasingly wide variety of popular entertainments had to vie for the short attention span of its mass public.

Plautus's comedies, known primarily for the fast traffic of their comic plots and low antic business, turn the traditional Roman values of patriarchal order and *gravitas* on their heads. Those with the least power in the Roman hierarchy – slaves, wives, and sons – are often those who win out (albeit the stakes are not large). The reference to the rod and whippings for slaves in the prologue to *Poenulus* cited above reflects the reality that Roman slaves were the lowest among the low in Roman society – objects with no rights who could be tortured or killed. In Plautus's plays, the clever slave often outsmarts his master. This is an example of "comic inversion" (discussed in the case study below) or the carnivalesque (discussed in Chapter 3). The plays depicted silly or impossible events and were not meant to criticize society (see Figure 2.2).

The later comedies authored by Terence were more constrained than those of Plautus. Because Terence had been a slave brought to Rome from northern Africa and educated by a wealthy family, some scholars suggest that he may have been black or Arab. From his first production in 166 BCE, Terence followed the model of the Greek New Comedy, with four of his six extant plays based on Menander's. He often combines plots and characters from several Greek sources into one play. Compared with Plautus's stock characters, the characters in Terence's plays are somewhat more complex. Terence's language is often elegant and witty, and less bawdy than Plautus's.

Despite or perhaps because of these characteristics, Terence at times had trouble holding the attention of his Roman audience. At the first performance of *Hecya*, written for the *Ludi Megalenses* in 165 BCE, the audience left to go and see the rope dancers. At a second staging, they left to see the gladiators fight. These examples suggest that not all of his plays successfully competed with other, more popular entertainments in the Roman marketplace. Nevertheless, in terms of the history of European theatre, his plays are crucial. They became key texts in Latin education during the medieval period, and they influenced the development of drama and performance during the early Renaissance.

CASE STUDY: Plautus's plays: What's so funny?

Gary Jay Williams, with Carol Fisher Sorgenfrei

Comedy has always been difficult to define. As soon as you explain why a joke is funny, it stops being funny. In addition, critics and theorists throughout the world have tended to value "serious" drama and literature over comedy; however, it is comedy that audiences more often prefer.

There are various types of comedy, not all of which can be considered here. Satire, for example, often has a serious or even political purpose, since it uses exaggeration to point out the flaws, foibles, and even the corruption of powerful people or institutions. Parody takes on familiar artworks or their genres and twists the originals to make fun of them. Farce focuses on wildly improbable characters and situations, fast-paced action and dialogue, and often involves mistaken identity and sexual situations. Some forms of comedy are only comic to specific audiences but are deeply offensive to others. An example is comedy that uses sexual, physical, or racial stereotypes. Some people find such comedy liberating and harmless ("Can't you take a joke?"), while others feel that it is hurtful to both individuals and to society ("That's mean [or racist, sexist, etc.]. It's not funny.").

Aristotle's *Poetics* (*c.*330 BCE), which focuses on Greek tragedy, only briefly mentions comedy. Nevertheless, what he did say about comedy has influenced subsequent Western criticism.

Aristotle's critical method was inductive, reasoning from a number of specific Athenian examples toward what he believed to be general principle of drama. Distinguishing between tragedy and comedy, he reasoned that comedy will be populated by "characters of a lower type," while tragedy's chief characters will be from great and "illustrious" families (nobility or ruling families) (Else 1957: 376; Aristotle 1984: 2319, 2325). Aristotle suggests that comic characters, not unlike their tragic counterparts, are obsessed by some all-consuming idea that leads to their downfall, but in comedy, this defect is neither painful nor destructive. Comedy's home, it follows, is not the court but the domestic household or neighborhood street. Comedy's plots usually involve food, money, sex, or social status. For the Greeks and Romans, all comedies had a happy ending.

Most comedies share at least some of the following elements: incongruity, reversal, repetition, misunderstanding, and mistaken identity. Some of these elements also appear in tragedies, but in comedy, potentially tragic events are reversed into happy results, leading to laughter and emotional release (and psychological health) for the audience. The founder of psychoanalysis, Sigmund Freud (1856–1939) is among those who have written about how laughter and comedy can have beneficial psychological effects. In the mid-twentieth century, critic Northrop Frye observed that many comedies end with some festive ritual, such as a dinner or wedding, signaling the formation of a stable, new society.

Following Aristotle's mode of formal analysis, later Western theorists made distinctions between high and low comedy. High comedy, also called comedy of manners, generally concerns (and appeals to) aristocrats or the economically privileged, and it features clever ideas and witty language. In low comedy, such as farces and the plays of Plautus, the humor derives from fast-developing events and physical action, with the body being a major player. The erect phallus is a standing joke in the oldest of Western comic forms – built into the costumes of the characters in the Greek satyr plays.

In 1900, French philosopher Henri Bergson (1859–1941) summarized various theories of comedy. Many of his examples still seem to make sense. His main idea was that comedy results from incongruity – especially when our expectations differ from reality. Bergson wrote that the comic character is usually comic in proportion to his ignorance of his own faults, and noted that the comic character continually repeats his mistakes in a mechanical way. For example, the central character of Plautus's *The Braggart Soldier* (*Miles Gloriosus*, 205 BCE) is totally infatuated with himself, bragging about his victories, his strength (he says he killed an elephant with his fist), and his sexual prowess. His slave, who struggles to carry his master's oversized shield, feeds his ridiculous appetite for flattery, describing his master as "Destiny's dashing dauntless debonair darling" (Plautus 1963: 9). Late in the play, the vain soldier flatters himself preposterously and demonstrates his ignorance of Roman religion by saying that he was born only one day after Jupiter and that he is the grandson of Venus. His servant's scheme, and the play's whole purpose, is to wind him up to strut like this. When a collaborating servant girl greets him with "Hail, you gorgeous creature! / Oh, man of every hour, beyond all other men / Beloved of two gods –" he interrupts her to ask, "Which two?" (1963: 90).

Another character who behaves mechanically (which, according to Bergson, is always comic) and who is unaware of his faults appears in Plautus's *The Pot of Gold*. Here, the miserly old Euclio is obsessed with money. He so fears that someone will steal the pot of gold he has hidden that he suspects everyone, including the rooster he finds scratching near it, which he instantly kills. The clever slave of his daughter's suitor manages to steal Euclio's gold, resulting in Euclio giving the suitor permission to marry his daughter, but only because that means he will get his pot of gold back. By ending in a marriage, this play conforms to Northrup Frye's idea of the festive. The play also demonstrates how serious issues (the cruelty of a father who refuses to allow his daughter to marry for love, or how excessive greed can destroy life's pleasures) can be twisted from potential tragedy to comedy.

According to Bergson, we laugh when "the history of a person or of a group . . . sometimes appears like a game worked by strings, or gearings, or springs" (Bergson 1956: 116). Plautus's *The Menaechmi* fits this description. It features another typical aspect of comedy – mistaken identity – by focusing on identical twin brothers (a happily practical idea for a theatre in which all characters wore masks). Long lost to each other by misfortune, neither knows for sure if his brother is alive, or where he might live. The plot of *The Menaechmi* is a calculus of complications set off by the presence of the twins. Menaechmus II, who is from Syracuse, has been searching the world for his brother. (In grief over the loss of one of the twins when the boys were seven years old, his family had renamed the remaining boy Menaechmus, the name of his missing brother.) He happens to arrive in Epidamnum where his brother, Menaechmus I, lives. The mistress of Menaechmus I, Erotium, mistakenly invites Menaechmus II into her house, supposing him to be her lover. So, too, the angry wife and all the servants of Menaechmus I mistake Menaechmus II for Menaechmus I. Each twin concludes that the world around him has gone mad. Everyone else believes the twins to be mad, including the doctor who is called in by Erotium's father. In exasperation at one point, Menaechmus II feigns madness to be rid of them all.

Plautus multiplies the confusions by repeatedly having one twin exit by one door just as the other enters by another. All the characters revolve in and out of the doors of the houses of Erotium and Menaechmus I like figures on a mechanical clock gone haywire. The audience is always in on the joke because Plautus is always careful to have the entering twin identify himself clearly. At the play's climax, the twins finally meet at center stage, mirroring one another, and to the relief of everyone, they sort out the confusion. Since these characters are not nobles, and their main preoccupations seem to be sex and food, we can see a connection to Aristotle's concepts of comedy.

Like his plots, Plautus's dialogue is full of comic devices. Near the end of *The Rope*, Daemones and the slave Trachalio, who serves the suitor of Daemones's daughter, have a rapid-fire exchange of lines in which the response "All right" is repeated seventeen times. After Trachalio exits, Plautus caps the sequence:

DAEMONES: All right, all right, nothing but "all right." He'll find all right's all wrong one of these days, I hope.

[*Enter Gripus, another slave*]

GRIPUS: Will it be all right [*Daemones jumps*] if I have a word with you, sir?

(Plautus 1964: 145–6)

A moment later, Trachalio has a series of exchanges with his young master, Plesidippus, who is in love with Daemones's daughter:

PLESIDIPPUS: Do you think we shall be betrothed today?
TRACHALIO: I do.
PLESIDIPPUS: Do you think I should congratulate the old man on finding her?
TRACHALIO: I do.
PLESIDIPPUS: And the mother?
TRACHALIO: I do.
PLESIDIPPUS: And what do you think?
TRACHALIO: I do.
PLESIDIPPUS: You do what?
TRACHALIO: I think.
PLESIDIPPUS: You do think what?
TRACHALIO: I do think what you think.
PLESIDIPPUS: Don't you think you could think for yourself?
TRACHALIO: I do.

(Plautus 1964: 147–8)

In both cases, the robotic responses of the slave, Trachalio, produce a comic momentum that threatens to unravel language itself. Once again, we see an example of Bergson's idea that comedy results when humans act like wind-up mechanical dolls rather than living beings. Bergson called this type of momentum "the snowball effect," which occurs when some tiny thing (in the plot or even in dialogue) gets totally out of control and becomes a gigantic problem. (Compare Abbot and Costello's famous skit "Who's on First?" in which the two men are using simple words and names to mean very different things, producing comic frustration over a simple baseball game.)

Plautus also employs parody and irreverence. He uses theatre to mock its own conventions, and makes fun of supposedly "superior" types of performance and even of the gods. Consider the following lines in Plautus's prologue to *Amphitryo*, which is delivered by the god Mercury in disguise as a lowly servant:

But I still haven't told you
About this favor I came to ask of you –
Not to mention explaining the plot of this tragedy.
I must get on . . .
What's that? Are you disappointed
To find it's a *tragedy*? Well, I can easily change it.
I'm a god after all. I can easily make it a comedy . . .

(Plautus 1964: 230)

Overall, this prologue suggests Plautus's familiarity with comic performance, a fact that would support the speculation that Plautus was himself a comic actor. The middle name that he took, Maccius, may be derivative of Maccus, the name of a clown figure in the ancient Atellan farces who was greedy and gluttonous, the type of character that Plautus might have played (see Figure 2.3).

Figure 2.3
Statue of a masked slave character from Roman comedy, leaning casually on a pillar. Archaeological Museum, Istanbul.

Photo: © Gary Jay Williams.

Plautus's plays have had staying power. One century after his death, the critic M. Terentius Varro put together a collection of 20 of his 21 plays that survived. Since Plautus borrowed many stock characters and plots from the prolific Greek comic playwright Menander, he is responsible for the survival of many classical prototypes. Among the many descendants of Plautus's *The Braggart Soldier* (*Miles Gloriosus*) are the Capitano and Scaramouche of the *commedia dell'arte* (see Chapter 4) and Shakespeare's Falstaff in *Henry IV, Part 1* (1598). Plautus's *The Menaechmi* is the source of Shakespeare's *Comedy of Errors* (1598), to which Shakespeare added a second set of identical twin slaves from Plautus's *Amphitryon*. *The Comedy of Errors* was the source for Richard Rodgers and Lorenz Hart's musical comedy *The Boys from Syracuse* (1938), with a script adapted by George Abbott. *Amphitryon* was the source for no fewer than 38 versions down to Jean Giraudoux's *Amphitryon 38* (1929), and Plautus's *The Pot of Gold* was the source of Molière's *The Miser* (1668). The 1962 American musical comedy *A Funny Thing Happened on the Way to the Forum* (by Burt Shevelove, Larry Gelbart, and Steven Sondheim) was a long-running concoction derived from Plautus. If we look at even the most contemporary comedy, we will find themes and devices that remind us of this ancient comic master.

Key references

Aristotle (1984) *Poetics*, trans. I. Bywater in J. Barnes (ed.) *The Complete Works of Aristotle*, rev. edn, vol. 2, Princeton: Princeton University Press.

Bergson, H. (1956) "Laughter," in *Comedy*, Garden City, NY: Doubleday Anchor Books.

Else, G. (1957) *Aristotle's Poetics: The Argument*, Cambridge, MA: Harvard University Press.

Frye, N. (1957) *Anatomy of Criticism*, Princeton: Princeton University Press.

Janko, R. (1984) *Aristotle on Comedy, Toward a Reconstruction of Poetics II*, Berkeley: University of California Press.

Plato (1942) *Symposium*, in Plato, *Five Great Dialogues*, trans. B. Jowett, Roslyn, NY: Walter J. Black.

Plautus, T.M. (1958) *The Pot of Gold*, trans. Peter Arnott, New York: Appleton-Century-Crofts.

Plautus, T.M. (1963) *The Braggart Soldier*, trans. Erich Segal, New York: Samuel French.

Plautus, T.M. (1964) *Amphityro*, in *The Rope and Other Plays*, trans. E.F. Watling, Baltimore: Penguin Books.

Plautus, T.M. (1974) *The Twin Menaechmi*, trans. Edward C. Wiest and Richard W. Hyde, in O.G. Brockett and L. Brockett (eds) *Plays for the Theatre*, 2nd edn, New York: Holt, Rinehart and Winston.

Slater, N.W. (1985) *Plautus in Performance*, Princeton: Princeton University Press.

Seneca's tragedies and Horace's Ars Poetica (The Art of Poetry)

It is perhaps surprising that so few Roman plays, other than the comedies, have survived. What little we know of serious or tragic plays comes primarily from the works of Seneca and Horace.

Lucius Annaeus Seneca (*c*.4 BCE–65 CE) was born in Spain and educated in Rome. He became a well-known politician, philosopher, and teacher who authored nine tragedies loosely based on Greek originals, including *Medea*, *Phaedra*, *Oedipus*, *Agamemnon*, and *Thyestes*. Unlike popular comedies, Roman tragedies were not performed in the marketplace. In fact, it is not clear if Seneca's tragedies were actually staged; they may have been merely recited at small, elite gatherings. Seneca's tragedies reflect the philosophy of Stoicism, which taught self-sufficiency and the avoidance of high emotion. Nevertheless, his plays are characterized by sensational violence and horror, far more than the Greek originals. This apparent contradiction may suggest a desire to condemn excessive emotion by demonstrating its horrific consequences. Alternatively, the gruesome violence depicted in Seneca's plays may suggest that even high-minded patricians enjoyed the bloody spectacles beloved of the plebeians, showing how the tastes of lower classes influenced those of the upper class.

Like Terence, Seneca had a great impact on the Renaissance. His philosophical essays influenced the French humanist and essayist Michel de Montaigne (1533–92), who is often cited as the "father of modern skepticism" and who himself influenced many later writers, including French philosopher Réné Descartes (1596–1650), American essayist Ralph Waldo Emerson (1803–82), and American science fiction writer Isaac Asimov (1920–92). As we will see in Chapter 5, Seneca's plays were the only Roman tragedies to survive the Middle Ages. As such, they were carefully studied as models of drama by scholars in the early Renaissance, since the language of learning in Europe was Latin. Consequently, Shakespeare and other English playwrights of the period were greatly influenced by Senecan tragedy and its often gruesome sensationalism.

Quintus Horatius Flaccus, generally known as Horace (65–8 BCE), was an important poet whose *Ars Poetica* (*Art of Poetry*, published 18 BCE, also known as *Letters to Piso*) makes several demands on playwrights that have come to represent what we call "neoclassicism" in Western drama. While generally agreeing with Aristotle in most matters, his work is prescriptive while Aristotle's is descriptive. In other words, Aristotle looked at existing plays and tried to figure out what worked; Horace imagined unwritten plays and told playwrights what they should do. He set down some of what came to be known later as "the rules." (For sixteenth/seventeenth-century misunderstandings of Aristotle and Horace, and the controversies regarding "the rules," see Chapter 5.) Among other things, Horace maintained that the five-act structure was the only correct one for tragedy and insisted that drama should entertain and educate, ideally simultaneously. Drama should not mix styles or genres (for example, no comic relief in a tragedy) and characters must be both consistent and recognizable (for example, playwrights should not deviate from the traditional image of well-known characters, such as Medea or Oedipus). Horace said that dramas should begin *in medias res* ("in the middle of things"), that is, not at the beginning of the story but closer to the climax. He disapproved of Plautus's bawdy language and plots, maintaining that drama must adhere to socially acceptable propriety, language and what he termed "decorum."

Like the structure and style of Senecan tragedy, the principles of drama explicated in Horace's *Ars Poetica* (although often misinterpreted) had a profound impact on subsequent playwrights and theorists. Because learning to read Latin was considered significant for educated Westerners until the mid-twentieth century, it may not be an exaggeration to suggest that the history of Western playwriting and dramatic theory owes at least as much to the influence of these two Roman authors as to the ancient Greeks.

Imperial spectacles: Performance during the Empire

During the late Republic, dramatic performances had been sponsored by wealthy men who sought to enhance their reputations, but by the end of the first century BCE, both comedy and tragedy had ceased to be viable dramatic forms. Rather than new plays, popular entertainment focused on spectacular re-stagings of extant dramas and on other events such as bloody contests.

The powerful patriarchy operating throughout the Roman Republic eventually gave way to a centralized authoritarian state with the establishment of the Roman Empire in 27 BCE, when Caesar Octavian (63 BCE–14 CE) received the honorific title of Augustus. Absolute power was surrendered by noble/landed families to a now all-powerful emperor, later called the father of the country (*pater patriae*). The service due to one's family was now to be extended to the state. As we will see, the values and tastes of the masses had effectively replaced the older ideals that the patricians had once hoped to spread throughout the Roman world.

Rome's first permanent theatre was not built until 55 BCE by Pompey the Great (106–48 BCE) (Figure 2.4). This grand building sat 20,000 spectators and featured a stage 300 feet in width, backed by an architecturally elaborated three-story façade (*scaenae frons*), decorated with statues. It was constructed less to serve the art of drama than to be a highly visible platform where Pompey (and subsequent rulers) could preside over the gathered populace, displaying the ruler's authority and the grandeur of Rome. Although a large temple was incorporated into the outer wall of the auditorium (*cavea*) for Venus Victrix, it seems evident that the *ludi* had lost almost all connection to religion.

Mime continued to be popular, as well as a relatively new art called **pantomime**. In panto-mime, a chorus and/or musicians accompanied a solo, masked, non-speaking actor who played all the roles in a lavishly staged myth or the re-staging of a drama. In the second century CE, Lucian wrote of the pantomime actor:

> You will find that his is no easy profession, nor lightly to be undertaken; requiring as it does the highest standard of culture in all its branches, and involving a knowledge not of music only, but of rhythm and meter, and above all of your beloved philosophy, both natural and moral. . . . The pantomime is above all things an actor; . . . success, as the pantomime knows, depends . . . upon verisimilitude . . . : prince or tyrannicide, pauper or farmer, each must be shown with the peculiarities that belong to him.
>
> (Nagler 1952: 28–9)

Like actors, pantomime and mime artists were often controversial figures denied citizenship but who nevertheless gained a large public following and were treated as stars. When Julius Caesar served as dictator of Rome (48–45 BCE), the noted producer and actor of mime, Laberius, was called out of retirement by Caesar himself to celebrate Caesar's victories. When Laberius appeared as a beaten slave in one mime performance, he dared to say on stage, "Henceforth, O citizens, we have lost our liberty!" And when Laberius said, "He must fear many, whom many fear," it is reported that the entire audience of 20,000 turned to see Caesar's

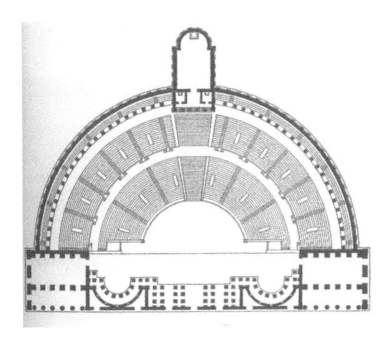

Figure 2.4
Ground plan of the Theatre of
Pompey (55 BCE), Rome, as
reconstructed in the Renaissance.
Connected to the rear of this theatre
was an enormous public plaza with
open colonnaded structures, which the
Greeks had called a *stoa*.

Source: Margarete Bieber, *The History of the
Greek and Roman Theater*, Princeton, NJ,
Princeton University Press, 1961, p.181.

reaction to the words. While Caesar awarded the palm of victory for acting to Laberius's rival, Publilius Syrus, he nevertheless treated Laberius genially and tolerantly. Not all performers were so lucky. It is said that the Emperor Nero, who loved to perform, became so jealous of the skill of a pantomime dancer called Paris that he ordered the young dancer's execution.

Increasingly popular and bloody spectacles took place in specially built circuses. The word "circus" in this context means a large, oblong or rectangular stadium-like building with open-air seating used for entertainment. Rome's Circus Maximus was originally built during the second century BCE. Julius Caesar expanded it to 1,800 feet long and 350 feet wide, with wooden seating over arched stone vaults for around 150,000 spectators. Although destroyed by fire, when reconstructed in 200 CE, it had a seating capacity of 250,000. Spectacles included chariot racing, animal fights (*venationes*), gladiatorial contests (*munera*), and *naumachiae* – the staging of sea battles in the flooded circus, based upon episodes from Greek history, and performed by slaves, prisoners of war, or criminals condemned to death. They were schooled in specialist forms of combat – some heavily armed wearing helmets, others lightly armed with sword and shield, and still others with net, dagger, and trident – usually with all fighting to the death. One of the sea battles (*naumachia*) staged in 46 BCE and commissioned by Julius Caesar re-enacted the battle between Tyre and Egypt on an artificial lake in Rome. In 52 CE, Claudius staged a fight between Rhodes and Sicily using 19,000 prisoners.

In some *naumachiae* – as in some gladiatorial contests – those who had demonstrated great courage might be saved from death. It is estimated that about 50 percent of all human participants in these events were spared. Those who lived often became "stars." Some gladiators were in fact volunteers who craved the spotlight and, if victorious, were rewarded for their bravery and military skill. Female gladiators, often as highly trained in arms as the males, sometimes participated in the games. However, they were not always taken seriously and might be pitted against dwarves. The games were free – all citizens had a right to attend.

Animal fights included animals in combat with armed men, animals fighting animals, and condemned men and women exposed to animals that had been starved – such as individuals tied to a stake who were wheeled into an arena in which a hungry lion had been set loose to devour them. During the reign of Augustus Caesar, 3,500 animals were killed in the course of 26 different festivals. To celebrate the completion of the Colosseum in 80 CE, 9,000 animals were killed in such games.

Roman society at this time was deeply divided between wealthy aristocrats and the rest of society, many of whom were very poor. Although legislation and official and semi-official educational propaganda attempted to constrain behavior and encourage a return to ancient virtues founded on "the way of the fathers" during the mid-Republic, the bawdy plays of Plautus and bloody, public spectacles at the amphitheatres remained popular. Spectacular entertainments such as those noted above may have helped to keep the poorer members of society occupied. Such events may have been seen as a way for the populace to "let off steam," since Romans were typically expected to subordinate their individual personalities to the larger social good. Although virtues such as honor, dignity, and uprightness were valued, the writer Pliny the Younger (c.61–c.113 CE) complained that the uneducated mob lived only for "bread and circuses."

Debating the ludi: Did violent spectacles serve a purpose?

Historian Paul Plass's analysis of the Roman games can help us understand how and why such massive public bloodshed with its "hideous damage done to men or animals" had both social and symbolic meaning. He makes several key points:

(1) The games and their bloody entertainments permitted daily "routines to be routinely broken" at festival time.
(2) The "intensity and scale" of violence made the games seem extraordinary.
(3) The public nature of the games allowed extreme violence to become the norm.
(4) Since they were mass public events, probably no individual felt responsibility for the lethal spectacles taking place. Rather, all citizens present participated in a new and separate "mass identity" that gave them a sense of "power and gratification at survival."
(5) The spectators were as important as the spectacle in that "their attendance in great numbers at a public event *was* the show in a political and social sense" (Plass 1998: 43). Therefore, the games proclaimed the fruits of building the Empire, the breadth of its world conquest, and the extent of its prosperity.
(6) The very extravagance of the games demonstrates an excess of "conspicuous consumption" that was fed by "copious supplies of [human and animal] blood." They indicated the "unrestrained power" of the emperor and the state (Plass 1998).

(For a view of how another culture used such displays, see the discussion of Mayan human sacrifice in Chapter 1.)

However, not everyone supported these events. The games and the theatre had long been opposed by the growing Christian community, not only because Christians condemned to death had sometimes been thrown to wild animals. By the end of the second century, the Christian writer Tertullian (c.160–c.240) had urged Christians to avoid theatre and the spectacles at the amphitheatres. He objected because the *ludi* were dedicated to pagan deities, were filled with unchaste and inhumane activities, and did not offer viewers a chance to practice Christian virtues. Attending them, he maintained, would pollute the viewer.

In 312, the Emperor Constantine converted to Christianity and in 313, the practice of Christianity ceased to be a crime in the Empire. A decade later, it became the official religion of the Roman Empire. In 398, the Church decreed excommunication for anyone going to the theatre rather than church on holy days. Actors were forbidden the sacraments unless they renounced their profession, a decree that remained in force into the eighteenth century. Nevertheless, Roman *ludi* continued, with festivals in the fourth century lasting as long as 100 days. By the early fifth century, there was some decline in the more excessive blood spectacles. With the economic and political decay of the Empire and its division into independent parts ruled by Rome and Constantinople, a weakened Rome fell to the Visigoths in 476. The last record of a Roman theatre performance is dated 549 CE.

As we will see in Chapter 3 and subsequent chapters, many religions continued to have conflicted attitudes toward theatre. The apparent contradictions (such as medieval Christianity's embrace of performance as a key element of certain religious observances versus the disdain for theatre by the reformers who created Protestantism) are examples of the twisting roads theatre historians must navigate.

Drama and theatre in early India

Although the Roman Empire was huge, it did not reach as far as India. However, Alexander the Great had previously extended Hellenic influence to the northwest of the Indian subcontinent, and mutual influences can be discerned in Greek and Indian sculpture and painting during the Hellenic period. The Roman Empire traded extensively with India and China, importing luxuries such as spices and silk. Sanskrit (a language of ancient India) is linguistically related to Greek, Latin, and most European languages. To some theatre historians as late as the mid-twentieth century, such facts suggested possible connections between ancient Greek and Indian performance. However, with the exception of some stories that traveled between cultures, there is no evidence of influence in either direction in this early period.

When we speak of Sanskrit drama, we are referring to a specific style of performance that originally used the Sanskrit language. The Sanskrit word for "story," *katha*, also means something "which is true" – that is, a story involving consequences that reverberate throughout cosmic history. It can also be translated as "telling or narration" (Lutgendorf 1991: 115). The performance of Sanskrit storytelling – and later, of Sanskrit drama – was always concerned with teaching moral lessons.

The great pan-Indian epics, both of which are sacred to Hinduism (the major but not the sole religion of India), are the *Mahabharata* and *Ramayana*. Both are important examples of *katha*. They began as narrated tales, and both have various written versions. The most respected Sanskrit version of the *Ramayana* dates from between 200 BCE and 200 CE. When regional languages developed, this version was replaced with easily accessible vernacular versions. The same is true of the *Mahabharata*, which dates back to at least the mid-first millennium BCE. Many other compendiums of stories exist, forming a storehouse of sources for drama.

All traditional forms of Indian theatre (that is, everything prior to the importation of European-style spoken drama) include complex dances, music, and detailed, conventionalized eye and hand gestures (*mudra*) that can be "read" almost like sign-language. Most also feature colorful, elaborate, non-realistic costumes and makeup.

The Natyasastra

The **Natyasastra** [NAH-tyah-SHAS-tr] – an encyclopedic work on all aspects of drama (*natya*) – dates from between 200 BCE and 200 CE. The author or authors are unknown. The *Natyasastra* relates the story of how the gods created drama as a pastime for humans, to give them visual and auditory pleasure. According to the *Natyasastra*, there were originally only four Vedas (books of hymns sacred to Hinduism), but the god Brahma created the *Natyasastra* as the fifth Veda. This Veda of drama is thus considered a holy book of Hinduism. According to the origin tale, Brahma gave the *Natyasastra* to the human sage Bharata, and also gave Bharata's hundred sons the task of putting it into practice.

The *Natyasastra* maintains that drama was to represent people from all walks of life and be accessible to all. Its aim was to teach by offering "good counsel" and "guidance to people" (Ghosh, intro. to Bharata 1967: 2–3, 14–15) using interesting stories of life in all its diversity, from war to sexual sensuality. The audience would "taste" (*rasa* [RAH-seh]) the states of being/doing (*bhava* [PHAH-vuh]) conveyed by the characters.

The *Natyasastra* is composed of 36 chapters. It traces the origins of drama and explains how to construct an appropriate theatre building. It explains how to worship the gods prior to performance, discusses types of plays, playwriting, costuming and makeup, character types and behavior, movement, gesture, and internal methods for acting the moods and states of being of characters. Even today, the *Natyasastra* continues to be honored as a divine gift, like a respected elder, but not slavishly imitated.

Early Sanskrit dramas

The scripts of Sanskrit plays reflect the social hierarchy of the period. Thus, only high-status male characters speak Sanskrit, while all women, children, men of inferior status, and a stock comic character (the *vidusaka*) speak in various dialects evolved from Sanskrit. The most common types of plays are heroic dramas, such as *Sakuntala* (sometimes written *Shakuntala*) by Kalidasa (*c.* late fourth century–early fifth century CE), a seven-act play based on well-known epic sources; invented dramas such as *The Little Clay Cart* by Sudraka (active sometime between the third and sixth century CE); along with one-act farces (for example, *Hermit/Harlot*) and other minor forms. All Sanskrit dramas begin with an invocation, followed by a prologue, and conclude with a benedictory prayer. Since the early nineteenth century, translations and adaptations of Sanskrit plays (for theatre, ballet, and opera) have been performed in Europe and North America.

Sakuntala is the name of the heroine of the play of that name. The original story appears in the *Mahabharata*. A king who is out hunting meets her by chance and falls in love. They marry, and he gives her a distinctive ring. He leaves for the palace, promising to return for her. However, a curse has been laid upon them and he forgets all about her. She decides to go to the palace herself, but during the journey, the ring slips off her finger and falls into a river. Because of the curse, the king does not recognize her without the ring. Many years later, a fish with the ring inside its belly is caught. When the king sees the ring, the evil spell is broken, and the lovers are reunited.

In *The Little Clay Cart*, a poor but generous man, although happily married with a son, falls in love with a courtesan. At one point, she piles rich jewels on his son's humble toy cart made of clay. Through a series of complications and misunderstandings, her lover is accused of her murder. Just as he is about to be executed, it is revealed that she is not dead. The actual

Figures 2.5 and 2.6
The *Bhagavan* or Hermit (Figure 2.5), and his wayward student, Shandilya (Figure 2.6), played, respectively, by Raman Cakyar and Kalamandalam Shivan, in a *kutiyattam* production of *The Hermit/Harlot* in Thiruvananthapuram, Kerala, in 1977. From a reconstructed staging based on traditional acting and staging manuals, under the supervision of Ram Cakyar of the Kerala Kalamdalam. Shandilya's costume is the traditional one worn in *kutiyattam* by the stock comic character, the *vidusaka*, who plays Shandilya here.
Photo © Phillip B. Zarrilli.

murderer of the real dead woman is arrested, the poor man and his lover are reunited, and the man's first wife and son happily welcome her into the family.

The one-act farce *The Hermit/Harlot* contains much witty dialogue and slapslick comedy. It was written by King Mahendravarman in the seventh century (see Figures 2.5 and 2.6). The plot revolves around a learned and austere yogi (the hermit) who attempts to teach his comically wayward disciple correct yogic practice. But the disciple can never learn correctly. In order to make his points, the yogi substitutes his own soul for that of a recently deceased prostitute (the harlot) with whom his disciple has fallen in love. Unbeknownst to the yogi, the harlot's soul had been mistakenly taken by the bumbling servant of the God of Death. The plot turns on farcical mistaken identities, ending with the souls being returned to their proper bodies.

More than 500 Sanskrit dramas exist today, composed in alternating simple prose and ornate verse, and chanted and/or sung to musical accompaniment, though some small prose sections may be spoken. The verse passages allow reflection, commentary, and a deepening of the state of mind of the main character(s) rather than forwarding the narrative.

Highly professional companies were composed of families that included male and female performers specializing in specific role-types, led by a male manager/actor (*sutradhara*). As described in the *Natyasastra*, actors followed a rigorous training regime that included a special diet, full body massages, yoga, and extensive training in "dance postures, physical exercise . . . [and] rhythm" (Kale 1974: 57–8). Their regimen included training in body movement, the language of hand-gestures, voice, emotional expression, and costumes and makeup. Actors

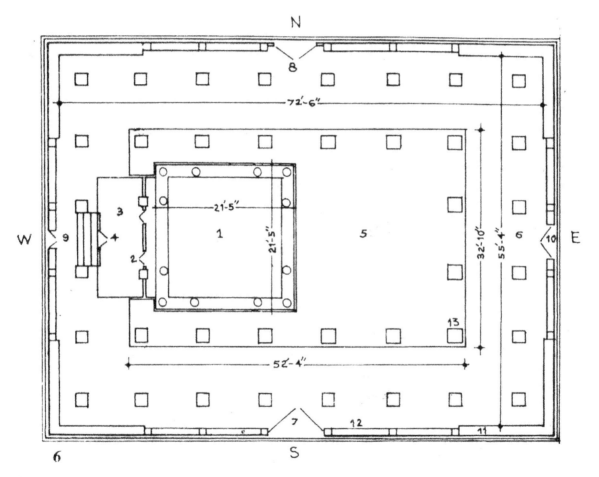

Figure 2.7

Floor plan of a playhouse for Sanskrit theatre in India, as described by Bharata in the *Natyasastra*, to be constructed on a consecrated piece of land on an east–west axis, and divided into equal halves for dressing room and acting areas. The audience is to be seated on the floor or a raked bank of seats in the east half.

Source: Line drawing. After Sketch No. 3, p. 47 in Tarla Mehta, *Sanskrit Play Production in Ancient India* (1995) New Delhi: Motilal Banarsidass.

learned physical vocabularies for representing both the ordinary things in nature, such as a deer or a flower, and for abstract concepts. Actors moved from one part of the stage to another to indicate a shift in locale. This convention also allowed the action to shift back and forth between two groups of actors on stage. Scenery was minimal.

Performances took place either in specially constructed theatres near temples as part of religious festivals (see Figure 2.7), or in small, intimate halls at court for other special occasions. The oldest outdoor spaces devoted solely to theatre were built between 300 and 50 BCE. Although they resemble Greek theatre architecture, their locations (in central and eastern India) are well beyond the areas invaded by Alexander the Great in 325 BCE. Consequently, the similarity may be coincidental, and later theatres did not follow this pattern. Rather, theatres for Sanskrit drama were built according to descriptions in the *Natyasastra*, and were either square, rectangular or triangular. Because none has survived, we don't know how many viewers these theatres held, but we do know that audiences came from all castes.

A person's caste indicted his or her hereditary place in society, including profession and level of ritual purity. Some contemporary scholars maintain that prior to British colonization, it was relatively easy to move between the castes, but that the British solidified the system for their own political ends (Dirks 2001). Such an interpretation would accord with our knowledge that people of all castes attended theatre. Audience members included experts in various fields (such as archers, grammarians, actors, courtiers, kings, musicians, and courtesans) who were seated at the front of the stage. They gave criticism and awarded prizes based on their area of expertise.

Kutiyattam: A new way to stage Sanskrit drama

After the tenth century CE, the Sanskrit language became increasingly restricted to members of the priestly castes. New forms of regional performance using local languages appeared. One of these, *kutiyattam* ("combined acting") [KOO-tee-ah-TAHM], emerged in Kerala (in south India). The *kutiyattam* version of the Sanskrit play *The Hermit/Harlot* (discussed above) is one of the oldest plays in the *kutiyattam* repertory. For more information on staging and performing this play, see "*The Hermit/Harlot* as an Example of Sanskrit Drama" on our website.

It is said that King Kulasekhara Varman became the patron of *kutiyattam*. He was actively involved in the performances and introduced several controversial innovations to the staging of Sanskrit dramas:

(1) the use of the local language, Malayalam, by the main comic character (the *vidusaka*) to explain key passages;
(2) the introduction of each character with a brief narration of his past;
(3) permission for the performance to deviate from the script in order to elaborate the meaning and/or a character's state of mind/being; and
(4) the development of manuals for staging and acting in this emergent style.

Although it was written in the local dialect, *kutiyattam* was originally not "popular" drama meant for ordinary audiences. Instead, *kutiyattam* during this period was exclusively performed within a small number of high-caste temples in Kerala; the performance was a "visual sacrifice" to the deities of these temples (see Figures 2.8 and 2.9). Other changes included performing only sections of the full play. These sections have become dramas in and of themselves, with

Figure 2.8
A temple theatre, known as a *kuttampalam*, built for *kutiyattam* in the Lord Vadakkunnathan (Siva) temple in Trissur, central Kerala. The temple compound containing this one is set apart from the outside world by high walls and massive gates. The main shrine housing Vadakkunnathan is to the right.
© Phillip B. Zarrilli.

lengthy preliminaries and elaborations of the story featuring one of the main characters on each night. Performing a single scene of a drama in the *kutiyattam* style can take from 5 nights to as many as 41. During the final one to three nights, all the actors come on stage to perform the act or scene. The term "combined acting" (*kutiyattam*) derives from this group appearance.

Not everyone approved of these innovations. Sometime in the fifteenth century, for example, a highly educated local connoisseur/scholar, writing in Sanskrit, attacked the "unfounded foul practices" of male and female *kutiyattam* actors. In his "Goad on the Actors," the unknown author wrote:

> Our only point is this – the sacred drama [*natya*], by the force of ill-fate, now stands defiled. The ambrosial moon and the sacred drama – both are sweet and great. A black spot mars the beauty of the former; unrestrained movements that of the latter. "What should we do then [to correct these defilements]?"
>
> Listen. The performance should strictly adhere to the precepts of Bharata [author of the *Natyasastra*]. Keep out the interruption of the story. Remove things unconnected. Stop your elaboration. . . . Reject the regional tongue. Discard the reluctance to present the characters.

Figure 2.9

Cross-section of the interior of the theatre in a temple in Trissur, central Kerala. Inside the high-ceilinged *kuttampalam*, the audience sits on the polished floor, facing the roofed stage. A drummer sits upstage, behind the actor. The dressing room is through two entry/exit doors behind the drummer.

Source: Line drawing No. 14 located on p. 79, from *Kuttampalam and Kutiyattam* by Goverdhan Panchal. New Delhi: Sangeet Natak Akademi, 1984. The author indicates that "most of the drawings in this book are based on my own drawings and sketches" and then rendered by Shri Ajit Parikh and Shri Ajit Joshi of the School of Architecture, Ahmedabad.

> . . . Always keep the self of the assumed character. This is the essence of acting. One follows the principles of drama if things are presented in this way.
>
> (Paulose 1993: 158–9)

Despite such attacks, *kutiyattam* survived, and continues to be performed today.

Rasa-bhava *aesthetic theory and the actor/audience relationship*

The *Natyasastra* states, "nothing has meaning in drama except through *rasa*" (Bharata 1967: 105). *Rasa* means "taste." The analogy to tasting or savoring a meal explains how a theatrical performance is experienced by the audience. "The 'taste' of the various ingredients of a meal is both their common-ground and organizes them as its end" (Gerow 1981: 230). The "various ingredients" include each character's state of being/doing (*bhava*), which is specific to the ever-shifting context of the performance and the specific actor. As each *bhava* is embodied and elaborated in performance, the accompanying *rasas* are "tasted" by the audience.

The *Natyasastra* identified eight permanent states of being/doing, each with its accompanying *rasa* (see diagram). These basic states are enhanced by many other transitory and involuntary states.

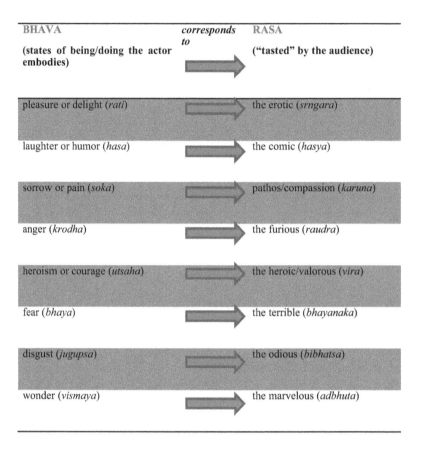

BHAVA	corresponds to	RASA
(states of being/doing the actor embodies)		("tasted" by the audience)
pleasure or delight (*rati*)		the erotic (*srngara*)
laughter or humor (*hasa*)		the comic (*hasya*)
sorrow or pain (*soka*)		pathos/compassion (*karuna*)
anger (*krodha*)		the furious (*raudra*)
heroism or courage (*utsaha*)		the heroic/valorous (*vira*)
fear (*bhaya*)		the terrible (*bhayanaka*)
disgust (*jugupsa*)		the odious (*bibhatsa*)
wonder (*vismaya*)		the marvelous (*adbhuta*)

Rasa theory operates simultaneously on two levels:

(1) the audience's experience of the various states or moods arising from the actor's embodiment of the character; and

(2) the process of aesthetic perception of the whole. Playwrights and composers structure their work around those modes most useful for elaboration, and the actors bring these modes to life.

Although the emotions we experience in everyday situations (becoming angry or guffawing with laughter) form the basis, they differ from the ultimate aesthetic experience of *rasa*. To understand this dimension of *rasa* theory, we must go beyond Bharata's *Natyasastra*, which focuses pragmatically on the means for evoking *rasa*.

The most influential later theorist is the Kashmiri philosopher Abhinavagupta (tenth to eleventh century). For him, the ideal spectator is one whose heart/mind is "attuned" to appreciate the performance. He wrote that *rasa* is

[b]orn in the heart of the poet, it flowers as it were in the actor and bears fruit in the spectator.

THINKING THROUGH THEATRE HISTORIES

Responding to theatre

Dramatic theories derived from Aristotle generally assume that the skillful playwright (rather than the actual performance) controls audience response. Such a view means that the written word ("the text") is the most important thing. However, as we will see in later chapters, many avant-garde theatre artists in the twentieth century rebelled against this concept.

Until the mid-twentieth century, theatre criticism and dramatic theory was considered to be a subset of literary theory. Beginning in the 1960s and 1970s, literary theorists began to consider the relationship of the reader or viewer to a work of art. Canadian scholar Susan Bennett is generally considered to be the first to apply these ideas to theatre (Bennett 1990).

Audiences (like readers, viewers of art or architecture, or people trying to interpret history) who share a common cultural background will interpret (receive) the art or event based on that shared background. If the artist and the audience (or reader, viewer, or interpreter) don't share a cultural or social heritage, then the cues for understanding meaning may be lost. Similarly, two audience members from divergent cultural backgrounds will react differently to the same performance (or artwork or historical event).

Unlike reading or going to a museum, where the individual reader's or viewer's imagination creates meaning from a fixed text or painting, viewing a performance involves both the imagination of the viewer and the contributions of actors, designers, choreographers, dancers, singers, composers, musicians, and directors in addition to playwrights. The "text" is expanded from the written script to include all elements of the specific performance. The so-called "original meaning" put into it by the playwright is transformed first by the artistic team in performance, and then by the audience who receives it. Thus every play has multiple potential meanings, depending on the performance elements, the audience, the historical moment, and the location of performance. This concept is especially important in thinking about theatre or other arts that originated in a culture very different from one's own.

The shift from trying to understand the intent of the originating artist to what the audience perceives transforms the audience from passive observer to active participant (or "agent"). However, the audience can only interpret what is offered on stage. Thus the artistic team (who are by definition active agents) are responsible for one half of the interpretation; but each audience member is responsible for the other half by being an active observer.

Rasa-bhava theory shifts our attention away from the written text and toward the role of the actor and the elements of performance; however, unlike contemporary theories, it assumes that if the actor fully embodies a specific *bhava*, then the attuned audience will inevitably "taste" a specific flavor.

If the artist or poet has the inner force of the creative intuition, the spectator is the man of cultivated emotion, in whom lies dormant the different states of being, and when he sees them manifested, revealed on the stage through movement, sound and decor, he is lifted to that ultimate state of bliss, known as *ananda*.

(Vatsyayan 1968: 155)

The birth of kathakali

Although Sanskrit drama died out in most of India, its legacy is evident in regional genres that appeared between the fifteenth and seventeenth centuries. One of these is Kerala's *kathakali* [kah-TAHK-ah-lee] dance-drama, which is performed in a highly Sanskritized form of the local language, Malayalam – the same language used for *kutiyattam*. *Kathakali* developed from several earlier genres in the mid-1700s under the patronage of local rulers and wealthy landholders; performances were held in temporarily defined public spaces just outside local Hindu temples during annual festivals, making them accessible to a broad-based, popular audience. Over the years, *kathakali* was further refined until it became the form that is seen today.

The actor-dancers of *kathakali*, accompanied by vocalists and percussionists, create their roles using choreography, a complete gesture language to visually "speak" their character's lines, and expressive use of the face and eyes to communicate the characters' internal states (*bhava*). Performances begin at dusk and last all night. Costuming and makeup begin the process of transforming the actors into idealized, archetypal character types, each of which is individualized by the dramatic context and the actors' choices. An example of green (*pacca*) makeup, used for divine characters or epic heroes, appears in Figure 2.10.

While not an ancient genre, *kathakali* demonstrates many characteristics typical of Sanskrit performance. Since the 1960s, *kathakali* has participated in many international cultural exchanges. Controversial experiments have included a play about Adolf Hitler at the end of the Second World War and leftist *kathakali* dramas such as *People's Victory* (1987). A *kathakali King Lear* was performed throughout Europe and at international theatre festivals such as Edinburgh, Scotland, in 1989 and at Shakespeare's Globe (London) in 1999.

For further information on *kathakali*, see the case study "*Kathakali* Dance-Drama: Divine 'Play' and Human Suffering on Stage" on our website.

Figure 2.10

The Progeny of Krishna, Scene 2. With the body of his eighth son lying before him, the Brahmin (M.P. Sankaran Namboodiri) pours out his tale of woe at court. Arjuna in green (*pacca*) makeup observes in the background.

Photo © Phillip B. Zarrilli.

Early Japanese performance and the development of *nō*

Until the fourth century CE, Japan had no system of writing, despite having a sophisticated culture. Compared with many areas of the world, this is exceptionally late. All aspects of life – including law-making, religion, commerce, and art – had to be memorized and passed on via one-to-one personal teaching. Some scholars feel this helps explain the continuing dominance of the oral tradition in Japanese performance.

After Japan invaded Korea in 370 CE, Korean scholars fluent in Chinese writing and literature were brought to Japan to educate the Crown Prince. Since Japanese and Chinese are not related linguistically, Japanese scholars were forced to learn Chinese in order to read and write. However, Chinese ideograms did not permit the voicing of grammatical changes, which are crucial in understanding Japanese. Therefore, they also created a system of phonetic symbols that made Japanese grammar clearer. Eventually, a complex system of writing developed that combined Chinese characters and two types of Japanese phonetic writing.

Japan's native religion was Shinto, in which it is assumed that everything – trees, birds, seas, animals, mountains, wind, and thunder, etc. – has its own soul or spirit, called *kami*. *Kami* are the natural energies and agents understood to animate matter and influence human behavior, and are sometimes identified as gods or goddesses. Chinese Buddhism became the official religion of Japan during the mid-sixth century, but it did not displace Shinto; rather, Buddhas and *kami* were and are often worshipped side by side. Interaction with China also brought the influences of Confucianism and Taoism (also called Daoism). Confucianism is not a religion, but a philosophy and system of ethics emphasizing maintenance of social harmony through hierarchical relationships in which the subordinate person (such as a child, wife, or servant) remains obedient and loyal to the higher-ranked person (such as a father, older brother, husband, or master) who behaves beneficently to the individual below. By 645, Japan had established a Confucian-based central administration. Taoism is a mystical religion that emphasizes harmony and balance in the universe. The ideologies of Buddhism, Confucianism, and Taoism joined with Shinto belief systems, and all can be found in various aspects of Japanese life and art. In theatre, we see their combined influence in stories, costumes, masks, makeup, theatre architecture, and staging.

In Japan, many ancient theatrical and proto-theatrical genres are still performed. Every December in Nara, a festival that lasts for several days is devoted to presenting these early types of performance, as well as related martial arts such as sumo wrestling and horseback archery. The oldest performance genres are Shinto-inspired, shamanistic ceremonies and dances intended to harness *kami*. Various proto-theatrical court performances, including masked dance-dramas such as *bugaku* and *gigaku* that were originally introduced from mainland Asia in the sixth century, are also performed at this festival and in special concerts. Masks dating from the Nara period (710–84) that depict warriors, gods, and semi-mythical beasts are preserved in temple collections.

Probably the greatest flowering of Japanese art and literature occurred during the Heian period (794–1185), after which the emperors, while still rulers in name, were gradually replaced by powerful warriors (samurai), and eventually by a single military leader called the shogun. Historical tales about the warring clans during the Heian period (such as *The Tale of the Heike*) were often chanted by blind musicians traveling the land. Such narrated stories joined literary fiction written by court ladies (such as *The Tale of Genji* by Murasaki Shikibu), folk tales, religious stories, and even contemporary events, as key sources for playwrights in subsequent eras.

Zeami and nō

After 1185, the rulers were brash samurai warriors rather than elegant aristocrats, and they soon realized how important it was for them to demonstrate their legitimate right to rule. With this in mind, they moved the seat of government from Kamakura back to the old imperial capital of Kyoto, where the emperor still lived, and began to adopt the tastes and practices of the aristocrats they replaced. Thus their rule gradually reunified the cultural and political centers. However, this transformation did not happen overnight. As we will see, the creation of *nō* [noh] demonstrates some of the ways that the arts are intertwined with political power.

The once-powerful aristocrats feared dispossession. One of these, the court poet Nijō Yoshimoto, tried to retain power by transforming the military court into a bastion of cultural refinement. In 1374, he encouraged the 16-year-old shogun Ashikaga Yoshimitsu (1358–1408; ruled 1367–1395) – famous for his wild excesses and vulgar taste – to attend a performance of popular *sarugaku* [sah-roo-gah-koo] ("monkey music"). The troupe he took the shogun to see was headed by Kan'ami (1333–1384) and featured Kan'ami's talented, 11-year-old son Zeami (1363–1443). Nijō hoped to wean his master from *dengaku* [dehn-gah-koo] ("field music"), the more shocking type of performance he usually patronized.

By Zeami's time, masked *dengaku* was performed by both males and females. It had become associated with political turmoil and recurring bouts of mass hysteria called "*dengaku* madness." People of all classes would commit acts of larceny or lewdness, dance semi-naked in the streets for weeks on end, and dress in clothing forbidden to their class or gender. *Dengaku* actors were accused of being animal spirits disguised as humans. An eyewitness to a 1349 *dengaku* performance described golden curtains, exotic animal skins, and actors dressed in embroidered, silver brocade. The huge audience caused the wooden stands to collapse. The eyewitness wrote:

> The number of those who died among the great piles of fallen timber is past all knowing. In the confusion thieves began stealing swords. . . . Cries and shouts rose up from people who had had limbs broken or slashed; from others, stained with blood, who had been run through with swords or halberds . . . and from others still who had scalded themselves with the boiling water used for making tea. . . . The *dengaku* players, still wearing devil masks and brandishing red canes, gave chase to thieves escaping with stolen costumes . . . Young servants unsheathed their weapons and went after men who had carried off their masters' ladies. . . . It was as if Hell's unending battles and the tortures of its demons were being carried out before one's eyes.
>
> (O'Neill 1958: 75–7)

Because *dengaku* had originated in native Shinto fertility dances, it was also tied to supernatural female powers and unbridled female sexuality. In contrast, *sarugaku*'s origin is connected to

---

Asian names

Chinese, Korean, and Japanese names (as well as names in some other languages) are written with the family name first. Although some publications in Western languages (especially newspapers) use only Western name order regardless of the original language, we will use the original name order unless the person has chosen to use Western order – usually because she or he was born and raised in a Western country and is considered to be Western.

As in the West, it is most common in scholarly writing to refer to people by their family name. However, some famous Japanese artists and historical individuals are routinely referred to by their given name only or even by a well-accepted nickname (similar to the way we might say "Elvis" or "Beyoncé"). For example, the *kabuki* actor Bandō Tamasaburō V is generally called Tamasaburō, because there are many actors in the Bandō family but only one Tamasaburō in any generation.

calm Buddhist burial rites. Nijō and others hoped the samurai could be weaned away from the irrational by associating it with female madness and the agony of the dispossessed, and made to embrace rational, "masculine" values, so that they would become less of a threat to the status quo that the aristocrats embodied. As we will see in the case study that follows, *sarugaku* (and eventually *nō*) would suggest victory over unruly, emotional female forces by calm, "rational" Buddhism and stoic male warriors.

When Yoshimitsu saw Zeami perform, he was so overwhelmed by the young actor's beauty and skill that he invited the entire troupe of rough and tumble, wandering, outcast performers to live in his court. Since sexual relations between males were not uncommon, Zeami became the shogun's lover.

Seeing the power of Zeami's position as the shogun's favorite, Nijō took Zeami under his wing and tutored him in the aristocratic arts, which were often associated with Buddhist meditation. He hoped his efforts would result in imbuing aristocratic tastes in Zeami, who might be able to influence the shogun. Nijō understood that Yoshimitsu and the other samurai felt culturally inferior to the aristocrats, but wanted to learn how to behave like them; he also understood that the aristocrats felt threated by the samurai, so they wanted to become indispensable to them. At the same time, the actors, due to their outcast status, needed to find a way to please both of these masters if they were to remain at court. Therefore, this project could ultimately benefit everyone.

Under Nijō's guidance, Zeami gradually altered the popular street entertainment *sarugaku*, into the stately, poetic, all-male, Buddhist-oriented genre later known as *nō*. After his father's death, Zeami continued to refine artistic practice. As he matured, he wrote many *nō* plays and a series of sophisticated treatises on acting and playwriting. These were meant for his descendants, and only came to public attention in the early twentieth century. Today, Zeami is acknowledged as one of the world's most important dramatic theorists.

Performing and staging nō

Nō was originally performed in circular spaces similar to those used in sumo wrestling. As the *nō* stage evolved, it began to be modeled on the architecture of Shinto shrines (see Figure 2.11). In contrast, much of the philosophy in the plays is Buddhist.

The stage is a raised wooden platform covered by a roof held up by four pillars, even when indoors (see Figures 2.11 and 2.12; see also Figure 2.15). The main acting area is about 15

Figure 2.11

A Japanese *nō* stage. It achieved the shape shown here by the sixteenth century. At first a separate structure, located in a courtyard, as seen here at the Buddhist temple of Nishi Honganji in Kyoto, it was housed within a larger building by the late nineteenth century. The stage proper remained covered by its own roof and linked to the green room by a raised passageway (*hashigakari*).

Source: Figure 1.9, p. 14 in *Dance in the Nō Theatre: Volume One. Dance Analysis* by Monica Bethe and Karen Brazell. Cornell University: China-Japan Program. Ithaca, 1982. The Cornell East Asia Papers series. Published with permission. © Monica Bethe and Karen Brazell.

Figure 2.12

Nō stage plan, indicating locations of musicians, chorus, and attendants. The painted pine and bamboo on the upstage wall and the three pine trees arranged along the passageway reflect the outdoor origins of the theatre. Stage and passageway are separated from the audience by a strip of sand or gravel.

Source: Bethe and Brazell (as in Figure 2.11 above) Figure 1.11, p. 151. © Monica Bethe and Karen Brazell.

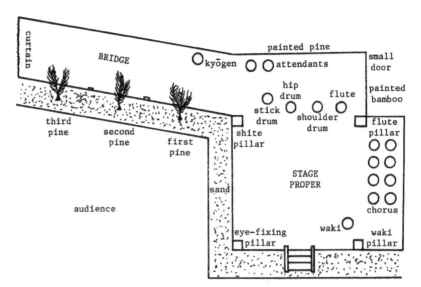

feet on each side. Beneath the floorboards, ceramic jars enhance the sound of the actors' stamping feet. The only décor is a painted pine tree on the back wall and a bamboo clump painted on the side. There are no special settings or lighting, and only minimal stage properties. A bridgeway (*hashigakari* [hah-shee-gah-kah-ree]) connects the stage with the curtained "mirror room" where the actors prepare; the *hashigakari* is seen as a passage from this world (the realm of the audience) to the world of spirits (embodied by the actor who crosses this bridge). The audience, usually about 400 people, sits on two sides of the stage. Steps lead from the stage into the auditorium, a vestige of the Tokugawa era (also called the Edo era, 1603–1868) when actors would descend them to receive valuable gifts from the shogun and his entourage. The steps are not used today.

Since Zeami's time, almost all professional *nō* actors have been male, training from childhood with older relatives. The main character, called the *shite* [sh-teh] (literally "the doer"), and the secondary character, the *waki* [wah-kee] (meaning "the listener" or "sideman"), may have companions called *tsure* [tsoo-reh]. In reading *nō* plays, you will notice that some translators use the characters' names to indicate who is speaking, but others use only the traditional titles of *shite*, *waki*, or *tsure*.

Three musicians (flute and two drums) and eight to fifteen chorus members enter in full view of the audience. The chorus kneels on the stage at the audience's right (opposite the *hashigakari*). Unlike the Greek chorus, they do not dance and have no specific identity. The musicians sit upstage, in front of the painted tree. They vocalize rhythmical sounds (*kakegoe*) as part of the musical score. Stage assistants (*kōken* [koh-kehn]) handle props, straighten costumes, or prompt actors. They are unobtrusive but clearly visible to the audience.

In most plays, after the chorus and musicians are in place, the *waki* enters on the *hashigakari* and establishes the situation; then the *shite* enters. The *shite* dances while retelling and reliving past woes; the *waki* is often a traveling Buddhist priest who is asked to pray for the release of the *shite*'s suffering soul. While the *shite* dances, the chorus chants his words.

When masks are used, they are worn only by the *shite* (and sometimes the *shite*'s companion). Smaller than the adult male face, they allow the audience to see simultaneously the role portrayed by the mask and the actor's living flesh. *Nō* masks, carved of light wood and carefully painted, are valued works of art handed down through the generations (see Figures 2.13 and 2.14). Costumes are elegant, costly, and conventional rather than realistic – even beggars are dressed in silks. The scripts are in an archaic language, using a "brocade style" that weaves together well-known stories, poetry, and Buddhist references.

Zeami maintained that actors should gauge the style of performance to please the audience, changing it as needed. However, during the Tokugawa period, *nō* became a state ritual rather than entertainment, and no variations were permitted. Because *nō* was slowed down to satisfy ritual requirements, it is now performed about three times slower than it was during Zeami's day. In the past, a performance consisting of five *nō* plays with four short, comic plays (*kyōgen* [kyoh-ghen], literally "crazy words") in between them lasted all day. Today, most programs last two or three hours, and have one or two *nō* plays and one *kyōgen*.

Kyōgen actors belong to their own schools, and like *nō* actors, are traditionally male. Even today, only a few professional *nō* and *kyōgen* actors are female. In addition to performing entire comedies, *kyōgen* actors also perform minor roles during the interlude between two-part *nō* plays. *Kyōgen* plays emphasize comic inversions of social roles and stereotypical behavior. Unlike *nō*, *kyōgen* uses everyday speech, few masks, no chorus, and reserves song and dance for comic effect. Short, simple plots depict comic situations that are common to many cultures: powerless characters, such as women, thieves, servants, or sons-in-law, outwit masters, husbands, priests, or gods. They play practical jokes and are carried away by song, dance, and uncontrollable urges (for wine, food, prestige, mischief, or even cruelty). For example, in *Tied to a Pole* (*Bōshibari*), the master ties up his two servants to prevent them from drinking his wine. In a complex, physically comic sequence, they cleverly help each other get drunk anyway. Many of the Roman comedies discussed above feature a similar topsy-turvy world. As we will see in Chapter 3, such plots exist throughout the world, and are often called "carnivalesque."

Although the period of Ashikaga rule (1336–1573, also known as the Muromachi period) was created by samurai warriors, the *nō* plays they preferred seldom depicted military victory. Rather, in keeping with the tastes of the aristocrats they had displaced, the new rulers preferred plays dealing with tragic love affairs, unrequited passions, the agony of defeated warriors, the elegance of old age, or supernatural events. Most of the approximately 240 *nō* plays still performed were written during the Muromachi period.

Supernatural beings, ghosts, and traces of shamanic practices can be seen in many *nō* plays. An example is *Aoi no ue* (*Lady Aoi*), one of many *nō* plays

Figure 2.13

Each *shite* chooses the precise mask to wear from several possible ones. This *zo-onna* mask of a beautiful young woman is typical of what might be worn in the first part of *Dōjōji*.

© kvap/iStock.

Figure 2.14

This *aka-hannya* ("red demon") mask is typical of what might be worn in the second half of *Dōjōji*.

Source: De Agostini/G. Sioen/Getty Images.

derived from *The Tale of Genji*. It deals with the life-threatening attack on the pregnant Lady Aoi by another woman's jealous spirit that is so powerfully demonic as to require exorcism. The body of Aoi is represented by an empty kimono laid flat on the stage floor. Another famous *nō* play, *Dōjōji*, demonstrates similar concerns and is the focus of our case study.

CASE STUDY: The *nō* play *Dōjōji*

Carol Fisher Sorgenfrei

Dōjōji is one of the most popular and theatrically flamboyant *nō* plays. The author is unknown; it was formerly attributed to Kanze Kojirō Nobumitsu (1435–1516). It has a prop used only in this play: a huge, silk-covered bell. Prior to the beginning of the play, stage assistants rig the bell to the roof of the stage. The action begins when the *waki*, the male Buddhist Abbot of Dōjōji (Dōjō Temple), calls the priests of the temple together. He announces that although there has been no bell in this temple for many years, today a new bell will be raised and dedicated. He leaves, forbidding the priests to admit women. The *shite* – an elegant woman – appears, and convinces the foolish priests to let her enter in order to perform a celebratory dance at the dedication (Figure 2.15).

Figure 2.15

In a performance of the *nō* play *Dōjōji* at the Kanze Theatre, Tokyo, 1962, the ghost of the maiden, dressed as a beautiful *shirabyōshi* dancer, approaches the bell at Dōjō Temple. Here, the actor moves from the *hashigakari* (bridgeway) toward the main stage, symbolizing her passage from the spirit world to this world.

Photo © Gary Jay Williams.

Figure 2.16

The ghost maiden dances around the bell which then descends over her and then is raised to reveal, as seen here, the differently costumed and masked actor (who has done a quick change inside the bell) as a horned, demon serpent which is the true form of the ghost maiden. The abbot and the priests, standing, are attempting an exorcism.

Photo © Gary Jay Williams.

She dons a special hat normally worn only by male courtiers. Her dance gradually becomes chaotic and animalistic, entrancing the priests. The music, used only in *Dōjōji*, is a secular version of the music of a Shinto demon-quelling ritual. Her feet move in triangular patterns, mimicking the fish-scale triangles we will later see on the actor's inner robe. Finally, the dancer knocks the hat from her head, stamps her feet, and looks at the bell as she stands directly beneath it. She swings her fan back and forth like the ringing hammer of a bell, as the chorus sings: "This loathsome bell, now I remember it!" (Brazell 1998: 199). She leaps up, and the giant bell falls crashing to the ground around her.

In the interlude, the priests discover that the bell is red hot. When the Abbot returns, he angrily explains why women were forbidden. Long ago, a girl's father told her that a priest who often visited would be her husband. One day, she asked the celibate priest when they would marry, and he fled in horror. She chased him by transforming herself into a serpent and swimming across a river. On the other shore, she followed him to the temple called Dōjōji, where he had hidden beneath an unraised bell. The serpent-woman entwined her body around the bell. The heat of her passion was so intense that the bell metal became fiery hot, burning alive the priest inside. The Abbot now explains that the dancer is this woman's furious ghost.

During this interlude, the *shite* remains inside the giant bell and changes mask and costume. When the bell rises for the second part of the play, we see a female snake-demon, the dancer's true form (see Figure 2.16). The Abbot and priests battle her, attempting an exorcism, but they cannot overpower her; they can only chase her off. As the play ends, the chorus chants:

> Again she springs to her feet,
> the breath she vomits at the bell
> has turned to raging flames.
> Her body burns in her own fire.
> She leaps into the river pool,
> Into the waters of the river Hidaka,
> And there she vanishes.
> The priests, their prayers granted,
> Return to the temple,
> Return to the temple.
>   (Brazell 1998: 206)

In order to interpret this play, we must consider its cultural and historical context. Zeami did much to develop *nō* theatre, but he did not create it from thin air.

Zeami and the female origins of nō

Japanese performance is said to originate in the shocking dance of the goddess Uzume, a female Shinto deity. According to the myth, because the sun-goddess Amaterasu – the direct ancestor of the emperor and thus of the Japanese people – was angry with her trickster brother, she hid herself in a cave. Deprived of the sun's light and fertility, the world would have died. In desperation, the goddess Uzume leaped on to an overturned rain barrel, stamping her feet in dance and lifting her skirts to reveal her genitals. The other deities roared with laughter. The curious Amaterasu peeked out. The laughter caused by Uzume's sexy dance had saved the world from eternal death. In his secret treatises, Zeami wrote that this myth proved *nō*'s divine origin and relationship to the royal household. But is that all the myth tells us today?

Amaterasu is a female identified with the life-giving sun. Her emotional, irrational response to the bad behavior of an unruly male dangerously disrupts the balance of nature. She cloaks her body in darkness. In contrast, Uzume intentionally displays her body in a kind of divine striptease. She uses explicit nakedness to create a sexual spectacle that makes the gods laugh. She is in control of how she is viewed, and is in control of her passions. These two female deities are reverse images that complement each other: light and dark, anger and laughter, life and death. Females have the power to give and to withdraw life.

In the sixth century, Korean emissaries introduced the patriarchal religion of Buddhism to Japan, challenging the dominance of female-oriented Shinto. Powerful leaders allied themselves with these opposing religions, vying for political control. Many sects combined aspects of both religions. Eventually, Shinto rituals became associated with the female realm and with life-affirming acts (fertility, marriage, sex, and birth), while Buddhist rites were tied primarily to the male realm, death, and the afterlife.

Nō theatre reflects this history. The texts are primarily Buddhist, emphasizing that actions in one lifetime determine how a soul is reincarnated in the next. They also emphasize salvation in the afterlife. In contrast, performance elements derive from aspects of Shinto (or Shinto-Buddhism). These female-oriented elements include demon-quelling dances, stamping feet, ritual purifications, possession by gods, the stage architecture, and most importantly, the presence of spirits and ghosts.

Nō also incorporated elements of earlier female dances. Shinto shrine maidens (*miko*) performed sacred *kagura* dances as well as ritual dances meant to pacify angry ghosts. Female prostitute-entertainers performed Buddhist funeral rituals for the imperial family and entertained aristocratic male clients on river boats. Their outcast status diminished as their religious importance grew. Zeami's family may have belonged to their clan (Kwon 1998).

Dances called *kusemai* and *shirabyōshi* were popular, secular entertainments mainly performed by women dressed in male clothing. Critics feared that their unconventional, disturbing musical rhythms and dance styles were contributing to "an age of turmoil" and were a sign of "a nation in ruins" (O'Neill 1958: 43–4). Like Uzume, these female ritualists and performers disrupted notions of social and religious stability.

Zeami praised and valued his female predecessors. He wrote that his father, Kan'ami, had trained with Otozuru, a female *kusemai* dancer. The *shite*'s main dance is still termed *kusemai*, and many plays, including *Dōjōji*, feature characters who are female *shirabyōshi* or *kusemai* dancers.

The aesthetics of nō

Two of Zeami's most important aesthetic concepts are *monomane* [moh-noh-mah-neh] and *yūgen* [yoo-ghehn]. *Monomane* is the imitation of character. By imitating "the three roles" (male, female, or old person), the actor reveals the fictional character's invisible body. For Zeami, a mask allows the actor to become another character; his body becomes a vessel inhabited by another's "essence," which resides in the mask. According to Steven T. Brown, "Underneath the actor's costume and mask is the body of the actor transformed into the virtual body of the other" (2001: 26). *Yūgen* is a deep, quiet, mysterious beauty tinged with sadness. Zeami expands its meaning to refer to both text and performance, emphasizing the fleeting, melancholy nature of human existence. The greatest *yūgen* appears in plays about aged, dispossessed, or formerly beautiful women who are reduced to poverty, madness, or regret.

Symbolic capital in nō plays

When samurai warriors displaced the aristocrats, they needed to foster legal changes to centralize their military power and weaken the noble branch families. Among the new laws were those that shifted inheritance rights away from female aristocrats and toward first-born sons. Suddenly, a divorced or abandoned woman found herself dispossessed both financially and emotionally. Her fury at an unfaithful spouse would be intensified by the loss of property she would previously have retained. Many people believed that the angry spirits of such dispossessed females (along with those of the dispossessed male rivals of the ruling Ashikaga clan) were responsible for a century of natural disasters (earthquakes, plagues, typhoons, droughts, famines, fires, and floods) that devastated Kyoto.

Many *nō* plays, including *Dōjōji*, center on the anger or madness of dispossessed spirits (dead or alive). The great majority of *shite* are agonized females. Although Zeami's main patrons were male samurai, they preferred plays about emotionally distraught women. These characters probably reminded them of those formerly haughty aristocrats who were now poor and powerless. For the same reason, when *nō* plays deal with warriors, they focus on the agony of loss and defeat rather than the glory of victory. By displaying aristocratic female bodies in exquisite emotional agony, Zeami and his troupe could please all members of the shogun's court (Brown 2001: 30–3). By combining *yūgen* with *monomane* in plays about often Shinto-identified females in need of male Buddhist healing or exorcism, Zeami consolidated the position of formerly outcast actors in a changing court and paved the way for the creation of mature *nō* plays (Sorgenfrei 1998).

Conclusion

In *Dōjōji*, the body of the male actor portraying a female dancer "enacts a complex double masquerade of both masculine and feminine" (Klein 1995: 118). The male *nō* actor's body stands in for the absent female body of the *shirabyōshi* dancer, which stands in for the absent male monk as well as the invisible demonic snake. By leaping into the bell, the *shirabyōshi* dancer imitates what happened to the male. However, instead of being burned to death, she is revealed in her true form. The climax of the play becomes a cosmic battle between demonic, female forces and holy, male forces, but it is not conclusive – the demon will continue to lurk in the river, able to resurface at any time. Female sexual power (or the potential power of the defeated and dispossessed aristocrats) can be contained but not destroyed.

The fear of women displayed in *Dōjōji* reflects the historical fact that "the position of women at the elite levels of Japanese society was taking a distinct downward turn" (Klein 1995: 117). The ambiguous ending suggests that chaos could erupt if the rulers failed to guard against all those (male as well as female) they had dispossessed.

Key references

Brazell, K. (ed.) (1998) *Traditional Japanese Theater*, New York: Columbia University Press.

Brown, S.T. (2001) *Theatricalities of Power: The Cultural Politics of Nō*, Stanford, CA: Stanford University Press.

Klein, S.B. (1995) "Woman as Serpent: The Demonic Feminine in the Noh Play *Dōjōji*," in J.M. Law (ed.) *Religious Reflections on the Human Body*, Bloomington, IN: Indiana University Press.

Kwon, Y.-H.K. (1998) "The Female Entertainment Tradition in Medieval Japan: The Case of *Asobi*," *Theatre Journal* 20: 205–16.

O'Neill, P.G. (1958) *Early Noh Drama*, London: Lund Humphries.

Sorgenfrei, C.F. (1998) "Zeami and the Aesthetics of Contemporary Japanese Performance," in B. Ortolani and S.L. Leiter (eds) *Zeami and the Nō Theater in the World*, New York: CASTA.

SUMMARY

In this chapter, we continued our discussion of the interactions between oral tradition, writing, and factors such as politics and social conditions in three early literate cultures. We noted that not all cultures transform at the same speed or in the same way, and that depending on one's perspective, certain historical transformations may even appear reversed.

Roman theatre, especially during the Republic, valued the skills of rhetoric and oratory that were important in political and social life. The literate classes created both comedies and tragedies inspired by the theatre of ancient Greece. Although the upper classes valued decorum in theory, theatre tended to reflect the less-refined tastes of the lower classes. As the Republic declined and Rome became an empire, performance began to emphasize visual spectacle, including violent, bloody "games." In contrast, the Sanskrit theatre of India always retained a balance between aural and visual pleasures, and theatre expressing elite values dominated. The *Natyasastra*, a holy book of Hinduism, states that theatre and drama should be available to all people, but most Sanskrit plays were written by members of the upper classes and were often performed to exclusive audiences inside temples. Finally, we discussed the fact that literacy came very late to Japan, and first only in the form of Chinese. *Nō* developed as an art that could please both the dispossessed aristocrats and the brash, relatively uncultured samurai. It also combined elements of the native belief system (Shinto) with imported ideologies (Buddhism, Taoism, Confucianism). In the next chapter, we will continue our discussion of how theatre works to please various types of audiences. As we will see, even in highly literate societies, orality does not vanish.

★

CHAPTER 3

Commemorative drama and carnival

Tamara Underiner

Contributors: Phillip B. Zarrilli and Tobin Nellhaus

Virtually every society finds some way to keep its history alive by means of performance. In the theatres discussed in Chapters 1 and 2, such performances were drawn from events recorded in their great epics, the stories of their predecessors, and recent important events in the society's history. While these events may also have been passed down orally and in written form, performance helped to ensure the continuity of social memory and played an extremely important role in cultural preservation.

After writing becomes well established in a society, its relationship to oral culture can and often does change. In Chapter 2, we considered forms of performance that developed when writing had become socially prominent, even if it was still often limited to scribes, priests, and the elite. In the period we cover here, however, writing was attaining an even more central role in society – in fact, one or more texts had become fundamental to religion, and all people were expected to know their content, whether or not they could read. These were now manuscript cultures, in which handwritten texts (generally on parchment or paper, often bound into a book rather than a scroll) were critical for much of the society's functioning and culture. Nevertheless, there was considerable interaction between manuscript cultures' oral and literate realms. For that reason, performance played an extremely important role in cultural preservation. This chapter focuses on two genres of performance – commemorative drama and Carnival – that have helped to impart such cultural knowledge in Europe, the Americas, India, and the Islamic world.

Commemorative drama refers to a wide range of performance practices that share certain characteristics, all aimed at preserving and promoting some aspect of a society's heritage. While much commemorative drama is meant to promote deep reflection in a spirit of devotion or civic pride, another form of performance elicits a different kind of spirit: that of release from the constraints of civil and religious propriety, if only for a day or week. Such performances can be broadly grouped under the category of the carnivalesque, in which human nature is explored through the mingling of the sacred with the profane, often to hilarious and spectacular effect. (Recall our Chapter 1 discussion of the *Egúngún* ritual, which combines ancestor worship with improvisational play of a distinctly earthy nature – including Gorilla's sexual pursuit of women in the crowds.) Many of the commemorative performance traditions we discuss below incorporate and combine both devotional and carnivalesque aspects, revealing the multi-faceted nature of human and divine relationships.

We begin with a discussion of Carnival, a public celebration that may pre-date Christianity. Here we consider not only its history but also its spirit, asking what it is about "the carnivalesque" that seems to transcend time and place, and how its energies are constantly channeled anew into different forms. We then turn to a discussion of commemorative drama, a term which encompasses a variety of forms that can be formal and devotional, or can blend the serious with the carnivalesque. What they share is a commitment to preserving and performing the cultural and/or religious legacies of a society. Our discussion of commemorative drama centers on the dramas of Christianity, which gave birth to a plethora of performance forms, some of which persist today. But of course other religious and cultural traditions, before and after Christianity, also use performance to some degree. Thus we frame our discussion of Christian commemorative drama between two other traditions of such drama: the Jewish Purim play, which features both commemorative and carnivalesque aspects, and the Islamic *Ta'ziyeh*, a mourning ritual central to the Shi'ite faith. Our case studies consider how commemorative drama functions both to solidify and to challenge prevailing norms of belief and custom. One examines a dramatization of the historic conflict between Christianity and Islam, staged both as a straightforward commemoration and as a kind of allegory for more recent examples of cultural conflict. The other considers a commemorative drama based on a Hindu epic – the *Ramlila* of northern India.

Carnival and the carnivalesque

Carnival is a centuries-old tradition of lively, often rowdy public performance featuring deliberate misbehavior by masked characters in elaborate costumes. It may trace back to the Greek and Roman festivals of antiquity (e.g., the Dionysian celebrations in Greece, and the Bacchanalia and Saturnalia in Rome). By the twelfth century in Europe, this tradition came to be associated with the Catholic season of Lent preceding Easter. But we can detect aspects of a carnivalesque spirit in other traditions, such as Roman comedy and *kyōgen* (discussed in Chapter 2). Rooted in oral culture, the carnivalesque appears in all societies, including manuscript and print cultures (a matter taken up in more detail in the "Thinking through theatre histories" box).

Within Christianity, Easter marks the highest holy day, on which Jesus is believed to have risen from the dead. In order to properly prepare for this momentous day, every year early Christians were asked to observe a fast for a period of time, which by the fourth century had become known as the season of Lent. To inaugurate this 40-day period of self-denial and deprivation, they celebrated what has come to be known as "Carnival," which some say comes from the Latin *carnem-levare* or *carne vale*, both of which refer to a "farewell to flesh (or meat)"; other explanations suggest it is a reference to the elaborate floats (*carrus navalis*, or floating cars) of an ancient Roman festival, floats being a signal feature of Carnival then and now.

Before entering their season of self-denial, folks feasted heartily on meat and other good things, and began to stage their "farewells" to it in increasingly public fashion, especially just before the official start of the season (Ash Wednesday). The culmination of this period –

known as Shrovetide in English, *Mardi Gras* (Fat Tuesday) in French, and *Fastnacht* (Fasting Eve) in German – is still a time of highly theatrical celebration in Europe and throughout the Americas, and has itself been extended into its own season in some parts of the world. The famous *Carnaval* of Rio de Janeiro, Brazil, is the largest in the world. In Brazil and the Caribbean, as in the Mardi Gras of New Orleans in the United States, Carnival has been transformed by the influence of African music, dancing, costuming, masking, and puppetry traditions that arrived in the Americas with the slave trade.

Carnival in Europe likely began in the urban centers and at court, in response to the increasingly stringent rules of Lent, later spread to rural areas, and then spread again across the Atlantic with the arrival of the Catholic colonizers. In each of these regions, Carnival was flexible enough to incorporate the existing festival traditions of the local populations. There were differences as a result from place to place, and also within the various strata of society within a particular place. For example, among the European aristocracy and urban elite, Carnival included masked balls, comical theatrical performances, and public competitions. In the countryside events were organized by groups of friends, clubs, fraternities, and guilds, and often featured parades of peasants costumed as royalty. The well-known parades of today's Carnival celebrations

Figure 3.1
This painting of the *Battle of Carnival and Lent* (1559) by Pieter Bruegel the Elder illustrates the worldly and "world-turned-upside-down" aspects of Carnival, as revelers prepare to say their farewell to meat and other pleasures in the Lenten season of abstinence.

Source: Kunsthistorisches Museum Vienna.

have their roots in this period, which saw processions of costumed people on foot and on floats, performing masquerades in which they poked fun at certain segments of society.

In both rural and urban settings, Carnival was a time when normal social strictures were suspended: aggressive and promiscuous acts were permitted, and reversals of social standing were enacted – with men and women cross-dressing, or masquerading as members of a different social or professional class. Carnivalesque humor reveled in life's fecundity, in sexuality and all the irrepressible life forces of the material body; its humor was full of images of copulating, defecating, dying, and birthing, always expressive of life's regenerative processes. Images of

THINKING THROUGH THEATRE HISTORIES

Mikhail Bakhtin's theory of the carnivalesque

One of the most important theorists of Carnival is the Russian literary critic Mikhail Bakhtin, who wrote between 1919 and the early 1970s, barely escaping Stalin's infamous purges in the 1930s. His concept of Carnival folk humor was developed in his analysis of the evolution of the novel, but it is useful to theatre studies as well. Bakhtin sees Carnival as an elemental force, nurtured by a 1,000-year tradition of folk humor, from satyr plays to medieval fools, liberating language and literature from the "official" ecclesiastical and feudal cultures and surging into the Renaissance. The culture of folk humor finds opportunities for expression in popular festivals all over the world.

Bakhtin based his theories on the Carnival traditions of Christian Europe. At the center of such celebrations, he argued, was the false coronation and later deposing of a Carnival king (usually a slave or clown). His coronation is full of pomp and circumstance, his dethroning full of shame and disgrace. For Bakhtin, this duality, or embrace of contradictions, is what characterizes a "carnivalesque" view of the world: one in which the sacred mingles with the profane, the new with the old, the high-born with the low-born, the wise with the foolish, and so forth. All of this is meant to reveal the hidden sides of human nature – and thereby to expose how social structures are relative, and social orders contingent rather than natural or God-given.

Bakhtin argued that the "carnivalesque" was central to medieval consciousness up until the end of the sixteenth century, allowing Christians of the time to break free, for a time, from the many restraints upon their comportment that Church dogma demanded. As Carnival began to lose traction (at least in Europe) in the Enlightenment period, its dualistic impulses were channeled away from the public streets and into the realm of literature, formal theatre, and other forms of art and popular culture – extending to our own day, where it might be argued that some popular reality TV shows do the work of Carnival – conferring fame and glory on everyday people, if only for an episode or a season. Of course, the carnivalesque also wears its public face in the ongoing traditions of pre-Lenten Carnival and Mardi Gras parades; in gay pride parades; in public New Year's Eve celebrations; in the parades accompanying sports bowl games; and in Halloween parades and parties where disguise affords the possibility of experimenting with alternate identities. Often, civic parades combine solemn patriotism with boisterous clowning and plenty of spectacle; just as commemorative drama can include the carnivalesque, so can Carnival contain commemorative elements.

excessive eating and drinking were common (the clowns of early German farces, Hanswurst and Pickelhering, are named after folk foods). Images of the body, from nose to phallus, and lower bodily functions were writ large and grotesquely in Carnival folk humor; such representations, argued Mikhail Bakhtin, were not about the individual body/ego but about the irrepressible and regenerative body of the people. (See Figure 3.1 and the "Thinking through theatre histories" box.)

These "rites of reversal" or "rites of misrule" were not confined to the Lenten season; the Church calendar also accommodated, if uneasily, other festivals in which social expectations were temporarily turned on their heads. For example, during Christmas time in many European countries a "Feast of Fools" (sometimes called "Feast of Asses") was held in which the lower clergy mockingly impersonated their superiors (as well as women), played dice on the altar during the celebration of the Mass, and processed through town singing lewd songs. They may also have appointed a "Boy Bishop" from among the ranks of their choirboys, who performed a burlesque of the official Church service.

Not surprisingly, Church authorities were none too pleased with these annual celebrations of misrule, and Church records show numerous attempts at banning them, and Carnival as well (which serve as proof of their enduring popularity). This happened in some European cities, and frequently in the Spanish and Portuguese colonies of the Americas. Scholars speculate that in the Americas, Carnival was an upper-class event until after the various wars of independence from Spain and Portugal; this may explain why so many revelers in today's Brazilian *Carnaval*, for example, don the attire of eighteenth-century aristocracy.

Although the Church's concern about Carnival's excesses is well documented, many latter-day researchers of Carnival suspect that the Church needn't have worried. They argue that the chance to temporarily reverse the social order was in fact an important component for keeping it intact. Others want to see it for its imaginative and liberatory potential, as a rehearsal for a new world order rather than a safety valve that keeps the old one in its place, as discussed in the "Thinking through theatre histories" box.

Commemorative performances

While commemorative drama may contain carnivalesque elements, it always shares certain basic elements that fulfill a more serious function: that of helping participants and observers learn and remember something important about their religious, civic, or cultural heritage. Recall, for instance, *Rabinal Achi*, the Mayan drama introduced in Chapter 1. It is a performance of local history, but not in strictly chronological terms. Rather, it is more like a montage of many different historical events gathered into one central conflict between two rival warriors from the distant past. Its yearly staging is meant to commemorate the origins and resilience of the town of Rabinal over the centuries, which is one reason why UNESCO proclaimed it a masterpiece of the oral and intangible heritage of humanity. Both in its local meanings and in its more global UNESCO designation, *Rabinal Achi* highlights the notion of cultural heritage and continuity. As social anthropologist Paul Connerton argues in *How Societies Remember* (1989), such performances have in common a key element: "they do not simply imply continuity with the past by virtue of their high degree of formality and fixity; rather, they have as one of their defining features the explicit claim to be commemorating such a continuity" (48).

Rabinal Achi shares many features with commemorative drama in general:

- it tells a story that has been carefully preserved both orally and in manuscript form;
- it celebrates a moment in the past that is of great contemporary importance for the drama's audience;
- it is meant to be staged on a regular basis to preserve that heritage in social memory; and
- its aim is not necessarily a full realistic representation in historically accurate detail, but more a symbolic portrayal of people and events important to the community's sense of cultural continuity.

Commemorative performances often offer participants the chance to represent themselves and their *present* concerns within the performance, in order to show how their present relates to their past. In these kinds of performances the carnivalesque can make a memorable appearance. An example is the centuries-old tradition of the Mexican *Pastorela,* or Shepherd's Play. Annual *Pastorelas* offer latter-day communities the opportunity to inaugurate the Christmas season with a performance that both recalls the journey of the shepherds to the infant Christ's birthplace, and comically treats and often satirizes local events of politics and popular culture of the previous year. In doing so these communities demonstrate that "continuity" can both

Figure 3.2

Latter-day performers of the Guatemalan *Rabinal Achi* wear masks suggesting the features of sixteenth-century Spaniards, even though the characters they portray are pre-Columbian Mayans. As such these latter-day performances register both cultural continuity and change.

Photo: Photonica World/Holly Wilmeth/Getty Images.

accommodate, and actually depend upon, change. Seen this way, it is not surprising that the Mayan characters in contemporary productions of *Rabinal Achi* wear the masks of sixteenth-century Spaniards (see Figure 3.2). We consider another example of performance that foregrounds both continuity and change in our case study on the Moors and Christians.

Commemoration and the carnivalesque in the Jewish Purim *shpil*

One remarkable example of how commemorative drama can blend both the past and the present, and the serious with the carnivalesque, is the Jewish tradition of the Purim *shpil* [shpihl] (or play). This is a tradition that emerged to commemorate a great victory in a people's past, and is performed in the present with great joy and much laughter. Its source is the Book of Esther (a part of Judaism's central religious texts), which tells a story of a Jewish victory over religious persecution, when the Jews were in exile in Persia in the fifth century BCE. The spirit of this victory – of a religious and ethnic minority over a hostile majority – is what is commemorated in Purim *shpiln* (plays).

The Book of Esther is indeed rich in dramatic possibilities. The Persian King Ahasuerus (in Greek, Xerxes) orders his wife to display her beauty to his banquet guests. When she refuses, he makes a lesson of her to all women who would dare to disobey their husbands, and sets out on a search for a young and beautiful woman to replace her. The orphaned Esther is the one who catches his eye, but to keep his favor she must hide her own Jewish identity. Later, her guardian, Mordechai, saves the king from an assassination plot – a fact which is recorded, but not known to the king. On another occasion, Mordechai had refused to bow to the king's prime minister, Haman. As a result, when Haman later learns that Mordechai is Jewish, he hatches a genocidal plot, with the king's approval: on a certain day, everyone in the kingdom has the right to murder and pillage the Jews and their property. Eventually, two events transpire to mitigate the slaughter. First, King Ahasuerus discovers Mordechai's life-saving service to him. Second, in order save her people, Esther takes the risk of revealing her identity to her husband – and the threat to her life that Haman's plot represents. The king leaves her in a rage, but later returns to see Haman pleading with Esther to spare his life. Thinking Haman is assaulting her, the king orders him to be hanged – on the very gallows Haman had intended to be used for executing Mordechai. But the decree against the Jews cannot be rescinded, so the king allows the Jews to defend themselves. The result is that the Jews slaughter some 75,000 Persians, including Haman's ten sons.

Readings of the Book of Esther are meant to commemorate the events of that day (which usually corresponds to a date in March). As early as the 1400s, these readings were accompanied by what we might now call "audience participation," with congregants hissing and booing at every mention of Haman's name, and collateral performances of humorous monologues and skits loosely based on its events. Over time, the repertoire expanded to include carnivalesque elements in order to parody contemporary events in the local community, often relying on bawdy jokes and profanities. Troupes of Purim players would travel from home to home, collecting alms to support themselves and those less fortunate (Figure 3.3). Some towns supported only one troupe; larger towns, several. The actors, typically young, unmarried men and boys, might perform year after year, often disguising themselves in order to "protect their freedom to be licentious" (Kirshenblatt-Gimblett 1980: 6). In the eighteenth century, biblical content returned to the Purim *shpil*, and in some parts of Eastern Europe the form expanded to full-length dramas with musical accompaniments and large casts (often featuring professional entertainers).

Figure 3.3

Because Esther had to live in disguise as a non-Jew, Purim celebrations that commemorate her story often feature costumes and masks to hide one's identity – thus granting revelers license to behave in ways they normally would not at any other time of year.

Source: Courtesy of the Sherwin Miller Museum of Jewish Art.

According to performance scholar Barbara Kirshenblatt-Gimblett, in the nineteenth and twentieth centuries, Purim *shpiln* took place in both private homes and public settings, and a single play could last up to five hours. In homes, where they were performed during the festive meals, they were often abbreviated so the troupes could reach as many homes as possible and collect more alms (1980: 6).

For Jews around the world, the Purim *shpil* is still known for its entertainment value, allowing a commemoration of hope and humor in the face of adversity – not only the trials of the distant past, but all the tribulations faced by Jews between then and now. Today, video has become a new outlet for the mocking spoofery of Purim, and many "videoshpiln" have found their way to YouTube. Purim is often described as the "Jewish Carnival," for its ability to overturn the normal rules of acceptable behavior for a time.

Commemorative performance in medieval Christian Europe

Because the early Christian Church opposed the popular entertainments of ancient Roman times, viewing them as sinful and the work of Satan, by the fifth century CE theatre had been banned outright; actors were excommunicated and denied Christian burial and the Christian sacrament of marriage. Drama as literature, however, was not equated with the excesses of theatrical spectacle during the days of the Roman Empire. This is exemplified in the dramatic work of Hrotsvitha (c.935–73), a noble lay member of the all-female Abbey of Gandersheim, in Saxony (within what is now Germany). Her writings in Latin included six plays, based on the comedies of the Roman playwright Terence (discussed in Chapter 2). Her adaptations put them to use for the personal discipline of young Christian women, encouraging them to suppress their sexuality in favor of maintaining their virginity. The plays may well have been intended for reading, reflection, and semi-dramatic recitation, rather than performance.

Although a few small groups of traveling performers continued, theatre essentially ceased between the sixth and tenth centuries in Europe. When, where, and why it re-emerged at that point is a matter of debate. Some scholars see it as a re-emergence of older, pre-Christian rituals and performances, some co-opted by the Christian Church. Others have argued that it emerged under the auspices of the Church as a part of the monastic worship service – but have disagreed about whether it developed organically out of the worship format, or was deliberately introduced in order to restore a faith in decline due to the Church's increasing power as a private landlord and broker of medieval social relations. And others have argued for a parallel emergence in the public realms of courtrooms of law and chambers of rhetoric, where the performance of forensic oratory took on highly theatrical forms. These "origin stories" suggest a complex interplay between textual authority and embodied performance.

Considering the function of writing in Christian Europe in the centuries before the invention of the printing press, Elizabeth L. Eisenstein (1979: 271) notes an interesting dilemma, one that has particular relevance for the study of theatre and performance: if knowledge of the Church's most sacred mysteries was the domain of an exclusive society of literate scribes and priests, how then was it able to bring its doctrine to a population that was largely illiterate? Among the principal means were the "oral and visual propaganda" of sermons, stained-glass windows, and sculptures within the church buildings. But starting in the late fourteenth century, the Church also encouraged laypeople to perform religious drama. In the "age of scribes" and well into the era of the printing press, oral culture and its embodied enactments remained (and remain) lively and important, ultimately resulting in what theatre historian Ronald W. Vince has called a "bewildering array of performances of one kind or another that we find in medieval Europe" (1989: ix).

Turning first toward the religious aspects of such performance, we begin with the Christian ritual of the Mass, itself a performative commemoration, and continue with a discussion of the principal types of religious drama that emerged within Christendom: **cycle plays** or "mystery plays" based on the Bible; **Passion plays** devoted to the last days of Christ's life, his death, and resurrection; **saint plays** (sometimes called miracle plays) that commemorated the life and works of the Christian saints and martyrs; and **morality plays** that used allegorical devices to explore the human condition in terms of Christian values.

A brief overview of developments in Christianity and Christian ritual will help the reader understand the function of commemorative performance in both ritual and drama.

The Christian Mass as a performance of commemoration

When Jesus of Nazareth (4? BCE–29? CE) began to carry out his public ministry in Galilee (Palestine), he was one of a number of Jewish prophets declaring the imminent arrival of a "new" Kingdom of God, in territory then under Roman rule. His followers proclaimed him to be the Christ ("anointed one") or the new "messiah." When he arrived in Jerusalem to celebrate the Jewish Passover at a feast (*seder*) with his followers, he extended his teaching and healing into an aggressive public protest by driving traders and moneychangers out of the main Jewish temple. He was arrested by the Roman authorities, put on trial, condemned to death, and crucified – a common mode of execution.

To the authorities of the period, whether Roman or Jewish, Jesus was a minor figure, the leader of a band of superstitious followers, and his crucifixion as an "enemy of mankind" was only one of many similar public spectacles of execution under Roman law. To his followers, the period immediately after Jesus's death was fraught with uncertainty. Was the new "Kingdom of God" imminent? Thrown into turmoil by Jesus's death, his small group of disciples gathered to share a memorial meal that recreated their last supper with Jesus and commemorated his crucifixion and resurrection. Similar memorial meals were established among converts as the new religion was brought to Greece. The meal also featured communal singing, perhaps a commentary by an elder in the community, and the blessing and distribution of bread and wine, as Jesus had at his last supper with his disciples. These activities are still part of the Christian Mass.

The conversion of the Roman Emperor Constantine to Christianity in 312 CE ended the persecution of the Christians and made Christianity the official religion of the Roman

Figure 3.4

The Three Marys at the Tomb (1425–1435), an altarpiece by Jan and/or Hubert van Eyck, depicts the events commemorated in the *Quem quaeritis* tropes during the Easter service of the early Christian Mass.

© Corbis

Empire. There were separate forms of Syrian and Greek Orthodox worship in the East; by the fifth century, when the vast Roman Empire itself was beginning to crumble, the Latin Mass had come to prevail in the West. Perhaps it was in the face of the collapse of world order as they knew it that Christian leaders formalized the order of the Mass and their symbolic vestments over the subsequent two centuries.

The liturgy (or order of the Mass) began as a manifestation and commemoration of the sacrificial aspects of Christ's life; by the tenth century, inventive clergy in monasteries – the main centers of learning and the arts – began elaborating on key moments of biblical history during the Mass. Many biblical passages were sung or set to music, and eventually, further small pieces of text were added to expand a melody through chant-and-response singing; these were called "tropes." Over time, the tropes became increasingly dramatic, providing for the characterization not only of the emotional tone of the text being presented, but also of the personages being commemorated in the text.

Early troping practice in the tenth century set to music one biblical passage of key importance to Christians, for it commemorated the central event in Christian history: Christ's resurrection. It begins, "*Quem quaeritis in sepulchre, Christicolae*," meaning "Whom do you seek in the tomb, followers of Christ?" The words are those of an angel greeting three such followers, all of them women, who had come to Jesus's tomb in order to properly anoint his body (Figure 3.4). The women (performed by men or boys) reply, "Jesus of Nazareth who was crucified, heavenly one." The angel's reply is of supreme importance for Christians, then and now: "He is not here. He is risen." This is the first confirmation of Christ's resurrection from the dead, which for Christians carries with it the possibility of redemption for all humankind. Many versions of the sung text exist.

In the tenth century, the Bishop of Winchester wrote out detailed instructions for performing this scene in the all-male Benedictine monasteries. Tropes were soon used for other holy seasons, including the celebration of Christ's birth. While moving and dramatic, tropes were not plays as such, but were designed for a heightened experience of personal/collective worship and devotion commemorating Christ. It was not long, however, before a few stories associated with Christ's birth were being dramatized in Latin within churches, but perhaps not as part of the liturgy proper.

Biblical dramas in Latin

Throughout the Middle Ages, literacy was confined to the learned language of Latin, and reading itself was dominated by one important text: the Christian Bible. The elite, empowered to access its wisdom, found much to appreciate and interpret on both religious and formal grounds. Medieval readers, trained to look for signs and symbols everywhere in God's creation, applied this to their reading of the Bible as well, looking for connections between the Old and New Testaments in the stories and characters presented in both. They remarked on the similarities, for example, between the sacrifice of Isaac by his father, Abraham (a patriarch of the Old Testament), and that of Christ by his heavenly father in the New Testament, and came to see Isaac as an early "figure" for the later Christ. This figural turn of mind led readers to look for other kinds of patterns, such as symbolism, allegory, and analogy. In turn, these figurative devices informed literature, art, political thought, theology, oral and written sermons based on that theology – and dramatic performances, in both Latin and the vernacular.

Early biblical plays in Latin dramatized the visits to the manger to see the newly born Christ, by both shepherds and Magi (the wise men or Three Kings who bring gifts to the Christ child); they were performed respectively on Christmas morning and January 6, the feast of the Epiphany. By the end of the eleventh century, the *Procession of the Prophets* was being performed, based on a popular sermon from the fifth or sixth century. After the initial spectacle of a musical procession, costumed priests playing Old Testament prophets stepped forward to deliver their prophecies of the coming of Christ. The monastery of Benediktbeuern in Germany combined this so-called prophets play with its Christmas plays from the New Testament (which told of the life and works of Jesus and his earliest followers).

One of the most sophisticated examples of Bible music-drama is *The Play of Daniel*, derived from the Old Testament story of Daniel in the lion's den. It was performed during the Christmas season in the Cathedral of St. Peter of Beauvais in northern France, in the twelfth and thirteenth centuries. Here the Old Testament prophet Daniel prefigures the New Testament Messiah. In this play, there are at least nine opportunities for processions through the cathedral, making use of harps, zithers, and drums to accompany chant singing. Daniel sings a musically compelling passage in which he deciphers the mysterious handwriting on the wall that predicts the fall of King Belshazzar. (*The Play of Daniel* and *The Play of Herod*, another Latin music-drama based in scripture, were staged and recorded by the New York Pro Musica in the mid-twentieth century.)

The scenes in *The Play of Daniel* and other early music-dramas were staged on elevated platforms set up near the altar in the open spaces of the cathedral normally used by the priest and choir (there were no fixed pews). These platforms, sometimes designated as **mansions** ("stations"), were bare platforms with symbolic scenic devices rather than realistic settings.

Actors moved freely from one *mansion* to another, using the common floor area, or *platea* [plah-TEH-ah] ("open space"). This was, in effect, a neutral, unlocalized playing area, with *mansions* bordering it. The *platea* could be whatever the text required at a given moment; the actor's lines identified the locale and atmosphere for the audience. The idea of the *platea* carried over into the later vernacular Bible plays staged outside the church (see Figure 3.7). The fluid, open stage that Shakespeare later wrote for was somewhat indebted to this staging tradition.

Christian drama in the vernacular

Over the centuries, regional dialects of Latin formed the precursors to the modern languages of Italian, French, Spanish, and Portuguese; English developed from Celtic origins into a new language combining Latin and Germanic roots. While Latin remained the official written language of Christendom, the "Word of God" came to the vast majority of laypeople not via reading the Bible but through performative acts of worship and other activities. Homilies and visual iconography within the churches encouraged congregants to reflect on key events in the life of Christ, and worshippers participated in prayerful processions to the "stations of the cross" – depictions of episodes in the sequence of Christ's suffering (called his Passion), such as Christ carrying the Cross, his being nailed to the Cross, his death, and the removal of his body for burial.

By the late twelfth century, innovative plays based on these and other biblical events began to be written in vernacular languages and performed outside churches. An important early example is *The Play of Adam* (*c.*1150) from northern France. It dramatizes the Old Testament story of the expulsion of the two first humans, Adam and Eve, from the Garden of Eden, and of the rivalry between their sons, Cain and Abel. The detailed stage directions make clear that it was performed adjacent to a church or cathedral, and they provide many details about scenic décor, costuming, and acting.

The fourteenth through sixteenth centuries saw a flowering of vernacular religious drama in towns throughout England and the European continent, whose themes were drawn from the Bible and from Christian doctrine. Such drama flourished for three reasons: (1) the institution of the new Feast of Corpus Christi; (2) the growth of towns and municipal governments as entities independent of feudal lords; and (3) the gradual development within towns of the medieval trade **guilds**. These were associations of tradesmen, such as bakers, tailors, and goldsmiths, who trained apprentices and eventually regulated wages and working conditions – and who sponsored the staging of certain plays. Alan E. Knight asserts that while on the surface the dramas of the period re-enact biblical history, behind that surface late medieval social structures, values, and political realities were being mirrored (Knight 1997: 1–2). Indeed, the staging of late medieval dramas was thoroughly urban, bourgeois, and informed by constant trade and transaction between continental Europe and England.

Christian feast days and biblical dramas

Key to the development of vernacular drama in the Middle Ages was the institution of the Feast of Corpus Christi – Latin for the "body of Christ." The sacrifice of Christ's body is centrally commemorated in the climax of the Mass, when the Eucharist is celebrated: the priest raises bread and wine, and pronounces, as Jesus did during his last supper with his apostles, "This is my body" and "This is my blood." With these words, the bread and wine are believed to be transubstantiated into the actual body and blood of the risen Christ. Pope Urban IV instituted the Feast of Corpus Christi in 1264 in order to celebrate the redemptive power of this sacrament and the presence of Christ in the world in general; by 1350 it was widely observed, between late May and late June of every year. Because this festival celebrated the body of Christ, it invoked the theological doctrine of Incarnation. For Christians, the Incarnation refers to God being made flesh in the person of Jesus Christ. The doctrine of Incarnation also extends to the Word of God, known through the Bible, as well as embodied in Jesus. Thus the Feast of Corpus Christi is a celebration of a text turned into a performing body. Figuratively speaking, the Feast of Corpus Christi can be seen as a figure for theatrical performance itself, which also turns words (scripts) into flesh (actors acting).

In a common Corpus Christi ritual, priests processed through the city displaying the "Host," a consecrated wafer encased in an elaborate vessel that signified the real (not symbolic) presence of Christ in the world (Figure 3.5). The procession of the Host was often accompanied by tableaux of biblical scenes representing Christian sacred history and testifying to the humanity of Christ. In Paris in 1313, actors began to recite the story of the Passion as part of a living tableau. Short speeches were introduced in Innsbruck, Austria, in 1391 with the appearance of Adam, Eve, and the twelve disciples of Jesus.

Meanwhile, in England and elsewhere on the continent, sets of plays based on key biblical episodes providing a whole history of salvation were being performed; these were known as cycle plays (see Figure 3.6). Among the Bible stories dramatized in the cycle plays were those of the creation of the world; the building of Noah's Ark; Abraham's sacrifice of his son; the Nativity, with the visits of the shepherds and the Magi; Herod's attempt to slay the new child-king by dispatching his army to slay all newborn children; Christ's raising of his friend, Lazarus, from the dead; and Christ's crucifixion and resurrection.

Not being attached to the liturgy as such, vernacular Bible dramas of all types combined instruction with dramatic freedom, often incorporating carnivalesque elements, creating local characters, and providing comic relief. In some plays God talks like one's neighbor; in others, shepherds suffer from oppressive landlords; and in at least one other, Noah's wife seriously doubts her husband's big ark project. The plays are unlike Greek and Roman drama: episodic, mixing comedy and tragedy, and held together by the frame of God's plan of salvation rather than chronology. They abound in seeming anachronisms, introduced to make contemporary points. For example, at Christ's birth, King Herod can swear by "the Trinity," referring to God the Father, Jesus, and God the Holy Spirit, a concept not possible until after Christ's death – but useful to show how even a pagan tyrant like Herod can inadvertently pay homage to Jesus and God. Here anachronism links the present to the past as a strategy for showing the eternal truth of what is being commemorated. In a less sanguine version of such an alignment between past and present, some plays reflected the anti-Semitism common at the time; Jews were routinely blamed for Christ's death.

Figure 3.5

In this prayer book illustration of an early Corpus Christi ritual (c.1320), the priest holds high the Host toward the figure of Christ on the Cross. It is designed to illustrate the miracle of transubstantiation, whereby the bread of the Host becomes one with the body of Christ (here, shown bleeding on to the bread). Note the witnesses to this miracle are laypeople, demonstrating the message of this high holy day: Christ's redemptive sacrifice is available to all humankind.

Source: Michael Camille (1996), *Gothic Art: Glorious Visions* (New York: Abrams). Bibliothèque nationale de France.

Because of the later censorship of religious drama during the Protestant Reformation (see Chapter 5), the manuscripts of only four complete or nearly complete English cycles are extant: 48 individual plays in the York Cycle, 32 of the Towneley (sometimes called Wakefield) plays, 25 in the Chester Cycle, and 42 in the "N-Town" (unknown city) manuscript. We know an exceptional amount about the earliest of the four, the York Cycle; the evidence tells us much about its staging, the degree of civic involvement in performance, and the social and economic background to its production.

The first record of the York Cycle's performance is from 1376, but by then it was already a well-established part of York's civic and economic life. The extant scripts were written sometime between 1463 and 1477. The plays were performed on **pageant wagons**, which held the setting (such as Eden or the Nativity manger) and sometimes incorporated special effects. The wagons were pulled along a path starting from the outskirts of York and ending in the city center, stopping at "stations" to perform each play (or "pageant") before the audience gathered there. The number of stations isn't known for certain and probably changed now and then; estimates range from 8 to 16, but 12 seems the most likely. While a play was performed at a station, the subsequent wagon was queued up. Then when the performance was over, the first wagon was pulled to the following station and the next play was brought in. With 48 pageants (and possibly as many as 51), the York Cycle probably took around 20 hours to perform, though possibly not all plays were performed every year.

Usually the action was set on the wagon, but it's likely that once in a while an actor performed in the street in front of the wagon or strode in through the audience. Devils and evil characters were often played with masks, helmets, or frightening makeup; God and angels may have had their faces painted gold. Music accompanied the performances.

With a few exceptions these plays were sponsored and performed by one of the city's craft guilds; women did not perform. Often the guild had a connection to the biblical episode it performed: for example, the Shipwrights were responsible for "The Building of the Ark," the Fishers and Mariners performed "Noah and His Wife," and the Bakers dramatized "The Last Supper." Sometimes the connection lay deep in the play's production or symbolism: for instance,

Figure 3.6
Detail from a painting of a city procession honoring the visit to Brussels in 1615 of Spain's Archduchess Isabella, then Governor of the Spanish Netherlands. This pageant wagon carries a scene of Christ's Nativity with actors in tableau. Joseph and Mary hover over the Christ child at the corner of the stable; the scene includes admiring shepherds, animals, and apparently a blacksmith. This wagon was one of nine in the procession that represented subjects both religious and secular. The painting is an important source for our knowledge of medieval pageant wagons, although they are in use here to display tableaux rather than as stages for the performance of plays.

Source: Painting by Dennis Van Alsloot. © the Board of Trustees of the Victoria and Albert Museum, London.

the reason the Armourers produced "The Expulsion from Eden" may have been that in medieval art, the archangel Michael typically wielded a sword when driving Adam and Eve out of Eden. In France, and later in England, these plays were also known as "mystery plays," mainly because of their spiritual character; however, another explanation may be that craft guilds often treated their methods and tools as trade secrets, referred to as "mysteries" that were carefully guarded.

Inventive means were used to stage religious plays, at York and elsewhere. Where pageant wagons were used, they provided stages for the tableaux in the processions and/or for performances at certain stations along the way in the processions ("processional staging"). Occasionally, some of the wagons might have been moved into (or next to) an open area such as a city square, a green, or even a large platform that would have provided a neutral playing space. (The overall arrangement, in which a platform or wagon with a set representing a relatively specific location is surrounded by a general playing area, is usually called *locus* [LAW-koos] and *platea* staging.) Some Corpus Christi cycles evidently used no wagons; others included pageants so elaborate that two wagons were needed.

Our only visual record of a medieval play in performance shows fixed, raised scaffolds – mansions – bordering the *platea*. A hand-painted illumination in a fifteenth-century French prayer book shows a scene from the lost saint play *The Martyrdom of St. Apollonia*, with actors in the *platea* and up on the scaffolds, possibly along with audience members (see Figure 3.7, and the discussion of saint plays below).

The production of cycle plays was far more than a side activity or entertainment for the trade guilds that sponsored them; the annual cycles were highlights of a festive season that attracted numerous visitors and provided a major economic boost for the community.

Figure 3.7

A scene from a lost medieval play, *The Martyrdom of St. Apollonia*, as represented in an illumination by Jean Fouquet in a French prayer book, the *Livre d'Heures pour maître Etienne Chevalier* (c.1452–1456). According to legend, Apollonia was once tortured by the extraction of her teeth. Among the scaffolds around the *platea* or playing area are those representing heaven (left) with its angels, and hell (right) with its devils and a hellmouth into which the damned were to be shepherded. The king's throne is at the rear, and the figure with book and baton may be the director, in ecclesiastical dress. The raised scaffolds seem to form a semi-circle around the *platea*, but in this and other details we may be seeing the painter's compositional strategies for representation in a book.

Source: © Musée Condé, Chantille, France. Photo RMN.

Their staging was a major undertaking that required considerable financial resources and planning, organizational support and supervision by city officials. The York Cycle, for example, featured some 300 speaking parts. Due to the financial burden, sometimes two guilds had to combine their resources in order to produce one of the pageants. Why they chose to sponsor them at all is a matter of debate. Certainly piety played a role. But other pressures may have also been a factor. While the Feast of Corpus Christi and the cycles of plays appealed to all sectors of society, what emerges from recent studies of the historical records is the sense that it was the merchant/entrepreneurs who controlled, sponsored, and even initiated these great "annual feat(s) of corporate ritual within their cit[ies]" (Dobson 1997: 105). Probably a combination of civic authority, economic motivation, civic pride, and religious devotion compelled the guilds to underwrite these major annual productions.

Outside England, Passion plays were popular during the Lenten season. These plays treated the life of Christ in the days leading up to and including his crucifixion and resurrection. Some of these plays were performed over several days on fixed stages in which all settings were visible at once (a convention known as simultaneous staging). The illuminations and stage directions of the text for the 1547 performance of the *Mystère de la Passion* in Valenciennes, France, indicate elaborate fixed stage arrangements that allowed complex scenic spectacles, including the descent of an angel, flying devils, and the ascension of Christ into the clouds with angels (see Figure 3.8). The late sixteenth-century Passion play at Lucerne, Switzerland, was performed in the city's Weinmarkt over two days. The three-part Cornish play known as the *Ordinalia* used mansions in a circular arrangement, perhaps within a circular earthen embankment, and it played over three days.

In the face of disasters or the horror of a plague like the "Black Death" so common at the time, some towns organized Bible plays to give thanks for their deliverance. The Catholic community of Oberammergau in the Bavarian Alps began to perform its Passion play in 1634 in fulfillment of a pledge to God that if the plague would cease, they would perform a play on Christ's sufferings every ten years. This the village has done, with few exceptions, until the present, with various script changes since the 1960s to remove anti-Semitic passages.

Figure 3.8

The setting for a Passion play in Valenciennes, France, in 1547, as depicted by the production's designer, Hubert Cailleau, in 1577. Note heaven on one side of the stage, and the hellmouth on the other.

Source: Elie Konigson, *La Représentatcion d'un mystère de la Passion à* Valenciennes en 1547 (Paris, 1969). Bibliothèque nationale de France.

Saint plays, morality plays, and autos sacramentales

There were various other types of vernacular Christian dramas in this period. One was the saint play (also called miracle play), devoted to the lives of the saints, especially their miraculous works. One Spanish saint play, *El Misterio de Elche*, dates from the late fifteenth century, and is still performed annually in the Basilica de Santa Maria in Elche (Spain), to celebrate the miraculous Assumption (ascent) of Jesus's mother, Mary, into heaven. This event allows us both a glimpse into medieval European performance traditions, and a sense of how they have changed over time. The play is divided into two parts; the first, *La Vespra*, is performed on August 14, the eve of her feast day, and commemorates the death of the Virgin Mary surrounded by the apostles. It begins when Mary (still played today by a haloed boy in a curly wig, and accompanied by a wind band) progresses through the church door and announces that she is about to die. Not long after, high above the congregants gathered below, the dome of the church – painted to represent the sky and heavens – opens as if by magic, allowing five angels (two boys, three men) to descend to Mary. The apparatus transporting the angels is known as *la magrana* (pomegranate). It dates in its present form from the sixteenth century and is similar to other simple but effective theatrical mechanisms utilized during the period in Spain. On the following day, Part II, *La Festa*, commemorates the coronation of the Virgin after both her body and soul arrive in heaven. The body of the silk-clad Virgin is transported heavenward in "the pomegranate," surrounded by four of the angels. As she rises toward heaven the trap door opens once again, allowing the Holy Trinity (played by two boys and a man) to descend on a separate apparatus to the Virgin, so they may fix the crown of heaven upon her head. Witnessing the performance in 2006, David Ward describes how

[b]oth contraptions then rise and are steered carefully through the skycloth. . . . The audience holds its breath until the delicate double docking manoeuvre is complete. Then all heaven breaks loose: golden rain falls from paradise and again the organ plays, bells ring, fireworks bang and the audience claps and cheers.

There are cries from all around the church of "Long live the mother of God!" and everyone shouts "Viva!"

The apostles sing a Gloria of thanksgiving and we stagger out into the square, amazed.

(Ward 2006)

When amateur congregant singers took over the performance from the priests and choirboys in the nineteenth century, they preserved the all-male performance tradition. As performed today, *El Misterio de Elche* is a montage of religious as well as secular performance elements which have accrued over the centuries. Its music ranges from medieval plainsong to Renaissance and Baroque musical styles. Melveena McKendrick observes how this major Church feast combines the procession of the penitents, fireworks, and other secular revelry to create a "potent mix of public fiesta and religious piety" (1989: 239) for the local congregants and numerous tourists who attend each year.

Morality plays developed widely during the fourteenth century, and probably derived from sermons given by the clergy to elaborate important points from the day's scriptural readings. They were locally produced by groups of citizens, sometimes elaborately. Allegorical in nature, they usually focused on an "everyman" figure who faced a choice between good and bad behavior. Since God had given humankind free will to choose good or evil, the individual who chose badly would suffer the consequences – damnation and the fires of hell. Often the entrance to this place was represented by a monstrous, fanged, mechanical "hellmouth" which would consume the fallen and the damned during the course of a play, and was meant to frighten the audience into choosing virtue (the place of "Paradise" at the opposite end of the playing space) over vice (see Figure 3.8). (Often a hellmouth was included in the Corpus Christi cycles as well.)

One of the earliest morality plays was authored by Hildegard of Bingen (1098–1179), a gifted Benedictine mystic, abbess, healer, and author. Like the dramas of Hrotsvitha, Hildegard's musical morality *Ordo Virtutum* (or "Play of the Virtues," *c.*1155) was probably intended to be read or recited by nuns within her convent, not for a general public. It featured the battle for a human soul between the

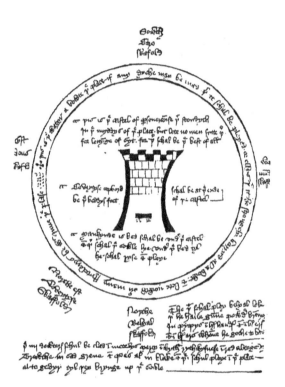

Figure 3.9

Plan of the mansions and playing area for the morality play *The Castle of Perseverance* (*c.*1400–1425), possibly for a performance in an ancient earthen round. Mankind's castle is at the center, the location of the five mansions is indicated outside the circle, and the direction within the double circles reads: "this is the water about the place [*platea*], if any ditch be made where it shall be played, or else let it be strongly barred all about."

forces of evil (the Devil) and 16 personified virtues like Humility, Charity, Fear of God, Obedience, and so forth.

Perhaps the most famous morality plays in English are *The Castle of Perseverance* (*c.*1400–1425, Figure 3.9) and *Everyman* (*c.*1495, likely based on an earlier Dutch version that was itself inspired by a Buddhist fable from a millennium earlier). In *The Castle of Perseverance*, the main character, Mankind, is seduced by the Bad Angel who tells him there will be time in old age to be virtuous. Mankind then encounters a wide range of allegorical characters who attempt to influence him. They include the Seven Deadly Sins (Wrath, Greed, Sloth, Pride, Lust, Envy, and Gluttony); the figures of Conscience, Confession, and Penance; and the Virtues, including Meekness, Patience, Charity, and Chastity. At Mankind's trial before God, Mercy and Peace plead for him against Righteousness and Truth. God judges mercifully in the end. In *Everyman*, the title character is faced with his impending death. Fearful of going to eternity alone, he asks one worldly character after another to accompany him; in the end, only Good Deeds can do so, thereby providing justification for Everyman's entry into heaven.

Within Spain, a new theatrical form, the *auto sacramental* [OW-toh sahk-rah-men-TAHL], began to develop once Spain became a unified Christian nation in 1492. Prior to that year, Spanish territory had been divided among separate kingdoms, and large portions had been inhabited by Muslims and Jews. When Isabella I, queen of the Spanish kingdom of Castile, married her cousin Ferdinand II of Aragon in 1469, they set about unifying Spain under Catholic rule, aided both by military campaigns and by the Spanish Inquisition. In 1492, they defeated the Moors at Granada, and passed a law requiring all Jews to either convert to Christianity or be expelled from Spain. Many Jews would decide to follow in Christopher Columbus's wake, once the Americas began to be settled.

As it had in other parts of Europe, theatre in Spain played its part in extending and solidifying Christian power. A unique form developed around the celebration of Corpus Christi that combined elements of the cycle plays and the morality plays; these one-act plays became known as *autos sacramentales* ("sacramental acts"). Like the cycle plays, the *autos* dealt with important stories from biblical history to culminate in a celebration of the mystery of the Eucharist. But they also bore traces of earlier morality play devices, which had been popular in non-Islamic Spain from the thirteenth century.

Mounted on portable, wheeled stages called *carros*, the plays were presented several times in different locations throughout the principal cities of Spain. Sometimes the city commissioned so many that performances took place over several days, for the benefit of the king, various governing councils, and the general public. The *carros* themselves were included in the Corpus Christi processions, where they were pulled along by bulls whose horns had been dipped in gold for the occasion.

Thousands of *autos sacramentales* were commissioned, to be staged and re-staged over the course of the centuries. As in England, they were under the control of trade guilds until the middle of the sixteenth century; after that, the city councils hired professional troupes to stage these plays, which were written by the peninsula's foremost dramatists, among them Gil Vicente, Juan del Encina, Lope de Vega, and Calderón de la Barca; these professional playwrights will be discussed further in Chapters 4 and 5. The most important of the *auto* authors was Calderón, who penned some 200, of which 76 survive. His work is remarkable not only for its quantity, but for its quality: Calderón is widely noted for his keen insights into human nature, which he viewed with great compassion, as well as his ability to blend serious religious philosophy and poetic language with inventive dramas embodying moral lessons. A fascinating example from his body of work is *The Great Theatre of the World* (1635), in which God is viewed as a kind of cosmic stage director, putting the characters of King, Beauty, Rich Man, Peasant, Beggar, and Child through their paces, noting that each has but one entrance and one exit from this particular "stage."

Interest in the *autos* began to wane after Calderón's death in 1681, but their influence was felt across the Atlantic as well. Perhaps the most famous is one that may never have been staged: the *Loa to the Divine Narcissus* by Sor Juana Inés de la Cruz, a Mexican nun who was also a celebrated philosopher, poet, and dramatist in the seventeenth century (see the case study in Chapter 6). "*Loa*" means an act of praise, and Spanish *loas* evolved from short monologues and dialogues that preceded a given work to a longer form resembling a one-act play in its own right, used to introduce a longer play with similar thematic material. Sor Juana's 1689 *loa* tells the story of the conversion to Christianity of the indigenous Mexicans by Spanish warriors and missionaries, and features such allegorical characters as Occident and America (a native prince and princess), Zeal (a Spanish soldier), and Religion (a Spanish lady), who argues that the "God of the Seeds" worshipped by the natives is an allegorical prefiguration of Christ himself.

Although the religious messages in the cycle plays and these other types of drama were strong, it is important to stress the entertainment value of these plays as well. The plots may have been familiar or didactic, but often carnivalesque elements of farcical and topical humor crept in to keep the telling fresh. The characters may have been non-human abstractions, but the allegorical figures were fully fleshed and often disarmingly human in their characterization. The sets may have been limited by pageant wagon constraints, but clever costumers devised ways to hold audience interest, including leather bodystockings meant to suggest nakedness (for the plays about Adam and Eve), and others rigged so as to shed blood, as in the case of a play from the Chester cycle about the risen Christ. In France, because the reputation of the guilds depended in part on the quality of their productions, a "mixture of personal showmanship and the desire to dress the sacred characters as icons could lead to extravagances of silk, satin, and jeweled embroidery which we might find more appropriate to the Follies than to sacred drama" (Vince 1989: 69). For a population not yet literate in their own spoken language, all of these elements worked together to ensure an experience of Christian doctrine and values they hoped literally never to forget. However, the Church's approval of religiously oriented performance did not necessarily extend to theatre generally: suspicion continued, and particularly after the Reformation, the Church again condemned actors and denied them sacraments.

Dramas of Christian crusade and conquest

While the Christian Church in Europe was busy reaffirming its central tenets for believers through drama, it was also busy both at home and abroad trying to win new souls for the Christian God, with means both military and theatrical. When medieval Christian power was eventually concentrated in Rome and in the figure of a pope, the Church constructed the idea of the "Holy Land," an area comprising the locations in which sacred history had unfolded (present-day Israel, Palestine, Lebanon, Syria, and Jordan). Soon, the Holy Land became a site of Christian pilgrimage. From the eleventh century, it also became a site of bitter, bloody struggles for power and ascendancy in a series of militarized engagements eventually described as the "crusades," or holy wars. (The term, which means "marked with a cross" – the key symbol of Christianity – first appeared in Spain in the thirteenth century.)

> There were holy wars against Muslim infidels [for the liberation of Jerusalem]; against heretics like the Albigensians of Provence; against recalcitrant Christian monarchs; even against humble towns that failed to toe the papal line. But the first category, war against the Muslim infidel, was always popularly regarded as the true war "for and by the Cross." Sanctified war was an innovation within the Christian Church, which had for centuries struggled to impose the peace of God upon adversaries.
>
> (Wheatcroft 2004: 187)

When Christian kingdoms began to colonize the world, a variety of dramas of conquest resulted. In some, Western Christian modes of performance were imposed on indigenous populations, as happened in Mesoamerica. In their American colonies, the Spaniards introduced all manner of Christian biblical theatre from medieval Europe, in service of teaching and converting the natives. The first European play performed in the Americas was a morality play: *Juicio Final* (*Final Judgment*), attributed to the Franciscan friar Andrés de Olmos, staged in Tlatelolco (*c.*1531–1533, in what is now Mexico City). Written as a warning against local customs of concubinage, it threatened natives with eternal damnation if they did not marry within the Christian Church.

It is impossible to know exactly how the indigenous peoples of the Americas understood these theatrical representations. Most scholars agree, however, that theatre played a strong role in the conversion project. As we noted in Chapter 1, early Spanish conquerors were quick to adapt existent forms of indigenous theatricality to their own ends. Plays were performed in local languages, and indigenous performers were recruited to fill the roles. The Crusades themselves were a frequent topic of such drama, as noted in the case study below, about the Moors and the Christians.

Figure 3.10
A scissors dancer from Peru. Some scholars trace this performance practice to a sixteenth-century "dancing sickness" performed as part of a resistance movement against Spanish occupation of Peru.
© Enrique Castro-Mendivil/Reuters/Corbis.

Mexican theatre scholar Maria Sten once noted that "theatre was to the spiritual conquest of Mexico what the horses and gunpowder were to its military defeat" (1982: 14). But other scholars have noted that indigenous peoples living in the early period of the Spanish conquest did not uncritically accept new performance forms and content, nor abandon completely their own, as we saw with *Rabinal Achi*, and as our case study on the Christians and Moors suggests. In the Andes, for example, a Spanish "extirpator," charged with stamping out idolatry in the 1560s, was outraged to report that followers of an indigenous resistance movement known as *taqui onqoy* (or "dancing sickness") had hidden an image of one of their local deities on the very vessel that displayed the Host during a Cuzco Corpus Christi celebration. Scholars of this resistance movement, which had at its center a form of deity-possession of dancing bodies, have suggested that its impulse to reclaim local cultural identity has never disappeared and may be visible in contemporary performance of the famous Andean *danza de las tijeras*, or scissors dance (see Figure 3.10).

CASE STUDY: Christians and Moors: Medieval performance in Spain and the New World

Bruce McConachie, with Tamara Underiner

To celebrate their conquest in 1598 of what is now the American southwest, Spanish *conquistadores* threw themselves a week-long party, which included a variety of performances. According to one participant, there were: "Tilts with cane-spears, bullfights, tilts at the ring, / A jolly drama, well composed, / Playing at Moors and Christians, / With much artillery, whose roar / Did cause notable fear and marveling, / To many bold barbarians . . ." (Harris 1994: 145).

How might we understand this important historical document? Many Spanish-speaking cultures continue to enjoy bullfights, of course, and "tilts with cane-spears" is easily explained as jousting matches on horseback with breakable lances (so as to avoid injuring the riders). Similarly, "tilts at the ring," another game dating from medieval tournaments, challenges the rider to thrust his lance through a small ring. But what was the "jolly drama" with "Moors and Christians" that involved noisy "artillery"? And why might a drama about Moors, the Spanish term for Muslims living in northern Africa, be performed to celebrate the conquest of land in North America?

At first glance, the answer to this last question might seem to be a simple one: why not? As we have suggested in this chapter, Spain carried the crusades to the Americas, where it sought to convert souls to Christ before the end-times came; the natives of the Americas, like the Muslims, can be seen as the "enemies" of Christianity who had to be defeated.

But upon closer examination, this explanation cannot account for the variety within and remarkable persistence of the tradition of the Moors and Christian dramas, both in Spain and in the New World, where the first record of such a performance dates back to 1538. At that performance, staged during a Corpus Christi procession in the town of Tlaxcala in central Mexico – by an all-native cast, in their native tongue of Nahuatl – the enemy "Sultan" was not an indigenous ruler but the Spanish conquistador Hernán Cortés himself, played by a native actor dressed as a Turk. At the end of the "play," he, along with all the other natives on stage and in the audience, were baptized in an act of compulsory conversion. What, exactly, was going on, and how do we understand such a performance?

To begin to answer it, we will cover the history of this genre of drama in both Spain and its colonies, and suggest an approach that will help to explain how this ancient dramatic form has survived half a millennium and more, on both sides of the Atlantic.

Historic background

By the time Spaniards in the New World crossed the Rio Grande to claim New Mexico, Christian kings, princes, and counts in Spain had been staging *moros y cristianos* spectacles for popular and aristocratic audiences for over 300 years. These choreographed battles typically pitted two groups of knights against each other – blackfaced Moors in exotic silk gowns and Christian crusaders in shining armor. Following exchanges of verbal abuse from both sides, the Moors usually won the initial battles, but the Christian knights always triumphed in the end, sometimes returning with facsimiles of Moorish heads on their lances. In other performances, the Moors would recognize the error of their ways, convert to Christianity, and bow down before a symbol of Catholic power.

Real battles between Christians and Moors began before Spain was even a country. At first of the Moors won most of them, in the early Middle Ages establishing a society in what is now Portugal and most of Spain that was more advanced and tolerant than Christian Europe. Over time, Christian forces prevailed; warfare lasted until 1492, when the Moorish port city of Granada fell (Figure 3.11). In that momentous year, as noted above, all Jews who refused

Figure 3.11
Map showing extent of Christian and Moorish territories in 1490.

to convert to Christianity were also expelled from the peninsula, and Columbus set sail under the flag of the new Spanish monarchs, Ferdinand and Isabella.

This 700-year crusade left an indelible impression on Spanish history and culture. Hardened by constant warfare, a newly united Spain forged a culture of religious fanaticism and military valor that shaped the Catholic Inquisition at home and conquest abroad. After 1492, the rulers of Spain expelled all infidels from the peninsula, tortured thousands of *moriscos* (Christians of Moorish background) and *marranos* (Christians of Jewish background) suspected of un-Christian belief, and extended their crusade of conversion or extinction to the natives of the New World. When the *conquistadores* of New Mexico performed the "jolly drama" of *moros y cristianos*, they were honoring a tradition of militant Christianity that had brought them victory for hundreds of years. There can be little doubt that the Spaniards rejoiced in the "fear and marvelling" that the spectacle produced among the Native Americans who were watching the show.

As in the Mexico and New Mexico productions of 1538 and 1598, performances of *moros y cristianos* in medieval Spain normally occurred in the midst of a festival. In 1461, for example, Count Miguel Lucas de Iranzo, the Castilian ruler of Jaen, threw a party for his town that lasted for 21 days. In addition to celebrating his wedding, the feast was designed to shore up his power and prestige in the wake of a recent plague and frequent attacks by the Moors. The count and his retinue claimed the blessing of God by dressing themselves in images of Christian power. Lucas transformed the entire town into a stage using an array of torches, symbolic tapestries, and musicians to heighten the effects of the processions, games, dances, and plays. Mock battles between Christians and Moors occurred in the midst of other dramatic spectacles. Like many of his subjects, Lucas appeared both as himself, a magnanimous ruler, and as a performer, enacting one of the kings who visited the Christ child in Bethlehem in a nativity play that was part of the celebration.

Figure 3.12

Stonework depicting a sexualized Lucifer tempting Christ. Carved on a capital of Autun Cathedral in France in the twelfth century by Gisilbertus.

Source: © Abbé Denis Grivot, Autun, France.

The "low other" in medieval performance

Performances in medieval festivals and religious holidays often defined proper Christian behavior by denigrating and defeating its un-Christian opposite. Because vertical relations of authority and belief were so important in medieval Christian culture, stereotypes of "low others" proliferated in European performances from the twelfth through the sixteenth centuries. Mummers plays, early Christianized versions of pagan rituals designed to ensure the return of spring after the winter solstice, often featured a blackened Turk as the antagonist of a white Christian knight. Another winter solstice performance, the Sword Dance, symbolically sacrificed a hairy wild man or a "greenman" from the forest to incite the resurrection of the springtime sun (and the Christian Son of God). In the cycle plays, Jews, Romans, and infidels were often characterized as buffoons, villains, or other "low" types. Characters associated with vice in morality plays – the female temptress, Sloth,

Gluttony, Pride, the rest of the Seven Deadly Sins, and Lucifer himself – were typically costumed and played in ways that aligned them with dirt, feces, and rampant sexuality (Figure 3.12). In medieval Spain, Moors and Jews became the primary symbols of the "low other" in festival performances. Medieval writers often characterized Moors as treacherous and cowardly in *moros y cristianos* plays, especially after 1492.

Moros y cristianos *in New Mexico today: Conquest and re-conquest*

The legacy of Spanish medieval theatre continues to shape popular and religious celebrations in Spanish-speaking countries today. For example, every year during a June fiesta about two dozen men and women of Chimayó, New Mexico dress in medieval costumes, mount horses, wield swords and scimitars, and engage in a symbolic battle. To create the illusion of darker skin, the Latinos playing Moors also wear black veils. As during the days of Spanish imperialism, the ideology of militant Christianity continues to shape the ending of the play. Convinced by the outcome of the battle that their own religion is false, the Moors convert to Christianity, and all performers join together in a hymn of praise to the Holy Cross.

Some Native Americans living in Mexico and the U.S. southwest also perform versions of *moros y cristianos*, partly to honor their conversion to Christianity under Spanish rule but also to gain a wry revenge against their historical persecutors. These performances typically involve Native Americans on hobby-horses

Figure 3.13

Drawing made in 1942 of a Native American as a Spanish Christian saint on a horse in a *moros y cristianos* production on Christmas day at San Felipe Pueblo. Anonymous artist.

From Papers of the Michigan Academy of Science, Arts and Letters. © The Michigan Academy of Science, Arts and Letters.

THINKING THROUGH THEATRE HISTORIES

Reading for the "hidden transcripts"

Religious theatre scholar Max Harris has studied a wide variety of *moros y cristianos* dramas, both historical and contemporary, and offers a way to explain them in terms of both their resistance and their persistence. Drawing on James C. Scott's *Domination and the Arts of Resistance*, Harris compels us to consider two kinds of "transcripts" at work in performances in which power imbalances figure strongly, as they do in this case study: the "public," or official message of the performance, its stated intent; and the "hidden" transcripts that both powerful and powerless might employ to critique the public transcript, behind its back, either consciously or unconsciously. In the case of the American variants on this drama, from the beginning – and despite how the Spaniards in Europe and New Mexico might have meant it – the *moros y cristianos* have been staged with multiple hidden transcripts that allow performers both to toe the official line of Christianity's triumph, and to stage its own critique of that victory. Today, in situations in which Native Americans control and perform the dance, the drama of the Moors and Christians is no longer a "military theatre of humiliation" (Harris 2000: 27); instead, they have turned white soldiers, saints, and traders into the "low others" that they themselves once had been.

playing, as they did in Tlaxcala in 1538, both groups of antagonists, with historic Native Americans on one side and Spaniards and "white" Americans on the other (Figure 3.13). Instead of dramatizing conquest and conversion, however, the performance points to the foolishness of the "whites," who, in this revised version of *moros y cristianos*, flee a symbolic bull, portrayed by a Native American.

Key references

Glick, T.E. (1979) *Islamic and Christian Spain in the Early Middle Ages: Comparative Perspectives on Social and Cultural Formation*, Princeton: Princeton University Press.

Harris, M. (1994) "The Arrival of the Europeans: Folk Dramatizations of Conquest and Conversion in New Mexico," in C. Davidson and J. Stroupe (eds) *Early and Traditional Drama: Africa, Asia and the New World*, Kalamazoo, MI: Medieval Institute Publications.

Harris, M. (2000) *Aztecs, Moors and Christians*, Austin, TX: University of Texas Press.

Holme, B. (1987) *Medieval Pageantry*, London: Thames and Hudson.

Scott, J.D. (1990) *Domination and the Arts of Resistance: Hidden Transcripts*, New Haven, CT: Yale University Press.

Shergold, N.D. (1967) *A History of the Spanish Stage from Medieval Times until the End of the Seventeenth Century*, Oxford: Clarendon Press.

Stallybrass, P. and White, A. (1996) *The Politics and Poetics of Transgression*, Ithaca, NY: Cornell University Press.

Stern, C. (1996) *The Medieval Theatre in Castile*, Medieval and Renaissance Texts and Studies, vol. 156, Binghamton, NY: Center for Medieval and Renaissance Studies.

Wickham, G. (1987) *The Medieval Theatre*, 3rd edn., Cambridge: Cambridge University Press.

Islamic commemorative mourning dramas: The *Ta'ziyeh* of Iran and beyond

Just as the life of Christ and biblical events played a central role in the development of commemorative liturgical and biblical dramas within Christianity, a major historical event in the history of Islam became the central inspiration for the development of the Islamic commemorative drama, *Ta'ziyeh* [TAH' zee-YEH].

"Islam" is an Arabic word meaning submission to God, or Allah. In the Islamic tradition, Allah revealed his message to Muhammad in a series of visions from 612 CE. Muhammad said he merely transmitted the message of Allah, adding and removing nothing. For Muslims the Qur'an (often rendered as "Koran") is nothing less than the transmission in simple, clear Arabic language of a divine archetype that is kept in heaven for eternity, and is graven on the "guarded Tablet." It was that archetype that was directly revealed to Muhammad. Muhammad, a merchant living in the city of Mecca, probably did not read and would have transmitted what he received orally. The word "Qur'an" is from a verb originally meaning "vocal recitation"; it was only after 622 that some of Muhammad's disciples began to inscribe fragments of what they heard on to bits of leather. After the Prophet's death, the Qur'anic revelations were gathered into a set of texts, collected by the first Caliph, Abu Bakr.

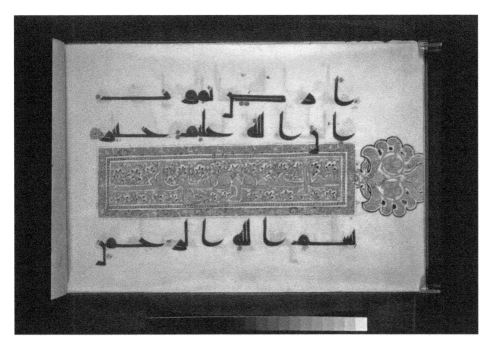

Figure 3.14
Qur'an fragment, showing the heading for Chapter 32, "The Prostration" (al-Sajda).
Arabic text in kufic script on vellum. Ninth century CE, Near East, possibly Iraq.
Source: © The Trustees of the Chester Beatty Library, Dublin

For several centuries, written versions provided little more than a guide to memory for repeating aloud a text already memorized. The writing of the Qur'an grew in significance, becoming a sanctifying act and done in elaborate calligraphy, the most esteemed art in Islam (Figure 3.14). Islam generally prohibits pictorial representation of the living or dead (people and animals) in order to maintain a clear distinction between the Creator and the created, but the Qur'an and other texts can be illuminated. Texts are often decorated with geometric and plant-like patterns. Each of the Qur'an's 114 chapters can be marked by a decorative heading, and special marks to guide one's reading, indicating places for required ritual prostration.

Sultans, shahs, princes, and members of the aristocracy or wealthy merchants throughout the Islamic world have also valued secular Islamic books and manuscripts highly. From at least the ninth century onwards, two attributes of royalty in Iran were maintaining a library and patronage of the making of fine manuscripts. Persian princes themselves were often artists or calligraphers. Other arts such as poetry, music, dance, storytelling (*Naghali*); shadow puppet theatre (*Khayal al-Zill* in Egypt, *Karagoz* in Turkey); storytelling in front of an illustrated backdrop (*Pardeh-khaani* and *Pardeh-dari*); and puppet theatre (*Aragoz* in Egypt; *Abderrazak* in Tunisia) also flourished under the patronage of Islamic rulers.

Commemorative mourning rituals and the development of Ta'ziyeh

When Muhammad died in 632, the Muslim community faced a crisis over his successor (or *Caliph*). Some of his followers believed that the Prophet passed special, divine knowledge to his son-in-law and cousin Ali (d. 661), as well as to his direct descendants, to serve as imams (prayer leaders and religious guides); these followers were called Shi'ites (members of the Shi'i sect). Others (members of the Sunni sect or Sunnis) held that the succession should fall to the best person, not necessarily to a direct relative of Muhammad. The two main branches of Islam – Sunni and Shi'i – reflect this historical and theological struggle over succession of the Prophet. The fundamental disagreement between Sunnis and Shi'ites was accentuated by both political and theological differences, which led to divergent legal and ritual practices. Most followers of Shi'i Islam live in present-day Iran, Iraq, Yemen, and Bahrain, with smaller communities in India, Pakistan, Bangladesh, and Afghanistan. The Sunnis constitute about 85–90 percent of the world's Muslim population and live throughout the Middle East, North Africa, Central Asia, Indonesia, and the Americas.

Among Shi'ites, a form of commemorative performance known as *Ta'ziyeh* (which in Arabic means expressions of mourning, sympathy, or consolation) became central to their version of Islam. The roots of today's *Ta'ziyeh* lie in the violent struggle over succession to the Prophet. When Ali's father and older brother were murdered, Hussein (Ali's son and the grandson of the Prophet) led a rebellion to regain control. But Hussein, his family, and followers were surrounded by the opposing army on the plain of Karbala (in present-day Iraq). On the tenth day of Muharram in the Islamic year 61 (October 10, 680), after ten battle-filled days without water in which all the males save a single small boy were massacred, Hussein himself was killed and the women taken captive. The battle became a source for most Shi'ite rituals because all those martyred modeled the ideal behavior in the struggle to follow the right path toward Allah.

The first month of the Muslim lunar calendar, Muharram, soon became a period for Shi'ites to perform mourning rituals to commemorate the moment when Hussein, his family, and followers were martyred. Since at least the tenth century, ritual processions in Baghdad have featured mourners with black-painted faces and disheveled hair, singing songs of lamentation and beating their chests in mourning. (Acts of self-flagellation have remained a central part of participants' identification with the martyred Hussein to the present day.)

Shi'ite practices were consolidated during the sixteenth century with the establishment of the Safavid dynasty on the Iranian Plateau. The popular orator, Hussein Vaiz Kashefi, composed *Rawzat al-shuhada* (*The Garden of Martyrs*) – a work which synthesized "various historical accounts, elegiac poems, theological tracts, and hagiographies into a chain of short narratives that together formed a much larger narrative" and which stressed "the courage, piety, and sacrifice of Hussein and his followers at Karbala." Reading it aloud at religious gatherings, orators improvised sermons based on the text whose intention "was to move the audience to tears through his recitation of the tragic deaths of the Battle of Karbala" (Aghaie 2005: 45–6).

Eventually, the events surrounding Hussein's martyrdom came to form the narrative core of an even more elaborate ritual performance called *Ta'ziyeh,* created during the Qajar period (1796–1925). A cycle of ten *Ta'ziyeh* plays is performed during the first ten days of Muharram, one each day (for a translation of one play, see Pettys 2005). Each chronicles a single episode of the brutal events, or focuses on the heroic deaths of specific members of Hussein's family and followers. The only prescribed play is the death of Hussein – always performed on the tenth day. Observances often continue through the remainder of the month of Muharram and into the month of Safar, specifically to mourn the torment of Hussein's female relatives taken as captives to Damascus. Some communities produce less ornate *Ta'ziyeh* performances throughout the year that are not necessarily about the events of Karbala.

Non-representational "reading" and representation in Ta'ziyeh

Ta'ziyeh was originally performed at a crossroads or in other outdoor areas. By the early nineteenth century, special performance spaces (*takiyeh*) were built for *Ta'ziyeh*. Some staging elements may be remnants of pre-Islamic entertainments and rituals, including a mourning ritual for the legendary Iranian prince Siyâvash, a sinless hero unjustly killed, like Hussein.

Ta'ziyeh is performed in the round, with a raised central platform surrounded by a huge circular, sand-covered space used for spectacular effects, such as equestrian events and foot battles. Additional raised stages erected around the edges of the circular space are used for subplots, enemy camps, or special scenes. These often extend into the audience area. Corridors stretch from the central stage through the audience so that messengers and processions of horses, camels, and vehicles can pass. Battle scenes can surround the entire audience. Audience and performers alike are immersed in a whirling, centrifugal experience of tumultuous action, songs, music, recitations, and battles (see Figures 3.15 and 3.16). Props and costumes are simple and sometimes symbolic. A basin of water represents the Euphrates River. Protagonists wear green or white and sing in lyrical Persian chants, while the antagonists wear red and declaim in a fierce, uncouth manner. Women's roles are played by veiled males dressed in black. Some characters, such as demons, are

Figure 3.15

A nineteenth-century performance of *Ta'ziyeh*. In the 1870s, the *Takiyeh Dowlat* shown here was erected in Tehran in the royal compound. Its walls, canvas ceiling, and circular stage were copied in *takiyeh* and *husseinyeh* (performance structures) all over the country.

Source: Photograph, Tehran 1976, of an original painting by Kemalal-Mulik. © Peter Chelkowski.

Figure 3.16

In a *Ta'ziyeh* commemorative performance, Nabiollah Habibabadi (on horseback) is seen in the role of Shemr, the general who beheads Imam Hussain. In the background is Yazid, the Umayyid Sultan who ordered the killing. In Habibabad near Isfahan, Iran.

Source: © William O. Beeman. All rights reserved.

masked. *Ta'ziyeh* participant-performers are not "actors" who represent characters. They do not memorize lines. Rather, they are "readers" who sing or recite in a non-realistic manner from segments of the script held in hand. Like many forms of commemorative ritual-drama, *Ta'ziyeh* has all the trappings of "theatre," as Westerners would understand the term, but in its most traditional form it is not theatre. Rather, it is a participatory, epic re-enactment of an historical event that makes the past present for Shi'ite participants and spectators.

To participate in *Ta'ziyeh* is to participate in a deeply religious event filled with intense grief, mourning, and lamentation. For his followers, Hussein's martyrdom at Karbala exemplified supreme self-sacrifice, human suffering, and a profound act of divine redemption. The pain participants inflict on themselves is the pain of Hussein.

Ta'ziyeh ties contemporary Shi'ites to their complex past, reminding them of their intimate connection with Hussein and the Shi'a battle of resistance against a powerful, alien invader. For those who participate, *Ta'ziyeh* brings the past into the present, and the site of performance becomes the physical locus of martyrdom. *Ta'ziyeh* remains of central importance in Iran, but is also performed today in South Asia, other parts of the Arab world, and the Caribbean. Secular versions of the *Ta'ziyeh* were performed at theatre festivals in Avignon in 1991, Parma (Italy) in 2000, and in New York in 2002 at Lincoln Center.

CASE STUDY: Playful gods: The *Ramlila* in north India

Phillip B. Zarrilli, with Carol Fisher Sorgenfrei and Tamara Underiner

In this case study we consider the Hindu commemorative devotional drama *Ramlila* [rahm-lee-lah] of north India. Unlike India's *kutiyattam*, considered in Chapter 2, which is patronized by relatively small, elite audiences interested in enhancing their aesthetic experience of performance, Hindu commemorative dramas are performed for mass, popular audiences. These dramas allow devotees immediate access to an encounter with one of many specific manifestations of the divine – an experience sometimes described as *bhakti rasa* (*bhakti* means devotion) – an aesthetic experience of deep devotion that is a creative interpretation of the *rasa* aesthetic considered in Chapter 2.

North India's *Ramlila* is an enormously popular, pluralistic form of open-air performance that re-enacts episodes from the life of Ram (also called Rama). Ram is considered to be one of the ten incarnations of the Hindu deity Vishnu (the preserver of the universe). *Lila* literally means an act of cosmic or divine "play"; that is, a moment when the divine interacts with the human world. In the case of *Ramlila* and its earlier quasi-dramatic precursors, the divine's vehicle for this interaction is Ram. The present form of the text used for the performance is called the *Ramcharitmanas* ("The Lake of Deeds of Rama," *c.*1577), attributed to the poet Tulsidas (*c.*1532–1623) or one of his disciples. Its plot is based on the main elements of the much earlier Sanskrit epic *Ramayana* (fifth to fourth century BCE). *Ramlilas* occur every year, usually in September and October. All *Ramlilas* involve role playing and the re-enactment of specific events from Ram's life. Some are brief, while others are elaborated at length.

Origins of Ramlila

Since its first telling, the *Ramayana* has been a source for performance. Norvin Hein (1972) postulates that the earliest forerunners of today's immensely popular *Ramlila* were dramatizations of parts of the *Ramayana* under royal patronage. One early source, the *Harivamsa* (no later than 400 CE) relates how part of the *Ramayana* was sung by a background chorus while actor-dancers in the foreground enacted the story. Hein suggests that this early form of dance-drama eventually died out in north India under Muslim rule (1200–1500), but that elements of the early performance were still reflected in the rebirth of devotional drama during the fifteenth and sixteenth centuries, when the popular Bhakti devotional movement swept across north India (Hein 1972: 124). The *Ramlila* makes a connection between performance and creation itself. The text of the most revered version of the *Ramayana*, that written by Valmiki (probably sometime between 200 BCE and 200 CE), makes it clear that the universe is a dramatic performance and that God is the writer, director, star, and even the audience:

> The world is a show and you are the viewer.
> You make Brahma, Vishnu and Shiva dance.
> . . .
> Putting on a man's body for the sake of gods and
>   saints,
> you talk and act like a natural king.
> Ram, when they see and hear your acts,
> the foolish are bewildered, the wise feel joy.
>
> (Quoted in Hess 2006: 130)

What happens at Ramlila?

Ramlila is a highly participatory form of drama in which the devotee enters into "the fabric of mythic narrative" (Lutgendorf 1991: 251). It draws millions of pilgrim-devotees from across India – especially the north and central regions. In the very geographical location where it is assumed that Lord Ram was born (Ayodhya) and lived in the distant past, *Ramlila* re-enacts the trials and tribulations of Ram. Some performances last three to five days and others for over a month. Audiences can exceed one hundred thousand – including not only Hindus, but (depending on the political climate) also minority Muslims and Christians. Performances culminate with the festival of Dussehra in which an effigy of the evil ten-headed demon-king, Ravana, is burned – a spectacular celebration of the victory of good over evil (see Figure 3.17). The performances are put on by amateur casts under the sponsorship of wealthy patrons.

In contrast to the highly decorative mode of composition of Sanskrit poetry still in use at the time he wrote, Tulsidas authored his version of the *Ramayana* in accessible language. In performance, Tulsidas's version of Ram's story is mapped

Figure 3.17

Ravana, the ten-headed demon-king as an effigy as part of the Ramnagar *Ramlila*.

Source: Photo © Richard Schechner.

on to the specific geographical locations understood to be dear to Lord Ram, so in effect, "the pageant came to express notions of cosmography and pilgrimage that aim at reclaiming and transforming the mundane world" (Lutgendorf 1991: 255). The entire performance becomes "a series of pilgrimages that re-enact the Lord's own movements and bring worshipers to the sites at which they reexperience his [holy] deeds" (1991: 250). Therefore, for the celebration of Ram and Sita's wedding anniversary, the ideal site is Mithila (Janakpur) in Nepal, the birthplace of Sita and the location of their wedding. Pilgrims who are able to travel there "identify themselves as members of Ram's . . . wedding party, and they trade humorous insults with the people of the bride's hometown" (1991: 250). For worshippers in Ayodhya, the birthplace of Ram, there are also festivities. According to scholar Philip Lutgendorf,

> On the marriage day in Ayodhya . . . wedding processions mounted by major temples wind through the city for hours. They consist of lampbearers, drummers and shehnai players, "English-style" marching bands (all requisites of a modern North Indian wedding), and of course the bridegrooms – Ram and his three brothers – astride horses or riding in ornate carriages. The grooms are usually *svarups* – young Brahman boys impersonating deities, but a few processions feature temple images borne on palanquins [see Figure 3.18]. After receiving the homage of devotees before whose homes and shops they briefly halt, the processions return to their sponsoring establishments, where a marriage ceremony is performed. The crowds of devotees attending these rites are not merely spectators; they are encouraged to take the roles of members of the wedding party.
>
> (Lutgendorf 1991: 251)

The Ramnagar Ramlila

Although hundreds of *Ramlilas* take place all over north India, the most famous (and the one that we will focus on) occurs in Ramnagar, which is across the River Ganga (Ganges) from the holy city of Varanasi (Benares). After a special set of offerings is given, Tulsidas's version

Figure 3.18

A Ramlila *svarup* on Hanuman's shoulders. Such young pre-pubescent boys play the holiest roles of Ram and Sita in performances where they are worshipped as the gods.

Source: Photo © Sam Schechner.

of Ram's sacred story is chanted/sung in its entirety by a group of twelve men, known as Ramayanis, who are accompanied by a drum. A prescribed number of couplets are sung daily. Only on the tenth day of recitation do the Ramayanis arrive at couplet 175, when the *Ramlila* re-enactment of scenes per se begins. Their singing is then incorporated into the larger context of the *lila*, and continues until they reach the last book of the epic poem, when the *lila* ends. But the recitation of the full text is not complete, so the Ramayanis continue their quiet reading until each word of the text has been read, so that the final ritual passing of a flame is held in Ayodhya, closing the full performance of 30–32 days.

Since the text is chanted, the actors do not simply recite the text of the drama, but rather, like the dancers of old, they "bring to life and . . . interpret the words of the recitation" (Hein 1972: 124). All actors are males, with the roles of Sita, Ram, and his brothers taken by prepubescent boys. They are worshipped as divine embodiments of those they impersonate (see Figure 3.18). Other characters such as Hanuman (the monkey king who helps Ram), and the ten-headed demon-king Ravana, wear masks, and all the performers are amateurs. Some actors of a specific *Ramlila* claim that their roles are inherited within their families. The performance style is a combination of wordless tableaux and processional drama, in which actors move from place to place with occasional dialogue that most of the devotees will not hear. Some locations are specially constructed for a *lila* while others are actual landmarks in the town.

The Ramnagar *Ramlila* is considered by many participants to be the most powerful. Why is this so? Among the reasons for this distinction is the belief that in Ramnagar, Lord Ram, his three divine brothers, and his wife (the goddess Sita) are literally present in the bodies of those who enact them, five boy actors, spectacularly attired, who are carried around (either by grown men or in palanquins), because the gods' feet must never touch the ground. At Ramnagar, the entire poem is presented, whereas some of the other productions used shortened texts. Another reason for the dominance of the Ramnagar version is the presence of thousands of *sadhus* (wandering, mendicant holy men) who camp out in Ramnagar for the entire month.

Pilgrims as participants, not spectators

What do the non-actor participants do? There are many ways that devotees can participate, but among the most common are some that are described by religious studies scholar Linda Hess (2006):

(1) When major characters begin to speak, the thousands of participants shout a set cheer. For example, when Ram speaks, they shout out "Bol! Raja Ramchandra ki jai!" ("Say it! Victory to King Ramchandra!")
(2) Many people carry the entire text with them and read it aloud along with the actors.
(3) At specific times in the performance, they sing out holy praises of the names of God in repetitive melodies.
(4) They offer flowers, sweets, fruits, or sacred basil leaves to the gods, touch the gods' feet whenever possible, and worship in other ways.
(5) They travel – by bike, boat, bus, horse cart, rickshaw, car, motorcycle, or on foot – both to Ramnagar every day and following the performers as the story unfolds. Each day's events may take four to twelve hours, and the most devoted participants follow along on foot, ideally barefoot.

(6)   They act out the drama, playing the roles of crowds and wedding guests, or reciting poems of praise from the rooftops. As Hess recounts:

> Again and again, the audience and citizens of Ramnagar act out what Tulsidas narrates. They drop their work and rush to gaze at the gods as they pass through town or village. They move with processions or climb on roofs to see. They illumine triumphant fireworks from their balconies as Ram's chariot returns slowly from exile. Some climb onto the chariot to make offerings. Others decorate their homes and shops just as the citizens of Ayodhya are said to have decorated theirs.
>
> (119)

(7)   People create special roles for themselves, such as making and donating flower garlands every year.

(8)   While most people come on and off, there is a core group who attend every day, basically taking a holiday (which may be part of every day, several days in a row, or even an entire month, if they can afford it). They come dressed in special costumes, wear distinctive holy makeup (red and yellow on their foreheads), carry special staffs, and so on.

Varieties of participant experience

A deep, personal piety and devotion is at the heart of the *Ramlila*, and motivates devotees to participate annually. In the past, the local Maharaja (the high king who sponsored and supported the performance) and Rama were considered "mirror images of each other, the twin heroes of the Ramnagar Ramlila" (Schechner and Hess 1977: 74). In modern, secular, democratic India the identification of the Maharaja as upholder of the cosmos is a vestige of the past. Since Indian independence in 1947, kings no longer have any political power at all.

The staging of *Ramlila* for mass audiences is, however, not simply a devotional experience. Given the thousands of pilgrims who inundate locales where the *Ramlila* is staged, the area of its staging becomes an economically important marketplace for traders and vendors. Wherever festival performances are held, and whoever patronizes such performances, pilgrim/devotees must be fed and provided for. Local merchants are more than happy to accommodate the influx of pilgrims.

Many participants have posted videos on YouTube, or have written about their experiences at the Ramnagar *Ramlila*. Hess, who has participated in several *Ramlilas*, notes that

> the Ramlila is what you make of it. If you come with devotion, you will see God. If you come with cynicism, you will see little boys in threadbare shorts. If you come looking for snacks, you will see refreshment stands. If you come for a spectacle, you will see fireworks. If you come with hostility or fear, that will also color what you see. "According to the feeling within, each one sees the Lord's form": such a statement admits the psychological nature of the Ramlila *darshan* ["vision" of the holy]. But it is not, as it might be in a different culture, "merely psychological." It is gloriously, cosmically psychological. Every witness-participant creates the drama in her own mind, and in this drama is at once creator, actor and viewer. Thus the Ramlila teaches by experience that our realities are mind-made.
>
> (2006: 135)

THINKING THROUGH THEATRE HISTORIES

Resurrective aspects of commemorative drama

Hess's description of the experience of the *Ramlila* for participants is interesting to consider in light of other commemorative dramas like the Catholic Mass, *Rabinal Achi*, and the *Ta'ziyeh* – all of which understand themselves to be, in some important way, re-enactments rather than representations of the past.

For believers attending the Catholic Mass, the priest does not represent the historical Jesus as would an actor in a realistic drama; rather, he serves as the agent for bringing the living Christ back to material presence in the form of bread and wine, miraculously transubstantiated into the actual body and blood of Christ. In *Rabinal Achi*, the audience is understood to include the ghosts of the individuals portrayed in the action, as well as those of all the performers who ever played them in the past; these ghosts are conjured forth by the staging of the drama. And in *Ta'ziyeh*, participant-performers do not understand themselves as actors representing characters; rather, they are literally making the past present, through the embodied experience of the pain of the slain Hussein.

For readers of this text who are accustomed to more secular or psychologically realistic kinds of performances, it may be difficult to understand the powerful effects of such performances on their participants, who would have no question that this is "only a play." For them, such performances – perhaps not quite literally but not merely symbolically either – have the power to raise the dead, and to bring the living face to face with their God.

Key references

Hein, N. (1972) *The Miracle Plays of Mathurā*, New Haven: Yale University Press.

Hess, L. (2006) "An Open-Air Ramayana: Ramlila, The Audience Experience," in J. S. Hawley and V. Narayanan (eds) *The Life of Hinduism*, Berkeley: University of California Press, 115–39.

Lutgendorf, P. (1991) *The Life of a Text: Performing the Ramcaritmanas of Tulsidas*, Berkeley: University of California Press.

Schechner, R. and Hess, L. (1977) "The Ramlila of Ramnagar," *The Drama Review* 21(3): 51–82.

SUMMARY

Paul Connerton suggests that "if there is such a thing as social memory, we are likely to find it in commemorative ceremonies" (1989: 71). As we have seen in this chapter, these ceremonies often take the form of theatrical performance – and these performances often combine elements of the serious and the comic, the devotional and the carnivalesque, the historic and the contemporary. They were particularly important in the medieval period, before literacy was widespread. We have focused primarily on religious observances that lend themselves to commemorative performances: the Jewish Purim *shpil*, the Islamic *Ta'ziyeh*, and the many forms of Christian ritual and drama designed to help followers of Jesus learn their religion's most important traditions and moral lessons. Of course, there are also many secular occasions for performances that honor a people's national or cultural heritage, some of which will form the basis of our discussion of theatre in Part II.

Throughout Part I, we have considered a number of performance traditions that depended for their continuance on oral and embodied "acts of transfer," even when a written text served as a basis, a referent, or a result. In so-called "traditional" or culturally homogeneous societies, the repetition of common values through regular, repeated performances serves a key purpose in fostering ongoing cultural cohesion. In the performances discussed in this Part of our textbook, the relationship between religion, power, and performance has been strong, with stagings occurring within sacred and shared civic spaces, under the watchful eye of authorities. Even so, the enthusiastic "amateurs" (lovers of the art) charged with maintaining and preserving cultural values in performance have always also appreciated its potential for transformation and critique.

In more Westernized societies, for which life is not necessarily seen as a "structure of celebrated recurrence," the urge to commemorate may arise out of a sense of nostalgia for a lost past (Connerton 1989: 64). For such societies, commemorative performances not only provide compensation for this loss, but keep the past in its proper place, so that the unfolding future can continue to be embraced.

The invention of the printing press will capture some of the energies formerly reserved for preservation and dissemination by means of performance, and the social energies thus released are channeled into an increasingly professionalized class of theatre makers, as we shall see in Part II.

★

Part I: Works cited

Other consulted resources and additional readings for Part I are listed on the **Theatre Histories** *website.*

Audio-visual resources

Yoruba performance

Drewal, M.T. (1992) *Yoruba Ritual: Performers, Play, Agency*, Bloomington: Indiana University Press. A video-tape companion to this book includes sequences from Agemo, *Egúngún*, and Jigbo masking and dancing; divination rituals; an Osugbo elder's dance; and a Muslim Yoruba celebration.

Awo Chief Ifakunle (2009) "Egúngún: Baba O, Yeye O!" Egúngún masquerade and procession during the 10th Annual Ile Eko Sàngó/Osun Milosa Rain Festival 2009 held in Santa Cruz, Trinidad. Procession led by Awo Oluwole Ifakunle Adetutu of NYC. Online. Available <http://www.youtube.com/watch?v=yGqCDExp4IM>.

French Egúngún video: <http://www.youtube.com/watch?v=Kb1TngCu0gc>.

Michael C. Carlos Museum of Emory University (n.d.) Page of masks, costumes, and very brief video of the *Egúngún* masquerade. Online. Available <http://www.carlos.emory.edu/ODYSSEY/AFRICA/AF_rit_cerem_mask_egungun.html>.

Rabinal Achi

YouTube videos: search for (1) Relato de Rabinal Achi; (2) Rabinal, Baile de la Conquista; (3) Baile del Rabinal Achi Feria de Rabinal.

Smithsonian Folkways sample recording at <http://www.folkways.si.edu/>: "Rabinal Achi: (a) Son del Quiche Achi; (b) Son del Rabinal Achi."

Audio recordings by P. Socub et al. Visit: <http://www.folkways.si.edu>. Recorded in Guatemala.

Greek and Roman theatre

Athens: The Dawn of Democracy, featuring historian Bettany Hughes, produced by the Public Broadcasting System, U.S.A., 2008. DVD 120 minutes, available from the PBS online shop: <http://www.shoppbs.org>. Click on the listing for all video titles.

Beacham, R. and Denard, H. "The Pompey Project," a paper, with computer graphic illustrations, on the digital research and reconstruction of Rome's first permanent theatre, the Theatre of Pompey. Online. Available HTTP: <http://www.pompey.cch.kcl.ac.uk/>.

Hines, T.G. (2003/2009) *The Ancient Theatre Archive: A Virtual Reality Tour of Greek and Roman Theatre Architecture*. Includes photos of the ruins and data on the later stone theatres of the Roman Empire: <http://www.whitman.edu/theatre/theatretour/home.htm>.

An excellent video, running 4:47 minutes, called *The Greatest Theatre* (produced by Discovery TV) about the history and acoustics of the ancient theatre at Epidaurus is available on YouTube at <https://www.youtube.com/watch?v=2CVO9Vd067U>.

Japanese theatre

The best single online source for *nō, kyōgen, kabuki*, and *bunraku* – video clips (*nō* and *kyōgen*), photos (*kabuki*), historical prints, and other materials – is provided by the National Theatre of Japan at: <http://www.ntj.jac.go.jp/english>.

Video introductions to these traditional forms are also available at: <http://www2.ntj.jac.go.jp/unesco/noh/en/>.

All U.S. Japanese Consulates (and the Embassy) have cultural attaché offices which lend out for free a wide selection of videos and DVDs about Japan, including excellent videos on *nō, kabuki, bunraku*, and modern theatre. The selection at each consulate varies. Contact the one closest to your physical location several weeks before planning to show the videos; they will ship them to you or you may pick them up personally. There are consulates in New York, Chicago, Los Angeles, and San Francisco as well as the Embassy in Washington, DC.

Many videos, including the brief sampling below of titles we recommend, are for sale from Insight Media: <http://www.insight-media.com>.

- *Bunraku: Classical Japanese Puppet Art* (28 minutes) #9AF905.
- *Kyōgen* classic: *Poison Sugar* (Busu) (28 minutes) #9AF733.
- *The Tradition of Performing Arts in Japan* (30 minutes) #9AF350.
- Overview of *nō, kabuki*, and *bunraku: Theatre in Japan: Yesterday and Today* (53 minutes) #9AF1899. Dated, but includes interviews with performers including Suzuki Tadashi on modern and traditional Japanese theatre.

Japanese Theatre 1: Nō <https://www.youtube.com/watch?v=_T5RqW8TWWY>. After a short general introduction to three classical forms, *nō, kabuki*, and *bunraku*, the video offers excerpts of a *nō* play with excellent commentary. The video is about 15 minutes.

A complete resource of factual material about *nō* is available at: <http://www.the-noh.com/>.

A 3 minute sequence of a fast-paced climactic dance: <https://www.youtube.com/watch?v=lu5Vn1vQ5i4 >.

Many videos of complete plays, in Japanese, without subtitles, are available online. For example:

- *Hagoromo*: <https://www.youtube.com/watch?v=aaFjFGrqMJ0>; starts at 2 min., 29 sec.
- *Aoi no ue*: <https://www.youtube.com/watch?v=1hI8edPXNS0>
- *Adachi ga hara*: <https://www.youtube.com/watch?v=I5j87foiwY0>

Kutiyattam

The following videos are available at <www.keralatourism.org/video-clips>. See the following videos on the *kutiyattam* temple-theatre tradition; enter the site and look for the complete list of clips.

(1) *Kutiyattam*
(2) *Koothiyattam* (a variant spelling of *kutiyattam*)
(3) *Chakyarkoothu* (solo performance of the *vidusaka* or clown-like comic figure)
(4) *Nangyarkoothu* (solo performance of the Nangyars or women who perform the female roles).

Kailasodharanam (Ravana: The Lifting of Mount Kailasa). On YouTube, search *kutiyattam* and then scroll for this title. This is a famous *kutiyattam* scene in which the actor playing the ten-headed demon-king, Ravana, mimetically enacts his tremendous power by "lifting" Mount Kailasa.

Richmond, F. (1999) *Kutiyattam: Sanskrit Theater of Kerala*, Ann Arbor: University of Michigan Press (CD-ROM). Audio and video clips. (See the University of Michigan Press listing online for computer requirements.)

Carnival

To "visit" carnivals from around the world, tour the New Mexico Museum of International Folk Art's excellent exhibition at <http://www.carnavalexhibit.org/>.

European medieval theatre

The Play of Daniel, New York Pro Musica, Noah Greenberg, musical director. Music transcribed by Bishop Rembert Weakland. Charles Bressler as Daniel and Russell Oberlin as the angels. Decca Records, DL 79402 (1958).

The Play of Herod, New York Pro Musica, Noah Greenberg, musical director. Scored by Noah Greenberg and staged by Nicholas Psacarpoulos. Brayton Lewis as Herod. Decca Records, DL 710,095–6 (1964).

Mystery of Elche (Misteri d'Elx), YouTube videos: (1) "Misteri d'Elx" (Part I: descent of the angels from heaven to Mary); (2) "Coronation of the Virgin Mary" and/or "Coronación Elche" (the conclusion of Part II); (3) "Misteri o festa" (series of images from Parts I and II).

There is an online simulator showing the path and the sequence of plays in the York Corpus Christi Cycle at <http://jerz.setonhill.edu/resources/PSim/applet/>.

For links to online resources, such as medieval play texts and bibliographies; to databases of research projects such as Records of Early English Drama; and to various groups devoted to research on and production of medieval plays, see: <http://www.netserf.org/Drama/>.

Ta'ziyeh

YouTube video: see "Persian Passion Play" at <https://www.youtube.com/watch?v=8aKAPL9 Fkz4>, which includes commentary. There are others as well; search for "Ta'ziyeh."

Purim shpiln

There are numerous YouTube videos that show homegrown versions of this "Jewish carnival" tradition. Enter the search term "Purim Shpiel."

Ramlila

There are many YouTube videos covering *Ramlila* performances, in Ramnagar and elsewhere, as well as other kinds of art inspired by *Ramlila*. For a compilation, visit <https://www.youtube.com/channel/UCnfMG94dQa7URGbE6bj8W8g>, or enter the search term "Ramlila."

Books and articles

Aghaie, K.S. (2005) "The Origins of the Sunnite–Shi'ite Divide and the Emergence of the Ta'ziyeh Tradition," *TDR: The Drama Review* 49(4): 42–7.

Ajayi, O.S. (1998) *Yoruba Dance*, Trenton, NJ: Africa World Press.

Akkeren, R. van (1999) "Sacrifice at the Maize Tree: *Rab'inal Achi* in its Historical and Symbolic Context," *Ancient Mesoamerica* 10: 281–95.

Bakhtin, M.M. (1981) *The Dialogic Imagination: Four Essays*, ed. M. Holquist, trans. C. Emerson and M. Holquist, Austin, TX: University of Texas Press.

Bakhtin, M.M. (1984) *Rabelais and His World*, trans. H. Iswolsky, Bloomington, IN: Indiana University Press.

Barish, J. (1981) *The Antitheatrical Prejudice*, Berkeley: University of California Press.

Bennett, S. (1990) *Theatre Audiences: A Theory of Production and Reception*, London: Routledge.

Bharata (1961, 1967) *Natyasastra*, 2nd edn, trans. and ed. M. Ghosh, vol. I, Calcutta: Manisha Granthalaya, 1961; vol. II, Calcutta: Asiatic Society, 1967.

Case, S.E. (1985) "Classic Drag: The Greek Creation of Female Parts," *Theatre Journal*, 37: 317–27.

Connerton, P. (1989) *How Societies Remember*, Cambridge: Cambridge University Press.

Connor, W.R. (1989) "City Dionysia and Athenian Democracy," *Classica et Mediaevalia* 40: 7–32.

Derrida, J. (1974) *Of Grammatology*, Baltimore: Johns Hopkins University Press.

Dirks, N. (2001) *Castes of Mind: Colonialism and the Making of Modern India*, Princeton, NJ: Princeton University Press.

Dobson, R.B. (1997) "Craft Guilds and City: The Historical Origins of the York Mystery Plays Reassessed," in A.E. Knight (ed.) *The Stage as Mirror: Civic Theatre in Late Medieval Europe*, Cambridge: D.S. Brewer, 91–105.

Drewal, M.J. and Drewal, M.T. (1983) *Gelede: Art and Female Power among the Yoruba*, Bloomington: Indiana University Press.

Drewal, M.T. (1992) *Yoruba Ritual: Performers, Play, Agency*, Bloomington: Indiana University Press. A video-tape companion to this book includes sequences from Agemo, *Egúngún*, and Jigbo masking and dancing; divination rituals; an Osugbo elder's dance; and a Muslim Yoruba celebration.

Duckworth, G.E. (1942) *The Complete Roman Drama*, vol. I, New York: Random House.

Eisenstein, E.L. (1979) *The Printing Press as an Agent of Change*, Cambridge: Cambridge University Press.

Else, G. (1965) *The Origin and Early Form of Greek Tragedy*, New York: W.W. Norton.

Fletcher, J. (2002) *The Egyptian Book of Living and Dying*, London: Duncan Baird Publishers.

Foley, H.P. (1981) "The Concept of Women in Athenian Drama," in H.P. Foley (comp.) *Reflections on Women in Antiquity*, London: Gordon and Breach.

Gaster, T. (1950) *Thespis, Ritual, Myth and Drama in the Ancient Near East*, New York: Henry Schuman.

Gellius, A. (1927) *The Attic Nights of Aulus Gellius*, trans. J.C. Rolfe, Cambridge, MA: Harvard University Press.

Gerow, E. (1981) "*Rasa* as a Category of Literary Criticism," in R. van M. Baumer and J.R. Brandon (eds), *Sanskrit Drama in Performance*, Honolulu: University of Hawaii.

Goldhill, S. (1990) "The Great Dionysia and Civic Ideology," in J.J. Winkler and F.I. Zeitlin (eds) *Nothing to Do with Dionysus? Athenian Drama in Its Social Context*, Princeton: Princeton University Press.

Hale, T.A. (1998) *Griots and Griottes: Masters of Words and Music*, Bloomington: Indiana University Press.

Harris, M. (1994) "The Arrival of the Europeans: Folk Dramatizations of Conquest and Conversion in New Mexico," *Comparative Drama* 28: 141–65.

Harris, M. (2000) *Aztecs, Moors and Christians*, Austin: University of Texas Press.

Harrison, T. (2000) *The Emptiness of Asia*, London: Duckworth.

Havelock, E.A. (1963) *Preface to Plato*, Cambridge, MA: Belknap Press of Harvard University Press.

Homer (1967) *The Odyssey of Homer*, trans. R. Lattimore, New York: Harper and Row.

Kale, P. (1974) *The Theatric Universe*, Bombay: Popular Prakashan.

Kirshenblatt-Gimblett, B. (1980) "Contraband: Text and Analysis of a 'Purim Shpil,'" *TDR: The Drama Review*, 24(3): 5–16.

Knight, A.E. (ed.) (1997) *The Stage as Mirror: Civic Theatre in Late Medieval Europe*, Cambridge: D.S. Grewer.

Lutgendorf, P. (1991) *The Life of a Text: Performing the Ramcaritmanas of Tulsidas*, Berkeley: University of California Press.

McKendrick, M. (1989) *Theatre in Spain 1490–1500*, Cambridge: Cambridge University Press.

Murray, P. and Dorsch, T.S. (trans.) (2000) *Classical Literary Criticism*, rev. ed., Harmondsworth: Penguin Books.

Nagler, A.M. (1952) *A Source Book in Theatrical History*, New York: Dover Publications, citing *The Works of Lucian of Samosata*, trans. H.W. Fowler and F.G. Fowler, Oxford: Clarendon Press, III, 249–63.

O'Neill, P.G. (1958) *Early Noh Drama*, London: Lund Humphries.

Paulose, K.G. (ed.) (1993) *Natankusa: A Critique on Dramaturgy*, Tripunithura: Government Sanskrit College Committee [Ravivarma Samskrta Grathavali–26].

Pettys, R.A. (2005) "The Ta'ziyeh of the Martyrdom of Hussein," *TDR: The Drama Review*, 49(4): 28–41.

Plass, P. (1998) *The Game of Death in Ancient Rome: Arena Sport and Political Suicide*, Madison: University of Wisconsin Press.

Rehm, R. (2002) *The Play of Space: Spatial Transformation in Greek Tragedy*, Princeton: Princeton University Press.

Roselli, D.K. (2011) *Theater of the People: Spectators and Society in Ancient Athens*, Austin: University of Texas Press.

Scullion, S. (2002) "'Nothing to Do with Dionysus': Tragedy Misconceived as Ritual," *Classical Quarterly* 52: 102–37.

Shah, I. (2000) *The Oxford History of Ancient Egypt*, Oxford: Oxford University Press.

Sten, M. (1982) *Vida y muerte del teatro náhuatl*, Veracruz, Mexico: Universidad Veracruzana.

Taylor, D. (2004) "Scenes of Cognition: Performance and Conquest," *Theatre Journal*, 56: 353–72.

Tedlock, D. (1985; 2nd edn 1996) *Popul Vuh: The Mayan Book of the Dawn of Life*, New York: Simon and Schuster.

Tedlock, D. (2003) *Rabinal Achi: A Mayan Drama of War and Sacrifice*, Oxford: Oxford University Press.

Vatsyayan, K. (1968) *Classical Indian Dance in Literature and the Arts*, New Delhi: Sangeet Natak Akademi.

Vatsyayan, K. (1996) *Bharata: Natyasastra*, New Delhi: Sahitya Akademi.

Versényi, A. (1989) "Getting under the Aztecs' Skin: Evangelical Theatre in the New World," *New Theatre Quarterly* 19: 217–26.

Vince, R. (1989) *A Companion to the Medieval Theatre*, New York: Greenwood Press.

Ward, D. (2006) "All Heaven Breaks Loose," *Guardian*, October 5, http://www.theguardian.com/music/2006/oct/06/classicalmusicandopera.

Wheatcroft, A. (2004) *Infidels: A History of the Conflict between Christendom and Islam*, New York: Random House.

Wiles, D. (2000) *Greek Theatre Performance: An Introduction*, Cambridge: Cambridge University Press.

Winkler, J.J. (1990) "The Ephebes' Song: *Tragoidia* and *Polis*," in J.J. Winkler and F.I. Zeitlin (eds) *Nothing to Do with Dionysus? Athenian Drama in its Social Context*, Princeton: Princeton University Press.

Wise, J. (1998) *Dionysus Writes: The Invention of Theatre in Ancient Greece*, Ithaca: Cornell University Press.

PART II

Theatre and performance in early print cultures

143

PART II TIMELINE

DATE	THEATRE and PERFORMANCE	CULTURE and COMMUNICATION	POLITICS and ECONOMICS
1266–1337		Giotto, artist	
1279–1368			Yuan dynasty, China
1279–1654	*Zaju*, China		
c.1300–c.1400	*Ramlila*, India		
c.1300–c.1500		Renaissance era begins in Italy	
1313–c.1600	Passion plays, continental Europe		
1343–1400		Geoffrey Chaucer, English writer	
c.1350–1569	Cycle plays, England		
1363–1443	Zeami, actor-playwright		
1368–1644	*Kunqu*, China		Ming dynasty, China
c.1374	*Nō* Japan		
1400–1500	*Rabinal Achi*, Mesoamerica		
1428–1521			Aztec Empire, Central America
c.1440		Movable type (printing press), Europe	
1452–1519		Leonardo da Vinci, artist	
1453			Ottomans capture Constantinople
1456		First printed Bible	
1468–1834			Spanish Inquisition
1475–1564		Michelangelo, artist	
1492			Spanish encounter with the Americas
1492–1898			Spanish colonization of Western Hemisphere
c.1500	Professional theatre companies begin to appear in various European countries		
c.1500–1600	*Kathakali* dance drama, India		
c.1500–c.1650	Classical humanist drama in universities, Europe		
c.1500–c.1650		Renaissance era spreads throughout Europe	
1517–1648		Protestant Reformation	
1530s–1790s			Ottoman–Habsburg wars
1540–1623		William Byrd, composer	
1545–1648		Catholic Counter-Reformation	
c.1545–c.1800	*Commedia dell'arte*, Europe		
1548–1783	Hôtel de Bourgogne, Paris		

PART II TIMELINE

DATE	THEATRE and PERFORMANCE	CULTURE and COMMUNICATION	POLITICS and ECONOMICS
c.1550–	*Kunqu*		
c.1550–c.1765	Spanish Catholic drama		
c.1550–c.1750	Court spectacles and masques		
1558–1603			Reign of Queen Elizabeth I, England
c.1560–			Bourgeoisie become increasingly significant
1561		Julius Caesar Scaliger, *Poetics*	
1562–1635	Lope de Vega, playwright		
1564–1616	William Shakespeare, playwright		
1567	Red Lion, earliest English theatre building		
1567–1643		Claudio Monteverdi, composer (some operas)	
1570		Lodovico Castelvetro, *The Poetics of Aristotle*	
c.1572–c.1632	Alexandre Hardy, playwright		
1571			London Stock Exchange founded
1572–1637	Ben Jonson, playwright		
1576	The Theatre, England		
1577–1640		Peter Paul Rubens, artist	
1585	Teatro Olimpico, first perspective stage scenery, Italy		
1588			English defeat the Spanish Armada
c.1590–c.1720s		Baroque era in Europe	
1598–1613; 1614–1642	The Globe Theatre, England		
c.1600	Okuni's performances begin *kabuki*, Japan		
1600–1681	Pedro Calderón de la Barca, playwright		
1602–1702		First newspapers – none are daily until 1702	
1603–1625			Reign of James I, England
1603–1868			Tokugawa (Edo) period, Japan
1606–1669		Rembrandt, artist	
1606–1684	Pierre Corneille, playwright		
1607			Jamestown, VA: First permanent English settlement in North America
1618–1648			Thirty Years' War, Europe

PART II TIMELINE

DATE	THEATRE and PERFORMANCE	CULTURE and COMMUNICATION	POLITICS and ECONOMICS
1618–1672	Madeleine Béjart, actor		
c.1620	Beginnings of neoclassicism in drama		
1622–1673	Molière, playwright		
1625–1642			Reign of Charles I, England
1631–1700	John Dryden, playwright		
1632		Galileo Galilei, *Dialogue Concerning the Two Chief World Systems*	
1632–1687	Jean-Baptiste Lully, composer (many operas)		
1633–1668	Mlle. Du Parc, actor		
1635–1710	Thomas Betterton, actor		
1637	*Le Cid* controversy establishes neoclassicism in France	René Descartes, *Discourse on the Method*	
1639–1699	Jean Racine, playwright		
1640–1689	Aphra Behn, playwright		
1640–1715	William Wycherley, playwright		
1642–1649	Suppression of theatre in England		English Civil War
1643–1715			Reign of Louis XIV, France
1644–1912			Qing dynasty, China
c.1650	Introduction of chariot-and-pole scenery system		
c.1650–c.1800		Enlightenment era in Europe	
1651		Thomas Hobbes, *Leviathan*	
1653–1729	Michel Baron, actor		
1653–1724	Chikamatsu Monzaemon, playwright		
1656–1743	Ferdinando Galli Bibiena, scenic designer		
1658–1713	Elizabeth Barry, actor		
1659–1695		Henry Purcell, composer	
1660			English Restoration; reign of Charles II (to 1685)
1660–1725		Alessandro Scarlatti, composer (some operas)	
1662	Re-opening of theatres in England; women begin to play female roles		
1662–c.1800	Neoclassicism in England, Germany, Russia		
1668–1733		François Couperin, composer	
1670–1729	William Congreve, playwright		

Introduction: performance, printing, and political centralization

Tobin Nellhaus

Part II covers the years from roughly 1250 to 1770. In the Western world, this era is sometimes called the "early modern" period, encompassing the Renaissance, the Baroque, and the Enlightenment. It was an age of massive economic, political, and cultural transformations. The system of agricultural production conducted by serfs laboring under a lord's power began to break apart, and the small-scale capitalist activities conducted by merchants living in the urban areas grew to economic and political dominance. The feudal political structure of the Middle Ages, which was structured around the lords' military duties and allegiances to kings and queens, was undermined as the royalty wrested power away from the nobility and placed legal, administrative, and sometimes religious functions into its own hands, establishing absolutist monarchies. To achieve both political and economic expansion, several of the absolutist regimes initiated explorations of the rest of the world, ultimately conquering huge parts of other continents and consolidating them within imperial power. A major schism arose in Christianity, followed by proliferating religious sects. The invention of the printing press around 1440, a means of mass-producing writing by using movable type (pieces with a single letter or word), facilitated or even provoked many of these upheavals, along with a variety of others.

In Asia too, the period was notable for political centralization and cultural flourishing. Economically and politically, the historical trajectories of Japan and

A woodblock print of a Western European printing shop.

China were long comparable to Europe's. Japan was in its own late medieval period in the mid-fifteenth century, similarly pairing a political structure founded on a hierarchy of warriors with an economic system based on peasant labor. Following over a century of social turbulence, the Tokugawa period (1603–1868) ushered in strengthened military political power and substantial governmental centralization, while merchants began to thrive. Japan's cultural activity centered on entertainment and leisure aimed at the merchant class (rather than the aristocracy), and some of its best-known cultural forms (including woodblock prints, the *geisha*, and *kabuki*) were born during this era. Japan had significant contact with Western merchants and missionaries, and it continued a practice of absorbing foreign elements into its culture rather than having them forced upon it. But troubled by the possibility of military incursions and ideological contamination, Japan's leaders decided to close off the country from most foreign contact.

Centralization, coupled with expansionism, began even earlier in China, during the Yuan dynasty (1271–1368). Unlike Europe and Japan, the massive state administration, staffed by highly cultured scholar-bureaucrats, possessed greater social esteem than the military. The earliest known Chinese theatre arose during this period as a kind of variety show, combining story with music and dancing. Many of these popular shows were written by scholar-bureaucrats who had lost their positions when the Mongols invaded China. State centralization continued further under the Ming dynasty (1368–1644), which is renowned as one of the finest periods of Chinese art and literature. However, the government grew increasingly dependent on the prospering merchant class. A peasant rebellion brought the dynasty to its knees and in 1644 it was replaced by the Qing dynasty (1644–1912), but China's economic and bureaucratic structures continued on roughly the same path as before.

China and Japan, like Europe, had printing with movable type. In fact movable type was first invented in China, around 1040 (the technique was developed further in Korea), and it was used extensively for bureaucratic functions; but for most other purposes, woodblocks were more practical – even money was printed using woodblocks. In Japan, there was some experimentation with printing with movable type during the early seventeenth century, but afterwards woodblock printing again became standard. In neither case, however, did printing with movable type instigate the sort of upheavals it brought to Europe. There are two basic reasons. First, Chinese and Japanese scripts utilize a large number of characters, since they are are logographic rather than alphabetic (Japan has two syllabic scripts as well). Thus printing with movable type required tens of thousands of type pieces, entailing a considerable financial investment. Printing with woodblocks was often more sensible because one needed to carve only the characters actually used. Second, all stages of printing in Asia were performed manually: paper was pressed on to the inked type or woodblock by hand, and sometimes rubbing was necessary in order to fully copy the page. In Europe, however, pages were printed by using a machine to press the inked type on to the paper, which involved less time and less labor. As media theorist Marshall McLuhan observed, printing probably gave Europe "the first uniformly repeatable commodity, the first assembly-line, and the first mass-production" (1962: 124). Printing in Europe may well be the earliest type of industrial capitalism.

Within theatre, the era covered by Part II is marked by three major transitions. One was the shift from performances connected with special events (such as festivals and commemorative occasions) or performed by touring companies, to professional theatre companies playing on a regular basis at permanent sites. Such companies arose in Europe, Japan, and China, often in connection with urbanization, which brought a large enough potential audience that permanent residence could make touring supplementary or supplant it altogether. By the end of the seventeenth century, theatre in many parts of the world had ceased being performed in the open air and moved indoors, partly to increase exclusivity, and partly because theatre-going became an ordinary leisure activity: during the daytime people worked, took care of their business, or tended to other duties, leaving the night free for entertainment. Chapter 4 provides an overview of these developments.

The two other major changes discussed in Part II occurred only in Europe. As we saw in Chapter 3, in the Middle Ages characters tended to be stereotypes, such as allegorical figures or simplified personages from religious history. Starting in the late sixteenth century, that approach to character construction began to be replaced by the creation of characters with a personal history and interior life – the bare bones of psychological realism. (Some *kabuki* "domestic" and historical plays had similar qualities.) Likewise, the tradition of having actors play multiple roles was superseded by having each actor perform only one role. Scenery shifted away from generalized or stylized settings, and became more elaborate and took major strides toward the lifelike depiction of places. In France, a dispute on dramatic form arose, and when the royal administration intervened, the resulting decision set "the rules" for dramaturgy throughout the European continent and to some extent in England as well. As Chapter 5 explains, these changes were closely tied to the formation of print culture.

Finally, during the seventeenth century, in tandem with their centralization of power in other areas, the absolutist monarchs of France and England began to wield control over theatre, in ways that reverberated through the following century. They licensed two or three specific companies, giving them not just favor but even exclusive rights to perform in the capital. Theatre buildings were designed to give the ruler special treatment – not just a particularly favorable view of the stage, but also well-positioned to be seen by the other spectators. The fact that the chief minister/cardinal who managed the reins of power in France interceded in a quarrel over dramatic structure sharply demonstrates the extent to which absolutism shaped theatre. Although the Japanese and Chinese governments also licensed theatres and imposed restrictions, these were generally meant to prevent disruptions in society, rather than to control aesthetics and ideology. Thus even though monarchs in Europe, China, and Japan all centralized power, only in Europe did the theatre become both controlled by and an actual instrument of the state. Yet, at the same time that the French state set the rules for good theatre in Paris and beyond, within its palaces the king and his retinue blithely ignored those rules for their own flamboyant entertainments, including opera. Chapter 6 discusses these developments and more.

The notion that plays should follow certain strict rules for dramaturgy and staging may seem odd from a modern perspective, when originality is prized and "breaking the rules" is occasionally touted as essential to art itself. But even though the rules were purportedly derived from Aristotle, his authority didn't automatically secure playwrights' obedience – in fact the rules were controversial until royal power stepped in. So something more was afoot when playwrights debated the rules.

The development of the rules was connected to the new approach to creating dramatic characters, acting a single role, and illusionistic scenery. At the heart of these trends was a new concept of realism – or rather, of reality – and how one obtains knowledge. This was the age of the "scientific revolution," which emphasized direct, individual observation of nature as the source of knowledge. Such observations eventually disproved various classical theories of nature, many of which derived from Aristotle. However, when the rules were first articulated – in Lodovico Castelvetro's commentary on *The Poetics*, published in 1570 – Aristotle's authority was still almost wholly unquestioned. But how Aristotelian were the rules?

Aristotle aimed mainly to describe drama, employing some "best examples" sometimes leading to recommendations. It was Castelvetro and his followers who contorted those descriptions into requirements, often twisting Aristotle's words in the process. But there is more to the difference than that. Castelvetro's argument has three striking features. First, it declared that the purpose of literature is to delight "the crude multitude and the common people" (Castelvetro 1570: 109). Second, it insistently constricted the imagination; for example, it asserted that it's impossible to write tragedies about a fictional king, only a real one, for a tragedy about a fictional king would "sin against the manifest truth" (Castelvetro 1570: 112). Third, it justified the rules by claiming that the ignorant commoners would never accept the notion that (say) several days had passed when the performance lasted merely a couple of hours (Carlson 1993: 48–9). As we can see, the rules' justification had nothing to do with Aristotle, who hadn't said any of these things. Instead, the basic theory was that drama (or at least serious drama) must only encompass what an individual can perceive or read from concrete reality.

Thus even though the rules claimed their authority from Aristotle, in actuality their underlying logic was founded on the same transformed concepts of knowledge and truth, hinged on the notion that reality must be observable and observed, that drove the scientific revolution – a revolution that included social conflict as well as ideas. The blatantly elitist emphasis on spectators' ignorance assumed that the upper classes possessed a superior type of knowledge, even though paradoxically the rules were necessitated by the lower classes' lack of knowledge. In other words, the elite required its own imagination to be restricted to what it believed the lower classes could understand, as classical authority ostensibly required. Both the rules' elitism and their prescriptiveness reveal an upper-class determination to establish those ideas throughout the culture. The alterations in characterization, acting, and staging arose from the same basic concepts. As Chapter 5 will explain, those shifts emerged from the changes in communication practices brought by printing.

The early modern period was not the first time Europeans wrestled with the connection between theatre and truth. As discussed in the introduction to Part I, the connection lay at the heart of Plato's antitheatricality, because in his view theatre purveys falsehoods and illusions. The issue would arise again repeatedly, such as in the nineteenth century with the movement known as Naturalism (to be discussed in Chapter 10). And Europe was not the only land where the question was ever considered important. For instance, as we pointed out in Chapter 2, the *rasa-bhava* aesthetic theory of early Sanskrit theatre relied on a particular understanding of reality, and *nō* had firm foundations in Buddhist philosophy. In fact, many theatre scholars today would agree that *all* theatre and drama – no matter where, when, or how performed – invoke concepts of reality, knowledge, and truth. Part II presents the history of theatre during an era when the use of printing in European society radically changed those ideas, but the issues are ever-present under the surface of performance.

★

CHAPTER 4

Secular and early professional theatre, 1250–1650

Tamara Underiner

Contributors: Carol Fisher Sorgenfrei and
Tobin Nellhaus

From the fourteenth to the seventeenth century, theatre outside of religious festivals, churches, temples, courts, and universities grew in popularity, eventually coming to serve as a livelihood for playwrights, performers, and theatre managers. In this chapter, we focus on the kind of theatre in Europe and Asia for which entertainment was at least as important as moral instruction, and for which troupes increasingly had to compete for audiences. To attract them, theatre artists deepened and extended their craft into new genres of drama and performance, for which new performance skills were required, and new buildings designed and constructed; women's roles were showcased more (even if women themselves were often still excluded from the stage); and enterprising managers developed new business models to sustain their companies. As we shall see, everywhere a secular and professional theatre developed, so too did suspicion about its power; we will also discuss how these developments were often accompanied by legal or religious edicts against theatre in general and actors in particular, by censorship of plays, and by numerous regulations and other forms of repression.

European societies that developed professional theatre during this period tended to have populous, concentrated urban centers. Of course, the introduction of the printing press played a key role in European theatre developments: theatre scholar Julie Stone Peters observes that "after print, performance was never the same" (2000: 4). As more books became available and literacy increased, so too did material available for adaptation into stage plays. The possibilities for dramatic exploration of secular topics, in plays written mostly by men who were university-educated or self-taught and eager to draw on literary sources, began to multiply. In Europe, the forms these plays took eventually would group themselves into recognizable genres that drew on classic notions of tragedy and comedy but also expanded into tragicomedy, pastorals or romances, and farce – as well as in various combinations of each in individual dramas.

Print had a different impact in East Asia (China, Korea, and Japan). Even with movable type, printing was done by hand – a laborious and expensive process; perhaps that is why few plays were printed. To enjoy drama, Asian audiences needed to attend live performances. The lack of widely distributed play scripts may help explain why the actor remained the primary theatre artist throughout Asia, while in Europe, by the end of the seventeenth century, the playwright's prestige and power began to increase.

The period covered in this chapter overlaps with those of the chapters before and after it. This calls attention to an issue facing all writers of history: that of chronological periodization, a topic we explore in our "Thinking through theatre histories" box. The key differences among these three chapters are thematic rather than chronological. Chapter 3 focused on theatre and

THINKING THROUGH THEATRE HISTORIES

The problem of periodization

One way to tell the story of theatre's past is to trace the key moments of its transformation and innovation as an art form. In such historiographies, various national traditions gave the world different signal contributions. For example, in France the contributions of this period in theatre history included the refinement of the ballet, and the advocacy of a tightly written form of drama that obeyed strict rules of structure, tone, and topic (the neoclassical drama discussed in the next chapter). In England, the great contribution of the age was Elizabethan theatre and its exemplar, William Shakespeare (the name of the era refers to its political ruler). In Spain, it was Golden Age drama (discussed in the next chapter as well). And most historians agree that this frenzy of innovation in Europe began in the courts of Italy, where an increased interest in ancient Greek and Roman culture led to the various "renaissances" both there and throughout the European continent; the specific and longest lasting contributions from Italy were in the opera and in the *commedia dell'arte*, discussed in this chapter.

Acknowledging these key moments, which are addressed in various ways by other theatre historians, we have turned our focus in this textbook more toward how they are related to changes in communication practices – in this period most notably the use of the printing press – and also in a shift in cultural dominance from orality to literacy enabled by it. In this chapter, for example, we focus on the theme of professionalization of the theatre and how it was informed by the wider circulations of texts available for staging – in Europe. But from a more global perspective, this approach ultimately rubs up against another problem in telling the stories of theatre history: that of dividing history into discrete periods based on more local developments. When we consider the histories of theatre throughout the globe, we must not assume that key historical moments of European (or Euro-American) performance are "normal." Rather, we must acknowledge that theatre exists in various cultures in various ways, that these cultures (and their theatres) change according to various timelines, and that each culture's theatre tradition is normal in its own context. Although changes in modes of communication did occur throughout the world in basically the same order, these changes often took place at different times in different cultures. For example, China and Korea developed movable print long before Europe. However, Europeans began using the mechanical printing press long before East Asians adopted the process. In Japan, writing was introduced centuries after it appeared in other parts of the world, and was largely used by the elite and administrative classes; this may be one reason that so many Japanese plays continue to include oral narration.

performance that was tied to some special occasion in the religious or civic calendar, or was used for the purpose of religious or moral instruction. Chapter 5 will focus on the development of print culture and its effects on the aesthetics and theories of theatre in the European Renaissance. In this chapter, we are more concerned with the "business" of the theatre, the various strategies undertaken to ensure its success – including the development of permanent playing spaces and an increased presence of female characters, actors, and audience members – and various countermeasures taken to restrict, regulate, and sometimes censor it. We also consider the opportunities the theatre provided for creating new social occasions and relations, and the plethora of new performance forms that emerged. We pay particular attention to Chinese Yuan drama and later *kunqu* opera, the *commedia dell'arte* of Italy (a physical form of comedy which influenced theatre throughout Europe), and the *bunraku* puppet and *kabuki* theatres of Japan. Our case study considers the essential *kabuki* role of the *onnagata,* a male specialist in female roles, and a boxed section discusses how European plays treated basic dilemmas facing women of the time.

Developments in Chinese drama, theatre, and performance

Sometime between *c.*1545 and 1500 BCE, China, a vast nation comprising many different spoken languages, developed a system of writing based on ideograms that could be read and understood by all these varied language speakers. Nevertheless, literacy remained the prerogative of a small, highly educated group of elite males. As the Chinese state solidified, literacy became more important for courtly success. Those elite males appointed to serve the imperial government needed to pass a difficult written exam based on Confucian ideology. Confucian philosophy (created by Confucius, 551–478 BCE) is a system of ethics that values righteousness, propriety, and mutual obligations to group and family. Many Confucian scholars also wrote poetry, fiction, history, and philosophical or scientific treatises.

Musical, sung, and acrobatic performances of all kinds had always been popular in China. During the Tang dynasty (618–907 CE), Emperor Xuanzong (685–762), commonly known as Emperor Ming Huang, had even founded a royal academy called the Pear Garden to train male and female actors, dancers, and singers to entertain at court. Even today, Chinese actors and actresses, especially those involved in traditional musical genres, are sometimes called "children of the Pear Garden." Such highly skilled, courtly performers were quite different from the low-status performers who entertained non-elite audiences.

When the Mongols, a non-Chinese people, invaded and conquered China, they founded the Yuan dynasty (1279–1368). These foreign military rulers distrusted the classically educated Confucian scholars and deprived them of their court positions. Some of these displaced scholars, seeking a means of employment, joined popular theatrical troupes as playwrights. Although doing so lowered their social status, the plays they created formed China's first significant dramatic musical performance with an extended narrative.

Yuan dramas (*zaju* [zah ju]) are popular variety plays featuring song, dance, monologues, and even farce, typically consisting of four acts, and sometimes including a shorter interlude called the "wedge" (occasionally two "wedges") (Figure 4.1). Each formal act features a single lead singing role with songs composed in a single musical mode based on standard patterns, though these modes might change for each of the four acts. In contrast, the "wedges" feature a secondary singer and may have alternative musical patterns. Wedges are placed either at the beginning of the play or between the acts. The songs in the wedge develop the plot. Male and

Figure 4.1

Thirteenth-century (Song dynasty) music drama (*zaju*). The period is just before the Mongol invasion that ushered in the Yuan dynasty. From a thirteenth-century tomb sculpture.

Source: William Dolby, *A History of Chinese Drama*. NY: Barnes and Noble, 1976, Figure No. 1 facing p. 100. Original source: Shao Jingshen, *Xiqu bitan*, Peking: Zonghua Shuju Publishers, 1962, p. 234.

female actors performed roles of either gender. Performances took place as part of temple or court ritual occasions, as well as in large urban theatres or public teahouses as commercial enterprises.

In composing their dramas, Yuan playwrights drew on literary tales, dynastic histories, and popular oral narratives in which Confucian values were embedded. Yuan *zaju* contain both highly literate and highly entertaining elements, including crusading bandits fighting corrupt officials, romantic adventures, and supernatural rescues. Many deal with lawsuits and justice (including murder cases), suggesting that the ousted scholars harbored and tapped into an undercurrent of dissatisfaction with the Mongol rulers.

One of the best plays to suggest distaste for the Mongol government is *Injustice Done to Dou E* (*Dou E Yuan*, also known as *Snow in Midsummer*) by Guan Hanqing (active in the late thirteenth century). It concerns a chaste young widow who is framed for murder by a man she refused to marry. At her execution, she calls on heaven to exonerate her, and indeed, the three miracles she prays for occur. After several years, her ghost appears to her long-lost father, now a righteous judge who is investigating corruption. The actual murderer is punished, and the girl's name is posthumously cleared. The play may be implying a connection between the corrupt government in the drama and the current Mongol rulers, as well as praising the moral superiority of the Confucian-trained, Chinese judge.

After the Mongols lost control of the country, plays seldom contained the kind of hidden political protest that characterized much of Yuan drama. Nevertheless, this type of music drama continued to be popular even after the Yuan dynasty ended in 1368, influencing the style of newer genres.

The growth of kunqu

One of these new genres was *kunqu* [kwin chu] ("kun opera"), the dominant form in China from the late fourteenth to the mid-eighteenth century. *Kunqu* remains highly popular today and is even often performed outside China. *Kunqu* focuses on beautiful singing but also includes dance and dialogue. In the mid-sixteenth century, *kunqu* was performed at public venues such as temples, teahouses, and brothels, as well as privately in the homes of wealthy aristocrats. Each aristocratic family supported its own troupe of about twelve actors, often buying children and training them. These private troupes maintained a higher level of sophistication and artistic skill than those performing in public venues.

Kunqu was originally performed on a square carpet, sometimes on a raised platform, with the audience on one side or surrounding the actors. While there was little or no set, *kunqu* plays featured lanterns and off-stage sound effects, as well as both real and symbolic props. For example, a real sedan chair might carry an actor, but horseback riding was mimed by an actor holding a riding whip. Both males and females performed. The most popular plays were romantic stories, often combining military, supernatural, judicial, historical, or other subjects. Comic and serious elements generally appear together in a single play.

Probably the most famous *kunqu* is *The Peony Pavilion* (*Mudan Ting*), written in 1598 by Tang Xianzu (1550–1617). *The Peony Pavilion* focuses on a young woman named Du Liniang who literally dies of love for a young man she has only seen in a dream. After her death, the dream lover – who is actually a real person – sees her self-portrait and immediately falls in love. With the intervention of the gods, he travels to the land of the dead and succeeds in having her resurrected, but her father refuses to believe in the miracle and has the young man beaten and imprisoned. In the meantime, there are political upheavals and military invasions. Eventually, the emperor intervenes, the lovers triumph, and harmony is restored. The play has 55 scenes and lasts about 24 hours when performed in its entirety. Typically, only selected scenes are produced at any one time, although in 1999, a "complete and traditional" 24-hour version, directed by Chen Shizheng (1963–), was presented over three days outdoors at New York's Lincoln Center. Other recent, internationally prestigious productions were a 1998 "contemporary opera" version, adapted and directed by Peter Sellars (1957–) with music by Tan Dun (1957–), and a nine-hour, three-evening "Youth Version" directed and adapted by Kenneth Hsien-yung Pai (also known as Bai Xianyong, 1937–) in 2004.

Early secular performance in Europe

There has probably never been a time in European theatre history in which people did not make a living as professional entertainers, offering their singing, dancing, or storytelling talents in return for coin, plying their trades on street corners and at village fairs, in princely banquet halls and in local pubs. Some scholars consider the precursors of the modern professional actor and actress to be the street mountebanks – men who sold remedies on street corners, often accompanied by a musician, and sometimes by a female accomplice as well, who helped to demonstrate the effectiveness of the remedies for sale (Figure 4.2). They enticed buyers through storytelling and theatrical devices such as feats of magic and physical prowess, making a living year-round as much from their performing talents as from the dubious health benefits of their products. (For a lively theatrical introduction to such a character in a play from this period, read Ben Jonson's *Volpone* [1606].)

But it was not possible to make a living through the more complex arts of the theatre, involving larger casts acting out plots that were either scripted or improvised, until the middle of the sixteenth century. It was then that theatre companies began to form, often under royal or ducal **patronage**, and permanent theatre structures were built to showcase plays all year long, and not just during religious occasions. The roots go a bit deeper back into the fifteenth century, when secular themes began to be introduced into religious and moral drama.

Religious plays such as the Corpus Christi cycles remained very popular well into the sixteenth century, especially in Catholic countries like Spain, Italy, and France. But over time, theatre began to be developed for occasions outside of the Church calendar from 1517 forward, when the **Protestant Reformation** began in Europe. This religious movement, discussed in more detail in Chapter 5, ushered in new varieties of Christianity that opposed the representations of divinity in any form; some were led to oppose theatre altogether (notably the Puritans and the Quakers). In England, religious and political controversy was the order of the day; as a result, Elizabeth I (born 1533; reigned 1558–1603) issued decrees constraining

Figure 4.2

"Mountebank distributing his wares on the stage." Some scholars speculate that men who hawked remedies on street corners and, later, stages, were the forerunners to modern professional actors. Artist unknown.

Source: From *The Book of Days: A Miscellany of Popular Antiquities* (published in the 1880s, with several reprints). Hulton Archive/Getty Images.

plays with religious and political subjects, ultimately succeeding in suppressing the cycle plays during the 1560s and 1570s. (Nevertheless, Shakespeare seems to be remembering a performance of a religious play – the *Play of Herod* – in Hamlet's advice to the players.)

The morality plays, lacking representations of God and Jesus, could more readily be converted to post-Reformation purposes, and contributed to the development of secular plays, written by individual authors for professional theatres, well into the **Elizabethan era**. Because morality plays were not tied to the Bible, they could explore moral themes in an adaptable, even non-sectarian manner that can be considered more or less secular. By the early sixteenth century, there were plays on frankly secular themes such as the importance of learning, nature, and so forth. For example, John Heywood's *The Play of the Weather* (published 1533) features a series of petitioners asking the Roman god Jupiter to provide the weather best suited to their needs. While such a plot may seem rather trivial, medieval studies scholar Pamela M. King (2012) argues that the play was actually a political satire about a tense moment in the reign of Henry VIII. Other morality plays were used to expose the alleged hypocrisies of the Catholic Church. But even in strongly Catholic countries, secular theatre developed in response to both increasing urbanization and new discoveries about the classical past, made possible by the rise of print culture.

In northern France and the Netherlands, "chambers of rhetoric" offer an example of a more clearly secular genre of performance we might call "pre-professional." These were societies devoted to the literary and dramatic arts, originally associated with the Church, which were pressed into service to help organize religious festivals, the entries of royal personages into the cities, and the performance of plays on festive occasions. Located in the urban centers, the chambers drew their members from the professional, merchant, and artisan classes, who were literate in French, Dutch, and/or Flemish. They originally met to exchange work; soon they began to hold literary competitions among themselves and, eventually, among different chambers, which led in turn to dramatic contests for public performance. There were prizes across a number of categories, including best play, best farcical entertainment, best actor, best singer, etc., suggesting an increased attention to the quality of the craft associated with theatre performance and production.

In Dutch-speaking countries these competitions were called *landjuweelen* [LAWHNT-yu-vay-lehn] ("jewels of the land"); the earliest of these was recorded in 1413, among six societies performing plays about the Holy Sacrament. They were typically held in large halls or public squares, to enthusiastic crowds; today, the village of Ruigoord in the Netherlands has revived the practice in an annual five-day *landjuweel* festival. Over time, the organization and artistry of these societies became ever more professionalized, with administrative and theatrical duties being differentiated among directors, writers, promoters, costumers – and fools, who could be counted on to entertain the crowds in processions and to perform in a chamber's farces. Few full-length scripts remain, but one features a husband whose wife is seduced by the local priest; other more serious dramas took on higher themes of the day, including the newer forms of Protestant theology sweeping through Europe. Such elements caused the plays to come under the scrutiny of Church authorities, especially during the **Counter-Reformation** (the period in which Catholic authorities

Figure 4.3

Scene from the 1457 French farce, *La Farce de maître Pierre Pathelin* (*The Farce of Master Peter Pathelin*), in which the self-proclaimed lawyer Pathelin cajoles a clothier into selling him six yards of cloth on credit, with no means of paying him back. Pathelin will eventually face the clothier in court, defending a shepherd who has been stealing the clothier's sheep, but his clever defense backfires on him.

sought to suppress the Protestant reforms, between 1545 and 1648). Some chambers were more radical than others in this regard, but historian Gary Waite (2000) suggests a connection between the chambers of rhetoric, theatre, and the growth of Protestant activism in the Low Countries.

Farces were another common form of secular performance, particularly in France. One of the most popular was *La Farce de maître Pierre Pathelin* (*The Farce of Master Peter Pathelin*), from the mid-fifteenth century (Figure 4.3). Like most medieval farces, it features a small cast of characters, in this case focusing on a lawyer and a merchant. Often the farces centered on professions, relationships (among family members, neighbors, servants, and illicit lovers), and various stereotypical figures who are driven by some basic need or desire, such as money, sex, or a cure for a disease. (Of course these weren't unique to medieval French theatre; recall our

Chapter 2 discussions of ancient Roman comedy and Japanese *kyōgen*.) Medieval theatre scholar Alan E. Knight suggests that, although the world of such farce in France seemed "governed by sensual desires and unconstrained by the requirements of reason" at its heart, even the bawdiest of farces functioned within a larger perspective of Christian morality, demonstrating "what the real world would be like without the guiding rudder of reason" (1983: 59).

Also important for the development of theatre in France were the traveling troupes, who often performed indoors at the Hôtel de Bourgogne (described in more detail below), and maintained a repertory dominated by farces with a smattering of serious plays mixed in. Some of the farce-actors became famous in their own day but usually performed under stage names such as Gros-Guillaume (Fat William) (Robert Guérin, 1554–1634), Jodelet (Julien Bedeau, *c.*1590–1660), and Valleran le Conte (?–1613). This group, under Valleran's leadership, became the first known *comédiens du roi* (King's Players) in 1598.

The *commedia dell'arte* in Italy and its influence in Europe

The scripted farces had much in common with another form of traveling professional theatre that emerged in this period from Italy, the *commedia dell'arte* [kohm-MAY-dee-ah dehl-AHR-tey]. In the *commedia,* however, the action was largely improvised, by troupes of professional actors highly trained in movement. Their performances were based on a repertoire of scenarios revolving around stories of love and money. The influence of these troupes was felt throughout Europe and made its way into the scripted drama of the other theatre capitals; even today, there are *commedia* troupes whose practice and rigorous training regimes are based in techniques developed some four centuries ago.

There is no exact English translation of the term *commedia dell'arte,* a form which most scholars trace back to the middle of the sixteenth century. (The term first appears in print some two centuries later, in Carlo Goldoni's 1750 play *Il Comico.*) The term *arte*, in Italian as well as in older English, can refer to a professional level of craft or technique, so it is usually left untranslated. *Commedia dell'arte* is distinguished by a number of features:

- Improvised playing based on a repertory of standardized plots, mostly having to do with matters of love and intrigue.
- A combination of stock characters, masked and unmasked according to type.

- The use of *lazzi* [LAH-dzee], or highly physical stage routines and comic bits that were often associated with the particular prowess of individual performers.
- Mixed-gender casts and companies.
- Professional companies with increasingly formal operations, providing the principal livelihood for their members, who performed year-round throughout Italy and Europe.

Origin theories

Although the form would have great influence on virtually every other European theatre tradition (and indeed, is still performed by specialized troupes in Europe and the Americas), no one can say with complete certainty where *commedia dell'arte* came from – or if indeed it had a single, linear genealogy. More likely a number of factors contributed to its development: the masked, improvised comedy of the Roman Atellan farces (discussed in Chapter 2) kept alive by traveling mimes; the jugglers, acrobats, singers, dancers, charlatans, and mountebanks of public life in medieval Europe; the circulation of plots and characters of ancient Roman comedies that were often also the subject of the learned Italian drama (*commedia erudita* [kohm-MAY-dee-ah eh-roo-DEE-tah]); and the farces of the earlier sixteenth century (which flourished in Italy as elsewhere throughout Europe from 1500 to 1550).

If its deeper origins are disputed, many scholars pinpoint the date of February 25, 1545, as the official "birthday" of the *commedia*. That was the date, in Padua, Italy, when director/manager Ser Maphio signed a letter of incorporation establishing his troupe of performers as the first known commercial theatre company, organized under a sharing system. Until then, there was, literally, no business like "show business" as we know it today. February 25 is still celebrated internationally as "*Commedia dell'arte* Day."

Conventionalized plots, individualized lazzi

Because the *commedia* was an improvised form, it relied on standard scenarios that were adapted in virtually limitless ways to accommodate topical themes and local realities, as well as to capitalize on the talents of individual performers. Once professional actresses took the stage – the first documented one, Vincenza Armani, appeared in 1566, but it is likely she had predecessors – these scenarios turned from conflicts between masters and servants to those of romantic intrigue.

A typical *commedia* scenario, like the Roman comedies that may have inspired it, featured two lovers who were prevented from being together, usually by a parental figure, sometimes inadvertently by the *innamorato* (m.; f. *-a*; pl. *-i*) [in-nah-moh-RAH-toh, -tah, -tee], or young male lead. To overcome this obstacle, comical servants (called *zanni* [ZAHN-nee]) are enlisted, or sometimes the *innamorata* in disguise enacts a plot of her own. This general plot outline was often complicated by subplots that could themselves be "dizzyingly complex, involving disguises, misunderstandings, plots within plots, impersonations, and magical deceptions" (Henke 2003: 14).

In addition to the masked servant characters and the young lovers (who played their parts unmasked), the other masked characters of the *commedia* included their parents and a variety of conspirators or unsuitable lovers who provided the central obstacles to their happiness. Isabella Andreini (1562–1604), of the Gelosi troupe, was the most famous of the *innamorati*; over time, young female leads came to be called, simply, "Isabellas." Of the *zanni*, the most famous was Arlecchino, introduced by Tristano Martinelli (*c*.1555–1630), whose characteristic motley costume would later be codified as "Harlequin" in seventeenth-century France. The elder characters were called *vecchi* [VEHK-kee] – usually men but sometimes their ambitious wives as well. They included Pantalone, a wealthy merchant with a healthy appetite for food and conversation, who was quick with advice, jealous of his fortune, and often after an inappropriately younger woman; Dottore, a learned, lustful philosopher given to propounding feats of virtuosic, if fatuous, punning, alliteration, and other forms of wordplay; Capitano, the soldier type whose arrogance outstripped his achievements (but who could, at times, be seriously in love); Pulcinella, the crafty beak-nosed and hump-backed clown who became "Punch" in the British "Punch and Judy" shows; and courtesans and procuresses who served as temptations and distractions for the *innamorati*. (See Figure 4.4.) A variety of supernumeraries drawn from other genres like the pastoral, tragicomedy, and even tragedy rounded out the cast, which could represent a dozen characters or more.

The various plots and subplots of the *commedia* can be considered scaffolds upon which to display the physical and verbal virtuosity of the most popular players, which they cultivated as

Figure 4.4
Late sixteenth-century engraving showing three stock characters from the *commedia dell'arte* – from left, Arlecchino, Zanni the cuckold, and Pantalone – serenading an unseen lady in her house on the right.
Source: National Museum, Stockholm.

their particular repertoire of *lazzi*. These bits often bore little relationship to the main action (indeed, they frequently interrupted it, but audiences loved them). One actor, for example, was known for his ability to do a somersault while carrying a full glass of wine, without a spill. Another could do whole scenes while standing on his hands. Acrobatics of all sorts, pantomimes, juggling feats, and elaborate word play were the order of the day in the *commedia*.

Verbal improvisation in relation to literacy

Within the basic situations provided by the plot scenarios, all the actors knew very well the relationships between their characters and the others in the troupe, and could draw upon repertoires of praise and compliments for some of them, insults, threats, and curses for others, depending upon the nature of those relations. It is important to remember that, although improvised, these speeches were themselves very formulaic and rhetorically coded, based on materials carefully recorded in the actors' commonplace books. These books were compendiums of important passages from longer works that literate people compiled and consulted for personal edification and as inspiration for writing essays and speeches in this period. Thus, although the *commedia* was and is known as an art of improvisation rather than textual interpretation, it was not because the actors couldn't themselves read. They were, in fact, highly literate, often more so than their audiences, and they drew on a variety of written and printed sources, everything from the *commedia erudita* to the latest jokes circulating in the city-state. One **actor-manager** of a *commedia* troupe, Flaminio Scala (1547–1624), published his troupe's scenarios – a risky venture for the time, since that meant any other troupe could appropriate them. His collection of 50 scenarios, published in 1611, tells us much about the state of the *commedia* in his time.

So, although the *commedia* seems to be a type of performance based in physicality and orality, in fact its relationship to literacy and textuality was strong; it was a form that combined low comedy with literary aspirations. Over the course of the seventeenth century, "a shortage of sufficiently educated *innamorati* and a large number of very talented servants and their prominence in performances tipped the scales in favor of the servants," and by the eighteenth century *commedia* had grown somewhat stale (Erenstein 1989: 133). As a result, the Italian playwright Carlo Goldoni tried to "elevate" the *commedia* by bringing the lovers back to center stage, reducing the number of comic masked players to four – and scripting the action in full. (We discuss Goldoni further in Chapter 7.)

Making a living through commedia

Commedia historian Robert Henke (2003) identifies a continuum of business models through which *commedia* performers made their livings. Most enjoyed some form of patronage by a ducal sponsor. Some individual performers may originally have performed regularly in the same designated time and spot, but without a formal contract with their patron; many others were part of *commedia* troupes established as fraternal societies under the seal of a duke. (Such seals functioned as passports and protected performers from imprisonment as vagabonds when they toured in Europe.) Troupes performed at courts and, often, in customs houses, where their audiences came from the growing merchant classes. Eventually, the most successful companies began to operate more independently and entrepreneurially; they were often headed by a *capocomico* responsible for both the business and artistic aspects of the companies, who came to epitomize the troupe itself. The famous Gelosi and Fideli troupes are examples; the former was headed by Giovan Battista Andreini (father-in-law to Isabella); after Isabella's death, her son and his wife left the Gelosi company to form Fideli.

So popular was the *commedia* throughout Europe that playwrights of scripted drama – notably Shakespeare and Molière – incorporated many *commedia* elements into their dramas, including character types, masked performances, and plot devices.

Urban growth and the new business of theatre in Europe

As social and political life came increasingly to be organized in the capitals of London, Paris, and Madrid, and in the Italian city-states (the largest being Florence, Milan, and Venice), so too did theatrical activity come to be centered there. The growing popularity of theatre led to several new developments, among them the professionalization of the various specializations associated with the theatre (actor, wardrobe manager, prompter, etc.); the increasing commercialization of theatre companies; and the development of permanent structures to house their work. These developments in turn had an effect on the social status and occasion of theatre, particularly as related to the participation of women on and off stage.

Legal records of English theatre companies show that as early as 1574, playing was referred to as an "arte and facultye," with "arte" signifying a level of technique necessary for belonging to a craft or profession. In 1581 this activity was called a "trade," and in the following year a "profession." It became increasingly possible to make something of a living in the theatre, albeit a difficult one. Audiences could demand a certain standard of craft and technique from performers, but this did not always translate into social respect, a carryover from the days when actors' legal status was "vagabond."

Although the professions of playwright, actor, and actor-manager emerged during this period in Europe, theatres were not a strictly entrepreneurial affair. In England, they depended reputationally, if not financially, upon sponsorship by the crown or the nobility or both, as actors without patrons were subject to severe penalties. In Italy, ducal patronage was important to the *commedia* troupes; in France and Spain, religious charities first ran the theatres as a way to raise money for their good works, and later the various cities took over the public theatre spaces. Almost everywhere, theatre companies needed official licenses to perform. In England, only two companies were granted direct royal **patents**; all others had to be licensed by the "Master of the Revels," an officer of the crown charged with authorizing the production of all plays. In Spain, his counterpart was called, simply, the "Protector." Three charitable organizations dominated public theatre in Spain until 1615, when entrepreneurs began to be granted leases for four years at a time; this practice lasted until 1638, when cities began to take over the licensing of theatres to companies. Typically only the largest cities had more than one officially licensed troupe. Meanwhile, France did not permit permanent theatre companies until well into the seventeenth century; after that, the companies at the Hôtel de Bourgogne and the Théâtre du Marais competed against each other.

Not only were authorities rather stingy in granting licenses, they also exerted some control over what could and couldn't be staged, and where. In England, for example, theatrical performances were banned inside the city limits in 1576, effectively removing public theatre to entertainment districts in the various "liberties," areas outside London proper which belonged to the city, but over which it exercised no real control. In Spain and England, there are numerous records of plays being banned or suspended on the very day of performance: in England, the reasons had often to do with suspicion of political sedition, while in Spain, the **Inquisition**, an office established to suppress religious heresy and subversion, cast its shadow over the Protector's shoulder, sniffing for more secular matters of scandal, indecency, and profanity as well. In France, a number of semi-professional troupes comprising student members performed primarily for the elite, but seized every opportunity to play for the common people as well. They generally had relatively easy access to performance spaces in town, but city authorities were often suspicious of the French and Italian professional troupes and sometimes forbade performance, or allowed it only under tight restrictions (not always obeyed).

England and Spain provide the best-documented examples illustrating how the business of theatre was conducted in this period in Europe. Two companies dominated London theatre at the end of the sixteenth and the beginning of the seventeenth century. Theatrical entrepreneur Philip Henslowe (*c*.1555–1616) backed the Admiral's Men, initially headed by the actor Edward Alleyn (1566–1626) and based at the Rose Theatre; the Burbage family, which owned The Theatre and later the Globe, ran the Lord Chamberlain's Men. (Theatre companies were named after the noblemen who sponsored them.)

Both companies were founded in 1594, but along very different business models. While the Admiral's Men relied from the outset on Henslowe and Alleyn to underwrite the company's activities, the Lord Chamberlain's Men was run according to the sharing system, by which actor-managers, leading actors, and financiers shared in the profits of a given run or theatrical season. Sharing systems were a common way of organizing theatre companies throughout Europe. Playwrights typically did not share in the profits but were paid on a per-play basis. In recognition of the importance of the English companies, King James I (b. 1566, ruled 1603–1625) put the Admiral's Men under the patronage of his son (renaming them Prince Henry's Men) and elevated the Chamberlain's Men to royal patronage (which changed them to the King's Men). Both companies, together with several minor ones, competed for plays and mounted them in outdoor and indoor playhouses as well as in "great rooms" at schools and courts. Rivaling the two companies in popularity during the first decade of the 1600s was the Children of the Queen's Revels (earlier known as the Blackfriars Boys), which produced a full range of dramatic genres performed entirely by boys whose voices had yet to change.

While the Admiral's Men produced Marlowe's popular tragedies, the Chamberlain's Men counted playwright William Shakespeare among its shareholders and controlled the rights to most of the successful plays co-authored by Francis Beaumont and John Fletcher. Co-authorship was a common practice in the 1590–1625 period; Fletcher probably collaborated with Shakespeare on the last three plays attributed to the "Bard of Avon" – Henry VIII (1613), The Two Noble Kinsmen (1613 or 1614), and the now lost Cardenio. Playwrights often wrote for several companies, crafting plays with specific actors in mind. Ben Jonson, for example, provided plays to all three of the major performing groups.

Most companies paid top dramatists up front for their work and divided the profits from any subsequent publication among their shareholders. The average payment per play until about 1603 was roughly 6 pounds sterling, a figure that had increased to 10 or 12 pounds by 1613 – or, by today's standards, approximately £2,600 to £3,200 (roughly U.S. $4,000–5,200).

The public appetite for dramatic variety was healthy, despite the competing attractions of other entertainment options such as sporting events (e.g., bear-baiting and cockfighting in England, bullfighting in Spain). The English companies maintained a repertory of up to 70 plays to satisfy this demand, with a different play being performed every day of their six-day week, repeated only once every month or so. Because plays weren't published until after they'd been performance-tested, and in many cases only when no longer being performed, actors were given only their own parts to memorize (on long strips of paper called "scrolls"), and must have worked hard between shows to refresh their memories for the next day's performance. In Spain, plays rarely ran for more than a half-dozen performances, and yet the theatres were never closed, except during Lent. As a result, Spanish playwrights like Lope de Vega (1562–1635) had to be prolific in order to keep up with the demand, since (as throughout Europe) they generally did not share in the profits unless they also acted. Lope de Vega, however, earned about twenty times what a lead actor would have earned for one day's work, and was the only Spanish writer to make his living exclusively in theatre; even so, Lope de Vega depended on private patronage to supplement his income and wrote until his death. In contrast, French playwrights received meager pay until the 1630s. Throughout Europe, when plays were eventually published, this often occurred without the playwrights' consent or compensation, and there were no copyright laws to protect their interests.

As companies grew more experienced in their day-to-day operations, professionalization may have led to certain modest economies such as the reuse of props, costumes, and scripts, which made it financially feasible to produce a season of plays, or to tour. While for playwrights and actors of principal roles it was possible to make a decent living in the theatre, that living was dependent on many factors that were outside anyone's control. For example, theatres were often closed due to weather, plague, and periods of royal mourning. In addition, in both Spain and England, anti-theatre sentiment occasionally forced the theatres to shut down.

The establishment of permanent theatre spaces

Noble, royal, and religious patronage may have given acting companies protection from being labeled vagabonds, but these sponsors only gave money to the troupes when they played before the monarch or at a private event such as a wedding. The rest of the time the companies were dependent on the box office. Thus some companies sought the benefits of having a permanent space in which to produce a full season.

Even though the ancient world had permanent theatres, in early Renaissance Europe and some parts of Asia, theatrical performance often took place in spaces originally created for other purposes (such as public squares, courtyards, tennis courts, or temple porches). When permanent structures devoted specifically to theatre were built, certain attributes of the original spaces remained. Theatre spaces were either converted from existing structures, or purpose-built to house professional touring companies.

While permanent theatre spaces are recorded as having been built in Italy as early as 1531, it is likely they were associated with private court more than public performances. An exception was the Teatro Olimpico (built 1580–1585 in Vicenza). Its interior was modeled on ancient Roman theatre and meant to stage classical Greek and Roman revivals. The Teatro Olimpico opened in 1585 with a production of *Oedipus Rex* to an audience of academics and nobility. Such productions, however, were mostly occasional, amateur undertakings intended for pedagogical, honorific, celebratory, and scholarly purposes. Renaissance academic theatre might employ professional actors, especially in Italy, but it never challenged the professionals' popularity with the public. Nonetheless, the literary resources of the academic theatre offered substantial opportunities to the early professional troupes. As we have already seen, two major theatrical traditions – *commedia dell'arte* and dramatic, text-based theatre – flowed from the intersection of amateur and professional theatre in the mid-sixteenth century. Teatro Olimpico remains a material manifestation of the age's fascination with the classical past; although it was abandoned soon after it was built, it is still standing after almost half a millennium, and since the mid-1990s has been active again in housing theatre productions.

The earliest of the permanent, public theatres in Europe was built in Paris in 1548, inside the Hôtel de Bourgogne. Its design followed the form of the tennis courts in which visiting troupes to the French capital were accustomed to perform, with seating arranged in galleries and boxes along three interior walls, for more than 1,000 spectators. As in Spain and England, multiple stage settings were conveyed more through language than set or scenery design.

 Permanent theatre structures soon appeared in all the major European capitals. In England and in Spain, early theatres – like the Red Lion (built 1567 in London) and the first Spanish *corral* [kohr-RAHL] (Seville 1574) – were built to imitate the spaces that had earlier been used for theatrical performances. Whereas in France the model was the indoor tennis courts, in England and Spain they were outdoor innyards or courtyards enclosed by the exterior walls of adjacent buildings (see Figure 4.5). Risers along three sides of the Red Lion allowed audience members to follow the stage action at one end of the space. In Spain, wealthy patrons used to rent the upper floors and balconies of the buildings surrounding the courtyards, making for a mixture of public and private seating; when designated theatres were built in the latter quarter of the sixteenth century, the custom of dividing the seating by class or occupation and gender carried over into the purpose-built structures, still called *corrales*. Between 1574 and 1628, eighteen such theatres were built in Spain and four in its American colonies; in England, between 1575 and 1623, thirteen new outdoor theatres were built.

One of the most important London theatres was called simply The Theatre, built in 1576. Unlike the Red Lion and its French and Spanish counterparts, which featured a stage at one end of a rectangular audience space, The Theatre's house was polygonal in shape. It included three galleries where some members of the audience stood or sat, an unroofed yard where others called the "groundlings" stood, a stage extending into the yard, and a "tiring house" (backstage area) – the first example of the distinctive architecture of the Elizabethan public

Figure 4.5

Artist's impression of the interior of the seventeenth-century Spanish playhouse, *El Corral del Principe* (c.1697).

Source: Drawing by Carlos Dorremochea in John Allen, *The Reconstruction of a Spanish Golden Age Playhouse* (1983). © University Press of Florida.

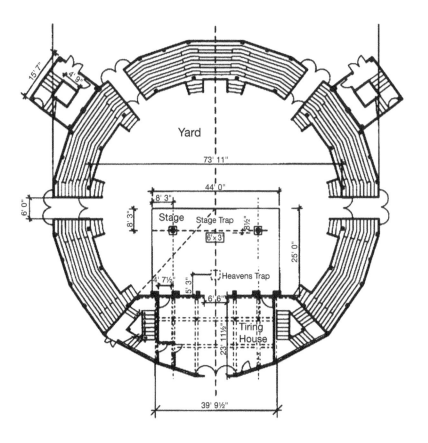

Figure 4.6

A plan of the new Shakespeare's Globe Theatre, completed in 1997, which sought to replicate the Globe of Shakespeare's day (with additional exits for safety reasons). See Chapter 14 for more information on the new Globe.

Source: Design by Pentagram Design Ltd. Reprinted in *A Companion to Shakespeare*, David Scott Kastan, ed. (1999, Oxford: Wiley-Blackwell), 370.

theatre. The design harked back to the Roman amphitheatre, which gave it some degree of classical cachet. But it also maintained some characteristics of the medieval *locus* and *platea* arrangement, with the audience surrounding a generalized acting area, and location suggested through words ("this is the forest of Arden") or context (a conference with the king might be in the great hall inside a castle), with an occasional set piece (like a throne). The Theatre eventually became home to several important theatre companies. In 1598, it was dismantled, rebuilt near the River Thames, and renamed the Globe. The Globe was home to the Chamberlain's Men (later called the King's Men), the company most associated with Shakespeare's plays. (See Figure 4.6 for a recent reconstruction.)

In England, The Theatre and the Globe were structures open to the air and known as "public" theatres. There were other theatres housed indoors which, although also open to the public, became known as "private" theatres, perhaps in order to skirt requirements that plays be licensed and their companies officially sponsored by the Crown. These theatres were most active in London during the 1570s and 1580s. After 1608 Richard Burbage, lead actor and manager of the King's Men company, took over Blackfriars Theatre, which soon became the company's winter home and the most important English theatre of its day. Although no illustrations or plans survive, contemporary accounts suggest the space was a large indoor hall, with a stage and tiring house at one end, benches for those seated in the pit, galleries on three sides above the pit, and boxes near the stage. Blackfriars, unlike the Globe, was an elite venue, intended for the most refined work of the best playwrights – but other more popular plays were staged there, and it wasn't unusual for spectators to sit or stand on the stage, perhaps showing themselves off. Also unlike the Globe, it was used in the evening, probably with the entire room illuminated by candles.

The growing popularity of theatre made it start to seem like a good business proposition, and this in turn made indoor theatres increasingly valuable: they allowed companies to perform, and therefore support themselves year-round. In an age increasingly dependent on selling theatre tickets, a dedicated theatre space allowed the companies to control the audience's entrance, thus assuring they paid the price of admission.

The social occasion of theatre

Early modern audiences in London could attend an outdoor, public playhouse most days of the year, except during the Lenten season and periods of intense heat (and possible plague) in the summer months. For Londoners, a trip to the Globe took them across the River Thames beyond the reach of a city government dominated by Puritans and into an area filled with taverns, brothels, bear-baiting arenas, and other playhouses. The theatres south of the Thames, like others north of the city, drew audiences of all classes. Apprentices, journeymen, soldiers, and others paid a penny (roughly the cost of a loaf of bread) for admittance into the yard of the playhouse, where they could stand to watch the show on the thrust stage, roughly four to six feet high (Figure 4.7). For an additional penny, merchants and their families, courtiers of both genders, foreign travelers, and others might purchase a bench seat in one of the galleries. If the Lord Chamberlain himself came to enjoy the troupe he sponsored, he and his retinue might sit in a lord's room behind and above the stage platform, an excellent location to see and be seen. Although the Globe could hold perhaps 2,500 spectators, the average crowd for most performances was probably around 600.

Daytime performances and the configuration of the theatre houses – rectangular as in Spain and France, or the polygonal "wooden O" of the English Globe – meant that audience members had as good a view of each other as they did of the stage action. In France, this view was probably better than that of the stage; perhaps that is one reason people tended to refer to "hearing" rather than "seeing" a play.

Audiences and seating in Paris during the early 1600s were roughly similar to London's. Theatregoers came from all social classes, but since ticket prices were linked to viewing privileges, seating became segregated by class and other social factors. Most spectators were male, but upper-class women began attending plays in the 1630s, when decorum in drama was becoming more important; however, women from the lower classes probably attended in small numbers long before then. The *parterre* [PAH(r)-tehr] (pit) was crowded mostly with spectators from the lower classes, who were often scorned by the elite for being noisy and quarrelsome. Nevertheless people from the upper classes could be found in the *parterre* as well,

Figure 4.7

A 1596 drawing of the interior of the Swan Theatre, London, probably generally similar to the nearby Globe Theatre. Note the figures in the gallery above the two stage doors; this area may have been used as a lord's room and as an acting space. The only picture of the interior of an Elizabethan public theatre, it is a copy by Arend von Buchell of a lost original drawing by his Dutch friend, Johannes DeWitt, who had visited London.

Source: E.K. Chambers, *The Elizabethan Stage* (1923). Buchell's drawing is in the Bibliotheek der Rijkuniversiteit, Utrecht.

especially writers wishing to be closer to the stage. The boxes were as usual more expensive and reserved for the elite. When *Le Cid* was performed in 1637, it was so popular that well-to-do audience members were allowed to sit on the stage itself, beginning a tradition that the theatres were unable to end for over a century. However, most playwrights of the early 1600s felt it was important to appeal to all tastes. That too began to change during the 1630s.

In Spain, the *corrales* similarly divided the audience by social class and therefore viewing privilege. Male and female audience members were strictly segregated, and women were not allowed to stand with men in the *patio*, or ground-floor area. Instead, they occupied an upper gallery called the *cazuela*, or "stewpot," where men were not allowed; women were, however, allowed to sit with male relatives in the *aposentos*, or boxes. Other galleries called *tertulias* were reserved for members of the clergy and intelligentsia.

Audiences in the public theatres were vocal and rowdy; theatre as a place of genteel sociability took some time to develop, as will be discussed further in Chapter 7. People ate fruit, nuts, pastries, and possibly fish and meat pies, and drank beer or ale. There were no restrooms. In England, "orange wenches" – young women who eked out a living selling oranges (and, often, themselves) – roamed among the spectators. Inter-act and post-show performances often featured highly physical song-and-dance routines.

Because both men and women attended, the theatre of this time afforded an opportunity for the public mingling of sexes outside the sanctioned religious holiday seasons, a matter of no small anxiety to the moral authorities. Throughout Europe, both official and self-appointed watchdogs inveighed against what they saw as the licentiousness and immorality of the stage. Actors themselves – whether male as in England or male and female everywhere else in Europe – were not held in general respect. Further, limited licensing opportunities made for a kind of hierarchical social ladder for actors everywhere: those associated with permanently licensed companies were at the top of this social schema; actors with touring companies lower down; and individual street performers who worked in the streets the lowest of all. But even actors associated with licensed companies were not granted full social esteem. They were banned from London's city limits in 1575; in Spain they were deemed "public sinners" and denied Christian sacraments.

Increasing importance of women in theatre

When a French theatre troupe featuring both male and female players toured to Blackfriars in 1629, they caused such a stir – being "hissed, hooted and pippin-pelted from the stage" – that the Master of the Revels reimbursed some of their license fees (Prynne, quoted in Adams 1904: 13). Although women frequently appeared in lavish royal court masques throughout Europe, their appearance on public stages was a more controversial matter. The reasons are complicated, and had much to do with a widely held belief that a woman's place was in the home, away from the gaze of men who had no legal claims on her – unless she was a prostitute. Nevertheless, despite widespread misperceptions of their virtue, women began to appear on stage throughout the continent: the first documented professional actress appeared in Italy, with the *commedia* troupes in the 1560s; in Spain in 1587 (although by 1599 actresses had to be the wives, widows, or daughters of company members); and in France in 1592. In England, boys and young men continued to play all female roles until 1662, when Charles II issued a royal warrant that only women should play women's roles (although there is some evidence that women started appearing on stage in 1660, and men still played older women for a time).

According to theatre historian Eric A. Nicholson, writing about the European context overall,

> Regardless of the country, period, and prevailing religious outlook, female roles distinguish both the drama and society of these centuries. Insofar as the postmedieval and preindustrial world categorized women almost exclusively in terms of their relationship to men, both normative roles – the virginal maid, chaste wife, and celibate widow – and transgressive ones – adulteress, prostitute, courtesan, and procuress or "bawd" – gave prominence to sexuality and the female body, precisely those entities that most demanded – and most threatened – patriarchal domination.
>
> (1993: 296)

The limited roles laid out by Nicholson nevertheless provided an opportunity for play-wrights (predominantly men) to expose, explore, exploit, and critique unequal social relations between the genders. Nicholson goes on to trace a number of European plays that treat the contradictory position of women in society in complex ways – at times rehearsing their limited social roles, at others reversing and transforming them (see "Women's roles in European drama" below).

In addition to having men playing the parts of women, Elizabethan England seemed particularly fascinated by the prospects of further cross-dressing within the action of the plays. In more than 80 plays, young male actors, playing the parts of women, cross-dress *back* into male clothing in order to pursue their female characters' various goals. Examples include Shakespeare's *The Merchant of Venice*, *As You Like It*, and *Twelfth Night*, where cross-dressing proves central to the dramatic action. These performances offered audiences the chance to witness the complicated representation of ambiguous sexual tension – between a male character and a female character dressed as and played by a male. A case study in Chapter 5 will discuss the issues raised by cross-dressing further.

Off-stage, however, sumptuary laws restricted clothing choices to their "proper" gender or social class, although some women chose to cross-dress in order to travel alone or pursue a trade. In Spain, prohibitions against cross-dressing extended to the stage as well. For parts requiring a young woman to dress as a man, actresses were required to wear male clothing above the waist, and a skirt below.

In Japan, as we will see below, female performers were at first central to *kabuki*, but they were eventually outlawed from performing in public. Similarly, cross-dressing (both across genders and across social classes) was banned. Even today, female roles in *kabuki* are played by males. The *onnagata* (female-role specialist) – one of the best-known features of *kabuki* – is discussed in more detail in our case study.

WOMEN'S ROLES IN EUROPEAN DRAMA

The dilemmas of social life for women in Renaissance society provided rich territory for dramatic exploration. Here we consider three common dilemmas facing women of the time, as they appeared in stage drama (adapted from Nicholson 1993).

The dilemma of the "fallen" woman

Some plays compelled audiences to respect and admire certain prostitutes, bawds, and courtesans whom society told them they *should* only despise.

Fernando de Rojas' *The Tragi-comedy of Calisto and Melibea* (1502) (also known by the name of the principal character, "La Celestina") was translated from the original Spanish into every major European language between 1515 and 1530. Based on the scheming madam stock character of ancient Roman comedy, in de Rojas' treatment her character is deepened to combine both "demonic corruption and versatile self-determination" (Nicholson 1993: 298). *La Lena* (1528) by Ludovico Ariosto takes the Celestina character even further, to offer both a critique of contemporary double standards in Italy, and a defense of learning and education for women. *The Alchemist* (1610) by Ben Jonson features a prostitute, Dol Common, bent on transforming her "common" status into royalty. Although Jonson does not expect the audience to admire this character, he does ask us to consider the theatricality of her profession and, by extension, Nicholson suggests, that of gender itself.

Some plays feature fully developed prostitute figures who are punished for their immorality, but whose characters are so well drawn that their choices seem justifiable, even when the playwright seems also to be judging against them. Examples include Thomas Heywood's *How a Man May Choose a Good Wife from a Bad* (1602) and John Marston's *The Dutch Courtesan* (1605). *La Cortigiana* (1533) by Pietro Aretino, *The White Devil* (1612) by John Webster, and *Women Beware Women* by Thomas Middleton (1621) all feature as secondary characters independent women of "ill fame" whose talents nevertheless are undeniable in aiding the more virtuous principal characters. Writing slightly after the period discussed in this chapter, Aphra Behn (1640–1689) was England's first professional female writer. Her *The Rover* (1677) features a lead character, Angelica, who self-transforms from "an artful courtesan to a constant lover" (Nicholson 1993: 301). However, the object of her affection (Willmore) is not so constant, choosing a chaste heiress over her. Four years later, Behn wrote a sequel, in which another courtesan, La Nuche, this time wins Willmore from the more conventional Ariadne.

continued

The dilemma of the "honorable" woman

Many plays featured maidens, wives, and widows who nevertheless find ways to transgress the limitations of these roles, often by resorting to disguise and transvestism.

At least two plays feature the attempts of an honorable widow to pursue her own love interests against the wishes of her jealous brothers. John Webster's *The Duchess of Malfi* (1614) does so at the cost of her own life, while Pedro Calderón de la Barca's *La dama duende* (*The Phantom Lady*, 1629) fares better.

Many more plays feature younger women who must disguise themselves as boys or men in order "to slip past a constrictive role model while appearing to obey it" (Nicholson 1993: 303). Examples include Dovizi da Bibbiena's *La Calandria* (1513), which later would influence William Wycherley's *The Plain Dealer* (1676); both plays feature heroines who cross-dress to escape the confines of maidenhood, pursuing love objects who seem hardly worth the effort. Calderón's Rosaura in *Life is a Dream* is another example, pursuing her honor after it has been ruined by a young man making false promises of marriage. The difficulties of her pursuit in turn become the key upon which the salvation of the principal "dreamer," Segismundo, depends. Shakespeare also used this device frequently, for the same purposes: examples include Portia in *Merchant of Venice* (1605) and Julia in *Two Gentlemen of Verona* (c.1590). Rosalind in *As You Like It* (1600) and Viola in *Twelfth Night* (1601) both cross-dress for defensive purposes, to travel alone in safety.

The dilemma of the unhappy marriage

In theory, patriarchy demands that husbands maintain control over their wives' bodies, since women themselves couldn't be trusted to do so. In practice, that rarely works, as these plays show.

Numerous plays explore what befalls a virtuous wife who, through no fault of her own, is accused of infidelity, often with tragic results. Perhaps the most famous is Desdemona in Shakespeare's *Othello* (1604). Other examples with happier, if ultimately not more satisfying endings, include Celia in *Volpone* (1605) by Ben Jonson, Hermione in Shakespeare's *The Winter's Tale* (1610), Imogen in Shakespeare's *Cymbeline* (1611), and Margery Pinchwife in William Wycherley's *The Country Wife* (1675).

The figure of the cuckold – the betrayed husband whose inability to control his wife was publicly symbolized by the horns growing out of his forehead – was a common figure in early modern drama. Whereas this figure appeared most frequently in satires, the specter of its particular kind of humiliation haunted more serious dramas, in which women paid dearly for choosing love outside their marriages. Examples of plays more seriously treating the double standard of sexual morality included Beaumont and Fletcher's *The Maid's Tragedy* (1611), Lope de Vega's *Castigo sin venganza* (*Punishment without Revenge*, 1631), and Calderón's *El Médico de su honra* (*The Doctor of his Honor*, 1635–1637).

Popular Japanese theatre in a time of cultural seclusion

Civil wars wracked Japanese society from 1467 until 1590. During this chaotic period, only *nō* could be considered professional, although not all *nō* troupes were connected to the court and many toured the country. Various other types of theatrical performance occurred as part of Shinto or Buddhist rituals, or at local festivals, but these were generally performed by the villagers themselves, as part of civic life. There were also troupes of itinerant entertainers – actors, dancers, storytellers, musicians, magicians, acrobats, and puppeteers – who roamed the land, but they were considered outcasts (officially classified as "non-humans") and were forbidden to reside in settled villages or towns.

Around 1590, one clan of samurai (professional warriors) gained military power and the long period of civil wars began to subside. In 1603, the Japanese emperor conferred the title of shogun (supreme military ruler) on Tokugawa Ieyasu, the leader of this victorious clan. This act established the Tokugawa shogunate, which enforced the peace until 1868. The period from 1603–1868 is therefore called the Tokugawa era. It is also sometimes referred to as the Edo era, because the seat of military government was moved away from Kyoto, where the emperor and many aristocrats resided, to a distant, unsophisticated town called Edo. Today, the city formerly named Edo is called Tokyo, the capital of Japan and a thriving metropolis.

The Tokugawa rulers, guided by neo-Confucianism, insisted on having an unchanging society divided according to hereditary class. As we saw with the sumptuary laws of Europe, each of the four social classes was permitted garments and adornments appropriate to them and forbidden to others. For example, only the topmost samurai could wear the double swords. Next in the hierarchy were the farmers, followed by artisans and craftspeople. At the bottom were the merchants, thought to contribute nothing to society, because they merely traded items grown or made by others. The three lower classes wore only cotton garments of blue and brown, with little or no pattern. In addition to these four classes, there were those who were outside and above all classes: the imperial family, the nobility, and Buddhist and Shinto priests. They could wear colored silks, embroidered and elaborately patterned. Similarly, there were others who were outside and below the class system, including hereditary outcasts, sorcerers, prostitutes, beggars, and actors. They were all forbidden to wear the trappings of those "inside society."

However, this supposedly inflexible hierarchy was turned upside-down in reality during the long period of peace of the Tokugawa era. Suddenly, money could be spent on leisure instead of war. The *daimyō* (feudal lords of the samurai class) actually became poor because they were forced to maintain two households: to prevent rebellions, they were required to have residences both in their home province and in the new capital of Edo. They, their families, and their retainers made the long journey back and forth several times a year, a very expensive and time-consuming practice.

Unemployed samurai (*rōnin*) sometimes became bandits or lived secretly among the merchants. In contrast, the despised merchants became rich. They secretly defied the law by wearing extravagant silks and bold colors beneath their simple cotton kimono. As many *kabuki* [kah-boo-kee] and *bunraku* [boon-rah-koo] plots demonstrate, the merchants embraced the virtues and values once appropriate to the samurai and feudal lords but which they no longer possessed.

The shogunate also feared foreign influences that might undermine their authority. European traders and Christian missionaries threatened to introduce new types of weapons, popular foreign goods (such as eyeglasses and clocks), and new ideas. To stem the flow of foreign influence, beginning in the early 1600s, the government enacted a series of laws forbidding contact with foreigners. By 1651, Japan had almost totally isolated itself from the outside world. This isolation (with the exception of a few Dutch traders who were limited to a settlement on the tiny island of Dejima, near Nagasaki in southwest Japan) continued for over 200 years, ending officially in 1868. It was during this period that *kabuki* developed and flourished.

The birth of kabuki

Around 1600, a female dancer named Okuni (d. 1610) and her mixed-gender troupe appeared in Kyoto, performing Buddhist dances in a dry river bed to raise funds for a temple. In addition to religious dances, they performed short skits – early plays that were vulgar, irreverent, and often lewd. Their performances became hugely popular, partly because the performers (both male and female) were also prostitutes. Okuni and her troupe ignored the laws against cross-dressing, with men playing women and women playing men. They defied rules against proper clothing, wearing forbidden foreign costumes and even Christian crosses. Woodblock prints from around 1600 depict Okuni dressed outrageously in male Portuguese garb, with a Christian cross around her neck and a samurai's double swords at her waist (Figure 4.8).

Like these outcast actors, wild young people also flouted the laws. They joined unruly gangs and sported outrageous costumes, shocking hairdos, large and extravagantly decorated swords, and four-foot long tobacco pipes. Like Okuni, they resisted legal dress codes and behaved in anti-social ways. All these counter-cultural people were termed *kabuki-mono*. The word *kabuki* derives from an old verb *kabuku*: "to tilt or slant dangerously to one side." In its origins, *kabuki* was shocking, off-balance, and inappropriate. As long as people performed and dressed outrageously, whether on stage or off, order could not be maintained. Today, however, *kabuki* is considered a "classical" art form, and the word itself is now written differently, using Chinese characters meaning "song-dance-skill."

Soon after Okuni's appearance, copycat *kabuki* troupes appeared, many composed of all women. At least as early as 1612, male prostitutes also formed *kabuki* troupes and competed with the women. By the 1620s, *kabuki* managers had established theatres linked to brothels in all of the major cities of Japan, an entrepreneurial strategy for boosting revenues from both endeavors. The government began to fear that the strict division of classes was breaking down as more and more people attended these outdoor performances and sought out the sexual

Figure 4.8

Detail from a painting showing Okuni, the Japanese female temple dancer/prostitute who originated the performance style eventually called *kabuki*, probably in the late sixteenth century. Note the Christian cross and double samurai swords. Other images show her in male Portuguese garb.

Source: © Tokugawa Reimeikai Foundation.

services of the actors. However, it was not prostitution itself that concerned the neo-Confucians who ran the government. Nor did they suggest that stage acting, cross-dressing, or imitation were inherently evil, as many Europeans opposed to theatre did. Rather, they feared class mingling and social rebellion.

The popular success of *kabuki* annoyed the samurai rulers, but also confirmed what they took to be their innate superiority to the rowdy culture of the cities. Although the regime could have stamped out *kabuki* when it first emerged, the shogun and his warriors chose to allow it to continue within limits, fearing that a total ban would lead to worse troubles. In a revealing document, one samurai official stated: "Courtesans, dancers, catamites, streetwalkers, and the like always come to the cities and prospering places of the country. Although the conduct of many is corrupted by them, if they are rigorously suppressed, serious crimes will occur daily" (Shively 2002: 41). This point of view, which underlay the Tokugawa shogunate's policy toward *kabuki* theatre for 250 years, rested on class disdain for merchants and city culture. The combination of traders and workers in wealthy towns, the samurai believed, would always breed criminality. Better for such potential criminals to be distracted by theatrical entertainment, they reasoned, than for these people to turn to "serious crimes."

At the same time, the samurai rulers worried that *kabuki*, if completely unregulated, would corrupt the soldiers and young men of their own class. Although samurai and aristocrats, including high-born women, were forbidden to attend, many flagrantly broke the law. Sometimes they came in disguise; in some periods, they were forced to sit behind screens where they were "invisible." Complaints against the *kabuki* performers in the 1600–1670 period centered on drunken fights and tales of young samurai losing their fortunes and ruining their reputations by chasing after a *kabuki* prostitute. In 1629, the government banned females from performing in *kabuki*. Despite the ban, similar laws were reissued in the 1630s and 1640s, indicating that it took several years for the shogunate to eliminate this popular form of *kabuki*. After 1652, young males were also prohibited from performing *kabuki*, again in an effort to prevent class mingling due to love affairs and prostitution. Henceforth only older males who shaved the forelocks of their hair were allowed to perform in the plays. It was assumed that the male actors would be less sexually appealing (to both males and females in the audience) without their forelocks. Eventually, the actors were required to use scalp coverings and wigs in an ongoing contest of regulation and innovation between the Tokugawa shogunate and the *kabuki* managers. The issue of hair is just one example of the kinds of restrictions and rules that the government tried to enforce.

Although this conflict between the samurai and the theatre managers continued until the end of the Tokugawa regime in 1868, *kabuki* troupes gradually won enough grudging legitimacy from the regime to allow them to elaborate an art form out of this sexually enticing entertainment. After 1652, audiences in Kyoto, Osaka, and Edo began to find more enjoyment in the extended performances by the mature male actors, who now played all the roles on the *kabuki* stage. *Onnagata* [ohn-nah-gah-tah], men who specialized in female roles, gained particular popularity among the merchant spectators (see our case study).

As star actors in the major cities sought better material, *kabuki* playwrights emerged to provide it. Many of the most famous *kabuki* plays began as puppet plays and were later adapted for actors. Many playwrights worked in teams, but a few, such as Chikamatsu Monzaemon (1653–1724), gained recognition for their singular excellence. Chikamatsu preferred writing for puppets rather than actors who might mangle his words.

Blurring performance genres: Puppets and actors

Japanese puppet theatre (also called *ningyō joruri,* which means doll theatre) has a long history, including connections to religious ritual. However, the most representative style, generally known as *bunraku,* is purely secular. Unlike much puppet theatre in the West, *bunraku* is not meant as children's entertainment. The histories of *kabuki* and *bunraku* are closely allied, and the two genres have many performance and script elements in common. Both reached their high points and solidified their most typical characteristics during the mid-seventeenth century, as entertainment for the newly wealthy merchant class. Since both were highly popular, each tried to out-do the other. For example, the puppets became more and more like humans, while the actors tended to mimic puppet movements.

Lifelike puppets can do things that living actors on stage cannot do as believably, such as cutting off heads, gouging out eyes, being eaten by a tiger, or walking to the stars on a rainbow. These effects charmed and thrilled audiences. Consequently, *kabuki* actors sometimes sought to rival the puppets by creating performance skills that were amazing because they seemed almost magical in showing off the actor's versatility. For example, to imitate puppet movement, the actor would perform *ningyō-buri,* a kind of dance in which black-robed stagehands (*kōken* [koh-kehn] or *kurogo*) acted as puppeteers, literally manipulating the actor as though he were a puppet.

Kabuki soon developed quick on-stage costume changes (such as costumes that seem to turn inside out or that fly off to reveal another costume beneath) that instantly transformed the character right in front of the audience's eyes. Doubles cleverly substituted for star actors so that the star could appear to play multiple roles in a single performance, even apparently acting with himself in the same scene. Special effects developed, such as an actor flying over the audience or appearing magically from a lantern, or a stage set depicting a rooftop that

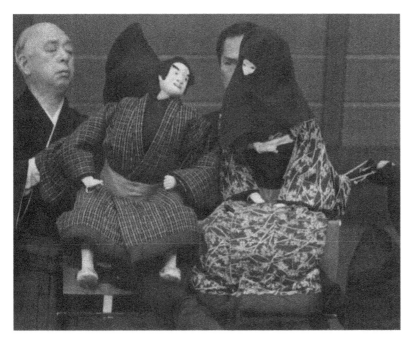

Figure 4.9

Japanese *bunraku* puppets. The head manipulator, without mask, controls the doll's head and right arm. The secondary manipulator, with face covered, controls the left arm. If needed, a third controls the feet.

Source: *Bunraku, The National Theatre of Japan* (Tokyo: Japan Arts Council, 1994), 7.

opened to reveal an interior. In response, *bunraku* puppets became more and more lifelike and believable, seeming to breathe, to cry, and to perform delicate, complex dances or activities such as sewing.

Today, *bunraku* puppets are three to four feet tall and highly realistic, with many movable parts – not only arms, legs, and bodies but individual fingers, eyes, and mouths. The puppet for a major character is manipulated by three operators who must work in perfect harmony. The main puppeteer manipulates the head and right arm; the secondary puppeteer manipulates the left arm; and the third puppeteer works the feet and legs. A puppeteer usually spends ten years working the feet and legs, then ten more years working the left arm. Only after 20 years is a puppeteer ready to manipulate the head and right arm (Figure 4.9). Minor puppets may only have a single puppeteer.

The puppeteers do not speak. A single narrator (the *joruri* or *gidayū*) voices the dialogue for all the characters, as well as all spoken and sung narration. The *joruri* is seated on a stage extension to the audience's right. He is accompanied by a *shamisen* (a three-stringed instrument). The musician sits next to the narrator, and both are in full view of the audience. In *kabuki* plays derived from *bunraku* scripts, a *joruri* narrator sometimes chants during certain parts of the play.

The *bunraku* stage is designed so that only the upper portions of the puppeteers' bodies are visible. The front screen covering their lower bodies sometimes serves as a floor for the puppets. The puppeteers often wear black hoods, unless the main puppeteer is especially famous. Even when the audience sees the puppeteer's face, he is considered to be "invisible" – the audience's attention is focused on the puppets and/or the *joruri* narrator. Generally, all manipulators are male; today, a few females perform as *joruri*, and both males and females play the *shamisen*.

Kabuki *and* bunraku *in performance*

 Early *kabuki* was performed outdoors in dry riverbeds. Later, it began to use a variation of the *nō* stage. After 1724, when indoor theatres became popular, the roof and pillars typical of the *nō* stage were eliminated, and the *hashigakari* (bridgeway) was moved to extend through the audience. The *kabuki* bridgeway, called the *hanamichi* [hah-nah-mee-chee], is used for major entrances and exits. Unlike its counterpart in *nō*, the *hanamichi* brings the actor into (and above) the audience, creating a highly theatrical and immediate effect. Some plays used two *hanamichi*, one on either side of the auditorium. Originally, the audience sat on the floor on *tatami* mats (woven from rice straw), either in two levels of galleries or in ground floor boxes (Figure 4.10). Soon, a front curtain of green, orange, and black stripes was added to hide scene shifts (although there had never been a front curtain in *nō*); today, at the play's opening, this curtain is pulled back to the sound of wooden clappers beating faster and faster. Still later, complex mechanical devices for spectacular effects appeared, including revolving sets, devices to fly actors, and traps in the stage floor and the *hanamichi*. Such machines were common in *kabuki* nearly a century before European theatre attempted to use them. Today, *kabuki* theatres can generally seat several thousand spectators.

There are several types of *kabuki* and *bunraku* plays: historical, domestic (about contemporary urban life), and dance plays lacking dialogue. The stories are usually derived from existing sources (legends, epics, novels, or *nō* and *kyōgen* plays), real or imagined history, or current events. Some of the most beautiful and poetic *bunraku* and *kabuki* dramas are Chikamatsu's double-suicide plays. These and other serious plays often focus on an impossible, ultimately tragic

Figure 4.10

A performance of the popular *kabuki* play *Shibaraku* (*Wait a Moment!*), in Tokyo's Nakamura Theatre in the mid-nineteenth century. On the rampway (*hanamichi*) leading to the stage at left, an actor in the robes of the Danjūrō line of actors portrays a commoner who enters to challenge the imminent execution on stage of innocent people by a powerful lord, uttering his famous fierce cry, "*Shibaraku*". The woodcut triptych by Utagawa Kunisada shows the traditional auditorium (note the seating arrangements) and stage, but with an additional *hanamichi* at right.

Source: Courtesy Gary Jay and Josephine S. Williams.

conflict between the demands of duty or loyalty to family or lord (*giri*) and personal, human feelings (*ninjō*). All plays are highly choreographed, often including dance or battle sequences and even acrobatics. The two main performance styles in *kabuki* are **aragoto** [ah-rah-goh-toh], or rough-house (popular in Edo), and **wagoto** [wah-goh-toh], or soft-style (popular in Osaka and Kyoto). The *aragoto* style features striking, non-realistic makeup, hugely exaggerated costumes, extreme vocal patterns, and powerful gestures that are based on images of the god Fudō, the patron deity of a Buddhist-Shinto sect of mountain ascetics, whose rituals include terrifying demon-quelling dances. At climactic moments, an *aragoto* actor may toss his head, raise his leg and stamp his foot, pose with open, outreached hand, grunt, and freeze his face in a cross-eyed grimace. Such "punctuation" in acting is called *mie* [mee-eh] (Figure 4.11). In these moments, the expressive body of the outcast actor incorporates both the Buddhist-Shinto deity and the samurai warrior, suggesting to the merchant audience that they, themselves, partake of both identities.

Music and sound effects are important elements. The vocalization of *kabuki* is unique. The language is old-fashioned and sometimes poetic, and the style of enunciation is highly elaborated and often artificial. *Onnagata*, the female-role specialists, speak in a rolling falsetto voice; villains often use a guttural, rough voice.

Figure 4.11

Danjūrō XII as Sukeroku, the commoner who is an aristocrat of the past in disguise, in the *kabuki* play *Sukeroku: Flower of Edo*. Here, Danjūrō is seen striking a typical *mie* pose.

Source: *Kabukiza* program, Tokyo, January 1995, p. 20.

Makeup and costumes are stylized, colorful, and sometimes fantastic, especially in the *aragoto* style. For example, the hero of the play *Shibaraku* (*Wait a Moment!*) wears a kimono with gigantic, stiff square sleeves. A high-ranking courtesan may wear many layers of colorful kimono, a wide, heavily brocaded and complex *obi* (broad sash) tied around her waist, an elaborate wig decorated with hairpins, jewels, and flowers, and tall, platform-style, lacquered sandals. In *aragoto* plays, everything is bigger than life. In *wagoto* plays, both costumes and makeup are closer to reality. (Chikamatsu's double-suicide plays are examples of the *wagoto* style.)

All actors in professional *kabuki* today are male. Most come from *kabuki* families and begin training and performing as children. Those who are not born into an acting family usually begin training at a special school at the National Theatre. If they exhibit sufficient promise, they will apprentice with an established actor and eventually will be adopted into the family. Actors are awarded new personal names as they progress in skill. Unlike most Japanese people, actors in *kabuki* and *bunraku* are known by these professional, personal names rather than their family name.

Many now-typical elements of *kabuki* came about as the result of attempts to stifle the art. For example, the *onnagata* developed because both women and boys were banned from the stage. Visual elements became more stunning to attract audiences. Scripts became more interesting and acting became more polished when the main reason for attending theatre was no longer finding an attractive prostitute. Keeping actors segregated from the rest of society meant that the children of actors would be forced to learn their craft at an early age. Ironically, official disapproval of *kabuki* actually contributed to its becoming more professional.

CASE STUDY: Realer than real? Imaging "woman" in *kabuki*

One of the most immediately recognizable features of *kabuki* is the *onnagata* (male actor specializing in female roles). In contemporary Japan, female actors perform in many types of theatre (even occasionally in *nō*), but *kabuki* remains an all-male genre. This case study will consider some of the historical and aesthetic arguments for and against female actors in *kabuki*.

Gender, visuality, and the onnagata

After 1868, when Western ideas such as feminism began to take hold, social and some theatre reformers wanted to replace the *onnagata* with actresses, while traditionalists were opposed. In 1914, a male Japanese theatre scholar wrote:

in Japan, males are superior to females in every way – from the shape of the face, eyes, nose, and mouth to body type and size. Females can be beautiful too, but they usually have some flaw: for example, a lovely face but a short body. Since these flaws do not allow an actress to complement a male lead, it is only obvious that males should continue to perform women onstage. (Quoted in Robertson 1998: 57)

On the opposite side, early Japanese feminists and their supporters felt that, as one put it, "Although the *onnagata* has the weight of history and tradition on his side, all I see is a middle-aged male wearing face powder trying to play the part of a young woman. It is in bad taste and wholly unconvincing. He doesn't even try to hide his Adam's apple!" (quoted in Robertson 1998: 58).

A great *onnagata* does not need to appear "beautiful" or even typically "feminine." Rather, he must be a skillful performer, creating a pleasing staged image of "woman." Some *kabuki* connoisseurs actually prefer *onnagata* who are physically unattractive, such as the extraordinarily talented Nakamura Shikan VII (1928–2011), because they feel that an actor's beauty distracts from his skill. One of the twentieth century's most beloved *onnagata*, Onoe Baikō VII (1915–1995) (Figure 4.12) was rather stout, not especially good looking, and behaved in a typically masculine way off stage. Others, such as the internationally renowned Bandō Tamasaburō V (1950–) (Figure 4.13), are quite beautiful on stage and off. Tamasaburō not only excels in *kabuki,* but portrays realistic, believable women in stage and film roles, such as Blanche DuBois in Tennessee Williams' *A Streetcar Named Desire* or Lady Macbeth.

Although all professional *onnagata* today are male, until the early twentieth century, some actresses – including

Figure 4.12

The well-known Japanese male actor Onoe Baikō in the *onnagata* (female) role in *Fuji Musume* (*The Wisteria Maiden*). He was considered one of the finest *onnagata* of the twentieth century.

Source: Program for Grand Kabuki Theatre, Los Angeles, September 1993.

female *onnagata* – did perform on stage, both in private mansions and in public theatres. Previously, scholars often dismissed them as amateurs, but feminist scholars have shown that this designation is inaccurate (Edelson 2009). One of the most famous female *onnagata* was Ichikawa Kumehachi I (*c*.1846–1913), who played both male and female roles in *kabuki*. In 1898, critics wrote that "on stage, nobody can tell that she is not a man. When she plays [female] roles. . ., she immediately transforms herself into a blooming beauty or a graceful, virtuous princess" (quoted in Isaka 2006: 111). Being indistinguishable from a man meant that her body performed in the "authentic" *kabuki* tradition, using the aesthetic ideals developed by male *onnagata*. Regardless of the biological sex of the performer, "the roles have been polished to the point where the mere pointing of a finger, swaying of a kimono sleeve, or exclamation of

Figure 4.13a and b

The *onnagata* actor Tamasaburō (left) as the courtesan Agemaki in the *kabuki* play *Sukeroku,* and as Lady Macbeth (right).

Source:
4.13a: Photo by Jack Vartoogian/Getty Images.

surprise has eliminated everything inessential to the communication of what is conventionally recognized as a womanly presence" (Leiter 2012: 118).

Historicizing onnagata aesthetics

However, some contemporary theatre scholars (both Japanese and non-Japanese) maintain that only a male *onnagata* can portray the "essence of femininity" and can seem more feminine than a "real" woman. Their comments often echo the 1939 Japanese scholar who maintained, "*onnagata* imparted a flavor that actresses could not hope to produce" (Robertson 1998: 58). In analyzing such comments, theatre historian James R. Brandon reminds us that:

> We should not forget the historical reason the *onnagata* became part of kabuki theatre . . . The *onnagata* was a political expedient and did not need justification on artistic grounds until the ban on actresses was repealed in the late nineteenth century. Then theatre scholars, performers, and culture managers were required to come up with reasons why the *onnagata* should continue. The result was the creation of unsubstantiated myths: only a

male actor can suggest the essence of a woman, only a man possesses the physical strength to wear a heavy wig and multiple kimono, and so on. These are not really artistic explanations; they are rationalizations for why the social institution of male-playing-female should continue undisturbed in the modern era when it was no longer needed or required.

(Brandon 2012: 122)

Although the *onnagata's* origin was political and not aesthetic, actors and other *kabuki* theatre artists did develop concepts of artistic beauty to justify their art. The great *onnagata* Yoshizawa Ayame I (1673–1729), maintained that the successful *onnagata* must behave like a woman both on stage and in real life, even in private and even if he is married with children. In daily life, he must practice a female's outward behavior and inner thoughts by eating, walking, and gesturing just like a perfect woman – but never copying any specific person. If someone mentions his wife and children, he should really blush in modesty. Even at the public bath, it is said that Ayame would use the women's section. No one objected, and no one was fooled.

According to Ayame, the *onnagata* is not "a male acting in a role in which he becomes a 'woman,'" but rather "a male who is 'a woman' acting a role" (quoted in Robertson 1998: 54). In other words, before playing a particular female role on stage, the male actor must transform his gender to "woman" (that is, to what society imagines "woman" to be, regardless of biological sex and regardless of specific circumstances). Because an actual woman would not be able to escape her own biological body, only a male, who was not hindered by biology, could hope to represent the ideal.

Ayame's ideas are related to certain Buddhist concepts of transformation (*henshin*), which state that females are inherently impure and can only reach enlightenment if their physical bodies are eliminated and they are reborn (after several reincarnations) as male bodies (Robertson 1998: 54). Women were in this view incapable of representing or becoming themselves; they were imperfect copies of an imagined ideal.

Official doctrine of the time concurred. For example, male educators and philosophers encouraged women to follow the Confucian precepts expressed in books such as *Greater Learning for Females* (*Onna daigaku*, 1672) which stated that possessing female sex organs and genitalia actually impeded the ability to be rational and to behave in an appropriately "chaste" fashion. As Jennifer Robertson points out:

Given the Kabuki theater's mixed reception by the Tokugawa Shogunate, and the low, outsider status of actors during the Edo period, basing the construction and performance of femininity on *Greater Learning for Females* quite likely added a modicum of legitimacy to the urban theatre. . . . An *onnagata*, then, according to Ayame, was . . . the embodiment of patriarchally inscribed, state-regulated "female" gender. The actor was unequivocally Woman, a model for females offstage to emulate and a sex object for males offstage to proposition.

(1998: 54–5)

Even today, contemporary Japanese women (who seldom wear kimono except for formal occasions) sometimes view the *onnagata* as "a model to emulate" – but only in terms of how to properly wear (and move gracefully in) kimono. However, even this emulation is not precisely photographic. In Ayame's time, real women performed a half-kneel with the right knee raised while men raised the left knee. Ayame noted that on stage, "it depended upon the look of the thing, and one should not raise the knee that is on the side of the audience. If one only went by consistency, it would not be *kabuki*"(Dunn and Torigoe 1969: 52).

Chikamatsu agreed. He maintained that "art is something that lies in the slender margin between the real and the unreal." When confronted with the argument that absolute realism was desirable, he asked, "would it prove entertaining if an actor, on the grounds that real [samurai] retainers do not make up their faces, were to appear on the stage and perform with his beard growing wild and his head shaven?" (Keene 1960: 389). He felt too much realism was repulsive; audiences would prefer the tension created by the actor's doubleness, an awareness of opposites in the same body (actor/character, male/female). In other words, aesthetic pleasure is more important than realism.

Some contemporary scholars suggest that the appeal of the *onnagata* results not from transformation into an ideal, but from the apparent incorporation of both genders within a single body by manipulating (usually visual) cultural gender codes, such as costuming, wigs, makeup, and movement patterns. The audience then "reads" the outer, clothed body as "woman" while simultaneously experiencing an acute awareness of the male/boy "body beneath" (Stallybrass 1992; Mezur 2001).

Although this perspective is both valid and helpful, one cannot help but ask why it doesn't work in reverse. In other words, why aren't male *kabuki* characters performed by biological females? To answer this question, we need to remember that we are speaking of a genre that originated in a time when the power to dictate artistic values – like other aspects of power – was controlled by males. Although *kabuki* has changed much over time, most fans think of it as a relatively unchanging historical treasure. Such fans agree that shifting the gender balance would destroy artistic pleasure. However, as we will see in Chapter 9, those who desire to view female bodies performing male roles have a brilliant outlet in the all-female Takarazuka Revue, established in 1914.

Conclusion

Like all vital arts, *kabuki* continues to grow and transform in response to changing times. Over the centuries, it has shifted from a disreputable come-on for prostitution to a classical, national form. Similarly, gender roles and identification differ widely depending on the specific time period and locale. Debates about *kabuki*'s *onnagata* can open diverse avenues to discuss gender and the position of women in various cultures throughout history.

Key references

Audio-visual resources

Tamasaburō talks about being an *onnagata*, in the interview and excerpts of several performances, in this 10 minute clip from the 1995 documentary *The Written Face*: <https://search.yahoo.com/search?fr=mcafee&type=B210US0D20110423&p=tamasaburo+interview>.

A 10 minute excerpt of Tamasaburō's performance of the *kabuki* dance *Sagi-Musume* (*The Heron Maiden*), with excellent commentary and example of *hikinuki*, quick on-stage costume change for character transformation: <https://www.youtube.com/watch?v=4q1MPwD7zCI>.

A 10 minute excerpt from a classic *kabuki* dance by Tamasaburō, *Fuji Musume* (*The Wisteria Maiden*): <https://www.youtube.com/watch?v=sPgtX-ljHi4>.

Books and articles

Brandon, J.R. (2008) *Kabuki's Forgotten War 1931–1945*, Honolulu: University of Hawaii Press.

Brandon, J.R. (2012) "Reflections on the *Onnagata*," *Asian Theatre Journal* 29(1): 122–5.

Dunn, C. and B. Torigoe (ed. and trans.) (1969) *The Actors' Analects*, New York: Columbia University Press.

Edelson, L. (2009) *Danjūrō's Girls: Women on the Kabuki Stage*, New York: Palgrave Macmillan.

Episale, P. (2012) "Gender, Tradition, and Culture in Translation: Reading the *Onnagata* in English," *Asian Theatre Journal* 29(1): 89–111.

Isaka, M. (2006) "Women *Onnagata* in the Porous Labyrinth of Femininity: On Ichikawa Kumehachi I," *U.S.-Japan Women's Journal* 30–31: 105–31.

Keene, D. (1960) *Anthology of Japanese Literature: From the Earliest Era to the Mid-Nineteenth Century*, New York: Grove Press.

Leiter, S.L. (2002) "From Gay to *Gei*: The *Onnagata* and the Creation of *Kabuki's* Female Characters," in Samuel L. Leiter (ed.) *A Kabuki Reader: History and Performance*, Armonk, NY: M. E. Sharpe, 211–29.

Leiter, S.L. (2012) "Is the *Onnagata* Necessary?" *Asian Theatre Journal* 29(1): 112–21.

Mezur, K. (2001) "Undressing the *Onnagata*: Kabuki's Female Role Specialists and the Art of Costuming," in S. Scholz-Ciona and S.L. Leiter (eds) *Japanese Theatre and the International Stage*, Leiden: Brill, 193–212.

Robertson, J. (1998) *Takarazuka: Sexual Politics and Popular Culture in Modern Japan*, Berkeley and Los Angeles: University of California Press.

Sorgenfrei, C.F. (2007) "Countering 'Theoretical Imperialism': Some Possibilities from Japan," *Theatre Research International* 32(3): 312–24.

Stallybrass, P. (1992) "Transvestism and the 'Body Beneath,'" in S. Zimmerman (ed.) *Erotic Politics: Desire on the Renaissance Stage*, London: Routledge, 64–83.

SUMMARY

The four centuries between 1250 and 1650 saw a tremendous expansion in the kinds and quality of theatre in Asia and Europe, as theatre grew ever more professionalized, secular, and independent of religious and civic cycles of performance. The "business" of theatre was born in this period, and was made possible in part because of the increasing urbanization of both Europe and Asia. Theatre first occupied outdoor public spaces that had often been designed for other purposes. Eventually purpose-built structures came to replace them, and then moved indoors to accompany a year-round calendar of performances.

An increasing demand for theatre resulted in a proliferation of theatre forms and thematic explorations. Increasing literacy meant actors were up to the demands of longer scripted drama, and some playwrights wrote their plays with specific actors in mind. Even in the *commedia*, an improvised form, the scenarios were often based on literary sources.

While in all periods in Europe, theatre had included female characters, it was not until this period that actual women began to take the stage and, in some cases, serve as managers of theatre companies. Educated women may have written plays for their own amusement and reading, but as we saw in the case of Hildegard of Bingen in Chapter 3, very little of their work was seen in public. Meanwhile, in Japan, actual women were forced off the stage and replaced by male *onnagata*.

Everywhere, theatre was held to be a powerful force in shaping public mores and values, and therefore was subject to careful scrutiny. The presence of actual women on stage, coupled with a growing sense of theatre as a rather rowdy social occasion, made theatre a matter of some concern to the authorities in both Europe and Japan. As a result, there were numerous attempts by authorities to control the theatre through regulations, censorship, and licensing restrictions. As in England, the Japanese shogunate segregated the theatre from other urban activities, and kept the official status of actors near that of thieves and prostitutes. The fact that women were either a principal attraction (as they were in the French, Spanish, and Italian stages) or forbidden from treading the boards at all (as they were in England and Japan) shows how these anxieties frequently were focused on the bodies of women.

And yet, these restrictions did not have a chilling effect on theatrical innovation, as professional troupes and actors found ever more inventive ways to circumvent or work within them. As we move to the next two chapters, we will deepen our exploration of the effects of a burgeoning print culture on both theatre and society. We will also consider the attempts of monarchs to influence or control drama and theatrical production. Whether theatre was constrained for its purported corruptive influence, or harnessed to legitimize the national interest and values (as was the case in neoclassical France), it could be argued that, without the restrictions of monarchy and shogunate, neither Renaissance/neoclassical theatre nor *kabuki* would have developed as they did.

★

CHAPTER 5

Theatre and the print revolution, 1550–1650

Tobin Nellhaus

Contributors: Bruce McConachie and
Tamara Underiner

The political, religious, economic, and cultural upheavals of Europe's Renaissance often placed theatre in contradictory circumstances. It drew support from monarchs and even religious authorities, often honored royalty, and sometimes partook in religious conflicts. But particularly where professionalization allowed theatre greater financial and intellectual independence from the aristocracy and clergy, sometimes it also clashed with the political structures or with religious doctrines, and it faced renewed opposition and even outright suppression. European drama during this period also fed off the influxes of knowledge about classical Greece and Rome in ways that shaped it for two centuries.

In this chapter we will focus on the impact of a fundamental change in communication in Europe, the invention of the printing press around 1440. As we will see, however, that development was closely entwined with the other changes transforming Europe. We begin by sketching the major transformations affecting Europe, including humanism and the Protestant Reformation, and the ways they were connected to the burgeoning print culture. We then look at how these changes affected theatre in England and Spain. Professional theatre in France got off to a later start, but during the 1600s the French developed a neoclassical approach to drama that came to dominate European playwriting for well over a century. Concurrent with all of these changes was the formation of new scenic practices, primarily in Italy, that shared many of the ideas behind neoclassicism. Our discussion includes case studies on sexuality in Shakespeare's play *Twelfth Night*, and on theatrical self-reference in the late Renaissance.

Social and cultural upheavals in early modern Europe

The rise of a commercial economy, which included international trade, was one contributor to the transformations that shook Europe. Global colonization was initially undertaken by monarchies, but it soon became the pursuit of private, profit-seeking companies. For example, the massive Dutch East India Company (established in 1602) obtained military, judicial, and diplomatic powers to support its mercantile ventures in Asia, including the establishment of colonies. It was also the first business in the world to issue stock, initiating the modern stock market. The profits from these colonial adventures fed the home economies. Domestically, a growing class of people drew their income from their business activities such as manufacturing, entrepreneurship, international trade, and banking, slowly forming the modern bourgeoisie – a "middle class" composed of businesspeople, property owners, professionals, and their families. And most importantly for theatre, in the wake of these economic changes came rapid urbanization, as cities became business centers and the source of work for former peasants: for instance, London and Paris more than doubled their populations. Establishing a permanent theatre became much more financially viable and led to the developments discussed in Chapter 4.

Another important change occurred in several countries' power structures, particularly after 1600: the monarch strove to wrest power from the nobility and place it directly in his or her own hands, and in the administrative, legislative, judicial, and sometimes even religious institutions that he or she controlled. Under this system, known today as absolutism, monarchs frequently claimed that their unilateral power was legitimate because they possessed a divine right to rule. Absolutism had important consequences for theatre, which we will touch on in this chapter and explore more fully in Chapter 6.

A third major force behind the social upheavals of this period was the rise of print culture. The printing press with movable type was invented in Germany around 1440. However, printing didn't have a substantial impact on social life for over 50 years. Printing was also a major commercial activity, which historian Benedict Anderson (1991) has called "print capitalism," and the organization of work in a print shop may have been the first production line. Although initially a printed book was quite expensive, it was less expensive than one copied by hand (a process that could take months or a year), so printing houses were able to serve the demands of a readership that was already beginning to grow during the late Middle Ages. Many of printing's effects would take centuries to develop, and they varied depending on social contexts and the ways in which people used print. Two of the first effects, however, were the broad dissemination of Greek and Roman classical texts, and of the Bible, especially in vernacular translations. Both of these had direct and indirect consequences for theatre and drama.

Printing, Renaissance humanism, and drama

During the fourteenth century, Italian authors began to view classical Roman texts as the epitome of literary style and elegance intended for the pursuit of moral good. Poet Dante Alighieri (*c.*1265–1321) exemplified this attitude toward Roman authors when he chose Virgil (70 BCE–19 BCE) as his guide in his trilogy *The Divine Comedy*. These admirers of classical culture were called "humanists."

But when the Turks conquered the Byzantine Empire in 1453, scores of scholars fled from the empire to Italy, bringing with them numerous classical Greek manuscripts. Among these writings were several works by Plato and Aristotle that were previously unknown in Western Europe – including a Greek text of Aristotle's *Poetics* (see Chapter 1), which until then was available only as a Latin translation of an Arabic translation and was virtually ignored.

Printing soon made these and other classical works widely available, not just in Italy but throughout the continent. Classical Greece and Rome became everywhere esteemed as the

Golden Age of culture and political glory. The wealthy and powerful often adopted imagery from those societies, and references to classical literature and art became a staple of European writing. During the century after the printing press was invented, the renaissance of classicism that began during the 1300s in a few Italian cities bloomed into a European Renaissance.

By 1520, editions of Aristotle's *Poetics*, the major plays of Sophocles, Plautus, Terence, and Seneca, and the illustrated discussions of theatre buildings and scenery by the Roman architect Vitruvius (first century BCE) were available in print. Fired by an interest in these ancient texts, Renaissance scholars and their aristocratic patrons began writing plays imitating the classics, and soon they sought to produce them. In Italy, Gian Giorgio Trissino (1478–1550) wrote and published the first classical-style tragedy, *Sofonisba* (1515). Italian political theorist Niccolò Machiavelli (1469–1527) borrowed the form of classical comedy to write *The Mandrake* (*La Mandragola*, c.1518). Like Machiavelli, university-trained Nicholas Udall (c.1504–1556) in England leaned heavily on Plautus to shape his *Ralph Roister Doister* sometime in the 1530s. Earlier in the century, classically based entertainments for Iberian royal courts were written by Juan del Encina (c.1468–c.1529) and Gil Vicente (c.1465–c.1536). Because of the religious strife that wracked France during these years, classically inspired plays and performances developed somewhat later in Paris, with the first of them coming to the French court in the 1550s.

However, playwrights were caught between the cultural value of printing and the drawbacks of the economic environment. On the one hand, along with classical drama, printers published local and foreign tales, myths, legends, chronicles, and histories which inspired many playwrights. Also, by increasing the number of texts available to read and learn from, printing helped to make education more affordable. This in turn meant more actors were available who could read and memorize lines for large numbers of plays.

On the other hand, playwrights had little incentive to see their own works in print. Philosophically, many considered the art of theatre to be something to be heard and seen, and not necessarily read on the page. More practically speaking, by the late sixteenth century, Europe's printers were keen to satisfy a growing public eager to read plays they had seen or heard about; but the playwrights themselves had reason to view the practice with some trepidation. There was no copyright protection or royalty system, so playwrights were paid only once: when they sold a play to a theatre. Theatres had a profit motive to guard their plays from piracy by other theatre companies and by publishers, and they seldom allowed a play to be published until it ceased to attract audiences. At that point they might sell the play to a printer in order to squeeze the final drop of money from it, none of which went to the playwright. But once a printer had his hands on a script, he reaped all the profit – which could be substantial. So unscrupulous printers stole or suborned the copying of prompt-books (the only "official" record of an entire play in performance, including stage directions), or published the remembered lines of actors that were not necessarily faithful to the playwright's intent. Thus printing under early capitalism threatened playwrights' demonstrations of their literary skill. Controversies over the "true" versions of Shakespeare's plays arise from the piracy that this business and legal environment encouraged. Only over the course of the seventeenth century did playwrights start to gain anything – whether money or status – by publishing their works.

Printing and the Protestant Reformation

In the Middle Ages, few people read the Bible, not least because it was normally in Latin, and Latin was the language of advanced education; in addition, Bibles were highly expensive. Ordinary priests in local parishes were themselves often ill-educated and lacked Latin. Most people received their religious knowledge primarily through sermons. But even among the elite, the most common religious books were breviaries, psalters, and similar materials for everyday devotional purposes.

Printing changed all that. Not only could a copy of the Bible be easily obtained, it was increasingly translated into the vernacular. Translations were highly desirable to a deeply religious laity: the book was the heart of Christianity. With a translation in hand, laypeople's beliefs were released from the interpretations and authority of the Church, and their practices took shape more nationally due to the connection with the vernacular – a tendency that gained strength with geographical distance from Rome. Some laypeople began feeling that individual and small-group Bible-reading could replace the ritual of the Mass.

Starting in 1517, Martin Luther (1483–1546) began to challenge the authority of the Pope. He protested against various Church practices, and taught that the Bible alone was the source of divine knowledge. Luther was not the first to have such ideas or instigate a popular movement to reform the Church: what most distinguished Luther's attack was that his words were rapidly printed throughout Europe, and thus reached a large discontented laity keen to read them. Within a few years a massive schism within Christianity ensued, known as the Protestant Reformation. The Roman Catholic Church responded with a Counter-Reformation (1545–1648) that sought institutional reforms but also aimed to revive Catholic faith. Both faiths quickly became intransigent.

Religious conflict became pervasive. It was central to the tumultuous succession of monarchs in England from Henry VIII to Elizabeth I, integral to England's frequent battles with Spain (including its defeat of the Spanish Armada in 1588), and a factor in the English Civil War that broke out in 1642. In Central Europe, the Thirty Years' War erupted in 1618 primarily on religious grounds, continuing non-stop until 1648. Conflict was not limited to Protestant vs. Catholic: Reformation Christianity promptly spawned numerous (and often antagonistic) denominations such as Lutherans, Calvinists, Puritans, and Anabaptists. This sectarianism was itself a product of print culture, as people developed their own interpretations of religious texts. The discord slowed the development of theatre in France, and as we will see, had an almost cataclysmic effect on English theatre.

Major characteristics of early European book culture

Due to the way books were used in early modern Europe, print culture developed a number of particular traits. One of them can be seen most clearly in religious practices. In the Middle Ages, people's relationship to the Bible was mediated by the Church through priests, pictures, and other avenues, which treated the Bible in piecemeal fashion as a compendium of stories. The mystery cycles and Passion plays, although generally organized independently from the Church, followed the same pattern. But under Protestantism, religiosity was exercised first and foremost by reading the scriptures oneself. Believers developed a personal relationship to the Bible, and read it whole. For Protestants, reading the Bible provided direct access to God's revealed truth, and their creed was that faith alone was sufficient for salvation.

People who intensively read books (whether scriptures, scholarship, or literature) tend to develop their interior life, and to define themselves in terms of their ideas, feelings, and beliefs. This is strikingly different from the classical era and the Middle Ages, when people were defined primarily by their outward relationships, such as social role or type (e.g., soldier, peasant, or merchant). Completing the shift from outward to inward conceptualizations of personhood took two centuries, but one can see it emerging as allegorical and stock characters such as Everyman, Avarice, and wily servant were replaced by more individualized figures such as Shakespeare's characters Hamlet and Viola.

Changes occurred in law too. Before print started gaining importance, contracts relied on oaths to guarantee validity. That was typical of oral culture, and in fact documents were often viewed with suspicion because of possible forgery. But with the rise of print culture, documents became more important, and lawyers sought written precedents in case law. In short, people began to assume that truth was to be found not in a person's word, but in writing.

In Protestantism these two tendencies – individuals' greater inward development and a strengthening view of writing as the embodiment of truth – tended to run hand in hand because faith was tied to reading the Bible and regarding it as the ultimate truth, although the linkage between the tendencies facilitated sectarian splits. In Catholic countries, however, the combination's impact was highly complex, and contradictory trends eventually came to a head in the 1630s when playwriting held Aristotle aloft, science rejected Aristotle in favor of direct perception, and philosophy turned instead to pure reason.

During the period covered by this chapter, then, theatre throughout Europe developed in the midst of enormous cultural, religious, scientific, and philosophical ferment and conflict, profoundly shaping society to the present day.

Elizabethan and Jacobean theatre in England, 1558–1642

When Queen Elizabeth I ascended to the English throne in 1558, the trends that would lead to a remarkable era of literature and performance were already beginning to coalesce – in particular, humanism fused with popular performance.

To help students learn their Latin, the universities and grammar schools had a 50-year-old humanist tradition of performing the works of Roman playwrights and eventually writing new plays in Latin. These plays, along with singing and other types of performance, were often presented for elite audiences, normally indoors. (Similar private performances date back to medieval times.)

Writing new plays in Latin led to new plays in English. Comedies in English had already begun to appear with *Ralph Roister Doister* in the 1530s. In 1561, school performances yielded the first blank (unrhymed) verse tragedy in English: *Gorboduc*, by Thomas Sackville and Thomas Norton. Modeled on Senecan tragedy, it foreshadowed the revenge tragedies that would frequent the English stage a few decades later.

Increasingly, university-educated playwrights turned to the professional theatres to have their plays performed. During the 1580s, most of the prominent Elizabethan playwrights came from the universities. One "university wit" was Thomas Kyd (1558–1594), whose *The Spanish Tragedy* (*c*.1587) opened the floodgates to murder-heavy revenge tragedies on the English stage. In this highly influential play, a man uses a play-within-a-play as cover to avenge the murder of his son. Another university wit was Christopher Marlowe (1564–1593), who mastered episodic

Figure 5.1

Faustus (played by Edward Alleyn) conjures a devil on this title page for a seventeenth-century edition of *The Tragical History of Doctor Faustus*, by Christopher Marlowe. Rumors that "one devil too many" had responded to Alleyn's black magic probably drew audiences to this popular play at the Fortune Theatre.

© Victoria and Albert Museum of Theatre History.

plotting in such popular tragedies as *Tamburlaine*, Parts I and II (1587–1588), and *Doctor Faustus* (1588) (Figure 5.1), in which a scholar takes up magic and makes a deal with the devil. The 1590s brought the first plays by the two greatest playwrights of the era: William Shakespeare (1564–1616) and Ben Jonson (1572–1637). Unlike their best-known predecessors, neither of them was university-educated: they began their careers as actors. Nevertheless, their grammar school education included Latin and possibly Greek. Thus the humanist tradition and the popular professional tradition merged in Elizabethan theatre.

According to historian Jeremy Lopez, during the English Renaissance most spectators, like television audiences today, cared little about who wrote the play as long as it met their expectations (Lopez 2003: 3–29). Spectators wanted dramas stuffed with sexual allusions and characters disguised as someone else. They expected frequent direct address, as in asides and soliloquies. The plays they applauded sometimes included such lurid (and Senecan) plot developments as incest and physical mutilations – in comedies as well as tragedies. Not disturbed by low comedy within tragedies (like the porter scene in Shakespeare's *Macbeth*, 1605) or mortally serious moments in comedies (such as the "Kill Claudio" scene in his *Much Ado about Nothing*, 1598), spectators enjoyed plays that jumped abruptly among scenes of lyricism, suspense, heroics, and grotesquerie. A good play, from their point of view, should also include several self-reflexive moments, in which the actors acknowledged the make-believe of their actions. Lopez argues that, to meet audience expectations, most comedies ended in marriage and/or reunion and tragedies ended with a stage full of dead bodies and order restored. For instance, in Shakespeare's comedy *As You Like It* (1599–1600), marriage piles upon marriage as four couples take vows in the final scene; *Hamlet* (1599–1601) concludes by killing four characters.

The growing prestige of well-written drama altered acting. In the past, talented performers had been known to go "off-script" because they had been accustomed to a more improvisatory form of theatrical performance. A frustrated reference to this continuing practice is made by Shakespeare's Hamlet, in his famous speech of advice to the players. (The problem was scarcely limited to England: for example, as we noted in Chapter 4, the popular Japanese playwright Chikamatsu Monzaemon is said to have become so angry at *kabuki* actors mutilating his scripts that he stopped writing for living actors and shifted to writing plays exclusively for *bunraku* puppets. Similar complaints go back to the Hellenistic age.) By the 1580s, however, performers who might have improvised their way through an evening's entertainment a generation before were increasingly expected to play "by the book." In *A Midsummer Night's Dream* (1595–1596), Shakespeare has even the "rude mechanicals" of his subplot memorize their lines before they mount their performance of "Pyramus and Thisbe" in the play-within-the-play. The expectation of the audience and actors that a script would be played as written led, in turn, to higher standards of playwriting. Better for actor-managers and their companies to memorize and perform several plays of high quality than to have to purchase and learn many mediocre scripts that would enjoy only limited popularity.

Although few contemporary plays were in print by 1600, humanists were convincing the literate public that dramatic theatre connected their own tastes with the superior culture of the ancients. After 1600, as more contemporary plays reached publication, acting companies and eventually playwrights reaped more direct benefits from the emerging print culture. By 1618, the shareholders of the Children of the Queen's Revels had published all of the extant plays performed by the boys' company, for example. Jonson, who won applause for satirizing the follies of the time through a strong dose of classical precepts and wit, was the first English playwright to edit and publish a collection of his own plays, in 1616. This was a major step toward recognizing newly written plays as having literary merit, like the classics. It was the crucial precedent for the publication of the "First Folio" in 1623, in which many of Shakespeare's plays, in authorized versions, were presented as literature. By the 1640s, it was increasingly common for companies and professional playwrights to arrange for the publication of their dramas. In addition, more dramatists were striking deals with their companies to maintain control of their publication rights.

When King James I (1566–1625) began his reign in 1603 – the Jacobean era – the countries of England and Scotland both came under his rule; English laws had been formally extended to Wales over 50 years earlier and Ireland had been ruled by the English king for about a decade longer than that, and so for the first time, the British Isles had a single monarch. Shakespeare's *King Lear* (1606), in which the king divides up his kingdom with disastrous results, alludes to King James's unification of the island. James, a firm believer in absolutism, had frequent conflicts with Parliament over financial matters, and he dissolved Parliament several times.

During James's and his Charles I's rule, drama continued to flourish. But tragedy became more sensationalist, dark, cynical, sometimes obsessed with (and terrified by) women's sexuality, but sometimes sentimental too. Revenge tragedies became more popular than ever. Strongly influenced by Seneca's morbid plays, they were often filled with gore and broken taboos, and almost specialized in body counts. One of the best known is *The Duchess of Malfi* (1612–1613) by John Webster (*c*.1580–*c*.1634), in which one of the Duchess's brothers has her murdered, along with her children, for marrying beneath her and sharing the siblings' inheritance; but then his spy turns the tables and avenges her death. Ten die in all. (*Hamlet* is considered a revenge tragedy.) Comedy tended toward satire, often turning toward London for its subjects. In Jonson's *The Alchemist* (1610), for instance, a trio performs preposterous con games that play on their marks' gullibility. Tragicomedies abounded too. John Fletcher (1579–1625) wrote many, including *A King and No King* (1619). In it, a young king and his sister, long separated, each feel intense incestuous desires which they struggle against, but all is resolved when they learn that actually they are unrelated.

Elizabethan and Jacobean drama – especially the plays by Shakespeare and Jonson – left long but shifting legacies. During the 1600s and early 1700s, although Shakespeare was much admired and performed, Jonson had greater influence on new plays. But during the eighteenth century Shakespeare's reputation as the world's greatest playwright began solidifying and Jonson passed out of favor. Nevertheless, Shakespeare's preeminence did not create many imitators.

Throughout the sixteenth and seventeenth centuries, many Protestant sects arose in England. One of them, the Puritans, slowly developed considerable clout within the Church of England, educational institutions, and city governments – and they abhorred theatre. Their religious objections to it were partly linked to Protestant print culture, in which morality was tied to reading the Bible. The Puritans feared that imitation and spectacle would turn people away from the biblical path to salvation, and thus corrupt their morals and reason, and teach them to delight in illusion and debauchery. Ordinary people (already inherently depraved, according to the Puritans) would be tempted to commit sinful behaviors such as robbery, sodomy, and even murder if they watched such activities or simply heard them discussed on the stage. Further, the Bible forbade transvestism, which was a regular part of English Renaissance theatre because (as we saw in Chapter 4) all female roles were played by boy actors, and many plot and character devices involved gender bending. In fact, panicked by the very notion of sexuality outside procreation, the Puritans damned every element of theatre as infested with deviance and effeminacy.

Playwrights returned the Puritans' animosity by poking fun at them. For example, the character Malvolio in Shakespeare's *Twelfth Night* is depicted as "a kind of Puritan," and other characters play a few mean practical jokes on him. The Puritans' objections to cross-dressing became the target of Jonson's satire *Bartholomew Fair*, in which a Puritan vehemently censures a hand puppet for wearing women's clothes, and loses the argument when the puppet lifts its skirt to reveal it has no sex at all. In the case study on *Twelfth Night* we discuss Elizabethan theatre and sexuality further.

However, deep trouble was brewing. When England's Charles I (1600–1649) succeeded James I in 1625, he married the youngest princess of France – a Catholic – raising fears that the Church of England might reunite with the Roman Catholic Church. Despite Charles's support for the Protestants during the Thirty Years' War, some of his actions seemed to justify those fears. Thus the Puritans began to conflict directly with the monarchy. Meanwhile, Parliament repeatedly clashed with the king, principally over financial matters, leading Charles I to dissolve it. In the late 1630s his religious measures provoked a rebellion in Scotland. To finance his battles with the Scots, Charles recalled Parliament, which refused to provide money except under its own terms. Conflict arose in Ireland as well, and ultimately spread to England. The English Civil War broke out in 1642. Led by Oliver Cromwell (1599–1658), opponents of the monarchy beheaded King Charles I in 1649 and declared a Commonwealth that lasted until 1660.

At the start of the Civil War, Parliament, controlled by Puritans, came fully into power in London and the surrounding areas. One of its first acts was to suppress all stage plays. The Puritans initially imposed the ban as a temporary safeguard against civil strife, but they later broadened and extended it. Some theatres managed to continue anyway, even as the Puritans tore down the Globe and all other playhouses. But by the end of the 1640s, theatre in England had effectively stopped.

CASE STUDY: Sexuality in Shakespeare's *Twelfth Night*

Bruce McConachie

Sexual desire has been a perennial subject of theatrical performance. Even during periods when only actors of a single sex appeared on the stage, audiences have applauded plays in which the anxieties, illusions, and expected pleasures of sexual desire took center stage. During the early modern period in England (1590–1642), cross-dressed boys between the ages of 8 and 18 performed all the female characters. The comedies, satires, and tragedies of numerous playwrights featured boys playing women involved in a range of sexual relationships, including conventional romance and marriage, potential lesbian affairs, prostitution, and even incest. The performance of Shakespeare's *Twelfth Night* at the Globe Theatre in London allowed audiences to explore, enjoy, and agonize about a range of sexual desires, including the desire for same-sex love.

The homoerotics of patriarchy

Most people in early modern England judged sexual urges and actions by patriarchal standards. Patriarchal ideology, the belief that males in superior social and political positions had an inherent right to their authority, generally elevated the expression of male over female sexuality. In this situation, a man's desire for a woman or for another man could be more ennobling than a woman's hetero- or homosexual desire. Patriarchy, however, needed women as a means of cementing alliances and accumulating property through marriage, as well, of course, as ensuring male heirs. The result was a social system and a dominant ideology that tied sexuality to class hierarchy and allowed for homoerotic acts that solidified or did not challenge the patriarchal order.

Within some early modern institutions – the Church, the school, the household – same-sex love initiated by men (and sometimes by women) in superior social positions was not uncommon. Male teachers might form liaisons with male students, and a master might act on his desire for a male apprentice living in his household without raising the neighbors' eyebrows. Likewise, powerful women might form homoerotic relationships with ladies-in-waiting or servants in their households. When these relationships threatened the procreation of patriarchy, however, society persecuted them. Although few instances of lesbianism ever came to court, occasional convictions for "sodomy" led some men to be imprisoned or hanged. In most of these instances, "sodomy" seems to have been broadly understood as an act that threatened the social order – not just sexual morality, but the hierarchy of class and gender.

Homoerotic desire and the boy actors

The convention of boy actors cross-dressed to play women's roles had been the norm in play productions throughout medieval Europe. This changed on the continent during the sixteenth century with the widespread touring of *commedia dell'arte* troupes, the first professional theatres to cast women in female roles regularly. Slowly, other continental theatres also began employing female actors, but English companies did not.

Historians and critics have suggested several reasons for the continuation of cross-dressed boys on the English stage. Fear of female sexuality may have played a part, as some historians

THINKING THROUGH THEATRE HISTORIES

Queer theory

Homoerotic activity sometimes endangered the social order, yet the historical evidence also shows widespread acceptance of homoerotic love in early modern England, a fact that raises significant questions for contemporary readers and critics. Most Westerners today draw a sharp distinction between hetero- and homosexuality and understand sexual orientation as key to a person's identity. Shakespeare's contemporaries, however, did not think about sexuality in these ways. For most Elizabethans, as for many people in other pre-modern cultures, there was nothing unnatural about a man desiring both women and other men; if he acted on these desires, he was not a "homosexual," a confused "heterosexual," or even a "bisexual," since identity was not tied to sexual expression. Of course there were many people then, as now, who preferred same-sex or opposite-sex intimacy and practiced it exclusively, but they did not classify themselves according to their sexual orientation. Most social and literary historians recognize that the homo-hetero binary used to categorize modern sexuality derives from the late nineteenth century and should not be read back into the sexual practices of early modern England.

Such insights help us today to better understand what we might call the homoeroticism of Shakespeare's England. Work by historians and critics in the field of "queer studies," so named to alter a formerly negative term into a positive one, has explored our critical assumptions about sexual desire and its expression. Much of this scholarship rests on the ideas of Michel Foucault, whose three-volume *History of Sexuality* developed the contention that sexuality varies from one culture to another. Following Foucault, Bruce Smith argued that we can distinguish between sex, the biochemical urge experienced by all humans, and sexuality, the cultural expression of that urge: "Sexual desire animates human beings in all times and places, but the forms that desire assumes, the objects to which it is directed, change from culture to culture, from era to era" (Smith 1991: 3). According to Smith and Foucault, sexual expression is tied to culture, not nature. Critics of this approach, however, argue that clear distinctions between nature and culture are impossible to make; both are thoroughly intermingled with each other where sexuality is concerned. Nonetheless, it is clear that all societies channel male and female sexual desires toward a hierarchy of approved subjects and away from subjects deemed inappropriate or immoral.

allege, although powerful men on the continent would have been no less wary of a woman's desire and procreative ability than the patriarchs of England. Then, too, few *commedia* troupes crossed the channel to perform in London; English audiences, consequently, had little familiarity with the possibilities of women on stage. Further, the practice of boys dressing as women was a theatrical convention of proven and continuing effectiveness. Even after the banning of all religious plays in 1559 and their complete suppression in the 1570s, boys continued to play female roles in fairground performances as well as in grammar school productions. In fact, plays written specifically for and performed by all-boy troupes were enormously popular in London after 1576. From 1600 to 1608, the all-boy Queen's Revels company at the Blackfriars Theatre did better business on average than any of the adult companies in London.

The popularity of the boy companies suggests a fourth reason for the continuation of boy actors in female roles: they may have provided a safe, conventional means of exploring the pleasures and anxieties of homoerotic desire on the stage – safe in most ways, at least. The Master of the Revels, a censor appointed by the royal household to guard against religious and political subversion in all dramas performed by licensed troupes, did not forbid plays on the basis of sexual suggestiveness, homoerotic or otherwise. Puritan critics of the stage, however, repeatedly pointed to the dangerous eroticism of beautiful boys. Opposed to any public displays of sexual desire, homo or hetero, Philip Stubbs, for example, singled out the "whoredome & unclennes" induced by the boy players in 1582:

> [For proof], but marke the flocking and running to Theatres and curtens . . . to see Playes and Enterludes, where such wanton gestures, such bawdie speaches; such laughing and fleering; such kissing and bussing; such clipping and culling; such wickinge and glancinge of wanton eyes, and the like is used, as is wonderfull to behold. These goodly pageants being done, every mate sorts to his mate . . . and in their secret conclaves (covertly) they play the Sodomits, or worse.

> (Brown 1990: 250)

Although their fear of the theatre made the Puritans biased reporters, Stubbs's description, echoed in less overheated phrases by more objective observers, does suggest that the boy actors were trained to make themselves objects of sexual desire on the stage.

The adult companies of Renaissance England generally employed four to six boys, both for female roles and for roles of their own age and sex. As in other master–apprentice relationships in early modern England, the boys lived in the household of the company member under whom they served, and the company paid the master a small fee for the boys' services. The Lord Chamberlain's Men probably employed four boys in the early 1600s, when they produced *Twelfth Night* at the Globe.

Historians know little about the acting style of adults on Renaissance stages and less about the techniques used by boys to impersonate women. The skimpy evidence does suggest that the boys playing major female roles attempted to fully embody the voice, movements, and emotions of their characters rather than merely indicate them. That Shakespeare wrote such complex psychological portraits as Juliet (*Romeo and Juliet*, 1594–1595), Rosalind (*As You Like It*, 1599), and Cleopatra (*Antony and Cleopatra*, 1606–1607) also suggests that his company had boy actors who could play these roles believably. For their part, spectators probably focused on either the female characters or the boy underneath during different moments of the performance. And Shakespeare, like other Renaissance playwrights, frequently reminded his audience of the sexual incongruity between the two.

Twelfth Night *at the Globe*

When *Twelfth Night* began near two o'clock in the afternoon, the audience heard the musicians – probably six instrumentalists in an elevated gallery – playing melancholy music as Duke Orsino and his court entered through the two doors at the rear of the stage. Music would have played a significant role in establishing the various moods of the comedy and the listeners' attitudes toward its major characters. No doubt the spectators also noted the lavish costumes worn by the duke and his court, costumes which gave important information about the social

Figure 5.2

Interior of the reconstructed Globe Theatre, London, which opened in 1997. Shown is a scene from an all-male production of *Twelfth Night*, with Mark Rylance as Olivia and Michael Brown as Viola/Cesario.

Photo by John Tramper, © Shakespeare's Globe Picture Archive.

class and gender of these and other characters (including the cross-dressed boys) at their entrance. A throne-like chair, placed center stage for the duke, was all the scenery needed to establish the setting of the first scene.

Twelfth Night tells the story of shipwrecked twins, a brother and sister, stranded in the fairy-tale land of Illyria. They eventually find their rightful, aristocratic place by marrying into the two powerful households of the country. In order to secure her livelihood, the female twin Viola dons male attire and apprentices herself to Duke Orsino as his page. Unknown to Viola, Sebastian, her twin brother, survived the wreck and also is seeking his fortune in Illyria. He is initially helped by Antonio, whose apparent homoerotic desire shapes their relationship. The plot focuses on Viola, who is soon caught up in the romantic intrigues of the two households. Duke Orsino is trying to gain the hand of the Countess Olivia, who disdains his love. When Viola, in male disguise as Cesario, goes to woo her as the duke's agent, Olivia falls in love with "him," not realizing Cesario/Viola's sex (Figure 5.2). Viola, meanwhile, is longing for the duke.

The character relationships in the secondary plot reflect the sexual "madness" of the major characters. Olivia's uncle, Sir Toby Belch, tricks Sir Andrew Aguecheek into believing that Olivia loves him. Knowing that Olivia's steward, Malvolio, also loves the countess, Sir Toby and his friends induce Malvolio into believing that she wants to marry him. Malvolio's attempts to confirm Olivia's love land him in prison for his "madness." After Viola (costumed the same as her twin brother, Sebastian) refuses to help Antonio, he also falls into a kind of "madness." Next, Olivia assumes that Sebastian is Cesario and promptly marries the amazed lad. In the end, the twins finally appear together on stage, the mistaken identities are resolved, and Viola reveals her male disguise. The countess reaffirms her marriage to Sebastian, and the duke, affectionate throughout with Cesario/Viola, pledges to wed her.

Staging homoeroticism

The double marriage at the end of *Twelfth Night* is a conventional comic ending that satisfies patriarchal values, but it does not resolve the homoerotic relationships hinted at and, arguably, even established during the play. The ending promises that both family households, once threatened by the narcissistic self-love of their heads and by eventual, childless dissolution, can flourish in the future. Threats to the aristocratic position of both families, such as Malvolio's desire for the countess, have been averted or punished. In the case of Orsino's love for Viola, however, the duke remains attached to the image of Viola as a boy. He even calls her "Cesario" in his final speech, perhaps reflecting his ongoing attraction to Viola's boyish role.

The marriage of Olivia to Sebastian may be based on a firmer heteroerotic desire, but ambiguities remain here as well. Olivia's former love for Cesario, a female character in boy's clothing, continues to shadow her attraction to her new husband, costumed identically to his sister. Her suggested desire for another woman is now channeled into a marriage with Viola's twin. And Sebastian's implied past homoerotic relation with Antonio may influence his marriage to Olivia. Sebastian's greeting to Antonio when they are reunited is: "How have the hours racked and tortured me/ Since I have lost thee" (5.1.211–2; all citations are from Greenblatt 1997). This might suggest that Antonio would be a welcome guest in Sebastian's new household. In short, the ending guarantees the reproduction of patriarchy, but it does not rule out the continuation of homoerotic desires and alliances. The finale puts potentially disruptive homoeroticism under the control of patriarchy.

Considered from a theatrical, rather than a simply dramatic point of view, the action of *Twelfth Night* allowed the audience even more opportunities to identify with homoerotic attractions. While dramatically the ending presents two opposite-sex couples united in wedlock, theatrically an adult male actor (who played Orsino) held the hand of a cross-dressed boy actor (Viola), while near them on stage two boys (Olivia and Sebastian) also posed as a heterosexual couple. Shakespeare frequently reminded his audience that boy actors were playing all the female roles by having Viola disguise herself as Cesario. This triple-level gender confusion entailed a boy actor playing a girl playing a boy. Shakespeare gave Viola several lines of dialogue that underscored these multiple layers of sexual identity: "I am not that I play" (1.5.164) and "Disguise, I see thou art a wickedness" (2.2.25), for example. The script also required the boy actor playing Viola/Cesario to change his voice in order to separate his two roles. Thus, every time the actor shifted from high-voiced Viola to boy-voiced Cesario (probably the boy actor's natural intonation), audiences were reminded of the boy actor underneath Viola and behind all the other female roles.

The intimate scenes between Viola/Cesario and Olivia – they are alone together on stage three times – consequently carried multiple homoerotic charges that may have created anxiety and pleasure in Shakespeare's audience. (For a modern all-male production of *Twelfth Night*, see the photograph in Figure 5.2.) Dramatically, Olivia's love for Cesario hinted at same-sex desire between two women, because of audience knowledge of Viola's disguise. Theatrically, one boy actor (Olivia) flirted with another boy actor, while the second boy (Viola/Cesario) demurred to profess his love for a man (Orsino). How could the need for patriarchy to reproduce itself find a way through the maze of homoerotic possibilities presented in the drama and theatre of such scenes? Shakespeare set up the situation and then relied on the comedy of "time" – "O Time, thou must untangle this, not I" (2.2.39) – to untie the knot, resolving in the end only the dramatic anxieties about the fate of these patriarchal families.

Some of this interpretation is speculative. What Elizabethan audiences made of these homoerotic possibilities can never be known with certainty, of course. Some may have understood but ignored the homoerotic enticements of the performance while a few of both sexes may have come to the theatre chiefly to be aroused by them. Given their familiarity with both homo- and heteroerotic desire, most early modern spectators probably feared for and enjoyed the performance of both sexualities. Clearly, the Lord Chamberlain's Men put both on stage in their Globe production of *Twelfth Night* in the early 1600s.

Key references

Brown, S. (1990) "The Boyhood of Shakespeare's Heroines: Notes on Gender Ambiguity in the Sixteenth Century," *Studies in English Literature* 30: 243–64.

Casey, C. (1997) "Gender Trouble in *Twelfth Night*," *Theatre Journal* 49 (May): 121–41.

Greenblatt, S. (gen. ed.) (1997) *The Norton Shakespeare*, New York and London: W.W. Norton and Company.

Howard, J.E. (1988) "Crossdressing, the Theatre, and Gender Struggle in Early Modern England," *Shakespeare Quarterly* 39: 418–40.

Jardine, L. (1992) "Twins and Travesties: Gender, Dependency, and Sexual Availability in *Twelfth Night*," in S. Zimmerman (ed.) *Erotic Politics: Desire on the Renaissance Stage*, New York and London: Routledge.

Shapiro, M. (1994) *Gender in Play on the Shakespearean Stage: Boy Heroines and Female Pages*, Ann Arbor, MI: University of Michigan Press.

Smith, B.R. (1991) *Homosexual Desire in Shakespeare's England: A Cultural Poetics*, Chicago and London: University of Chicago Press.

Thomson, P. (1992) *Shakespeare's Theatre*, London: Routledge.

Golden Age theatre in Spain, 1590–1650

The volume and variety of dramatic output during Spain's Golden Age was enormous, numbering in the tens of thousands of plays. In turn, Spanish drama of this period influenced numerous European playwrights of the time, many of whom borrowed its plots and themes.

While the presentation of religious drama (*autos sacramentales*) remained strong throughout the period, and despite Spain's reputation for being an overly zealous Catholic country, the drama of its Golden Age treated many themes central to a humanist understanding of the world. In such drama, the decisions made by everyday men and women – not God, not saints, not allegorical figures – drive the action of the play, as they face conflicts in love, honor, duty, valor, social standing, political power, and so forth.

In Spain as elsewhere in Europe, it took some time for theatre to separate itself from religious themes and contemporary issues to create a world apart from reality, or what Spanish Golden

Age scholar Melveena McKendrick calls "a self-contained world of its own, a world of the imagination" (1989: 11). Most scholars credit playwright Juan del Encina (c.1468–1529) with the beginnings of this movement, especially in his later plays introducing secular themes. Encina was a shoemaker's son who studied law, and his experiences at court in Spain and Rome likely influenced his later work.

Perhaps the principal inaugurator of a truly humanist impulse in Spanish theatre was Bartolomé de Torres Naharro (c.1485–c.1520). He consciously looked back to ancient models from Italy and Greece to derive principles for writing effective drama, both technically and thematically – principles meant to serve as guidelines, in contrast to the ways they became hardened into strict rules and regulations in places like France (discussed below). According to McKendrick, Naharro's plays may never have been staged in Spain, but they were widely read in printed editions and re-editions up until 1557, when they were banned in their entirety by the Spanish Inquisition (which enforced Catholic orthodoxy) for their irreverent themes. His popularity inspired many imitators in print, but it is not clear whether these dramas were ever performed.

As we saw in Chapter 4, once permanent theatres began to be established in the urban centers of Spain, especially in Madrid, the demand for new plays on all kinds of subjects was insatiable. Just as the public theatres accommodated popular and aristocratic spectators, so too did many of the new *comedias* [sing. *comedia*: koh-MEY-dee-ah] (plays) merge the tastes and values of both groups. (The Spanish term *comedia* refers to a wide variety of plays, both serious and comic, and should not be confused with *commedia dell'arte*.) The history plays and romantic dramas successfully fused these traditions, and are characterized by their blending of serious and comic elements, usually in a three-act structure. Frequently they featured plots in which a man's or woman's honor was at stake, and which often turned on such devices and developments as mistaken identity, the use of disguises, and swordfights. In fact, swordfights, or the threat of them among men of a certain social rank, were so common as to constitute a subgenre of *comedia* called the *capa y espada* [KAH-pa ee es-PAH-thah] (cape and sword) plays; other recognizable types included pastorals, comedies of manners, "noisy" plays featuring lots of spectacle and stage effects, and dramas based on myth and history.

The illusive nature of reality itself was a frequent preoccupation of Spanish Golden Age playwrights. Theatre and theatricality offered tempting ways for them to explore this theme, in works that staged plays-within-plays, or were themselves *about* plays, or in some other ways showed life itself to be highly theatricalized. Scholars refer to this as metatheatre, metadrama, or metatheatricality. So frequently was this device employed in Spanish Golden Age drama that some scholars claim it as a characteristic convention of such drama. In fact metatheatricality was commonplace throughout European drama during this era; we discuss it further in the second case study in this chapter.

Writing about Spanish Golden Age drama, Alexander A. Parker suggests that the plays operated on five basic principles:

> (1) the primacy of action over character drawing; (2) the primacy of theme over action, with the consequent irrelevance of realistic verisimilitude [appearance of truth]; (3) dramatic unity in the theme and not in the action; (4) the subordination of the theme to a moral purpose through the principle of poetic justice [where good is rewarded and evil punished], which is not exemplified only by the death of the wrongdoer; and (5) the

elucidation of the moral purpose by means of dramatic causality [i.e., all the principal events in the play follow a chain of cause and effect that culminates in the distribution of poetic justice].

(1971: 29)

Of the voluminous number of plays written and produced, the canon of Golden Age plays in English translation is small, but indicative and provocative. Perhaps the most famous plays of this canon are the historical play *Fuenteovejuna* by Lope de Vega; *The Trickster of Seville* by Tirso de Molina (which first introduced to the stage the legendary lothario, Don Juan); and the philosophical drama *Life is a Dream* by Pedro Calderón de la Barca (who you will recall from Chapter 3 was also the most famous author of *autos sacramentales* in Spain).

The most prolific and renowned playwright of the Golden Age, Lope Félix de Vega Carpio (1562–1635), wrote many *capa y espada* dramas among his more than 800 plays. Although a favorite of the aristocracy, Lope de Vega came from an artisan family, worked to gain more education throughout his life, and eventually became a priest. Two of Lope de Vega's history plays, *The Life and Death of King Bamba* (1597–1598) and *Fuenteovejuna* (1612–1614; the title refers to a town itself named after a watering hole for sheep), provide illustrative examples of how the *comedias* blended secular and religious elements. Both alter the historic record for dramatic effect, contrasting peasant wisdom, valor, and humility, backed by Catholic faith, against the foolish and villainous objections of a fractious nobility; both call on the Spanish nobility to draw on history and popular tradition to change their morality. The latter play is still frequently re-staged, for its view of community solidarity against a tyrannical overlord: when this overlord is assassinated, and the royal investigators come to ask "who did it," each community member proclaims, "Fuenteovejuna!" (In Spanish, the answer can become a play on words that further frustrates authority, for if the first syllable is drawn out, "Fue" also means "It was. . . .")

On one occasion, at the invitation of a learned contemporary, Lope de Vega also concerned himself with theorizing drama as well as writing it; the result was his *New Art of Writing Plays for Our Time* (1609), originally delivered in verse as an address to a literary assembly. An informal defense of popular taste as a valid measure of a drama, Lope de Vega's ideas, like Torres Naharro's before him, stand in contrast to the stricter neoclassicism of Italy and France (discussed below), and many scholars view his dramaturgical approach as more aligned with Shakespeare's than with his other European contemporaries.

The role of printing in this period was especially important to female writers, who only rarely, if ever, saw their plays staged, but who nevertheless wrote numerous and worthy dramas that circulated in print and have recently become fertile grounds for scholarship. These playwrights include Ana Caro Mallén de Soto (1590–1650), Leonor de la Cueva y Silva (1611–1705), Feliciana Enríquez de Guzmán (1569–1644), and María de Zayas y Sotomayor (1590–1661). What their plays share most strongly, writes Teresa Scott Soufas, "is an emphasis on male irresponsibility with regard to social mores and gender ideological demands" (1997: ix). These plays seem to ask of their readers: if Spanish society depends upon strict adherence to gendered categories of proper behavior and codes of honor, what happens to its women when the men don't hold up their end of the bargain? According to Soufas, most of these playwrights followed the principles of Lope de Vega's *comedia nueva* (new comedy), but Enríquez's work was consciously concerned with following the form of classical drama, and was meant to appeal to a more learned audience. The verse prologue to her *Tragicomedia de los jardines y campos sabeos* (*Tragicomedy of the Sabean Gardens and Fields*, 1624) called for a return to the formal unities of time and place in drama (as defined by neoclassicism).

During the reign of Philip IV (1621–1665), the Spanish monarchy asserted more control of its kingdom and colonies and also called more frequently on the theatre to bolster its absolutist claims to power. Calderón succeeded Lope de Vega as Spain's most successful playwright, but his energies were split between the public theatres and the court. Writing primarily between 1622 and 1640, Calderón continued and improved upon the previous genres, often blending religious and secular themes. His best-known secular play, *Life is a Dream* (*c.*1636), presents the absolute power and agency of kingship as the necessary answer for a royal prince who was imprisoned his whole life and does not know if his return to court has been a dream. After 1640, Calderón mostly abandoned writing for the public theatres so that he could create *autos* and devise entertainments with lavish spectacles to glorify Philip IV and his court.

When Spain began to colonize the Americas, learned men and women there also wrote plays in the tradition of the Golden Age. Perhaps the most important of these American playwrights were Juan Ruiz de Alarcón (whose work was less prolific but more consistently fine than those of his Peninsular counterparts) and Sor Juana Inés de la Cruz, whose importance for theatre history is discussed in a case study in Chapter 6.

French theatre before the triumph of neoclassicism, 1550–1637

As we saw in Chapter 4, theatrical performance in France began in much the same way as it had in Spain and England: traveling troupes, attracted by the rising population of Paris, eventually established permanent homes in existing buildings or even in purpose-built theatres. Broadly speaking, French playwriting charted a similar course, with the parallel development of popular and humanist plays, a significant number of them written by university students. But from there they diverge. The development of French theatre was slowed by the political and religious turmoil endemic in the country during the last third of the sixteenth century and continuing sporadically well into the seventeenth century. In addition, unlike England and Spain, popular performance was dominated for decades by Italian *commedia dell'arte* companies, often invited into France by the royalty itself. Touring troupes from other countries came to France as well, including some from England. Due to this competition, French popular drama was strongly shaped by *commedia dell'arte*, and its influence remained visible in French comedy past the middle of the seventeenth century.

Drama for the elite, as elsewhere, was mainly affected by humanism and its more exacting successor, neoclassicism; however, the latter increasingly pushed out popular approaches. By the mid-sixteenth century the schools and colleges began to generate plays imitating Roman drama but in French vernacular. The first humanist play in France was *Cléopâtre*, a tragedy by Étienne Jodelle (1532–1573), which appeared in 1552. It was a resounding success when performed before King Henry II. Comedies and tragicomedies followed, as did plays written in the classical mode but on biblical subjects. Sometimes students toured these plays to towns across France, where they were also warmly received. French humanist drama was spread throughout France through printed editions, which were usually read aloud. However, playwriting was a relatively minor literary activity in France until the 1630s, when it rapidly grew in both importance and quality.

The professional players customarily performed a serious play followed by a comedy or a farce, but the farces – often laden with coarse humor or outright obscenity – were by far the most popular with general audiences and at times dominated the repertory until the 1630s, when they fell from favor. In Paris, professional companies were occasionally summoned to perform in the palaces and estate houses, bringing exactly the same plays they staged at the Hôtel de Bourgogne. But in the early 1600s, the aristocracy began to turn away from farces and instead preferred serious drama and more tasteful comedy.

During the first quarter of the seventeenth century, the playwright who dominated the stage was Alexandre Hardy (c.1572–c.1632). Hardy was extraordinarily prolific, claiming authorship of at least 600 plays, although only 34 have survived (having been permitted publication by the acting companies). He wrote mainly for a popular audience, but increased characters' psychological depth. Although he adopted some of the Senecan style, he combined it with the multiple settings of medieval theatre. His plays frequently mixed genres and have often been disparaged. Nevertheless, as the first professional playwright he paved the way for the neoclassical playwrights who emerged in the coming decade; their works continue to be performed today.

During the 1630s, French theatre developed rapidly. Professional acting companies became increasingly well established in Paris. The Comédiens du Roi (King's Players, led by the actor Bellerose [1592–1670] after Valleran's death in 1613) secured permanent residence at the Hôtel de Bourgogne in 1629. In 1634, Montdory (Guillaume de Gilleberts, 1594–1654), who had been one of the leading actors of the Comédiens du Roi but left that company to start his own, settled his troupe in a new permanent space, the Théâtre du Marais – the first significant challenger to the Hôtel de Bourgogne. Tastes became more sophisticated; audiences probably became less mixed as class divisions took root in French theatre. And most importantly, humanist approaches to drama, which had continued since the mid-1500s, adopted a new, more rigid form now known as neoclassicism.

Neoclassicism, print, and the controversy over *Le Cid*

Italy – birthplace of the Renaissance humanism that printing helped sweep across Europe – also spawned neoclassicism, an effort to follow the drama theories of classical Greece and Rome as strictly as possible. Its main theorists were Julius Caesar Scaliger (1484–1558) and especially Lodovico Castelvetro (1505–1571), who set out to update and improve upon the discussions of drama found in Aristotle's *Poetics*, with some additions from Horace's *Ars Poetica* (see Chapters 1 and 2, respectively). But Aristotle's authority was appropriated to justify a dogma that actually drew rather little from the text of the *Poetics*.

Aristotle derived his recommendations from actual examples of what he considered excellent and lesser plays. Scaliger and Castelvetro reversed Aristotle's inductive method to create prescriptive requirements, or "rules," for future plays. The most fundamental requirement was Aristotle's concept of imitation (mimesis), which the neoclassicists developed into the concept of verisimilitude: the quality of appearing true to life, realistic, or dramatically probable.

From the concept of verisimilitude flowed further rules. Relying in part on several misunderstandings (and even willful distortions) of Aristotle's notoriously difficult text, Scaliger and Castelvetro required playwrights to maintain three unities – of action, time, and place – in constructing their dramas: a play should encompass only one major plot, its fictional time should last no more than a single day, and its scenes should occur in a single location.

The *unity of action* – the only one that actually came from Aristotle's text – prohibited multiple plots, such as those common in English Renaissance and Spanish Golden Age drama. Scaliger and Castelvetro devised the *unity of time* out of Aristotle's observation that the action in most tragedies occurs within a single day, although sometimes longer. Castelvetro not only made this comment an absolute rule, but also urged that 12 hours would better serve verisimilitude. The "ignorant multitude" attending a play, said Castelvetro, would not believe "that several days and nights had passed when their senses tell them that only a few hours have passed" (Carlson 1993: 48–9). Similarly, the *unity of place* was necessary because spectators would be bewildered if the stage in front of them portrayed several locations.

One further precept formed the main rules: decorum (or propriety), a rule which the neoclassicists took from Horace. It required that playwrights follow the tastes and morals of the day, and it slowly restrained all material that might shock audiences. Decorum preserved class lines by specifying behavior appropriate for each class: for example, in serious drama only lower-class characters could act foolishly. As we will see, one more requirement of neoclassicism would eventually descend from decorum: the principle of poetic justice.

Neoclassicism radically underestimated spectators' imaginative capabilities and flew in the face of most people's actual experience in the popular theatres. But the prejudices of early print culture, plus the current beliefs about social hierarchy, supported Scaliger and Castelvetro. Supposedly, only educated scholars and aristocrats whose imaginations had been stretched and tested by books might be able to understand plays that violated verisimilitude, whereas the "ignorant multitude," with merely their "senses" to guide them, would be lost. Ironically, it was the popular drama that freely presented multiple places, events covering sometimes years, and subplots along with main plots; the upper classes instead demanded plays that carefully narrowed imaginations.

In practice, moreover, the unities often conflicted with the goal of verisimilitude. It is extremely unlikely that the volume of action in most plays could actually happen in a single day, and that it would all occur in a single room or even building. Consequently, plays frequently stretched the rules and glossed over any contradictions. Today the rules are usually viewed as straightjacketing dramaturgy, and they are seldom considered, let alone obeyed.

However, as historian John Lough points out, the rules had a crucial result: neoclassical tragedy subordinated physical action to "psychological conflict portrayed at a moment of crisis" (1979: 106). Thus they were part of a general movement in Western drama – and print culture as a whole – toward a focus on personal internal struggles. Because it was tied to print culture, this orientation became a permanent part of mainstream theatre (and some outside the mainstream), leading for example to the psychological realism of the 1950s to be discussed in Chapter 12.

During the early 1600s, the impact of neoclassicism varied across Europe. Most French and Spanish scholars agreed with the Italian theorists, at least in principle, but several popular playwrights voiced objections from the start. As we have seen, Lope de Vega, for example, acknowledged the validity of the rules advocated by the Italians and admitted that his plays violated them, but he forthrightly stated his intention of continuing to please his audiences rather than bowing to the theorists. Alexandre Hardy also sought the vindication of public applause over scholarly praise. In England, playwrights almost completely ignored neoclassicism until after the ban on theatre was lifted in 1660. Overall, however, neoclassicism solidified a class division between types of performance: the rule-bound drama of the highly literate elite, and the popular drama which ignored most or all of the rules.

Eventually print culture developed to the point where some of the educated began believing that reading printed plays was superior to watching a live performance. Although that view had been directly contradicted by early neoclassicists like Castelvetro just a few decades previously, some elites developed an antitheatrical prejudice, claiming that the stage was, in effect, the place of bodies and mortality, while the page could attain immortality in the realm of the spirit. Even some dramatists writing for the popular stage supported this view.

The dispute between the popular stage and the academic theorists came to a head in France with the production of *Le Cid*, by Pierre Corneille (1606–1684), in 1637. The play concerned a soldier who, in order to defend his father's honor, is forced to kill the father of the woman he loves. But following victories in battle and a duel, he and his love will probably marry. The play generally accorded with the unities, but numerous actions were crowded into a single day and the locations were spread across the city, so that it was more like a popular play. Controversy arose quickly, and when it threatened to get out of hand, Cardinal Richelieu (1585–1642) called on the French Academy to settle the dispute.

Richelieu, who effectively ruled France in the 1620s and 1630s behind the throne of Louis XIII, used the controversy over *Le Cid* to position the monarchy as the final judge of French culture. Although the French Academy had originated as a private organization of scholars, Richelieu pressured its members to adopt state support and to take as its primary goal the codification and regulation of French language and culture. Like the publication of dictionaries and grammars that attempted to standardize Western European languages in the 1600s, the French Academy was itself a product of print culture. By referring the debate over *Le Cid* to the arbitration of the Academy, Richelieu ensured that the French state had control over the future of French theatre and culture, which became a pillar of French absolutism.

Six months later, Richelieu's appointee Jean Chapelain (1595–1674) delivered the Academy's verdict. Chapelain took issue with some of the criticism leveled against Corneille, but condemned the play for breaching verisimilitude and for its lack of ethics. Even though *Le Cid* observes the unity of time, Chapelain complained that Corneille had packed too many incidents into 24 hours to sustain the play's probability. The Academy argued that the play was particularly offensive because a young woman consents to wed her father's killer (a trumped-up charge: in actuality, she protests the marriage, which the king has decreed), and so the play transgressed the neoclassical precept of decorum. In his decision, Chapelain had vindicated the unities, upheld decorum, and went beyond the Italian critics in firmly tying the purpose of dramatic theatre to the ideal of poetic justice – evil characters should be punished and good ones rewarded – which became part of the neoclassical rules. The rules drove the older approaches to dramaturgy off the elite Parisian stage. In subsequent years, Richelieu and later Louis XIV built France into the main political and cultural force in the continent, and the neoclassical rules soon regulated drama across Europe, not to be toppled for nearly two centuries.

Scenic perspective in print and on stage

Print-influenced neoclassicism altered theatre architecture and scenic conventions as well as playwriting. In the early seventeenth century, scenic practices on the stages of public playhouses remained indebted to the *platea* and *mansion* arrangements of the medieval theatre (described

Figure 5.3

Sketch of a set by Laurent Mahelot for Pierre Du Ryer's *Poliarque et Argénis*. This example of simultaneous scenery shows a cave (left), an altar (center), and a ship (right).

Bibliothèque nationale de France.

in Chapter 3). Parisian theatre troupes continued to use small *mansions* or "simultaneous scenery" visible throughout the performance on an unframed stage into the 1630s, when for example it was used for *Le Cid*. The French scene designer Laurent Mahelot included many drawings of such settings in his memoirs (Figure 5.3). And in the open-air theatres of England and Spain, the *platea*-like platforms, backed with doors and perhaps an upper level, provided a fluid, unlocalized playing area that could be whatever the characters said it was. These scenic practices gradually gave way to a series of single settings that localized the dramatic action – settings that were organized according to the laws of perspective. This convention for staging appeared first in Italian courts and gradually altered public performances throughout Europe.

There are many reasons for the rise and eventual triumph of **perspective scenery**. One was the emergence of perspective in painting. European interest in perspective began in the fourteenth century as part of the Italian humanism discussed earlier in this chapter, stirred by an Arabic treatise on optics. Perspective became highly popular among Italian artists by the middle of the fifteenth century, when the printing press would carry their ideas across Europe. By 1500, Italian painters had perfected the geometry and graphics of single-point perspective. Soon this mode of illustrating depth on a canvas or on walls began to influence Italian scenographers. By the mid-seventeenth century, perspective scenery had become magic on stage.

But the move toward perspective was also part of a change *in* perspective. Medieval art often portrayed people and objects in terms of their religious significance (for example, by making them larger), or gathered them together primarily for allegorical or spiritual purposes, rather than for a naturalistic representation. An example of the medieval approach in theatre is *locus* and *mansion* staging, which presents many locations simultaneously. In a sense, this artistic strategy answers the question, "How do things appear in God's eyes?" But perspective painting is more concerned with how things look in a human's eyes – specifically, one's own. It is much more individualistically oriented. That orientation fits well with the interiorized individualism that print culture fostered. Print culture gave perspective painting a new meaning and importance.

Finally, perspective scenery began to appeal to dukes and monarchs for reasons other than their illusionistic and individualistic representations of reality: they noticed that perspective scenery also had a political meaning, since only one person in the theatre could sit where perspective scenery lined up perfectly. This and the techniques of perspective scenery will be taken up in Chapter 6.

Early print culture reaches a watershed

To paraphrase historian Elizabeth Eisenstein's observation about the impact of printing upon religion (1979: 366–7), print's effects on art and scholarship during the Renaissance pointed in two opposite directions: toward orthodoxies that leveraged their power by claiming the authority of ancient texts; and toward critical thought willing to start afresh, without the chains of classical views. Orthodoxies made a few books the foundation for all else. The trend toward critical thought was no less dependent on texts, but its dependence was in the form of collecting and comparing them, allowing thinkers both to discover errors and conflicts, and to gather resources and build on the work of others.

In the 1630s these trends reached a tipping point. Neoclassicism began its trek toward dominance in the 1560s with Scaliger, and it became orthodoxy in 1637 through the debate over *Le Cid*. Concurrently, paths within critical inquiry were being cut elsewhere in higher learning. In 1632, the Italian scientist Galileo (1564–1642) – arguably the greatest figure of the scientific revolution, and a frequent critic of Aristotle – published his major book on the heliocentric model of the universe, and in 1638, a pioneering treatise on physics and mechanics. His method of basing knowledge on the observation of nature is called empiricism. Along with the triumph of neoclassicism, 1637 saw a decisive text by French philosopher René Descartes (1596–1650), who held that reason is the sole means of producing truth, and that only absolute, mathematical certainty was acceptable. Part of his effort to establish knowledge independent of ancient opinion was his dictum, "I think, therefore I am" (*cogito ergo sum*): the proof of my existence is that I think. Descartes' rationalism was central to much philosophy in subsequent centuries.

Despite their disagreements on the value of ancient texts and the roles of observation *versus* reasoning, these developments had commonalities. One is the mathematical element in each. This is obvious in Galileo; Descartes was himself an important mathematician, and his desire for absolute certainty had mathematical laws as its model. Neoclassicism's rules are law-like in their apparent clarity (despite any breaches in practice), and the very term "unity" conveys a desire for invariance and the elimination of multiplicity and ambiguity. Although perspective painting arose earlier, its mathematical methodology accorded with these other cultural developments. Perspective organized art around individual perception – and here we find another commonality among these cultural developments. We observed in the Introduction to Part II that the neoclassical unities constrained drama to represent what an individual can perceive, and in this chapter we mentioned how they made psychological conflict the fulcrum of drama. Rationalism and the scientific revolution likewise depended on individual thought and experience as the means for producing knowledge. Print culture was at the heart of new reliance on individual consciousness and the orderliness of knowledge – two of the hallmarks of the next era of Western culture, the Enlightenment. Empiricism, rationalism, and neo-classicism would all become cornerstones of that epoch.

CASE STUDY: Early modern metatheatricality and the print revolution

Tobin Nellhaus

William Shakespeare's *Hamlet*, written around 1600, is famous for its play-within-a-play, "The Murder of Gonzago" (which Hamlet jokingly called "The Mousetrap") (Figure 5.4). His *Midsummer Night's Dream*, written sometime during 1590–1596, includes the playlet "Pyramus and Thisbe," performed (poorly) by a group of lowly artisans. Ben Jonson's *Bartholomew Fair* (1614) includes a puppet show.

Plays-within-plays are just one type of metatheatricality: theatrical performance that refers to or represents theatrical performance. It is a broad category that includes characters (or even actors) who talk to the audience, characters who observe that they're in a theatre, plays about actors, characters who play roles within the play, conversations about plays, and much more. During the Renaissance, metatheatricality was extraordinarily common – some scholars estimate that around 10 percent of the plays written in England during that period involved metatheatricality.

Figure 5.4

The "Mousetrap" scene (Act III, sc. 2) from the 2008 production of *Hamlet* by the Royal Shakespeare Company, with David Tennant as Hamlet.

Source: Getty/BBC Motion Gallery.

The interest in metatheatricality wasn't restricted to England, either. Numerous Spanish Golden Age plays had metatheatrical elements. Lope de Vega's *The Great Pretenders* (*c*.1608) has a play-within-a-play during which a Roman actor ridicules Christians on stage only to be converted while acting the role of a Christian. In Calderón's religious drama *The Great Theatre of the World* (1649), God is an author for whom the world is the stage for human actions. That play is also a prime example of the metaphor "All the world is a stage," which was a commonplace for centuries, yet never so salient as during this period.

In France too there were plays-within-plays, such as in Pierre Corneille's *The Theatrical Illusion* (1636) and Jean Rotrou's *The Genuine St. Genest* (1645), the latter on the same subject as *The Great Pretenders*. More frequent in French drama were "performances within plays," in which characters create scenes to dupe another character, often to reveal truths about the dupe. A famous example is in Molière's *Tartuffe* (1664), in which a woman pretends to be attracted to the ultra-religious Tartuffe in order to show her husband that Tartuffe is a lecherous con-man. (We will discuss Molière more fully in Chapter 6.)

Why were so many plays across Europe metatheatrical during this time? Metatheatrical techniques are available to all playwrights in every era, and one can find examples throughout theatre history. Yet only in a few eras has it been so frequent. The richest periods are those spanning roughly 1575–1675, and the period from around 1920 to now (although different metatheatrical techniques were often used). Perhaps these periods indicate no more than a passing fad — or perhaps there are deeper explanations about what makes metatheatricality exceptionally valuable during a time period. Given that people in the sixteenth and seventeenth centuries were wrestling with or even fighting over urgent questions about God, nature, thought, and knowledge, one suspects that large social and cultural forces had to be in play.

The years 1550–1650 saw numerous radical social changes – in political structures, economic systems, religious beliefs, and more. But as we have observed throughout this book, none of society's basic structures strikes so close to the inner workings of theatre as changes in communication practices. Theatre is, after all, a form of communication, so it makes sense that when printing became the dominant mode of communication, theatre would be strongly affected. It took generations for printing to become dominant, and in fact its dominance was never a foregone conclusion – China and Korea had forms of printing, but printing didn't become dominant there in the way it did in Europe. For any number of reasons the older mode of communication may remain dominant, and it can take many years before a new mode of communication has a significant cultural impact, because people must explore and absorb its possibilities (they may, for example, stop exploring its possibilities early, or never stop at all). In the case of the printing press, however, much evidence indicates that roughly 1550–1650 was the period when printing became culturally dominant in most European countries.

As we have seen, not long after the printing press became commonplace, it made the Protestant Reformation possible. Just a few decades later, a print-based scientific revolution unleashed new ideas about the world, particularly in such fields as astronomy, mechanics, mathematics, human physiology, and scientific methodology. Thus, between the Middle Ages and the early modern era, there was a radical shift in ideas about God and nature. In fact, both the old and the new ideas were active at the same time. Not only did different groups of people perceive things in different ways, but even single individuals could think about religion one way but understand nature in another, or see both perspectives on these subjects.

THINKING THROUGH THEATRE HISTORIES

Critical realism

When culture and society change, the natural question should be, why? Why was there a change, why did the change occur during one time span rather than another, and why was the change from *A* to *B* rather than *A* to *D*? Was something happening during the sixteenth and seventeenth centuries that made metatheatricality so frequent?

Critical realist historians approach these issues in a particular way. Critical realism is a movement in philosophy which in its current form began in the work of Roy Bhaskar (1944–2014) during the late 1970s. Since then it has attracted scholars in such diverse fields as philosophy of science, ethics, and especially the social sciences. (The phrase "critical realism" has also been used in entirely different fields, such as theology and aesthetics.) Two of critical realism's tenets are particularly important here. First, what is real isn't limited to what we can perceive (whether directly through our senses or through instruments such as a radio telescope): instead, something is real if it has the power to cause changes. That includes social relationships and thoughts, even though they aren't physical. Second, according to critical realism, reality is stratified. Most people are acquainted with this notion in the natural sciences: atoms can combine to form molecules, certain molecules create life, living beings evolved to a point where some animals can walk on land, and so forth.

According to critical realism, society is stratified too. It identifies three main "planes." One plane consists of social structures, such as the economic system. The second consists of agents, that is, people acting within society. Finally, there are discourses, a term encompassing ideas, values, words, images, and sounds. Society can't be boiled down to just one of these layers: all three are necessary, because history consists of their development and interplay. Distinguishing and untangling these planes helps to provide extensive explanations for historical events. In practice, many historians follow this approach, even if they are unaware of critical realism; but the philosophy establishes the theory behind the practice.

This case study uses critical realism to explore three questions about metatheatricality. One is how to explain why, even though metatheatrical techniques are always available, they're heavily used during some times, much less so in others. Next, since metatheatricality is particularly common during only certain eras, what is it doing then – what "cultural work" does it accomplish – that isn't as urgent in other periods? Last, there must be a reason why metatheatrical techniques are particularly effective for this work, otherwise they wouldn't be employed. Such questions concern complex, multi-leveled interactions and changes in society.

Consequently knowledge itself became a crucial issue, full of questions: questions about whether there can be any certainty or truth, and if so, what form it would take; questions about who has (or should have) knowledge; questions about whether the medieval or the early modern approach to knowledge is correct, or if neither one of them is; and many more. An example of the struggle can be seen in Descartes' effort to achieve absolute certainty, leading to his aphorism, "I think, therefore I am": to Descartes, an individual's own consciousness and self-awareness is all that someone can be categorically sure about. In theatre, doubts about knowledge appeared in the neoclassicists' belief that the lower classes could understand neither multiple plots and locations, nor plots that cover more than a day – a belief that in actuality shaped playwrights' ideas of what upper-class audiences could understand.

But there is only one way people can think about problems in thought and knowledge: in thought and knowledge themselves. In other words, during a crisis in knowledge, thought has to be self-consciously reflexive, so that people are aware that they are thinking through problems of thought through the medium of thought itself. "Thought," in this case, means any kind of intellectual activity, be it philosophy, religion, fiction, painting, dance, or theatre. The need for reflexivity is one reason behind the explosion of metatheatricality at the moment when print culture was becoming dominant.

There is another reason, too, but in order to understand it we need to consider some things about society. Imagine that you want to be an actor, and start auditioning for roles. When the economy is good, there may be lots of roles to audition for; but when the economy is poor, there may not be so many. Also, you may find yourself often being considered for certain kinds of roles, but not others. You might be a "character actor," a "romantic lead," a "heavy," or some other standard type, sometimes whether you like it or not. So you develop your career dealing with the economics of theatre on the one hand, and on the other, people's ideas about you and about what theatre should be.

The situation for actors is also true for every other person, no matter their age, sex, ethnicity, social class, or any other category. There is an important philosophical point here: people necessarily live within certain social preconditions for their actions. Some of these preconditions consist of the economy, political systems, gender-based social relationships, race relations, and so forth: generically, we refer to them as social structures. Other preconditions consist of ideas, beliefs, values, images, and the like that circulate in society through its various communications media; generically, these are called discourses. And then there are people themselves, managing their lives amid these circumstances. These are the three planes of society noted in the "Thinking through theatre histories" box. According to this view of society, people are social agents, who attempt to achieve their goals under the preconditions of whatever social structures and discourses surround them – and sometimes, in the process of achieving their goals, social agents change the surrounding social structures and discourses.

Theatre, from this perspective, is very similar to society. On the one hand there is the actor/audience relationship, which is shaped by the physical space of the performance, the existence or absence of an imaginary "fourth wall" preventing the actors from addressing the audience, and various other factors. This is theatre's structural level. On the other hand, there is either a script, a scenario, or at least a set of improvised character types or situation ideas that actors come up with while performing. These make up theatre's discursive level. The actor (the agent producing performance) is situated between these two elements. Theatre is actually more complicated still, because characters ("virtual" agents) act within their *own* (fictive) structural and discursive preconditions. Because the constituents of theatrical performance are so similar to what constitutes society, theatre can be described as a model of social agency.

Modes of communication such as printing are among society's structures. When communication structures change, however, it becomes deeply unclear what it means to take action in the world and to be situated in society – not only is knowledge thrown into crisis, but agency is too. New ways of thinking arise. In medieval society, people understood themselves as occupying a position along a vertical Great Chain of Being, which placed their existence and action in relationship with God, then to the monarch, the clergy, and continuing on down to lords of the manor, peasants, and serfs. But print culture brought a reorientation: relationships strictly among humans started to be foremost. Religious plays such as the mystery cycles and moralities were replaced by intrigues of murder, power, and romance. Hamlet struggles over the questions of whether, how, and when to act, and when he ponders whether to take his own life, what stops him is the fear of death: if hell is meant, it's only in the background.

Theatre, which is a model of social agency, is a vital arena in which to wrestle with the nature of social agency. That entails reflexivity about agency. But we can engage in reflexivity not just as individuals: we can also do it as a group, in a social or collective manner. That is what plays-within-plays achieve: a group of people watch a group of fictional people in a play, who watch another fictional group of people in a play. Often the inner play is a poorer form of theatre, for example, dumb shows (silent plays) like the ones in *The Spanish Tragedy* and *Hamlet*, the puppets in *Bartholomew Fair*, and clumsy performances like the one by the "rude mechanicals" in *A Midsummer Night's Dream*. The outer play usually presents a superior kind of social agency. Some of the other metatheatrical techniques mentioned earlier can also accomplish reflexivity about agency, but plays-within-plays present the clearest, most forthright approach.

According to this argument, then, behind the extraordinary increase in metatheatricality in Western drama around the year 1600 were the radical shifts brought about by print culture. Those shifts created a crisis in how to define knowledge and agency. Theatre's connections to communication practices and its multilayered structure made it an especially dynamic medium for embodying and working through this crisis through reflection, which took the form of metatheatricality.

Key references

Nellhaus, T. (2010) *Theatre, Communication, Critical Realism*, New York: Palgrave Macmillan.

SUMMARY

Western Europe in the late 1500s and early 1600s experienced enormous social transformations and upheavals. One of the most important changes was in communication. The printing press made books far more available and far less expensive than they were before. As a result, people of moderate means could afford to purchase Bibles in the vernacular for their religious practices. Reading itself altered, and fostered a new sense of interior selfhood, seen most clearly in the new Protestantism, but also evident in secular areas, such as the natural sciences and philosophy.

Printing also disseminated classical works, which became the foundation for most education. As a result, new plays were often written on classical models. In England, Spain, and France, university-educated playwrights began writing for professionals in the popular theatre. Simultaneously, acting troupes produced major writers, and because even grammar schools had a humanist curriculum, they too were influenced by the classics. Print culture affected playwriting in much the way it altered other areas of secular culture: dramatic characters became less like "types" and more like individuals, and plots focused on human activities, not on salvation. Playwrights sought to please a popular audience, but kept an eye on the tastes of their substantial aristocratic audience as well.

In England and Spain, playwrights often alluded to classical literature, and Roman drama frequently inspired their own plots. In France, humanism played an even deeper role, eventually pushing the popular tradition almost to the sidelines. The views of Aristotle and Horace were transformed (with considerable distortion) into strict neoclassical rules. Backed by the increasingly powerful French state, neoclassicism came to dominate playwriting throughout the continent for nearly two centuries. That story continues in the next chapter.

★

CHAPTER 6

Theatres of absolutism, 1600–1770

Bruce McConachie
Contributor: Tobin Nellhaus

As we will see in this chapter, neoclassicism was linked to the political ideology of absolutism, as well as to print culture, as noted in Chapter 5. Those who believed in absolutism advanced the new idea that the rightful monarch must monopolize the rule of law and the use of force within the lands that he (or she) controlled. This chapter will examine the rise of absolutism in Europe during the 1600s, its immense power on the European continent in the 1700s, and the kinds of theatrical entertainments that supporters of absolutism enjoyed. By the mid-eighteenth century, absolutism flourished throughout continental Europe. For more than 150 years, until the 1770s, the aristocracy and most of the rich merchants and professionals followed European monarchs and their courts in applauding festive entertainments, masques, operas, and finally neoclassical plays in court theatres and public playhouses. With few exceptions, these performances legitimated the values and beliefs of absolutism.

Nonetheless, as we will see, there were significant tensions between neoclassical entertainments and two other kinds of performances. The splendors and enchantments of Baroque opera regularly overwhelmed the rational strictures of neoclassicism in performances at court until the early 1700s. And carnivalesque entertainment, its low delights more popular in fairground theatres than in aristocratic playhouses, also subverted the didactic claims of neoclassicism. In the next chapter, we will discuss a third challenge to neoclassical forms and ideas – the sentimental theatre of the eighteenth century. Partly in response to these alternatives, neoclassicism became so intertwined with the ideology and institutions of absolutism by the 1770s that its theatrical genres would not survive the French Revolution of 1789, which beheaded the French king and threatened absolute monarchies throughout Europe.

The rise of absolutism

To some observers at the time, absolutism was a necessary response to a widespread political and ideological crisis during the early modern period of European history. From medieval times through the mid-1600s, several overlapping and competing centers of power co-existed within most countries in Europe. Kings and queens might assert their right to rule their kingdoms, but their actual powers were typically limited by local customs, traditional medieval privileges, strong regional noblemen, and occasionally by powerful churchmen. Most kingdoms (and dukedoms and church states) in Europe were little more than bundles of territories held together by allegiance to a ruler. This arrangement had worked well enough before 1500, but it came under pressure and sometimes fell apart during the religious wars caused by the Protestant Reformation, the economic shift from medieval guilds and serfdom to early capitalism, and political turmoil in Europe from the mid-sixteenth to the mid-seventeenth century. Rebellions marked the reigns of Henry VIII and Elizabeth I in England, where a Puritan revolution finally ended in civil war. When the French king tried to exert more direct control in the provinces, French noblemen rebelled twice against the crown in the 1640s and 1650s, even calling in Spanish troops to support them. In the present areas of Germany, Poland, and Scandinavia, the Thirty Years' War, fought mostly among Protestant and Catholic rulers, devastated populations, towns, and regional economies. It took much of northern and central Europe another 80 years to recover after the peace treaty of 1648, retarding the growth of theatre and other arts until the 1720s.

By the 1620s, many sovereigns and their ministers recognized that monarchy needed a firmer base of recognized authority to survive and flourish. The Catholic Church, which had mounted a Counter-Reformation (1545–1648) to fight the rise of Protestantism in northern Europe, provided a traditional source of legitimation by reviving the ideology of the divine right of kings. According to the Vatican, Catholic kings aligned with the teachings of Rome provided their subjects with a beneficent and infallible source of justice. Catholicism strengthened absolutist rule in Spain and Portugal and also aided the Austrian Empire. Cardinal Richelieu, who spoke for the French monarchy in the 1620s and 1630s, linked the crown to the power of the Catholic Church and paved the way for the absolutism of Louis XIV later in the century. Although Protestantism had made inroads in France, the Vatican could rejoice that Richelieu's policies had won another Counter-Reformation victory for Rome.

Among Protestants, the English political philosopher Thomas Hobbes (1588–1679) provided one of the best justifications for centralizing all power in the hands of the crown in his 1651 book, *Leviathan*. Hobbes pointed to recent history and the danger of continuous anarchy unless state power were vested in a centralized government that could override all customs, traditional immunities, and even the authority of what some churchmen might claim as the will of God. His treatise provided part of the justification for the Restoration, so called because it restored the institution of monarchy to England (in 1660) after the Commonwealth period of the Civil War. The ideas of Hobbes were influential, as well, in Protestant Scandinavia and northern Germany.

Absolutism reached its zenith in France during the reign of Louis XIV (1643–1715) and became the model (and the envy) of other monarchs in Europe. King Louis reputedly boasted, "*L'etat, c'est moi*" ("I am the state") and he set about elevating himself as the symbol and embodiment of France. Using the power of print, the king's ministers extended centralized rule into the French provinces through standardized weights and measures, new tax codes, and a disciplined royal army. Until the late seventeenth century, raising an army had been left to local noblemen, but Louis excluded the fractious aristocracy from that traditional right, made officers dependent on his government, and effectively mobilized the army as an extension of the state. To house his much enlarged civilian government and to bind provincial noble families

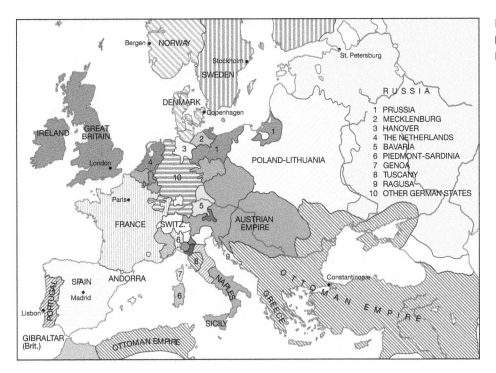

Figure 6.1

Political map of Europe, c.1730.

more closely to himself, Louis built a new city in the village of Versailles, about ten miles from Paris. The centerpiece of Versailles was the king's new palace, intended to embody the grandeur of his reign through neoclassical façades, extensive gardens, Baroque statuary and paintings, and the sheer size and extravagance of its public spaces and ballrooms. While holding court at Versailles, Louis XIV divided his daily routines into a series of ritualized acts to elevate his royal body and keep his noblemen envious of each other's privileges; one gentleman, for example, was accorded the honor of holding the right sleeve of the king's nightshirt as he took it off in the morning. The king's propagandists for absolutism advanced the Catholic belief that kings were God's representatives on earth. But they also wrote and preached that royal power, though necessarily absolute, was inevitably reasonable and just, because the king embodied God's will as well as his symbolic power. Because the French monarchy was the most powerful and influential in Europe from the mid-1600s through the 1770s, much of this chapter will center on French political and theatrical practices.

Recognizing that the theatre could influence rebellious aristocrats and wealthy merchants in their kingdoms, absolute monarchs usually sought to control theatrical expression. They used patronage, monopolistic regulations, state censorship, and sometimes personal interference to support and shape the kinds of theatre that would legitimate their regimes. In addition to paying directly for performances at court, some absolute monarchs provided subsidies to their favorite theatrical companies to finance their public performances. Absolutist governments also granted monopolies to some companies, giving them exclusive rights for the production of certain kinds of theatre; Louis XIV's bureaucrats, for example, restricted operatic, dramatic, and *commedia dell'arte* performances to three different companies and attempted to prohibit other troupes from producing these genres. Finally, believing these restrictions were not sufficient,

European absolutists also censored their regulated theatres. Companies performing dramatic theatre had to submit their scripts for approval and even operatic and *commedia* troupes performed their shows under the pricked-up ears and watchful eyes of censors, who attended to make sure that their pieces offered no offense to the crown. Nonetheless, as we will see, some approved authors managed to suggest subversive ideas and occasionally entire companies found ways to effectively challenge the monopolistic practices of absolutist regimes.

Entertainments at court

Despite the print-based victory of neoclassicism, most cultured opinion by the 1650s exempted monarchs and their court entertainments from neoclassical standards. This was a major tension in the theatre of absolutism. As we have seen, Louis XIV and other absolute monarchs endorsed neoclassicism – even to the point of censoring artists and theatres that did not meet its rigorous standards. Nonetheless, their major forms of entertainment at court mostly avoided its strictures. For their sumptuous performances, many royals, especially those in the Catholic courts of southern Europe, preferred the **Baroque aesthetic** of playfulness, allegory, metamorphosis, power, and sensuality to the rules of neoclassicism. Despite the extravagant and even voluptuous nature of much Baroque visual art, architecture, and performance, the Catholic Church was one of the most enthusiastic supporters of the Baroque, seeing in its emotional and public appeal a possible counter to the ascetic and private claims of Protestantism. After 1600, the Vatican paid many painters, sculptors, and architects to immerse Rome in the new Baroque style and it sponsored the operas of Claudio Monteverdi (1567–1643), whose lush music initiated Baroque opera with *Orfeo* in 1607.

Baroque aesthetics returned court life to the centrality of visual and oral culture that had predominated in Europe before the rise of print and the new standard of verisimilitude. Although our last chapter focused on the effects of print culture on European theatre from 1550 to 1650, it is important to emphasize that earlier forms of communication continued to instruct and delight court spectators during these years. Baroque performances borrowed from several of these traditions to flourish in absolutist courts during the 1600s and continued to undercut state-sanctioned neoclassicism into the 1700s. Our discussion of Baroque theatre for the first half of this chapter culminates in a study of the public career of Sor Juana Inés de la Cruz, who was writing Golden Age-style dramas inflected by Baroque playfulness in Spanish Mexico in the 1680s.

Typically, when a new medium of communication is introduced and gains cultural power, the old media, though generally less influential, continue to shape many cultural practices, often gaining new niches of authority. This was the case with Baroque spectacles at court, especially performances of seventeenth-century opera. Certainly the technologies of perspective scenery and the libretti and music for the new operas benefited from print culture; both circulated much more widely in print than would have been possible in a culture that rested on copying manuscripts. But the visual tropes and transformations that linked the power of a king or queen to the magnificence of a Christian God depended on a mode of visual allegory that derived from the manuscript cultures of ancient empires and can be easily traced from Roman times to the courts of medieval Christianity. Music, important to all cultures but diminished in the theatre with the rise of print, reasserted its centrality in the festivals and masques presented at court. As we will see, the values of playfulness and sensuality that the rules of rationalist, neoclassical thinking had shunted to the wings moved center stage in the spectacular performances of Baroque opera after 1650.

Indeed, similar kinds of delights had been a part of court-sponsored festive entertainments in Europe since the late medieval period and into the Renaissance. In addition to weddings and other dynastic events, late medieval rulers celebrated visits of foreign dignitaries, the signing of peace treaties, and the feast days of particular saints with dances, games, and performances throughout their capital cities. Medieval towns returned the favor, staging huge welcoming ceremonies when the monarch paid them a visit. Renaissance innovations in Italy, however, began moving European court entertainments from late medieval practices towards the Baroque era. Florentine artist and engineer Leonardo da Vinci (1452–1519), for instance, designed a glittering revolving stage that featured moving planets, fabulous beasts, and Roman gods and goddesses to welcome a new duchess to the court of Milan as part of a wedding ceremony in 1490. Called the *Festa del Paradiso*, the spectacle used visual symbols, poetry, and song to suggest that the rulers of Milan descended from a classical version of paradise. Da Vinci's *Festa* mixed pagan with Christian symbols and emphasized lavish display.

As in Milan, most pre-Baroque festivals opened the court to the populace of the city. The counts, dukes, and others who sponsored these events usually took an active part in several of the performances, demonstrating the stability and justice of their rule by the symbolic roles they played, as well as by their clothing, horsemanship, and retinue. In the largest of these festivals, the celebrations spread throughout the town, temporarily transforming its squares, churches, and palaces into festive spaces. Although usually centered on the ruler-sponsor, Renaissance festivals were public in the sense that they were accessible to most of the populace and their performances embodied mythic symbols and social relations that all understood to be necessary for the welfare of the whole.

After 1500, however, these festivals began to move indoors, into ducal and royal palaces that were off limits to the populace. Because European rulers had to impress a fractious aristocracy with their power, the audience for court festivities gradually changed from the populace as a whole to the nobility living at court. The shift to indoor spectacles also led court designers to turn increasingly to the wonders of Italianate perspective scenery in order to glorify the duke or monarch. By the middle of the century, scenographer Sebastiano Serlio (1475–1554) had designed several Italian court entertainments in large palace ballrooms and banquet halls. When Serlio depicted a series of tragic, comic, and pastoral stage settings using perspective in his *Architettura* (1545), this type of scenery had already been in use for performances at Italian courts for some years. To realize Serlio's conventional designs in production required a painter and carpenter to construct and hang a painted backdrop at the rear of the playing space and flank the drop with three sets of angled wings, each with two painted sides that receded symmetrically from the front of the stage (Figure 6.2). To contribute to the perspective effect, the upstage floor was sharply raked (sloped upward toward the backdrop). The actors had to perform far downstage on the level flooring, because if they performed within the upstage scenery, their bodies would appear out of proportion to the converging lines of perspective and spoil the illusion.

When the Teatro Olimpico (mentioned in Chapter 4) was opened in 1585, it integrated perspective scenery into its architecture. Its primary architect, Andrea Palladio (1518–1580), based much of his design on the architectural drawings of the Roman writer Vitruvius

Figure 6.2

The setting for a comic scene by Sebastiano Serlio, from his *De Architettura*, 1569 edition.

Courtesy Lilly Library, Indiana University, Bloomington, Indiana.

(first century BCE), from whom Palladio borrowed the look of the *scenae frons* from the Roman theatre (see Chapter 2) for the Olimpico's scenic façade. After Palladio's death, architect Vincenzo Scamozzi (1552–1616) completed the building's design. Behind each of the five entrances on the façade and two more on either end of the stage, Scamozzi placed perspective scenery. In effect, Palladio and Scamozzi had merged an ancient, Vitruvian design with the Renaissance innovation of perspective painting. However, this approach to putting perspective on stage was not pursued further; Serlio's approach remained predominant.

By the 1610s, court entertainers and musicians in Paris were using modified versions of Serlio's designs to mount lavish **ballet** spectacles – amateur performances featuring the king and court as powerful mythological and allegorical figures. From 1605 until 1640, Inigo Jones (1573–1652) designed Serlian scenery for the court masques of English kings, first for James I, then Charles I – entertainments similar to the expensive ballet spectacles in France. In these court masques, Jones typically positioned the king as the pivot around which the costumed courtiers danced (Figure 6.3). Jones convinced Charles I to convert two rooms at his court palace for masquing, an extravagance that angered the Puritans and helped to lead to the overthrow of the king and the English Civil War in 1642. Court entertainments in the Catholic countries of Europe, however, faced no such popular impediments and Baroque musical spectacles flourished in Madrid, Paris, and Vienna during the middle decades of the seventeenth century.

While royal families had continued to perform in many of the masques and ballet spectacles in London and Paris, they gradually withdrew from active participation in the festivities and into positions where they could appear as beneficent overlords to watch the performances of others. To ensure that the glorification of kingship continued to maintain its central focus, however, many Baroque court spectacles placed a symbolic representative of the monarch on stage. When Philip IV of Spain enjoyed *The Greatest Enchantment is Love* in 1635, he watched a symbol of himself as the protagonist of the entertainment. The musical extravaganza, penned by Golden Age playwright Calderón and produced by an Italian engineer, featured the temptation of Ulysses by the enchantress Circe, with characters and dramatic situations based on Homer's *Odyssey*. The lavish spectacle, intended to celebrate a saint and honor the opening of the king's new pleasure palace, placed ship-wrecks, triumphal chariots, and volcanic destruction on an island in the middle of a small lake within a garden of the new palace. From their seats on gondolas, the court could watch the king enjoy the show or attend to the songs and actions of his representative (Ulysses, in this case) in the entertainment.

Baroque aesthetics also influenced art and architecture in the Americas. As on the European continent, where the expansive visual culture of the Baroque allowed for the mixing of Spanish and Moorish elements, so in the Americas did artists mingle Spanish and Native American elements – not only in art and architecture, but also in music, theatre, and court entertainments. Among the American playwrights of this period, perhaps the most Baroque in sensibility was the Mexican nun Sor Juana Inés de la Cruz (1648/51–1695). She was known for her voracious intellectual appetite, unusual for a woman of her time – a matter the absolutist Mexican Church came to view with great suspicion. But before she laid down her pen for the last time, these appetites found outlets in virtually every literary form, including drama.

Figure 6.3

Costume designed by Inigo Jones for *The Masque of Queens* (1609), an antimasque written by Ben Jonson to celebrate heroic women. Intended to turn social norms upside down, antimasques often involved suggestions of cross-gender dressing. In this case, the costuming and the dialogue praise the female character of Penthesilia, partly dressed as a male warrior, for her masculine strength and virtue.

Source: © AKG-images, London.

CASE STUDY: Sor Juana Inés de la Cruz and the perils of print culture in New Spain

Tamara Underiner

Hardly anything about Sor Juana Inés de la Cruz's life was conventional, and much of it was controversial. Born in the mid-seventeenth century as Juana Inés de Asbaje y Ramírez de Santillana to an unwed mother and self-educated in the classics she found in her grandfather's library (at a time when only boys received formal education), by the time she was 16 she was as famous at the New Spanish court for her learning as for her beauty. Four years later, she took the vows of a Catholic nun in order to pursue a life of the mind – a profession impossible for married women in her day. (It is by her religious name, Sor Juana Inés de la Cruz – "Sister Juana Inés of the Cross" – that she is known.) While at the convent of San Jerónimo, she produced hundreds of written works in all literary genres, and wrote numerous philosophical,

Figure 6.4

Sor Juana Inés de la Cruz in 1666 as a lady-in-waiting for the viceregal court in Mexico City (left), and later in life as a nun in the Order of San Jerónimo (right).

Left: *Juana de Asbaje*, *c*.1666, signed J. Sánchez. © The Art Archive/Alamy Stock Photo. Right: *Portrait of Sor Juana Inés de la Cruz* by Miguel Cabrera, *c*.1750 (Museo Nacional de Historia, Castillo de Chapultepec, Mexico).

theological, and scientific essays. She earned a reputation for independent thought, rooted solidly in her understanding of canonical texts. Her cleverness with language and her fearlessness in the face of textual and religious authority both impressed and threatened her Church superiors, who eventually worked to silence her.

Sor Juana's work is important for students of theatre history in two ways. First, her plays are late examples of Spanish Golden Age and Baroque drama. Although she herself never went to Spain, she was familiar with the conventions of that form, and her works are notable for their gendered inversions of those conventions, as well as for her openness to incorporating elements of non-Spanish culture into her work. Second, she worked under what many scholars refer to as "the shadow of the Inquisition," an institution that, in Spain and its colonies, forged its own particular brand of absolutist authority. The central paradox of her life, which has perplexed scholars for more than 300 years, was her apparent capitulation to that authority when she was at the height of her fame and powers. This surrender was the culmination of a number of events that had caught Sor Juana up in a complex web of oral, written, and print culture.

Sor Juana's dramaturgy

For theatre history, Sor Juana's output is relatively small – three *autos sacramentales*, three *comedias* (two co-authored), and numerous short plays, some devotional, some farcical. Most of these were staged, if they were staged at all, behind convent walls or for the viceregal court in Mexico City. Nevertheless, her work for the stage, even if never realized on one, is noteworthy for its theatrical potential as well as its philosophical qualities. In Chapter 3 we briefly discussed Sor Juana's Corpus Christi *auto*, *The Divine Narcissus*, and its *loa* (one-act prologue, *c.*1688). Meant for performance in the court at Madrid, both play and *loa* combine the depth of medieval allegory with the height of the Baroque court masques described in this chapter. The *loa*, for example, opens with Native American song and dances in honor of the God of the Seeds. It features four elaborately costumed characters: the European Zeal and Religion and the Mexican Occident and America, who debate finer points of Christian and native theology; the characterization of Zeal as a blustering Spanish soldier suggests the playwright's opinion on the merits of force in the matter of religious conversion. The play proper reconfigures the Narcissus myth, with Christ as Narcissus falling in love with his own image in Human Nature, dying for that love and being resurrected in the sacraments; Echo is a fallen angel, jealous of that love. In *loa* and play together, Sor Juana figuratively aligns Christ with both the pagan Greek figure of Narcissus and the heathen American God of the Seeds – no small feat artistically, philosophically, and theologically. At the same time, she raises a subtle question about the actual success of the Spanish religious conquest of indigenous Americans.

If the subject of religious conversion sounds appropriately pious for a nun to have undertaken in an *auto sacramental*, her secular *comedias* were another matter entirely. Sor Juana was familiar with the conventions of the "cape and sword" plays of the Spanish Golden Age, which both circulated in print in Mexico and were staged at court. (In fact, both *The Divine Narcissus* and her most famous *comedia* seem to be directly inspired by Calderón's works.) But in her hands, the convention was transformed from *capa y espada* into what Mexican dramatist and scholar Guillermo Schmidhuber calls "*falda y empeño*" ("petticoats and perseverance"), wherein the perspectives of female protagonists are privileged, as are their "efforts to bettering the condition of women as thinking and social beings" (2000: ix).

The first *comedia* credited to her was actually begun by the Spanish Golden Age dramatist Agustín de Salazar y Torres to celebrate the birthday of the queen of Spain in 1676, but he died before it was completed. Schmidhuber has found evidence that it was Sor Juana who polished and completed the play. It is based on characters from the *Tragicomedy of Calisto and Melibea* by Fernando de Rojas, but whereas in the original Celestina (a woman versed in the arts of love) is murdered and the true lovers die, in this version Celestina survives, and the play ends with a triple marriage – an ending engineered through the cleverness of Celestina and, presumably, Sor Juana herself. Her third *comedia* was also co-authored, this time with the Mexican lawyer and intellectual Juan de Guevara: *Love is the Greater Labyrinth* (written in 1689, first published in 1692). It was an adaptation of the Greek tale of the Labyrinth of Crete, inspired by her reading of Ovid's *Metamorphoses*. Sor Juana was responsible for the first and third acts, while Guevara wrote the second. It features the metatheatricality discussed in Chapter 5, as well as a hint of Sor Juana's autobiography in the complex character of Ariadna.

But it is Sor Juana's solo-authored *comedia* that is best known among theatre scholars and producers, for it is still being written about and staged: *Los empeños de una casa*, translated literally as *Pawns of a House*, and more figuratively as *House of Trials* or *House of Desires*. It appears to be a take-off of or response to Calderón's *Los empeños de un acaso* (*Determinations of a Chance Happening, c.*1631).

Like the best of the Golden Age dramas, Sor Juana's features the familiar devices of mistaken identity, love triangles, and plenty of swordfighting, by candlelight. The low light of the candles serves at first to mask, and then reveal, a clever plot twist: the person the rivals are fighting over is not the beautiful Doña Leonor, but the clownish manservant Castaño, dressed in her clothes. The men are the "pawns" of the title, masterfully manipulated by the mistress of the house, Doña Ana, for the benefit of Leonor. The language of the scene is full of *double entendres* meant for the pleasure of the knowing audience. It is not clear who actually acted these parts in the original production, but had it been staged in Spain, it would have presented a spectacle of mistaken same-sex desire that reversed the usual set-up for cross-dressing on the Spanish stage, where normally it was actresses who dressed as young men in order to move freely through the world of the play. Scholar Julie Greer Johnson suggests that in *Los empeños de una casa*, Sor Juana argues theatrically that "a woman is suited to other social and cultural roles than the ones she currently occupied, and she demonstrates this by testing, transgressing, and transforming the skewed, conventional spatial boundaries on stage" (Johnson 2001).

Sor Juana herself was a transgressor of social norms – cloistered as a good nun should be, but working as a public intellectual by virtue of her writings. Her relations with her superiors were often fraught, but for a time she enjoyed the protection of the viceregals for whom she wrote this play: the Marquis of la Laguna and his wife María Luisa, countess of Paredes, to whom Sor Juana also addressed many poems of gratitude, admiration, and love. During their term in New Spain (between 1680 and 1688), Sor Juana produced the majority of her work, and they were responsible for its eventual publication in Spain – two volumes of her collected works during her lifetime, and one after her death, as well as numerous individual works, some of which circulated in Mexico as well. (The strict censorship of books in New Spain would have made their publication there impossible, but copies found their way to the Americas with Spanish travelers.) Under the protection of the viceregals, she was relatively safe from the Inquisition in New Spain. When they left for Spain in 1688, she came under the increasing scrutiny of Church authorities at home. Dorothy Schons (1949) has suggested that one of her "crimes" was that she was a dramatist at all – let alone a published one who happened to be not just a woman, but a nun – in a period when Mexico City was ruled by an archbishop who did his best to prevent the publishing and staging of theatrical works in Mexico.

A sermon, two letters, and a famous Reply

The story of the end of Sor Juana's life and career revolves around tensions between oral, written, and print cultures. In 1690, at the request of her friend, the Bishop of Puebla, Sor Juana hand-wrote a private letter formalizing comments she had made in conversation with him, about an oral sermon delivered at the Portuguese court and published some 40 years earlier by a Portuguese Jesuit priest. Without her knowledge or permission, she later claimed, the bishop transcribed and printed her letter as a pamphlet entitled *Carta Atenagorica* (*Letter Worthy of Athena*), introducing it with a letter of his own under the feminine pseudonym "Sor Filotea de la Cruz." The bishop's intentions in printing the letter were, ostensibly, to acknowledge Sor Juana's intellectual gifts in a public way. But hiding behind his pseudonym, he actually spent much of his own letter warning her of the dangers to her soul, as a woman, for pursuing humanist learning, and urged her to focus more on the study of religious works in a manner more befitting her vows of obedience as a devout nun.

Within three months, Sor Juana had composed a response, the famous *Respuesta a Sor Filotea*, or *Reply to Sor Filotea*, in which she defended the rights of women to knowledge and learning, in the process writing her own spiritual and intellectual biography. Hailed by some as the first feminist manifesto in the New World, it was not published until after she died (and then only in Spain). But her prior work had already brought her under the scrutiny of Church authorities in New Spain, and the Archbishop of Mexico began to issue public calls in support of "Sor Filotea's" position that Sor Juana abandon her worldly studies.

In 1693 she came under investigation by the Church authorities. In 1694, celebrating the twenty-fifth anniversary of her vows, she signed certain documents that may have been conventional acts of repentance, or may have been deliberate renouncements of her past life, made under pressure. While her motives may be opaque to us now, it is certainly true that, with the departure of her patrons, her public voice was effectively silenced, since it would have depended upon access to print. We know that she stopped writing in 1694, sold a great number of her books and scientific instruments to help the poor who had suffered through three years of floods, famine, and disease in Mexico City, and devoted her last year of life to nursing ailing nuns in the convent. In 1695, she herself succumbed to the plague that had swept the city.

Feminist scholars have long appreciated the sophistication of Sor Juana's rhetorical strategies in negotiating the various levels of Church and civic power with which she regularly had to contend. As a result, it is difficult to interpret the events of her final year: was she forced by these authorities to abandon all she had once valued, or did she do so of her own choice? Perhaps a clue is in her "Reply":

> But in truth, my Lady, what can we women know, save philosophies of the kitchen? It was well put by Lupercio Leonardo [*sic*] that one can philosophize quite well while preparing supper. I often say, when I make these little observations, "Had Aristotle cooked he would have written a great deal more." And so to go on with the mode of my cogitations: I declare that all this is so continual in me that I have no need of books.
>
> (De la Cruz 1999: 75)

Not content merely to argue for women's place at the table of learning, Sor Juana suggests that Aristotle himself could have learned and written more had he ventured into the kitchen, that primal domain of women. In this context of her life and work, her claim now to "have no need of books" is a complex statement indeed. For it can be argued that her life and career were both made possible and undone by print culture itself, in a period of religious absolutism.

Key references

Bemberg, M.L. (2003 DVD, dir.) *I, the Worst of All/Yo, la peor de todas*, First Run Features.

De la Cruz, J. (1997a) *Poems, Protest, and a Dream*, trans. M.S. Peden, New York: Penguin Books.

De la Cruz, J. (1997b) *House of Trials/Los empeños de una casa*, trans. D. Pasto, New York and Oxford: Peter Lang Press.

De la Cruz, J. (1998) *The Divine Narcissus/El divino Narcisso*, trans. P.A. Peters, Albuquerque: University of New Mexico Press.

De la Cruz, J. (1999) *The Answer/La Respuesta*, 2nd edn, trans. E. Arenal and A. Powell, New York: Feminist Press.

De la Cruz, J. (2005a) *House of Desires/Los empeños de una casa*, trans. C. Boyle, London: Oberon Books.

De la Cruz, J. (2005b) *Los empeños de una casa/Pawns of a House*, trans. M. McGaha, Tempe, AZ: Bilingual Review Press.

Johnson, J.G.(2001) "Engendered Theatrical Space and the Colonial Woman in Sor Juana's *Los empeños de una casa*," *Ciberletras* 5 (August). Online. Available HTTP:<http://www.lehman.cuny.edu/ciberletras/v05/johnson.html> (accessed Dec. 5, 2015).

Merrim, S. (1999) *Feminist Perspectives on Sor Juana Inés de la Cruz*, Detroit: Wayne State University Press.

Paz, O. (1990) *Sor Juana: or, The Traps of Faith*, trans. M.S. Peden, Cambridge, MA: Belknap Press.

Schmidhuber de la Mora, G. (2000) *The Three Secular Plays of Sor Juana Inés de la Cruz*, trans. S. Thacker, Lexington: University Press of Kentucky.

Schons, D. (1949) *Book Censorship in New Spain*, Austin: University of Texas.

Realizing absolutism in stage design

Writing late in the Baroque era, Sor Juana intended her plays for a proscenium stage. The proscenium arch, a conventional feature of many theatres today, provides a formal barrier between the area for the spectators and the stage and backstage areas for the actors and technicians by providing two side walls and a horizontal wall that joins them above, creating an opening through which spectators may enjoy the stage action. Because court spectacles before 1640 generally involved scenery in a room used for other purposes, prosceniums were a late addition to the perspective stage. Serlio's angled wings, for example, usually stood alone on temporary platforms without a downstage proscenium to frame them. The move from temporary to architectural prosceniums began in 1587, when the ruler of Florence approved a permanent proscenium for his spectacle room at the Uffizi Palace. After that, as Baroque opera designers and librettists invented more opportunities for elaborate scenic display – such as lavish throne rooms that could be quickly transformed into a scene of pastoral bliss and Olympian gods perched in a cloud machine that gradually descended to the stage – they increasingly relied on permanent proscenium arches to hide and house the machinery that could produce these magical effects.

Theatre historians have examined several reasons for the gradual incorporation of proscenium arches into stage productions at court, among them the suggestiveness of printed illustrations. More quickly than on the stage, the organization of space on an illustrated page in a book shifted historically from the simultaneous representation of several images on a manuscript page to a unified image on a printed one that could take advantage of the discoveries of single-point perspective. Like printers, scenographers thought about space in graphic terms; they shaped the vision of the viewer through unity, symmetry, and the illusion of depth. By the 1540s, printers were using tall arches, modeled after the triumphal arches of Roman times, as a common motif to organize the title page in a book. And even when no printed symmetrical frame dominated the page, the sides of its paper created a visual frame that established every page as a quasi mini-proscenium. By the 1640s, literate Europeans had been looking for 100 years at the pages of books and pamphlets that organized their vision according to a framed perspective. How "natural," then, to expect that a proscenium arch framing perspective stage scenery should mirror this reality.

The proscenium arch formalized an aspect of the Baroque stage that linked the aesthetics of perspective scenery to absolutism. When Serlio and other designers drew and painted three-dimensional scenery on to two-dimensional flats, they needed to fix a vantage point in the auditorium to figure out the mathematics from which it would appear that the perspective on stage was correct. Soon after perspective was applied to scenery, designers began using the vantage point of the ruler, seated in the center of the auditorium (later, at the rear center), to organize the visual scene. That is, the designer figured out where in the auditorium the ruler's eyes would gaze on the scene and drew his perspective lines for painting the scenery from that single point toward the vanishing point. This meant that only one person seated in the auditorium had a "perfect" view of the scenery; from every other point, the painted perspective looked skewed. For those seated on the side, the perspective was completely awry. The implicit visual demand on the other spectators in the auditorium, of course, was to imagine how the scene looked from the ruler's point of view. This visual power play suited the political dynamics of ruling Italian families in northern Italy, where it was first introduced. As the proscenium arch and single-point perspective scenery spread from Italy to the rest of Europe, this practice also served absolutism at the royal courts of Spain, Austria, and France.

One reason for the relatively quick adaptation of proscenium and perspective staging was the success of the **chariot-and-pole system** of scene changing, invented by Giacomo Torelli (1608–1678), dubbed the Great Sorcerer for his scenic wizardry. Working in Venice, the center of operatic innovation in Europe, Torelli was hired in 1641 to design the stage machinery for the Teatro Novissimo, the only Venetian theatre at the time built solely for operatic production. Torelli got the idea for his new technology from the complex rigging in use by Venetian sailors on their ships. In brief, the chariot-and-pole system involves flat wings mounted on the downstage side of long poles, which pass through slots in the stage flooring to small two-wheeled wagons, or "chariots," that run on tracks under the stage. Through a series of ropes, pulleys, winches, and counterweights, all of the chariots under the stage – perhaps as many as ten on both sides for each pair of five wings – could be made to move simultaneously. As one flat moved into view, the flat behind or in front of it receded off stage. The counterweighted flats and drops were linked, as well, to painted borders hanging from the flies. Chariot-and-pole rigging could also include special upstage effects in perspectival miniature and the descents of deities on cloud machines from the heavens. Much as sailors could reorient the

Figure 6.5

Cut-away drawing by Gustaf Kull of the chariot-and-pole machinery for changing flats at the Drottningholm Court Theatre in Sweden. From Per Edstrom, "Stage Machinery," in Ove Hidemark et al. (1993), *Drottningholm Court Theatre*.

© Gustav Kull, Jr.

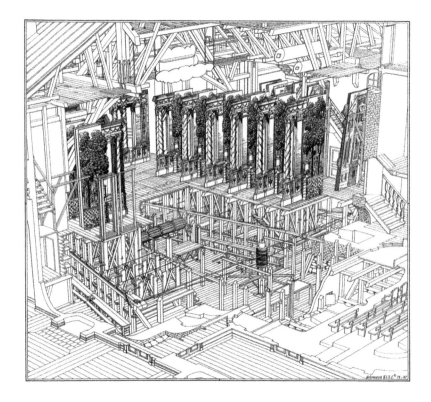

sails of a large vessel by turning a few master winches on board, so stagehands could effect a complete scenic transformation from one setting to another in less than a minute through hidden ropes, pulleys, and winches. Cut-away line drawings of Sweden's Drottningholm Court Theatre, built in 1774 and still in use today, provide a good illustration of the workings of the chariot-and-pole system (Figure 6.5).

In 1645, Cardinal Mazarin brought Torelli from Venice to Paris to transform the scenic and playing spaces of French court theatres into fully-rigged machines for the production of Baroque opera. Knowing the spectacular marvels that Torelli's accomplishments had facilitated for opera in Venice, Mazarin expected the Great Sorcerer's scenic wonders to glorify the new French king, Louis XIV, and to make French theatre the envy of absolutist Europe. Torelli remodeled two royal theatres in 1645 and 1646 and gradually won over the French court to the new mode of scene shifting and design (see Figure 6.6). By the early 1700s, court and public theatres throughout Europe were struggling to catch up with the French mode.

Among the successes of chariot-and-pole staging was the Baroque opera *Hercules in Love*, performed in 1662 for Louis XIV at the new Salle des Machines theatre, built especially to house single-point perspective scenery changed through Torelli's ropes, winches, chariots, and counterweights. Cardinal Mazarin had helped to orchestrate the defeat of those aristocrats who mounted uprisings against royal absolutism between 1648 and 1653. To celebrate this triumph of the king, his recent victories over the Spaniards in war, and his impending marriage to Maria Theresa of Austria, Mazarin spent several years organizing the production of *Hercules in Love* (Figure 6.7). The opera celebrated the suffering of a lustful hero (a stand-in for Louis), who

Figure 6.6
Giacomo Torelli's setting for Act II of Pierre Corneille's *Andromède* at the Petit-Bourbon Theatre, 1650, in which Torelli's chariot-and-pole scene-shifting machinery was used. Engraving by François Chauveau.
© Bibliothèque Nationale de France.

must sacrifice the love of his mistress for the good of the state. According to historian Kristiann Aercke, the court had no difficulty reading Mazarin's allegory as a congratulatory commentary on the well-known political and amatory machinations of the cardinal and the king (Aercke 1994: 165–220). By featuring the changeable qualities of nature through the spectacle of moving scenery – raging storms at sea, the fires of passion, and frequent interventions from classical gods – the production highlighted the changeable characteristics of the sovereign. Although several viewed the production of this six-hour opus as an artistic failure, Aercke argues that *Hercules in Love* helped to vivify Louis XIV's growing reputation as the Sun King, the embodiment of heavenly power and natural majesty.

The Baroque aesthetics of *Hercules in Love* massively contradicted the neoclassicism that French absolutists had embraced in the controversy over *Le Cid* just 25 years earlier. As noted in the last chapter, Cardinal Richelieu's new French Academy severely criticized Corneille's play on the basis of the neoclassical principles of the three unities, verisimilitude, decorum, and poetic justice. Arguably, *Hercules* ensured justice through its glorification of monarchy and preserved some decorum by insisting that the king's rule was absolute in the bedroom as well as in matters of state, but it trashed the rest of neoclassicism. *Hercules* ignored the unities of time, place, and action; most of its allegorical scenes were set in no particular time or place and the opera featured the character of Hercules in a variety of suffering situations and noble deeds that defied any cohesive plot or logic. Whereas neoclassicism had endorsed verisimilitude, the notion that dramatic scenes should generally mirror situations that could occur in real life, music pervaded the action of *Hercules*, cuing the songs of characters and choruses and the descent of gods from stage machines. *Hercules* broke the neoclassical rules, but (unsurprisingly) no one from the French Academy stepped in to correct the cardinal or the king. Absolutism allowed the monarchy to make theatrical rules for everybody else, but also to violate them when Baroque aesthetics suited their propagandistic goals better than neoclassical restraint.

Operatic scenery on the continent gained more Baroque grandeur and monumentality in the eighteenth century. This was due, in part, to the pan-European success of an extended family of architects and designers, the Bibienas. Patriarch Ferdinando Bibiena (1657–1743) gained initial success in Italy and rose to fame in Barcelona and Vienna, where he designed theatres and the scenery for several operas after 1711. His brother Francisco (1659–1739) also enhanced the family's reputation through his international architectural and design work. Three second- and third-generation Bibienas continued the family business: Giuseppe (1696–1757), Antonio (1700–1774), and Carlo (1728–1787). By the time of Carlo's death, the Bibienas had planned theatres in Italy, Austria, and France and had worked as designers with major opera companies in Vienna, London, Paris, Lisbon, St. Petersburg, Berlin, Dresden, and Stockholm. Perhaps the Bibienas' most famous innovation was angle perspective (*scena per angolo* [SHAY-nah pehr AHN-goh-loh]), which visually opened up the operatic stage by creating diagonal vistas on the sides of the stage rather than restricting the vista to a central alley, a requirement of single-point perspective. By using two (or more) vanishing points, Bibiena designs could suggest that the palace interiors and garden exteriors of European rulers continued forever. The vertical thrust of the architecture painted on their flats and drops, which might fly upwards beyond the proscenium arch, also increased the magnificence of their designs. In theatres that were still lit by candles and mirrors, diagonal vistas and vertical columns or arches could appear to recede and tower into infinity (Figure 6.8). What better way to tie the absolute will of the monarch (or even the desires of a local duke) to the will of God!

The chariot-and-pole system deployed by the Bibienas and other designers remained the European standard among premier theatres on the continent until the late nineteenth century. These new technologies allowing for easy and flexible scene changes were a triumph for Baroque opera over neoclassical drama. According to neoclassical rules, plays were supposed to occur in one place; one set of stage flats that could suggest a single room or outdoor space was all that was needed. There was little point in putting neoclassical dramas on stages that were built for elaborate and magical transformations. For much of the eighteenth century, however, many European spectators watched neoclassical plays on the

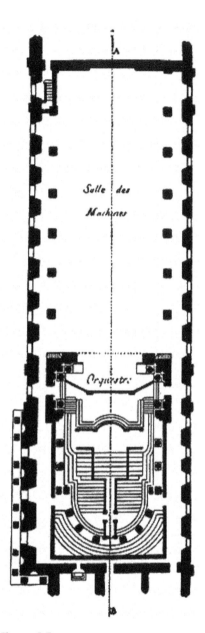

Figure 6.7

Plan of the Salle des Machines, designed by Gaspar Vigarani (1586–1663) for the 1662 Baroque opera *Hercules in Love*, an allegorical tribute to Louis XIV. The stage, 140 feet deep, accommodated six sets of side flats and flying machines. At one point in the opera, the entire royal family and attendants were flown in on one machine, 60 by 45 feet wide. The settings, organized around a single, central vanishing point, offered monumental images of a rationally ordered world, seen to fullest advantage by the king seated in his throne front and center.

From L.P. de la Guepière, *Théâtre et Machine* (1888).

Figure 6.8
Scena per angolo stage setting designed for a chariot-and-pole theatre by Giuseppe Galli Bibiena. The flats and drop were initially used for an opera produced to celebrate a betrothal between members of the ruling families of Saxony and Poland in 1719.
© AKG-images, London.

same stages that also housed lavish operatic productions. Although most probably grew accustomed to the contrast in production styles and values, the possibilities for more elaborate scenic display put pressure on neoclassical staging that could not be accommodated within the rigid rules of the aesthetic. It was not until the early nineteenth century, with the rise of melodrama and romantic theatre, that non-operatic drama would enjoy the full scenic possibilities of chariot-and-pole staging.

Louis XIV and Molière

Nonetheless, despite its paucity of stage scenery, neoclassicism for spoken drama thrived in France in the 1660s and 70s. One of Louis XIV's most reliable court entertainers was Jean-Baptiste Poquelin (1622–1673), better known by his stage name, Molière. Molière and his company had been performing in the French provinces when a message from the king's younger brother brought them to Paris in 1658 for their debut at court. Their success with a farcical afterpiece won them permission from Louis XIV to share a Parisian theatre with an Italian *commedia* troupe. Other farces and comedies followed, both at court and in their public theatre, and soon Molière had established himself and his troupe as a royal favorite. But the king kept his popular actor-playwright on a short leash. From 1661 until his death 12 years later, Molière devised, directed, and performed several court entertainments, mostly comedy ballets (which alternated scenes of dialogue and dance), to please his royal patron and ensure the continuing employment and success of his company. Molière's relations with the Sun King cooled over the years, however, especially during the long controversy that surrounded one of his most famous plays, *Tartuffe* (1664–1669).

CASE STUDY: Molière and carnival laughter

Gary Jay Williams, with Bruce McConachie

> Carnival laughter . . . builds its own world versus the official world, its own church versus the official church, its own state versus the official state.
>
> Bakhtin (1984)

This case study uses the concept of carnival folk humor proposed by Mikhail M. Bakhtin (1895–1975) to suggest a deep connection between the comic and the controversial sides of Molière's theatre. (For previous commentary on Bakhtin's concept of the carnivalesque, see Chapter 3.) In addition to reading *Tartuffe*, students using this case study may also wish to read one of Molière's short plays, such as *The Precious Damsels* (1659) or *Love's the Best Doctor* (1665), and one of his other five-act verse comedies, such as *The School for Wives* (1659), *The Miser* (1668), or *The Imaginary Invalid* (1673).

Molière's full-length verse plays are regarded as the cornerstone of French comedy. They have been staples in the repertoire of the Comédie Française, France's national theatre, for over three centuries and are revived often in the Western world. Molière served Louis XIV as playwright, actor, and courtier for 15 years, but his middle-class background and profession as an actor set him apart from the court in important ways. He excelled in the leading roles of his own comedies, but also suffered the social stigma attached to the profession. Although the Parisian literati characterized his plays as trifles, some of his satires on the fashionable and foolish made him powerful enemies.

In general, it is not difficult to understand Molière's later five-act plays as comic examples of neoclassicism and many critics have noted his adherence to decorum and the neoclassical unities. Yet, surely as important is the fact that Molière never abandoned the kind of disruptive comic elements that are in the spirit of the carnivalesque. Especially important for this study, his plays and performances were strongly influenced by the popular comic theatre traditions of (1) French farce, which had roots in medieval comedy; (2) *commedia dell'arte*, which had plots and character types similar to French farce; and (3) the kind of street medicine show that Molière knew well, in which hawkers sold potions they bragged could cure anything.

In previous chapters we have already noted that the traditions of medieval farce, *commedia*, and medicine shows have strong links to what Bakhtin calls the spirit of the "carnivalesque" (Figure 6.9). This case study argues that, despite Molière's ties to an absolutist monarchy, the subversive qualities of the carnivalesque spirit are at work in many of his plays. As we have seen, folk festival entertainments often "marked the suspension or inversion of hierarchical rank, privileges, norms, and prohibitions," according to Bakhtin. In the case of *Tartuffe*, there are key instances of such challenges and inversions. From this point of view, it is not surprising that the French Catholic Church, allied with the absolutism of the monarchy, believed it had to suppress a play that was so close to the seat of power in France.

Elements of carnival humor deriving from oral culture are present throughout Molière's work – early, middle, and late. Molière's early one-act farce *The Precious Damsels* (*Les Précieuses ridicules*, 1659), for example, has many attributes of the carnivalesque. It is a broad parody of the affectations of the salons of fashionable court women (*précieuses*) who were setting the protocols for aristocratic manners, courtship, language, and literature. Two affected young

Figure 6.9
In this farce at a
country carnival,
a husband is
being cuckolded
by a monk.
Detail from the
painting *Village
Festival in Honor
of St. Hubert and
St. Anthony* by
Pieter Brueghel
the Younger
(1564?–1637).

© Fitzwilliam
Museum, Cambridge
University/
Bridgeman Art
Library.

women turn away two potential suitors for lacking faddish manners and language. The young men then contrive a hoax. They send their valets, Mascarille and Jodelet, to visit the young women in the guise of fashionable courtiers, and the foolish women take them to be genuine. According to a surviving account of the performance, when Molière entered as Mascarille in marquis disguise, he wore a hyperbolic parody of a courtier's apparel. His powdered wig (topped by a tiny, fashionable hat) was so large that it swept the area around him every time he made a bow. His lace collar was huge and so were his breeches, the pockets of which sprouted colored tassels. He wore six-inch heels on his beribboned shoes and was carried on stage in a sedan chair by porters, whom he tried to avoid paying (Dock 1992: 53; Molière 1971: I, 1008). Molière's scale of exaggeration here is beyond satire; it has the overflow of the carnivalesque about it. It is a festive undoing, a parodic uncrowning of established order writ large on the body. Molière's performance as Mascarille made him a larger-than-life comic icon who bursts the seams of both salon decorum and the neoclassical rules for plays that required the restraint of verisimilitude. While his marquis represents an original departure from the stock characters of the *commedia dell'arte*, he functions in the same iconic way: the bold extravagance of the figure testifies to a force of elemental comic energy that explodes the world of over-rationalized drama. Without this kind of elemental comic force, without the precedents of the *commedia dell'arte* and old French farces, it is hard to imagine this performance.

In the original production of *The Precious Damsels*, a comic icon descended from the carnivalesque world was also on stage with Molière. Jodelet (Julian Bedeau), Paris's most famous actor of old French farce and Italian comedy, played the other valet, a character who impersonated an old viscount. Known as a good-natured clown, Jodelet always wore clown-white face makeup (probably a vestige of the flour-faced millers of old farce). Mascarille tells the young women, "Don't be surprised at the Viscount's looks. He just got out of bed from an illness that left him so pale" (Molière 1957: 23). Jodelet had recently left a rival theatre company, and Molière jumped at the chance to hire him. Jodelet would have brought with him plays written for him by Paul Scarron (1610–1660), whose parodies Bakhtin cites often, and who influenced Molière. The two comedians go through some ribald jokes involving sexual anatomy under the guise of talking about old war wounds and then they call in musicians for a dance – both typical bits of *commedia* business. Their masters enter to put an end to the deception and the play, beating and stripping their valets of their aristocratic clothes. Bakhtin speaks of thrashings and clothes-changing as a part of the cycle of crownings and uncrownings in carnivalesque fun (Bakhtin 1984: 197). No one gets to lord it for long in festive humor.

Such analysis could be extended through most of Molière's comedies, but a sampling must suffice here. Two obvious instances of the parodying of "official" language occur in *The Bourgeois Gentleman* and *The Imaginary Invalid*. In the first, a servant dupes Monsieur Jourdain into believing that a long, burlesque ceremony, conducted in an amalgam of pseudo-Latin and pseudo-Turkish, is conferring on him the noble title of "mamamouchi." In *The Imaginary Invalid*, in which Molière satirizes the medical profession (as he does in at least five other plays), an elaborate ceremony ends the play that parodies the granting of degrees to medical doctors. In this case, the profession's Latinate language grants a dunce of a new doctor the right to slash, purge, bleed, and kill his patients at will. The mocking of the "official" language suggests that it has no more truth-value than any other language.

Carnival humor's uncrownings of authority also take the form of cuckoldry. A wife's sexual deception of her husband uncrowns his domestic authority, while at the same time parodically crowning his head with horns (Bakhtin 1984: 241). A commonplace in medieval farces and *commedia*, cuckoldry or near-cuckoldry is a feature of several of Molière's plays, notably *The School for Wives*, *Don Juan* (1665), and *Amphitryon* (1668). In *The School for Wives*, the foolish Arnolphe has had his prospective young wife raised in the country in convent captivity on the theory that she will be too ignorant to know how to be unfaithful to him, a proposition the play gaily unravels. Carnivalesque sexuality often erupts in this play. Arnolphe, justifying to a doubtful friend his expectation of success in his training of Agnes, says he was delighted when Agnes once came to him much troubled to ask, "In absolute and perfect innocence,/ If children are begotten through the ear!" (Molière 1957: 37). Earlier in the same scene, when the zealous Arnolphe is fantasizing about his control of his prospective young wife, a *crème tarte* figures as a salacious sexual reference (Molière 2001: 5; 1971: I, 548). These and several other such moments have the comically subversive merit of suggesting that very powerful sexual forces are surging just below the surface of Arnolphe's selfish, rational social engineering. Predictably, such bawdiness disturbed decorous court audiences. But Molière went on to mock them further in his *Critique of the School for Wives* (1663), one of several episodes in a year-long controversy over the play.

In another variation on carnival humor's upside-down world, the servants in Molière are often wiser than their masters and mistresses (much like those in Plautus's comedies, from which Molière borrowed directly for his *Amphitryon* and *The Miser*). Dorine in *Tartuffe* and Toinette in *The Imaginary Invalid* challenge their masters' delusions to a degree that borders on comic domestic anarchy. Similarly, in *Don Juan*, Sganarelle directly challenges the right of his master to seduce women. Street-smart underclass characters in Molière are frequent foils to the self-deluding bourgeoisie. In many of the plays, folk wisdom comes from the servants in the form of proverbs as Molière mines another vein of popular culture.

Finally, let us look through the carnivalesque lens at Molière's *Tartuffe*, in which a clergyman preaches holiness but practices seduction, almost with impunity. It was his most controversial play and, ultimately, the most profitable in his lifetime. Molière first staged it as part of Louis XIV's lavish entertainments at Versailles in 1664, in a version now lost. The king enjoyed it but suppressed it in deference to the outrage of a sect of zealously devout Catholics. The play has many strains of popular folk humor inherited from farce and *commedia*, including Tartuffe's near sexual overpowering of Orgon's wife on top of the table under which Orgon is hiding (Figure 6.10). But let us focus here on one profound example of carnival humor in the play.

In the comic spectacles of popular festivals, travesty – the mocking appropriation of the costumes and insignia of authority and identity – was typical. Travesty suggests a slippage between the ideal and the real, between symbol and truth, between the sign and what it signifies – an effect which, for Bakhtin, nourishes positive social change. Molière's plays are full of imposters and poseurs, such as his affected courtiers, his bourgeois would-be gentleman, and all of his mock doctors. Disguised in the vestments and language of authority, such imposters create comic havoc. Tartuffe, as a sexual predator in the guise of a devout, creates more. Molière's play, like theatrical art itself, raises the question of whether we can ever know where the performance of the self ends and a true self begins. Taken seriously, a question about the stability of our knowledge of truth is not one an absolutist church or state can long entertain. Molière's play could be seen not only as irreverent but as a strike at the heart of the Church's authenticity. It is this,

Figure 6.10

Orgon catches Tartuffe (standing at left) in the act of trying to seduce his wife in Act IV of Molière's *Tartuffe*. Engraving by François Chaveau from the 1669 edition of the play.

© Bibliothèque Nationale de France.

perhaps more than the sexuality, that would account for the deep wrath of the powerful conservative cabal that insisted that the king, who had been Molière's protector in controversies up to this time, suppress the play. One Catholic curate raged in print against *Tartuffe*, saying the author was "a demon . . . dressed like a man," that Molière had held Christ's Church in contempt, and that he should be burned at the stake as a foretaste of what he would surely suffer in hell (Molière 1971: I, 1143–4). When Molière tried to produce a revised version in 1667, the Bishop of Paris closed it down, threatening the excommunication of anyone who performed or read it.

A very persistent Molière finally got his play to the public stage in 1669 in the version that survives today. The ending probably represents his revising process and has been the subject of much debate; it features the last-minute intervention of an emissary from Louis XIV to save Orgon and his home from Tartuffe's grasp. This scene may be understood as a conventional, obsequious compliment from Molière to the king, represented in the emissary's speech as Orgon's omniscient, all-wise sovereign. But some in the original audience may have read this last-act dénouement as an ironic *deus ex machina* [deh-oos ex MAH-khee-nah], which is to say as a carnivalesque parody of power. At the very least, two language zones, as Bakhtin would call them, were in play in the ending – the official and the unofficial – each offering different reception possibilities. The result would have been the kind of dialectic celebrated by Bakhtin that promotes ambivalence and subverts orthodoxy.

In their ribald humor and theatrical artifices drawn from street theatre traditions, Molière's plays, at least momentarily, critiqued decorum and absolutist control. Whether instinctively or consciously, Molière persisted in deploying carnivalesque humor throughout his career, as if his integrity as an artist depended on it. Molière, the carnivalesque comic actor and writer, was never elected to the classically rigorous, decorum-conscious French Academy, guardian of French language and literature, a fact that the Academy never has lived down.

Key references

Bakhtin, M.M. (1984) *Rabelais and His World*, trans. H. Iswolsky, Bloomington, IN: Indiana University Press.

Dock, S.V. (1992) *Costume and Fashion in the Plays of Jean-Baptiste Poquelin, Molière*, Geneva: Editions Slatkine.

Gaines, J.F. (ed.) (2002) *The Molière Encyclopedia*, Westport, CT: Greenwood Press.

McCarthy, G. (2002) *The Theatres of Molière*, New York and London: Routledge.

Molière (1953) *Molière, Five Plays*, trans. J. Wood, Baltimore: Penguin Books.

Molière (1957) *Eight Plays by Molière*, trans. M. Bishop, New York: Modern Library.

Molière [Poquelin, J.B.] (1971) *Oeuvres completes*, ed. G. Couton, Paris: Gallimard. (Scholarly French edition of all the plays and related documents referred to in this study.)

Molière (1993) *Tartuffe*, trans. R. Wilber (1961) in W.B. Worthen (ed.) *The HBJ Anthology of Drama*, Fort Worth: Harcourt Brace Jovanovich. (Includes English translations of Molière's important preface and other documents.)

Molière (2001) *The Misanthrope, Tartuffe, and Other Plays*, trans. M. Slater, Oxford: Oxford University Press.

Scott, V. (2000) *Molière, A Theatrical Life*, Cambridge: Cambridge University Press.

Absolutism and neoclassicism in France and England, 1660–1700

By 1660, the French crown was providing financial assistance to four theatre companies that primarily performed neoclassical plays. This practice had begun in the 1630s when Cardinal Richelieu initially arranged subsidies for the acting troupe at the Théâtre du Marais and then extended similar treatment to the other major troupe in Paris performing at the Hôtel de Bourgogne. As other troupes in Paris vied for royal support with the ascension of Louis XIV to the throne in 1643, the new king and his ministers took advantage of the monarchy's position in French culture to continue to tie theatre to the power of the crown. A *commedia dell'arte* company from Italy under the management of Tiberio Fiorillo (1608–1694), which enjoyed the support of several influential courtiers, gained a subsidy in the mid-1640s that was renewed from 1653 onwards. As we have seen, the king also lavished financial assistance on Molière and his company in the 1660s.

Royal support of French neoclassical theatre was capricious and haphazard, however, leading both theatre artists and state bureaucrats to attempt to regularize the arrangements. When Molière died in 1673, rivalry among the Paris acting troupes created a period of flux, with several actors leaving one company to join another. In 1679, the crown forced an end to the conflicts by ordering the two remaining major acting troupes in Paris to combine into one – the Comédie Française. Further, the king's edict also granted a monopoly over spoken drama in French to the new company. (An exception was soon made, however, when Fiorillo's *commedia* troupe won the right to continue to use French in their performances.) Louis XIV's 1679 decree continued the traditional organization of French acting companies, by which the actors shared in the profits of the troupe, but he fixed the number of shares so that no new members could be admitted to the Comédie Française until an old one retired or died. The edict also regulated how actors might be elected as sharing members and the authority the members possessed in selecting plays for production. Finally, the king took control of the internal affairs of the troupe; his decree established his First Gentleman of the Chamber as the arbiter of disputes within the company. Later, in 1701 and 1706, the king imposed censorship on the troupe; the new rules mandated that all scripts be read and approved by a censor in the police department before a public performance in Paris would be allowed. Although members of the Comédie Française enjoyed state support and might benefit from generous pensions on retirement, they had become bureaucrats of the monarchy.

Not surprisingly, perhaps, the triumphs of French neoclassicism in playwriting came before the absolutist consolidation of French dramatic theatre in the Comédie Française. During the 1660s and 1670s, the counterpart in tragic playwriting to Molière's success in comedy and farce was Jean Racine (1639–1699); both were popular in public theatres and at the court of Louis XIV. Following several successes beginning with *Andromaque* in 1667, Racine penned what most critics agree was his masterpiece, *Phèdre*, in 1677. Like several of Racine's tragedies, *Phèdre* plays out the consequences of a maxim by the philosopher René Descartes: "Our passions cannot be directly aroused or removed by the action of our will" (quoted in Sayer 2006: 258). Proposing a strict separation between human emotions and rational thought – between the needs of the body and the logic of the mind – Descartes and the other rationalists of his day believed they could offer little help to men and women in the grip of "passion." In *Phèdre*, based on an ancient Greek myth, Queen Phèdre is passionately in love with her stepson Hippolyte. Nonetheless, in accordance with neoclassical decorum, Racine spares Phèdre the loss of dignity evident in his play's sources. But the moral code of neoclassical decorum prevents her from acting on her desire. Following the constraints of the three unities, Racine constructs a tightly woven, psychologically driven plot in which Phèdre struggles to express and finally to extricate herself from her passion, only to bring on the wrath of her husband, the death of Hippolyte, and her own shame and suicide. As in *Phèdre*, the precepts of neoclassical rules and Cartesian rationalism provided sharp conflicts between duty and desire in many tragedies of the seventeenth century. Long a favorite of French audiences and female tragedy actors, *Phèdre* continues to thrill spectators today.

In England, regular performances by professional companies did not return until 1660, after the Civil War, with the Restoration of Charles II to the throne. While living in exile at the court of the French monarch, Charles had come to appreciate the control that Louis XIV and his ministers were exercising over French performance. Charles did not want to pay the direct theatre subsidies that allowed the French throne to enjoy entertainments that reflected its absolutist goals, but he did believe that he needed to control the stage to legitimize his fragile hold on power. Consequently, Charles awarded royal **patents** to two playwright-impresarios, making them the only men allowed to produce plays in London, an unprecedented theatrical monopoly in England. Thomas Killigrew (1612–1683) became the manager of the King's Company, which soon floundered. A better theatrical manager, William Davenant (1606–1668), supervised the Duke's Company more closely until his death in 1668, when the actors Thomas Betterton (1635–1710) and Henry Harris assumed artistic control. With the imminent failure of Killigrew's company, the king allowed the two troupes to merge in 1682.

During the reign of Charles II, which lasted until 1685, the London companies generally performed at two indoor theatres, Drury Lane and Lincoln's Inn Fields. Both playhouses accommodated small audiences of mostly aristocratic spectators, who enjoyed bawdy comedies and heroic plays featuring royalist propaganda. Built for wing-and-drop scenery with side flats that slid in grooves on the floor and painted drops lowered from the flies above (the **wing-and-groove system**), these proscenium theatres did not deploy the more expensive chariot-and-pole rigging of many continental playhouses. When the king decided he needed a theatre in which he could

Figure 6.11

The stage of Dorset Garden Theatre, London, with the setting for Act I, sc. 1 of *The Empress of Morocco*, by E. Settle, produced in 1673. King Charles II's coat of arms is at the center of the proscenium arch. Designed by Christopher Wren, the theatre featured London's best-equipped stage at the time. Engraving by William Dole in the 1673 edition of the play.

© Gary Jay and Josephine S. Williams.

entertain foreign dignitaries, he advanced funds from the royal treasury for the completion of a new playhouse in Dorset Garden, which was equipped with a modified version of the chariot-and-pole system for the staging of European opera (Figure 6.11). For ten years after its opening in 1671, the king used Dorset Garden as an extension of his royal power, even though it remained primarily a commercial operation.

Until 1685, the desires and values of King Charles and his aristocratic favorites dominated the English stage. Soon after his return to power, the king had decreed that English companies should now employ women as professional actors, a casting convention he had enjoyed while watching French theatre. Called the "merry monarch" for his sexual affairs, Charles extended his royal prerogatives to taking actresses of his choice as his bedmates. The new female actors were an instant hit on stage (and the convention of men playing young women soon died out). Several women achieved artistic stature, including comedy actor Nell Gwyn (1650–1687), who became Charles's mistress, and tragedian Elizabeth Barry (1658–1713). Although a new law (passed as a sop to the Puritans) made it illegal to produce plays that offended "piety and good manners," many Restoration productions paraded lusty actions and explicit sexual innuendos.

Playwriting between 1660 and 1680 generally reflected royalist values. John Dryden's (1631–1700) *Indian Queen* (1664) and his two-part *The Conquest of Granada* (1669–1670) followed neoclassical patterns and focused on competitive royal heroes and heroines caught in conflicts between romantic love and duty to the state. Like Racine, his contemporary in France, Dryden attempted to reconcile the philosophy of Descartes with the morality of his heroes and their tragic decisions. Influenced by his correspondence with political philosopher Thomas Hobbes, Dryden celebrated the rational and even contemptuous power of absolute rulers in his early plays.

In the 1670s, however, he began to search for a dramatic vehicle that would allow his spectators to understand greatness through the standard of "generosity," as Descartes had defined it in his writings. According to Descartes, a king could attain "generosity" when he resolved "to undertake and carry out what he judges best" (quoted in Fletcher 2011: 105). The playwright believed, with Descartes, that such self-esteem allowed the virtuous ruler to rise above his contempt for lesser mortals and judge them with compassion. Dryden reworked Shakespeare's *Antony and Cleopatra* to express these Cartesian values, changing the title (and emphasis) of the tragedy to *All for Love* (1677). In Dryden's neoclassical version of the final days of these two heroes from Roman times, Antony gradually forsakes the competitive masculinity of Shakespeare's character and eventually finds "generosity" in his continuing concern for Cleopatra, even when both are near their deaths. States critic Angus Fletcher, "[Antony] discovers a greatness that takes others into account but does not depend upon them, that is grounded in the self but does not devolve into solipsism. Following Descartes' own progression, he discovers generosity" (Fletcher 2011: 111).

Restoration comedies, such as William Wycherley's (1640–1715) *The Country Wife* (1675), George Etherege's (*c*.1634–1691) *The Man of Mode* (1676), and Aphra Behn's (1640–1689) (Figure 6.12) *The Rover* (1677), featured witty language and titillating sexual intrigue among the beautiful and privileged. At the center of *The Rover*, for example, are four "Banish'd Cavaliers" (the subtitle of the play), who have

Figure 6.12
Aphra Behn, the first woman in England to earn her living as a writer, wrote several plays during the Restoration period, featuring women as central characters. She also wrote novels, poetry, and translations, and served as a spy for Charles II. Sketch by George Scharf from a portrait believed to be lost.

traveled to Naples for pleasure and adventure. The subtitle sets the play in the 1650s, when many royalists moved to the continent to escape Puritan rule during the English Civil War. Chief among them is Willmore, who pursues many women, two of whom – Hellena and Angelica – fight for his affections. Behn weaves two more love plots into the action, which involve an English colonel and Florinda, Hellena's sister, and a foolish Cavalier who falls for an Italian prostitute. Because Behn's female characters are nearly as sexually voracious as her male Cavaliers, a disguised Florinda is nearly raped and Angelica almost shoots Willmore in a jealous rage. In the end, the prostitute robs the Cavalier, the colonel gets Florinda, and Willmore reluctantly agrees to end his roving and marry Hellena.

Other comic writers followed the example of Molière, whose neoclassical comedies provided models on both side of the English Channel. These and other dramatists wrote for a coterie audience that usually mirrored the king's taste for heroic grandeur and salacious sexuality. While a few playwrights, including Nahum Tate (1652–1715) in his adaptations of Shakespeare's *King Lear* and *Richard II*, attempted to articulate anti-absolutist positions through allusive language, most bolstered royalist prejudices. By 1680, it seemed to many that the English theatre was going the way of its French absolutist cousin.

The political crisis of the 1680s, however, cut short the drift toward absolutism in England. Anti-royalist factions in London took to the streets to perform massive Pope Burning pageants and other demonstrations that linked royal absolutism to the power of Rome. These and other political actions led in 1688 to increased power for Parliament and less overt support and control by the crown over the theatre. The two patent companies continued to dominate theatrical production in London for another ten years, even though they lacked the legal authority of the Comédie Française to enforce their apparent monopolies. When in 1695 the legal validity of the patents expired, the English throne, which no longer claimed absolute authority, did not revive them. After 1700, although the crown continued to license theatres, it did so unevenly, with the consequence that many kinds of theatre flourished in England in the early eighteenth century. Soon, neoclassical comedies and tragedies were living, cheek by jowl, with satires and ballad operas as the popular theatres at the Hounslow, Southwark, and Bartholomew fairs competed with the regular London playhouses catering to aristocrats and wealthy merchants.

Reforming Baroque opera

As we have noted, Italian librettists and composers in the 1600s favored the extravagance of the Baroque over the restraints of neoclassicism for their operas. This began to change in the 1690s, however, as many Italians turned away from the Counter-Reformation ideology of the Vatican, which had pushed the emotional and flamboyant style of the Baroque for over a century, to embrace the Cartesian rationality that Racine, Dryden, and other Europeans had explored and advanced in neoclassical literature and drama. Led by the Arcadian Academy, a group of intellectuals and wealthy patrons in Rome set on modernizing Italian culture, the reformers drew on Aristotle and Renaissance ideals to restore older modes of artistic expression and to urge that artists take up more rational and simplified forms as models for their work. One later Italian critic, looking back on Baroque opera from the perspective of the 1780s after the Arcadian reforms were complete, painted a sharp contrast between the enlightened qualities of present opera and the musical contraptions of the previous century. Baroque opera, he said, presented "an enormous chaos, a concoction of sacred and profane, of historical and fabulous, of mythology, ancient and modern, of true and allegorical, of natural and fantastic, all gathered together to the perpetual shame of Art" (quoted in Kimbell 1991: 182). As we shall see, however, this critic exaggerated the differences between seventeenth- and eighteenth-century opera.

The reformers of Italian opera began by separating serious from comic opera, establishing two major genres that would endure for the next 80 years – *opera seria* [OH-peh-rah SEH-ree-ah] and *opera buffa* [OH-peh-rah BOOF-fah]. *Opera buffa* drew much of its energy, many of its plots, and most of its stock characters from *commedia dell'arte*, which remained popular among all classes of Italians during the eighteenth century. Our next chapter traces major changes in *commedia dell'arte* during the 1700s, changes that were also reflected in the libretti and music of *opera buffa*. Although reformers also altered *opera seria* (serious opera), the changes were less substantial, primarily because this genre was dominated by one man, Pietro Metastasio (1698–1782), for much of his career as a librettist. Metastasio gained initial fame as a poet in Rome, where he soon turned to writing libretti for operas under the initial sponsorship of the Arcadian Academy. In response to the increasing popularity of *opera seria* among royals and aristocrats in the Austrian empire, Metastasio moved to Vienna in 1730 and produced several of his most famous libretti, including the words for *Olympiade* and *Clemenza di Tito*.

Bowing to some of the constraints of neoclassicism, Metastasio's libretti reduced the spectacular and allegorical elements of Baroque opera and emphasized intrigues and mistaken identities among historical rulers that turned on conflicts between duty and expediency or virtue and passion, much as the plots of Racine and Dryden had earlier. Unlike their tragedies, however, Metastasio resolved most of his dramatic conflicts comically, often through a change of heart by the hero and the general reconciliation of the principal characters. His libretti suggested that the world of his virtuous aristocrats and royals was more benign than cruel or tragic, if looked at through an enlightened perspective. From the 1730s into the 1770s, many composers found Metastasio's poetic libretti so elegant and captivating that they returned to several of them again and again to re-set them to different music. *Opera seria* in the form and style of Metastasio took much of the pomposity and religiosity out of Baroque opera, but his lyrical libretti departed significantly from the verisimilitude and rational rigor of the neoclassical plays of Racine and Dryden. Regarding the difficulties of European absolutism for its rulers and subjects, the pleasant endings of *opera seria* made these problems seem resolvable. Metastasio's neoclassical libretti may have simplified the plot contortions of Baroque opera, but most of the operas based on his words were performed against the soaring magnificence of Bibiena-designed or -inspired scenery.

Metastasio also regularized the scene structure of *opera seria* by moving most of the action between characters to recitative (dialogue sung in the simple rhythms of natural speech with only slight melodic variation) and leaving the arias of his major characters to mark the ends of scenes. Given this placement of their arias, it was probably inevitable that operatic stars would push composers to lengthen and elaborate their difficulty. The primary stars of *opera seria*, inspiring devotion in many as well as contempt in a few, were castrati [kahs-TRAH-tee], male singers who had been castrated in their youth to preserve the purity of their boyish voices in the hope that their adult bodies could deliver *opera seria* arias with supreme virtuosity. Once castrated, a boy's voice does not deepen by an octave, as normally occurs in males in early adulthood, but usually stays in the soprano range, with a tonal quality half-way between a child's and a woman's. The Catholic Church had been practicing the castration of vocally promising boys (following the dubious consent of their parents) to produce singers for the Papal Choir since the 1500s and castrati sang in Baroque opera in the 1600s.

During the eighteenth century, as *opera seria* spread through Italy and north into the rest of Europe, the practice of castration increased and several more castrati moved from church choirs to operatic stages. Although less than one in a hundred castrati gained a career as a singer, operatic fame meant substantial wealth and aristocratic connections. Among them, Carlo Broschi (1705–1782), who took the stage name Farinelli, was the most popular (Figure 6.13). Following his debut in Naples, Farinelli performed throughout Italy, then toured Europe in the 1720s and 1730s, with stops in Munich, London, and Paris and extensive stays in Vienna, where he befriended Metastasio. Like other castrati, Farinelli primarily performed the masculine heroes of *opera seria*, endowing their arias with intensity, tenderness, force, and passion. While most audiences fawned over castrati opera stars, their few critics pointed to the hypocrisy underlining the fact that an elite that called itself "enlightened" believed in the need to castrate boys to enable their operatic enjoyment. The critics also noted that castrati performing the roles of powerful rulers were an affront to neoclassical verisimilitude.

For the aristocrats, royal ministers, wealthy merchants, and famous professionals who purchased a box at the theatre for the season, however, opera-going was primarily a social rather than a musical or dramatic occasion. The regularities of *opera seria* and the fact that so many of its stories were repeated enabled spectators to ignore much of what was happening on stage (usually until a castrato began an aria) and to focus, instead, on social interests and desires. Eighteenth-century architects built opera houses to emphasize the dominance of the boxes, which generally ringed a "U"-shaped auditorium and might be stacked four high, allowing the elite of a city to view the social hierarchy at a glance, to parade

Figure 6.13
Portrait of Carlo Broschi (Farinelli), soon after the king of Spain made him a Knight of the Order of Calatrava in 1750. Farinelli proudly displays the insignia of the Order on his coat.

Painting by Jacopo Amigoni, *c.*1750–1752.© Classic Image/Alamy Stock Photo.

their wealth and family, and to use their opera glasses to get a good look at each other's affairs (Figure 6.14). Most opera houses featured a royal or ducal box, much larger than the others, at the "bottom" of the "U," from which the king (or the local duke, count, or margrave) might watch his subjects and set the social tone for the evening. The best boxes, usually placed on the lower levels of the "U" near the royal box, were actually small parlors, built to accommodate socializing, card playing, and even dining during the performance. (When not serving their masters, servants might stand in the pit area below the boxes, which sometimes doubled as a ballroom, or perch on a bench in a cramped balcony above the royal box, if such a gallery had been built for them.) In Italy and in many of the small states of Germany, wealthy merchants shared the social ostentation of the opera with local rulers. In eighteenth-century Lisbon, Vienna, Madrid, and Paris – the capitals of empires – absolute rulers made sure that operatic spectacle and sociality reflected and enhanced their power.

The Paris Opéra in the 1750s provides a good example of the link between absolutism and opera-going. As music historian James H. Johnson notes, "At mid-century, the Opéra . . . was a royal spectacle, tailored to fit the tastes of the king's most distinguished subjects: his closest

Figure 6.14

The Margrave's theatre in Bayreuth, Germany. Designed by Giuseppe and Carlo Galli
Bibiena and built in 1748, this small Baroque opera house features the typical "U" shape
for its auditorium with a large opera box for the local ruler at its apex. The chairs in the
pit below the boxes were added in the nineteenth century. In the eighteenth century, the
pit probably accommodated temporary benches for servants and others.

© Theatermuseum, Munich

relatives held their boxes in the most visible rows, royal administrators and palace functionaries
seldom missed performances, and Louis XV himself came with some regularity" (Johnson 1995:
10). Despite the drone of conversations during performances, critics complained that the court
etiquette of Versailles prevailed, with many spectators watching the king to see how they should
respond. Indeed, in his examination of the records of annual subscribers for first-level boxes
over an eight-year period, Johnson found that over 90 percent of them were aristocrats and
most of those held high positions in the regime. During the 1750s, Louis XV took a personal
interest in the affairs of the Opéra, which, like the Comédie Française, had lost most of its
artistic freedom to gain monopolistic privileges. The king established budgets, interfered in
personnel decisions, selected operas for performance, and occasionally gave advice during
rehearsals. In addition to *opera seria*, the king enjoyed opera ballets (which featured more dancing
than singing), pastoral operas (which idealized rural peasant life), and revivals of the lyrical operas
of Jean-Baptiste Lully (1633–1682), who had turned Baroque opera away from Italian modes
toward French tastes soon after the establishment of the Paris Opéra. Because these operatic
genres were royal favorites, they dominated the repertoire in the 1750s. When they were not

Figure 6.15

Touring players on their temporary stage (left) before an audience in a market square in Munich in 1780. From a painting by Joseph Stephan.

© Bayerisches Nationalmuseum, Munich. Photo Courtesy of the Deutsches Theatermuseum.

socializing or watching fights among drunken servants in the area for standees in front of their boxes, the aristocrats might occasionally turn their attention to the stage to enjoy what the king had chosen for them to see and hear.

Absolutism and neoclassicism in the German states and Russia, 1700–1770

While some of the larger courts among the German states and cities in the early 1700s could afford to subsidize regular operatic productions, most of the dukes, counts, princes, and others who ruled in Germany got by with occasional visits from traveling operatic troupes. With regard to public performances, small *commedia dell'arte* companies toured the area and home-grown fairground troupes set up temporary stages for seasonal performances. Still recovering from the devastations of the religious wars, most of German society could afford little more than such offerings, which were nonetheless enjoyed by peasants, workers, burgers, and a few aristocrats (Figure 6.15). Although these troupes performed a variety of genres, the star of most of them was a carnivalesque clown, who generally enacted a character called Hanswurst. This fun-loving, hard-drinking, and often devilish figure combined attributes from several previous clown-figures seen in Germany, including medieval fools, Falstaffian characters (introduced by English actors who played in Germany during the English Civil War), and Harlequins (known to German audiences from *commedia* tours).

Despite these difficult circumstances for neoclassical theatre, two reformers, Johann Christoph Gottsched (1700–1766) and Caroline Neuber (1697–1760), used their combined companies to introduce several neoclassical innovations into the German theatre after 1727. Gottsched translated and adapted French plays into German, and Neuber staged them and polished their troupe's performance style. Although the Gottsched–Neuber company made some allies among the German aristocracy, the troupe never found a large audience for their neoclassical plays in Leipzig and Hamburg, their primary sites for performance. Both had hoped to banish Hanswurst and the kind of theatre he represented from the stage, but Hanswurst plays at fairground theatres remained popular when their troupe broke in two in 1739. Once again, as in the theatre of Molière, the carnivalesque had successfully undermined neoclassical restraint – at least with popular audiences, if not with many German aristocrats, educated to believe in the superiority of French culture.

Folk and fairground theatrical traditions existed in Russia as well and continued throughout the eighteenth century. But neoclassical ideals, if not direct subsidies for theatrical production, had received a boost during the reign of Tsar Peter the Great (1682–1725), who campaigned to Westernize Russia. By the 1740s, the Russian court was enjoying Italian *opera seria* and French neoclassical plays, produced by troupes of Italian singers and French actors on a chariot-and-pole court stage in St. Petersburg. During the next decade, Alexander Sumarokov (1717–1777) was writing successful Russian tragedies and comedies on the French neoclassical model and the empress established and subsidized a state theatre for Russian plays and actors. Russian neoclassical theatre expanded substantially during the reign of Tsarina Catherine II (1762–1796), with more Russian dramas, better subsidies, and the establishment of an acting school. French theatre remained the ideal, however, with translations of neoclassical French plays dominating the repertoire and the French crown's rules for the regulation of the Comédie Française serving as the model for the tsarina's control of the state-supported theatre and opera companies. By 1770, public as well as court theatres had gained a foothold in Russia, but the policies of Catherine II, as well as the domination of theatrical life by the aristocracy and court, ensured that upstart theatre companies would not use their performances to challenge her absolute rule.

The limits of neoclassicism and absolutism in France, 1720–1770

Theatrical neoclassicism spread from Paris throughout France in the 1700s, as large and medium-sized French cities competed with each other to build playhouses that could support touring and eventually permanent companies. About 20 cities enjoyed public performances at their theatres by 1750 and that number jumped to 71 by 1790. By 1789, the date of the French Revolution, France could boast more public theatres outside its capital than any other country in Europe. Funded mostly by local aristocrats and entrepreneurs, these theatres usually housed operatic as well as spoken performances and might also include *commedia dell'arte* troupes and fairground entertainers. Their managers primarily served local nobles, merchants, regional representatives of the crown, and other provincial elites, who socialized and conducted business at the playhouse. Not surprisingly, they looked to Paris for their models of acting, staging, and dramatic or operatic repertoire, which meant in practice that the traditional neoclassicism of Corneille and Racine in playwriting and Lully in opera pervaded the French provinces. Although some Parisian artists challenged neoclasssical restraints, the power of the French Catholic Church, the French Academy, and the direct control of Parisian theatre and opera exercised by the French monarchy silenced or sidelined much of the opposition. Officially, all of France was becoming more neoclassical during the 1700–1789 period, even though, in retrospect, neoclassical forms could no longer contain the energies and concerns of the time.

In the 50 years between 1720 and 1770, the most renowned and one of the most popular playwrights of the period was Voltaire, the pen-name of Francois-Marie Arouet (1694–1778). Dramatist, pamphleteer, novelist, historian, and cultural gadfly, Voltaire corresponded with many of the rich and powerful throughout Europe to urge reforms in a range of areas, from established religion to absolutist government. Although his plays occasionally took liberties with the three neoclassical unities and with class-bound notions of decorum, Voltaire defended the rules of neoclassicism in several essays. Historian Bettina Knapp calls Voltaire "an innovative theater traditionalist" (Knapp 2000: 80); she recognizes the tension between Voltaire's push for reforms in staging and costuming (plus his campaigns against arbitrary rules in many areas of French life) and his continued support of neoclassicism.

In part, this tension resulted from the peculiar public position of Voltaire and the other French *philosophes* [fee-loh-zohf], those journalists, encyclopedia writers, and cultural critics of the period who were advocating for reform, but who also believed that they must work within the present absolutist system of government and culture to achieve it. As a leading *philosophe*, Voltaire hoped to influence the powerful to change French life from the top down, and part of this campaign involved a commitment to preserving what he took to be the high moral ground of elite French culture. In addition to attacking the Church, the academy, and other bastions of reactionary power, Voltaire and the other *philosophes* criticized those whom they accused of trivializing the culture of France. This included the popular playwright Pierre Marivaux (1688–1763), whose love comedies, the *philosophes* believed, appealed to the vain and frivolous. Hoping to educate the public through elite networks of patronage and sociability and also recognizing that French neoclassical taste was becoming European taste, Voltaire clung to the ideas and forms of neoclassicism and shunned what he saw as the decadence of newer, more popular artistic movements. While a few of the *philosophes*, such as Denis Diderot, believed that some new dramatic genres could be encouraged without compromising traditional standards, all of the reformers saw themselves as the guardians of superior culture. By writing plays for the elite, the *philosophes* ensured that theatrical neoclassicism would stay wedded to the politics of absolutism.

Voltaire's point of view about the need for elite power to effect top-down reform is evident in many of his dramas. Although his essays and histories were often didactic and ironic, most of his 52 plays were packed with emotion, often concerning conflicts involving absolutist power and religion. Voltaire understood that emotional appeal was probably the best way to convince the audience at the Comédie Française and local elites in the provinces of the reasonableness of his ideas. In *Zaïre* (1732), one of his most successful tragedies, for example, Christian intolerance leads a Moslem Sultan to kill the Christian heroine, Zaïre, whom he loves, and then to take his own life. Voltaire's critics correctly saw his *Mohammed, or Fanaticism* (1741) as a veiled attack on all religions, including Christianity, that spread their gospel through the sword. He had to withdraw this play from production at the Comédie Française after three performances in order to avoid censorship. Both *Zaïre* and *Mohammed* demonstrate the need for rulers to separate religion from the power of the state; the plays suggest that only a virtuous monarch might be able to free humanity from the thrall of religious intolerance.

Like other *philosophes*, Voltaire believed that the rational and progressive values of the French Enlightenment could lead all of humankind out of superstition and misery. Indeed, many educated people in Europe spoke of the eighteenth century as an "Age of Enlightenment" and foresaw inevitable progress – in the economy, science, religion, the law, and even in governance – for the future. They based their hopes on the scientific and philosophical advances from the previous century, the appearance of rational discourse in public affairs, and on the growing prosperity for some Europeans in the 1700s.

Voltaire's confidence in Enlightenment values helped him to succeed as a dramatist and polemicist, but they also left several of his plays open to the charge of ethnocentrism. With little interest in Chinese theatre, Voltaire adapted a Yuan *zaju* (see Chapter 4), translated initially by a Jesuit missionary, as *The Orphan of China* for the French stage in 1755. Although hailed as the first Chinese play to appear in any European language, *The Orphan of China* deleted the songs, changed the verse structure, and telescoped the plot sequence to comply with neoclassical rules. In Voltaire's play, Genghis Khan has recently conquered China, but has also fallen in love with a beautiful Chinese woman. Through her influence, the conqueror decides to spare the life of a royal Chinese orphan, despite the political risks, because nature has taught him tolerance and love. Voltaire believed that established religion undercut morality; in the absence of Christianity and other religions, he held that natural morality would triumph. In *The Orphan of China*, Voltaire altered a traditional Chinese play to preach what he believed was a universal human value.

The *philosophes* hoped that such plays and similar reformist efforts could convince European rulers to set aside many of their policies and abide by rational notions of public morality. In brief, Voltaire and the *philosophes* tried to use the power of print and performance to turn the absolutist rulers of their day into enlightened monarchs. Voltaire had lived in London as a young man and admired the limited monarchy that was beginning to emerge in Great Britain. He tried to advance these and other reforms at the court of Louis XV in the 1740s, but the king and his ministers ignored him. Soon after, Voltaire accepted an invitation from King Frederick II of Prussia to join him in Berlin. Voltaire had corresponded with Frederick over the years and hoped that Prussia might become a model of enlightened monarchy. Again he was disappointed; King Frederick sponsored the arts and sciences and supported religious toleration, but refused to give up any of his power. Undaunted, Voltaire continued to write to the royals of Europe with ideas for reform. He corresponded with Catherine II of Russia in the 1760s, even after it was obvious that she was using him (and Diderot) as convenient press agents for her consolidation of power and for Russian expansion in Europe. In short, the Enlightenment principles of Voltaire and the other *philosophes* did little directly to change the political realities of European absolutism, at least before the French Revolution in 1789.

Between 1789 and 1792, French revolutionaries turned many Enlightenment principles into national laws, including the disestablishment of the Catholic Church in France, which Voltaire had fought for nearly all of his adult life. Although theatrical neoclassicism, including the plays of Molière, enjoyed a brief resurgence in the 1790s, the turmoil of the Revolution and the Napoleonic wars that followed rechanneled the broader cultural energies that had sustained neoclassicism from the 1500s to the 1720s.

SUMMARY

The absolute monarchs of Europe encouraged two very different styles of dramatic theatre and opera between 1600 and 1770 – Baroque aesthetics and neoclassical restraint. Initially a product of the Renaissance and print culture, neoclassicism had helped many artists to move past the legacies of medieval entertainments and to reimagine how theatre might better serve the needs of elite cultures eager to embrace a new orderliness in their lives. Nonetheless, European rulers favored the power and playfulness of Baroque masques and operas for most of the 1600s. Despite challenges from Baroque allegories and carnivalesque entertainments, theatrical neoclassicism reached the pinnacle of its cultural success in the plays of Molière, Racine, and Dryden between 1660 and 1680. Later, in the hands of the Roman Academy and Metastasio, neoclassicism mustered enough cultural prestige to reform some the excesses of Baroque opera. If we can speak of a tragic flaw in the history of neoclassicism, however, it was its marriage to political absolutism. After 1720, despite the continuing power of neoclassicism in the reformist plays of Voltaire and others, theatrical neoclassicism was doomed to go the way of absolute monarchy in Europe.

★

Part II: Works cited

Other consulted resources and additional readings for Part II are listed on the **Theatre Histories** *website.*

Audio-visual resources

Commedia dell'arte

The National Theatre offers a series of informational and instructional videos on the history, art of, and training for *commedia* performance. Visit <http://www.nationaltheatre.org.uk/backstage/commedia-dellarte> for more information.

Kunqu

"*Kunqu*: The Mother of All Chinese Drama" short introduction and except from *Peony Pavilion* <https://www.youtube.com/watch?v=qNGUhRTfBhE>.

Japanese theatre

See listings in Part I for overall material on classical Japanese theatre (*nō*, *kyōgen*, *kabuki*, and *bunraku*). Many of these include all or several of these genres. Specific material for *kabuki* and *bunraku* follows.

Kabuki

Japanese Theatre 3: Kabuki: 13 minute introduction with excellent excerpts from plays and commentary <https://www.youtube.com/watch?v=F3IHdm2Tf8g>.

Ennosuke III: Kabuki Actor: a brilliant documentary, made in 1984, about an important and innovative *kabuki* actor (now retired), including backstage scenes as well as excerpts of plays <https://www.youtube.com/watch?v=kEUQNvn8EJQ>.

Bunraku

Titled "Japanese Theatre 2: *Bunraku*": an introduction to *bunraku* with excerpts from plays and excellent commentary, total running time 9.5 minutes: <https://www.youtube.com/watch?v=4TKt67ouaqM>.

Another excellent introduction to *bunraku* with excerpts and excellent commentary, with a total running time of 4.45 minutes: <https://www.youtube.com/watch?v=kEUQNvn8EJQ>.

Printing press

The Atlas of Early Printing has animations showing how the printing press worked and the spread of printing during the fifteenth century: <http://atlas.lib.uiowa.edu>.

There is a brief video on the history of the printing press at <http://www.history.com/topics/middle-ages/videos/mankind-the-story-of-all-of-us-the-printing-press>, and a demonstration at <http://youtu.be/ksLaBnZVRnM>.

Renaissance and Baroque theatre

Scene design and machinery: *The Development of Scenic Spectacle*: <http://spectacle.appstate.edu/>. Dr. Frank Mohler provides reliable explanations and basic demonstrations, with virtual moving models (using *Quicktime*) of scene-changing machinery. Click "Scene Changes" for *Florimene*.

Molière's Tartuffe, video recording of the Royal Shakespeare Company production, directed by Bill Alexander, with Antony Sher as Tartuffe (1984).

The original Globe Theatre: informational website about its history and design, with interesting excerpts from primary sources: <http://www.shakespeare-online.com/theatre/globe.html>.

Books and articles

Adams, W.D. (1904) *A Dictionary of the Drama*, Philadelphia: J.B. Lippincott.

Aercke, K.P. (1994) *Gods of Play: Baroque Festive Performances as Rhetorical Discourse*, Albany: State University of New York Press.

Anderson, B. (1991) *Imagined Communities*, London: Verso.

Carlson, M. (1993) *Theories of Theatre*, expanded edn, Ithaca and London: Cornell University Press.

Castelvetro, L. (1570 [2000]) *The Poetics of Aristotle*, selections, in D. Gerould (ed.) *Theatre/Theory/Theatre: The Major Critical Texts from Aristotle and Zeami to Soyinka and Havel*, New York: Applause.

Eisenstein, E.L. (1979) *The Printing Press as an Agent of Change*, Cambridge: Cambridge University Press.

Erenstein, R.(1989) "The Humour of the Commedia dell'Arte," in C. Cairns (ed.) *The Commedia dell'Arte from the Renaissance to Dario Fo*, Lewiston/Queenston/Lampeter: Edwin Mellen Press, 118–41.

Fletcher, A. (2011) *Evolving Hamlet: Seventeenth-Century English Tragedy and the Ethics of Natural Selection*, New York: Palgrave.

Henke, R. (2003) *Performance and Literature in the Commedia dell'Arte*, Cambridge: Cambridge University Press.

Johnson, J.H. (1995) *Listening in Paris: A Cultural History*, Berkeley: University of California Press.

Kimbell, D. (1991) *Italian Opera*, Cambridge: Cambridge University Press.

King, P.M. (2012) "John Heywood, *The Play of the Weather*," in T. Betteridge and G. Walker (eds) *Oxford Handbook of Tudor Drama*, Oxford: Oxford University Press.

Knapp, B.L. (2000) *Voltaire Revisited*, New York: Twayne Publishers.

Knight, A.E. (1983) *Aspects of Genre in Late Medieval French Drama*, Manchester: Manchester University Press

Lam, J.S.C. (n.d.) "*Kunqu*: The Classical Opera of Globalized China: A Long Story Briefly Told." Online. Available HTTP: <http://www.confucius.umich.edu/uploads/HcHLEQLsVE6yBvqVb726.pdf>.

Lopez, J. (2003) *Theatrical Convention and Audience Response in Early Modern Drama*, Cambridge: Cambridge University Press.

Lough, J. (1979) *Seventeenth-Century French Drama: The Background*, Oxford: Clarendon Press; New York: Oxford University Press.

McKendrick, M. (1989) *Theatre in Spain, 1490–1700*, Cambridge: Cambridge University Press.

McLuhan, M. (1962) *The Gutenberg Galaxy: The Making of Typographic Man*, Toronto: University of Toronto Press.

Nicholson, E.A. (1993) "The Theater," in N.Z. Davis and A. Farge (eds) *History of Women in the West, Vol. III: Renaissance and Enlightenment Paradoxes*, Cambridge, MA: Belknap Press, 295–314.

Parker, A.A. (1971) *The Approach to the Drama of the Spanish Golden Age*, London: Hispanic and Luso-Brazilian Councils.

Peters, J.S. (2000) *Theatre of the Book, 1480–1880: Print, Text, and Performance in Europe*, Oxford: Oxford University Press.

Sayer, J. (2006) *Jean Racine: Life and Legend*, Bern: Peter Lang.

Shively, D.H. (2002) "*Bakufu* versus *Kabuki*," in S. Leiter (ed.) *A Kabuki Reader: History and Performance*, Armonk, New York: M.E. Sharpe.

Soufas, T.S. (ed.) (1997) *Women's Acts: Plays by Women Dramatists of Spain's Golden Age*, Lexington: University Press of Kentucky.

Waite, G. (2000) *Reformers on Stage: Popular Drama and Religious Propaganda in the Low Countries of Charles V, 1515–1556*, Toronto: University of Toronto Press.

PART III

Theatre and performance in periodical print cultures

PART III TIMELINE

DATE	THEATRE and PERFORMANCE	CULTURE and COMMUNICATION	POLITICS and ECONOMICS
1644–1912			Qing dynasty, China
c.1650	Introduction of chariot-and-pole scenery system		
c.1650–c.1800		Enlightenment era in Europe	
1653–1724	Chikamatsu Monzaemon, playwright		
1656–1743	Ferdinando Galli Bibiena, scenic designer		
1660			English Restoration; reign of Charles II (to 1685)
1662	Re-opening of theatres in England; women begin to play female roles		
1662–c.1800	Neoclassicism in England, Germany, Russia		
1670–1729	William Congreve, playwright		
1670s	Beginnings of the *aragoto* style of *kabuki* acting, Japan		
c.1675–c.1800			Height of Atlantic slave trade
1680	Comédie Française founded, France		
1685–1750		Johann Sebastian Bach, composer	
1694–1778	Voltaire, playwright and writer		
1697–1764		William Hogarth, artist	
c.1700–c.1750	Sentimental drama in England and France		
1702		First daily newspaper, *Daily Courant*, England	
1705–1782	Farinelli, singer		
1707–1793	Carlo Goldoni, playwright		
1709–1712		*The Tatler* and *The Spectator*, English periodicals	
1712–1778		Jean-Jacques Rousseau, writer	
1717–1779	David Garrick, actor		
1729–1781	Gotthold Ephraim Lessing, playwright and dramaturg		
1732–1799	Pierre-Augustin Caron Beaumarchais, playwright		
1737	Licensing Act imposes censorship on drama in England; censorship continues until 1968		
1741–1806	Ichikawa Danjūrō V, actor		
1749–1832	Johann Wolfgang von Goethe, playwright		

PART III TIMELINE

DATE	THEATRE and PERFORMANCE	CULTURE and COMMUNICATION	POLITICS and ECONOMICS
1756–1791	Wolfgang Amadeus Mozart, composer (many operas)		
1759–1805	Friedrich Schiller, playwright		
c.1760–c.1830			Industrial Revolution
c.1760–c.1880			Rise of nationalism in Europe, North America, and South America
1767–1769	Hamburg National Theatre		
1770–1827		Ludwig van Beethoven, composer	
1775–1783			American Revolutionary War
c.1780–c.1870		Romantic era	
1781		Immanuel Kant, *Critique of Pure Reason*	
1789			French Revolution
c.1790	Beginnings of *jingju* (Beijing Opera)		
c.1800	*Ta'ziyeh*, Muslim performance		
c.1800–c.1900	Melodrama in Europe and the U.S.		
c.1800–c.1900		Development of steam-powered railways and ships in Europe and North America enables faster trans- and intercontinental communication	
1807		Georg W.F. Hegel, *Phenomenology of Spirit*	
1813–1883	Richard Wagner, composer (many operas)		
1826–1914	Georg II, the Duke of Saxe-Meiningen, producer-director		
1828–1906	Henrik Ibsen, playwright		
1830			U.S. begins removing Native Americans to western parts of North America
1830–1962			French colonial rule in North and West Africa, Southeast Asia, and elsewhere
c.1830		Beginnings of modern photography	
1833			U.K. abolishes slavery
1833–1893	Edwin Booth, actor		
c.1835–c.1940	Minstrel shows		
1837		Commercial telegraph	
1840			Modern women's suffrage movement begins
1844–1900		Friedrich Nietzsche, philosopher	
1844–1923	Sarah Bernhardt, actor		
1845–1853			Major U.S. expansion westward

PART III TIMELINE

DATE	THEATRE and PERFORMANCE	CULTURE and COMMUNICATION	POLITICS and ECONOMICS
1848–1849			Revolutions throughout Europe
1848–1947			British rule in India
1849–1912	August Strindberg, playwright		
c.1850	Rise of realist stage settings, directors, and playwrights		
c.1850		Copyright laws begin to be passed; enforcement difficult	
c.1850–c.1900	Rise of realism in drama, stage design, and directing		
c.1850–c.1960	Variety shows (e.g., music hall, vaudeville, revues)		
1851		First World Fair	
1854			External and internal pressures force Japan to open to foreign trade
1856–1950	George Bernard Shaw, playwright		
1858–1943	André Antoine, director		
1859		Charles Darwin, *On the Origin of Species*	
1860–1904	Anton Chekhov, playwright		
c.1860–c.1925		Impressionism in painting	
1861–1865			U.S. Civil War
1862–1928	Adolphe Appia, stage designer		
1863–1938	Konstantin Stanislavsky, director		
1864–1911	Kawakami Otojirō, actor-playwright		
1867		Karl Marx, *Capital* vol. I	
1867–1936	Luigi Pirandello, playwright		
1868			Meiji Restoration in Japan
c.1870–c.1900	Rise of the director		
1871		Charles Darwin, *The Descent of Man*	
1872–1946	Kawakami Sadayakko, actor		
1872–1966	Edward Gordon Craig, theatre theorist		
1876		Electric telephone Phonograph	
1877–1927		Isadora Duncan, dancer	
1879		Electric light bulb	
c.1880–c.1900	Avant-garde theatre, first generation		
1880–1914			"Scramble for Africa": European powers divide Africa among themselves

PART III TIMELINE

DATE	THEATRE and PERFORMANCE	CULTURE and COMMUNICATION	POLITICS and ECONOMICS
1881–c.1914	Naturalist movement		
1881–1973		Pablo Picasso, artist	
1882–1971		Igor Stravinsky, composer	
1884–1885			First Sino–Japanese War
1885		Automobile	
1886–1919	Matsui Sumako, actor		
1887–1896	Théâtre Libre		
1889–c.1930	Symbolist theatre		
1895		First public motion picture screening, France	
1895		Radio	
c.1895–c.1930	*Shimpa*		
1898			Spanish–American War
1898–	Moscow Art Theatre (various name changes after 1932)		
1900		Sigmund Freud, *The Interpretation of Dreams*	
1903		First successful airplane	
1904		Vacuum tube: beginning of electronics	
1904		Sigmund Freud, *The Psychopathology of Everyday Life*	
1909–	*Shingeki*		
c.1910–c.1925		Cubism in art	
c.1910–c.1930	Avant-garde theatre, second generation		
1914–1918			The Great War (aka the First World War)
1914–	Takarazuka Revue		
c.1915–		Jazz	

Introduction: Theatre for bourgeois civil society

Tobin Nellhaus

The SPECTATOR.

Non fumum ex fulgore, fed ex fumo dare lucem Cogitat, ut fpeciofa dehinc miracula promat. Hor.

To be Continued every Day.

Thurfday, March 1. 1711.

I Have obferved, that a Reader feldom perufes a Book with Pleafure 'till he knows whether the Writer of it be a black or a fair Man, of a mild or cholerick Difpofition, Married or a Batchelor, with other Particulars of the like nature, that conduce very much to the right Underftanding of an Author. To gratify this Curiofity, which is fo natural to a Reader, I defign this Paper, and my next, as Prefatory Difcourfes to my following Writings, and fhall give fome Account in them of the feveral Perfons that are engaged in this Work. As the chief Trouble of Compiling, Digefting and Correcting will fall to my Share, I muft do my felf the Juftice to open the Work with my own Hiftory.

I was born to a fmall Hereditary Eftate, which I find, by the Writings of the Family, was bounded by the fame Hedges and Ditches in *William* the Conqueror's Time that it is at prefent, and has been delivered down from Father to Son whole and entire, without the Lofs or Acquifition of a fingle Field or Meadow, during the Space of fix hundred Years. There goes a Story in the Family, that when my Mother was gone with Child of me about three Months, fhe dreamt that fhe was brought to Bed of a Judge: Whether this might proceed from a Law-Suit which was then depending in the Family, or my Father's being a Juftice of the Peace, I cannot determine; for I am not fo vain as to think it prefaged any Dignity that I fhould arrive at in my future Life, though that was the Interpretation which the Neighbourhood put upon it. The Gravity of my Behaviour at my very firft Appearance in the World, and all the Time that I fucked, feemed to favour my Mother's Dream: For, as fhe has often told me, I threw away my Rattle before I was two Months old, and would not make ufe of my Coral 'till they had taken away the Bells from it.

As for the reft of my Infancy, there being nothing in it remarkable, I fhall pafs it over in Silence. I find, that, during my Nonage, I had the Reputation of a very fullen Youth, but was always a Favourite of my School-Mafter, who ufed to fay, *that my Parts were folid and would wear well.* I had not been long at the Univerfity, before I diftinguifhed my felf by a moft profound Silence: For during the Space of eight Years, excepting in the publick Exercifes of the College, I fcarce uttered the Quantity of an hundred Words; and indeed do not remember that I ever fpoke three Sentences together in my whole Life. Whilft I was in this Learned Body I applied my felf with fo much Diligence to my Studies, that there are very few celebrated Books, either in the Learned or the Modern Tongues, which I, am not acquainted with.

Upon the Death of my Father I was refolved to travel into Foreign Countries, and therefore left the Univerfity, that had a great deal of unaccountable Fellow, that had a great deal of Learning, if I would but fhow it. An infatiable Thirft after Knowledge carried me into all the Countries of *Europe*, where there was any thing new or ftrange to be feen; nay, to fuch a Degree was my Curiofity raifed, that having read the Controverfies of fome great Men concerning the Antiquities of *Egypt*, I made a Voyage to *Grand Cairo*, on purpofe to take the Meafure of a Pyramid; and as foon as I had fet my felf right in that Particular, returned to my Native Country with great Satisfaction.

I have paffed my latter Years in this City, where I am frequently feen in moft publick Places, tho' there are not above half a dozen of my felect Friends that know me; of whom my next Paper fhall give a more particular Account. There is no Place of Publick Refort, wherein I do not often make my Appearance; fometimes I am feen thrufting my Head into a Round of Politicians at *Will's*, and liftning with great Attention to the Narratives that are made in thofe little Circular Audiences. Sometimes I fmoak a Pipe at *Child's*; and whilft I feem attentive to nothing but the *Poft-Man*, over-hear the Converfation of every Table in the Room. I appear on *Sunday* Nights at St. *James's* Coffeehoufe, and fometimes join the little Committee of Politicks in the Inner-Room, as one who comes there to hear and improve. My Face is likewife very well known at the *Grecian*, the *Cocoa-Tree*, and in the Theaters both of *Drury-Lane*, and the *Hay-Market*. I have been taken for a Merchant upon

The first page of the first issue of *The Spectator*, 1711.

Source: Hulton Archive/Culture Club/Getty Images.

During the period spanning roughly 1700–1930, the Western world underwent profound transformations. For two millennia, merchants, tradesmen, manufacturers, and various types of professionals had only modest social and economic power and virtually no cultural influence. Often they were the butt of humor, such as the unintelligible lawyers and quack physicians of *commedia dell'arte* (see Chapter 4) and the ridiculous would-be aristocrat of Molière's *The Bourgeois Gentleman*. Because they lived mainly in the urban centers, this social class was called the bourgeoisie, derived from a French word for "city." (The term "capitalists" refers to part of the bourgeoisie: the owners of assets used to create private profits, such as industrialists and financiers.) But starting in the seventeenth century, the bourgeoisie became increasingly affluent and started exercising political power. In England, their rise to power was achieved by Parliament progressively whittling away at the monarch's rule via legislation, starting in 1689; elsewhere it occurred violently, most conspicuously in the American Revolution of 1775–1783, and the French Revolution of 1789–1799. By the nineteenth century the bourgeoisie was politically ascendant throughout Europe and North America. Absolutism reached its end, and the nation-state came into being.

A development within print culture played a pivotal role in this upheaval. During the seventeenth century, there were various efforts to establish regular newspapers (published weekly or every few days), but these attempts were short-lived. Around 1700, the growth of business and transportation networks made daily newspapers sustainable. As Chapter 7 explains, the development of reliable periodical publication had deep cultural, social, and political effects. The most salient was the formation of what philosopher and social theorist Jürgen Habermas (1989) described as the social and political "public sphere" and historian Benedict Anderson (1991) conceptualized as the "imagined community": the unification of a people, or more precisely a country's bourgeoisie, into a political identity – a nation. Anderson described nations as "communities" because within their borders, their members were portrayed as equals; but they were "imagined" communities because individuals could never know or even hear about everyone in the nation. Newspapers built nationhood because they put a country in conversation with itself and provided an image of the country as a whole.

The shift from purely oral to literate culture and the later rise of print culture involved new technologies; this time, however, dramatic changes in politics and culture arose through a change in how the existing technology was used. Print culture now possessed two main forms: the book and the periodical. Chapter 7 describes how theatre in the Western world participated in these eighteenth-century developments. Sometimes the theatre satirized people and activities which threatened to undermine the premise of equality within the public sphere. But more often, it sought to foster a sense of fellow-feeling (termed "sentiment") among people – the spirit of the public sphere's opposite, the private sphere. Together the public and private spheres define bourgeois society. Theatre was increasingly recognized as a profession, and actors could be lionized as public figures and their techniques studied. Yet "low" forms of entertainment also thrived, much to the consternation and scorn of the bourgeoisie.

Nationhood was quickly, often simultaneously, accompanied by nationalism. Nationalism asserts that only those people born within a geographic region have the right to govern it, and they must be independent of "foreign" powers. Nationalism is complex, and Chapter 8 distinguishes between three kinds. The earliest, which expanded the ideas guiding the early eighteenth-century public sphere, emphasized Enlightenment ideals of equal rights and rational discourse. Ironically, these genial ideals became fodder for two revolutions. The American Revolutionary War joined separate British colonies to produce the United States under a constitutional democracy. (Interestingly, one of the revolution's leaders was a newspaper publisher and editorialist: Benjamin Franklin.) However, in the French Revolution, years of political turmoil culminated in a coup led by Napoleon Bonaparte, who soon proclaimed himself emperor and launched a series of wars in a quest to rule Europe. The second form of nationalism focused on the supposed native characteristics of the land and its people's spirit, which were shaped by their history – both its glories and tragedies. This cultural nationalism rebuffed the universality claimed by the Enlightenment in favor of each country's uniqueness. But in some cases it putrefied into racial nationalism, the third type, which replaced unity through shared territorial history with unity through shared genealogy or "blood." Implicitly undermining the nation-state itself, racism denied the rights of some of the country's residents and sought to unite members of a "ruling race" within an imagined community of common racial descent. As a result, the pursuit of equal rights that had fueled eighteenth-century revolutions was sometimes ousted by an ideology of superiority which, well into the twenty-first century, could erupt into state-sanctioned genocides and racial or ethnic civil wars. Chapter 8 traces the rise of these three nationalisms and theatre's place within them, such as national theatres, Romanticism, melodrama, and minstrel shows.

Napoleon's campaign to conquer Europe was a form of imperialism. Imperialism – the formation of empires controlled by a central power – has been part of history for millennia. In modern Europe it began in earnest with the absolutist monarchies discussed in Chapter 6. The Spanish conquest of the Americas during the sixteenth century is an example. Starting in the eighteenth century, imperialist expansion was increasingly tied to capitalism; in the nineteenth century, driven forward by industries' demands for raw materials and foreign trade, European imperialism massively intensified. Ideologies of bestowing civilization upon "backward" people played a role as well. By the early twentieth century, the British Empire ruled about a fifth of the world's population and a quarter of its land. With these expansions of power came complex attitudes toward foreign cultures, including paternalism, fear, and exoticism. Chapter 9 describes some manifestations of the West's imperialist fascination with (and terror of) foreign cultures, such as World Fairs which exhibited "specimens" of non-Westerners, and theatrical performances which showcased the sometimes frightening, sometimes appealing character of foreign peoples.

During the same period, in China – another huge but much older empire, with a quite different social structure – this process was inverted. Far from being intrigued by the provincial cultures, the upper classes in the urban centers at first disdained them. The lower classes, however, were captivated by the unfamiliar performances brought by touring companies. Eventually several genres of provincial performance fused and established an enduring form – *jingju*, often called Beijing Opera – that slowly gained upper-class acceptance.

While the modern nation came into being in the late eighteenth century, an Industrial Revolution also began. Steam-powered machines increasingly replaced the hands that produced commodities. Over the course of the nineteenth century, industrial capitalism expanded throughout the Western world and became the dominant economic system. Railways connected cities within and between countries; steamers shipped goods, raw materials, and people all over the world; electric power started to light the cities. Industrialists profited handsomely while also bringing significant improvements to urban life – but the working class found themselves stripped of control over their existence and lived hand to mouth, working 12 or more hours a day, six or seven days a week. Whole families, including children, had to work for their meager living, amid highly dangerous conditions where even death was not uncommon. Not surprisingly, the bourgeoisie's industrial revolution was soon met with workers' labor unions and efforts at political revolution. Many workers sought a socialist economy, in which manufacturing would be taken over by the laborers and would produce goods to serve needs rather than profit. German philosopher and economist Karl Marx, a major advocate of socialism, developed highly influential (and to the bourgeoisie, highly subversive) analyses of how capitalism operated and how economic classes struggled for power across history. In the early twentieth century, the pressures of nationalism, capitalism, and imperialism exploded into a world war, followed by a revolution in Russia (eventually creating the Soviet Union) and a failed one in Germany.

These economic and political developments form the background to late nineteenth-century European theatre and its two major legacies. One was the producer-director, who wrested financial and artistic control from the actors. This was the first version of the modern director, who determined how (and often, by whom) a play would be performed, and insisted that actors and designers adhere to those ideas. Although the theatre was certainly no factory, such rigidity and centralization of decision-making was similar to the control that factory bosses had over their workers.

From the beginning, producer-directors pursued aesthetic realism – the second major legacy of the nineteenth century, which was already developing at the middle of the century. Realism fit well with the concept of a public sphere that was rooted in periodical print culture. It also dovetailed with the scientific objectivity needed in designing machinery and pursuing profits. Before long, realism was adopted in North America and Japan. Chapter 9 discusses the major varieties of nineteenth-century realism; more would develop in the twentieth century.

At the end of the century, alternatives to realism began to arise. They substituted the objectivity assumed by realism with subjective or spiritual perspectives (a good fit with the private sphere), and they rejected realistic aesthetics. Realism and the early "avant-gardes" overlapped chronologically so closely that some realist playwrights also wrote in the alternative genres. Chapter 10 surveys the highly diverse first-generation avant-garde movements that developed in the early twentieth century. A cultural separation between mainstream and avant-garde theatre began to take shape, an early twentieth-century legacy continuing today.

The proliferation of stylistic genres had its roots in both book and periodical print culture, and also (as Chapter 10 observes) in the impact of photography, telephones, and phonographs – heralds of new forms of communication. Yet the diversity didn't reflect unfettered imagination: the fact that playwrights could readily switch from an objective to a subjective style hints that there were hidden connections between realism and its opposition. As discussed in Chapter 5, early print culture positioned the individual as the source of perception and knowledge. The seventeenth-century scientific revolution was founded on individuals taking the evidence of their own senses or their own reason as the source of verifiable truth. By the late seventeenth century, science's use of sense experience had ripened into a philosophy called empiricism; Descartes' focus on reason developed into rationalism. However, both philosophies had an objective cast: objects are perceived and logic is conducted by individuals, but they are independent of individuals as such – anyone else can check their accuracy.

But as we've noted, periodical print culture – an organ of bourgeois society – created a division between a public sphere and a private sphere. The latter was the realm of the individual's home and heart, faith and feeling, and only the individual could attest to his or her own emotions and beliefs. With this division, a true contrast between the objective and the subjective arose – a polarity founded on the bedrock of individualism. The notion that individual experience was the foundation for all knowledge (whether that experience consisted of objective observations or subjective perceptions) provided the fundamental contrast between the realisms and the avant-gardes. This polarity suggests one reason why a dramatist might readily switch from writing highly realist plays to symbolically oriented drama: in many ways, they are the sides of a single coin.

Both the realistic and the avant-garde styles arose out of efforts to define and represent truth, whether that truth was objective or subjective. For example, in 1881 French playwright Émile Zola wrote that "environments, the study of which has transformed the sciences and humanities, must inevitably assume an important place in theatre," because "environment should determine character" (Zola 1881: 365). Likewise, the Belgian Maurice Maeterlinck, considered a Symbolist, wrote in 1896 that "in the ordinary drama, the indispensable dialogue by no means corresponds to reality; and it is just those words that are spoken by the side of the rigid, apparent truth . . . that conform to a deeper truth" (Maeterlinck 1897: 112).

There is yet a third characteristic shared by the realists and the avant-gardes, closely tied to their concern with the presentation of truth on stage: a strong ambivalence toward theatricality, and sometimes even outright antitheatricality. One advocate of realism held that the goal of presenting environments in minute detail is to replace theatrical artifice with "a near-perfect reality, in other words, to drive the 'Theatre' gradually from the theatre" (quoted in K. Williams 2001: 285). Within the early avant-gardes, hostility to theatricality was sometimes equally strong. In 1907, avant-gardist Edward Gordon Craig complained that the actor's inescapable, unreliable body and emotions eliminated the possibility of exact reproduction and perfection, and so he proclaimed, "The actor must go, and in his place comes the inanimate figure – the *Über-marionette*," which he described as a "symbolic creature" (1911: 81, 84). Citing Plato, he criticized the actor as merely "an imitator" who "cannot convey the spirit and essence of an idea," but only "a facsimile of the thing itself" (63). The premises born within literate culture two thousand years earlier about the nature of truth and representation still generated misgivings about theatre.

The director, realism, avant-gardes, and antitheatricality within theatre are still with us. As we will see in Part IV, during the twentieth century all of them would undergo alterations, sometimes putting into question the idea of individualism and the supposed opposition between theatre and truth. Nevertheless they persist, shaping the majority of theatre today. The path from sentimentalism to realism and avant-gardes presented in Part III is the story of contemporary theatre's beginnings.

★

CHAPTER 7

Theatre and sentiment: newspapers, private lives, and the bourgeois public sphere, 1700–1785

Tobin Nellhaus

Contributor: Bruce McConachie

As the Introduction to Part III observed, European print culture began to change around 1700 with the publication and wide dissemination of newspapers, magazines, journals, and other periodicals. Unlike books, which were printed "for the ages," periodicals were "of the day," like blogs and Twitter, intended to bring current news to a broad readership with common interests. Where early book culture generally helped to legitimize absolutism, periodical print culture after 1700 enabled the new bourgeoisie to solidify its values and to enlarge the arena of public discourse. Periodical culture also promoted a sense of private life that helped to underwrite a "sentimental" theatre embracing the morality and feelings of the emerging middle class. We open this chapter by discussing the connection between the periodical press and sentiment, which will allow us to explore the development of sentimental drama.

That was not the only type of theatre to thrive during the eighteenth century. Particularly in England, satire played an important role in both the theatrical offerings and the political discourse of the day. In addition, throughout Europe forms of performance arose that attracted all classes, especially the lower ones. Many of these popular genres involved music and song, which heightened their appeal and, perhaps more importantly, sometimes allowed the theatres to escape the stranglehold that the officially sanctioned theatres had through their monopolies over tragedy and comedy. In England, however, popular performance often included political satire so biting that a system of censorship was imposed which lasted until 1968.

In Japan, too, theatre was continually scrutinized by the shogunate. In our first case study, we discuss how the shoguns regulated *kabuki* as a way to control its potential for social disruption. There were strict limits on intermingling between actors and the public, sometimes attended by harsh punishments for infractions, as well as censorship on the political and moral content of *kabuki* performances.

By the last third of the eighteenth century, sentimentalist thought developed an extreme form more deeply opposed to rationalism, especially the Enlightenment rationalism that dominated continental thought and drama. These ideas particularly influenced German drama.

Most of the plays of eighteenth-century Europe did not survive the test of time, even if they were enormously popular in their own day. Often what captured the audiences was the power of the acting. Although to us, eighteenth-century acting seems stylized and presentational, to the audiences of the time it broke new ground in realism. Many actors became renowned not only in their own countries, but throughout Europe.

The most famous of all was David Garrick, the premier English actor of the mid-eighteenth century. In the second case study, we explore how Garrick encouraged the use of prints and even commissioned paintings in order to strengthen his standing as a lead actor of the age and make him a popular star.

Sentiment and periodical print culture

Although "sentiment" bears negative connotations today, many eighteenth-century playwrights, actors, and spectators in Europe valued sentiments for the refinement, knowledge, and moral uplift they might provide. Sentiments were not the syrupy emotions that today we associate with "sentimentality": the term invoked a view of human nature and cultured behavior. A sentimental play (or poem or novel) could evoke feelings of sympathy, joy, and sorrow for worthy others that allowed genteel spectators (and readers) to test the depths of their own emotional responses and to broaden the reach of their moral concerns. Those who embraced sentimental culture believed that humans were innately good, and that personal and social bonds would thrive if individuals were true to their "natural" virtues. As we shall see, a significant school of philosophy endorsed this moral and aesthetic point of view in the eighteenth century. Bourgeois sentimentalism helped to drive Baroque culture out of favor and challenged aristocratic neoclassicism in the theatre throughout Europe during the 1700s.

The culture of sentiment did not appear out of thin air: it was created and fostered by a new type of print culture based in the periodical press. Efforts to publish periodicals began as far back as 1600, but most of the earliest newspapers struggled to survive and did not last long. Generally they were published once a week or every few days, and offered only business information or official government records. It wasn't until the early 1700s that urbanization, business demands, political activity, cultural desires, city and inter-city postal systems, and growing maritime trade made it financially and logistically feasible to sustain daily publication, and to expand coverage to include topics with broad appeal.

One thing periodicals did *not* require was any change in technology: periodical print culture arose because people utilized the existing technology in a new way. The development of periodical print culture is an example of how important changes in communication practices are not always tied to changes in communication technology. Economic, political, and other factors play a role in changing communication practices and ways of thinking. For their financial survival, periodicals needed a method for sustaining interest. Books are generally read by solitary individuals at whatever day and time is convenient. A single printing of a book may satisfy reader demand for decades. But newspapers, magazines, and other periodicals are meant to be read by many people throughout a significant geographical area, more or less at the same time, and with each new issue. The challenge in publishing a periodical is ensuring that readers return for subsequent issues. One way a periodical can achieve that goal is by concentrating on a particular subject, such as ever-changing business news, fashion, or celebrity activities; or conversely, by giving a picture of the entire society by covering all subjects. Another way is to create a sense of narrative, so that the reader wonders what will happen next.

England was at the forefront in developing daily periodicals. Among the reasons were politics and economics. In 1688 and again in 1714, problems of religion and royal succession led Parliament to install kings of its own choosing from the royal lineage, making absolutism on the French model impossible. Merchants, traders, and investors gained more power in England. The top tier of the English bourgeoisie, who were growing rich on colonial domination, expanding domestic markets and the international slave trade, sought a government that would protect and expand its interests. They required daily newspapers with important business and political news; and as their public roles advanced, they demanded intense partisanship as well. They and other middle-class men and women sought periodicals that would keep them up-to-date on social affairs and culture in London, and justify their emerging cultural values.

Social life, family, fellowship, and culture were the subjects of two early periodicals: *The Tatler*, published three times a week during 1709–1711 and edited by Richard Steele (1672–1729); and *The Spectator*, a daily edited by Steele, and Joseph Addison (1672–1719) from 1711 to 1712. Despite the brief spans of their existence, they were enormously important: often distributed in coffeehouses, issues of *The Tatler* and *The Spectator* were read by perhaps 80,000 Londoners and many beyond London, and frequently they were read aloud for others' enjoyment. The two papers present superb examples of how a periodical can unite readers across space and time, creating a social ambience by focusing the papers on the readers themselves, encouraging them to share the paper and eagerly anticipate what might come next. The editors strived to create the sense of a benevolent community among their readers. Addison and Steele published essays advocating mutual trust and self-disclosure within circles of families and friends, and they invited letters to the editor to foster such a circle of affection within their readership. In contrast to aristocratic culture, which emphasized a hierarchical order and the public projection of social status, Addison and Steele underlined the importance of social bonds and fellow-feeling in public communications. Unlike today's *Us Weekly*, which celebrates celebrities, *The Tatler* and *The Spectator* were truly about "us." As the models for hundreds of subsequent periodicals, *The Tatler* and *The Spectator* broadcast the principles of sentiment in the early eighteenth century. The form as well as the content of the new periodicals thus underwrote the legitimacy of bourgeois sentimentalism and broadened its reach.

English sentimental culture drew on the principles of "moral sense" philosophy, which was closely tied to Enlightenment values. Liberal thinkers of the age distinguished their ideas from those of previous philosophers, who had advocated absolutism. For example, in 1651 Thomas Hobbes had written that a strong monarchical government was necessary to control the problems created by rapacious individual interests. In contrast, in 1690 John Locke (1632–1704) – one of the luminaries of the Enlightenment – urged that free individuals in a state of nature might form civil governments that could channel competing interests toward socially beneficial results. Locke, immersed in print culture, also believed that people were like blank pieces of paper when they were born, awaiting the "imprint" of their parents and society.

Locke's ideas about the association of free individuals became a concrete reality through papers such as *The Tatler* and *The Spectator*. These periodicals relegated politics to the margins, contained little or no news (they even ridiculed "newsmongering"), and focused instead on human foibles and promoted a culture of politeness. Their efforts to form a polite society founded on personal character and sensibility helped to create a bourgeois distinction between the public sphere (where issues of politics, economics, and culture are debated) and the private sphere (the realm of the home, family, and friends). The distinction was brought into sentimental drama, and as we will see, it was not the only theatrical genre that contributed to separating the public and private spheres.

Later moral sense philosophers built upon Locke's premises to argue that humanity had an inherent sense of right and wrong and would generally choose the right for its natural beauty and worth. A bad environment, however, could "impress" other values on children, they believed. According to moral sense philosopher Adam Smith (1723–1790), all people had within them an "ideal spectator of our sentiments and conduct" (Kramnick 1995: 287), who, awakened by social pressure, would ensure that each person does his or her moral duty. Like friendly conversation and the sight of strangers in distress, watching the right play could awaken that "ideal spectator" in the mind and steer the playgoer toward affection and beneficence. For the moral sense philosophers, morality was inherent and natural; doing the right thing flowed from emotional sensitivity, not abstract reason.

Sentimental drama in England

Just as periodical publication flourished earliest in England, so too did sentimental theatre. It was in part a response to criticism of the often racy Restoration plays. Early advocates of sentiment found temporary allies among the Puritans. Puritan attacks on the wickedness of the London stage increased in the 1690s, culminating in Jeremy Collier's (1650–1726) *A Short View of the Immorality and Profaneness of the English Stage* in 1698. Beginning with the neoclassical precept that "the business of plays is to recommend virtue and discountenance vice," Collier castigated several comedies from the aristocratic Restoration era for "their smuttiness of expression; their swearing, profaneness, and lewd application of Scripture; their abuse of the clergy; and their making their top characters libertines and giving them success in their debauchery" (Collier 1974: 351–2). Collier's attack aroused indignation in some, struck home for others (a few playwrights even apologized), and garnered public support that altered playwriting. For example, one of Collier's targets was William Congreve (1670–1729), who published an impassioned retort; but stifled by the changed atmosphere, after writing *The Way of the World* (1700) – considered a jewel of Restoration comedy – Congreve left the stage. Both Collier's reproach and the playwrights' reactions were motivated by the rise of bourgeois culture throughout Europe. Even before Collier's *Short View*, some playwrights were already softening Restoration cynicism and arranging sentimental endings for their plays. In *Love's Last Shift* (1696), for instance, actor-playwright Colley Cibber (1671–1757) celebrated several characters for their inherent goodness and featured a rakish hero, Loveless, who gladly repents of his compulsive woman-chasing in the last act. While Cibber was writing popular variations on this formula in the first decade of the eighteenth century, playwright George Farquhar (1678–1707) took several of his dramatic characters and conflicts out of London into the more sentimental air of the English countryside.

Steele often campaigned in *The Tatler* and *The Spectator* to replace the wittiness and eroticism of Restoration comedy with sentiment. His play *The Conscious Lovers* (1722) demonstrated what he had in mind. Its plot centers on young John Bevil, Jr., who has ensconced a mysterious female stranger in rooms that he is paying for. However, he promised his father that he will wed a girl of his father's choosing. Although Bevil loves the beautiful stranger, Indiana, whom he treats with courteous respect, he obligingly prepares to marry his father's choice, Lucinda. Lucinda's father, a rich businessman, suspects Bevil of duplicity and investigates the relationship between Bevil and his mysterious beauty. This sets up a recognition scene in which the businessman discovers that Indiana is his long-lost daughter. Bevil can now marry Indiana, who is suddenly rich, and still meet his father's approval. (Steele's plot conveniently provides a suitor for Lucinda.) Eleven years before in *The Spectator*, Steele had announced his belief that "A man that is temperate, generous, valiant, chaste, faithful, and honest, may, at the same time, have wit, humor, mirth, good breeding, and gallantry" (*The Spectator*, April 28,1711, in Dukore 1974: 392). He created Bevil partly to prove his point. *The Conscious Lovers*, which was wildly successful, drew sympathetic tears as well as laughter from English audiences for the rest of the eighteenth century.

Notions of sentiment affected tragedy as well as comedy during the 1700s. Early in the century, Nicholas Rowe (1674–1718) wrote several tragedies featuring pathetic heroines that partly broke the mold of neoclassical tragic form. With *The London Merchant* (1731), however, playwright George Lillo (1693–1739) crafted a tragedy that dispensed completely with the idealized aristocratic heroes and constraining unities of neoclassicism. Its naïve protagonist, the apprentice George Barnwell, is enthralled by the prostitute Sarah Millwood, who entices him into stealing money from his bourgeois master, Thorowgood, and later into murdering his rich uncle as well. Throughout the play, Lillo contrasts the optimistic and benevolent sentiments of the merchant, with Millwood's deep-rooted resentments (based, interestingly, on her misuse by men, providing the audience with a moment of psychological understanding). Despite Thorowgood's attempts to save him, a repentant Barnwell dies on the gallows – but not before Lillo props him up as an example of the destructiveness of unbridled sexual passion that threatens the social stability that the merchant economy has built. *The London Merchant* achieved immense popularity and inspired several imitations. Real-life London merchants, who expected the morality of the play to produce wholesome and profitable results, sent their own apprentices to see the show during the Christmas season for a century.

Watching *The Conscious Lovers*, *The London Merchant*, and other sentimental plays, spectators generally expected to immerse themselves in the feelings of sentimental heroes and those with whom they sympathized. The objects of sympathetic concern in sentimental plays ranged from slaves, to the poor, to distraught maidens, all the way to general pity for suffering humanity. According to sentimental aesthetics, exposure to such feelings on stage would spark a sentimental response in the genteel viewer, who might then use this response to improve his or her own sensitivity and morality. Like *The Tatler* and *The Spectator*, sentimental plays sought to evoke a benevolent community in the audience. In this manner, sentimental drama contributed to the establishment of the bourgeois private sphere, which along with the public sphere was a major byproduct of periodical print culture. Book-oriented neoclassicism instead generally kept spectators at a greater emotional distance and involved them more typically in feelings of awe, disdain, and suspense rather than sympathy, sorrow, and generous good humor.

The helpless heroines of sentimental drama were a far cry from the smart, urbane women sparking the stage just a few years before. They reflected the etiquette of the bourgeois private sphere, which restricted women to the domain of gentle domesticity. Similarly, women effectively vanished again from the ranks of new playwrights. In the first decades of the 1700s, a few women had stood as successors to Aphra Behn (discussed in chapters 4 and 6), such as Susanna Centlivre (*c.*1667–1723); but after 1725, new plays by women were rarely performed, and none would achieve popular success for another 50 years.

In contrast with neoclassical drama, sentimental drama chose middle-class figures rather than aristocrats as its heroes, endorsed benevolent paternalism instead of royal absolutism for its ethics, and emphasized empathetic responses over judgments. By the mid-eighteenth century, the ethos of the private sphere had reconfigured the traditional forms of tragedy and comedy on the London stage. The neoclassical tragedies that had dominated the repertory were fading in popularity for new tragic performances that featured more pathos and tears, and comedies featured sententious moralizing and few laughs. Bourgeois sentimentalism had become firmly entrenched in the dominant culture of England.

Pantomime, satire, and censorship in England

English sentimental drama, including both comedy and tragedy, supported the values of the rising merchant class and the minor aristocracy, the prime constituents of the public sphere. Other types of performance sought to entertain a broader audience, including those at the margins of the bourgeois public sphere, such as tradesmen, workers, soldiers, small-scale shop-keepers, and others from outside the elite. Dances and pantomimes were the most important during the early eighteenth century, but there were also songs, performances of instrumental music, acrobatics, and other entertainments. Most of these diversions were performed between acts of a play; the pantomimes usually appeared as afterpieces.

Pantomime had originated during Roman imperial rule (see Chapter 2). It re-emerged in fifteenth-century Italy as part of the *commedia dell'arte* tradition. When illegal fairground performances of *commedia* were suppressed in Paris in 1702, a number of performers from the *commedia* tradition sought work in London. Some of *commedia*'s non-verbal comic scenes were set to music and dance, and performed with a few of the key *commedia* characters in a transposed English context as "Italian night scenes."

At the beginning of the eighteenth century, pantomimes often had a serious intent or segment. In 1717 the dance master at London's Drury Lane Theatre, John Weaver, created *The Loves of Mars and Venus* featuring dancers impersonating Roman gods. It was advertised as a "new Entertainment in Dancing after the manner of the Antient [*sic*] Pantomimes" (of Rome). Rivaling it, John Rich (1692–1761), dancer, actor, and manager at the Lincoln's Inn Fields theatre, created his own pantomime with characters from Roman mythology, who were magically transformed in the second part of the performance into characters in a knock-about comedy. Rich, known by his stage name Lun, further developed and popularized this earliest form of British pantomime as "harlequinades" – spectacular performances in which the *commedia* character, Harlequin, magically underwent self-transformation, or transformed the scenery with a touch of his magic sword or wand. In the 1720s spectacle and farce became increasingly prominent. But to appeal to every type of audience, serious scenes based on mythology came to alternate with episodes of farce, fantasy, or intrigue, with plenty of spectacle to go around.

The pantomimes became enormously popular, often more popular than the plays, and they elicited plenty of complaints from the upper-class audience, who felt they degraded the dignity of the stage. The pantomimes also stirred intense competition between the foremost theatres, Drury Lane and Lincoln's Inn Fields.

Some pantomimes enjoyed long runs, and they became a staple of London's theatrical offerings. Although scorned by critics, who described them as "irrational entertainments," the pantomimes were a major source of revenue for the theatres. In the middle of the eighteenth century the eminent actor David Garrick (1717–1779), who distanced himself from pantomime and even sought to undercut Harlequin's appeal, nevertheless produced his own pantomimes at Drury Lane, primarily at Christmastime. It was in Garrick's productions that Harlequin first began to speak. His costume of various colored patches also became a literal map for portraying his emotions. Touching red meant love, blue was truth, yellow indicated jealousy, and, to become invisible, Harlequin pointed to a black patch and "disappeared" in order to work his magic. The popularity of pantomimes never abated, and they continue in England to this day. (To read about the later history of pantomime, see the case study "British Pantomime" on the *Theatre Histories* website.)

Pantomime arose in part because theatrical licensing was allowed to slide, allowing four unlicensed theatres to operate in London in 1730, openly competing with the two major theatres, which were Drury Lane and (after 1732) Covent Garden. Aside from pantomimes, the patent theatres had little interest in innovation, and the most exciting developments were at these unlicensed theatres. The English merchant class, which was replacing the aristocracy as the dominant group both in the government and at London playhouses, approved of the fairground theatres no more than the monarchy had, and tried to shut them down, without success. By the middle of the decade, there was regular traffic between the fairs and the London theatres. London actors performed frequently at the fairs, and theatre managers borrowed rope dancers and jugglers for *entr'acte* entertainments and incorporated into their plays the political jibes that were common at the fairs.

In fact political satire appeared frequently at the unlicensed theatres. The taste for it became especially strong with the production of *The Beggar's Opera* (1728) by John Gay (1685–1732). In an era when opera meant imports from Italy, *The Beggar's Opera* achieved popular appeal by setting new words to popular songs, creating a genre called "ballad opera." Gay's play also parodied sentimental comedy, in part by up-ending the sort of characters it presented: rather than wealthy merchants, honorable shopkeepers, and urbane aristocrats, *The Beggar's Opera* was peopled by thieves, beggars, and prostitutes. Gay's travesty had a political point: by inverting the social pyramid, he implied that the upper classes were no better than robbers, mobsters, and other social leeches. Chief among his targets was the Prime Minister, Robert Walpole (1676–1745).

Walpole was at the opening night performance and seemed to take the digs with good humor. But he had the play's sequel *Polly* (published 1729) banned from the stage, and later, after almost a decade of increasingly savage theatrical attacks on his political manipulations, he lowered the boom and rushed the Licensing Act of 1737 through Parliament. The act strengthened the censorship exercised by the Lord Chamberlain (to whom the Master of the Revels reported) by requiring companies to submit all scripts for approval before performing them. It also limited to two the theatres authorized to perform plays: Drury Lane and Covent Garden in London (which paid sizable fees for the privilege). Requiring prior approval for all plays put an end to these attacks on Walpole, and it also ingratiated him with the royal family, whose troubles had led to some theatrical jabs as well. Limiting the number of theatres had an even more drastic effect on performance in London, since it removed all incentive for the licensed theatres to present almost anything but tried and true older plays and farcical afterpieces.

Although the 1737 act drove overt satire off the stage, its restrictions also forced some playwrights to couch their criticisms in subtler and more psychological forms. For the most part, though, the Licensing Act transformed London playhouses from arenas of debate and political dissension into models of decorum and false consensus. Walpole had succeeded in pushing the bill through primarily because others in the governing classes also preferred censorship to derisive laughter. English theatre's participation in the public sphere through satire effectively ceased until the Licensing Act was repealed in 1968.

Derisive laughter was nevertheless part of the new distinction between the public and private spheres. As one of the main sites where people gathered, theatre was embedded in the public sphere and played an active role in the political discourse of the time, no less important than the partisan editorializing that crowded the era's newspapers. William Hogarth (1697–1764), one of the leading artists of the eighteenth century, was especially well known for his satirical engravings caricaturing the politics and morals of the time. Hogarth, who was friends with Gay, even depicted a scene from *The Beggar's Opera* in one of his paintings (Figure 7.1). Walpole showed that although politics in the theatre can have a particularly powerful impact, it is much easier to censor than the press. But sometimes suppression creates interest, as Gay found when the banned *Polly* became a top seller when published. Satire off stage contributed to the vitality of the British public sphere.

Despite its short-term success, the 1737 act proved unwieldy over time. Designed to protect Walpole and the monarchy, the act made no provisions for theatre outside of London. Troupes and towns in the rest of the country simply ignored its strictures. Its numerous loopholes also allowed fairground managers and other theatre entrepreneurs to produce plays for lower-class patrons that encouraged a range of antisocial behavior. This led the governing classes to pass the Disorderly Houses Act of 1751, a new strategy in social control that lay responsibility for restraining the masses on those who owned and operated theatres. After 1751, all places for

Figure 7.1
A Scene from The Beggar's Opera (1729) by William Hogarth. The painting depicts a moment in Act III, sc. 11.

Courtesy of the Yale Center for British Art, Paul Mellon Collection.

entertainment of any kind within a 20-mile radius of London had to display a license that certified that the managers were liable for the good conduct of their patrons. The local constabulary might revoke the license if order were not maintained. Intended to cut down on the rioting that sometimes accompanied lower-class theatre, the 1751 act implicitly acknowledged that the Licensing Act of 1737 had not restricted all forms of theatre in the London area. The 1751 law admitted that it would be more effective to make managers responsible for the behavior of popular audiences than to try to dictate the form and content of their entertainments.

CASE STUDY: Censorship in eighteenth-century Japan

Carol Fisher Sorgenfrei

If a historian of Japanese theatre with no prior knowledge of the West suddenly discovered eighteenth-century English theatre, she might be amazed by its uncanny parallels to *kabuki* of the same period. *Kabuki* historian Samuel L. Leiter has noted the following, among others. In England and Japan, theatre was a successful, commercial business controlled primarily by actor-managers but under strict government surveillance, including licensing only a limited number of theatres. Theatre in both countries relied heavily on print media to advertise – in Japan, this included both woodblock prints of famous actors and critical commentary on *kabuki* (see Figure 7.2). The repertories in both nations were non-religious, popular plays, including many revivals, and audiences were both male and female, primarily from the urban, merchant class with some aristocrats also attending. Some spectators sat on the stage in both cultures; others observed from boxes, galleries, or a pit. Both *kabuki* and English stages had a front curtain, an apron extending into the audience, and complex machinery for rapid, sometimes spectacular scene shifts. Actors in both countries were highly paid, hugely popular stars who nonetheless were considered socially inferior. Acting was modeled on tradition and actors performed specialized role-types. Music and dance were often important elements in plays. In Japan as in England, all theatres had fairly recently been allowed to reopen after government closure, albeit subject to careful scrutiny and censorship (Leiter 2002: 297–8).

Such parallels would remind the scholar of a key issue often noted in this book: throughout the world, different cultures and different theatres develop in various ways, sometimes in tandem, sometimes sharply diverging. Of course,

Figure 7.2

A *kabuki* actor, from an *ukiyo-e* woodblock print by Utagawa Kunisada (1786–1865), a pupil of Toyokuni and famous for his prints of actors and courtesans.

© AKG–images, London.

she would also note many factors specific to each, such as *kabuki*'s *hanamichi* and England's (still relatively new) use of female actors.

In this case study, we focus on one aspect of Japanese theatre history: government control and censorship of eighteenth-century *kabuki* scripts. As we will see, the political and cultural situation in Japan led to somewhat different results from those in England.

As noted in Chapter 4, *kabuki*'s relation to the authorities was fraught from the start. *Kabuki* had always been a counter-cultural enterprise. The government had made many attempts to suppress or destroy it, primarily to discourage upper-class samurai and aristocrats from mingling with lower-class merchants and virtually outcast actors. Those who violated the laws were punished severely. An extreme example occurred in 1714, when a raucous theatre party revealed the nine-year love affair between the popular, handsome actor Ikushima Shingorō (1671–1743) and Ejima, a high-ranking lady in the women's quarters of the shogun's castle. Everyone who participated in the party or the love affair was punished. Ikushima was banished to a remote island for 18 years. Ejima was banished to another locale and her brother (who it was felt should have controlled her) was executed. The theatre where the party took place – the most popular of the four licensed theatres in Edo – was demolished and its assets and those of its owner were auctioned off. The other theatres were closed for three months, and major actors and managers were required to state in writing that they would abide by all laws. For the remainder of the Tokugawa period, there were only three licensed *kabuki* theatres in Edo.

Despite such measures, many samurai and aristocrats secretly attended *kabuki*, sometimes in disguise. The authorities understood that they could not completely destroy theatre. As pragmatic neo-Confucianists, they believed that limited access was preferable to a total ban. The government felt that "*kabuki* was, like prostitution, a necessary evil. These were the two wheels of the vehicle of pleasure, useful to assuage the people and divert them from more serious mischief" (Shively 1955: 41). Ironically, many of the attempted suppressions forced actors and managers to find creative ways to circumvent the laws, ultimately enhancing the art. Examples are the 1629 ban on female actors and the subsequent 1652 ban on handsome young males portraying females, both of which encouraged the creative development of the *onnagata*. Similarly, sumptuary laws, including restrictions and requirements for hair, wigs, and clothing/costumes (both in and out of the theatre), were partly responsible for the *kabuki* actor's distinctive visual style. Playwrights, too, found imaginative ways to avoid censorship.

In eighteenth-century Japan, scripts were censored only after the play opened, since there was no equivalent to England's Walpole or his 1737 Licensing Act. (Japan created an office similar to that of Lord Chamberlain, including the power of prior restraint, in 1875.) Japanese theatre of the time, unlike British theatre, did not attempt to satirize or critique the government. When Japanese authorities sought to censor scripts, it was because they presented content that was deemed socially unacceptable or politically dangerous. For example, in 1723, love-suicide plays (often based on actual events) were banned because it was felt they glorified and encouraged such behavior. Despite the ban (which lasted only a few years) and harsh punishments for survivors of attempted love-suicides, such works continued to be written, and actual love-suicides continued to occur. Other forbidden subjects were overt sexuality (despite the many references to both same-sex and heterosexual love), using the real names of living samurai or aristocrats, and dramatizing actual events after 1600 that involved samurai.

One method for circumventing the law was to substitute the facts and character names in a contemporary event with those from a well-known historical or legendary "world." Such substitution is called *mitate.* An example of how playwrights used *mitate* to avoid censorship is the play *Sukeroku: Flower of Edo* (1713). Sukeroku is a rowdy commoner in love with a gorgeous courtesan who refuses the advances of an evil samurai named Ikyū. The action takes place in Yoshiwara, Edo's "pleasure district," where theatre, teahouses, and brothels were located. In Sukeroku's danced entrance on the *hanamichi,* he wears a purple headband (a color permitted only to the upper classes), suggesting disdain for society's rules. (For a photo of Sukeroku's entrance, see Chapter 4, Figure 4.11.)

Like the merchants' ideal self, Sukeroku is brave, clever, funny, and a great lover. However, the contemporary surface is revealed as false. He is in disguise, and the time is not the present. He is actually one of the Soga brothers, historical samurai who avenged their murdered father in 1193. He typifies both the pluck of the Edo townsman and the samurai class's abandoned ideals. Sukeroku comically insults and picks fights with various samurai; when the evil Ikyū finally draws his sword, Sukeroku recognizes it as his father's, proving that Ikyū is the murderer. His character seems to suggest that common people, not actual samurai, possess the values and behaviors of *bushido* (the traditional "way of the samurai") which, due to a century of peace, seem to have been discarded by the upper classes.

Mitate is crucial in the period's most significant example of script censorship. The actual events took place between 1701 and 1703 and show how deeply the public revered the concept of *bushido.* A young, untutored samurai failed to bribe an elegant superior samurai, who mercilessly taunted him until the younger man drew his sword while in Edo castle, wounding the bully. In punishment, he was ordered to commit *seppuku* (suicide by disembowelment), his lands were confiscated, his retainers became *rōnin* (masterless samurai), and his family line was to be stamped out. On January 30, 1703, his former retainers, who had secretly plotted to avenge his death, attacked and murdered their lord's tormentor, aware that for this act of loyalty, they would be executed.

Their deeds polarized society. Numerous poems and essays glorified their act as an example of loyalty to their master and a heroic demonstration of apparently lost ideals. Others expressed more complex feelings. The Confucian philosopher Ogyū Sorai wrote that because they pursued the vendetta to avenge their lord's shame, and because

> they have followed the path of keeping themselves free from taint, their deed is righteous. However, this deed is appropriate only to their particular group; it amounts therefore to a special exception of the rules. . . . [T]hey deliberately planned an act of violence without official permission. This cannot be tolerated under the law. . . . If [they] are pronounced guilty and condemned to commit *seppuku,* in keeping with the traditions of the samurai, the claim of the [wronged] family will be satisfied, and the loyalty of the men will not have been disparaged.
>
> (Keene 1971: 2–3)

Seppuku, unlike simple execution, was an honorable death. The 46 who were ordered to commit *seppuku* (plus the 47th, admitted to the group posthumously after proving his loyalty) were buried in the same graveyard as their master; their burial place remains to this day a venerated pilgrimage site.

The rapid publication of materials dealing with the incident and subsequent trial ensured a well-informed population. Twelve days after the mass suicide, the first play based on the vendetta was staged, set (like *Sukeroku*) in the medieval world of the Soga brothers. Despite the substitutions, the government closed it after only three performances. Three years later, in a new third act tacked on to an existing play, Chikamatsu set the events in yet another historical era. Probably because it was staged in Osaka, this production was not closed down. It provided the standard "world" for later versions of the tale, including the one that became definitive: the 1748 puppet play *Chūshingura: The Treasury of Loyal Retainers*, subsequently adapted and performed as *kabuki*. Between 1706 and 1748, new versions were staged almost yearly, some with differing interpretations of the characters' motivations, others using new, spectacular staging. As long as the outer form did not violate the law, clever playwriting and staging could appease the censors while pleasing the audience. Even today, new versions continually appear, not only on stage, but as films and even year-long television series.

Key references

Brandon, J.R., ed. and trans. (1975) *Sukeroku: The Flower of Edo*, in *Kabuki: Five Classic Plays*, Honolulu: University of Hawaii Press, 49–92.

Keene, D., trans. (1971) *Chūshingura: The Treasury of Loyal Retainers*, New York and London: Columbia University Press.

Leiter, S.L. (2002) "From the London Patents to the Edo *Sanza*: A Partial Comparison of the British Stage and *Kabuki*, ca. 1650–1800," in *Frozen Moments: Writings on Kabuki, 1966–2001*, Ithaca, NY: Cornell University East Asia Program, 297–320.

Shively, D.H. (1955) "*Bakufu* versus *Kabuki*," *Harvard Journal of Asiatic Studies* 18 (December), reprinted in S.L. Leiter, (ed.) (2001) *A Kabuki Reader: History and Performance*, Armonk, NY: M.E. Sharpe, 33–59.

Shively, D.H. (1978) "The Social Environment of Tokugawa Kabuki," *Studies in Kabuki: Its Acting, Music and Historical Content*, Honolulu: University of Hawaii Press, 1–61.

Sentiment and satire on the continent

Sentimentalism emerged on the European continent as well as in England. French playwright Pierre Marivaux (1688–1763) injected subtle expressions of feeling into his love comedies, most of which he wrote in the 1720s and 1730s, although his heightened prose style kept his plays much less sentimental than Steele's. Nonetheless, beginning in the 1730s French sentimental comedy, called *comédie larmoyante* [koh-meh-dee LAHR-mwah-yawnt] (tearful comedy) became popular, such as with *The False Antipathy* (1733) and other plays by Pierre Claude Nivelle de la Chaussée (1692–1754). Some of these plays were often performed for the rest of the century. The phrase "tearful comedy" was literally true: throughout the 1700s, French audiences loved to cry at both comedies and tragedies, and plays that failed to elicit tears seldom received favor. Anne Vincent-Buffault observes that the audience's weeping served not only emotional purposes, but also a socio-political one:

> Tears shed in company sealed a kind of social pact of sensibility which turned the theatre into a sort of political assembly. . . . In this unanimous assembly of tears, the man whose eye remained dry . . . [was thought to] hold himself outside not only the rules of society but those of humanity.

(1991: 68)

In the 1750s, *philosophe* Denis Diderot (1713–1784) urged the adoption of "middle" genres between comedy and tragedy that would encompass sentimental notions of morality and domesticity. As editor and chief writer of the *Encyclopédie*, the first modern compendium of knowledge and a triumph of Enlightenment culture (which valued individual liberty and rationality), Diderot won many readers throughout literate Europe. He argued for a type of comedy emphasizing tears and virtues, domestic tragedy centered on bourgeois family problems (*drame*), and more realistic dialogue in all plays. Diderot's interest in realism extended to staging as well: he was the first to propose that there should be an imaginary fourth wall separating the actors from the audience, requiring the actors to perform as though there were no spectators peering in; but this idea was not put into practice for over a century. A few *drames* based on Diderot's ideas saw production in some French theatres, but the actors at the Comédie Française saw little in the new genre that would advance their careers, and interest in it faded in France. Although the country had a large bourgeoisie by the middle of the eighteenth century, state monopolistic theatres retarded the growth of a sentimental, bourgeois theatre in France until after the Revolution. Consequently, despite the emergence of sentimentalism and *drame*, neoclassicism and its absolutist values remained firmly entrenched in France's official theatres until the 1789 Revolution.

But, as in England, the royally approved theatres did not go unchallenged. A variety of alternative genres and performance venues began developing late in the seventeenth century at the fairgrounds in Paris. Originally the fairs were known for coarse farces, jugglers, pantomimes, dancers, puppeteers, and similar entertainments (the sort of carnivalesque entertainments discussed in Chapter 6), but theatre became increasingly popular. When the Comédie Italienne was expelled from Paris in 1697, some of its actors probably began performing at the fairgrounds; it's clear that *commedia dell'arte* was adapted for performance there. Soon plays were being performed in theatre buildings fully equipped with stage machinery for scenery and special effects.

The fairground theatres posed strong competition to the monopoly theatres. The Comédie Française and the Opéra succeeded in closing them down from time to time, usually by imposing restrictions against spoken drama or the use of music. (However, when the Opéra needed money, it lifted restrictions in exchange for payments.) The fairground theatres soon found ways around the proscriptions, such as using mime, monologues, marionettes, invented languages, and even by having characters pretend to whisper into the ear of an actor, who would then say aloud what the character had said. Perhaps the most striking method of evading the monopoly theatres' prohibitions aimed to circumvent the ban on actors singing: when a song was supposed to occur, placards were lowered from the flies with lyrics set to a popular tune, and the audience sang the songs. The stratagem soon developed into a new genre, *opéra-comique* (comic opera), which became the most popular type of fairground theatre offering (see Figure 7.3). The adversarial relationship with the official theatres also formed part of the repertory: the fairground theatres produced numerous plays about their difficulties with their rivals, and they parodied nearly every production at the Comédie Française and the Opéra, sometimes just days after their openings – which could only work if much of the audience had seen the original shows. Voltaire's plays were skewered repeatedly, and he disdained the theatres of the fairs. However, despite the popularity of the plays engaged in the battle with the monopoly theatres, the majority of the plays at the fairground theatres were fantasies, often with characters from *commedia dell'arte*.

Figure 7.3

Scene from a Parisian fair theatre play,
The Quarrel of the Theatres, which satirized two
state-supported theatres for stealing from the
fair theatres: the Comédie Française, represented
by the player on the right, and the Comédie
Italienne, represented by the player on the left,
which performed the *commedia dell'arte*
repertoire and a mix of other works.

From Alain René Le Sage and Jacques Autreau
d'Orneval, *Le Théâtre de la Foire l'Opéra Comique* (1723).
© Bibliothèque Nationale de France.

The conflict between the conventional and the alternative theatres did not lead to completely polarized
encampments: like the audiences, actors and genres crossed
over between them, and several playwrights, including
Marivaux, wrote for both. Even so, the fairground theatres
held a special attraction for their audience. Their incessant
attacks on the Comédie Française and the Opéra established
the fairground theatres as contributors to a burgeoning
public sphere. There were few explicit criticisms of the
monarchy and its government, but as Derek Connon points
out,

> One of the pleasures for audiences in supporting the
> underdogs lies in the frisson of danger in doing
> something that is almost illegal (and may slip over into
> illegality), in getting one over on the authorities and,
> ultimately, the monarch who is the source of the laws
> which are being bent to breaking point. Hence, even if
> the original reasons for the ban on these theatres is not
> fundamentally political, the reaction of audiences to it
> certainly is.

> (2012: 191)

In the mid-1700s, Paris's fairgrounds started to decline,
and the theatres began seeking alternative locations. In the
early 1750s a new area for popular entertainment developed
in the north of Paris on the Boulevard du Temple, closer to
the fairground theatres' audience. The locale arose with
cabarets, cafés, and marionette booths; soon trained animals,
acrobats, and other types of street performance arrived as
well. Eventually full-length plays were performed there. In
1759, a permanent theatre was built on the Boulevard; many
more soon followed. Over the course of the eighteenth
century, these boulevard theatres became home to middle-
class dramas of various types.

Italian theatre in the early eighteenth century was in a
contradictory state. On the one hand, Venice (the center of
theatre in Italy) was able to sustain more theatres than either
London or Paris. On the other hand, theatrical performance
was still dominated by *commedia dell'arte*, which had long fed
theatre everywhere else in Europe, but had deteriorated at
home, unable to create new situations or *lazzi*. Sentimental
drama did not arise in Venice, although French sentimental
plays eventually reached there in translation during the

1770s. But two major playwrights – who were mutual antagonists – brought new life to the Venetian stage. Carlo Goldoni (1707–1793) accommodated *commedia* in some respects (he was employed by various *commedia* companies), but at a fundamental level he transformed it. His early play *The Servant of Two Masters* (1745), perhaps his best-known work outside Italy, is in the *commedia* style and was initially written as a scenario. But breaking from *commedia* traditions, Goldoni later eliminated improvisation and insisted that the actors work from the script. These changes switched priority from the actor to the playwright. In pursuit of a more intimate acting style, in 1754 he eliminated masks from his plays altogether. Like reformers elsewhere in Europe, he also banished spectators from the stage. Most of Goldoni's work centered on middle-class characters and values. His greatest innovation was his attention to everyday life, introducing a sense of realism and observation. Many of his plays focused on a new, bourgeois sense of morality which sometimes challenged his audience. An unusual number of his lead characters were female.

Carlo Gozzi (1720–1806) vehemently resisted Goldoni's innovations and passionately defended the older approach to performance. His earliest play, *The Love for Three Oranges* (1761), used a fantastical fable in order to satirize Goldoni. Placing fantasy on stage also contrasted with Goldoni's turn toward everyday life, so Gozzi's next several plays continued in that vein. Yet despite his reactionary approach to theatre, soon even Gozzi adopted some of Goldoni's reforms, such as requiring actors to work from the script and (at his actors' insistence) removing some of the masks. Gozzi's plays outstripped the popularity of Goldoni's for a time, which probably contributed to Goldoni's decision to leave Italy in 1762, but they soon faded from fashion. Several, however, were later adapted into operas and new scripts. In the early twentieth century Gozzi's plays inspired many anti-realist playwrights and directors.

The turn to sentimentalism in Germany came with the popularity and influence of Gotthold Ephraim Lessing (1729–1781). Lessing was one of the first writers in Germany to make his living from his pen and he gained success as much from his criticism as his plays. Influenced by Diderot, he advocated domestic tragedy in his writings in the 1750s and used these ideas for his middle-class play, *Miss Sara Sampson* (1755). By 1759, Lessing was attacking Gottsched (see Chapter 6) and French neoclassicism, and advocating Shakespeare as a better model for German theatre. The literary advisor for the Hamburg National Theatre (discussed in Chapter 8, where we address nationalism), Lessing used his *Hamburg Dramaturgy* (1767–1769) to offer a non-neoclassical interpretation of Aristotle's *Poetics* and to urge the writing and production of more sentimental plays. He put this criticism into practice with *Minna von Barnhelm* (1767), a romantic comedy that unites lovers from two sides of a recent war that divided Germany. Like his model, Diderot, Lessing was critical of aristocratic privilege and morality and attacked both in his next influential drama, *Emilia Galotti* (1772). Although Lessing did not intend *Nathan the Wise* (1779) for the stage, his dramatic demonstration of the wisdom of tolerance and understanding among representatives of Judaism, Islam, and Christianity became one of his most widely produced plays in the German theatre. Together with other playwrights and companies after 1750, Lessing had helped to ensure that German drama would gravitate more toward sentimentalism than neoclassicism for the rest of the century.

A German composer, Christoph Willibald Gluck (1714?–1787), was primarily responsible for turning *opera seria* away from the neoclassicism of Metastasio and toward European senti-mentalism. Like many composers of his time, Gluck traveled to Italy to learn the rudiments of operatic dramatic form and used the libretti of Metastasio for several of his early operas. Influenced by French *opéra-comique* and by a desire to free serious opera from the weight of recitative, Gluck broke with Metastasian tradition in 1762 with the production of *Orfeo ed Euridice*. When composing for the Paris Opéra in the 1770s, Gluck also challenged the domination of operatic castrati, writing lead roles for tenors instead of castrati in a few of his works. According to several Parisian operagoers, Gluck's gloomy and intense operas caused a flood of welcome and sentimental tears, affecting everyone from the king to the *philosophe* Jean-Jacques Rousseau.

Although generally more neoclassical than sentimental in his style, Wolfgang Amadeus Mozart (1756–1791) benefited from the freedom in operatic composition that Gluck's reforms had effected. Born in Salzburg, Mozart worked there as a court musician for most of the 1770s, finally fleeing to Vienna in 1781, where his operatic career took off. His first production at the court of Emperor Joseph II, *The Abduction from the Seraglio* (1782), an *opera buffa* with a German libretto, was an enormous success. Mozart began collaborating with court librettist Lorenzo da Ponte in 1786; two of their works together, *The Marriage of Figaro* (1786) and *Don Giovanni* (1787), continue to be enjoyed by operagoers today for their compelling drama and emotional range. Through his travels as a child prodigy, his amazing musical memory, and his fluidity and daring in composition, Mozart was able to weave into his mature operas a range of styles from the eighteenth century – the Baroque power and contrapuntal techniques of Bach and Handel, the optimism and charm of Metastasio and his composers, Haydn's astringent clarity and sinuous surprises, and the emotional fervor of Gluck and his imitators – that was unsurpassed in its time. Mozart's final opera, *The Magic Flute* (1791), demonstrated that he could also use German folk tunes and fairy tales to brilliant effect.

Changes and challenges in sentimentalism

In the last third of the eighteenth century, some English playwrights grew impatient with sentimentalism's tepid humor and began to write "laughing comedies," the first significant departure from sentimentalism's velvet grip. Nonetheless, even comic playwrights who disliked sentimentalism still bowed to most of its precepts. Oliver Goldsmith (*c*.1730–1774), for example, provides much robust humor in *She Stoops to Conquer* (1773), but arranges a sentimental ending for his lovers. Richard Brinsley Sheridan (1751–1816), parliamentarian, theatre manager, and playwright, tweaks the excesses of sentiment and derides those who pose behind a sentimental mask in *The School for Scandal* (1777). But he comes down firmly on the side of paternalistic benevolence and morality in wedlock. A few women were finally able to provide plays that proved highly popular, such as Hannah Cowley's (1743–1809) *The Belle's Stratagem* (1780), which joined the drive for "laughing" romantic comedies.

Although the French Revolution would shatter genteel sentimentalism irreversibly in Europe, there were several deep cracks in the sentimental vase before 1789. At one extreme of eighteenth-century sentimentalism was the cult of sincerity that drew its ideas from Jean-Jacques Rousseau (1712–1778). In his writings, Rousseau criticized Enlightenment rationalism and celebrated an image of natural, sincere, authentic humanity, unencumbered by social masks. These ideas eventually led Rousseau to damn the theatre because acting necessarily trades in what he took to be duplicitous role-playing. Despite Rousseau's antitheatrical prejudices, his ideas carried wide influence in the theatre and culture of his time, both before and after the Revolution, and shaped the work of several playwrights.

Rousseau's extreme version of sentimentalism fired the imagination of a young generation of German playwrights, loosely grouped together as the Storm and Stress movement. Friedrich Maximilian Klinger's (1752–1831) *Sturm und Drang* (1776), which posed Rousseau's natural, sentimental humanity against the restrictions of rationality, gave the movement its name (Figure 7.4). Not all in this rebellious generation of playwrights embraced Rousseau, but most rejected Lessing's synthesis of sentimental and Enlightenment values and challenged conventional social norms. Recognizing the natural sexual desires of young soldiers, for example, Jakob M.R. Lenz's (1751–1792) *The Soldiers* (1776) advocated state-sponsored prostitution. Although many Storm and Stress plays, including *The Soldiers*, never made it past German censorship into performance, several circulated in print. Three plays from this movement, however, gained some productions and are still in the standard German repertory: *Goetz von Berlichingen* (1773) by Johann Wolfgang von Goethe (1749–1832); and *The Robbers* (1782) and *Fiesko* (1783) by Friedrich Schiller (1759–1805). We will discuss Goethe and Schiller further in Chapter 8.

Rousseau's ideas were important to several of the Storm and Stress playwrights, but their plays also reflected the political situation in Germany – which was that there was no "Germany" at this time. There were over 300 German-speaking principalities, autonomous cities, and bishoprics, but they lacked the political unity that defines a nation. "National" theatres such as Hamburg's strove to create a nation or the idea of a nation, not to represent it. Under King Frederick II (called Frederick the Great, 1712–1786), Prussia began seizing large swaths of German-speaking lands,

Figure 7.4

A scene from Friedrich Maximilian Klinger's *The Twins*, a Storm and Stress play, in a contemporary engraving by Albrecht.

© Osterreichische Nationalbibliothek, Vienna.

many of them scattered about toward the west. Frederick both militarized and bureaucratized his lands, beginning the formation of a modern state. His rule did not extend to most of what is now Germany: Hamburg, for example, was not in Prussian control. Prussia was not the nation "Germany," it was one of many German lands. Despite his support for Enlightenment values and his personal military valor, Frederick didn't embody an ideal to the Storm and Stress playwrights: most of them despised his despotism, regimented governance, and power politics. Storm and Stress plays often sought to develop German nationhood as a feeling (not as a state), with a culture that didn't imitate French neoclassicism, but instead developed on its own terms. Rousseau's ideas of untrammeled genius dovetailed with these goals; in drama, the protagonist's strength of character and underlying freedom were essential.

Another German playwright, August Friedrich von Kotzebue (1761–1819), avoided the dramatic and social excesses of the Storm and Stress movement, but popularized its rejection of rationalism and its general embrace of Rousseau. Kotzebue's first hit, *Misanthropy and*

Repentance (1787) – a pot-boiler stuffed with Rousseauian sentiments, pathetic situations, comic relief, romantic love, and moral didacticism – set the formula for his later successes. Several of Kotzebue's more than 200 plays retained popularity for the next 70 years in translations and adaptations in Russia and the United States as well as in Western Europe. Among his most successful plays were *The Stranger, Pizarro in Peru*, and *Lovers' Vows*. Kotzebue explored the democratic potential of Rousseau's philosophy in theatrical terms. Where most previous sentimental plays had invited middle-class audiences to test their sentimental feelings and ethics within a genteel and rational framework, Kotzebue's dramas appealed to a wider audience by encouraging spectators to believe that all people, with or without enlightened reason, were already natural, ethical, and authentic human beings. By downplaying rationality and democratizing sentiment, Kotzebue's plays anticipated a significant aspect of nineteenth-century melodrama.

Acting in the eighteenth century

Most of eighteenth-century European drama has dropped into obscurity. Tearful comedy and moral sentiment lived on, but in other genres. However, in performance, sentimental characters' inward feelings and experiences needed to take outward form. Acting became one of the great attractions of the theatre. With it, actors increasingly played a role in public life as representatives of a nation's culture – a function which rapidly developed into star power. Although actors performed both sentimental and neoclassical plays during the century, and necessarily adapted their playing styles to suit each type of production, progressive changes from grand rhetoric toward everyday speech and from heroic to more homely emotions occurred between 1700 and 1790. Acting remained idealized and presentational from today's perspective, with performers striking poses, playing directly to the spectators, and inviting applause in the middle of scenes. Nonetheless, the new emphasis on affecting audience emotions gradually pushed the playing style toward more intimacy and vulnerability.

Print played an important role in turning acting styles toward sentimental culture. Actors continued to rely on their voices to express the dialogue, of course, but after about 1660 they paid as much or more attention to the poses and gestures that made them visually expressive and interesting to spectators. Since the arrival of printing, speech had gradually declined as the culturally dominant mode of communication in Western Europe; sight became more significant than sound. Where previously music and voice had been the path to spiritual transcendence, critics now feared that mere sounds could too easily seduce the other senses. Further, many commentators were laying more emphasis on the importance of gestures in human communication. One treatise written in 1644, for example, suggested that human gestures were a kind of universal alphabet of nature; preachers, actors, and orators must know this alphabet to communicate effectively. Increasingly in society, people were "reading" the appearances of others in addition to listening to their voices to understand human behavior and emotion. To be legible, a character on the stage (like a print "character" on the page) had to look right.

By the eighteenth century, actors were striving to please a print-soaked public eager to read the gestures and poses of their performances. Many treatises and manuals instructed actors in the proper embodiment of their characters' "passions" (emotions). Perhaps the most systematic of these in England was *The Art of Speaking* (1761), by James Burgh. For Burgh, speaking was a whole-body activity that included gestures. The manual offered a series of illustrated "lessons," some of them drawn from plays, demonstrating which pose should accompany each passion so that the audience could understand the desired "affect." By reading books like *The Art of Speaking*, actors learned how to register the progression of poses involved in "Awe – Horror – Fear," for example, with their spectators (Figure 7.5). In addition, the theatre-going public praised actors who could hold these poses believably for an extended moment. Not only was it important for actors to model the right attitude, they also had to manage a believable transition from one to the next. As Lessing explained in his *Hamburg Dramaturgy*, the actor must prepare for each of his poses "gradually by previous movements, and then must resolve them again into the general tone of the conventional" (Roach 1985:73). The result in performance was a kind of garlanded effect that alternated between static poses and graceful movement as the actor used a character's lines and emotions to transition from one tableau to the next. It was crucial that each pose make an "impression" on the minds of the spectators before the actor moved on – a printing metaphor widely used in the eighteenth century to describe theatrical communication.

Several significant performers after 1740 embodied the audience's increasing interest in sentiment. On the London stage, for example, Charles Macklin (1699–1797) altered the traditional clownish interpretation of Shylock in *The Merchant of Venice* to emphasize the character's domestic affections and fierce ambition. In the 1770s, Friedrich Ludwig Schröder (1744–1816) performed the major plays of Lessing and Shakespeare with his company in Hamburg,

Figure 7.5
The passions classified: "Terror." From J.J. Engel, *Ideen zu Euer Mimik* (1812).
© P.M. Arnold Semiology Collection, Washington University Libraries.

Germany, with greater attention to his characters' emotions than had been common in the past. At the Comédie Française in the 1750s, Mademoiselle Clairon (Claire-Josèphe-Hippolyte Léris de la Tude, 1723–1803) challenged the traditional rhetorical force of French heroic acting by adopting more conversational tones for her tragic roles. Lekain (Henri-Louis Cain, 1729–1778) followed in her footsteps in the 1760s and garnered applause for his more restrained style in neoclassical tragedy. Because leading actors usually chose their own costumes during this time, Macklin, Schröder, Mlle Clairon, and Lekain also won acclaim for their costuming innovations, which generally shifted stage dress from lavish toward domestic. Together with Macklin, David Garrick revolutionized acting on the English stage by discarding the oratorical style of the past and introducing a more natural style (although still with stylized elements). Garrick rapidly became the most renowned actor of his era, and we discuss him in depth in the case study that follows.

CASE STUDY: Theatre iconology and the actor as icon: David Garrick

Gary Jay Williams

Theatre is a transitory art that thrives in the immediacy of the cultural moment that performer and audience share, most especially, it seems, at times of dynamic cultural change. Past performances cannot be hung in a museum or replayed from a score. To appreciate performances of the past, theatre historians turn to several kinds of primary sources – among them, pictorial representations. These pose both intriguing opportunities and problems. This case study offers examples of iconological analyses of such images. We will discuss four pictorial representations of the famous English actor David Garrick, emphasizing the relation between these images and two culturally important issues for eighteenth-century England: sentimentalism, and England's reinvention of its national identity. Garrick was a significant – and richly signifying – figure in England's construction of itself.

THINKING THROUGH THEATRE HISTORIES

Cultural studies and theatre iconology

Theatre **iconology** is the interpretive analysis of theatre and performance-related pictorial representations, such as prints, paintings, and photographs, to better understand the cultural work the images were doing and so to better understand the theatre of the past. We use "iconology" here, following Erwin Panofsky (1955), rather than "iconography," a term that is often associated with the work of documentation, such as the thematic cataloging of paintings. Recently scholars have used pictorial sources aware that any representation of performance will itself be the product of many forces at play in the culture of the time. Such images tell us much about the social formations in which actor and audience, painter, and viewer participated, often more than they provide literal depictions of performance.

Analyzing images in this way will involve, as Christopher B. Balme notes, the interpretive task of "uncovering the semantics of a painting's 'sign language' and its relation to the larger social formation" (Balme 1997: 193). Doing so means approaching the image as a system for making meaning within a particular culture that operates with both explicit and tacit conventions and codes. Pictorial representations are always embedded with value choices (Barthes 1973: 117–74). The cultural historian's task may involve some demystification in order to understand the cultural forces at work in an image.

Among the sign-systems in a painting to be considered are the usual compositional ones: choice, size, and placement of the main figure and its spatial relation to other figures, the relation between the figure(s) and their environment, or their clothing, gestures, or postures – but as matters not just of form but as revealing social relations. (The discussion that follows of Hogarth's *Mr. Garrick in "Richard III"* offers examples of this kind of analysis.) Such analysis draws on the field of semiotics, the study of signs, which began with linguistics but expanded to consider how meanings inhere in all kinds of human endeavor, from the use of colors in

continued

military uniforms to the rules for social rituals or athletic games. Not only the painting or print itself, but also the circumstances of its production and distribution can tell us what cultural work it was doing. For example, the analyses here point to the fact that the Garrick images were produced in response to a new market for accessibly priced prints of popular actors. This is a symptom of middle-class economic development to which enterprising artists responded, a variation on print capitalism.

The analysis of a painting and print representing a performance may also involve examining it in relation to all the other theatrical primary sources on the performance, such as eyewitness accounts and promptbooks (play texts annotated by those involved in the production), or other related paintings and prints. The analysis of such visual resources requires some understanding of the conventions of the art. For example, portraits of actors in Garrick's day reveal more about individual personalities than did those in the preceding period, which were in the French neoclassical mode that monumentalized actors. To take an eighteenth-century example from Japan, the study of *kabuki* theatre using the contemporary color prints of *kabuki* actors would need to consider the conventions of this special genre of *ukiyo-e* woodcuts. Also, artists derive some of their compositional vocabulary from the works of other artists, as will be seen below in the discussion of Hogarth's composition.

Artists of Garrick's time drew on a widely known illustrated book that offered a science of archetypal facial expressions of emotions (horror, anger, surprise, grief), *Methode pour apprendre à dessiner les Passions* (*A Method for Learning to Delineate the Passions*) by Charles Le Brun (1619–1690), President of the French Academy. Both Hogarth and Garrick knew the work. In Hogarth's painting, *Mr. Garrick in "Richard III"* (Figure 7.6), Garrick's expression of horror and amazement is closer to Le Brun's sketch of an archetypal expression of horror than to a likeness of Garrick. Denis Diderot described Garrick doing a demonstration of Le Brun-like expressions when Garrick visited Paris in 1764 (Diderot 1957: 32–3) (compare Figure 7.5).

Iconological studies may also look at scenery, costumes, and staging arrangements. Pierre-Louis Ducharte's *The Italian Comedy* (1929) draws on 259 prints, paintings, and drawings as sources for the costumes, properties, and poses typical of each of the stock characters of the *commedia dell'arte*. Martin Meisel's *Realizations* (1983) explores relations between nineteenth-century fiction, painting, and drama.

As a gifted actor, manager, and playwright, Garrick dominated the British stage and became a focal point in British culture across the mid-century. In his debut, he astonished London as Shakespeare's Richard III in a small, unlicensed theatre in 1741. His first biographer, Thomas Davies, wrote: "Mr. Garrick shone forth like a theatrical Newton; he threw new light on elocution and acting; he banished ranting, bombast, and grimace, and restored nature, ease, simplicity and genuine humor" (Davies 1780: I, 43). All of fashionable London turned out to see him; poet Alexander Pope went three times. Garrick became the leading actor at Drury Lane Theatre, where, within a few years, he won extraordinary acclaim for his performances in his signature roles, tragic and comic, including Hamlet, King Lear, Macbeth, Archer in George

Farquhar's *The Beaux' Stratagem* (1707), and Abel Drugger in Garrick's own adaptation of Ben Jonson's *The Alchemist* (1743). As artistic manager of Drury Lane from 1747 to 1776, Garrick was especially dedicated to Shakespeare, staging 26 of the plays and playing leading roles in 14. With his 1769 Shakespeare "Jubilee," he made Stratford-upon-Avon a site for literary pilgrimages, capping his long promotion of Shakespeare as the national poet. In effect, this dedication to Shakespeare and to Enlightenment England was framed as one and the same.

His successes derived from his genius in the performance on stage and off as the new "natural man" of reason and moral sensibility. Easy and graceful in motion, with a quick intelligence, Garrick offered a nimble, fluent model of the century's ideal of the rational mind and natural sensibility in the confident governance of the self. He planned his performances meticulously, blending physical and vocal grace with the virtuous responses of the Lockean "natural man," which is to say, the self-possessed man of vital moral sympathy, in whose bosom was the potential for the virtue and the benevolence toward others that the new social order required. Garrick, who had been born of a relatively poor family, thus offered the persona of a gentleman by nature more than by class, a persona seen in some of the key plays of the period, such as *The Beaux' Stratagem*, and promoted by the periodicals *The Tatler* and *The Spectator*. This made the actor an appealing figure for an England still negotiating its transition from an old social order, which had its roots in the concept of a divinely ordained, absolutist monarchy, toward a relatively democratized monarchy and a new social order based on civic and personal virtue across the middle class. The middle, merchant class saw itself as the keeper of the moral and economic foundation of a stable society.

Garrick is an ideal figure for iconological studies; portraits of him have been the subject of many articles and exhibitions. The number of engraved portraits of Garrick in the British Museum is exceeded only by those of Queen Victoria. The painting of him as Richard III by William Hogarth is probably the most famous portrait of a Western actor ever done (Figure 7.6 is the engraving). But many other major English artists painted portraits of him, in his roles or in private life, including Joshua Reynolds, Thomas Gainsborough, Johann Zoffany, Benjamin Wilson, Nathaniel Dance, and Angelica Kauffmann. Louis François Roubiliac created busts of Garrick in marble and bronze, and images of him appeared on porcelain dishes, silver tea caddies, enameled boxes, and medallions. Garrick was arguably the West's first modern, commodified celebrity.

He himself did much to bring that about. He commissioned many paintings and prints of himself in his most successful roles, the prints being intended for wide circulation. Visiting Paris in 1764 as England's most famous actor, he wrote back urgently requesting prints for distribution to friends and fans. He also commissioned portraits of himself in his off-stage role of the natural gentleman, a role that straddled old and new ideas of class.

Moreover, he conceived his performances with a visual acuity that intersected perfectly with trends in English art. Garrick was among the first of a younger generation of actors with a freer physical style and more appeal for the eye than had been the case in the older, declamatory school, which emphasized classical, rhetorical music for the ear. He was, as Michael Wilson has suggested, well aware of the visual lexicon of painters of the time for portraying the passions. Applying this knowledge to his acting, Garrick aligned his performances with the legitimacy of art. Hogarth expert Ronald Paulson makes an acute point about Hogarth's painting of Garrick as Richard III: "If Hogarth tended to make his painting look like a play, Garrick made his play look like a painting" (Paulson 1992: III, 250). Garrick might be described as an iconic

Figure 7.6
Mr. Garrick in the Charakter of Richard the 3rd (1746), engraving by Charles Grignion, after a painting by William Hogarth. This popular image of Shakespeare's version of the English king served several narratives of English national identity in the mid-eighteenth century.

Source: © liszt collection/Alamy Stock Photo.

actor in his use of visually arresting poses, which he planned carefully – his acting choices being influenced by his media consciousness, as we shall see. He then had these images popularized through paintings and prints – the visual media of his time. In so doing, he advanced his career and inscribed his performances on the national social consciousness.

Four Richards III

In Hogarth's *Mr. Garrick as "Richard III,"* there is Garrick and more. Garrick debuted in 1741 in the Shakespearean role, as compelling a protean character as any in Western drama. Plotting his ascent from Duke of Gloucester to King of England, Richard vows (in an earlier Shakespeare play that includes him) to deceive everyone like a good actor and to kill anyone between himself and the throne:

> Why I can smile, and murder while I smile,
> And cry "Content" to that which grieves my heart,
> And wet my cheeks with artificial tears,
> And frame my face to all occasions.
> [. . .]
> I can add colours to the chameleon,
> Change shapes with Proteus for advantages,
> And set the murderous Machiavel to school.
> Can I do this, and cannot get a crown?
> Tut, were it farther off, I'll pluck it down.
>
> (*Henry VI*, Part 3, Act III, sc. 2: 182–95, in Greenblatt 1997)

His deception and murders bring him to the throne, but they finally result in his overthrow and death in battle at the hands of the decent Earl of Richmond, Henry Tudor.

Hogarth's painting represents the moment when, on the night before the battle, Richard wakes in his tent from a dream in which he has been visited by the ten souls of those he killed, including his king, his brother, his two young nephews, and his wife. Awaking terrified, he cries out, "Give me another horse! Bind up my wounds! / Have mercy, Jesu! – Soft, I did but dream. / O coward conscience, how doest thou afflict me?" (*Richard III*, Act V, sc. 5: 131–3). The adaptation of the play by Colley Cibber that Garrick used stressed Richard's villainy heavily, and, in this scene, Cibber added the ghosts' demand that Richard "wake in all the hells of guilt," which he does, though he goes on to fight to his death.

For a mid-eighteenth-century English audience, this anguished recognition of his sins by this, the most evil of men, would have been a critical moral turn, and Garrick turned it into a moral awakening of great visual power, meticulously arranged. Arthur Murphy, a contemporary playwright and Garrick biographer, wrote, "His soliloquy in the tent scene discovered *the inward man* [italics added]," a code phrase in England's age of moral sensibility signifying the natural, inner potential for good in humankind. Hogarth renders Richard's expression of horror in the wide eyes that stare out over the shoulder of the viewer of the portrait and in the outstretched arm and extended fingers. However, Hogarth does not render Garrick's face with individualized particularity, nor are the figure and costume in the more natural mode of that in his earlier theatrical paintings of *The Beggar's Opera* (Figure 7.1). Rather, the painting of Garrick as Richard III is rendering the theatrical moment in the grand manner of history painting, a genre in which Hogarth had worked in the previous decade. Hogarth took his general composition from Le Brun's *Tent of Darius*; the voluminous flowing robes and other fabrics were painterly strokes to convey nobility. The painting's huge size – over eight feet long and six feet high – is in the mode of history painting, and here it magnifies and ennobles the figure of King Richard. This Richard is, then, a combination of four Richards III: the Richard of Garrick – meticulous master of the morally iconic moment for the age of sensibility; the Richard of English history; the Richard of Shakespeare, the great national poet (whom Garrick was promoting in his playhouse); and the Richard of Hogarth, by then the great English artist. Each presence complements the other. Together they constitute a national narrative aspiring to the status of myth. The buyer, Thomas (William?) Duncombe, paid 200 pounds sterling for the painting, more than had ever been paid to an English painter for a portrait (Paulson 1992: 3, 256–7). The engraving that followed shortly after served the interests of both Garrick and Hogarth. Analyzing the work and its cultural valences today, we can see not only a vestige of Garrick's iconic performance but the ways in which the image was speaking from, and to the English people's construction of their national identity in the eighteenth century.

Two rivals, two prints

Many of Garrick's other performances resulted in images suitable for framing, including those of his Hamlet and Lear, considered briefly here (Figures 7.7 and 7.8). James McArdell did mezzotints of him in these roles. Published in 1754 and 1761, respectively, they were based on paintings (both lost) by Benjamin Wilson (1722–1788). (Zoffany also painted the same scene from *Hamlet*.) Both images seem to aspire to the effects of Hogarth's hugely successful portrait of Garrick as Richard III. Both advance Garrick's moral agenda. Collaboration among actor, painter, and printmaker on both is very probable.

The very method of these prints – the mezzotint – represented a new media technology. A special engraving tool was used to create surface texturing on the paper that allowed inking in gradations of shading and subtle chiaroscuro effects. This allowed the capturing of subtler, more emotional facial expression or more emotionally charged landscapes. Both prints also served Garrick's media campaign. Spranger Barry, the "silver-tongued" actor who was a close competitor of Garrick, was playing these same roles at the rival theatre, Covent Garden, at about the time that these Garrick images were published – likely in order to imprint Garrick's triumph in these roles in the public mind.

Garrick had taken special visual care with both scenes. He was proud of the scene from *Hamlet*, performing it in private for friends. He reportedly used a mechanical wig that he could manipulate to make his hair rise in fright, the better to capture Hamlet's horror, as Cartesian mechanics said it should. The effect seems to be apparent in McArdell's print (Figure 7.7). The print is corroborated by a detailed description of the scene by Georg Christoph Lichtenberg, who saw a performance. Garrick's sentimentalized Lear, seen in Figure 7.8, is frail and vulnerable in the storm scene. Consistent with the Nahum Tate adaptation that Garrick used, his Lear is the sentimentalized father of the family whose demise is tragic in the domestic sphere, that sphere where eighteenth-century Britain had now relocated its national moral center. Tate has Cordelia live to marry Edgar, assuring succession to the throne and a stable future for kingdom and family more than Shakespeare's play does. Both of McArdell's prints were among those Garrick sought supplies of for distribution to friends in Paris.

Figure 7.7
Mr. Garrick in Hamlet, mezzotint print by James McArdell, 1754, after a painting by Benjamin Wilson, depicting Garrick at the moment of Hamlet's encounter with his father's ghost.

Figure 7.8
Mr. Garrick in the Character of King Lear, hand-colored mezzotint by James McArdell, after a painting by Benjamin Wilson. With the mad Lear are Kent behind him (Astley Bransby) and Edgar (William Havard). The Fool is missing because the role was eliminated in Nahum Tate's sentimental adaptation. Neoclassicism dictated that comedy and tragedy should not be mixed.

Thirty Garricks

A century after his Hamlet, Garrick still figured prominently in the British imagination. One comic color print made in the mid-nineteenth century serves both as an amusing index to the Garrick image industry and as an insight into the long English fascination with him. *Garrick and Hogarth or The Artist Puzzled* (1845) by R. Evan Sly was based on an amusing anecdote about a Hogarth–Garrick skirmish that had appeared in a London newspaper several years after Garrick's death (Figure 7.9). Reportedly, every time Hogarth thought he had captured Garrick's likeness in a painting session, the actor mischievously changed his expression; by all accounts, Garrick's expressive face was famously mobile, never at rest, even off stage. Discovering the trick, Hogarth drove Garrick from his studio in a hail of brushes (Paulson 1971: 285–6). Sly used a clever mechanical device to capture the mercurial Garrick face. He placed a rotating wheel on the back of the print so the viewer could change the face of Garrick on Hogarth's canvas and also the face on the seated actor, bringing into view 30 different likenesses of Garrick. These likenesses are, in fact, caricatures of other artists' portraits of him. The faces in the sketches on the floor – caricatures of other Hogarth works – also change with a turn of the wheel. (You can see all the 30 likenesses on the Folger Shakespeare Library's website by visiting www.folger.edu and searching for "Thirty Different Likenesses.") The dog on the left, whose knowing look at the viewer heightens the joke on Hogarth, is borrowed by Sly from a Hogarth self-portrait with his own dog, Pug (1745).

Figure 7.9

Garrick and Hogarth, or The Artist Puzzled. Color print by R. Evan Sly, 1845. The face on Hogarth's canvas and the face of the seated David Garrick can be changed by rotating a wheel on the back of Sly's print, bringing into view 30 different likenesses of Garrick. The print is based on an eighteenth-century anecdote about Hogarth painting the actor which is evidence of the public fascination with the protean Garrick.

The tale on which this print was based was probably an embellished one; its construction and repetition (there was a Gainsborough version) suggest some complexity in the fascination with Garrick. Behind the tale and the print was a paradox that began in his own time: the figure who had become an exemplar of a natural gentleman was an actor, a very adroit member of a profession that was historically suspect, morally and socially. Eighteenth-century English audiences with a hunger for outward signs of interior moral sincerity were enthralled with a talented professional who was skilled in creating meticulous semblances of sincerity. Could an actor adroit with images be a national model of the sincere, natural, virtuous man? Horace Walpole seems to have been aware of the problem when he warned his friend Sir Horace Mann, the British Envoy in Florence, "Be a little on your guard, remember he is an actor" (Shawe-Taylor 2003: 11).

In summary, this case study provides examples of theatre iconology that reads pictorial representations not only for what they might tell us as depictions of performance but for what they tell us about the social formations in which the actor and audience, and painter and viewer all participated. Garrick's performances and the making of the theatrical images of him are parts of a large historical picture, albeit one in which his uses of the media of his time are very recognizable today.

Key references

Audio-visual resources

For many images of David Garrick from the Folger Shakespeare Library exhibit, "David Garrick (1717–1779) A Theatrical Life," go to <http://www.folger.edu> and search for "Garrick."

Shakespeare Illustrated. Website in progress by Harry Rusche on nineteenth-century paintings, criticism, and productions, listing and reproducing illustrations by play: http://shakespeare. emory.edu/illustrated_index.cfm.

Books and articles

Aliverti, M.I. (1997) "Major Portraits and Minor Series in Eighteenth Century Theatrical Portraiture," *Theatre Research International* 22: 234–54.

Balme, C.B. (1997) "Interpreting the Pictorial Record: Theatre Iconography and the Referential Dilemma," *Theatre Research International* 22: 190–201. (This issue is devoted to articles exploring different possibilities and problems in pictorial analysis.)

Barthes, R. (1973; 1st edn 1957) *Mythologies*, London: Paladin.

Davies, T. (1780) *Memoirs of the Life of David Garrick, Esq.* (2 vols), London: Thomas Davies.

Diderot, D. (1957) *The Paradox of Acting* [*c*.1778], trans. W.H. Pollock, New York: Hill and Wang.

Ducharte, P.-L. (1929) *The Italian Comedy*, London: Harrap.

Greenblatt, S. (1997) *The Norton Shakespeare*, New York and London: W.W. Norton and Company.

Highfill, P., Jr. and Burnim, K.A. (eds) (1978) *A Biographical Dictionary of Actors, Actresses, Musicians, Dancers, Managers, and Other Stage Personnel in London, 1660–1800*, Vol. 6, Carbondale: Southern Illinois University Press. (The Garrick entry includes an annotated iconography of Garrick portraits.)

Lennox-Boyd, C. and Shaw, G. (1994) *Theatre: The Age of Garrick*, London: Christopher Lennox-Boyd. (English mezzotints from the collection of the Hon. Christopher Lennox-Boyd, published in conjunction with an exhibition at the Courtauld Institute Galleries.)

Mander, R. and Mitchenson, J. (1980) *Guide to the Maugham Collection of Theatrical Paintings*, London: Heinemann and the National Theatre. (Somerset Maugham's collection, which he gave to London's National Theatre, includes several important Garrick paintings.)

Meisel, M. (1983) *Realizations: Narrative, Pictorial, and Theatrical Arts in Nineteenth-Century England*, Princeton: Princeton University Press.

Panofsky, E. (1955) "Iconography and Iconology: An Introduction to the Study of Renaissance Art," in E. Panofsky, *Meaning in the Visual Arts*, New York: Garden City.

Paulson, R. (1971) *Hogarth: His Life, Art, and Times* (2 vols), New Haven and London: Yale University Press.

Paulson, R. (1992) *Hogarth* (3 vols), New Brunswick: Rutgers University Press.

Shawe-Taylor, D. (2003) *Every Look Speaks, Portraits of David Garrick*, Bath: Holbourne Museum. (Catalog for the Exhibit at the Holbourne Museum of Art, Bath, England.)

Wilson, M.S. (1990) "Garrick, Iconic Acting, and the Ideologies of Theatrical Portraiture," *Word and Image* 6: 368–94.

Performers and the public

Few Europeans thought of acting as a profession until print helped to elevate it in public esteem. When the public could read about actors in weekly newspapers and monthly journals and began to understand the difficulties of actor training, the past mystery and opprobrium surrounding their work began to dissipate. The press began its long love affair with actors. In addition to theatre reviews and manuals, actors' pictures appeared in printed plays, in theatre almanacs and books of anecdotes, and in collections of engravings and illustrations, where performers often posed in costumes in evocative moments of their most characteristic roles. Soon after the press began to use actors, actors found ways of using the press – to puff their latest role, to create printed programs that boosted their reputations, and to write articles and memoirs that shaped their recollections of "great" performances. Without the actor–press mutual admiration society, theatrical "stars" could not have been "born."

One of the first things that actors did with their newfound authority was to remove spectators from the stage. At various times throughout Europe, the audience sat on public stages and occasionally interrupted the performers – a legacy of the easy flow between spectators and actors in medieval festivals. From the 1600s into the late 1700s, this was an elite practice. Male aristocrats eager to display their wits or wigs often chose to sit among the performers and draw occasional focus from their efforts. With help from the actors, Voltaire pushed for architectural reforms at the Comédie Française that removed Parisian spectators from that stage in 1759. Garrick effected this reform at the Drury Lane Theatre in London in 1762.

The relative ease with which performers were able to claim the stage as their own space reflected their increasing social status in Europe. In subsequent centuries, aided by improved transportation, imagery in printed publicity helped actors become local, national, and ultimately international stars.

Theorizing acting

The eighteenth-century bourgeoisie, many of them new to the pressures of social performance, welcomed actors as models for enacting their own emotions in public life. Their social anxiety prompted a wide range of investigations into all manner of public performances, the first general outpouring of interest in the topic since classical times. Given the broad interest in acting, it is not surprising that some writers pushed beyond generalities to analyze how actors accomplished their artistic work. Among the most significant writings were reflections by Aaron Hill (1685–1750), an English playwright and critic who published them primarily in his theatrical journal *The Prompter* (1734–1736), and *The Paradox of the Actor*, written by Diderot in 1773 (published posthumously in 1830). Both dealt creatively with problems that still concern actors today.

Hill examined the process used by actors for producing emotion and based his conclusions on the mechanistic assumptions about the body that Cartesian philosophy had made popular among many literate Europeans. For Descartes, the body was a machine, following the laws of mechanics. Denouncing those who advocated mere rhetorical technique, Hill depicted a three-step process that involved the will operating the body almost as though it were a computer game. First, the actor's imagination was to generate an image of the body expressing a specific emotion. Or, as Hill put it in a poem in *The Prompter* (where he deployed a print metaphor to capture his Cartesian idea): "Previous to art's first act – (till then, *all vain*) / Print the *ideal pathos*, on the *brain* . . ." (Roach 1985: 81, Hill's italics). Next, the actor was to allow the "impressions" of the emotion in his mind to play out in his face. Third, facial expression would impel what Hill took to be the "animal spirits" of the mind and nerves to affect and shape the muscles, so that the actor would fully embody the emotion he had first imagined and thus could speak and act accordingly. In the end, wrote Hill, "the *mov'd* actor *Moves* – and passion shakes" (Roach 1985: 81, Hill's italics). Hill's ideas are similar to modern theories that assume that the actor's mind can trick the body into automatically producing the necessary emotions for a role.

Diderot also built his ideas upon mechanistic Cartesian assumptions, but broke with Hill (and most other acting theorists of his time) to argue that emotion actually got in the way of good acting technique. Like Hill, Diderot believed that the actor must use observation, imagination, and rehearsal to create an inner model of the character, but this preparation provided the basis for enacting an illusion of that character, not embodying the figure's actual emotions in performance. From Diderot's point of view, actors who relied on spontaneity and emotion rather than study and technique reduced the character to themselves, undercut the illusion of the character's emotional life for the audience, and compromised the range of characters they could create. In *The Paradox of the Actor*, Diderot praised performers who could marry a flexible vocal and physical technique to a perfect conception of the role and its emotional dynamics, thus enabling them to present their character in exactly the same way at every performance. Aware that enacting even the illusions of various emotions would tend to involve the actors in experiencing them directly, Diderot drew on Enlightenment science to argue that actors could effectively separate their minds from their bodies and control themselves on stage, much as a puppeteer controls a puppet. As we will see in Chapter 11, Diderot's cool-headed, self-manipulative actor might be compared to the ideal actor of Meyerhold and Brecht in the twentieth century.

Diderot held up Mlle Clairon and David Garrick as exemplars of his theory. He had watched Garrick perform a parlor entertainment in which the great actor shifted his facial expressions instantly to embody a wide range of characters, much to the amazement and delight of his Parisian hosts. Diderot published his *Observations on Garrick* in 1770, and it is clear that the English star significantly influenced his thoughts on acting.

Public interest in acting continued well into the nineteenth century. For example, the elocutionary movement of the mid-1800s in Britain excited numerous lectures and publications that engaged a range of professions from lawyers and merchants to preachers and politicians. In general, the advice given to these budding public speakers was the same as that given to actors: coordinate your words with your gestures, express emotions through the attitude of your body as well as your voice, and pause to "impress" your listeners. Attentive readers and listeners also learned to avoid accents and affects that would mark them as Scottish or Irish and how the voice and body could be pressed into the service of marking oneself as a member of a higher social class.

SUMMARY

In early eighteenth-century Europe, the development of the periodical press led to profound changes in print culture. Periodicals played a key role in creating the bourgeois division between the public sphere that concerned politics, economics, and cultural interests such as fashion and entertainment, versus the private sphere where family, friends, and feelings abided. Popular magazines established the concept of sentiment, through which refined members of society experienced fellow-feeling, sympathy, and moral improvement. Sentimentalism oriented drama throughout the century. In England, where the public sphere was able to develop with little interference from the monarchy, satire became prominent as well, until it was suppressed by the government. Censorship was also imposed in Japan, but there the motives concerned class intermingling and morality rather than political control. Both there and in Europe, audiences' imaginations were captured by actors and acting. In Europe, this interest was configured according to the public/private distinction as the visual, public enactment of private sentiments. Theatre stars fascinated the nation – or more precisely, the emerging nation-state.

★

CHAPTER 8

Nationalism in the theatre, 1760–1880

Bruce McConachie

Nationalism is relatively new in world history. The idea that a people, a nation, loosely united by a common language or culture, has an inherent right to its own geographical and political state would have seemed absurd to most of humanity before 1700. Most people owed allegiance to distant rulers or local chiefs and their cultural lives were bounded by spoken, topographical, and regional differences. As historian Benedict Anderson notes, the imagined fellowship that undergirds nationalism has to be invented and continuously reaffirmed. Nations, as gatherings of strangers, must both build upon and surpass the affiliations that draw people together as families, townspeople, and social classes. According to Anderson, a nation is "an imagined political community – and imagined as both limited and sovereign" (Anderson 1991: 6). That is, the nation, with its accompanying political state, is imagined as limited with regard to its territorial expanse and sovereign in terms of its ability to take independent political action within its boundaries and against other countries.

Citizens in France, England, and the Netherlands were the first to successfully transform their states into national "imagined communities," and this development gave their bourgeoisie a decided advantage in international politics and economics over other countries after 1760. As we have seen, King Louis XIV facilitated this process in France and the middle classes consolidated nationalism in England after 1688. In the towns and villages of the Netherlands, the Dutch began to embrace nationalism in 1609, after winning independence from Spain. In 1760, however, these nation-states remained the exception in Europe and throughout the world. Despite some commonalities of language and culture, Italy and Germany were divided into small states, and the Austrian Empire encompassed a patchwork of national cultures, including Polish, Hungarian, and Czech. Absolutist emperors or monarchs, together with landed aristocrats, ran things in Russia, Spain, and Portugal, where the bourgeoisie were second-class citizens and enjoyed little economic power. People in the rest of the world mostly owed their loyalty to distant monarchs, emperors, war lords, and tribal chiefs, not to an "imagined community" of other people that they assumed were like themselves.

Much of this would change in Europe by 1880. During the nineteenth century, Italian politicians and patriots brought most of Italy under one rule (in 1861) and the Chancellor of Prussia, together with the Prussian army, united most German-speaking lands within the German Empire (in 1871). Meanwhile, in the Americas, the United States established nationhood in the late eighteenth century and most of what is now Latin America had gained independence from Spain and Portugal by 1825. While the push for freedom from colonial rule in the Americas was not based initially on nationalism, it led to the creation of nation-states that became nationalistic in the nineteenth century. The primary matches that lit the flames of nationalism in Europe were the French Revolution of 1789 and the Napoleonic wars that followed until 1815. Unlike earlier European wars, much of the combat after 1795 involved citizen-soldiers who believed they fought to defend people like themselves, not to advance the interests of a king or emperor. As in subsequent wars involving nation-states, the bloodshed of the revolutionary era required justification, and the ideology of nationalism provided ready answers.

This chapter primarily examines the kinds of theatre that helped to legitimate Western nationalism between 1760 and 1880. Unlike today, the theatre participated directly in debates about nationhood and occasionally influenced the rise and fall of governments. Specifically, we will examine three varieties of nationalism and the types of theatre intertwined with each that flourished during these 120 years. The first is *liberal nationalism*, which began in the eighteenth century and involved a commitment to the Enlightenment ideals of individual liberty, private property, and constitutionalism. Although its legitimacy suffered from the wars of the revolutionary era, liberal nationalism continued to inform bourgeois notions of the nation-state during the nineteenth century. The basic idea of *cultural nationalism* may also be found in the Enlightenment, but it only emerged politically after 1800 as a defensive response to Napoleon's universalizing claims of a benevolent French empire. During the war years of the revolutionary era, roughly 1775–1815, many European and American peoples adopted a version of cultural nationalism, a belief in the uniqueness and greatness of one's language-based culture. It flourished, for disparate reasons, in all Western countries for the rest of the century. As we will see, *racial nationalism* mixed traditional notions of racial superiority with cultural nationalism to produce a brew that was particularly potent in Germany, Brazil, and the United States. Although our chapter ends at 1880, it will be evident that these three varieties of nationalism played significant roles in the twentieth century and continue to shape theatre and politics today.

Print, theatre, and liberal nationalism, 1760–1800

Before the French Revolution, print periodical culture helped some bourgeois Europeans to envision themselves as a potential governing class. As literate Europeans read more about current affairs and shared ideas for improving their societies, they developed a sense of themselves as a public, with interests separate from the dukes, kings, and emperors who ruled most of them. As explained in Chapter 7, the news press was especially important in forming this notion of a "public sphere," but so was the theatre. By 1760, many of the same people in Paris, Vienna, London, Hamburg, and other large cities went to the theatre, read plays, and gathered in coffeehouses and salons to discuss developments in science, the arts, and current events. As the press and the theatre influenced each other, both helped to shape an emerging public sphere in their countries.

After 1760, these publics increasingly thought of themselves as national audiences, with rights that all theatrical spectators could expect to exercise. Royal and aristocratic patronage had waned, especially in England and Germany, and the bourgeoisie had partly taken its place. As theatrical benefactors, they strove to cultivate a theatrical public that might rise above the petty emotions of the aristocracy to sustain a theatre that could explore many of their new, enlightened ideas. Most of the literate bourgeoisie looked to the power of rational public opinion expressed in print to regulate behavior in the theatre. Stung by the response of a small group of critics to his *The Barber of Seville* in 1775, lawyer-playwright Pierre-Augustin Caron Beaumarchais (1732–1799), for example, addressed a "Temperate Letter" to the reading public of France. "I recognize no other judge than you," wrote Beaumarchais, "not excepting Messieurs the spectators, who – judges only of first resort – often see their sentence overturned by your tribunal" (Peters 2000: 249). Although Beaumarchais might distrust, he knew he could not dismiss theatrical spectators. Nonetheless, he believed that the reading public, with more time for rational reflection, could gradually educate the theatrical public. Although the state might be mired in royal monopolies, such as the Comédie Française, the public sphere of the nation could support a kind of theatre that could move France toward the political ideals of the Enlightenment. Beaumarchais' views were shaped by the rise and influence of periodical print culture. As we saw in the last chapter, newspapers and other periodicals were leading to the standardization of national languages, which facilitated communication among groups within that nation. In effect, print allowed the literate classes in Europe to imagine the existence of other nationals like them as they read their books, newspapers, and journals. Liberal nationalism, with its commitment to freedom of the press and other Enlightenment values at this time, rested on the imagined coherence of a reading nation.

Influenced by this belief, German critic Johann Friedrich Löwen (1729–1771) published his hope that his new theatre in Hamburg could help to unify the German-speaking-and-reading nation. In the eighteenth century, most Germans lived outside of Prussia and the Austrian Empire, in small states, duchies, and principalities. Löwen's manifesto called for a theatre that would "raise the dignity of German drama" and "inspire the nation's authors to [the writing of] national dramas" (Sosulski 2007: 16). The Hamburg National Theatre opened in 1767. Löwen induced critic-playwright Gotthold Ephraim Lessing to join his troupe as a literary advisor. Lessing thereby became the first dramaturg in Europe, an in-house critic in charge of recommending plays and advising the company on artistic matters (see Chapter 7 on Lessing and sentimentalism). In effect, the German tradition of dramaturgy grew out of the eighteenth-century bourgeois goal of educating a rational theatre public for national responsibilities; dramaturgy was initially a part of liberal nationalism.

Löwen and Lessing's repertoire did not change Hamburg audience preferences for farces and ballets, however. Attendance declined and the idealistic enterprise closed after two seasons. Although Lessing had rejected French neoclassical plays as models for German drama, major problems of audience education and taste remained. Lessing's final essay in his *Hamburg Dramaturgy* expressed his deep disappointment that the public had not supported the theatre. More importantly to Lessing, the public apparently had no desire to create something distinctly German (Lessing 1962: 262). Nonetheless, Lessing's dramaturgical memoir provided an inspirational model for the more than a dozen "national" theatres that flowered in other German-speaking cities before 1800.

Friedrich Schiller, a celebrated historian as well as a playwright and director, shared many of Löwen's and Lessing's hopes for an enlightened national theatre. Following his early plays and his tenure as a professor of history at the University of Jena, Schiller returned to the theatre in 1799 in the German principality of Weimar. Like the poet and playwright Johann Wolfgang von Goethe, the director of the Weimar Court Theatre, Schiller had reassessed his earlier embrace of Storm and Stress anarchy; his late plays reflect an interest in classical restraint and Enlightenment morality. Indeed, many Germans would later celebrate the "Weimar classicism" that Schiller and Goethe achieved in their productions at the Court Theatre as models of enlightened nationalism in opposition to the xenophobia that more fervent German nationalists expressed during the nineteenth century. Our first case study for this chapter tests the Weimar experiment against Schiller's concept of a transformative aesthetic experience that could help to shape his ideal of a German nation.

CASE STUDY: Friedrich Schiller's vision of aesthetic education and the German dream of a national theatre

Gary Jay Williams

> . . . if we had a national stage, we would also become a nation.
>
> Friedrich Schiller (1784)

In recent years, theatre historians have been exploring the relations between theatre/performance and national/cultural identity. This has been fruitful because of theatre's conspicuous place as a mirror of culture in the public sphere. German-speaking peoples, more than most, have pursued aggressively the idea that theatre and the other arts are necessary to the health of a society. In fact, the effort may be rightly characterized as having become an attribute of German culture.

The ideas of playwright, historian, and theorist Friedrich Schiller are significant in that pursuit. This case study explains Schiller's vision, advanced in his *Letters on the Aesthetic Education of Man* (1795), in which he proposes that aesthetic experience can contribute to the social good in its power to better integrate human sensibility. Basing his ideas on Immanuel Kant's (1724–1804) Enlightenment philosophy of art, Schiller argued that dramatic art could heal the eighteenth-century division between reason and feeling. His proposition is located in the context of the efforts of other German artists, including Löwen and Lessing, to create a theatre that would be both a voice of German culture and a force in shaping it. This case study speculates on whether Schiller's tragedy for the Weimar stage, *Mary Stuart*, probably his finest play, contributed to the kind of aesthetic education he hoped would make humankind whole. In doing so, it raises one of the questions that studies in theatre and national identity often do: Did *Mary Stuart* fulfill the mission of a theatre that aspires to form the life of a nation?

Schiller's vision and its context

Dreaming of a theatre that would be a voice of German culture and a force in shaping it, Schiller wrote in his 1784 essay, "The Stage as a Moral Institution": "If all our plays were governed by one principle, if our poets were agreed and allied to this end, if a rigorous selection

THINKING THROUGH THEATRE HISTORIES

Studies in theatre and national identity

The scholarly work in this field is related to the larger issue of how nations define themselves, an interest spurred by many contemporary developments. Among them have been the struggles of once-colonized nations to reshape their identities, "ethnic cleansing" in Europe and Africa, the long, violent antagonism between Israelis and Palestinians, and, of course, globalization, which implicitly challenges notions of national identity. Studies in theatre and national/cultural identity draw on a range of late twentieth-century works in cultural history and philosophy. For example, Raymond Williams and Fredric Jameson articulated the implications for literature and the arts of the classical Marxist critique of capitalism and the oppressive social structures it creates, in which nation-states have been complicit. Eric Hobsbawm and others have shown how nations reinvent their "traditions" to try to produce a coherent national narrative. And Benedict Anderson's *Imagined Communities* (1991), much used by theatre historians, offered the concept of nations as imagined political communities.

Scholarly investigations of theatre and national/cultural identity often carry contemporary significance. Patricia Ybarra, for example, has shown how the excavated ruins of Meso-american civilizations in Mexico have been used in performances for Mexican audiences of tourists to suggest an imaginary national heritage (Ybarra 2005). Loren Kruger's *The National Stage: Theatre and Cultural Legitimization in England, France, and America* (1992) shows the contradictions between the pretexts and the actual practices of three distinct twentieth-century national theatres. In the process, Kruger raises important questions about the funding of theatres in democracies. In 1988, the Royal National Theatre in the U.K. won the crown's permission to describe itself as "Royal" as well as "National." But what is the cost of their tickets today, who attends their productions, and how else are they funded?

guided their work and their brushes were dedicated only to national matters – in a word, if we had a national theatre, we would also become a nation" (Schiller 1985: 217–18).

Dismayed by the French Revolution, especially its Reign of Terror that guillotined thousands of French citizens in 1793–1794, Schiller believed that the savagery of the masses after the Revolution showed that the Enlightenment had failed to touch the heart and make humankind whole. In his letters *On the Aesthetic Education of Man* (1795), Schiller looked to the potential of art to heal what he believed to be the fragmented psyche of modern humankind, to restore the once natural balance between reason and feeling, between intuitive and rational processes. This harmony, he asserted, would never be restored by political means or by revolution. Only through aesthetic experience can modern man become whole: "it is only through Beauty that man makes his way to Freedom" (Wilkinson and Willoughby 1967: 9, Letter 2; Sharpe 1991: 146–8). Kant's philosophy provided the credible base for this theory, and Schiller, working especially from Kant's *Critique of Judgment*, hoped to make a case that art could renew the social order.

In Kant's quest to articulate the first principles of human understanding (*Critique of Pure Reason*, 1781), the philosopher argued that through the use of reason any individual will be able to understand and can live up to the basic principles of knowledge and moral action, without recourse to any metaphysics or the divine. Rather, it is through the data of our experience that our reason derives the laws of nature and human conduct. In his *Critique of Judgment* (1791), Kant argues that our aesthetic judgments, though free expressions of individual autonomy, must also be based in cognitive capacities we share with others if such judgments are to have any claim on their assent (Kant 1971: Sections VII, VIII). Yet this pleasurable exercise is not constrained by rules. It involves "free play" between the imagination and understanding in a process in which, as Paul Guyer summarizes it, "the imagination satisfies understanding's need for unity by presenting a form [to us] that seems unitary and coherent" (Guyer 2004: section 12). The aesthetic work of artistic genius cannot properly be judged by how well it conforms to external standards (such as neoclassical rules). Nor can art be judged by whether it fulfills some external, pragmatic purpose (moral instruction). The aesthetic object has an internal purposiveness, stated Kant, a "purposiveness without purpose" (Kant 1971: xv, 386–7).

Schiller wanted to take this idea further and attempted to show that high art had the potential to do work in the world, that the aesthetic experience could reintegrate reason and feelings. Schiller certainly agreed with Kant that art should not attempt direct moral instruction. He and Goethe disapproved of the domesticated moralizing of eighteenth-century sentimental drama, and his plays of the 1780s, such as *Passion and Politics* and *Don Carlos*, have a complexity that does not allow them to be reduced to simplistic lessons. Schiller believed the theatre should have the poetic dimension of transcendent, classical art; this would give theatrical productions social efficacy, but of a higher order. Influenced by Kant's notion of the "play-drive" in humankind, Schiller contends that the ultimate form of play is the contemplation of beauty. "Man only plays when he is in the fullest sense of the word a human being, and he is only fully a human being when he plays" (Wilkinson and Willoughby 1967: 107, Letter 15). It is this "play," this contemplation of the beautiful, that will restore in humankind that lost unity of sensibility. Schiller's reference point here was an idealized vision of ancient Greece that had allowed for the development of the balanced individual.

Schiller joined Goethe at the Weimar Court Theatre in 1799 for their legendary artistic partnership (Figure 8.1). They made "an open declaration of war on naturalism in art" and sought to create a poetic theatre where spectators could have the kind of aesthetic experiences that would refine and educate their audiences (Sharpe 1991: 253). Their plays and their carefully disciplined production style became known as "Weimar classicism." Schiller wrote five historical verse dramas for Weimar: *Wallenstein's Camp* (1799), *Mary Stuart* (1800), *The Maid of Orleans* (1801, his St. Joan play), *The Bride of Messina* (1803), and *William Tell* (1804). "For only great affairs will have the power / To stimulate mankind's first principles," wrote Schiller in his prologue for the reopening of the remodeled Weimar with his *Wallenstein's Camp* (Schiller 1991: 9). Goethe staged all of these history plays with historically accurate settings and costumes, the better for audiences to contemplate the magnitude of the issues.

Schiller's vision for German nationhood was probably best expressed in *Mary Stuart*, one of his most enduring works. The playwright creates his tragedy out of the conflict between the famed queens of English Renaissance history, depicting Mary's final days leading up to her execution by her cousin, Queen Elizabeth. He invents a one-on-one meeting between them for his capstone scene and renders Mary younger than she was in the 1580s. He characterizes Elizabeth as the woman who has a clear understanding that the throne will often require her to sacrifice herself in order to rule with an iron will. Schiller's Catholic Mary is a charismatic and sometimes impetuous woman who, following her strong passions, has inspired devotion

Figure 8.1

The Weimar Court Theatre interior in 1798. Prosperous bourgeoisie sat on red-covered benches in the orchestra, poorer spectators upstairs in the side galleries, and the duke in the rear center of the gallery. On this stage (approximately 38 feet wide), Schiller and Goethe staged their plays with historical period settings and costumes, an innovation that had wide influence.

Drawing by Alfred Pretzsch in Philipp Stein, *Deutsche Schauspieler, Eine Bildnissammlung*, Berlin, 1907, reproduced in Michael Patterson, *The First German Theatre*, Routledge, 1990.

in her followers but also made profound moral errors. Taking the queens symbolically, as Schiller surely intended – which points to his high expectations of spectators in a theatre – the women might be said to exemplify Schiller's view of the modern splintered psyche. Neither character is whole – Elizabeth, the rational, political pragmatist or Mary, the emotionally alive, charismatic spirit. Mary, confronting the inevitability of her execution at Elizabeth's hand, achieves grace and serenity at the end. Schiller attempts to embody this spiritual transcendence by having Mary receive the sacraments from a priest before going to her death. At the end of the play, Elizabeth, victim of the necessity of being the guardian of order and power, is left on stage alone. Her elder counselor, Shrewsbury, says to her before he leaves, "I could not / preserve the better part of you . . . Your rival's dead. You have from this day forward / no more to fear, and no more to respect" (Schiller 1998: 615).

The tragedy was reported to have been successful at Weimar, as were all of Schiller's plays. But if we are to hold Schiller to his vision, we must ask if his theatre produced the kind of transformative aesthetic experience for spectators that he envisioned would result in the healing of the divided modern sensibility. German theatre historian Erika Fischer-Lichte thinks this unlikely, arguing that few audience members at Weimar would have been able to resist emotional identification with the major characters. This would have prevented them from achieving the kind of distance that is implied in Schiller's characterization of the contemplative aesthetic experience from which a balanced self would emerge (Fischer-Lichte 2004: 197–9). To this, we may add that Goethe's occasional autocratic scolding of Weimar audience members from his box and his heavy fining of actors for "extemporizing" and for unrefined comic business in violation of his stringent *Rules for Actors* suggest that audiences were not always experiencing aesthetic contemplation (Schwind 1997: 100, 98). In addition there is the fact that during Goethe's administration of the theatre until 1826, pieces by August von Kotzebue and A.W. Iffland (1759–1814), plus melodramas, comedies, and other lightweight works, were staged twice as often as plays by Lessing, Goethe, Shakespeare, and Schiller (Sosluski 2007: 27–8). The idealistic Weimar theatre had to offer popular fare to make its budget, only a third of which was covered by its patron, the duke.

Schiller's dream of an aesthetic experience that could heal the modern psyche probably was never realizable. Nonetheless, many Germans today see a vital connection between the productions of their government-funded theatres, whose work is often challenging and controversial, and their lives as engaged citizens.

Key references

Anderson, B. (1991) *Imagined Communities*, 2nd edn, London: Verso.

Fischer-Lichte, E. (2004) *History of European Drama and Theatre*, trans. J. Riley, London and New York: Routledge.

Guyer, P. (2004) "Kant, Immanuel," in E. Craig (ed.) *Routledge Encyclopedia of Philosophy*, London: Routledge. Online: www.rep.routledge.com/article/DB047 (accessed May 12, 2009).

Hobsbawm, E. and T. Ranger (eds) (1983) *The Invention of Tradition*, Cambridge and New York: Cambridge University Press.

Kant, I. (1971) *Critique of Judgment*, trans. J.H. Bernard (1931), in H. Adams (ed.) *Critical Theory Since Plato*, New York: Harcourt Brace Janovich.

Kindermann, H. (1961) *Theatergeschichte Europas*, Vol. IV, Salzburg: Otto Müller Verlag.

Kruger, L. (1992) *The National Stage: Theatre and Cultural Legitimization in England, France and America*, Chicago and London: University of Chicago Press.

Lessing, G.E. (1962) *Hamburg Dramaturgy*, trans. Helen Zimmerman with a new introduction by Victor Lange, New York: Dover Publications.

Patterson, M. (1990) *The First German Theatre, Schiller, Goethe, Kleist and Büchner in Performance*, London and New York: Routledge.

Schiller, F. (1962) *Love and Intrigue*, English version by Frederick Rolf with an introduction by Edmund P. Kurz, Great Neck, NY: Barron's Education Series.

Schiller, F. (1971) *Letters on the Aesthetic Education of Man*, in H. Adams (ed.) *Critical Theory Since Plato*, New York: Harcourt Brace Janovich.

Schiller, F. (1985) "Theatre Considered as a Moral Institution," trans. J. Sigerson and J. Chambless, in *Friedrich Schiller, Poet of Freedom*, New York: Schiller Institute, New Benjamin Franklin House.

Schiller, F. (1991) *Wallenstein* and *Mary Stuart*, ed. Walter Hinderer, trans. C.E. Passage, New York: Continuum Publishing.

Schiller, F. (1998) *Schiller: Five Plays*, trans. R.D. MacDonald, London: Oberon Books.

Schwind, K. (1997) "'No Laughing!' Autonomous Art and the Body of the Actor in Goethe's Weimar," *Theatre Survey 38* (Nov. 1997).

Sharpe, L. (1991) *Friedrich Schiller, Drama, Thought, and Politics*, Cambridge: Cambridge University Press.

Sosulski, M.J. (2007) *Theater and Nation in Eighteenth Century Germany*, Williston, VT: Ashgate Publishing.

Wilkinson, E.M. and Willoughby, L.A. (eds) (1967) *Friedrich Schiller: On the Aesthetic Education of Man in a Series of Letters*, Oxford: Oxford University Press.

Ybarra, P. (2005) "Staging the Nation on the Ruins of the Past: An Investigation of Mexican Archeological Performance," in K. Gounaridou (ed.) *Staging Nationalism: Essays on Theatre and National Identity*, Jefferson, NC and London: McFarland.

The French Revolution, melodrama, and nationalism

Before the Revolution of 1789, many looked to France as the most prosperous and civilized country in the world. The Revolution and the chaos that followed in France during the 1790s, however, shocked the European bourgeoisie. The civil strife and international wars of the late 1790s brought more bloodshed and confusion, and many Europeans were relieved when Napoleon Bonaparte emerged as a strong leader in 1799. Although Napoleon's rule ensured stability in France, his imperial ambitions soon brought parts of the Revolution to the rest of Europe and the Americas. The turmoil engulfed the entire Western world in intermittent warfare until 1815 and lasted through 1825 in Latin America. We will examine the ramifications of the revolutionary era for the Americas later in this chapter.

These political transformations reconfigured the predominant genres of Western theatre. Pre-revolutionary aristocrats and bourgeoisie in France, Great Britain, and Germany had been applauding neoclassical and sentimental comedies and tragedies, together with several minor genres. Twenty years later, by 1810, most European theatregoers in these countries were thronging to see nationalistic spectacles, gothic thrillers, and melodramas. In theatres where heroic virtues or genteel pathos had inspired neoclassical or sentimental responses, the emotions of rage, fear, and panic now stirred audiences. For spectators who had weathered the turmoil of the Revolution, either directly or vicariously, the temperate values of pre-revolutionary times seemed quaint and uninteresting. Some pre-1789 plays continued to be performed, of course, but few dramatists after 1800 wrote popular plays within the old conventions. In short, the revolutionary era had transformed the dramatic genres of European theatre. How had this happened?

We need to focus primarily on the shattered expectations of theatregoers in Paris during the Revolution to understand this transformation. According to historian Matthew S. Buckley, several events occurred between 1791 and 1794 that alienated Parisian playgoers from the kinds of enjoyments that they had come to expect from the old genres. Consequently, the Revolution, says Buckley, "became a nightmarish, originary drama of modernism, a material, historical experience of [traditional] drama's failure that could be neither reversed nor banished from cultural awareness" (Buckley 2006: 6). By the start of 1791, many in Paris (including several revolutionaries) expected that the antipathy between the people and the French crown would soon play out like a sentimental comedy, with the king and the revolutionaries agreeing to a constitutional monarchy. After all, the first stages of the Revolution had witnessed the Declaration of the Rights of Man, the abolition of state monopolies, and attempts to separate the French Catholic Church from the power of Rome. In line with such progress, it seemed to many Parisians that King Louis XVI might decide to accept a limited role in ruling, much like the king of Great Britain.

Instead of a reconciliation involving tears of gratitude from the people and smiling beneficence from his majesty, however, King Louis attempted to flee the country with his family in June of 1791. This revealed to many Parisians that the hope of a sentimental ending had been a seductive fiction all along and it set the stage for the king's execution, which followed in 1793. During the so-called Reign of Terror in 1793–1794, when the revolutionary leader Maximilian Robespierre and his Committee of Public Safety were attempting to purge the Revolution of its enemies, many Parisians looked upon this lawyer-turned-politician as an "incorruptible" hero in a neoclassic tragedy and they cheered his attempt to form a republic of virtue. But again their hopes were dashed. Instead of sacrificing himself to establish an era of peace and goodness in the neoclassical mode, Robespierre's Terror petered out and his botched attempt at suicide revealed him to be more of a fool than a tragic hero. Further, the Terror, in which Enlightenment ideas were deployed to justify the legal execution of over 40,000 citizens in France, led many Parisians to conclude that the enlightened principles behind many sentimental and neoclassical plays could only end in chaos and horror.

In Buckley's interpretation, then, crucial events in the Revolution radically undercut the believability of two of the major genres that had sustained French culture in the decades leading up to 1789: sentimental comedy and neoclassical tragedy. Throughout his discussion, Buckley emphasizes that these traditional genres were not simply abstract devices of literary discourse. For literate Frenchmen, they were narratives about the shape of events that rested on reliable historical knowledge and evoked deep-seated expectations for the future. When the events of the Revolution spun away from the reassuring contours of these narratives, many citizens could no longer give form to their experiences. Similar to the events of September 11th for many U.S. citizens, the events of 1791–1794 unhinged their worldview. With their old dramatic genres rendered unreliable and irrelevant, Parisians sought new ones.

Many traumatized by revolution, terror, and war found a hopeful replacement for the old plays in the genre of melodrama. This genre stirred up the memorable emotions that Parisians had experienced during of the Terror but provided a safe and moral resolution. Melodrama as a distinct genre emerged in 1800 with the production of *Coelina, Or the Child of Mystery*, by Guilbert de Pixérécourt (1773–1844). Soon, several other playwrights were writing melodramas and the new genre was all the rage in the boulevard theatres of Paris for the rest of the decade.

For evidence of the connection between the experience of the Revolution and the new genre, theatre historian Buckley cites an introduction to the published plays of Pixérécourt written by his friend, Charles Nodier:

> The entire people had come into the streets and the public space to perform the greatest drama in history. Everyone had been an actor in this bloody play, everyone had been a soldier, a revolutionary, or an outlaw. To its solemn spectators who had smelled gunpowder and blood, there was a need for emotions analogous to those from which they had been cut off by the re-establishment of order. . . . There was [also] a need to be reminded anew of the framework, always uniform in its result, of this great lesson that comprehends all philosophies, supports all religions: no matter how low, virtue is never without recompense, crime never without punishment. . . . This was the morality of the revolution.
>
> (Nodier, quoted in Buckley 2006: 66)

Buckley recognizes that the narrative of early melodrama as described by Nodier provided a form of cultural wish fulfillment. Nodier's belief that the "morality of the revolution" proffered a kind of poetic justice experienced by many between 1789 and 1799 was far from the truth, however. Melodrama may have reassured a traumatized people, but it could never fully allay the gut-wrenching fears or soothe the moral panic undergone by many Parisians.

Had it not been for the network of periodical print culture in Europe, the traumas of the revolutionary decade in Paris might have remained relatively isolated. Most of Europe, however, still looked to Paris as the center of the enlightened world. Journalists, poets, travelers, and others soon spread the word about the events of the Revolution, first to the French provinces and then to all of the capitals of Europe. Although print was slow by today's standards of instant reporting, the news stories in London, Berlin, and elsewhere (which included many exaggerations and rumors) swept up many literate Europeans in the emotions and politics of the Revolution. For them, too, reading about the events in Paris in the early 1790s produced the feeling that the bottom had dropped out of their world. After such vicarious experiences, many European playgoers, like their counterparts in Paris, also sensed that the older forms of comedy and tragedy could no longer accommodate what they were reading about in their newspapers. In the wake of the Revolution and especially during the European and American wars that followed, melodrama claimed more and more adherents.

Although few of the early melodramas were overtly nationalistic, most undercut the rational and ethical basis of liberal, enlightened nationalism. The Revolution, coupled with the Rousseauian thinking of the previous decade (see Chapter 7), had induced a desire for utopia, the conviction that naturally good people might create a society in which evil could be banished from the world. *Coelina* and other plays in the new genre often depicted such a utopia, typically finding it in idealized visions of traditional peasant life (Figure 8.2). Lessing, Schiller, and other liberal nationalists had been more politically realistic; they knew that utopian nostalgia for the old order ignored the problems of absolutist rule and blind religious faith. Similarly, the early melodramas enjoined Europeans to make firm distinctions between hero and villain, French and Prussian, "us" and "them." Such black-and-white morality might be the ethics of fairy-tale allegories and simplistic nationalisms, but it avoided the kinds of hard choices that Schiller dramatized between his two queens in *Mary Stuart*. Enlightenment nationalists believed that all peoples needed

Figure 8.2

This print depicts a scene from Pixérécourt's *The Forest of Bondy*, still popular in 1843 when this illustration (known as a "penny character print") was published. For this exciting melodrama, a dog was trained to jump at the throat of the actor playing the villain, the killer of the dog's master. Penny character print, Mr. Cony-Landri-Webb.

HTC 28, 321. © Harvard Theatre Collection.

national theatres to elevate their nations; they did not assume that some national peoples had already arrived at the pinnacle of Kantian morality. Revolution and war also degraded the value of enlightened reason, which many believed had led to the trauma of the Terror. Like the plays of Kotzebue, melodrama elevated nature and intuition over reason as better guides to morality and possible utopia. This assumption, of course, contradicted much that Schiller and other liberal nationalists held dear. Without rationality, the liberals believed, humankind might never heal the breach between reason and feeling.

Melodrama flourished on European and American stages for the rest of the nineteenth century, reshaping much of Western theatre. Because audiences enjoyed melodramatic spectacles, the genre helped to transform the two-dimensionality of chariot-and-pole staging into more realistic scenic illusions. As the size of stages expanded to accommodate the increased demand for spectacle, playwrights called for more three-dimensional scenic units – fortresses that could collapse in an explosion and a mountain which a horse and rider could ascend to near the top of the proscenium, for example. By the 1880s, melodramatic ice floes, steaming trains, and galloping horses – the last done with treadmills and revolving scenery – were stretching the ingenuity and endurance of technicians and stagehands. The wide appeal of melodrama also broadened theatrical audiences. In addition to the middle class, which continued to provide the core audience for melodrama, working-class spectators began attending the theatre in increasing numbers after the 1820s, enjoying plays like *The Carpenter of Rouen* (1837) that pitted plebeian avengers against decadent aristocrats. Moral reform melodramas such as *The Bottle* (1847) and *Uncle Tom's Cabin* (1852) even converted some sober, antitheatrical Protestants to playgoers. After 1840, many star-struck spectators enjoyed their favorites in melodramatic spectacles. English star Henry Irving's (1838–1905) most famous melodramatic role was Mathias in *The Bells*, for example, a haunted figure who robbed and murdered to gain success early in his career (Figure 8.3). Melodrama organized the dramatic plots of many nationalistic war plays and also mixed easily with Romantic drama, as will be seen.

Figure 8.3
Henry Irving in his production of *The Bells* at the Lyceum Theatre, London, 1871.

© V&A Images, Victoria and Albert Museum.

European cultural nationalisms, 1815–1848

After 1815, versions of cultural nationalism flourished in most European countries (Figure 8.4). When Enlightenment thinkers looked at history in the eighteenth century, they tried to deduce universal principles about human behavior from the past that they could apply to all nations in the present and future. Historian Johann Gottfried von Herder (1744–1803), however, denied that this was possible. In his *Ideas on the Philosophy of the History of Mankind* (1784), Herder argued that everyone's understanding of the past was necessarily subservient to a *Volksgeist* [FOYLKS-gahyst], a German word that means the spirit of a national people. Not even well-trained historians could transcend their particular *Volksgeist* to write universal history because the history of each national people was unique, said Herder, and historical interpretation was necessarily tied to the ideas and values of the *volk*, the nation. Although Enlightenment notions of the potential universality of historical interpretation remained dominant in much of the West during the eighteenth century, modifications of Herder's ideas shaped most discussions about cultural nationalism throughout the nineteenth. Napoleon's armies had conquered in the name of universal Enlightenment principles, and Europeans oppressed by the French looked to Herder and his followers to justify their nation's opposition to French imperialism. Although Herder himself never argued that one nation or racial group might be superior to others, several of his later disciples claimed that his historicism justified their sense of national and/or racial superiority. In general, Herder's legacy animated historians and others to search for the origins of their nation's *Volksgeist*, to explore what they took to be the unique features of their "imagined community," and to celebrate their own national heroes. Many of Herder's ideas continue to be influential today.

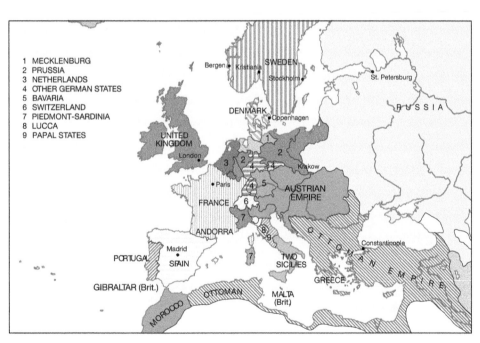

Figure 8.4
Political map of Europe in 1820.

Depending on the national political context, cultural nationalism based on a version of Herder's ideas played out differently in various European countries. In Great Britain, victorious in the fight against Napoleon, conservative cultural nationalists mostly relived past glories. On the London stage in the 1820s and 1830s, for example, star actor T.P. Cooke (1786–1864) presented the manly and sentimental virtues of an idealized English seaman. Cooke had actually served in the British navy against the French and used this experience to promote his image as the archetypal British sailor. Among his favorite starring roles were Long Tom Coffin and Harry Hallyard in two nautical melodramas. As the beleaguered seaman hero in Douglas Jerrold's *Black-Ey'd Susan* (1829), Cooke found his most popular vehicle, performing it 785 times in his long career. Jerrold's melodrama, awash with nautical metaphors, led to several other plays featuring heroic sailors – and eventually to W.S. Gilbert's brilliant parody of the character type in the operetta *H.M.S. Pinafore* (1878).

Also in the 1820s, British theatre artists began working with historians to mount more accurate productions of national historical plays, principally the dramas of Shakespeare. This was a part of the movement known as **antiquarianism**, which aimed to immerse spectators in the spirit of past and exotic cultures through an accurate rendering of their details. Under antiquarianism, Shakespearean productions in England became a means of honoring the genius of the national poet and a conservative understanding of the national past. English antiquarianism began with Charles Kemble's (1775–1854) production of *King John* in 1824.

Figure 8.5

James Robinson Planché's antiquarian design for the king's costume in Charles Kemble's 1824 production of Shakespeare's *Henry IV, Part 1*.

From Planché's *Costume of Shakespeare's King Henry IV, Parts I and II* (1824). © Lilly Library, Indiana University, Bloomington.

James Robinson Planché (1796–1880) based his costuming of Kemble's actors on scrupulous research into medieval dress, an innovation welcomed by Kemble's bourgeois audience. Planché, a leader in antiquarianism, costumed subsequent Shakespearean productions with attention to historical detail and provided managers with extensive information on the banners and insignia of medieval heraldry (Figure 8.5). William Charles Macready (1793–1873), who dominated the English stage from the 1830s into the early 1840s, popularized the goals of antiquarianism by aiming consistently for historical accuracy in costuming, props, and painted scenery for his major productions. Eighteenth-century nationalists like Beaumarchais and Löwen had hoped that nationalism would teach their countrymen rational deliberation and liberal values. Later cultural nationalism in England, however, pushed conservative values and emotional attachments to historical artifacts and ancient customs.

In contrast, most French cultural nationalists split into radical, conservative, and reactionary factions, with each group claiming to represent the true identity of France. In addition, liberal nationalists hoped to revive the French constitutionalism of the first three years of the Revolution. After 1815, these factions clashed in several areas of French culture, including the advent of Romanticism on the French stage. **Romanticism** had already triumphed in England and

Germany, and even penetrated Austria and the Italian states, but political opposition impeded its realization in France. In brief, Romanticism celebrated artistic genius and ambitious action. In the music of Beethoven and the poetry of Wordsworth, Romanticism marked a new point on the continuum of cultural modes for gaining knowledge about the self. In medieval and early modern times, Western culture taught people to look primarily to external entities – the feudal order, the Church, the logic of absolutism – for self-understanding. Beginning with the Protestant Reformation and moving to the Enlightenment, to sentimentalism, and then to Romanticism, Western culture increasingly invited humans to discover purpose and understanding from within. Most French radicals and liberals supported Romanticism, although the liberals were skeptical that heroic action could provide much of a basis for political legitimacy. French reactionaries, however, yearned for a return to a Catholic and absolutist Europe and modeled their hopes for French theatrical culture on the neoclassical era of Molière and Racine.

Leading the liberals was novelist and playwright Victor Hugo, who had announced the goals of a Romantic theatre in his preface to the play *Cromwell* in 1827. He and others pointed out that a few Romantic productions had already achieved some success at the Comédie Française. The French reactionaries took their stand in 1830 at the Comédie's production of Hugo's *Hernani*. Hugo had added some political conservatives to the liberals among his supporters for *Hernani*, a play that intentionally violated many of the rules of neoclassicism and incorporated several scenes of melodramatic action. After an initial three nights of calm, a shouting and shoving match raged for the remaining 36 performances between the Romantics and the reactionaries in the audience, drowning out the actors (Figure 8.6). In the end, most of the Parisian press hailed the Romantics as the victors, chiefly for outlasting their opponents. Following the riots, French Romanticism, with frequent injections of melodrama, achieved widespread success in the 1830s and 1840s. These included the generally liberal plays of Hugo and the conservative costume dramas of Alexandre Dumas (1802–1870), such as *Henri III and His Court* and his adaptation of *The Three Musketeers*.

There was also a radical side to French cultural nationalism, exemplified in the theatre by the career of actor-playwright Frederick Lemaître (1800–1876). Through the roles he played, Lemaître came to embody the revolutionary values of heroic freedom and working-class grit denied to most French citizens by a conservative French state between 1815 and 1848. Whereas most liberal and conservative artists and critics understood the state and the nation as one, Lemaître's vehicles implicitly divided the French state from the nation of French people in order to criticize the repressive regime installed in Paris after Napoleon's defeat. Lemaître played a wide variety of melodramatic roles between 1825 and 1850, the era of his greatest renown. These included a moody and violent gambler, a scorned

Figure 8.6

Contemporary illustration of the *Hernani* riots, showing the audience and the final scene of Hugo's play on stage at the Comédie Française in 1830.

Bibliothèque nationale de France.

lover who throws himself into the Seine River, and the English star Edmund Kean (1787–1833), played by Lemaître as an erratic and tempestuous melodramatic actor. Many critics favorably compared Lemaître to the English celebrity. Novelist Victor Hugo, for instance, praised Lemaître as "capable of movements, utterances, cries that could cause an audience to shudder violently, and of astounding flashes which transfigured him and made him appear in the dazzling halo of absolute greatness" (Hemmings 1993: 221).

Lemaître gained fame initially in 1823 when he played the dashing thief Robert Macaire. Although he used the character to parody the style of early melodrama, he also aimed some pointed barbs at the current French state for its graft and greed. Lemaître worked with the authors of the original piece to fashion a new play in 1834, called simply *Robert Macaire*. In this vehicle, Lemaître's anti-hero attacked the villainy and hypocrisy of the wealthy, especially those who had profited from the short-lived and largely futile Revolution of 1830 in Paris. Not surprisingly, the authorities eventually banned all melodramas about Macaire, including several other plays that only hinted at the character type. This censorship, of course, helped the star to seal his image as the defender of France's revolutionary heritage. In the 1840s, Lemaître chose several vehicles that also positioned him as a champion of the poor. He appeared, for instance, in a feature role in a stage adaptation of *The Mysteries of Paris* in 1844, an exposé of Parisian poverty. Like the Macaire plays, these and several other melodramas performed by Lemaître mixed cynicism about wealth and exploitation with popular notions of revolutionary outrage and hope. Lemaître inspired cultural nationalism in many of his spectators by contrasting present corruption with the remembered glories of 1789.

In Germany and Eastern Europe, nationalism tended to unite radical cultural nationalists and liberal constitutionalists in plans for transforming groups of language-based peoples into nation-states. Earlier German attempts to establish national theatres and write national history plays set the precedent for later cultural nationalists among the small German states and within the Austrian and Russian empires. Polish nationalists throughout the nineteenth century also pushed for a return to independence of their native lands. Several Hungarian-language plays in the 1840s dramatized the plight of Hungarian peasants under the rule of Austrian aristocrats. In Prague, cultural nationalists published articles, books, and plays arguing for the independence of Czech lands from the Austrian Empire.

These and other national aspirations exploded in the revolutions of 1848. In that year, radicals demanding constitutional rights, the independence of national groups, and an end to remaining feudal privileges staged revolts in Paris, Copenhagen, Budapest, and Palermo (Sicily). Revolution spread to other cities, gained support among many liberal groups, and soon much of Central and Eastern Europe was in turmoil. In France, Parisians rallied to the barricades to oust an unpopular king, but ended up with the nephew of Napoleon for an emperor. Although Polish, Czech, and Hungarian nationalists threatened for a short time to pull apart the Austrian Empire, the emperor's army routed the rebels and suppressed calls for separate constitutions and independence. An assembly of liberal German delegates met for nearly a year in Frankfurt to form a unified, constitutional German state and offered to make King Frederick of Prussia its constitutional monarch, but he refused, dashing hopes for a liberal German nation. By 1850, serfdom had been abolished throughout Europe (except in Russia) and a few small states had gained more liberal constitutions. None of the stateless European national groups had gained independence, however, and many of their leaders were dead or in prison. Only after the Great War, also known as the First World War (1914–1918), and the dissolution of several European empires would cultural nationalists climb to political power within the new nation-states of Ireland, Czechoslovakia, Poland, Finland, and several others. Although the radicals and liberals of 1848–1849 mostly failed to achieve their goals, they did validate the continuing desire for popular liberty and equality and also demonstrated the political power of cultural nationalism

Nationalism in Russia and Italy, 1848–1880

Despite their defeat, most cultural nationalists in Central and Eastern Europe went underground and vowed to fight on. Many disappointed liberal nationalists, however, abandoned their hopes in the wake of 1848 or traded in their Enlightenment values to side with the cultural nationalists. Meanwhile, some in Italy began looking for more direct political and military ways to unify their disparate people.

Before turning to developments in Italy, however, we should focus briefly on Russia. Although this most economically underdeveloped and politically repressive of European empires had been nurturing pockets of cultural nationalism, both among the majority of Russian-speaking peoples and within its many ethnic minorities, Russia was virtually untouched by the revolutions of 1848. This was partly due to poor communication among rival minority peoples, but also the result of the regime's censorship of all printed material. With regard to the theatre, Tsar Alexander I (1777–1825) clamped down on performed as well as printed drama and mandated a monopoly on theatrical production, which lasted until 1882. As such laws had done in France before the 1789 Revolution, Russian censorship severely restricted theatrical expression, fostered cynicism about the regime, and spawned numerous ways to evade imperial regulations. For most of the nineteenth century, the theatre continued to be enjoyed primarily by aristocrats and the imperial court; few in the Russian bourgeoisie thought of themselves as constituting a possible public sphere with their own theatre and an imagined national community.

Given these circumstances, traditional beliefs and loyalties – to a local nobleman, to the aristocratic class, to the tsar, to the Russian Orthodox Church – remained stronger than the pull of Russian nationalism for most theatregoers until the 1870s. From 1815 into the 1830s the court and the aristocracy cheered a spate of conservative and reactionary plays in the wake of the tsar's victory over Napoleon's invading army in 1812. Still influenced by French fashions, however, Russian theatregoers applauded conventional melodramas and historical pageants in the middle decades of the century. But the regime did not allow playgoers to see the work of many Russian Romantic playwrights. Like the French Romantics, Russian poet Alexander Pushkin (1799–1837) turned to history for inspiration, but the radical politics of his play *Boris Godunov* (1825), a sprawling masterpiece, kept it out of publication until 1831 and off the stage entirely until 1870. Censorship eased somewhat in the 1850s, allowing the staging of Mikhail Lermontov's (1814–1841) *Masquerade*, inspired by Shakespeare's *Othello*. However, his play *The Spaniards* (1830) – exposing the similarities between Tsar Nicholas I's reign (from 1825 to 1855) and the Spanish Inquisition – was published but not performed during the nineteenth century. Russian comic satirists A.S. Griboyedov (1794–1829) in *Woe from Wit* (1824) and Nikolai Gogol (1809–1852) in *The Inspector General* (1836) had more success with their attacks on individual bumblers, embezzlers, sycophants, and hypocrites, in part because their generally conservative politics offered little offense to the ideology of the regime.

With the loosening of censorship, the freeing of the serfs in 1861, some modest reforms, and the playwriting of Alexander Ostrovsky (1823–1886), Russian theatre began to change in the 1860s. Ostrovsky wrote in a variety of genres, but found his greatest success in dramas of domestic realism for and about the Russian middle class. *The Thunderstorm* (1859), for example, explores the tragic results of a parent's oppression, while *Enough Stupidity for Every Wise Man* (1868) follows the comic success of a man who manipulates the foibles and stupidities of others. Ostrovsky, whose often ironic tone and focus on domestic situations influenced the plays of his countryman Anton Chekhov (discussed in Chapter 9), encouraged other realist writers to turn to the stage. Given the constraints of tsarist absolutism, Ostrovsky steered clear of politics, including the exploration of possibilities for Russian nationalism. But by welcoming the emerging Russian bourgeoisie into the theatre with his plays, Ostrovsky ensured a wider, more public audience for future dramatic discussions about Russia. This conversation began to occur with productions of the historical dramas of Aleksei K. Tolstoy (1817–1875), second cousin to Leo, the great novelist. In his trilogy of plays about three Russian feudal monarchs, *The Death of Ivan the Terrible* (1864), *Tsar Fyodor Ivannovich* (1868), and *Tsar Boris* (1870), Tolstoy focused on the psychological and ethical ramifications of political rule. Most historical plays, however, like many operas and ballets popular with the regime, continued to conflate tsarist rule, Christianity, patriotism, and imperialism until the Russian Revolution of 1917.

In significant ways, southern Italy and Sicily were just as tradition-bound as Russia at mid-century; as a result, few Italians in Naples or Palermo had any interest in nationalism. But patriots in the north were agitating for Italian unification and insurrections broke out in 1848 in several northern cities and in Rome, where a constitutional republic lasted for three months. After the failures of 1848 in Italy, patriots looked to the king of Piedmont, in the northwest corner of Italy, as a potential standard-bearer for the military unification of the country. Led by the Piedmontese prime minister and aided by Giuseppe Garibaldi's rag-tag army in the south, the state of Piedmont unified most of Italy in 1861, later adding Venice and Rome to its territory. Italy in 1870 was a nation in name only, however. Culturally, socially, and economically, the north and south had few interests in common and centuries of warfare had kept alive regional fears and antagonisms that mere political unity could not erase. Lacking a common language, written or spoken, most Italian subjects could not easily communicate across regions; what is now standard, modern Italian only emerged and began to spread in the twentieth century. These divisions undercut Italian nationalism and hobbled the development of all of the arts, including the theatre.

Despite their divisions, Italians in all regions did share a love for opera and many nationalists celebrated the works of Giuseppe Verdi (1813–1901) for their apparent endorsement of national unity. Ironically, though, Verdi's operas actually had very little to say about Italian nationalism. Verdi was a patriot, but he stayed in Paris during the uprisings of 1848 and for most of the 1850s; despite his reputation in Italy, he never considered himself "the maestro of the revolution." Most of his operas center on love triangles among historical characters. His one vaguely nationalistic opera was *The Battle of Legano* (1849), set in the twelfth century, which did praise Italy as "a single people of heroes" in its opening chorus and featured a second act that heaped scorn on Austria (Gilmour 2011: 170). Perhaps because the opera was staged in Rome during its short-lived days as a republic, Italian nationalists seized on *Legano* as a symbol of Italian independence and unity. It would not be the first (or last) time that nationalists imagined more patriotism and glory for their communities than their national symbols could sustain.

Star tragedian Tommaso Salvini (1829–1915) provided a more genuine nationalistic symbol of Italy than Verdi. In 1849, he fought the Austrians in defense of the Roman Republic and later welcomed Garibaldi and his army into Naples when they overthrew the Neopolitan kingdom. Salvini's political and cultural nationalism remained a part of his public image and colored his international reputation. After performing in Italy for most of the 1860s, Salvini embarked on a series of tours in the 1870s and 1880s to South America, the United States, England, France, and even Russia (where a young Konstantin Stanislavsky, to be discussed in Chapter 9, marveled at his power). In addition to a few Italian vehicles, Salvini played Othello, Macbeth, King Lear, and other Shakespearean tragic heroes, performing them all in Italian. Salvini's Othello (Figure 8.7) overwhelmed American novelist Henry James:

> His powerful, active, manly frame, his noble, serious, vividly expressive face, his splendid smile, his Italian eye, his superb, voluminous voice, his carriage, his tone, his ease, the assurance he instantly gives that he holds the whole part in his hands and can make of it exactly what he chooses, – all this descends upon the spectator's mind with a richness which immediately converts attention into faith and expectation into sympathy. He is a magnificent creature, and you are already on his side.
>
> (quoted in Carlson 1985: 61)

For James and for many other spectators around the world, Salvini's Othello, his most popular role, was more Italian than African. Cultural nationalism was in the business of propagating positive stereotypes and Salvini's passionate, tragic Othello fit the bill. If the new Italian nation-state could produce such a combination of pathos, passion, and power, admirers, both in Italy and abroad, believed that its national pride was surely justified.

Figure 8.7
Tommaso Salvini as Othello. Despite his darkened skin and Moorish headdress and costume, Salvini retained his own Italian-style moustache for the role, perhaps to emphasize his Italian heritage.

© Folger Shakespeare Library, Washington DC.

Wagner and racial nationalism in Germany, 1848–1880

Nineteenth-century nationalism in many German-speaking areas turned toward racism. To some extent, racial nationalism exaggerates a major tenet of cultural nationalism; it proposes that the dominant cultural group in a nation is not only different from, it is also superior to minority groups. Racial nationalism breaks with cultural nationalism, however, to claim that the essence of a *volk* is in the blood. By conflating culture with a racist notion of biology, the full assimilation of minority Others as equal citizens into the nation becomes impossible. Racism, according to the comparative historian George M. Fredrickson, "has two components: *difference* and *power*. It originates in a mindset that regards 'them' as different from 'us' in ways that are permanent and unbridgeable. This sense of difference provides a motive or rationale for using our power advantage to treat the ethnoracial Other in ways that we would regard as cruel or unjust if applied to members of our own group" (Fredrickson 2002: 9).

Although in general Herder's cultural nationalism was neutral about the superiority of one culture over another, Herder himself hoped that Jews and other minorities would alter their identities when Germany became a state and seek to assimilate to what he believed was superior German culture. This prejudice against minority cultures in German-speaking areas in Europe festered and grew in the nineteenth century; many Germans attacked the arid rationalism of the "French people" as inherently inferior, for example, or sought to elevate the essence of "Germanness" over "Jewishness." Opera composer Richard Wagner (1813–1883) shared these prejudices and advanced them in his political and artistic attempts to facilitate German unification. Like many other German Romantics, Wagner imagined a unified, utopian Germany based in traditions of language, mythology, and ethnic origin and these ideas shaped his operas. As Wagner scholar Hannu Salmi asserts, "Wagner's national thinking became a unity fusing art and politics" (Salmi 1999: 195).

Although several of Wagner's operas before 1848 celebrated German tradition, they did not push cultural into racial nationalism. Wagner set *The Flying Dutchman* (1843) in Nordic legend, for example, and *Tannhäuser* (1845) featured Wartburg castle, a celebrated site for German nationalistic pride. Involved in the idealistic attempt to forge a German nation during the uprisings of 1848–1849, Wagner wrote patriotic poetry, edited a radical newspaper, and aided others in the fight against Prussian domination. Barely escaping arrest, Wagner fled Germany and spent the next eleven years in exile. In 1864, Ludwig II, the new king of Bavaria, which was then the second-largest state in Germany, invited Wagner to join his court and the composer accepted. Both men understood the German *Volksgeist* as an unchanging essence and a possible force in history, if only the right political opportunity combined with musical genius to inspire the nation.

Despite the later political friction between them, King Ludwig's support of Wagner allowed him to envision and complete several operas, facilitated the realization of a national theatre for the production of his works, and also encouraged Wagner to shift his nationalism from a cultural toward a racial definition of the German people. During his exile, Wagner had begun *The Ring of the Nibelungen*, his immense tetralogy of operas, which would be completed in 1874. Pushed and pulled by various influences over the years, especially by the pessimistic philosophy of Schopenhauer, the vast work nonetheless attempts to distill the destiny of the German people in what Wagner believed was a truthful fusion of myth and history. The final opera, *Götterdämmerung*, stages the destruction of a decadent order of states, forces, and laws so that a new, utopian Germany might emerge. Throughout, Wagner distinguishes between superior German characters and others who represent corrupt, non-Germanic influences. In one scene in *Siegfried* (1871), the third opera in the cycle, for instance, Wagner signals his rejection of what he had termed "Jewishness in Music" by having his hero, Siegfried, turn away in contempt from a dwarf characterized as a Jew. At other points, blood purity plays an important role in the plots of the four operas.

Wagner finished *The Mastersingers of Nuremberg* (1868) at a crucial time in the push for German unification. Under the leadership of Chancellor Otto von Bismarck, Prussia had won a short war against the Austrian Empire in 1866 and was poised to unite Germany under Prussian leadership. Wagner, despite his previous alliance with the king of Bavaria and antipathy toward Prussia, now sought to gain influence with the stronger power. While composing *The Mastersingers*, Wagner wrote a series of periodical articles that attacked the French people for their effete and imitative nature; at one point, Wagner calls them apes in contrast to the inventive Germans. Similarly, in the opera, Wagner depicts a medieval master singer in Nuremberg fighting against foreign influences and winning the singing contest (and the girl) in the end. After the success of *The Mastersingers* in Munich, Wagner toured the opera to Berlin in 1870 and scored a triumph in the Prussian capital. In effect, Wagner's nationalistic opera helped to fan the flames for the Franco-Prussian War (1870–1871).

The Prussian victory in that war established a German Empire that facilitated the incorporation of Bavaria and the smaller German states under Prussian rule (Figure 8.8). In response, Wagner composed the "Kaiser March" and conducted it in Berlin, hoping for an appointment in the new regime. But Bismarck had no interest in identifying the German Empire with Wagner's visions, and the composer turned his attention to fundraising for his Festival Theatre at Bayreuth in Bavaria.

Although announced to open in 1867, the first festival did not occur until 1876. Wagner designed the Festival Theatre to achieve his aesthetic and nationalistic goals. Believing that his epic music-dramas could transport his listeners to a spiritual realm of imagined aspiration and unity, Wagner aimed for the total immersion of his audience in his fictions. Accordingly, he attempted to weave together music, drama, singing, scenery, lighting, and all of the other theatrical arts into what he called a *Gesamtkunstwerk* [ghe-ZAHMT-koonst-vehrk], a totally integrated and unified production. Interested in solidifying the unity of the *volk*, Wagner designed a proscenium theatre that did away with architectural social distinctions in the auditorium, such as private boxes and an upper gallery, and arranged all seats facing the stage (Figure 8.9). In his attempt to ensure that all spectators would sit in rapt attention to the stage illusion, Wagner even eliminated the sight of the pit orchestra, placing it well below the lip of the Bayreuth forestage. In other ways, though, Wagner continued mid-nineteenth-century

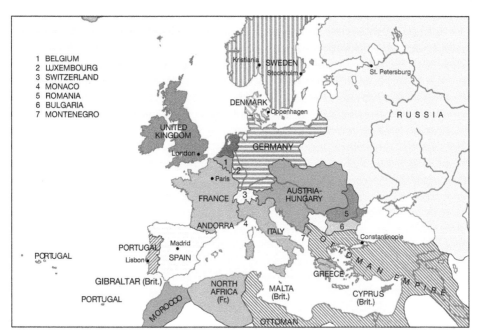

Figure 8.8
Political map of Europe in 1880.

Figure 8.9

Floor plan for Wagner's Festival Theatre at Bayreuth. Notice the fan-shaped seating, with side entrances, the forestage, and the ample depth of the stage area for scenic illusion.

From E. O. Sachs, *Modern Opera Houses and Theatres* (1896–1898).

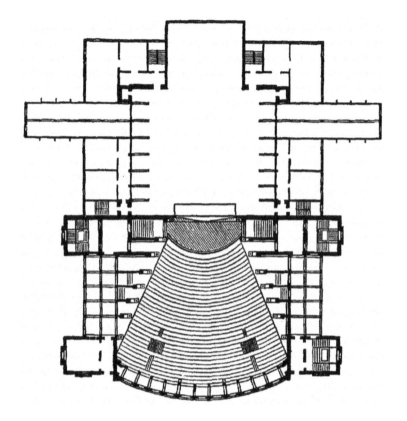

staging conventions. His theatre relied on painted flats and backdrops, trap doors, gas lighting, and spot lights. After the composer's death in 1883, Bayreuth became a pilgrimage site for ardent Wagnerians for the next hundred years. Wagner's auditorium design, though not his staging practices, would continue to influence the Western theatre well into the twentieth century.

Wagner staged *Parsifal*, his final opera, at Bayreuth in 1882. While *The Ring* and other of his operas were based on pagan myths, Wagner imported specifically Christian ideas and images into *Parsifal*, apparently to support his claim that belief in Germanic nationalism should be understood as a mode of spiritual redemption. In *Parsifal*, religion merges with racism through a plot in which the racial degeneration of the German people must be countered by racial purity so that Germany may be saved from interbreeding and decline. Wagner mixes images of the blood of Christian sacrifice with the blood of racial exclusivity. Even as he was composing his opera, Wagner was writing articles in anti-Semitic periodicals that sounded the alarm about "racial miscegenation." With *Parsifal*, Wagner made the complete shift from cultural to racial nationalism. As is well known, the Nazis adopted Wagner and his operas as cultural avatars of the Third Reich; Hitler himself was particularly fond of *Parsifal*. While this does not mean that Wagner would have approved of Nazi Germany's policy of racial extermination, it should alert us to the long-term political effects that popular theatrical works can unknowingly help to legitimate.

Liberal and racial nationalisms in the Americas

The new nation-states of North and South America emerged during the revolutionary era when notions of liberal nationalism, based on principles from the Enlightenment, predominated. These ideals continued to shape the United States and the countries of Latin America through the 1870s. Herderian cultural nationalism played a small role in the American nation-states. Racial nationalism, however, though substantially different from the German version, developed throughout the Americas and became predominant for a short time in Brazil and for much longer in the U.S.

Late medieval Spain and Portugal had practiced a version of racist Christianity that carried over into their colonies in the New World. Officially, Catholicism recognized that Christ had died for the sins of all humanity and that all people might be saved. In practice, however, many Spaniards believed that those Jews and Moors who had converted to Christianity were actually incapable of becoming true Catholics; only those who could claim *limpieza de sangre* (purity of blood) through Christian family descent might gain salvation. When they took this belief to their new colonies, the Spaniards and Portuguese usually distinguished between the native populations, who were deemed capable of salvation, and the slaves imported from Africa, who, like the Moors before them, became racialized Others. In addition to blood purity, the pigmentation of the Africans signified to many Catholics that they were descended from the biblical Sons of Ham and therefore, as in the Bible, destined by God for slavery. Despite other factors that slowed the development of racism in Latin America, Frederickson concludes, "What we have here, therefore, is a quasi-racialized religious nationalism and not a fully racialized secular nationalism of the kind that arose in Germany" (Fredrickson 2002: 41).

Napoleonic imperialism in Europe ignited the Latin American patriotism that led to the wars of independence. Following Napoleon's invasion of the Iberian peninsula, the king of Spain abdicated in 1808. Latin American creoles, those white Americans of direct Spanish descent, rebelled against the Spanish-born viceroys and bureaucrats sent by the king to rule the Spanish colonies. A series of patriot victories and political arrangements, some involving *mestizos* (those of mixed Spanish and indigenous heritage) and Native Americans, eventually gained freedom from Spain for nearly all of its former American colonies by 1825 (Figure 8.10). In contrast, the white population of Portuguese Brazil, united but vastly outnumbered by African slaves and Native Americans, welcomed the king of Portugal and his court, who had fled from Napoleon's armies. In 1822, the prince regent of Portugal, in alliance with the white Brazilian elite, declared Brazil an independent monarchy. Creole Brazilians had won independence without bloodshed and also without disturbing white rule.

After independence from Spain, the white elites in most of the new countries established liberal constitutions based on the principles of the Enlightenment and the early French Revolution. With the exception of Brazil, most of the new states gradually abolished slavery soon after independence. The new constitutions typically granted universal suffrage to all males in the country, but in practice few people of indigenous, African, and mixed descent participated as citizens. Until the 1850s, the politics in most of the new nations veered between ineffective republican assemblies and strong-man dictatorships. Nonetheless, the creole elites in most countries continued to honor the principles of liberal constitutionalism, a commitment that would eventually open a path to fuller citizenship for the non-white majority.

Regarding the theatre, traditional songs and dances continued unchanged among Native Americans and Africans, while the creoles, as they had done during colonial times, primarily

looked to trends in European theatre as the model for their entertainments. Despite the turmoil of the early national years, Spanish and French companies were touring to major Latin American cities with some regularity to entertain mostly white audiences by the mid-1830s. In Mexico City, the most populous and liberal of the post-colonial capitals, entrepreneurs built several new theatres in the 1840s and 1850s to accommodate these companies, as well as for local Mexican troupes and their occasional playwrights. Like Manuel Eduardo Gorostiza (1789–1851), who wrote neoclassical plays and satirized Romanticism, several of these Mexican dramatists continued the traditions of the past. Others turned to penning sketches for the musical and variety entertainments that were growing in popularity. Manuel Ascensio Segura (1805–1871) gained a reputation for his popular comedies of manners among the more conservative creoles of Lima, Peru. Segura was one of several Latin American dramatists who worked in the general style of *costumbrismo* [kos-toom-BREES-mo], plays that featured picturesque places, exotic peoples, and curious customs. Although *costumbrista* theatre – popular in Argentina, Chile, Nicaragua, and Mexico as well – encouraged the elite to patronize their less fortunate countrymen, it generally paraded social rather than racist stereotypes.

Figure 8.10
Political map of South America in 1825.

According to historian Will Fowler, "the rise of a neo-colonial order" marked the 1850–1880 period in Latin America. Great Britain, and later the United States, folded the economies of these countries into the emerging global order of nineteenth-century imperialism (Fowler 2008: 59–83). In exchange for bank loans, transportation, communication, and manufactured goods from the industrialized countries, whites and *mestizos* in Latin America supplied raw materials, mining and farm products, cheap peasant labor, and willing consumers to foreign capitalists. Many Latin American landowners and merchants worked to integrate their operations with the Europeans and North Americans. After 1850, some of this new wealth was flowing to *mestizos* and others of mixed descent. These groups joined with some of the rich creoles to push for more stable societies based on liberal constitutions and, by the 1870s, liberal versions of nationalism flourished among participating citizens in most of the former Spanish colonies.

Neo-colonialism, however, also created vast disparities of wealth. In each country, the rich enjoyed privileged lives at the expense of the majority of Native Americans and peasants, most of whom had lost control of their lands to the huge farms, mines, and oil fields that dominated the land and politics of each nation-state. These new elites purchased extravagant houses in their capital cities, adorned themselves with the latest European fashions, and, says

Fowler, built "lavish theatres and opera houses" for their enjoyment (Fowler 2008: 74). For the most part, this shift in the economic and political basis of Latin American life produced more European theatrical imports, especially operas, but left relatively unchanged the comedies, variety entertainments, and *costumbrista* productions of the past. By 1880, most Latin American theatre reflected the values of liberal nationalism and imperialistic capitalism, but it would not begin to critique the social and political realities of its nation-states for another 20 years.

Although foreign capital reshaped the economy of Brazil as well, its society and politics remained more traditional than most of the rest of Latin America during the nineteenth century. The emergence of Brazil as a monarchy after independence and its relative stability compared with the rest of the continent sparked a surge in conservative nationalism among the court and the group of white creoles who ruled the country in the 1830s. Proponents of nationalism, however, had to justify or ignore Brazil's huge investment in slavery, which at the time constituted roughly half of the population (not counting the indigenous tribes in the Amazon interior). Portuguese colonial policy had turned Brazil into a sugar plantation dependent upon slave labor and the growing industries of coffee and rubber, which were also labor-intensive, increased the demand for more slaves. While Catholicism had long supported African slavery, the new monarchy and its plantation elite, despite its continuing ties to Portugal, needed to believe that an independent Brazil was somehow different from and superior to its colonial past.

They found such justification in the conservative Romantic works of Domingos José Gonçalves de Magalhães (1811–1882) and his circle, which included several other Brazilian poets and playwrights as well as supporters in the monarchy. The Brazilian Romantics promoted a mix of Catholicism and *indianismo*, a Rousseau-inspired belief in the primitive simplicity and natural virtue of Brazil's many indigenous tribes. Magalhães wrote plays and poetry in a neoclassical style and argued for the creation of a Brazilian national theatre. In his most famous play, *Antonio José or the Poet and the Inquisition* (1838), still celebrated as the first Brazilian tragedy, Magalhães took on the purity of blood prejudice that prevented some Jews and Moors in Portugal from becoming full Catholics. The historically based tragic hero of the piece is a converted Jew who, though tried and condemned by the Portuguese Inquisition, nonetheless affirms his Catholic faith in the end and dies a martyr for the more open kind of Catholicism endorsed by Magalhães. Along with other Brazilian Romantics, Magalhães affirmed that the Catholic faith in Brazil could embrace Jews and natives – especially those idealized tribes in the interior that might inspire Brazilian nationalists to similar virtues. Although the play is not directly racist, it ignores slavery in order to celebrate a notion of Catholicism that is marginally more liberal and might be fused with essential Brazilian qualities for the future of the nation. By idealizing the Amazonian peoples, Magalhães and the Romantics embraced a kind of cultural nationalism, but one that could have no political consequences for the elite. In the 1840s, the emperor of Brazil officially endorsed these ideas and awarded Magalhães with a series of prestigious diplomatic appointments. Conservative Romanticism allowed the Brazilian elite to turn its back on the racist basis of its power.

Brazil's conservative Romantics, however, could not paper over other problems in the monarchy. A lost war with Argentina, economic disarray, and fragmentation within the ruling elite opened up some political opportunities for Brazilian liberals and led to the abdication of the first emperor. Fearing massive slave revolts, the elite finally closed ranks and backed a new emperor in 1840. Meanwhile, British warships were dramatically curtailing the slave trade. Great Britain had prohibited the Atlantic slave trade in 1807 and stepped up its naval patrols after 1834; Brazil finally ended the slave trade in 1853. Although most elite Brazilians favored the continuation of slavery, a few Brazilian dramatists and poets, including Castro Alves (1847–1871), advanced the cause of abolitionism through their work. By the mid-1870s, the neo-colonial order had brought a new generation of liberals to power in Brazil who sought to modernize the nation and viewed slavery as a reactionary holdover from the old days. It was not until 1888, though, that slavery itself was finally abolished; the republican movement ended the Brazilian monarchy the next year. Brazil had joined the other Latin American nation-states in basing most of its nationalistic values on liberal rather than racial principles.

In contrast, it took the United States a bloody Civil War (1861–1865) to reverse its slide toward racial nationalism and, even after that, white racism would continue to the present day. U.S. racism was partly due to its colonial legacy. In contrast to most of Latin America, the British encouraged their subjects to emigrate to their American colonies to begin agricultural and (later) commercial ventures that could profit the mother country through trade. Nor did British culture condone racial intermarriage. Unlike the Spanish and Portuguese, British imperialists did not set out to exploit natural resources and force the natives to work for them, even though all three colonial powers encouraged African slavery. Although British settler colonialism proved much more stable and profitable than the Iberian model of European imperialism, its success also made slavery more difficult to eradicate in the nineteenth century.

The society and culture of the new United States reflected its origins as a settler colony. The nation-state inherited slavery, white male supremacy, bourgeois capitalism, and Western expansionism from its imperial past. In addition, the legacy of Puritanism, which preached that America might separate itself from the decadence of Europe and lead the world to salvation, reinforced American self-righteousness and the claim of moral exceptionalism. Given this perspective, few Americans for most of the nineteenth century understood their conquest of other peoples as imperialism. Although the U.S. was continuing to practice settler colonialism in its western territories, most citizens believed that the incorporation of new lands into their nation-state expanded freedom and democracy, even when these acquisitions and wars increased the reach of chattel slavery and deprived Native Americans of their homelands. Although the Revolution and the Constitution had been fought and ratified primarily on the basis of Enlightenment values, liberal nationalism vied for dominance with racial nationalism in the beliefs and major institutions of many citizens, especially after 1830.

Until about 1800, many Americans, North and South, believed that slavery would gradually fade away. On stage, citizens of the new country saw both sympathetic and buffoonish characterizations of black slaves and free people of color and they applauded some plays that endorsed slavery and others that opposed it. Outside of a few elite groups in the South, however, white racism, though often a personal prejudice, was not a widespread nationalistic ideology. In 1800, most northern states in the U.S. were gradually abolishing slavery and individual manumissions were increasing in the South. The rising profitability of cotton, however, encouraged many southern planters to double down on their commitment to slavery. A series of southern presidents who held slaves and professed racist views, including Thomas Jefferson and Andrew Jackson, also increased the legitimacy and spread of racial nationalism.

British pressure to end the slave trade, attacks by northern abolitionists, and Nat Turner's slave revolt in Virginia (1831) led many southerners in the 1830s to reframe their defense of slavery; what had been understood by many as a necessary evil they now proclaimed as a positive good. Many southern ideologues proclaimed that black people were biologically incapable of rational action, and ought to be thankful that they had been brought to the U.S., where they could learn civilization from a superior race. Some workers in northern cities resented competition from free black people for scarce jobs and a series of riots occurred in the 1830s that pitted working-class racists against black citizens and abolitionists, scorned by many as advocates of racial mixing. Racial nationalism was making inroads in the North, motivated as well by capitalists who depended upon southern cotton for their profits. The popular genre of Yankee theatre during the 1830s, which often featured a droll New England character in comic opposition to a free black figure (always played in blackface by a white actor), also increased racial nationalism.

Divisions among groups of liberal and racial nationalists increased dramatically in the 1850s. The so-called Compromise of 1850, which guaranteed slavery in several western territories, also included a Fugitive Slave Act. This allowed southern masters to pursue their runaway slaves in the free states of the North, partly nationalizing the rights of slave owners. Outraged by this attack on black slave families, Harriet Beecher Stowe penned *Uncle Tom's Cabin*, which was quickly adapted for the stage after its appearance as a complete novel in 1852. Although an early adaptation preserved Stowe's abolitionist views, most stage versions of *Uncle Tom's Cabin* compromised her religious and sentimental depiction of slave families; some adaptations even endorsed slave holding as a paternalistic institution. Abolitionist objections to slavery were winning more converts in the 1850s, but few commercial theatres in the North were willing to risk their profits to stage abolitionist dramas. In the infamous *Dred Scott* decision of 1857, the Supreme Court gave southern slaveholders the right to take their "private property" with them anywhere in the U.S.; the decision implicitly countermanded the ability of Congress to restrict the spread of slavery at all. The rise of the new Republican Party, which opposed extending slavery in the West as a threat to white male farmers who could not afford slaves, divided the country and alarmed the South. Believing that a Republican presidential victory could limit slavery's national expansion, several southern states seceded from the United States to form their own white supremacist nation after the election of Abraham Lincoln in 1860. The new Confederate States of America, which began the Civil War in 1861, had shredded liberal principles to embrace racial nationalism.

As we will see in the case study on blackface minstrelsy that ends this chapter, there were plenty of racists in the North, as well. Abolitionism remained a small political movement with little clout at the start of the war; very few northerners joined the Union army to free black slaves in the South. Knowing that many conservatives in his party feared abolition, President Lincoln initially fought the war on narrow constitutional principles. As the casualties mounted, however, it became apparent to many that abolishing slavery in the ten rebel states would shorten the war and Lincoln issued the Emancipation Proclamation (1863). In 1865, with the end of the war in sight, Lincoln and the Radical Republicans pushed the Thirteenth Amendment through Congress, abolishing slavery forever in the U.S. The amendment did not kill racism, of course, but it ended one of its institutional bulwarks. The failure of Reconstruction in the 1870s led to new forms of racial nationalism, which continued to insist that the U.S. should guarantee whites preferential treatment over non-white citizens because of their race. Racial nationalism would continue into the twentieth and twenty-first centuries.

CASE STUDY: Imagining a white nation: Minstrelsy and U.S. nationalism, 1840–1870

Bruce McConachie

As is evident throughout this chapter, nationalism depends upon the imaginations of its citizens. Those nationalists who lived in a nation-state could usually validate their feelings of patriotism and community by invoking the glories of their national past, whether real or mythical. People without a national state but who shared a language and some culture, such as Germany for much of the nineteenth century, had a more difficult time finding imagined common ground and sometimes turned to racial difference as a means of invoking in-group sameness. The question of who rightly belongs within a national community could be especially problematic for diverse groups that shared the same geography and some past traditions but were riven by deep internal divisions legitimated by long-standing institutional practices, such as slavery. As we have seen in Brazil and the United States, imagining others in your nation-state as inherently inferior and unqualified for citizenship has been a strong incentive for excluding them from full participation in your nation.

Minstrel shows, the most successful form of popular entertainment in the northern cities of the U.S. in the decades before and after the Civil War, provided apparent "evidence" that black people, freed or enslaved, could not participate as the equals of white citizens in a liberal and democratic United States. This case study investigates minstrelsy as a significant source of racial imagining and white nationalism in the northern United States during the middle decades of the nineteenth century. Popular culture studies provides a good approach to the history of blackface entertainment in the U.S.

Although blackface minstrelsy emerged as a cross-class entertainment in the 1850s, it never lost its working-class roots. Thomas Dartmouth Rice (1806–1860) was performing minor

---

THINKING THROUGH THEATRE HISTORIES

Blackface entertainment as popular culture

For most historians, definitions of "popular culture" depend upon the audience for this form of entertainment and the means used to gather and communicate with them. In this sense, live performances that appeal to cross-class audiences in complex societies through commercial means are "popular" ones. They reach a broader audience than "elite" or "working-class" entertainments and rely on marketing strategies that "folk" theatre cannot employ. Entrepreneurs pushing popular shows may draw on these older traditions, but they transform them in the attempt to generate as big an audience as possible. The period between 1820 and 1920 was the "golden age" of popular culture on stage, after print media could be used to generate big audiences and before films and the radio changed many live, popular entertainments into mass mediated images and sounds.

Historians usually credit English circus entrepreneur Philip Astley (1742–1814) with two key innovations that began popular entertainment. In 1768, Astley required attendees to pay an

---

continued

entrance fee to enable them to watch his feats of horsemanship, instead of hoping that they would drop money into a hat before they wandered away. Second, Astley advertised his skill. He and his wife dispersed handbills around London and paid for ads in the press to lure the crowds. Circus acts had long been popular at fairs in Europe, but Astley's innovations transformed the circus from a series of folk practices into a commercial business. Following his success in London, Astley added several more acts, housed his circus in an amphitheatre, and opened similar shows in Dublin and Paris. By the 1820s, Astley's Amphitheatre was mounting grand equestrian dramas such as *The Battle of Waterloo*, a nationalistic celebration of the British victory over Napoleon that ran for 144 performances in 1824.

In the U.S., P.T. Barnum (1810–1891) followed Astley's example of commercializing entertainment and also strived to elevate his popular performances to respectability. Although now chiefly remembered as a circus impresario, Barnum was best known in the 1850s as the tireless promoter of his "museum," the American Museum in New York City. Before museums were public institutions, private businessmen owned and operated them. In addition to featuring several exhibits of natural history, fine art, circus animals, and mechanical wonders, Barnum also touted such "freaks" of nature as the "Feejee Mermaid" and the "What Is It?", a black man presented as an evolutionary "missing link" to his astonished customers (Figure 8.11). He outfitted the dwarf Charles Stratton in bourgeois elegance as the gentleman "Tom Thumb" and even arranged for Tom's introduction to Queen Victoria. Through such humbugs and self-aggrandizing strategies, Barnum succeeded in making his exhibits and performances respectable as well as popular.

In his *Inventing Popular Culture* (2003), historian and cultural theorist John Storey draws on the British tradition of cultural studies to analyze popular culture. In general, scholars in cultural studies such as Stuart Hall and Raymond Williams revised orthodox Marxism in the 1960s and 1970s to enable them to understand how relations of class, race, gender, and ethnicity were structuring all kinds of cultural production, including popular culture. Storey is particularly interested in applying Williams' notion of cultural hegemony to understand the experiences of audiences while they are enjoying popular books, visual arts, and performances. In brief, historians who view popular performances through the lens of cultural hegemony attempt to understand how such entertainments position spectators to accept or reject prevailing arrangements of power in their historical societies. In applying this approach to the popular entertainments of Astley or Barnum, for example, Storey would ask what these businessmen did to induce people to attend their performances, what social categories of people (according to class, race, gender, etc.) enjoyed them, and how did their engagements with these performances probably shape their beliefs and practices? Finally, which significant ideologies and institutions did these beliefs and practices support or undermine?

While Storey does not look specifically at blackface shows in the U.S., other historians have provided copious insights into minstrelsy that encourage scholars to pursue a popular culture approach to study them. These, plus Storey's *Inventing Popular Culture*, will serve as our primary guide in the following case study on blackface minstrelsy and racial nationalism in the U.S. between 1840 and 1870.

Figure 8.11
Henry Johnson posed as Barnum's "What Is It?"
Photograph by Mathew Brady (c.1872).

From Robert Bogdan's *Freak Show*, University of Chicago Press (1988).

roles in the frontier theatres of the Mississippi valley when he invented or stole from a slave – the historical record is unclear – the song and dance that would make him famous:

> Come listen all you galls and boys,
> I'm just from Tuc-ky hoe;
> I'm goin' to sing a leetle song,
> My name's Jim Crow.
> Weel about and turn about,
> And do jis so;
> Eb'ry time I weel about,
> I jump Jim Crow.

(Lott 1994: 23–4)

Dressed in rags with burnt cork covering his face, neck, and hands, Rice performed several verses of the song, jumping with agility and variety on each chorus. When he danced as part of a comic afterpiece at the New York Bowery Theatre in 1832, the young, mostly male working-class audience gave him a tumultuous reception. Rice wrote several one-act plays that featured his Jim Crow character and his famous dance and performed them successfully at the end of a regular evening's entertainment for the next 20 years.

The verses of his song, which were taken up by mobs destroying symbols of elite privilege during urban rioting in the 1830s and 1840s, celebrated white working-class victories over their social and economic oppressors. Rice's rough-music and violent gyrations likely reminded his spectators of their own raucous parades through town during holidays, when they blackened their faces to entertain and alarm friends and enemies with scurrilous antics and the noise of tin kettles and cow bells. This European tradition of blackface dated from medieval mummers plays at Christmastime and continued into the nineteenth century; it encouraged traditional male forms of merrymaking and celebrated the rights of the common man. When Rice began jumping "Jim Crow," most of his spectators no doubt thought about holiday fun and working-class freedom; initially, despite the blackface, the antics of "Jim Crow" were about political and physical liberation, not race.

By the early 1850s, however, blackface performance had grown from occasional afterpieces by Rice and others into full evenings of entertainment presented by an all-male minstrel troupe of four to ten performers. Dozens of minstrel companies played throughout the urban northeast, paying top salaries to their headliners and composers, among them the popular songwriter Stephen Foster. White performers borrowed some of their material from slave festivities in the South, including musical instruments (the banjo and bones), slave dances ("patting juba"), and the comic exchanges typical of corn-shucking rituals on plantations. They also relied on the musical traditions of Irish folk songs and grand opera, which they parodied with abandon. Minstrel shows usually featured jokes and musical numbers, specialty acts, and a concluding one-act comedy, parody, or farce. While Rice's "Jim Crow" afterpieces were not overtly racist – some of the verses of his song even called for the abolition of slavery – most minstrel troupes of the early 1850s pandered to groups of poor white urban workers who needed to be assured of their racial superiority. These were frequently Irish immigrants escaping from the potato famine and newcomers to city life fresh from the farm. To please these spectators, minstrels generally portrayed black characters as inept fools, grotesque animals, or sentimental victims.

By the end of the 1850s, minstrel entrepreneurs had increased their audiences to include a substantial number of middle-class males, plus some female and elite spectators. Minstrel troupes were also touring beyond northern cities into medium-sized towns and parts of the South. Looking for topics that could appeal to and further broaden this mixed, cross-class audience, the troupes settled on the southern plantation as an idealized site for white enjoyment; its sentimental Old-Folks-at-Home masters and humorous black folks, from sly tricksters to foolish Jim Crows, could provide a soothing contrast to the violence, crowding, and confusion of northern city life and national politics in the 1850s. In addition, the image of the happy plantation featured Earth Mother mammies, feminized old uncles, and "yaller gals" (played by a male in drag), a light-skinned slave whose beauty and allure motivated incidents of victimization and sentimentally mournful songs.

Not surprisingly, mid-century minstrelsy parodied abolitionism and anti-slavery productions of *Uncle Tom's Cabin*. One typical version, titled "Happy Uncle Tom," depicted Stowe's exemplar of self-sacrificing morality and vigorous spirituality as a decrepit old uncle meant to be laughed at for his grotesque jigs and foolish dialogue. Minstrel plantation skits and musical numbers avoided the realities of slavery – exhausting work, the forced separation of families, and the ever-present threat of violence and death – to deliver its audience to a never-never land of domestic warmth, sentimental love, and easy power in which whiteness provided the ticket to security and fun. For many northerners on the eve of the Civil War, the minstrel depiction of black people, white southerners, and slavery was all they knew about the South. From this perspective, it was difficult to see what could be so bad about the extension of slavery in the west. Why fight a war about that?

Minstrel shows had always professed a generalized, flag-waving patriotism, but the outbreak of war in 1861 forced the minstrel troupes to choose racial over liberal nationalism as the key to national unity. White performers in blackface praised the bravery of Union soldiers, anguished over the suffering of the wounded and women on the home front, and pushed for a compromise that might end the fighting – a compromise with southern advocates of slavery that would restore the Union to the racial basis of U.S. nationalism in the 1850s. "To go in for de Union," observed one performer, "ain't nigger abolition" (Toll 1974: 113). Accordingly, minstrels continued to attack abolitionists, but generally avoided the topic of emancipation after Lincoln's proclamation. When the North began recruiting and training black soldiers, minstrelsy portrayed the black troops as buffoonish dandies and ignorant cowards, unfit for fighting next to their white superiors (Figure 8.12).

After the war ended in 1865, minstrel skits demanded that the newly freed slaves stay in the South, as wards of their former masters. The failure of Reconstruction to educate black people and find them good jobs was a foregone conclusion in minstrelsy, which also mocked

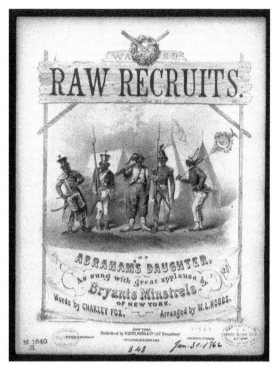

Figure 8.12

"Raw Recruits." This cover for sheet music performed by Bryant's Minstrels in an 1862 minstrel show in New York City mocks the presumed incompetence, foolishness, and fear of newly enlisted black soldiers.

Library of Congress.

the black quest for political and economic equality in the post-war South. Despite the end of slavery, minstrelsy found new strategies for relegating black people to second-class citizenship and maintaining the racial basis of nationalism. Imagining a U.S. nation-state in which blacks and whites could work and prosper together in the same community was not an option in the racist world of minstrelsy.

Minstrel shows were gradually incorporated into American vaudeville, but individual minstrel acts continued to amuse white audiences into the 1950s, when African-American activism and cold war concerns exposed the racism under the burnt cork for most citizens. Until then, though, some of the premier performers of popular and mass entertainment on stage and screen paraded their talents in blackface – including Al Jolson, Eddie Cantor, Mickey Rooney, and Judy Garland. Further, there are some who would argue that the continuing rumors concerning the true citizenship of President Barak Obama may be traced to the legacy of racial nationalism in the United States.

Key references

Adams, B. (1997) *E. Pluribus Barnum: The Great Showman and U.S. Popular Culture*, Minneapolis: University of Minnesota Press.

Cockrell, D. (1997) *Demons of Disorder: Early Blackface Minstrels and Their World*, Cambridge: Cambridge University Press.

Frick, J.W. (2012) *Uncle Tom's Cabin on the American Stage and Screen*, New York: Palgrave.

Jones, D. (2014) *The Captive Stage: Performance and the Proslavery Imagination of the Antebellum North*, Ann Arbor: University of Michigan Press.

Lott, E. (1994) *Love and Theft: Blackface Minstrelsy and the American Working Class*, New York: Oxford University Press.

McConachie, B. (1992) *Melodramatic Formations: American Theatre and Society, 1820–1870*, Iowa City: University of Iowa Press.

Mahr, W.J. (1999) *Behind the Burnt Cork Mask: Early Blackface Minstrelsy and Antebellum American Popular Culture*, Urbana: University of Illinois Press.

Nathans, H. (2009) *Slavery and Sentiment on the American Stage, 1787–1861: Lifting the Veil of Black*, Cambridge: Cambridge University Press.

Roediger, D. (1991) *The Wages of Whiteness: Race and the Making of the American Working Class*, London: Verso.

Storey, J. (2003) *Inventing Popular Culture*, Oxford: Blackwell Publishing.

Toll, R.C. (1974) *Blacking Up: The Minstrel Show in Nineteenth-Century America*, New York: Oxford University Press.

SUMMARY

In Europe and the Americas, numerous theatrical performances reflected and legitimated varieties of nationalism from 1760 to 1880. Liberal nationalism began with the Enlightenment in the eighteenth century and continued to animate peoples who regarded (or hoped to regard) their country as the home of individual rights and constitutional government. Schiller's plays can stand as a good example of liberal nationalism on stage. The basis for cultural nationalism, which inspired many Europeans after 1800, was pride in the distinctiveness of their heritage, language, and customs. Cultural nationalists celebrated their traditions through such varied fare as nautical melodramas, comic operas, and antiquarian revivals. Racial nationalists, especially numerous in Germany, Brazil, and the United States, emphasized the superiority of their ethnoracial group; they believed that their inherent greatness was a biological gift which elevated them over other groups within their nation-state and over rival nations outside of it. In the theatre, racist nationalism ranged from Wagnerian opera to blackface minstrelsy. All three of these fusions of nationalism and performance helped to shape the theatre and general culture of several nation-states during the nineteenth century. After 1880, these forms of nationalism influenced historical developments in parts of the world beyond Europe and the Americas, such as Japan and other sovereign countries. In the twentieth century, varieties of nationalism and nationalistic theatre swept the globe, as many nations gained independence from the empires that had dominated them.

★

Performing "progress": From imperial display to the triumph of realism and naturalism, 1790–1914

Carol Fisher Sorgenfrei

Contributors: Bruce McConachie and
Gary Jay Williams

When the "imagined communities" called nation-states (as discussed in Chapter 8) forcibly transform or absorb other peoples or geographical areas into colonies through military and/or economic force, the result is imperialism. In other words, nation-states transform into imperial empires through the practice of colonialism.

Empires see themselves as the locus of truth, rationality, science, civilization, maturity, and the life of the mind; the rest of the world as the realm of ignorance, child-like naivety, mystical forces, irrationality, and sensuality (all of which can be desirable, especially with the lingering Romantic imagination typical of Rousseau, discussed mostly in Chapter 7). In this chapter, we examine the rapid, profound shifts in theatrical expression that resulted from modern imperialism, guided by this perception of "rational self" vs. "irrational Other." The "rational/ irrational" dichotomy extends to race/ethnicity, class, philosophy, science, and artistic expression. In Chapter 8, we saw how theatre bolstered the development of a sense of self for the nation-state; in this chapter, we will discover how artistic practices from colonized or alien areas ("irrational Others") impacted performance in the "rational" imperial heartland.

After a discussion of imperialism, we will explain and expand the concept of Orientalism. We consider how international expositions and world fairs showcased overseas colonies and imperial wealth while introducing new visual and aural experiences. In the West and Japan, artists began to incorporate foreign imagery in their work, creating new genres. At the same time, consumers saw and desired exotic items that were formerly available only to the wealthy. In contrast, Chinese imperial expansion resulted in a new genre incorporating the "irrational" performance styles of internal "Others" that were initially outlawed but eventually replaced older, aristocratic styles. In all imperialist nation-states, the middle and upper classes at first disdained "irrational" lower-class entertainment, but in each case, these popular genres were eventually embraced, as were "irrational" experimental or alien forms.

Modern imperialism developed side-by-side with new concepts and technologies, including the invention of photography, the philosophy of positivism, and scientific innovations such as the theory of evolution, enunciated in Charles Darwin's (1809–1882) *On the Origin of Species* (1859). Such innovations and inventions challenged long-held religious and spiritual beliefs (seen as "irrational"), fostering an emphasis on the material world. Progressive theatre artists in Europe, the U.S., and Japan advocated these new ideas, but many religious and government leaders feared change and attempted to censor the resulting plays. Aesthetic realism and the Naturalist movement, which grew from these concepts, often featured unorthodox or shocking material. Daring European theatre managers such as André Antoine (1858–1943), stage designers, and playwrights such as Henrik Ibsen (1828–1906) and Anton Chekhov (1860–1904) embraced these new modes of perception, foreshadowing the kinds of dramatic structures and theatrical practices that would dominate much of the twentieth century.

Modern imperialisms

Imperialism has existed in many periods of history, including the ancient Roman Empire, the Mongols under Genghis Khan, the Persian Empire, the Ottoman Empire, various Chinese dynasties, the Aztec Empire, the Ethiopian Empire, and many others. In contrast to these earlier empires, modern types of imperialism flourish partly due to technological advances in travel and communication, the development of international capitalism, and more powerful military resources.

By the late nineteenth century, British and other European imperial expansion, which had begun in the 1600s with state-supported private investment by entities such as the British and Dutch East India Companies, had reached its peak. In addition to parts of Africa and Asia, Britain had occupied Afghanistan and other areas to prevent Russian expansion. In 1894–1895, European imperial nations (Britain, Germany, France, the Netherlands, Portugal, and others) organized the Berlin Conference to divide the colonized world (especially Africa) into zones to lessen economic competition. They imposed artificial linguistic and cultural boundaries without consulting African or other colonized peoples.

The reasons for imperialism are complex, but overall there are three basic rationales that often overlap.

(1) *Economic or commercial gain*: the previously foreign areas have something valuable that the imperialists desire. Examples include spices, gold, minerals, oil, water, land, slaves, cheap laborers, or a convenient route to other parts of the world. Usually, large businesses or corporations work hand-in-hand with the imperial government to maintain economic control and to obtain wealth, often preventing colonized areas from achieving further economic development.

(2) *Military advantage*: the imperialists may want to gain military advantage over the foreign country, or fear it as a potential enemy or the ally of enemies. They feel a need to protect themselves or to prevent future attacks. In such cases, military forces remain in the colonized areas, often controlling or "advising" the local government, or acting as emissaries of the imperium.

(3) *Ideological arrogance*: the imperialists believe their culture, religion, language, and/or way of life is superior to that of the colonized people. They may believe they have a "destiny" to rule others. They may try to convince their own population and the colonized foreigners that incorporation into the imperial whole (and elimination of cultural differences) will offer the colonized peoples opportunities for "modernization" or other

advantages, such as material gain, spiritual or religious enlightenment, advanced scientific education, or access to artistic or cultural treasures. In such cases, the imperialists often impose their language and culture on the colonized. However, belief in the imperialists' superiority sometimes translates into hatred of the colonized, resulting in racism, massacres, or even attempted genocide.

One example of these overlapping rationales occurred in the mid-1800s, when European nations and the U.S. used their military power, desire for economic advantage, and belief in their cultural superiority to force Japan to end its long isolation, allowing Western access and trade. The result, however, was not colonialism. Rather than being colonized, Japan rapidly learned from the West how to be an imperialist nation.

A different example is the U.S. concept of "manifest destiny." Many white settlers in the United States argued that they were fulfilling "manifest destiny" by expanding the nation westward, even though expansion entailed exterminating Native Americans and extending areas of African-American slavery. Partly believing that the U.S. had an inevitable right to expand, and partly to end economic depression, the U.S. militarily took control of Cuba, Puerto Rico, the Philippines, and Guam in the Spanish-American War of 1898.

In the three decades between 1868 and 1900, Japan had incorporated nearly all of the scientific, technological, social, economic, artistic, and other innovations that had occurred in the West since the 1600s (when Japan had begun to close itself off from the world). Japanese imperialism began in earnest when Japan gained control of Taiwan from China in 1895. In the Russo-Japanese War of 1904–1905, Japan decisively defeated Russia – a European nation – shocking the West. In 1904, Japan made Korea a protectorate and formally annexed it in 1910. That same year, the Japanese play *Korean King* suggested that all Asians would welcome Japanese imperial conquest as progress. By the 1930s, the Japanese Empire included a large number of Asian and Pacific colonies, under the euphemistic heading of "The Great East Asia Co-Prosperity Sphere."

THINKING THROUGH THEATRE HISTORIES

Orientalism

In 1978, Edward Said (1935–2003), a professor of comparative literature, published a landmark study of primarily British and French imperial practices, focusing on how intellectual traditions about the "Other" are invented and transmitted. The book, titled *Orientalism*, reconsiders the underlying meaning of visual, aural, literary, and theatrical imagery. Although most people today think of "the Orient" as meaning Asia, in earlier eras the term referred primarily to the Islamic Middle East.

Said defines Orientalism as:

> the corporate institution for dealing with the Orient – dealing with it by making statements about it, authorizing views of it, describing it, by teaching it, settling it, ruling over it: in short, Orientalism is a Western style for dominating, restructuring, and having authority over the Orient.

> (1978: 3)

continued

Orientalist representations take two basic forms. The first is to represent the Other as weak, childlike, uneducated, naïve, submissive, and sexually available. In this view, the Other needs (and even wants) to be saved, educated, uplifted, or seduced by a morally, spiritually, and physically superior power. Often, the Other is depicted as female, childish, or feminized, while the Self is envisioned as male, mature, or masculinized.

The second type of representation portrays the Other as uncivilized, barbaric, powerful, sexually terrifying, scheming, and intellectually incomprehensible. Here, the Other threatens to devour, attack, murder, rape, or destroy the Self. He does not value human life, is a crazed killing machine, and, in contrast to the first version, is usually seen as male. This version of the Other needs to be dominated, controlled, and prevented from undermining the civilization of the Self. Fear and hatred of this version of the Other can lead to war, mass murder, or attempted extermination of the Other.

Often, both versions of Orientalism exist simultaneously in regard to a specific culture.

Non-Western cultures can also harbor Orientalist views about the West, about neighboring countries, or about minority populations within their own lands. Nor is Orientalism only a modern phenomenon, as Euripides' *The Bacchae* demonstrates. In that play, a Greek leader fears and hates the "Eastern" or "Asiatic" god Dionysus, whom he views as both feminized and dangerously powerful. He is simultaneously repelled and fascinated by this exotic Other.

Orientalism should not be confused with racism, although often these two ideologies go hand-in-hand. Racism is defined as prejudices against, and practices aimed at, a specific group of people, defined as "inferior" due to their genetic characteristics. Although racism certainly exists, most scientists today deny the biological validity of distinct races. The targets of Orientalism, on the other hand, may include people of one or of many so-called "races" who share some other characteristic in common, such as nationality, gender, or religion.

Orientalist representations can be found in educational, historical, political, or artistic works. According to Said:

> The things to look at are style, figures of speech, setting, narrative devices, historical and social circumstances, *not* the correctness of the representation or its fidelity to some great original. The exteriority of the representation is always governed by some version of the truism that if the Orient could represent itself, it would; since it cannot, the representation does the job, for the West, and *faute de mieux*, for the poor Orient.
>
> (1978: 21)

Although Said's book dealt exclusively with Euro-American images of the Islamic world, Orientalist attitudes are not confined to works produced in the past, or to images of another country. An understanding of Orientalism can be a valuable tool for unearthing subtle prejudices or underlying attitudes about ethnicity, gender, disability, class, and so on in a play's script, costumes, settings, style of acting, musical score, or other aspects of performance, or in the way these things have been analyzed by critics or scholars.

Performing imperialism and Orientalism at the great expositions

The London Exhibition of 1851 was the first of many world fairs and expositions presenting the non-Western world as a marketplace for Western tourists and capitalists. Between this exhibition and 1920, world fairs and expositions attracted more spectators than any single genre of popular diversion, including the circus. At such events, imperial nations celebrated their conquests by showing off the riches of colonial goods and people, and demonstrated their architectural and technological prowess by erecting mammoth buildings and fabulous arcades. The Eiffel Tower, for example, was built for the 1889 Paris World's Fair.

At the Great Crystal Palace Exhibition in London, 1851, millions of visitors gasped at wonders such as huge steam engines, Indian miniatures, giant lumps of coal, classical sculptures, and the interior of a palace identified as a "Nubian Court." Housing many of these spectacles was the Crystal Palace itself, covering almost 19 acres in Hyde Park. The Great Exhibition's success led other imperial nations to present their own events. The Paris *Exposition Universelle* took place in 1855. The Philadelphia Centenary of 1876 celebrated one hundred years of U.S. independence. Although originally organized to glorify the progress and superiority of their nation-states, world fairs and expositions soon settled into promoting national empires. For example, in reaction to the loss of two French provinces after the Franco-Prussian War (1870–1871), the French increasingly turned to imperial glory abroad and expositions at home to emphasize their greatness (see Figure 9.1).

Figure 9.1
A view of the buildings and grounds for the Paris Exposition of 1867. Note the nearby barges in the River Seine for popular amusements. From the *Art Journal Illustrated Catalogue of the Universal Exhibition*.

Paul Greenhalgh, *Ephemeral Vistas*, Manchester University Press, 1988, Figure 2.

In fairs from 1889 to 1914, entire "villages" were erected, in which colonized peoples from Africa, Asia, the Middle East, the Pacific Islands and the Americas were displayed like animals in a zoo. They wore native costume and demonstrated local crafts, traditional dances, food preparation, and so on in carefully recreated surroundings, supposedly presenting a "realistic" image of daily life. Of course, it was all a performance. The imported natives were seldom offered decent pay or housing, they did not speak the language, and many suffered severe culture shock and terrible homesickness.

At the 1893 Chicago Columbian Exposition, colonial subjects from the British and French empires were housed in 17 native settings near the Midway Plaisance, an area that also featured "freak" shows and other carnival acts. At the Pan-American Exposition in Buffalo, NY in 1901, Native and African-Americans were exhibited along with other "primitive" peoples of the world. Native Americans performed war dances in traditional attire, and African-Americans were hired to portray happy antebellum slaves in a popular exhibit called "The Old Plantation."

The organizers claimed that these events offered educational opportunities and promoted international understanding. Indeed, most of those attending were simply out for an enjoyable day, hoping that they or their children had learned something about distant lands. They probably thought that the native peoples on display were benefiting from being part of the imperial whole.

Although these expositions and fairs were sponsored by and took place in Western empires, other nations often participated. Japan had been exhibiting its success as a modernizing nation in U.S. and European fairs since the 1860s. After its takeover of Taiwan, its defeat of Russia, and its annexation of Korea, Japan mounted an impressive display of its imperial possessions at the Japan-British Exhibition of 1910. At that time, the Japanese believed that their imperial conquests demonstrated their superiority over other Asian peoples, because Japan had never been conquered or colonized by the West. In addition, a common ideology held that Japan preserved the artistic and cultural treasures of once-powerful Asian nations such as China and India which were now laid low by Western imperialism. Japan clearly desired to control its neighbors and their resources, but it also saw itself as the savior of all Asian civilization.

In addition to touting the superiority of their nation, race, and empire, the British deployed strategies solidifying their imperial hold around the globe. Between 1851 and 1914, Britain organized 33 major expositions in India, Australia, and Great Britain. India, symbolizing British subject colonies, usually provided traditional performers, craftspeople, and models of ancient monuments. Australia, symbolizing all white settler societies, celebrated its progress under the empire through its rising cities and manufacturing. As the "mother country," Great Britain displayed its noble traditions, royal munificence, ships, armaments, and its imperial leadership.

All these identifiably British events cemented the interconnections made possible through empire. As one historian notes,

> Participation at the exhibitions as visiting tourists and actors in pageants was part of the process of building [national and imperial] communities. This was not fantasy as escapism, but the fantasy which integrated experience and imagination, thereby linking citizens and subjects together in a seemingly viable, tangible way.
>
> (Hoffenberg 2001: 243)

Such events were the forerunners of the mass spectacles and rallies that would sweep millions into the political enthusiasms of the twentieth century.

Distorting science to justify imperial entertainments

Charles Darwin and others who had examined scientific evidence concluded that humans evolved from and are related to animals, and that evolution results from successful adaptation to the environment. Darwin found that the forces driving evolution were complex and mostly due to variations that arise from generation to generation and their suitability to the natural environment. Although today his theories are widely accepted, they were, and continue to be, controversial because they conflict with biblical accounts. They were also adopted and twisted to support ideologies such as Social Darwinism, with which Darwin sharply disagreed.

Social Darwinism argues that all human life is a ruthless competition for material goods, leading to "the survival of the fittest." From a Social Darwinist point of view, white Westerners had proven themselves to be the most "fittest," but their morality also instructed them to save more "primitive" peoples from extinction. British poet Rudyard Kipling's 1899 poem "The White Man's Burden" had insisted that Euro-American imperialism would help "civilize" colonial subjects. The poem obliges the world's "white men" to assist "Your new-caught, sullen peoples, / Half-devil and half-child." (Because non-Western peoples were supposed to be inferior, Social Darwinists were impressed and surprised by Japan's rapid modernization and military prowess.)

In the U.S., the St. Louis World Fair of 1904 featured several tribes of Philippine villagers "scientifically" classified as representing different stages of civilization. Fresh from their victory in the Spanish–American War, U.S. imperialists could now boast that they had joined Great Britain and France to shoulder "the white man's burden." (No mention was made of the ongoing military campaign to suppress factions of rebellious Filipinos.) While a number of prominent Americans had actively opposed the trend, by 1900 the United States, a former settler colony which built a nation through slavery and the acquisition of aboriginal lands, had joined the ranks of imperialist nations.

Other popular events such as the "Ethnological Congress" at P.T. Barnum's circus encouraged a "scientific," Social Darwinist view of non-Western peoples as savages in need of imperial civilizing. (For more information on Barnum and the circus, see the website.)

Social Darwinism is related to "Orientalism" because both see the "rational Self" as a positive, forward development from a lesser or "irrational Other." Both buy into the idea of inevitable progress. As we will see below, these ideas are crucial to the philosophy of positivism and the development of Naturalism.

Imperialism and Orientalism in British theatre

The English actor Edmund Kean starred in many plays set in the Middle East. During the 1810s and 1820s, Kean performed Turkish kings, Saracen warriors, Arab princes, and half-Greek, half-Turk heroes, as well as an exotic, Moorish Othello, and what critics termed an "Oriental" Shylock, the Jewish money-lender in Shakespeare's *The Merchant of Venice*. Several of Kean's star vehicles, including *The Bride of Abydos* (1827) which was adapted from a poem by Romantic poet George Gordon Byron (generally known as Lord Byron, 1788–1824), featured scenes in a harem. Watching such scenes permitted male viewers the pleasure of seeing skimpily clad actresses; simultaneously, male and female viewers could imaginatively participate in the Western imperialist dream of rescuing exotic maidens (symbolizing feminized, weak "Others") from the control of evil, "irrational," Muslim rulers. Just as romantic, pictorial, scenic antiquarianism was reshaping London's Shakespearean productions, Orientalist scenery helped unify English audiences in regard to British imperial conquests in the Middle East.

Melodramas such as these also celebrated the technology that made imperialism possible. For example, *Freedom* (1882) depicts the British invasion of Egypt as a quest to end the slave trade and save a British financier's daughter from sexual slavery in a harem. Such plays suggest that introducing steamships, railroads, and international trade to Egypt more than made up for the unfortunate deaths of a few Egyptians. In *Khartoum* (1885), a newspaper reporter uses the telegraph and other new modes of communication to tell English imperialists about the dire circumstances in that Sudanese city. The melodrama actually reversed the loss of Khartoum to rebelling Islamic tribesmen the year before. Like later adaptations of *Around the World in Eighty Days* and other plays, these melodramas presented British domination as the forward march of white progress and civilization. Such works were patronized by the middle-class and higher.

Variety theatre and music hall

While such plays explored the exotica of foreign lands, new types of popular entertainment developed, catering to a predominately working- and lower-middle-class audience. To these audience members, imperial expansion was less important than making it through everyday life. In some ways, they were "internal Others," perceived by the upper classes in the same negative terms as colonial aliens. Sometimes, members of the upper classes would "go slumming" and patronize lower-class entertainments; consequently, aspects of popular entertainment seeped into more aristocratic styles, just as foreign elements had done. At the same time, lower-class audiences both aped and made fun of aristocratic passions.

One major form that proliferated after 1850 was variety theatre. Variety is simply a series of light entertainments unconnected by any overriding theme, story, or major star. Since the Renaissance, theatre in Western cultures had often incorporated singers, acrobats, performing animals, and other diversions between the acts of a regular drama. In the mid-nineteenth century, however, showmen strung together a series of such "numbers" without providing a regular play as the main attraction. Variety took numerous forms after 1850. One was the blackface minstrel show, which began in the U.S. (as discussed in Chapter 8) but quickly spread to Europe and to European colonies.

Another form of variety was the burlesque show, which began with female performers doing a parody, or "burlesque," of a popular play or work of literature. Eventually the parodic elements dropped out, and by 1900 the typical burlesque show in England and the U.S. featured a male comic, several comic sketches, dance acts, and musical pieces, plus scantily clad females in all of the numbers. The striptease, now identified as the central act of a burlesque show, did not make its appearance in the U.S. until the 1920s.

Concert saloons, which peddled beer and food along with entertainment, appeared in industrializing cities in Britain during the 1850s. They led to the most resilient and significant form of popular variety theatre, the music hall. Although "music hall" is an English Victorian term, it may designate any series of unconnected entertainments on an indoor stage. Music hall entertainment, lacking the coherence of "blacked-up" white performers or the presence throughout of a male comic and pretty girls, typically had even less aesthetic unity than a minstrel or burlesque show. In the U.S., this form of variety was called vaudeville.

In England, the music hall lasted longer than variety in other countries and probably had a more enduring effect on the national culture. In 1866, London had over 30 large music halls and more than 200 smaller ones; a few of the larger halls seated over 3,000 spectators. Most English music halls in the 1870s provided entertainment, food, and drink to a predominately working- and lower-middle-class audience. During the 1880s, some music hall entrepreneurs, seeking higher profits through increased respectability, opened new halls in middle- and upper-class neighborhoods. The halls reached their high point of popularity around 1910, when competition from silent films began to erode their numbers, which further declined in the 1930s and 1940s as the radio brought entertainment into homes. In the 1950s, television delivered the deathblow to the English music hall. However, aspects of music hall performance found their way into the plays of authors such as Samuel Beckett (1906–1989) and Harold Pinter (1930–2008), both discussed in Chapter 12.

Until the 1890s, the English music hall provided an alternative, both in its environment and its entertainment, to the strictures of Victorian life for many working-class families. While many music hall songs sentimentalized romantic love, others delighted in sexual pleasure, a taboo subject for proper Victorians. Several songs also derided the entanglements of marriage. Policemen, government clerks, and other figures of authority provided frequent butts for music hall humor. Nonetheless, the music hall generally remained culturally conservative. Entertainers might poke fun at factory discipline and lambaste politicians caught up in scandals, but they usually applauded English victories in war and the racism that accompanied English imperialism. Amidst the acrobats, magicians, performing animals, and human "freaks," early music hall variety preserved aspects of traditional English customs that provided workers and others with strategies for enduring and occasionally countering a culture that oppressed them.

By the 1890s, many halls, even in working-class neighborhoods, no longer allowed patrons to eat and drink while watching the show. They also featured more homogenized acts that would not offend Victorian tastes. Although gentrification and standardization drained the class-based vitality from music hall entertainment after 1890, its anti-Victorian legacy had wide ramifications in the twentieth century – from satiric popular songs and a scandal-mongering penny press to the electoral success of socialism in English politics.

For a discussion of another form of British popular entertainment, pantomime, see the case study on the website.

Figure 9.2
George Leybourne, a *lion comique* of the music hall stage, who wrote and sang "Champagne Charlie" (c.1867).

© V&A Images. Victoria and Albert Museum.

"Internal imperialism" and the origins of *jingju* ("Beijing Opera")

Modern Chinese imperialism focused on expanding into areas already within China's sphere of cultural and linguistic influence. The Chinese Qianlong Emperor (1711–1799; reigned 1735–1796) consolidated power and wealth, expanding his hegemony by using military force and by massacring and/or incorporating several minority ethnic groups, including Tibetans, Uyghurs, Kazhaks, Mongols, and others.

During the late eighteenth century, toward the end of his reign, local or regional styles of performance favored by peasants and/or recently colonized groups began to replace the dominant Chinese genre of *kunqu* (see Chapter 4). Roving troupes of low-status performers (all of whom were male) had begun to cater to the tastes of a far-flung population composed of ordinary people, rather than the elite literati, scholars, and aristocrats of big cities. At first disdained and ignored by the upper classes, hundreds of local and regional performance styles developed throughout China, often using stories derived from novels and earlier types of performance such as *zaju* and *kunqu*. These local styles used local languages in performance, which (although all written the same) when spoken are often mutually incomprehensible. Among the most important regional styles at this time were "clapper operas" (*bangzi qiang*).

Clapper operas feature musical instruments such as stringed fiddles, side-blown flutes, drums and cymbals, and blocks of wood (clappers) called *bangzi* that the players strike with a stick. The rhythm is fairly constant regardless of the region of origin. All clapper operas divide the music into "happy sounds" and "weeping sounds." Like other forms of traditional Chinese music theatre, clapper operas are divided by content into "civilian" plays (often love stories) and "military" plays (about heroic actions and battles).

In 1779, Wei Changsheng (1744–1802), a famous clapper actor from Sichuan Province (but who was born in Shaanxi Province), brought his troupe to Beijing, hoping to participate in upcoming celebrations for the emperor's seventieth birthday. Wei was a *dan* (male actor specializing in female roles) who was also an accomplished acrobat skilled in male martial roles. He was the first to use "false feet," stilted shoes tied to the feet of actors playing female roles, in order to mimic the appearance and walk of women with bound feet. His troupe's new, exotic style of performance captured people's imagination. They remained in Beijing for six years despite official attempts to censor them. In 1785, they were banned from the stage due to Wei's excessively bawdy acting style. Nevertheless, scholars have called the troupe's arrival and impact "the prelude to the birth of Beijing opera" (Mackerras 1983: 103).

In 1790, additional actors from far-flung corners of the empire came to Beijing for the emperor's eightieth birthday. Like the celebrations a decade previously, events were held in public locales – they were intended not for the emperor to see or hear, but to keep the general populace occupied. The court and other aristocrats disdained these popular genres and patronized the more elegant *kunqu*. Troupes from Anhui Province performed in two distinct styles. Eventually, elements of each were combined into a new genre uninfluenced by non-Chinese sources. The new genre became extremely popular, and is known as *jingju* [jing ju] or *jingxi*. Both terms mean "drama of the capital." In English, the genre is generally termed "Beijing Opera."

Seventy years would pass after *jingju*'s inception before an emperor would invite a performance at court (in 1860). In 1884, the Empress Dowager Cixi (1835–1908) requested *jingju* performances for her own birthday. Subsequently, *jingju* – once a lower-class, alien genre – began to enjoy imperial patronage.

During the first half of the twentieth century, *jingju* became an internationally acclaimed genre, primarily through the world tours of Mei Lanfang (1894–1961), a *dan* actor. Mei's performances influenced the ideas of Western theatre artists, including Bertolt Brecht (see the discussion of Brecht in Chapter 11). At that time, all roles were still performed by males, although prior to the Ming dynasty (1368–1644), both male and female actors had performed either gender. With the exception of specially trained girls who performed in private mansions, female actors did not perform publicly in Chinese traditional genres until the mid-twentieth century.

During the nineteenth and early twentieth centuries, China's empire was ravaged by both Western and Japanese imperialists, as well as by civil war. Mei's tours helped increase awareness of China's complex situation and reinforced the significance of Chinese performance.

Western artists appropriate non-Western imagery

In the West, the popularity of world fairs, exhibitions, and Orientalist plays increased demand for exotic items. While the wealthy continued to collect Asian art and antiques, the middle class desired inexpensive objects such as ceramic tea sets, decorative fans, wall hangings, folding screens, paper lanterns, rattan furniture, and "native" costumes to be worn as lounge wear at home or at "fancy dress" and masquerade balls. In an earlier craze that began in the seventeenth century, Westerners collected Chinoiserie, that is, items that looked Chinese or were supposedly of Chinese origin. Voltaire's *The Orphan of China*, discussed in Chapter 6, is an example of Chinoiserie in theatre.

Both popular entertainers such as magicians and serious artists rushed to add Orientalist imagery to their acts. For example, seeing an advertisement for cigarettes depicting an Egyptian dancer inspired Ruth St. Denis (1879–1968), one of the pioneers of modern dance, to create her "Oriental" dances (Figure 9.4).

Despite their infatuation with the exotic, most serious artists did not harbor imperialist or Orientalist goals. Instead, many were rebelling against rapid industrialization/modernization, wishing to "revitalize" what they saw as a dying Western culture by an infusion of something new. They felt non-Western art had more sensual beauty than Western art, and were often drawn to an imagined "purity" or "spirituality" that resonated with older, Romantic ideas celebrating a lost "Eden." Although in hindsight some of their work may seem naïve or even racist, in the context of their time and place, their art was both innovative and influential, planting the intellectual and artistic seeds for the emergence of later twentieth- and twenty-first century avant-garde and intercultural artists.

Figure 9.3
Jingju actor as Xiangyu, the king of Chu in *The King's Parting with His Favourite*. Costume and makeup denote character type.

The Image Bank/Tuul and Bruno Morandi/Getty Images.

Figure 9.4
Ruth St. Denis performing *Egypta*, one of her "Oriental dances."
Source: New York Public Library.

CASE STUDY: Inventing Japan – *The Mikado* and *Madama Butterfly*

Carol Fisher Sorgenfrei

Japonisme is a French term used by art historians to discuss the influence of Japanese art on Western art beginning in the 1850s, after Japan began to trade (however reluctantly) with the West. Painters such as Vincent Van Gogh, Pierre-Auguste Renoir, Claude Monet, and Édouard Manet first encountered Japanese art by seeing *ukiyo-e* (woodblock prints). Although today these prints are highly valued, when Japan began to modernize, the prints were used as wrapping paper or packaging (as we use newspaper today) for shipping inexpensive souvenirs to the West. These Western artists became excited about Japanese artistic style. Elements such as asymmetry, irregularity, lack of perspective, lack of shadows, use of flat, empty space, bright colors, and contrasting patterns were in direct opposition to traditional, academic Western design (Figures 9.5a and 9.5b).

Figures 9.5a and 9.5b

Two examples of *Japonisme* in art: Vincent Van Gogh's *La Courtisanne*, after Eisen (1887), and Claude Monet's *Madame Monet in a Japanese Costume* (1885).

9.5a: © Heritage Image Partnership Ltd/Alamy Stock Photo and 9.5b © 2015 Museum of Fine Arts, Boston. All rights reserved/Bridgeman Art Library.

Unlike Orientalism, *Japonisme* does not attempt to represent, control, or authorize the Other. Rather, *Japonisme* is an artistic strategy by which artists incorporate or borrow elements of Japanese origin into their own art, often creating entirely new styles. Japanese art historian Okakura Kakuzō (1862–1913) applauded *Japonisme* as proof of Japanese art's international significance. Okakura's opinions were later distorted by ultranationalists to support their view of the superiority of Japanese culture.

All artistic borrowing (sometimes called "appropriation") has the potential to become problematic. For example, if an artist appropriates aspects of another culture that are sacred to that culture's religion, or that represent things the other culture feels should not be shown in public, the result may be offensive. Critics and historians of the arts must understand what elements were borrowed from other cultures, what those elements mean in their original context, and how they are understood in the new context. Part of the theatre critic or historian's task, then, is to accept the possibility that even great art might contain aspects of Orientalism or even racism. At the same time, she must be able to determine when and why artistic appropriation enhances art without insulting or harming the original culture.

In an 1891 essay framed as an imaginary discussion, playwright, novelist, and essayist Oscar Wilde (1854–1900) archly wrote:

> No great artist ever sees things as they really are. If he did, he would cease to be an artist. Take an example from our own day. I know you are fond of Japanese things. Now, do you really imagine that the Japanese people, as they are presented to us in art, have any existence? . . . The Japanese people are the deliberate self-conscious creation of certain individual artists. . . . In fact the whole of Japan is pure invention. There is no such country, there are no such people.
>
> (1969: 315)

For this case study, we consider two of the most enduring examples of an invented "Japan" in Western performance. One, the comic operetta by Gilbert and Sullivan, *The Mikado* (1885), "straddles the porous boundary between art and popular entertainment" (Lee 2010: xiv). In contrast, many people consider Puccini's tragic opera *Madama Butterfly* (1904) one of the pinnacles of Western "high art." Both works remain hugely popular, despite critiques that they perpetuate Orientalist practices.

The Mikado, or The Town of Titipu

Opening in March 1885 at London's Savoy Theatre, this ninth comic operetta by librettist William S. Gilbert (1836–1911) and composer Arthur Sullivan (1842–1900) played for 672 performances – up to that time, the second longest run of any musical theatre piece produced in London. By the end of 1885, over 150 companies in Europe and North America had performed it. *The Mikado* has been translated into many languages and continues to be performed all over the world.

All Gilbert and Sullivan operettas are comedies, usually set in some fantastic "topsy-turvy" world filled with absurdities. *The Mikado* is a satire of British politics and culture set in an imaginary, exotic time and place called "Japan." Like other Gilbert and Sullivan operettas, it includes many clever "patter songs" satirizing British society. In the play, the Mikado (another name for Japan's emperor) has made flirting a crime punishable by death. To sidestep this decree, his counselors have appointed a poor young man, originally sentenced to die for flirting, to be Lord High Executioner. Since they know he will not decapitate himself, they assume that everyone is safe. Meanwhile, Nanki-poo, the Mikado's heir, has been traveling in disguise to avoid marrying an ugly, mean woman. He is in love with a schoolgirl named Yum-Yum, who is engaged to the Lord High Executioner. Further complications arise when the Mikado demands at least one execution. After many satirical jibes at corrupt politicians and absurd plot twists – including letting the young lovers marry for one month, after which the husband, Nanki-poo, will have his head cut off – true love triumphs.

The visual aspects of the production demand familiar Japanese commodities, such as Japanese costumes, makeup, swords, wigs, fans, parasols, scenery, and so on. The operetta opens with the following stage directions and lyrics:

> SCENE: Courtyard of Ko-Ko's palace in Titipu. Japanese nobles discovered standing and sitting in attitudes suggested by native drawings.
>
> CHORUS OF NOBLES:
>
> If you want to know who we are,
>   We are gentlemen of Japan;
> On many a vase and jar –
>   On many a screen and fan,
>   We figure in lively paint:
>   Our attitude's queer and quaint –
>   You're wrong if you think it ain't, oh!

The audience is alerted from the start that the play is only as real as the painted images on fans and vases. This is not Japan, and the actors are not Japanese. The action and even the names of the characters are so comical that no one could possibly imagine that the play was meant to represent Japan. Nevertheless, the original production took pains to be "authentic" by having Japanese people from a "native village" in Knightsbridge, London teach the actors how to gesture and walk "like real Japanese." Some of the music was inspired by Japanese tunes, and the actors dispensed with corsets (normally worn on stage by both males and females), instead wearing the looser Japanese kimono. Such uncorsetted costuming was considered quite shocking.

Despite the obviously comic exaggerations that were evident to the original audience, some late twentieth- and early twenty-first-century Asians and some scholars find the work offensive and Orientalist. They point to the repetition of negative Japanese stereotypes, such as numerous vows to commit suicide, childish, vulgar, or silly women, foolish men, and incomprehensible, primitive behavior. Even more disturbing is the practice of Caucasian or other non-Asian actors performing in "yellowface" makeup (Figure 9.6).

Yellowface performance is related to American minstrel shows of the same period, which involved white performers "blacking up" to embody childish images of African-Americans (see the case study in Chapter 8). The minstrel show spread from the United States, where it originated in the 1840s, throughout the British Empire. In many instances, minstrelsy helped to confirm the racism that justified imperialist oppression. In 1853, when the American Commodore Matthew C. Perry's ships (with their superior cannons) arrived in Japan to force trade with the West, white crew members performed blackface minstrelsy for the Japanese court. The Japanese assumed that blackface performance was a "normal" practice by Western imperialists. Even today, Japanese actors "black up" when performing African or African-American roles, and some Japanese rappers and hip-hop musicians have been accused of wearing darkening makeup. In contemporary China and Japan, actors portraying Caucasian characters typically don red or blond wigs and use pale makeup. Do such practices mean that the Japanese and Chinese are racist, imperialist – or merely naïve? Scholars disagree about how to interpret such facts.

Despite the negative connotations, many famous Caucasian actors have performed in yellowface for the sake of greater realism. For example, Marlon Brando (1924–2004), who was strongly opposed to racism, spent two hours each day donning prosthetics and makeup to portray an Okinawan in the film *Teahouse of the August Moon* (1956). David Carradine (1936–2009) wore yellowface makeup and prosthetics in his *Kung Fu* TV series (1972–1975 and 1993–1997), in various martial arts films, and in *Crank: High Voltage* (2009).

Yellowface remains a controversial practice. Asian actors and those of Asian descent feel they – not Caucasians – should be cast as Asian characters. In 1991, protests erupted over the choice of a Caucasian actor to portray the half-Vietnamese narrator in the Broadway musical *Miss Saigon*, a contemporary retelling of *Madama Butterfly*. David Henry Hwang, a Chinese-American playwright who led the protests, wrote about the controversy in his Obie-winning play, *Yellow Face* (2007).

Figure 9.6

English actor/singer George Grossmith in "yellowface" makeup, as Ko-Ko in the original 1885 production of *The Mikado*.

© Victoria & Albert Theatre Collection.

Madama Butterfly

In contrast to the clearly invented, comical, and commodity-laden Japan of *The Mikado*, Puccini's opera strikes most viewers as believable, moving, and beautiful. Nevertheless, some contemporary people are troubled by the opera's depiction of Japan, and especially of Japanese women. In its own time, however, the opera was controversial for a very different reason: because it pushed the boundaries of the art.

Composer Giacomo Puccini (1858–1924) wrote his early operas in the style of nineteenth-century Romanticism, but later became a passionate advocate of operatic realism (in Italian, *verismo*). *Verismo* stressed violent, sometimes sordid aspects of life, often depicting lower-class characters. Although it remains one of the world's most widely produced and popular operas, Italian audiences booed the first performance. Both score and libretto were modified several times over the next few years, until the opera's initially "unconventional structure was replaced by the more usual framework of Italian opera of the period. The uncompromising, harsh, moral view of the original version was diluted until a soft-grained, sentimental atmosphere pervaded the opera" (Smith 1984: 18).

Madama Butterfly (two-act version, 1904; revised three-act version, 1907) was based on an American play by David Belasco (1853–1931), which had been inspired by John Luther Long's short story, and possibly by a novel by Pierre Loti. There is some evidence that all versions may have been based on actual events in Nagasaki, Japan, in the early 1890s (Groos 1994: 169–201).

A fifteen-year-old Japanese woman named Cio-Cio-san (pronounced "*chōchō*," Japanese for "butterfly"; "*san*" is a Japanese suffix used with names) is about to marry American Navy Lieutenant Pinkerton. She is in love, has renounced her family, and has secretly converted to Christianity. For Pinkerton, however, this "marriage" is a sham. He merely wants a mistress while he is stationed in Japan. When his ship sails away, Cio-Cio is convinced that he will return someday. She gives birth to his son and faithfully waits for three years, refusing marriage to a worthy Japanese suitor. When Pinkerton does return, he brings along his American wife, who has agreed to raise Cio-Cio and Pinkerton's son in the U.S. Cio-Cio agrees to give up the child only if Pinkerton comes to see her. She believes the boy will have a better life in America. Before Pinkerton arrives, she offers Buddhist prayers, blindfolds the child, puts an American flag in his hand, and then uses her father's knife to cut her own throat in a ritual suicide. Pinkerton arrives too late.

What are we to make of her passionate actions? Is she merely the victim of cruel American imperialism, a noble child-woman who dies for love and for the benefit of her child? The question becomes more complicated as we learn about the opera's history. In addition to the Western sources noted above, Puccini was influenced by the Italian tour of the Japanese Kawakami acting troupe, especially by Sadayakko's depiction of ritual suicide. (Kawakami and Sadayakko's tour is discussed later in this chapter.) The Japanese actress's death scenes impressed him so much that he referred to them in justifying his revisions (Groos 1999: 53). On the one hand, Cio-Cio and Sadayakko's other roles repeat the Orientalist stereotype of the victimized, self-sacrificing woman, an image the Japanese actors fostered in order to please a Western audience. At the same time, these women's brave decision to die reinforces the willpower associated with Japanese *bushido*, the code of the samurai. Kawakami's troupe intentionally stressed these contradictory images in order to remind the West of Japan's imperialistic triumphs and patriotic fervor. In Puccini's opera, Cio-Cio is a complex contradiction who embodies the imperial fantasies of both Japan and the West. Joshua Mostow, an expert on Japanese culture, calls her

the tragic artefact of a traditional Japan sacrificed on the altar of masculine modernity. And yet, women are by this sacrifice mobilized . . . and become the exemplars of self-abnegation, a model for patriotic bushido. . . . We miss a great deal then, if we see Cio-Cio-San's destruction by Pinkerton as nothing more than the heartless exploitation of a woman of color by a white male. The woman's self-destructive sacrifice is overdetermined by both the Western imperialist *and* the Japanese imperialist subtexts, despite the fact that those subtexts are at cross-purposes, the one defending the Western subjugation of non-European sites, the other an expedient means to avoid such subjugation.

(Mostow 2006: 193–4)

Unfortunately, many reviewers miss this complexity. Consider the career of the great Japanese soprano Miura Tamaki (1884–1946), who performed Cio-Cio-san throughout the world starting in 1915. She began a tradition of "attempts at realistic casting, by using Japanese singers in the lead" (Groos 1989: 182). Ironically, ethnically correct casting was not appreciated by the early critics. One wrote, "though there is an ethnographic truth in some details, Mme. Miura had to divest herself of most of the artistic traditions of her own land before she could *impersonate* the character imagined by an American novelist and set to music in Italy" (Browne 1996: 232). Is the critic suggesting that only a non-Japanese singer can "realistically" portray a Japanese character? How might such ideas relate to concerns about yellowface?

Conclusion

When *The Mikado* and *Madama Butterfly* were created, audiences were relatively unfamiliar with, but intrigued by, Japan and its culture. Gilbert and Sullivan used this lack of familiarity to create a "topsy-turvy," satirical portrait not of Japan, but of England. They employed Orientalist imagery that was popular at the time, when the British Empire was at its height. They also used the styles and forms of popular British entertainment to satirize aspects of British society. In contrast, the depiction of the arrogant Pinkerton and the tragic Cio-Cio in Puccini's opera appears to critique U.S. imperialism. However, the controversies over its musical form and libretto demonstrate both an artist's desire to move toward realism and Naturalism, and the audience's preference for a less strident style. By analyzing these works historically, we see some of the differences between what viewers in the past saw and what those in the present see. We discover that the Other is continuously being reinvented.

Key references

Browne, N. (1996) "The Undoing of the Other Woman: *Madame Butterfly* in the Discourse of American Orientalism," in D. Bernadi, ed., *The Birth of Whiteness: Race and the Emergence of U.S. Cinema* (New Brunswick, NJ: Rutgers University Press), 227–56.

Groos, A. (1989) "Return of the Native: Japan in Madama Butterfly/Madama Butterfly in Japan," *Cambridge Opera Journal* 1(2): 167–94.

Groos, A. (1994) "Lieutenant F.B. Pinkerton: Problems in the Genesis and Performance of Madama Butterfly," in W. Weaver (ed.) *The Puccini Companion*, New York: Norton.

Groos, A. (1999) "Cio-Cio-San and Sadayakko: Japanese Music Theatre in Madama Butterfly," *Monumenta Nipponica* 54(1): 41–73.

Lee, J. (2010) *The Japan of Pure Invention: Gilbert and Sullivan's* The Mikado, Minneapolis: University of Minnesota Press.

Mostow, J. (2006) "Iron Butterfly: Cio-Cio-San and Japanese Imperialism," in J. Wisenthal, S. Grace, M. Boyd, B. McIlroy, and V. Micznik (eds) *A Vision of the Orient: Texts, Intertexts, and Contexts of* Madame Butterfly, Toronto: University of Toronto Press.

Smith, J. (1984). "Tribulations of a Score," in N. John (ed.) *Opera Guide 26: Madam Butterfly/Madama Butterfly*, London: John Calder and New York: Riverrun Press, in association with English National Opera.

Wilde, O. (1969) "The Decay of Lying," in R. Ellmann (ed.) *The Artist as Critic: Critical Writings of Oscar Wilde*, New York: Vintage.

New media and new ideologies: Photography, science, and positivism

While Western and Japanese imperialists, driven by the need for raw materials and new markets, were conquering native peoples around the world, their photographers were publishing images of "primitive" peoples from distant lands. Photography was as much a tool of imperialism as were print media, steamships, high explosives, and machine guns. For example, numerous photographs depicting a supposedly corrupt and backward Korean people in need of Japanese civilization preceded the Japanese annexation of Korea.

Henry Fox Talbot invented photography in Britain in 1839, and by the 1860s photographic studios were flourishing throughout Western Europe and North America. By 1900, photography was ubiquitous in Japan as well. While people immersed in a world of orality, writing, or print could easily imagine spiritual and mental realities without material form, viewers of un-retouched photographs were encouraged to believe that the real world "out there" was limited to what they could see with their eyes or capture on film. In other words, photography helped shift many people's perspective of the world, from an emphasis on the immaterial (or "irrational") to a new focus on the material (or "rational").

The widespread experience of taking and viewing photographs suggested an "objective" and materialistic understanding of reality that helped move mainstream playwriting, acting, and design toward aesthetic realism. In contrast, non-visual new media (telegraph, telephone, and phonograph) gradually excited an interest in the "subjective" and spiritual side of reality that sharply conflicted with the photographically inspired realism, a trend in twentieth-century avant-garde performance that will be considered in Chapter 10.

THINKING THROUGH THEATRE HISTORIES

Positivism

Positivism is a philosophy introduced by Auguste Comte (1798–1857) that insists that only those things that are experienced by the senses and can be measured are real; intuition and subjective feelings are not external behaviors and cannot be measured, and thus they cannot provide truth. This concept was expanded to include the idea that societies are also subject to natural laws that work in a way similar to scientific laws, such as the law of gravity.

Positivism maintains that human intellectual development progresses to a high point that is defined by scientific knowledge. It implies that humans can (and will) ultimately understand everything. Clearly, imperial nations with superior weapons and advanced technologies imagined themselves to be closer to knowing the "truth" than those they conquered. Critics of positivism point out that universal understanding is impossible to achieve, since each new scientific breakthrough leads to others, without end.

For the theatre historian, the most important aspect of positivist philosophy is the way that it ties ideas of "truth" and "reality" to a narrow view of science. The aesthetics of Naturalism and realism could only develop in an intellectual climate that supported such ideas. Positivism and theatrical realism continue to be influential – even dominant – in much of the world today.

The rise of realist staging

After 1850, Western theatre artists gradually adapted their techniques to incorporate the new interest in photographic realism. For example, in American Dion Boucicault's (1820?–1890) *The Octoroon* (1859), a photograph taken by accident reveals the murderer of a slave boy. In England, the plays of Thomas W. Robertson (1829–1871) revealed character through the actors' handling of realist stage properties. Robertson's "cup and saucer plays" (as they were called), such as *Society* (1865) and *Caste* (1867), also suggested a less romantic style of acting (Figure 9.7). In Vienna, Ludwig Anzengruber (1839–1889) turned the peasant play, formally a romantic piece meant to evoke nationalistic pieties, toward realist purposes in the 1870s. As noted in Chapter 8, in Russia, Ostrovsky's *The Thunderstorm* (1859) and *Enough Stupidity for Every Wise Man* (1868) demonstrate a realist handling of melodrama and comedy, and keen attention to the details of middle-class life. Because early nineteenth-century actors usually chose and purchased their own costumes (a costly expense for female actors especially), productions usually lacked a unified appearance. By the 1880s, however, most producers provided costumes for their entire casts to ensure a measure of uniformity and/or authenticity.

After encountering the "box set" in continental Europe, producer/manager, actress, and opera singer Madame Vestris (Lucia Elizabeth Vestris, 1797–1856) introduced it to London in 1832. The box set permitted greater photographic realism by creating the illusion of three walls

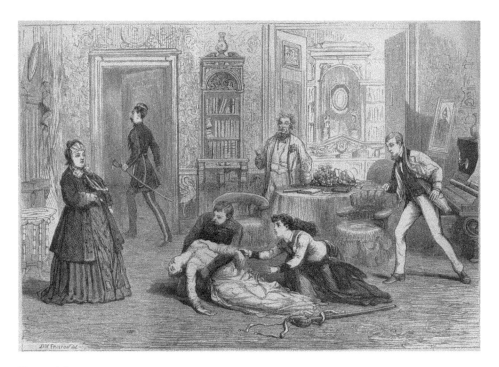

Figure 9.7

An 1879 print illustrating a scene from Thomas W. Robertson's *Caste*, at the Prince of Wales Theatre, 1879. Notice the stage properties on the central table.

© Enthoven Collection, V&A Images, Victoria and Albert Museum.

(with the audience peering in through an imaginary **fourth wall**), real doors and windows, and actual furniture.

When electrical stage lighting began to be used in the late 1870s, the unreal appearance of painted, two-dimensional scenery became evident. Consequently, improved methods of shifting three-dimensional units and real props and furniture were developed. In 1879, for example, Madison Square Theater in New York rigged elevators for two complete stages, one above the other, to allow one stage to be changed while the other stage served as the playing area. At Henry Irving's Lyceum Theatre in London, workers ripped out the grooves for sliding flats to allow for the "free plantation" (*ad hoc* placement) of scenic units. Less commonly, theatre architects and managers began to abandon the older systems of scene changing, dominant in the West since the seventeenth century, to offer increased off-stage storage space for furniture and three-dimensional units, and clear access from the wings.

Other innovations followed. For example, by 1914, technicians lighted concave, plaster cycloramas in the upstage area to create a variety of outdoor realist illusions. Several German theatres had installed elaborate revolves to wheel on the cumbersome materiality of stage realism. Despite all the interest in Asia, European technicians were unaware that in Japan, revolving stages and other mechanical devices for creating sophisticated stage illusions had been common in *kabuki* since the 1750s.

The American actor William Gillette (1857–1937) performed his star vehicle *Sherlock Holmes* (1899) using realistic properties, costumes, and scenery that looked as though they had been whisked from Victorian London into the United States. British star actor Herbert Beerbohm Tree's (1853–1917) London production of *A Midsummer Night's Dream* in 1900 featured real flowers, mechanical birds, and fairies with battery-operated glow lamps. For its revival in 1911, Tree added live rabbits. In Boucicault's *The Vampire* (1852), thrilling melodramatic staging included a supernatural, instantaneous rescue of the heroine by the use of a "vampire trap" from which actual red flames and smoke spewed, along with the evil vampire himself.

In Japan, realism had never been of interest to artists. However, the shock of superior Western technology and fear of potential colonization forced attitudes to change. Accepting the ideology inherent in positivism, Japan embarked on massive and rapid modernization, including attempts to make Japanese theatre more like Western theatre. Although Japan had been forced to trade with the West, the West had not imposed its own aesthetics on Japan, as it typically did in colonized areas. Rather, the Japanese themselves chose to adopt realism and other Western artistic modes in order to "join" the modern world. Experts in science, technology, education, government, and the arts were sent all over the world to learn the latest Western ideas.

Simultaneously, some theatre artists and managers tried to make *kabuki* more realistic. In 1872, *kabuki* actor Ichikawa Danjūrō IX (1839–1903) appeared in formal Western attire (white tie and tails) instead of traditional Japanese kimono to inaugurate a new theatre that he promised would cleanse *kabuki* of bawdiness and – in a move that paralleled Western antiquarian Shakespearean performance – would present *kabuki* history plays with authentic-looking costumes, properties, and scenery. *Nō*, in contrast, did not attempt to modernize or to add realistic elements, and was almost extinguished due to its connections with pre-Meiji feudalism. However, when former United States president Ulysses S. Grant visited in 1879, he recognized the value of this ancient genre and successfully urged his Japanese hosts to preserve it without change.

The Japanese government soon embraced the practices of capitalist imperialism perfected by the West. Like the West, Japan rationalized its imperialistic ventures by telling its own people and those it colonized that Japanese expansionism was a positive force that would improve lives by offering the benefits of modern science, technology, and so on. As we will see, Japanese imperialism was closely tied to the development of realism.

Among Japan's first imperialistic ventures was the invasion and defeat of northern China in 1894–1895. This invasion offered a pretext for a group of brash young theatre reformers, led by Kawakami Otojirō (1864–1911), to sidestep attempts to alter *kabuki* and instead, to create something entirely new, more closely allied to Western models of playwriting and production. They produced *shimpa* [sheem-pah] – literally "new style" – dramas that adapted aspects of nineteenth-century Western dramatic forms to Japanese tastes, but continued the use of an all-male cast. The acting was a cross between highly stylized *kabuki* gesture and vocal patterns, and the comparatively realistic Western acting of the period. One of the earliest *shimpa* plays was *The Sublime, the Delightful Sino-Japanese War* (1894), which was presented like a series of journalistic reports from the front. Like popular historical melodramas in Europe, Kawakami used photographically authentic military uniforms and makeup to depict realistic battle scenes, including heroic re-creations of actual battles.

The introduction of female performers in Japan

After *shimpa*'s successes, the Japanese government sent Kawakami's troupe on a fact-finding and performance tour of the West. While touring the United States, the lead *onnagata* in *The Geisha and the Knight* (1900) became ill. Although women were still not permitted to perform professionally in Japan, the desire of U.S. audiences to see females playing women's roles prompted Kawakami to allow his wife, Kawakami Sadayakko (1872–1946), a former geisha [geh-sha] and thus a trained dancer, to perform instead. Audiences adored her, and she continued to play the female lead in subsequent tours of Europe, to great critical acclaim.

The content of plays and dance-dramas such as *The Geisha and the Knight* – and especially the critical and popular praise heaped on Sadayakko – helped create simultaneous and apparently contradictory images of Japan, as suggested in the case study of *The Mikado* and *Madama Butterfly*. These plays presented Japan as part of the exotic Orient filled with sexually alluring women and fierce male warriors; at the same time, however, they offered the vision of a successful, modern nation that should be considered the military, economic, and cultural equal of the West. In this way, Kawakami and his troupe helped transform Western Orientalist perceptions to Japan's advantage, presenting a revised image of a new, modern Japan to the West. In 1908, Sadayakko founded the Imperial Actress Training Institute, Japan's first acting school for women. *Shimpa* eventually incorporated female actors performing on the same stage as *onnagata*, a practice that continues when *shimpa* is performed today.

One indicator of the growing acceptance of female actors – as well as an example of how aspects of Western realism supported Japanese imperialism and were transformed to conform to Japanese tastes – was the creation of the all-female Takarazuka Revue. In 1914, a Japanese entrepreneur, hoping to lure tourists to his spa in Takarazuka City (near Osaka), offered the first performance of a family-friendly "all-girl opera troupe" attached to a music school. Eventually, the music school became a kind of finishing school for girls who were taught not only singing, dance, and music, but how to become "good wives, wise mothers." The phrase indicated women's preferred role in Japan's growing imperialist ventures. They would give birth to and raise strong, patriotic Japanese citizen-soldiers.

At first, the school presented operettas deemed suitable for family entertainment. Later, musical plays often based on Parisian revues (and, after the Second World War, on Broadway musicals) and exotic, Orientalist tales were joined by elaborately costumed and be-feathered chorus lines, something like a cross between a non-sexualized Las Vegas Revue and the Radio City Music Hall's Rockettes. The word "Takarazuka" now indicates both the city and this unique, all-female performance genre that originated there.

Today, the Takarazuka Revue's school is one of Japan's most competitive and professional performance training institutions. The students, carefully selected young women, are trained in almost militaristic fashion as professional singer-dancer-actors. In addition, as originally envisioned, the school teaches skills such as house cleaning, patriotism, and proper etiquette. The Takarazuka Revue is wildly popular with teenage girls, housewives, and lesbians. Actors specialize in either male or female roles, but male impersonators are the biggest stars. Spectators

Figure 9.8
Kei Aran performs as Oscar François de Jarjayes, a female captain of the royal guards of French Queen Marie-Antoinette during the Takarazuka theatre's *The Rose of Versailles* final rehearsal in Tokyo. The rigorously trained company, which has performed for nearly a century starring young single women, has drawn generations of devoted, yet decidedly mild-mannered, fans.

Source: Toshifumi Kitamura/AFP/Getty Images.

enjoy the gender ambiguity and idealization of masculinity embodied in the performance of male characters – an idealization that is as much a female fantasy of ideal masculinity as *kabuki's onnagata* is a male fantasy of ideal femininity. In the Takarazuka Revue, the entire world is transformed into an exotic image, an alien world of Otherness that rejects photographic realism and embraces the irrational.

With few exceptions, Takarazuka Revue actors do not perform for more than a few years after graduation. Consequently, almost all are young, usually under 30, enhancing the fantasy element of the performances. Former Revue stars have gone on to successful careers in film and music; most, however, follow the traditional path to marriage. Some men believe that having played males on stage, the male impersonators make ideal wives, because they have learned to "understand" the male psyche.

Scripts, which often foreground gender disguise, range from historical romances set at the time of the French King Louis XIV to spectacular productions of Broadway musicals, original works, and adaptations of Western and Japanese novels, including a musical based on *Gone With the Wind*. Shows are seldom overtly political, but often convey subtle suggestions of Japanese cultural superiority, including the ability to perform "the West." The Takarazuka Revue maintains two major theatres (in Takarazuka City and Tokyo), six permanent touring companies, and its own TV station (Figure 9.8).

Naturalism on stage

The gradual shift toward theatrical realism after 1850 reached its apex in the West in the movement known as Naturalism. While absolute distinctions between realism and Naturalist aesthetics are probably impossible, realism may be understood as a general style that remains pervasive today, while Naturalism can be seen as a movement that influenced theatre between 1880 and 1914, but then disbanded. Committed Naturalists joined Émile Zola (1840–1902), their leader, in asserting that heredity and the social-economic environment are the primary causes of human behavior. Zola argued in *Naturalism in the Theatre* (1881) that play productions must demonstrate the effects of these visible causes (Figure 9.9). In the theatre, stated Zola, "[W]e would need to intensify the illusion [of reality] in reconstructing the environments, less for their picturesque qualities than for dramatic utility. The environment must determine the character" (Zola 1881: 369). Further, photography provided reliable, objective evidence about a character's social-economic environment: "You cannot claim to have really seen something until you have photographed it," wrote Zola in 1901 (Sontag 1977: 87). Zola and the Naturalists were well-educated writers, privileged members of the middle and upper classes. Zola's manifestos insist on the use of "rational" or "scientific" methods (including photography) to depict characters who were decidedly Other and "irrational": women forced into prostitution, beggars afflicted with incurable diseases, the uneducated and unemployed, or homeless, hopeless characters addicted to drink or drugs. Although such plays may seem to suggest social protest and calls for reform, viewing the plays, their authors, and their audiences in historical/social context suggests that, instead, they may have been exploitative fantasies.

As we have noted, photography helped push realism toward positivism, the claim that scientists could discover an objective reality by dispassionately observing nature. Naturalism joined positivism and photographic realism to Social Darwinism. The Naturalists believed that an accurate rendition of objective, external realities was required to explore positivist and Social Darwinist causation, which, as we saw, has ties to notions of the rational Self and irrational Other.

Figure 9.9

Emile Zola's naturalistic *The Earth*, directed by André Antoine at the Théâtre Antoine in Paris, 1902.

© Biliothèque Nationale, Paris.

Although Zola strove to meet his goals by dramatizing his novels, the plays of Henri Becque (1837–1899) were more successful on stage. Becque's *The Crows* (1882) and *La Parisienne* (1885) nearly abandon conventional plotting to present everyday situations in which greedy characters prey on the weak, and a "respectable" wife sleeps with other men to advance her husband's career. The German playwright Gerhart Hauptmann's (1862–1946) influential *The Weavers* (1892) focuses on the exploitation and rioting of German workers in 1844.

Like Hauptmann, an increasing number of theatre artists urged moderate or even radical reform, often focusing on liberalism or socialism. Many of them saw Naturalism as the most powerful genre for impressing their views on their audiences. However, neither liberalism nor socialism meant what most Westerners understood by these terms after 1917. Liberalism – defined as the right of individuals to pursue their interests unrestrained by aristocratic privileges or state regulations – had been the banner of reformers since the French Revolution. The bourgeoisie throughout Europe had largely secured these rights by 1850. From the liberals' point of view, the laws of the marketplace and individual effort, if unimpeded, should guarantee economic progress and social justice. However, it had become evident (partly through photographs of slums) that social reforms were needed. Some liberal, Naturalist plays after 1880 railed against social injustice. *A Man's World* (1910) by U.S. playwright Rachel Crothers (1878–1958) critiques the double standard that condemns women for sexual behavior that is accepted in men. In Britain, John Galsworthy's (1867–1933) *Justice* (1910) pleaded for more humane prisons. In *Damaged Goods* (1902), French playwright Eugene Brieux (1858–1932) campaigned against the ignorance and fear that led to the spread of syphilis.

In contrast, socialism argued that social needs and equity, rather than private interests, should drive economics. By the late 1800s, many socialists throughout the world had turned to the economic ideas of Karl Marx (1818–1883), who maintained that although capitalism might produce some forms of progress, exploitation of the working class was intrinsic to capitalism. However, large numbers disagreed with his call to revolution; the revolutionaries became known as communists. The dramas by Russian socialist Maxim Gorky (1868–1936) include *The Lower Depths* (1902), which centered on tramps and impoverished workers living in a Moscow flophouse. Like most Naturalist plays, *The Lower Depths* dramatized a photographic "slice of life," with all of its banality, cynicism, sentimentality, and violence (see Figure 9.10).

Women, whether socialists or not, were demanding more equality, including the right to vote, the right to wear less restrictive clothing, safer working conditions, and even the right to birth control. One of the earliest and most radical socialist feminists was Finnish playwright Minna Canth (1844–1897). Her *Children of Misfortune* (1888) depicted the diseases, drunkenness, crimes, and death that degraded the lives of the unemployed, especially women and children.

State censorship throughout much of Europe before 1914 prevented the production of many Naturalist plays. The authorities objected to the plays' offensive language and feared their political implications. To avoid censorship and produce Naturalist plays, independent (or private) theatres appeared in several countries, offering subscriptions to members. In Paris, André Antoine began the Théâtre Libre (Free Theatre) in 1887 when the censors denied permission for a short season of new plays, including an adaptation of a Zola novel (see Figure 9.11). One of Antoine's early productions was Ibsen's *Ghosts* (1881), forbidden by the censors because it depicts previously taboo subjects, including sexually transmitted disease. The Théâtre Libre also produced several of Becque's plays, *The Power of Darkness* (1886) by Russian novelist Leo Tolstoy (1828–1910), and *Miss Julie* (1893) by Swedish dramatist August Strindberg (1849–1912).

Antoine's theatre provided a model for other free theatres in Europe, and eventually in Japan. For example, the Freie Bühne (Free Stage) in Berlin produced predominantly Naturalist plays by Ibsen, Becque, Tolstoy, and others and created the first audience for Hauptmann's dramas. London's Independent Theatre, modeled on the other "free" theatres on the continent, opened in 1891 with a production of *Ghosts*. It continued until 1897, mostly showcasing Naturalist plays. Because the Freie Bühne and the Independent Theatre used professional actors who were simultaneously involved with other productions, they could not mount the kind of

Figure 9.10

The Moscow Art Theatre production of Maxim Gorky's *The Lower Depths*, 1902, with Stanislavsky as Satin (center).

© Society for Cooperation in Russian and Soviet Studies, London.

Figure 9.11
André Antoine as old Hilse next to his loom in the Théâtre Libre's 1892 production of Hauptmann's *The Weavers*. Color lithograph by Henri-Gabriel Ibels (1893), on the cover of a portfolio for Antoine's Théâtre Libre programs, all of which featured prints by Parisian avant-garde artists.
© Gary Jay and Josephine S. Williams.

fully integrated productions that marked the success of the Théâtre Libre, where Antoine relied on trained amateurs. Nonetheless, all three theatres played a significant role in introducing Europe to the possibilities of stage Naturalism.

Realism and the rise of producer-directors

In Central and Eastern Europe, where subsidized theatrical institutions predominated, a few strong producers championed realism in state- and city-supported theatres. In Western Europe and the United States, by contrast, some producers gradually wrested economic control of commercial theatrical production from the stars, which allowed them to shape both the economic and the artistic fortunes of their theatres. By 1900, both routes had led to the emergence of a new figure who specialized in staging realism: the producer-director. In Japan, the producer-director appeared a few years later, and his appearance highlighted the struggle between those who advocated a contemporary, literary, playwright's theatre and those who wished to modernize *kabuki*'s actor-driven theatre.

The first producer-director to exercise near total control over his productions was Georg II (1826–1914), the Duke of Saxe-Meiningen (an independent duchy in Germany before 1871). The duke designed all of the costumes, scenery, and props, even insisting on genuine materials and period furniture for historical authenticity. When the company toured throughout Europe between 1874 and 1890, it set new standards for the aesthetic integration of realist productions, especially in ensemble acting. Most members of Saxe-Meiningen's company played both leading roles and supernumeraries; there were no stars. For the first time on a European stage, mob scenes featured individuals with their own character traits speaking intelligible lines, and the mob itself was choreographed to move with a level of reality and power that audiences had never witnessed before (Figure 9.12). The duke achieved these effects by rehearsing for several months, frequently with full sets and costumes, until he believed his productions were ready for the public. By 1890, the troupe had given over 2,500 performances of 41 plays and the duke had demonstrated how an authoritarian producer-director could integrate realist productions.

Konstantin Stanislavsky (1863–1938) saw the Meiningen troupe perform in Moscow in 1890. The ensemble acting and realistic, off-stage sound effects especially impressed him. As he developed his own mode of directing, he would recall the highly disciplined control of this company, and would merge that discipline with an emphasis on non-egotistical, creative, emotionally honest acting that contrasted with the more typical strutting and posturing of the day. The desired result would be a fully organic production (Benedetti 1999: 40–2). Along with

Vladimir Nemirovich-Danchenko (1858–1943), Stanislavsky brought high standards of realist production to Russia after founding the Moscow Art Theatre (MAT) in 1898. He insisted on long rehearsal periods and the presence of all actors. Although somewhat less powerful than similar producer-directors, he carried substantial authority due to his membership in the Moscow business elite, connections to wealthy patrons, and growing eminence as an actor and director. The MAT produced the four major plays of Russian playwright Anton Chekhov (1860–1904): *The Seagull* (1896), *Uncle Vanya* (1899), *Three Sisters* (1901), and *The Cherry Orchard* (1904). Stanislavsky paid scrupulous attention to the realities of Russian provincial life on which these plays are based, encouraged ensemble acting, and used a "fourth wall" performance style (Figure 9.13).

After 1906, Stanislavsky began working on a "system" to help actors develop commitment to their characters' realities – work he would continue for the rest of his life. Today, most scholars agree that his system combines devotion to finding the character's (not the actor's) personal, emotional truth with intense, physical control of the voice and body. In Chapter 12, we discuss how American interpretations sometimes shifted emphasis away from Stanislavsky's insistence on physical control and toward the actor's (rather than the character's) emotional truth.

Figure 9.12

A crowd scene in the Duke of Saxe-Meiningen's staging of Shakespeare's *Julius Caesar* at Drury Lane Theatre, 1881.

© V&A Images, Victoria and Albert Museum.

In France, for productions at the Théâtre Libre, André Antoine's actors observed the realist convention of the imaginary "fourth wall," occasionally delivering lines with their backs to the audience. Antoine also used the conventions of realism for a different effect in later productions of French classical plays at the state-subsidized Théâtre Odéon. For example, to re-create historically accurate productions of Molière's comedies, he placed costumed actors playing spectators on the stage and hung chandeliers over them. Antoine's productions toured widely in Western Europe and, like Saxe-Meiningen's, shaped a generation of theatre artists.

Emotional and physical truth were also important in Japan. Sadayakko's success challenged the exclusion of women from female roles and professional actor training. Some traditionalists feared that replacing *onnagata* would destroy aesthetic pleasure and encourage female sexual promiscuity. Even Osanai Kaoru (1881–1928), whose production of Ibsen's *John Gabriel Borkman* (1909) is considered the first *shingeki* [sheen-gheh-kee] ("new theatre," i.e., modern, Western-style theatre), urged *onnagata* to learn to play modern women. Nevertheless, Osanai's Free Theatre (*Jiyū gekijō*), named after Antoine's Théâtre Libre, sought to emulate its ideals.

In contrast, literary critic Tsubouchi Shōyō (1859–1935) argued that realist representation demanded women on stage. In 1906, he founded a Theatre Institute to train actors and mount private *shingeki* productions. His 1911 *Hamlet* featured his student Matsui Sumako (1886–1919),

Figure 9.13
V.S. Simov's 1898 naturalistic design for Act I of the Moscow Art Theatre's production of Anton Chekhov's *The Seagull*. Note the painted backdrop.
© The Society for Cooperation in Russian and Soviet Studies, London.

Japan's first professionally trained female actor. Later that year, Matsui performed her most famous role, Nora in Ibsen's *A Doll House*, with another *shingeki* troupe. The content of the play, Matsui's performance, and her personal life shocked the country, seeming to crystalize the fears of the traditionalists. However, women acting in realistic plays could not be stopped. Although *shimpa* continued to use both female actors and *onnagata*, by 1930 women routinely performed female roles in *shingeki*. Today, *shingeki* is virtually indistinguishable from contemporary Western theatre.

In China, the humiliations of European imperialism and military defeat to Japan encouraged a shift toward Western culture ("The May Fourth Movement"). Wishing to modernize, progressive Chinese students studying in Japan discovered Harriet Beecher Stowe's novel *Uncle Tom's Cabin*. The theme of freedom and the style of modern Western drama (as they imagined it) resulted in the creation of *The Black Slave's Cry to Heaven* (*Heinu yutian lu*, 1907), the first *huaju* (Chinese spoken drama). Many important Chinese authors wrote for *huaju*, including Cao Yu (1910–1996), whose influential *Thunderstorm* (*Leiyu*, 1934) is a psychologically based family drama.

THINKING THROUGH THEATRE HISTORIES

Ideology, realism, and the well-made play

How "real" is realism? With its selective focus, its unobtrusive exposition, its appearance of real time, its linear sequences of cause-and-effect actions that lead (seemingly) to a third-act crisis, and its careful construction of credible character psychology, realism tries to hide the fact that it is a carefully crafted fiction designed to keep the viewer inside the ideology of the middle-class world it represents. Because it emphasizes individual character psychology, it is not well suited to showing how social formations are constructed or how they might be dismantled. In other words, realism encourages an acceptance of things as they currently are.

Raymond Williams has shown that modern realist tragedy, from Ibsen's *A Doll House* through Arthur Miller's *Death of a Salesman* (1949), tracks the struggle and ultimate defeat of the individual who attempts to fulfill her or his desire, but who is ultimately the victim of social formations that are never addressed (Williams 1966: 87–105; 1969: 331–47). Williams shows the inherent contradictions between all the talk of social reform in such plays and the invisible limitations of realism. Williams' one-time student, Terry Eagleton, summarizes the argument:

> The discourse of the play [the liberal tragedy] may be urging change, criticism, rebellion; but the dramatic forms – [that] itemize the furniture and aim for an exact "verisimilitude" – inevitably enforce upon us a sense of the unalterable solidity of this social world, all the way down to the color of the maid's stockings.
>
> (Eagleton 1983: 187)

Consequently, realist plays – even those that appear to be highly critical of society – ultimately support the status quo. The form itself implies that revolutionary change is not possible.

In many ways, realist play structure derives from the very "unreal" structure of "the **well-made play**," a suspenseful genre that had proven its believability for bourgeois audiences since the 1820s, when French playwrights Eugène Scribe (1791–1861) and, later, Victorien Sardou perfected it. Although the term is usually used in a derogatory sense, the well-made play's structure is central in every significant playwriting and screenwriting textbook in English today.

The well-made play derives from French neoclassicism. The plot results from events happening prior to the play's beginning, demanding much exposition. The plot must follow a strict cause-and-effect pattern, including a series of escalating complications with a final reversal (and/or revelation) that returns the world to a state of order. Well-made plays typically use devices such as letters or other props that are at first misunderstood, but are later revealed as proof of a character's true identity or as a way to unravel plot complications. This structure is also typical of farce. As we will see later in this chapter, Ibsen's plays use techniques derived from farce and the well-made play, but they refuse endings that return the world to a socially acceptable order.

Ibsen and Romantic idealism

Norwegian playwright Henrik Ibsen published his first play in 1850, and remained active in the theatre until his death. His career can be seen as a microcosm of the shifting genres of theatre during the late nineteenth and early twentieth centuries. Most of his early dramas were written in verse and set in the Scandinavian past. With *Pillars of Society* in 1877, Ibsen altered the form and style of his plays from Romanticism to realism, while retaining strong philosophical ties to Romantic idealism. During the 1870s and 1880s, Ibsen was often considered either a realist critic of contemporary society or even a Naturalist, intent on revealing the ways in which heredity and environment determined human fate. As noted earlier, many independent theatres, including Antoine's Théâtre Libre, produced his *Ghosts* (1881) as a demonstration of Naturalism. But Ibsen's theatre consistently moved beyond the limitations of realism and the ideology of Naturalism. Rather, Ibsen was drawn to Romantic idealism, a worldview directly influenced by the philosophy of Georg Wilhelm Friedrich Hegel (1770–1831), especially *The Phenomenology of Spirit* (1807). For Hegel, natural and human existence consisted of the process of self-governing and self-developing reason; in humans (both individually and socially), reason seeks self-fulfillment and free spirit. Hegel's view is called idealist because it places ideas as the fundamental element or driving force of reality. (Many other thinkers, such as Plato and Kant, are also idealists.)

Two Romantic plays of Ibsen's mid-career, *Brand* (1865) and *Peer Gynt* (1867), endorse Hegel's commitment to the individual's search for transformational self-fulfillment. Brand is a symbolic Everyman who struggles to transcend earthly fragmentation and live up to the idealist claims of his imagination. Peer Gynt is the comic opposite of Brand, a figure who prefers indirection and compromise to Brand's direct pursuit of perfection. In effect, Peer's foolish, futile life confirms the superiority of Brand's flaming idealism (Figure 9.14). In both plays, Ibsen recognized that self-fulfillment was necessary to strive for but impossible to achieve. As we will see in the case study of Ibsen's *A Doll House* (1879), he merged Hegel's idealism with a notion of liberal tragedy.

Despite the surface realism of Ibsen's later plays, they continued to affirm Hegelian idealism and (as we will see) attacked the limitations of photographic realism. In doing so, they also questioned the representational basis of the theatre. The plot of *Hedda Gabler* (1890), for example, rests on several clichés that had come to be associated with melodramatic versions of the well-made play: a *femme fatale* (Hedda herself, who threatens to lure two good men

Figure 9.14

A scene from an Indian adaptation of Ibsen's *Peer Gynt* called *Gundegowdana Chaitre*, directed at the Rangayana Theatre in Mysore in 1995 by Rustom Bharucha. Hulugappa Kattimani as Peer, in the white suit, and Manjuatha Belakere, as an Indian folk version of the Button Moulder. The Button Moulder, a messenger of Yama, god of death, in the adaptation, warns Peer of his approaching mortality. Partly because of its universal implications, *Peer Gynt* continues to be performed around the world.

Source: Kennedy, D. (ed.) *The Oxford Encyclopedia of Theatre and Performance*, Vol. 1, Oxford University Press, 2003, p.615.

to their doom), a pair of sensational pistols (which spectators know will be fired), a Mephistophelean figure (who attempts sexual blackmail on Hedda), and the evils of drink, leading to a misplaced manuscript (which nearly drives one man to suicide). Ibsen invites his spectators both to enjoy the operation of these mechanical contrivances of character and plot and to look through them to his language for the more essential action of the play. Mostly through its imagery, *Hedda Gabler* suggests an idealist battle between the forces of light and the forces of darkness.

In contrast to most realist playwrights' emphasis on photographic reality, Ibsen relied on language rather than spectacle to express his ideas. In *The Master Builder* (1892), he traces the spiritual regeneration of Halvard Solness, a disillusioned middle-aged architect-builder. Solness is urged on a quest for spiritual awakening by Hilde Wangel, a girl in her twenties who shares in his drive for self-perfection. At the end, Solness climbs to the top of an off-stage tower that he built, symbolizing his quest for transcendence, but once there, he falls to his death.

Ibsen was interested in dramatizing the conflict between imaginative vision and practical reality, the spiritual needs that drive individuals and the limitations of material possibility that constrain and can finally kill them. The problem with staging this conflict in the 1890s (and a problem that remains today), however, is the impossibility of realizing purely spiritual realities on a materialist stage. During the era of classical Greece or Baroque opera, writers could lower gods on to the stage to represent spiritual needs and possibilities. But Ibsen, writing for a more realist theatre, can only arrange for his characters to talk about their spiritual yearnings. Consequently, *The Master Builder* is necessarily dense with dialogue.

Ibsen wrote in many styles. His late, non-realistic plays seem to foreshadow such twentieth-century experiments as Expressionism. This aspect of his career will be considered in Chapter 10.

Chekhov undermines nineteenth-century theatre

Anton Chekhov, while studying to become a medical doctor, wrote sketches, short stories, and one-act plays – several of which were performed in the popular variety theatres of Russian cities. Despite a growing reputation as a dramatist, Chekhov almost abandoned the theatre after the failure of *The Seagull* in 1896. However, Stanislavsky convinced him to allow the Moscow Art Theatre to mount a revival of the play and, following its success, Chekhov composed three more full-length pieces for the MAT. Despite his small output, Chekhov's plays are second only to Shakespeare's as the most produced in the world.

Chekhov, who was interested in the materiality of psychology and history, generally looked with amusement or compassion on people who professed to believe in spiritual realities. Unlike Ibsen, Chekhov relied on dramatic action and gesture, rather than on speech, to reveal characterization and to undermine the usual genres of nineteenth-century theatre. In the third act of *Uncle Vanya* (1899), for example, Chekhov has his middle-aged protagonist enter a room intending to present a bouquet of flowers to a married woman he is desperately in love with, only to find her in the arms of his best friend. Later in the same act, Vanya chases the woman's husband (an ailing, selfish professor) around the house with a pistol, finally corners him, then shoots at him and misses, twice. Earlier in the play, though, Chekhov paints a sympathetic portrait of Vanya as a man who has wasted his youth and happiness to help others by managing a country estate.

Figure 9.15
Sonja (Patti Love) comforts Uncle Vanya (Michael Bryant) in the final scene of Chekhov's *Uncle Vanya* in the 1982 production in the Lyttelton Theatre, the National Theatre, London, directed by Michael Bogdanov.

Photo by Laurence Burns, courtesy National Theatre Archive.

Uncle Vanya combines the genres of French farce and realistic psychological melodrama, making the character of Vanya both ridiculous and pathetic for much of the play (Figure 9.15). Where Ibsen's dramas might use nineteenth-century dramatic genres to indirectly criticize the representational possibilities, Chekhov's plays radically rework and sometimes parody them. For Chekhov, the usual dramatic frames for representing reality could not probe the major psychological and historical conflicts of the modern age.

In *The Cherry Orchard* (1904), Chekhov subverts both tragic and comic expectations. The play asks its spectators to respond to a family of aristocrats who return to their debt-ridden estate, waste their time when they should be saving the family legacy, then lose and finally abandon the estate. Should they be understood as tragic or comic figures, or both? Chekhov provides ample possibilities for either interpretation and directors have chosen both extremes, as well as mixing them together in various combinations. Despite Chekhov's objections, for example, Stanislavsky staged the play as a tragedy.

Whatever the tone of a production, Chekhov's works undermined conventional dramatic forms of representation to theatricalize the downfall of the Russian aristocracy and the rise of the bourgeoisie.

Ibsen, Chekhov, and the critique of photography

Although theatre historians hail the influence of photography on the development of realism in the theatre, both Ibsen and Chekhov – two of the most significant playwrights identified with early realism – believed that photography had little to reveal about human experience.

Chekhov sets up photography for ridicule in the first act of *The Three Sisters*, when a minor character, Fedotik, has everyone pose for a photograph. Of course, photos freeze the flow of life in a static pose, and Chekhov uses this fact to explore the changes that actually occur. The happy faces frozen in the Act I photograph are no longer possible by the play's end. In Act III, a fire burns up all of Fedotik's photos, and by Act IV, taking photos has become a sour joke.

Similarly, Ibsen sets much of *The Wild Duck* (1884) in a photographer's studio, but his photographer, Hjalmar Ekdal, is a fool who cannot see beyond the surfaces of his photos. Like many photographers in the 1880s, Ekdal's clients want him to retouch his photos to conform to their sentimental self-images. His clients actually reject the documentary evidence of photography, wanting the images to be more like idealized paintings. Ekdal gives much of this retouching work to his adolescent daughter, even though the strain on her eyes is gradually blinding her. The implications are clear: those who believe that photographs are truthful may lead themselves and others into sentimentality and moral blindness. Thus, while working within the conventions of realism, both playwrights questioned the psychological effects and social uses of photography.

CASE STUDY: Ibsen's *A Doll House*: Problems in Ibsen's problem play

Gary Jay Williams, with Carol Fisher Sorgenfrei

Although often heralded as a play about women's liberation at a time when that concept was still very new, Ibsen himself denied that such was his intent. Rather, he said the play was about the struggles of all humankind. Nevertheless, when the play premiered in 1879, its story of a wife abandoning her husband and children shocked audiences in Scandinavia, Germany, and England.

The controversy over *A Doll House* even caused Ibsen to write an alternative, sentimental ending for the German premiere. In this version, Nora, after looking in on her children one more time, falls to her knees, unable to leave. Ibsen despised this ending but wrote it to insure the play's production. This ending, emphasizing the power of "mother love," was also used in Japan when the play was first translated and performed there in 1911. Revisions that softened the ending were being made throughout the world as late as 1976.

But the play has continued to present serious problems of its own making. Actors playing Nora struggle to make credible the journey of the obedient Victorian wife of the first part of the play to the independent woman at the end. In addition, many critics see a still more profound question, one that Ibsen did not really allow his audiences to dwell on: will Nora's leaving her home result in her liberation in the society she lives in?

Ideology and A Doll House

Although Ibsen unfolds with sophisticated craft the economic, cultural, and social forces entrapping Nora, the play does not consider what might happen to her if she actually left her husband and children. Rather, Ibsen presents us with Nora's miraculous transformation from a child-like wife, imprisoned in a Victorian culture where she has long been infantilized by her father and husband, into a budding, self-reliant woman.

As the play opens, we see Nora as a homemaker, blissful shopper, and practiced manipulator of her husband – using the only powers and making the only choices that she has within her culture. Nora still seems emotionally childlike at times, secretly eating her macaroons. Torvald refers to his wife in trivializing diminutives, as "my little squirrel," and his "little lark" (Ibsen 1978: 125–6). Nora, however, uses her sexuality and takes advantage of the inconsequentiality men assign to her, as she does when she manipulates her husband to get the extra money that she will use to pay off her secret loan. She takes pride in having secretly saved Torvald's life when his health broke from overwork. However, since married women were not permitted to get such loans without their husband's signatures, she had planned to ask her father to sign for it. When her father died, she forged his signature – a criminal act.

Figure 9.16

Nora (Betty Hennings), dancing the tarantella for her husband, Torvald (Emil Poulsen), with Raphael's portrait, *Madonna and Child*, in the background (above the piano) in the premiere production of *A Doll House* at the Royal Theatre Copenhagen, 1879, directed by H.P. Holst. At the piano, Dr. Rank (Peter Jerndorff), with Mrs. Linde (Agnes Dehn) in the doorway.

© Teatermuseet i Hofteatret, Copenhagen.

Nora may believe she has "worked the system," but like many women, she is working around ideologies long in place that she cannot change. Her husband is sovereign in the household; on his side are the full force of tradition, state law, and Christian religious passages on wifely obedience by St. Paul (*Ephesians* 5: 22–33). What marginal power Nora has she derives from the ways in which a male-dominated culture constructs her: she is sexualized on the one hand and idealized on the other, subject in both to the pleasure and convenience of men.

The play takes place during Christmas, a traditional Christian family feast day. In the setting of the premiere production in Copenhagen in 1879, a copy of Raphael's portrait of the Madonna and Child hung over the fireplace, reinforcing the "natural" order of things (Figure 9.16).

The disgraced lawyer Krogstad knows her secret and knows how to ruin Nora. When first confronted with the question of illegality, she naïvely assumes that the law would understand her motives. Once she realizes the seriousness of her situation, she becomes desperate in the face of Krogstad's blackmail. She briefly considers suicide but lacks the courage. She resorts to sexually tantalizing the dying Dr. Rank, trying to extract money from him (the silk-stocking scene in Act II – once omitted by some translators who felt it was too blatantly sexual). Beneath the painting of the Madonna and Child (the religious and social framing of woman in her acceptable role), she raises her tambourine and wildly dances the exotic, wild tarantella in an attempt to prevent Torvald from seeing Krogstad's incriminating letter (Figure 9.16).

When Torvald finally learns the truth of the forged signature, he shatters Nora's last desperate illusion. Rather than realizing that her action was for his sake, Torvald explodes in rage about the loss of *his* honor. The "miracle" Nora hoped for did not happen and never could have.

While Ibsen has revealed a great deal about Nora's material circumstances, he also gives Nora her famous exit. He asks us to believe that Nora evolves in this crucible of three days and three acts to the point that she can sit her husband down and begin her discussion with three shattering insights: "I've been your wife-doll here, just as I was Papa's doll-child. And in turn the children have been my dolls" (Ibsen 1978: 191) (Figure 9.17). This, in effect, deconstructs her social identity.

However, such a transformation would never have been possible in the real world. True, as feminist critic Annelise Maugue writes, Ibsen's play had important symbolic value for women. Late nineteenth-century feminists predicted that the play would have reformative effects. However, Maugue adds that Nora's leaving "is precisely the step that real women could not imagine, let alone take" (Maugue 1993: 523).

Material conditions in the real world

Had Nora been a real woman in nineteenth-century Norway, it would have been very difficult for her to have supported herself on the other side of Torvald's door. Job prospects for real Noras were very poor. Census data for four French cities at the end of the nineteenth century show that one out of every two women was single, widowed, or divorced, and therefore seeking employment. In England in 1851, 40 percent of the women who were working were domestic servants; 22 percent were textile factory operatives. A London shirt-maker told an interviewer in 1849 that her normal hours were from five in the morning until nine at night, and in the summer she often worked "from four in the morning to nine or ten at night – as long as I can see." Still she was barely able to support herself (Yeo and Thompson 1972: 122–3). The low wages – not the hard work – drove many such women to prostitution.

Ibsen briefly focuses on the material circumstances of two other women in his play. Mrs. Linde married her husband not for love (which astonishes Nora) but because she needed to support her bedridden mother and two younger brothers. Now widowed, she seeks a clerical job, which she gets only through Nora's strenuous intercession with Torvald. Anne-Marie, the

Figure 9.17

In the mid-1890s, a canned food company in Paris, the Compagnie Liebig, offered this pocket-size trading card depicting the final scene from Ibsen's *A Doll House*, with the purchase of one of its products.

Courtesy Gary Jay and Josephine S. Williams.

children's elderly nurse (who years ago had been Nora's nurse), had to give her own illegitimate child away in order to get employment: "A girl who's poor and who's gotten into trouble is glad enough for that" (Ibsen 1978: 155). Nora hears this when she is glimpsing the unspeakable consequences of Krogstad's blackmail. But when she walks out the door, she will be subject to the same employment conditions. In the late 1870s, courageous women were leading movements in Europe and the U.S. to improve women's working conditions and change the laws, but Nora would not have benefited from them for another decade. A real Nora in Japan would have had to wait even longer for such changes. Ibsen's Nora has no ties to a feminist sisterhood, nor would she have thought to seek them.

Ibsen based Nora's situation on real life. However, Laura Kieler (the inspiration for Nora) did not slam the door. Like Nora, she had secretly obtained a loan to save her husband's life by financing a trip to a warm climate, but was unable to repay the interest, so she forged a check. After her forgery was revealed, she had a nervous breakdown and her husband committed her to a mental asylum. Later, she begged him to take her back for the sake of the children, which he grudgingly did. When he was forced to change the ending to "soften" it, Ibsen was actually going back to what happened in the real world. Not to examine the ideology embedded in the play is to risk perpetuating it.

Ibsen's American translator, Rolf Fjelde, preferred the title *A Doll House* to the more common *A Doll's House* as the translation of Ibsen's title, *Et Dukkehjem*. He believed the title

Figure 9.18
In this 1991 staging of Ibsen's *A Doll House* at Center Stage, Baltimore, Maryland, the child-like Nora (Caitlin O'Connell) has just returned home from her Christmas shopping spree to be treated patronizingly by her husband, Torvald (Richard Bekins). In the final act, both were in anguish when the newly strong Nora determined that she must leave their home. Directed by Jackson Phippin and designed by Tony Straiges.
© Center Stage.

without the possessive points not just to Nora, as the doll, but to the entire household – husband, wife, servants, and the whole set of social formations to which all are subject (Ibsen 1978: 121) (Figure 9.18).

In the late 1970s, Austrian playwright and Nobel Prize winner Elfriede Jelinek (1946–) offered her own dark answer to the question of whether Nora will be a liberated woman once she leaves her home. Jelinek wrote a sequel to Ibsen's play, entitled *What Happened after Nora Left Her Husband, or Pillars of Society*. In it, Nora works in a factory after leaving home, marries an industrialist, is eventually forced to become a high-class prostitute, and then turns to anarchism, which fails. At the end, she is back in her stifling home with Torvald, who clearly will soon become a Nazi.

Ibsen was a pioneer reformer in bringing substantive ideas to the theatre. It is not to detract from his historical achievement to understand how the ideologies of his plays (which continue to have a powerful presence even today) and the complicit mode of realism work in *A Doll House*.

To read a longer version of this case study, including a discussion of the theory of cultural materialism that guides it, please see the *Theatre Histories* website.

Key references

Audio-visual resources

A 1973 Paramount film of the play, directed by Patrick Garland with Claire Bloom and Anthony Hopkins, is available in a video recording. The opening scene (highly recommended) of this film is available on YouTube: search "Ibsen Hopkins Bloom."

Books and articles

Eagleton, T. (1983) *Literary Theory, an Introduction*, Minneapolis: University of Minnesota Press.

Foucault, M. (1969) "What is an Author?" in H. Adams and L. Searle (eds) (1986) *Critical Theory since 1965*, Tallahassee: Florida State University Press.

Foucault, M. (1972) *The Archaeology of Knowledge*, New York: Pantheon Books.

Ibsen, H. (1978) *A Doll House*, trans. R. Fjelde, in *Henrik Ibsen, The Complete Major Prose Plays*, New York: Farrar Straus Giroux.

Marker, F.J. and Marker, L.L. (1989) *Ibsen's Lively Art*, Cambridge: Cambridge University Press.

Marx, K. (1950) "Preface" to *A Contribution to the Critique of Political Economy*, in K. Marx and F. Engels, *Selected Works*, Vol. 1, London: Lawrence and Wishart.

Maugue, A. (1993) "The New Eve and the Old Adam," in G. Fraise and M. Perrot (eds) *Emerging Feminism from Revolution to World War*, Vol. 4 of G. Duby and M. Perrot (gen. eds) *A History of Women in the West*, Cambridge, MA: Harvard University Press.

Meyer, M. (1971) *Ibsen, a Biography*, Garden City, NY: Doubleday & Company.

Shepherd-Barr, K. (1997) *Ibsen and Early Modernist Theatre, 1890–1900*, Westport, CT: Greenwood Press.

Williams, R. (1966) *Modern Tragedy*, Stanford: Stanford University Press.

Williams, R. (1969) *Drama from Ibsen to Brecht*, New York: Oxford University Press.

Williams, R. (1977) *Marxism and Literature*, Oxford: Oxford University Press.

Yeo, E. and Thompson, E.P. (eds) (1972) *The Unknown Mayhew*, New York: Schocken Books.

SUMMARY

In the West and Japan, imperial expansion joined forces with new ideologies to create the notion of inevitable progress. In order to justify this concept, nation-states and their upper classes needed to see themselves as rational and mature, while seeing those they colonized and their lower classes as irrational and childlike. The concept of Orientalism clarifies how these distinctions are made and how they function in works of art, theatre, and historical writing. International fairs and expositions demonstrated imperial power and progress, while exposing artists and audiences to the unfamiliar and exotic, creating desire for new material goods and new theatrical imagery.

Imperialism and Orientalism were aided by the development of new technologies such as photography, new philosophies such as positivism, and new scientific discoveries such as Darwin's theory of evolution. Social Darwinism developed as a distortion and misinterpretation of Darwin's ideas. Positivism encouraged imperialists to believe that colonization led to progress, which included not only economic or military advantage, but spreading "civilization." Even in areas like China, untouched by such ideologies and technologies, an internal form of imperialism created distinctions between Self and Other. Such distinctions include economic class, gender, disability, etc. as well as race and ethnicity. Throughout the world, modern imperialism resulted in new theatrical genres. Realism (the most widespread new genre) developed simultaneously with imperialism, and the two are closely allied.

At first, Western and Japanese theatre reflected and gloried in the biases of imperialism. As economic and social disparities grew wider and the plight of the poor and marginalized became more visible, theatre artists began to create works reflecting the changes in reality. Theatre staging and design developed methods to enhance the photographic reality of plays, and powerful stage directors emerged who championed these new ideas. For example, Stanislavsky worked to make acting more believable by de-emphasizing the actor's performance of herself, and emphasizing instead performance of the character's inner life through vocal and physical means. Naturalism, created by middle- and upper-class authors, emphasized perversions, poverty, and other dark aspects associated with "irrational" or unfortunate Others. Naturalists embraced Social Darwinism, believing that the ills of the world are the result of one's inborn nature and environment. In contrast, realism offered a more balanced perspective and remains the dominant genre today. Realist authors (including early feminists) who depicted life's ills suggested that these might be mended if the causative economic or social factors improved. In Japan, debates about Westernization resulted not only in the creation of the new genres of *shimpa* and realistic *shingeki*, but in the gradual acceptance of women on stage. The great masters of realism, Ibsen and Chekhov, wrote plays demonstrating the complexities and confusions not only of society, but of theatre in a process of transformation.

★

CHAPTER 10

New media divide the theatres of print culture, 1870–1930

Bruce McConachie

As we saw in the last chapter, the cultural effects of photography pushed Western theatre toward the embrace of positivism, which validated visibility and materiality as the defining features of the real. This communication process within print-based culture led many to the practice and enjoyment of theatrical realism, and, for a few, to the embrace of Naturalism. In this chapter, we will first explore some of the ramifications of these positivist effects on mainstream theatre around 1900, including the emergence of musical comedy and theatrical revues and the influence of performances featuring international stars. In addition to positivism, these trends reflected the triumph of industrial capitalism, evident in the fashion shows in the new department stores that joined the glamor of revues to consumer desires. Then we will look at the rise of avant-garde movements that opposed realism and Naturalism by countering their positivist assumptions. Instead of upholding an "objective," materialistic understanding of reality, the avant-garde artists of the new movements – Symbolism, Aestheticism, and Expressionism – told audiences that reality was actually "subjective," spiritual, and more immaterial than photography seemed to show. This embrace of subjectivity had emerged earlier in Romanticism, but the influences of positivism and industrialism heightened its importance. Finally, this chapter will examine playwrights, directors, and other theatre artists who took themes, styles, and theatrical forms from both sides of this division in Western theatre. Playwrights like August Strindberg and Eugene O'Neill, plus directors such as Stanislavsky and Max Reinhardt (1873–1943), attempted productions that borrowed from realism and from the new avant-garde movements to acknowledge both the "objective" and "subjective" sides this ongoing theatrical conflict.

Western theatre makers who clung to the forms and traditions of print-based theatre could not resolve this division, however. As noted in the last chapter, this tension was already apparent in the final plays of Ibsen, who had embraced the apparent objectivity of realism in the middle of his career with *A Doll House* and *Ghosts*, but moved to the subjective spirituality of Symbolism of *When We Dead Awaken* at the end of it. Driving the objective/subjective conflict was the underlying tension between the effects of print, now broadened to include photography, and the newer effects of telephones and phonographs on perception. As we will see, these audiophonic (i.e., sound-based) media, increasingly influential after 1900, validated realities that could not be photographed – sounds, voices, and music. Inventive dramatists and directors might offer productions that explored both "objective" and "subjective" realities, but as long as Western culture insisted that philosophers, scientists, and thinkers must choose between one or the other – that both versions of reality could not, ultimately, be true – traditional modes of making theatre could not overcome the division. By bringing this conflict to a kind of boiling point, however, many theatre productions between 1890 and 1930 undermined the believability of both the "objective" and "subjective" traditions of print-based theatre.

As often occurs in history, cultures and their theatres do not usually resolve such problems. Instead, they put them aside when other difficulties thrown up by circumstances that no one anticipated grab their attention and demand action. As we will learn in the next chapter, the cultural fragmentations caused by the immense popularity of film and by the catastrophe of the Great War (1914–1918) sparked new insights and innovations that no one could have predicted before 1914. (Many Europeans continue to call the First World War the "Great War," the name given to it initially, because they have come to understand that the conflict was a significant turning point in world history and not simply the first of two similar disasters for Western culture.) Film, the first mass medium of the twentieth century, was almost as culturally disruptive as the war, though for different reasons. Together with radio and other electrically powered media, it helped to catapult the theatres of the twentieth century toward the use of multi-media in theatres today. Print-based theatre would continue throughout the twentieth century and into the next – Western culture was too steeped in its assumptions, procedures, and protections for it to disappear quickly – but as we will see, the 1920s mark the beginning of its decline.

Spectacular bodies on popular stages

Audiences have always enjoyed spectacular bodies – bodies that are meant to be looked at – but the proliferating photographs of these bodies excited this interest even more so. Strongmen, burlesque queens, contortionists, exotic dancers, "freaks" of all kinds, and other spectacular bodies peopled the variety stages, circuses, and festivals of all the major cities in the world (see Figure 10.1). As we saw in the last chapter, these types of entertainment drew vast audiences into huge auditoriums at world fairs, music halls, and other forms of variety theatre in the urban centers of the industrializing world.

Photography also advanced musical theatre, which featured spectacular female bodies and handsome male stars, in addition to hummable music. Although musical theatre traditionally meant opera in the West, light operatic entertainment (operetta) emerged in the mid-nineteenth century in Vienna, Paris, and London to amuse mostly bourgeois spectators. In London in the 1890s, musical comedies challenged and soon replaced operetta in popularity – including the delightful, "topsy-turvy" concoctions of William S. Gilbert and Arthur Sullivan, discussed in the last chapter. While there is no firm distinction between operetta and the musical, pre-1910 musicals typically featured a script with a girl-gets-boy love story, songs that could be marketed by the new popular music industry, and a chorus line of beautiful women. Indeed, the first important impresario of musicals was George Edwardes (1852–1915), who made his initial reputation through shows highlighting the Gaiety Girls chorus at his theatre in London. Audience interest in the chorus girl rose with the influence of photography and by 1900 her sexual allure was a chief feature of the musical stage. Not surprisingly, perhaps, photographs of chorus girls and other spectacular females of the theatre, in various states of undress, were popular pornographic items after 1870.

A variety of musicals flourished on U.S. and European stages from 1895 to 1930. An outgrowth of print-based theatre, musicals were built upon the same economic foundation as spoken-language dramas; musical composers joined writers and occasionally other authors to claim copyright and production privileges. Several U.S. musicals, such as Victor Herbert's (1859–1924) *Babes in Toyland* and the first of several versions of *The Wizard of Oz* (both 1903), mixed whimsy and fantasy with light satire. Austro-Hungarian composer Franz Lehar's (1870–1948) *The Merry Widow* (1905 in Vienna and 1907 in London) reminded audiences of the soaring musical tones of operetta. Others, like George M. Cohan's (1878–1942) *Little Johnny Jones* (1904), made a splash with catchy tunes ("I'm a Yankee-Doodle Dandy," for example), wise-cracking humor, and polished dancing. London saw a run of musicals with "girl" in the title – *The Earl and the Girl, The Girl in the Taxi, The Shop Girl,* and *The Quaker Girl,* for instance. In New York, African-American artists wrote and performed in several successful musicals, from *A Trip to Coontown* in 1898 to *Shuffle Along* in 1921. These London, Viennese, and New York musicals, as their titles suggest, accommodated contemporary beliefs about racial and gender roles to win popularity.

Figure 10.1

U.S. vaudeville star Eva Tanguay, in a publicity photo for a 1908 performance in Kentucky.

© Special Collections, University of Iowa Library, Iowa City.

Theatrical revues also flourished on Western stages for mostly bourgeois audiences between 1900 and 1930. This genre mixed chorus girls with the musical, comic, and sketch traditions of the variety stage. As in many other forms of variety, Paris led the way with spectacular revues at the Folies-Bergère and elsewhere in the 1880s that involved dancing girls and glamorous tableaux. By 1900, high-priced variety shows in Germany and Austria typically ended the evening as spectacular revues. Florenz Ziegfeld (1869–1932) popularized revues in the United States with his lavish *Follies,* staged yearly between 1907 and 1931. The "follies," "shows," "scandals," "vanities," and "revues" of these years in U.S. entertainment typically featured top talent, from Eddie Cantor (1892–1964) to Bert Williams (1874–1922), and exciting music by the likes of George Gershwin (1898–1937) and Irving Berlin (1888–1989). The legacy of these spectacular revues may be seen today in the night club acts at Las Vegas and on the Takarazuka stages of Japan. Our first case study in this chapter examines the intersections of the *Ziegfeld Follies* with pictorial magazines, high fashion, and the growth of consumer culture in the U.S.

CASE STUDY: Retailing glamor in the *Ziegfeld Follies*

Bruce McConachie

Florenz Ziegfeld and his *Ziegfeld Follies*, produced almost every year between 1907 and 1931, had enormous influence on American society, especially in forging a link between female beauty and consumer culture. Miss America pageants, Macy's Thanksgiving Day Parades, Busby Berkeley film musicals, *Playboy Magazine*, baton twirlers at football games, fashion shows in department stores, and many other institutions and events in American life between the 1920s and the 1960s – all owe much of their popularity to Ziegfeld's success in promoting high fashion and glamorizing what he called "the American Girl." This case study will primarily focus on fashion shows in department stores and their similarity to Ziegfeld's staging of women in his revues. Together, fashion shows and the *Follies* changed American culture.

Much of the initial influence of the *Ziegfeld Follies* rested on the ties between periodical print culture, touring Broadway shows, and department store marketing that had emerged in U.S. cities by 1900. Publishers of high-gloss photo magazines had discovered that pictures of star actors and expensive shows could attract readers to their journals. The new department store capitalists needed to reach high-end consumers with their magazine advertisements. And Broadway producers knew their productions could make more money on the road (i.e., outside of New York) if they arranged for tie-ins with local businessmen. This network of mutual needs took shape as U.S. capitalism began to require a mass market of consumers. The merchandisers who organized some of the world's first department stores, together with their allies in journalism and showbiz, were leading the transition toward consumer capitalism, a gradual change that would utterly transform the economy of the United States by 1990. After 1900, some already understood that consumerism demanded a new ideology. In 1912, for example, a merchant admitted that the department store "speaks to us only of ourselves, our pleasures, our life. It does not say, 'Pray, obey, sacrifice thyself, respect the King, fear thy master.' It whispers, 'Amuse thyself, take care of yourself.' Is not this the natural and logical effect of an age of individualism?" (Leach 1993: 3). For many U.S. consumers around 1900, the desire to amuse and take care of yourself, animated by photo magazines and Broadway musicals, now seemed to be within easy reach, a mere trolley ride away at a downtown department store.

The notion that shopping could lead to happiness – a truism for many living in the West today – was a novel idea for most Americans in 1900. Traditional culture had preached that hard work, sacrifice, family attachments, and civic and religious commitments were the roads to salvation, in this world as well as the next. After 1880, however, writes historian William Leach,

> American capitalism began to produce a distinct culture, unconnected to traditional family or community values, to religion in any conventional sense, or to political democracy. It was a secular business- and market-oriented culture, with the exchange and circulation of money and goods at the foundation of its aesthetic life and of its moral sensibility. . . . The cardinal features of this culture were acquisition and consumption as the means of achieving happiness; the cult of the new; the democratization of desire; and money value as the predominant measure of all value in society.
>
> (1993: 3)

THINKING THROUGH THEATRE HISTORIES

Linking causalities

Many theatrical events have helped to cause later developments within the same culture. Because theatrical performances usually worked with similar activities that were popular with many of the same spectators, theatre historians often seek to demonstrate how these activities were moving the culture in the same direction. Had the run of the *Follies* existed in a cultural bubble off by itself, it probably would have had little influence on the future of U.S. culture. Because the productions were similar to fashion shows, beauty contests, parades, and other entertainment and journalistic events, they promoted many of the same desires and values. The *Ziegfeld Follies* joined with these other events to change American culture during the first three decades of the twentieth century.

In 1900, these pleasures were unavailable in farming villages and small towns; to enjoy them, you had to move to the city.

In addition to better access to print journalism and touring shows out of New York, U.S. cities after the turn of the century could offer hotels, dance halls, restaurants, amusement parks, and new department stores. Most middle-sized cities had at least one such store – a retail outlet that concentrated merchandise from several departments (children's clothes, furniture, kitchen goods, ladies' fashions, etc.) under one roof. Most of the major department stores that would dominate U.S. retail sales in cities for the next 70 years were founded between 1890 and 1910: Wanamaker's in Philadelphia, Marshall Field's and Carson, Pirie, Scott in Chicago, Filenes' in Boston, Macy's and Bloomingdale's in New York, Hudson's in Detroit, and the Lazarus store in Cincinnati, for instance. (In contrast, most European department stores opened after 1920.) U.S. department stores increasingly used shop windows, sumptuous surroundings, print advertising, and fashion shows after 1900 to draw people into their environments, where their images and events could serve up visions of an ever-new Land of Oz for consumers. As Leach explains, "Cultures must generate some conception of paradise or some imaginative notion of what constitutes the good life. They must bring to life a set of images, symbols, and signs that stir up interest at the very least, and devotion and loyalty at the most" (1993: 9).

"Fashion!" wrote one store display manager, "there is not another word that means so much to the department store as *Fashion*" (Leach 1993: 91). The modern fashion show – female models parading the latest clothes up and down a runway to the admiring gaze of buyers and shoppers – probably began in 1903, although varieties of the ritual had flourished before. The larger department stores had special theatres, equipped with electric lights and stylish décor, built solely for the fashion parades which typically attracted thousands of spectators. Hooking American consumers – especially women – on fashion was becoming a capitalist necessity after 1900. The clothing trade was America's third largest industry by 1915 and one of the best ways to move garments off the racks was to declare last year's fashions obsolete. Fashion awareness persuaded consumers to buy new clothes, wear them a few times, and throw them out when they were no longer *à la mode*. This is not to say that all women could afford to purchase the latest in Parisian gowns. Through yearly marketing campaigns, however, department stores succeeded in getting millions of consumers to buy mass-market versions of the upper-class French trade. As a part of these campaigns, fashion shows participated in the cult of the new, inducing feelings of restlessness, envy, and desire in the minds of fashion-conscious Americans.

Merchandisers of fashion typically accorded a unifying theme and style to their shows. The "lure of the Orient" (discussed in Chapter 9) provided a tantalizing topic for several fashion shows in department stores before 1915; its themes of primitivism, luxury, and immediate self-gratification also spoke directly to American consumerist fantasies. After the Wanamaker family opened a department store in New York City, for example, they staged a *Garden of Allah* fashion show in their store theatre in 1912. The show was based on a 1904 popular novel of the same title by Robert Hitchens that had spawned a successful Broadway show and national tour in 1907. The plot of both features a young, unmarried woman aching for a connection to the supposedly primitive passions of the Muslim natives of North Africa. Wanamaker decided to adopt the *Garden of Allah* name for his show soon after a revival of the lush musical appeared in New York. The merchandiser's director and designer staged the spectacle against a star-lit African sky. According to press reports, they recruited six "Arab men and two women" from the Broadway show (Leach 1993: 110) for their afternoon production, decorated the theatre in Oriental motifs, and hired a string orchestra to play appropriate music. Thirty-six models sashayed to the alluring music as they paraded down the promenade, showing off U.S. adaptations of Parisian fashions based on Algerian originals. Wanamaker's *Garden of Allah* attracted thousands of women, many of whom (according to the press) gawked from the back of the auditorium or did not get in at all. The New York Wanamaker's was not the only department store to "tie in" its products to the theatrical popularity of *Garden of Allah*; Marshall Field's also borrowed some cast members and the title of Hitchens' show from the touring production in 1912 in Chicago. The *Garden of Allah* invited Americans to connect the consumer-capitalist dots joining department-store fashion shows to commercial Broadway productions.

By 1912, Florenz Ziegfeld had been popularizing this marketing strategy in his revues for five years. For his first *Ziegfeld Follies* in 1907, Ziegfeld secured a "tie-in" to the image of "the Gibson Girl," Charles Dana Gibson's drawings of upper-class young women who enjoyed civilized sports and respectable fun. Ziegfeld staged his *Follies* girls in bathing suits of the era in exchange for advertisements drawn by Gibson for his revue. A song in the show featured the girls pleading with Mr. Gibson to take them out of their elegant clothes and draw them instead in bathing suits to display their "dimpled knees . . . and plenty of rounded limb" (Mizejewski 1999: 77). Even before his 1907 *Follies*, Ziegfeld the impresario understood the lure of flesh. His first successful promotion featured "Sandow the Magnificent" (1867–1925), a weight lifter, who displayed his well-muscled body in little more than a leopard skin loincloth. Sandow's physical feats on stage provided the initial titillation for the real act that followed, when audience members, including women, were invited backstage and encouraged to touch the arm muscles of the strong man. His next promotion was Anna Held (1872–1918), a music hall comedian advertised by Ziegfeld as a naughty Parisian singer. Ziegfeld hyped her arrival in New York City, dressed her in suggestive and expensive attire, put her in intimate theatres in close proximity to the audience, and encouraged her to flirt with the spectators in such songs as "Won't You Come and Play Wiz Me."

Ziegfeld continued to mix flesh and fashion for his 22 revues between 1907 and 1931. Typically, he opened most of his *Ziegfeld Follies* on Broadway in the summer time to garner New York reviews, then took his productions on the road in the fall, touring to the best theatres in major American cities. His "front men" preceded the show, scouting for publicity and tie-ins with local journals and department stores. Initially, Ziegfeld's emphasis on high fashion earned him the reputation in New York of refining the image of the low-class chorus girl, whose general social status was barely above that of a prostitute. Several New York reviewers noted with approval that Ziegfeld's girls often looked more like department-store mannequins than typical chorines. And several similarities were apparent: all of Ziegfeld's showgirls were white, of Nordic-looking ethnicity (no Jews or Eastern Europeans allowed), and they usually performed a number in which they showed off fashionable gowns. In the "Palace of Beauty" show-stopper of the 1912 *Follies*, for example, spotlights picked up each dress as the women paraded them across the stage to the tune of "Beautiful, Beautiful Girl." The effect, however, was to turn the models into the same kind of objects as the gowns. The notion that the costumes were just as important as the bodies underneath had already been a feature of Ziegfeld's 1910 *Follies*. In a number entitled "A Woman's Necessities," the showgirls' bodies were outfitted with corsets, furs, jewels, and even lingerie. As feminist scholar Linda Mizejewski points out, this conflation of women and clothes was an early version of what another scholar has called "The Girl," an image that confuses "the abstract consumable and the abstract consumer" (Mizejewski 1999: 97).

With his 1915 *Follies*, Ziegfeld pushed the image of showgirl-as-mannequin even further. He hired trend-setter Lady Duff ("Lucile") Gordon (1863–1935) to design his fashionable costumes and choreographer Ned Wayburn (1874–1942) to teach his performers how to walk in them. The 1915 show depended on a clear distinction between the tall, languid fashion models, some of whom had worked for Gordon in department store shows, and the smaller chorines, who performed the dances and acrobatics. Wayburn taught the showgirl models a mode of erect posture and slow gait that came to be called "the Ziegfeld Walk" (Figure 10.2). From the 1915 revue onwards, the fashion mannequins generally paraded down a steep, curved staircase, moved to the down-center area of the stage where they turned on their charms for the spectators, and then moved to the side to make way for the next model. As Wayburn explained it, the women needed to practice a difficult thrust of the hip and shoulder in order to avoid falling over; "the Ziegfeld walk" could cause broken bones.

Although Duff Gordon was known for her erotic fashions, her designs for Ziegfeld apparently balanced the sensual with the refined. One reviewer of the 1915 *Follies* credited Ziegfeld's set designer, Joseph Urban (1872–1933), with creating an environment in which the mannequin models could, as he said, "titillate the senses in really artistic fashion" (Glenn 2000: 162). The reporter concluded that the show avoided "blatant, obvious display of nudity" by placing the women in the midst of "a cleverly designed background for the pulchritude on view." On the whole, Ziegfeld was probably more interested in marketing fashion to women than he was in inflaming the desires of men. Despite his later reputation for female sexual display, Ziegfeld's revues never featured erotic exhibition for its own sake nor the dangerous sensuality of a salacious dancer. As feminist historian Susan A. Glenn concludes, female eroticism in the *Ziegfeld Follies* "was understood to be artfully managed by men, and in the place of the passionate abandon of female self-expression, revue choreography emphasized impersonality, control, and repetition" (2000: 162).

Figure 10.2

Dolores (Kathleen Mary Rose Wilkinson), originally a Duff Gordon mannequin model, who became a Ziegfeld star. In "The Episode of Chiffon," one of Ziegfeld's most celebrated spectacles, Dolores portrayed the Empress of Fashion.

Billy Rose Theatre Collection. New York Public Library for the Performing Arts.

Those models who could master the Ziegfeld walk to become the masters of impersonal glamor appeared in photos in national and local fashion magazines. They also served as social models for thousands of ordinary women who were invited to dream of marrying millionaires. Although few Ziegfeld models actually married wealth, press releases perpetuated the myth of the gold-digging chorine who trapped a rich man's son into marriage. "Mr. Ziegfeld has difficulty keeping his beauties because the millionaires persistently carry off and marry them," was a typical by-line in the press (Mizejewski 1999: 102). By joking about it, American culture refused to face the kind of objectification that the image of woman-as-mannequin entailed. In her study of department store practices in the first three decades of the twentieth century, Rachel Bowlby notes the importance of well-dressed mannequins in shop windows for the average consumer. The mannequin in the display window, says Bowlby, was intended to reflect "an idealized image of the woman . . . who stands before it, in the form of the model she could buy or become. . . . [T]he woman sees what she wants and what she wants to be" (Bowlby 1985: 32).

Most of the women in Ziegfeld's audiences were not average consumers, of course; tickets for the *Ziegfeld Follies* cost more than the average couple usually spent on entertainment. Nonetheless, the message was the same: regardless of wealth and social class, women should aspire to dress with the taste and expense of a Ziegfeld mannequin. For the men in the audience, the *Ziegfeld Follies* may have made such mannequin women more sexually desirable, but they also set an impossible standard of beauty, elegance, and cool reserve for their girlfriends and wives. For both sexes, the *Follies* led them to believe that sophistication, class, and glamor could be acquired through money and enjoyed at leisure. Ziegfeld positioned the women and men in his audience as consumers of beauty; like shoppers watching a department store fashion show, his spectators saw woman and costume as one in the *Follies*, a single object of envy and desire.

Key references

Bowlby, R. (1985) *Just Looking: Consumer Culture in Dreiser, Gissing, and Zola*, London: Methuen.

Davis, L. (2000) *Scandals and Follies: The Rise and Fall of the Great Broadway Revue*, New York: Limelight Editions.

Glenn, S. (2000) *Female Spectacle: The Theatrical Roots of Modern Feminism*, Cambridge, MA: Harvard University Press.

Leach, W. (1993) *Land of Desire: Merchants, Power, and the Rise of a New American Culture*, New York: Random House.

Mizejewski, L. (1999) *Ziegfeld Girl: Image and Icon in Culture and Cinema*, Durham, NC: Duke University Press.

Mordden, E. (2008) *Ziegfeld: The Man Who Invented Show Business*, New York: St. Martin's Press.

Print culture for stars and playwrights

As we saw in the case study, photographs worked in conjunction with other printed materials to sell department store fashion and Ziegfeld's *Follies*. Within the theatre, international stars and popular playwrights also benefited from this mode of marketing performances. Photography widened the appeal of theatrical stars and the prestige of print helped to win playwrights international copyright protection.

After 1870, it was common for stars to arrange for the sale of small pictures of themselves in their performances, typically costumed in the roles of their favorite characters. By 1900, photographic images splashed on posters and throughout newspapers told the public that a star had hit the town. Photos helped make possible the great era of international stars that toured from Tokyo to New York to St. Petersburg from the 1870s into the 1920s. National-turned-international stars Tommaso Salvini and Eleanora Duse (1858–1924) from Italy, Henry Irving (1838–1905) and Ellen Terry (1847–1928) from England, Kawakami Otojirō and his wife Kawakami Sadayakko from Japan, and Edwin Booth (1833–1893) and Richard Mansfield (1857–1907) from the United States performed (in their native languages) before millions of fans. International starring on this scale had not been possible before telegraphs, railroads, and steamships allowed agents to schedule theatres, plan mass publicity campaigns, and transport their precious cargoes to the desired site on the right night with efficiency and economy. Photography and newspaper stories, among several other technologies, helped make the international star a possible and very profitable commodity.

From among these luminaries, most critics around 1900 would likely have ranked Sarah Bernhardt (1844–1923) at the top of the firmament (Figure 10.3). Following her success at the Comédie Française and elsewhere, Bernhardt quit the Comédie at the height of her popularity in 1880 to form her own company for a series of international tours, primarily to England and the U.S. During a career of more than 60 years, Bernhardt performed over 130 characters, nearly half of them written specifically for her. Twenty-five of her 130+ roles were male, Hamlet among them, her cross-gender role-playing facilitated by her thin body and flexible, yet powerful voice. Novelist Anatole France suggested some of the chief reasons for her magnetic attractiveness in male roles in a comment about her performance as a young poet in Alfred de Musset's (1810–1857) *Lorenzaccio* (Figure 10.4):

> We know what a work of art this great actress can make of herself. All the same, in her latest transformation, she is astounding. She has formed her very substance into a melancholy youth, truthful and poetic. She has created a living masterpiece by her

Figure 10.3

An 1880 photograph of Sarah Bernhardt as Marguerite Gautier in *The Lady of the Camellias,* one of her greatest romantic roles.

© V&A Images, Victoria and Albert Museum.

sureness of gesture, the tragic beauty of her pose and glance, the increased power in the timbre of her voice, and the suppleness and breadth of her diction – through her gifts, in the end, for mystery and horror.

(quoted in Gold and Fizdale 1991: 261)

Bernhardt, who played more male roles later in her career, once said that a woman was better suited to play roles like Hamlet than a young man who could not understand the philosophy or an older man who does not have the look of the boy. "The woman more readily looks the part, yet has the maturity of mind to grasp it" (Ockman 2005: 41–2).

Her millions of devoted fans returned often to enjoy *la divine Sarah,* not only for her latest physical and vocal transformations, but also for her conscious sculpting of self and role into a "living masterpiece" of art. Further, Bernhardt found numerous ways of sharing her emotions with the audience, inducing them to feel the same "mystery and horror" experienced by herself as the character. Due to a backstage accident, Bernhardt had to have her right leg amputated in 1915, at the age of 70. Nonetheless, she continued to perform, often seated or completely static, still thrilling spectators with her vocal power, range, diction, and emotional expressiveness. Despite her many photogenic qualities, Bernhardt may be best remembered for her voice. In many ways, she was the perfect star for a culture that was becoming more aware of the potential mystery and lumin-escence of the human voice.

While Bernhardt and other international stars could hire and fire directors, designers, and promoters at will, by 1900 they had to pay for the right to perform the plays of living dramatists upon which their stardom depended. Around 1870, most dramatic authors, like other self-employed writers, had gained legal copyright protections for the publication of their plays. Control over performance rights, however, remained elusive. For much of the eighteenth and nineteenth centuries, stars and acting companies could purchase plays outright from their authors, perhaps paying them an additional sum after the third night of its opening performance if the play were a success. After that, the performance rights normally belonged to the company or star and the playwright received no royalties.

This began to change in the 1850s, when powerful playwright-producers such as Dion Boucicault secured some legal protection for future performances of their plays. Nonetheless, it remained a common practice for managers to pirate published and unpublished plays from other theatres, make a few minor alterations, and pay nothing to the original playwrights when they produced the piece under a different title. The international traffic in pirated plays was even higher because, prior to 1886, no treaties protected the rights of non-national authors. By 1900, although Western dramatists continued to have difficulties collecting payments due from theatre managers, they had won the cultural and legal battle for full copyright protection. The prestige of print had trumped business-as-usual in the theatre. As a result of these developments, which by the turn of the century were a part of the general victory of liberal capitalism, dramatists after 1900 had the right to claim a share of the profits from performances as well as from the publication of their plays.

Authorship would continue to be a significant keystone of theatrical power. Despite the rise of star actors, producers, and directors after 1870, the playwright, designer, and choreographer could claim legal protection for his or her work, but actors and (until very recently) directors could not copyright their work. Under print-based theatrical capitalism, authored plays became the metaphorical "land" upon which stars and producers could build their shows by investing capital and hiring labor. This sense of the economic utility of copyrighted plays survived in the lingo of Broadway; stars and producers buy "options" on "properties" they are considering for future "development." In addition, most playwrights in the West extended their authority over producers by retaining a veto power over the choice of a director and sometimes over the casting for their plays. Despite their increasing artistic importance during the twentieth century, stage directors in the West could not challenge the legal power of dramatic authors. When a U.S. director around 1900 tried to claim copyright protection for a bit of stage business he had invented, for example, the courts did not allow it. As we will see in Part IV, the power of authorship continued as an important economic foundation of the theatre, even as new media began challenging the persuasiveness of print-based theatre.

Figure 10.4
Poster of Sarah Bernhardt in the title role of the young male poet in Alfred de Musset's *Lorenzacchio*. Bernhardt played 25 male roles during her career, including Hamlet and the Hamlet-like Lorenzacchio. The poster is by Alphonse Mucha, the Czech artist whose distinctive style heralded Art Nouveau. Bernhardt signed a six-year contract with Mucha for a now-famous series of posters.

Courtesy of FulcrumGallery.com.

Audiophonic media after 1870

Despite this triumph of print in the theatre, other media were beginning to alter, narrow, and divide older modes of dramatic communication. Two audiophonic (sound-based) media, the telephone and phonograph (invented in 1876 and 1877 respectively), initially appeared to complement and extend the power of print-based theatre. Before 1900, from the point of view of most theatre makers, telephone conversations and the ability to record the human voice simply made it easier to produce, manage, and publicize all theatrical productions.

But telephones and phonographs did more than serve practical purposes. The new audiophonic media excited an interest in the "subjective" and spiritual sides of reality and began to challenge the implicit positivism of photography. The telephone and phonograph separated the human voice from the materiality of the body. Apart from their wires and machinery, these media carried the intimacy and immediacy of music and the human voice on sound waves that lacked the visibility and concreteness of previous media. In the past, "hearing voices" had been a sign of religious possession or mental instability, and these traditional attributes clung to the affects (and the socio-cultural effects) of these new media. Conversing on the phone and listening to music and voices from strange new machines revived an interest in religion, altered musical composition, and played on age-old fears of alien "others." It also tended to validate belief in the new psychoanalytic techniques of Sigmund Freud (1856–1939) and his followers. Freud, in fact, understood phonographic recording as a metaphor for part of the work of the analyst. Convinced that sound revealed the realities of the unconscious mind, Freud urged the accurate recording of patient vocalizations as the first step in a psychoanalytic session. He advised psychoanalysts to transcribe all of the vocal mistakes of the patient in order to understand her or his psychological problems. Freud's view of vocalization was part of a wider notion that, as we will see, would have a formative influence on the early avant-garde movement known as Symbolism.

The emergence of avant-garde theatre

As we saw in the last chapter, stage realism generated many of the innovations of late nineteenth-century theatre in the West and altered theatrical practices in countries touched by imperialism in Asia and Africa. With its ability to focus attention on the mundane realities of everyday life, the spread of photography helped to generate enthusiasm for the realism of Ibsen, Chekhov, and other playwrights. Likewise, photography influenced producers, directors, and designers to transform Western stage technology and adopt realist conventions for costumes, décor, and stage properties. By 1900, even the spectacular theatres of musicals, revues, and star-centered performances had adopted a patina of realism to acknowledge popular expectations concerning the photo-like look of what most people understood as "the real." Bernhardt, for example, insisted on photographically accurate costuming and props for her historically based productions and the latest fashions, lavishly displayed in magazine photos after 1900, for her contemporary shows. And the Naturalists, of course, pushed beyond realism, demanding that reality be limited to positivism and Social Darwinism. Not surprisingly, perhaps, this narrowing of possible contents and styles in print-based theatre led to a reaction. In the 1890s, a small minority of artists began demanding that the theatre must not ignore the spiritual and subjective qualities of reality most evident to them in poetic and aural symbols. These artists called themselves Symbolists and many theatre historians point to Symbolism as the first movement of the avant-garde.

"Avant-garde" was originally a French military term referring to the forward line of soldiers – those leading the charge into battle. Likewise, avant-garde artists thought of themselves as marching in the front ranks of artistic progress, fighting bourgeois propriety to expand the boundaries of the possible. Avant-garde movements proliferated in the theatre between 1880 and 1930. Both first- and second-generation avant-garde movements began in small groups of artists and spectators who reinforced each other in their rebellion against established cultural institutions and their desire for change. They published manifestos to proclaim their ideology and elevate their work over that of conventional artists and rival avant-garde groups. While some of these movements flamed out within a few years, others burned for two decades or longer and exerted a significant impact on twentieth-century theatre.

Avant-garde theatre did not exist before the end of the nineteenth century. Innovative theatre artists in earlier times might have rejected the prevailing norms of artistry, but they did not form movements, write manifestos, and attempt to set the terms by which their art should be understood. Avant-garde movements began to flourish in all of the arts after 1870, partly as a result of industrial capitalism, but also due to the traditions of revolutionary Romanticism, still a usable past for artists in the West. In earlier decades and centuries, most artists had worked directly for rich patrons, whose interests partly sheltered them from direct competition for survival. Nineteenth-century capitalism forced many artists to compete in the marketplace, however, where they found a bourgeoisie eager to purchase "art" but unsure of its own artistic taste. This situation and their newfound freedom, by turns both liberating and terrifying, led many artists to mine the legacy of Romanticism for sensibilities, values, and roles, including the role of the Romantic rebel.

Avant-garde innovators in the theatre after 1880 exploited a brand new technology to alter stage production – electricity. Electrical illumination allowed for the full dimming of house lights during performances, which left audiences, for the first time in theatre history, in the dark. When spectators could no longer communicate visually with each other during performances, theatre-going shifted from a generally social to a much more individualistic experience. Increasingly, modern audiences after 1880 no longer started a riot if the show displeased them; nor did they often interrupt the show to applaud star actors after an impressive speech. Musical performers still gained applause at the end of a song or dance number, but musicals, too, kept the house lights turned off except during intermissions. This more private mode of spectating generally suited the goals of the Naturalists, as we have seen, and also heightened the kinds of effects sought by the Symbolists and by other movements in the first generation of the avant-garde. (We will examine second-generation avant-garde movements, which roughly spanned the years from 1910 to 1930, in Chapter 11.)

Despite significant differences between the two generations of the avant-garde, they shared a common cultural situation. With the questioning of traditional religious faith and the rise of positivism, some Westerners were beginning to suspect that all values might be relative. The influential philosopher Friedrich Nietzsche (1844–1900) held that all ethical truths were illusory and that modern people had progressed no further than savages in moral understanding. Perhaps, as some linguists, anthropologists, and philosophers were beginning to affirm after 1900, this cultural relativism extended to all claims of truth; maybe there was no position beyond human language and culture that allowed for objectivity. Complementing this cultural relativism was the recognition that human subjectivity was much more complex and irrational than people had realized. Could it be that humans were chiefly animated by a "will to power," as Nietzsche thought? Or perhaps an unconscious sexual drive motivated humanity, which meant that bourgeois society was little more than a clanking, ridiculous machine for sexual repression? This, in more scientific language, was the pessimistic conclusion of Freud's *Civilization and Its Discontents* (1930). Maybe Westerners needed to cut loose from their restraints and gain liberation through war, the electric dynamo, or even "primitive" (usually colonized) peoples! Avant-garde innovators would explore these and other possible paths for the next 40 years.

Most of the avant-garde movements could claim some legitimacy for their work within their national cultures. Since the eighteenth century, French culture had provided public forums for debates among the intelligentsia (a recognized elite of artists, academics, critics, philosophers and others) on topics ranging from the nature of art to the nature of being. This tradition spread to other national cultures strongly influenced by France or containing a significant level of public debate about the arts – notably Italy, Germany, Poland, and Russia. England and the U.S., in contrast, lacked a recognized intelligentsia, with the consequence that theatre artists did not have an established public forum in which to discuss new work. Although avant-garde artists were active in all of the major cities of the West between 1880 and 1930, avant-garde movements tended to flourish best in cities that supported an influential intelligentsia.

On the European continent, the intelligentsia often gathered in cabarets. "Bohemians," typically university-educated members of the urban youth culture, plus artists and other intelligentsia, constituted the primary participants and spectators for cabaret entertainment, which emerged in Paris in the 1880s. After 1900, cabarets in several major European cities – the Mirliton in Paris, Motley Stage in Berlin, The Green Balloon in Krakow, The Stray Dog in St. Petersburg, and The Cabaret Voltaire in Zurich – hosted artists in many of the avant-garde movements of the twentieth century. Performances at these venues might include puppet shows, poetry readings, political skits, art songs, satirical and literary tableaux, and occasionally one-act plays. In general, cabarets provided a hot-house environment where avant-gardists could explore new performance ideas with little risk before sympathetic audiences.

Symbolism and Aestheticism

Exulting in what they took to be subjective experience, the Symbolists urged viewers to look through the photo-like surface of appearances to discover true realities within – spiritual realities that they believed the realists and Naturalists had ignored. Seeking to advance a theatre of immanent spirituality, Gustave Kahn (1859–1936) wrote the first manifesto of theatrical Symbolism in 1889. Other manifestos followed. According to Symbolist Pierre Quillard (1864–1912) in 1891, "The human voice is a precious instrument; it vibrates in the soul of each spectator" (Schumacher 1996: 87). Quillard advised artists to avoid the trap of material décor on the stage, so that the chanting of verse could be "freed to fulfill its essential and exclusive function: the lyrical expression of the characters' souls" (90). The early Symbolists, who also included the French poet Stephane Mallarmé (1842–1898) and Belgian playwright Maurice Maeterlinck (1862–1949), drew inspiration from the gothic mysteries of Edgar Allan Poe, German idealist philosophy, the imagistic poetry of Charles-Pierre Baudelaire (1821–1867), and the myth-laden music-dramas of Richard Wagner. Many Symbolists praised Wagner's aesthetic goals (discussed in Chapter 8) and attempted to mount similarly integrated works of art in their own productions.

The Théâtre de l'Oeuvre, begun in Paris in 1893 and run by Aurélien Lugné-Poe (1869–1940), became the center of Symbolist performance in Western Europe. (Lugné-Poe added the "Poe" to his name in honor of the American author.) Lugné-Poe opened his theatre with Maeterlinck's *Pelléas and Mélisande*, written in 1892. Like other of his early plays, *Pelléas and Mélisande* evokes a mood of mystery through multiple symbols, eerie sound effects, and ominous silences. With little overt action, *Pélleas and Mélisande* relies as much on sound as sight. Following Quillard's advice to avoid realist décor, Lugné-Poe produced Maeterlinck's play on a semi-dark stage with gray backdrops and gauze curtains separating performers and spectators. In accord with the Symbolists' desire to foreground the aurality of language, the actors chanted or whispered many of their lines, and they moved with ritual-like solemnity. Maeterlinck's Symbolist plays mystified and irritated some spectators, but they also fascinated others. In his theatre, Lugné-Poe also experimented with synesthesia (the combination of distinct senses, as in "hearing green") in an attempt to engage all of the senses in the theatrical experience. Although the Théâtre de l'Oeuvre produced plays in many styles and from many periods (including translations of Sanskrit dramas from India) until its demise in 1929, it continued to be known for its Symbolist experiments.

The Parisian Symbolists influenced two centers of Symbolist production in Russia. In Moscow, Valery Bryusov (1873–1924) argued that the naïve lyricism of Russian folk drama made it appropriate for the Symbolist stage. Viacheslav Ivanov (1866–1949) led the St. Petersburg Symbolists with manifestos calling for a theatre in which actor-priests would facilitate the creation of mythic dramas with audience-congregants, primarily through the chanting of archaic language. Although Stanislavsky produced several Symbolist pieces at the Moscow Art Theatre, Vsevolod Meyerhold (1874–1940) had more success with Symbolism in St. Petersburg. Meyerhold's production of *Hedda Gabler*, for example, ignored Ibsen's realist stage directions and deployed bold colors and sculpted, repetitious movements to evoke the claustrophobia of Hedda's world.

Although Ibsen never endorsed the principles of Symbolism, his final four plays of the 1890s investigated many of the interior and spiritual themes of the Symbolists. The first of these, *The Master Builder* (1892), discussed in Chapter 9, uses a variety of symbols to contrast vaulting spirituality with earthly cowardice, old age, and death. Despite its realistic settings, the overt symbolism of the play moves it sharply toward a dream-like allegory. *When We Dead Awaken* (1899), the last drama of the playwright's career, depicts the evolution of human spirituality through the works of a sculptor, Rubek, who began by crafting half-human, half-animal shapes and finally created an idealized nude of a young woman. After many years, the artist and his former model meet again when both are much older, with Rubek weighed down by guilt and Irene, the model, now looking like a corpse. Nonetheless, the statue they created together, "Resurrection Day," continues to inspire others with its universal sublimity, a sharp contrast to their shattered lives. The play, which ends ambiguously, opposes spirituality to physicality, art to life, without embracing either side.

Two theatrical visionaries, Adolphe Appia (1862–1928) and Edward Gordon Craig (1872–1966), borrowed many of their ideas from the Symbolists. Both urged a radical break with the pictorial illusionism of the past through the innovations made possible by electricity. They understood that the new lighting could add dynamism to the image of the actor moving within sculpted scenery rather than pasted against stage flats. Eager to perfect a scenic equivalent to the soaring music of Wagner's operas, Appia published *The Staging of Wagner's*

Figure 10.5

Adolphe Appia's design for Christoph Willibald Gluck's opera, *Orpheus and Eurydice*, 1913, at Hellerau, as realized through computer-assisted design.

© 3D Visualization Group, School of Theatre Studies, University of Warwick.

Musical Dramas in 1895 and *Music and Stage Setting* in 1899. In these and later works, Appia agreed with Wagner that the aesthetic unity of opera depended on synthesizing all of the stage elements – crucially the music, scenery, lighting, and the performers. This led him to recommend steps, platforms, vertical columns, and other non-realist, three-dimensional units in scenic design (Figure 10.5). Appia emphasized musical rhythm as the key to aesthetic coherence, following the ideas of the "Eurhythmics" movement. Eurhythmics, begun by Émile Jaques-Dalcroze (1865–1950), trained musicians and dancers to learn music through movement. For Appia, audiophonic communication was the proper basis for artistic unity and the key to true reality. Most theatre practitioners ignored Appia's ideas before 1910, but his precepts exerted significant influence after the Great War, when German Expressionist experiments with sound, scenery, and light gave his ideas new cogency.

Craig's visionary statements about the need to revolutionize the stage were harder to ignore than Appia's, primarily because Craig never ceased to publicize them. In a series of books beginning in 1905 and in a periodical, *The Mask*, which he edited sporadically between 1908 and 1929, Craig argued for aesthetic and atmospheric coherence through designs that integrated the actor with three-dimensional, abstract set pieces through the bold use of light and sound. Unlike Appia, Craig favored a single setting for an entire performance to evoke the spirit of the play, with minor changes effected through the movement and lighting of towering, vertical screens. Craig also urged that the theatre – which he believed was an individual, not a collective art – must bow to the control of a master-artist. Influenced by Wagner's call for stage production as a *Gesamtkunstwerk* and by Nietzsche's desire for a superman who could bear the burden of life's contradictions, Craig sought a total artist of the theatre who could combine playwriting, designing, and directing. At one point, Craig proposed that this directorial superman might even control the acting during performances. Despairing of the intransigence of stars and the materiality of actors' bodies, he suggested that live performers should be replaced by large puppets – *Übermarionettes* [EW-behr-marionettes] he called them – that could evoke spiritual realities and would be easier to control. Like Appia, Craig prefigured the film era of theatrical art. Both advocated abstract scenery and flexibility in lighting, and pushed the stage director toward the role of an *auteur* [OH-tur], a figure (like some film directors) who takes author-like control of all the elements of a production.

Appia and Craig shared some commonalities with the Aestheticist movement, which also praised the artistic unity achieved by Wagner in his music-dramas. In general, though, Aestheticism turned its back on the spiritual yearnings of the Symbolists; the Aestheticists attempted stage productions that encouraged spectators to escape the workaday world and revel in heightened aesthetic sensations. Believing in "art for art's sake," they often chose contents and styles from the theatrical past to inspire new emotional responses. In his Aestheticist drama *Salomé* (1893), for example, Oscar Wilde hoped that his imagistically charged dialogue and tension-filled stage pictures would move his audience to experience the anger, lust, cruelty, and revenge of his major characters from the biblical story. Aestheticism also shaped the neo-romanticism of Hugo von Hofmannsthal (1874–1929) in Germany. The playwright and poet invited a meditative response from audiences with a group of short plays in the 1890s, including *Death and the Fool* (1893) in which allegorical characters speak a poetic language. The French dramatist Edmond Rostand (1868–1918), best known for the lyrical poetry of his *Cyrano de Bergerac* (1898), also embraced the goals of the Aestheticists early in his career. Sarah Bernhardt lent her soaring, lilting voice to the lead character in Rostand's *La Samaritaine* (1897), a biblical drama inspired by the story of a woman from Samaria.

Aestheticism traveled under the name of Retrospectivism in Russia. Aleksandr Blok (1880–1921), earlier hailed as a major Symbolist poet and dramatist, came to reject Symbolism for what he took to be its empty mysticism. Meyerhold, too, moved beyond Symbolism after 1905. His 1906 production of Blok's tragi-farce, *The Puppet Show*, combined *commedia dell'arte* comic techniques with grotesque effects to underline Blok's poetic and absurdist vision. In addition to its satirical intent, the aim of this production, and of cultural Retrospectivism in general, was to recover older forms of theatre as a means of transporting audiences into heightened aesthetic experiences. Like the Aestheticists, the Retrospectivists believed in immersing themselves in artistry for relief and enjoyment. Nikolai Evreinov (1879–1953) became the major proponent of Retrospectivism in Russia. He drew on Nietzsche's praise of the aesthetic life to propose that the artist-hero transform his own life into a work of art. In a series of manifestos, essays, and plays, Evreinov urged the production of monodramas – monologues about the self – to externalize the consciousness of the artist-protagonist. He co-founded a theatre in St. Petersburg to explore his ideas and later served as artistic director at the Maly Theatre in Moscow, where he directed harlequinades, pantomimes, and monodramas.

German Expressionism

While German Expressionistic theatre has its roots in the first generation of the avant-garde, it also extends into second-generation concerns centered on utopian hopes and social transformation. For ease of comprehension, we will present an overview of the complete movement in this chapter and then refer back to several key elements of Expressionism after 1918 in Chapter 11. As will be apparent, German devastation in the wake of the Great War substantially altered the movement.

The term "Expressionism" was initially used by François Delsarte (1811–1871), who attempted to systematize the actor's physical and vocal expression of ideas and emotions related to what he conceived to be the physical, mental, and spiritual parts of the performer's body. By the end of the nineteenth century, Delsarte's system had become the basis for many programs of actor training. The theatre artists in Germany who began calling themselves Expressionists around 1910 were especially interested in the spiritual dynamics of Delsarte's system. After 1900, art critics also used the term to denote a non-realist painting suffused with the subjective emotions of the artist; this general connotation also applied to the new theatrical movement.

The late plays of August Strindberg (1849–1912) provided several significant models for Expressionism as well. Following such Naturalistic dramas as *Miss Julie* and a difficult period of mental instability the dramatist called his "inferno," the Swedish playwright strove for a theatre that he hoped might synthesize the objectivity of Naturalism with the spirituality of the Symbolists. His post-inferno plays, notably *To Damascus*, a trilogy (1898–1901), *A Dream Play* (1902), and *The Ghost Sonata* (1907), attempted to embody the experiences of mythical journeys and spiritual dreams. Strindberg's interests in spirituality, strong emotions, the tricks of perception, and grotesque sounds and images were given fuller rein in theatrical Expressionism.

Early German Expressionist plays called for such anti-realist techniques as grotesquely painted scenery, exaggerated movement, and "telegraphic" dialogue, so named because it copied the abbreviated, mechanistic quality of a telegraph message. These features were evident in several Expressionist plays, including Walter Hasenclever's (1890–1940) *The Son* (1914), and *From Morn to Midnight* (1916) by Georg Kaiser (1878–1945). While both plays invite spectators to view the distorted dramatic action through the fevered eyes of the protagonist (who also represents much of the author's point of view), neither drama ignores the very real material factors that constrain the protagonist's spiritual longings. The younger generation's revolt against the restraints of bourgeois society in *The Son*, in fact, acknowledges that the title character cannot realize his ecstatic hopes without killing his father, a symbol of conventional order and repression. Like Strindberg, the early Expressionists explored the tensions between spiritual desires and material constraints.

Although censorship before and during the Great War prevented most Expressionist plays from reaching the stage, Expressionism flourished in German theatre immediately after the war. Optimism about the imminent overthrow of conventional German society after Germany's defeat and the 1917 revolution in Russia turned some Expressionists toward utopian socialism. When *The Son* finally reached the stage in 1918, the director's statements about the production summed up the goals of the movement for the public. Expressionism, he said, was "the exteriorization of innermost feelings," a "volcanic eruption of the motions of the soul"; it involved "the boundless ecstasy of heightened expression" (Berghaus 2005: 85). Georg Kaiser's vision now embraced pacifism in his anti-war play *Gas* (1918), which took the poison gas used

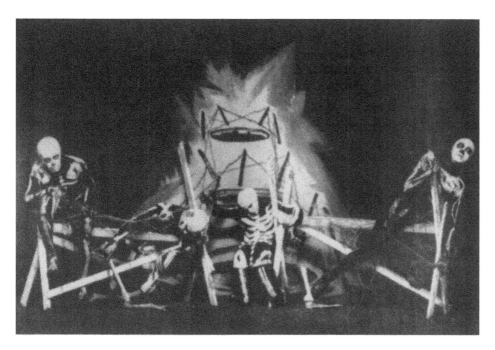

Figure 10.6

Contemporary print of a scene from the 1919 Expressionist production of *Transfiguration* (*Die Wandlung*), 1918, by Ernst Toller.

C. Oskar Fischel, *Bildernerische der Scene* (1931), Abb. 125. Photo courtesy of the Deutsches Theatermuseum, Munich.

by troops in the Great War as a metaphor for the spread of social corruption. In the same year, with some Germans still inspired by the news of the Russian Revolution, Ernst Toller (1893–1939) advocated a revolution in Germany in *Transfiguration* (1918) (Figure 10.6). Other Expressionists combined the generational rage that had fueled several prewar plays with a more general call for the spiritual and material regeneration of German society. To model their hoped-for utopia, several productions sought to forge a spiritual union between actors and spectators by abolishing the proscenium arch, eliminating illusionistic scenery, and mounting direct calls for a new world. Ecstatic acting often powered Expressionist performance with revolutionary urgency. According to one review praising actor Fritz Kortner, for example: "Words coagulate and dissolve in a rhythmic fashion. Screams erupt and vanish again. Movements surge back and forth. . . . Kortner's playing pushed himself beyond the limits of the stage and made him burst into the auditorium" (Berghaus 2005: 87).

Revolutionary fervor was short-lived in German Expressionism, however. Kaiser ended *Gas II* (1920), his sequel to the 1918 play, with the apocalyptic destruction of the world to indicate his growing despair with politics. Toller, initially a more politically radical writer than Kaiser, used irony to express his disillusionment with socialism in *Hurrah, We Live!* (1927). The uneasy fusion of subjective vision and revolutionary politics in postwar German Expressionism quickly faded in the theatre after 1924. More so than Symbolism or Aestheticism, German Expressionism had explored the relativity of extreme perceptions and emotions on the stage.

At the same time, however, most Expressionists tried to claim that the objective, material world was just as real as inner, subjective feelings. Although today we might say that these two realities actually met in the bodies of Expressionist actors, such a synthesis seemed fleeting or even impossible to most Germans in the 1920s. Pulled between the effects of audiophonic and photographic media, most Westerners believed that they must ultimately choose between what they took to be objective and subjective realities. These competing perceptions generated by the new media fatally undermined the coherence of German Expressionism and narrowed possibilities for the future of print-based theatre.

CASE STUDY: Strindberg and "The Powers"

Bruce McConachie

As noted, several of the late plays of August Strindberg were forerunners of German Expressionism. Strindberg – essayist, painter, novelist, photographer, and playwright – was among the most tormented of artists by what he and his contemporaries understood to be the divisions between objective and subjective realities.

Scholars have examined Strindberg's many plays from several points of view – as experiments in avant-garde playwriting that challenged his theatrical contemporaries, as probing analyses of the inequalities and class conflicts of his era, as testaments to his difficulties with the women he knew and to his personal misogyny, as intended affronts to the Victorianism of late nineteenth-century Swedish life, and as points of crisis in his psychological and religious journey. While each of these approaches to Strindberg's drama has been rewarding, this case study will focus on his personal beliefs, both secular and religious, as an important key to two of his most famous plays, *Miss Julie* (1888) and *The Ghost Sonata* (1907). Although these dramas rest in very different belief systems – atheism and Social Darwinism for *Miss Julie*, and theism mixed with the "theosophy" of H.P. Blavatsky for *The Ghost Sonata* – both also display Strindberg's unchanging assumption that "powers" beyond human control invariably intervene to shape our actions. Strindberg generally explained these "powers" in "objective," positivist terms before 1896 and switched to "subjective," spiritual explanations after that date.

Strindberg's change in belief occurred in the middle of his "inferno" period. Most biographers and critics divide Strindberg's life and work into two periods – pre- and post-inferno. Between 1895 and much of 1897, Strindberg suffered a series of psychotic attacks that disabled his playwriting, led him to experiment with alchemy and the occult, and finally drove him to write *The Inferno*, an autobiographical novel that helped him to resolve many of his torments. Although raised in a strict Christian home, Strindberg proclaimed himself an atheist when a Swedish court tried (and acquitted) him for blasphemy in 1884. From that date until 1896, Strindberg published several Naturalist plays and novels, including *Miss Julie*. Then, with the onset of his inferno period, Strindberg returned to a kind of Christianity. Between 1896 and his death in 1912, he wrote stories and plays, such as *The Ghost Sonata*, that attested to his faith in theism, but his was a god that had made it impossible for humans to find happiness. Two quotations from *The Inferno* indicate not only Strindberg's shift in belief, but also his continuing sense that "unseen Powers" remained in control. Commenting on his pre-inferno

---

THINKING THROUGH THEATRE HISTORIES

Exploring extreme examples

Historians always hunt for salient examples to demonstrate the main points of their narratives, whether they are writing detailed historical studies or broad textbook histories. As we have seen, Chapter 10 is about a crisis in belief in Western culture, a crisis that was particularly acute in the theatre between 1880 and 1920. More than most theatre artists, Strindberg suffered psychologically from his inability to resolve this crisis between "objectivity" and "subjectivity" and the two plays chosen for this case study demonstrate his vacillation. Consequently, Strindberg's changing beliefs provide us with an excellent possibility for exploring one key example that is relevant to the main content of this chapter.

It is important to emphasize, though, that Strindberg was not a typical artist of his era; no person who excelled in a variety of professions, hated several women, delighted in causing so many of his fellow countrymen to fear him, and suffered a nervous breakdown will ever be "typical" of his time. As in all historical periods, most people living in Europe around 1900, including theatrical artists, led humdrum and predictable lives; they were the typical ones. Theatre historians can and do focus on typical people, often when they write about the social dynamics of the theatrical past. We must pay attention to representative artists and spectators in every period because these average people sustained the major theatrical institutions of their day. But this is not a usual strategy for historians who are interested in exploring avant-garde artists and events. Because the theatrical past often best reveals the tensions and conflicts within a culture through its non-mainstream productions, theatre historians sometimes look for unique, even extreme playwrights and their dramas to write about to explore those cultural fissures. The example of Strindberg points to the tension between what historians can learn about the theatrical past from extreme examples versus more representative artists and spectators.

---

life, he remarked, "The fact is, that in the course of years, as I came to notice that the unseen Powers left the world to its fate and showed no interest in it, I had become an atheist" (Malekin 2010: 18). Later in *The Inferno*, these "unseen Powers" became "an intelligence superior to our own": "It is the earth itself that is Hell, the prison constructed for us by an intelligence superior to our own, in which I could not take a step without injuring the happiness of others, and in which my fellow creatures could not enjoy their own happiness without causing me pain" (Malekin 2010: 20). Whether because of an amoral nature or caused by a malevolent god, humanity for Strindberg was doomed to unhappiness and pain.

Miss Julie focuses on the degeneration and eventual suicide of a young aristocrat during Midsummer Eve festivities on her father's estate in rural Sweden. Attracted to Jean, the Count's handsome valet, Julie flirts with him and he reciprocates until the approach of dancing peasants drives them out of the downstairs kitchen and into an adjacent bedroom. Following their off-stage intercourse, Jean plans for their escape from the estate while Julie remains paralyzed with guilt and shame. The sudden return of Julie's father (who is heard upstairs but never seen on stage) forces a resolution. In a kind of stupor, Jean scurries to answer the Count's demands while Julie, her will hypnotized by Jean, takes his razor and walks slowly to the barn to kill herself. *Miss Julie* caused a minor scandal in Sweden when it was published in 1888; although staged in Paris in 1887, it was not produced in Strindberg's home country until 1906.

In a preface written after he finished the play, Strindberg aligned *Miss Julie* with Naturalism. According to the preface, "an abundance of circumstances" led to Julie's fate, including

> her mother's "bad" basic instincts; her father's improper bringing-up of the girl; her own nature; the festive occasion of Midsummer Night; her father's absence; her period; her preoccupation with animals; the intoxicating effect of the [peasants'] dance; the light summer night; the powerful aphrodisiac influence of the flowers; and finally chance that drives these two people together in a room.
>
> (quoted in Szalczer 2011: 76)

In Zola's manifesto for Naturalism, the French author made it clear that playwrights and other authors should depict characters that have very little control over their behavior. According to the Naturalists, heredity, environment, and immediate circumstances should drive a character's actions. Although modern readers would reject Strindberg's reduction of female sexuality to instincts, bad genes, poor nurturing, animality, the smell of flowers, and menstruation, many scientists (and probably Zola) would have agreed with this list of causes in 1888.

While Strindberg's exposition for the drama does make it clear that the factors mentioned in his preface are at play in determining Julie's behavior, Julie is also engaged in some conscious role-playing with Jean. Both, in fact, enjoy pretending to be people of a different class while they are flirting with each other – Jean the servant plays at being an aristocrat while Julie the mistress occasionally comes on like a sexually available peasant. It is difficult to read *Miss Julie* without concluding that their conscious role-playings, as much as unconscious factors related to heredity and environment, helped to produce their sexual attraction. Consequently, the reasons behind the events of the play are more complicated than Strindberg's preface allows for and than the Naturalists would have favored.

Nonetheless, two other aspects of the plotting of *Miss Julie* keep the play firmly within the orbit of Naturalism. Many Naturalists, following tenets of the Social Darwinists, believed that certain powers were built into nature; so did Strindberg in 1888. One was the inevitability of a "battle between the sexes," a battle that men were naturally more "fit" to win. Jean and Julie battle frequently in *Miss Julie*, both before and after intercourse, but Jean alone survives, even though his survival returns him to his status as a servant. Second, the ending of the play asks the audience to believe that Jean, who has violated all of the rules of the patriarchal Count through his behavior with Julie, will suddenly be paralyzed by his master's voice upstairs in the estate. They must also believe that Jean, despite his weakened state, can hypnotize a weaker Julie to kill herself. Interested in many scientific topics, Strindberg also studied hypnotism; he, like other scientists of the time, believed that hypnotism could compromise the individual will of another person. Both of these plot devices combined – male victory in the battle of the sexes and, in the end, through hypnotic power – reveal Strindberg's belief in "unseen Powers," powers that might be explained objectively as natural, but that generally lay beyond the exercise of human will.

André Antoine directed *Miss Julie* at the Théâtre Libre in Paris. As with his other Naturalistic productions, Antoine filled his stage with the details specified in the playwright's script – a large basement kitchen on a rural Swedish estate with upstage doors leading to the outside and entrances on both sides of the stage. Placing the mutual seduction of a mistress and her servant in the middle of an environment of work, food, and sweat underlined Julie's degradation. The actors, even the peasant dancers who break into the kitchen midway into the play, observed the convention of the "fourth wall," never acknowledging the presence of the audience. Although few details about the production survive, Antoine's amateur actors apparently performed the play successfully for the conventional three-night run at the theatre; the production enhanced Strindberg's reputation among the Parisian Naturalists.

By 1907 when he wrote *The Ghost Sonata*, Strindberg was linking "unseen Powers" to the work of a malicious god, rather than to nature. One of his initial titles for the play was "Kama-Loka: A Buddhist Drama" (Malekin 2010: 131). And on a draft page for *Ghost Sonata*, Strindberg wrote, "Maya = the World-weaveress, the Spider, the Illusion, the Folly, Matter" (Malekin 2010: 134). These notes reveal that Strindberg had been reading some of the works of H.P. Blavatsky, whose "theosophical" ideas in the 1880s mixed together Buddhist and Platonic beliefs in ways that many turn-of-the-century thinkers found convincing. In brief, Blavatsky taught that humankind inhabited what she thought the Buddhists called "Kama-Loka," a kind of limbo or Hades, in which human desire forever doomed people to continued cycles of reincarnation. The power of Maya, who wove the illusions of the world like a spider, made sure that humanity remained trapped in Folly and Matter. In contrast, believed Blavatsky, perceiving true reality, which was spiritual and immaterial, could only occur when humanity forsook desire and allowed its spirit to draw the mind to transcendence.

In *Ghost Sonata*, the material world is indeed a place of illusions, where webs and traps ensure that humanity cannot escape from the pull of its desires until death brings peace. Near the start of the drama the audience meets a young male student who is attracted to a girl he sees in the window of an elegant mansion. Like the student, the audience is led to believe that the people inside must lead happy and enlightened lives. Visions of the material world are deceiving, however, especially when prompted by desire, and Act II reveals that the family within is enmeshed in webs of crime and deceit that are poisoning them. Hummel, a vampire-like villain whose power represents the workings of a malicious universe, brutally unmasks the lies and crimes upon which the reputation and wealth of the family have been built and effectively drives the family patriarch to suicide. By the end of the act, however, Hummel himself has been killed by an aging woman that he had earlier seduced. As new agents of evil replace previous powers of wickedness in the play, the vengeance that Hummel pursued finally traps him as well. Through these repetitions, Strindberg is suggesting that malevolence is recycled through never-ending reincarnations.

Act III begins with the student expressing his ardent love for the girl in the Hyacinth Room, which also contains a harp and a prominent statue of Buddha. Both complain that the odor of the enveloping hyacinths, a symbol of the couple's blooming sexuality, is suffocating their senses. Despite the girl's interest in him and her apparent beauty, she tells the student she is dying because a vampire cook is robbing the family of life-giving food. When the audience meets the cook later in the act, it is apparent that the cook and her masters are locked in a situation of mutual exploitation; both are sucking the life out of each other. While the girl is dying, the student ends the play with a long poetic monologue which begins as a denunciation of the deceptions of the world and then shifts to become a kind of ritual chant. At this point, the student takes on the role of a priest who blesses the dying girl and attempts to mediate between the illusory world of the living and the approaching world of the dead. Strindberg's final stage directions indicate that the room fills with white light and then vanishes, replaced by distant harp music and a painting called "Isle of the Dead" revealed on a backdrop. According to critic Theo Malekin, Strindberg probably intended the elements of his ending, especially the statue of the Buddha, "to open up a level of reality, or rather a level of the self beyond egoic [i.e., egocentric] identification with life's surfaces . . ." (2010: 143). After two acts of crimes and illusions, the ending of the third act is meant to point the way toward possible transcendence.

Strindberg had written *The Ghost Sonata*, along with several other plays, for production in his Intimate Theatre, a company of actors in a small playhouse that he had helped to start in Stockholm in 1907. The director and actors could not manage the complexities of the script, however, and the 1908 premiere production was not a success. Strindberg had partly modeled his Intimate Theatre on director Max Reinhardt's Kammerspiele, a small playhouse in Berlin where the German director had already staged several successful productions. Strindberg hoped that Reinhardt would direct some of the plays he had written for his Intimate Theatre at the Kammerspiele and sent copies of them (translated into German) for his perusal. Although the author and director corresponded, Reinhardt would not direct *The Ghost Sonata* until four years after Strindberg's death.

Reinhardt's 1916 *Ghost Sonata*, staged initially at the Kammerspiele and then in Stockholm and elsewhere in Sweden, came as a revelation to the German and Swedish theatre-going public. In Germany, Reinhardt's Expressionist-style production caused more of the Berlin public to investigate this still new avant-garde movement, while many Swedes recognized belatedly that "their" Strindberg had been a theatrical genius. Reinhardt's production of five of Strindberg's post-inferno plays between 1913 and 1921 led to a burst of international fame for the Swedish playwright, aligned Strindberg's goals in the public mind with those of the Expressionists, and drew particular attention to the dramatist's post-inferno experiments.

Produced amidst the horrors of the Great War, Reinhardt's *Ghost Sonata* enthralled audiences with its nightmarish evocation of evil and grotesquerie. Following his understanding of Expressionism, Reinhardt staged the play as though the audience were seeing and experiencing it through the eyes of the student protagonist. He ignored Strindberg's initial stage directions, for example, and began the performance in total darkness, which only gradually eased into a dim grey dusk when the student (the only figure on stage in full light) began to see figures around him slowly coming to life. In keeping with this style, the vision of the student guided the actions of the other characters, which often caused the student-as-dreamer to pass his hand over his eyes or to shake his head in disbelief. Reinhardt characterized the family inside the house as a group of half-human marionettes, whose voices and actions confused and terrified the student. The actor playing Hummel began his portrayal as a shrunken, crumpled old man who gradually gained in size and demonic power as he fed on the strength of others before exiting to his death. As have most subsequent directors of *The Ghost Sonata*, Reinhardt did not display the "Isle of the Dead" at the end of the performance, as per Strindberg's stage direction. Instead, he had the student throw open a window to cut through the hyacinth room's claustrophobia and reveal a star-studded night, suggesting to some the possibility of eternity and peace after death.

Strindberg remains a popular playwright in his native Sweden as well as throughout the German-speaking world. Some of the most daring productions of his works in recent times have been directed by Ingmar Bergman (1918–2007), well known in Europe for his theatrical as well as his filmic productions.

Key references

Brandell, G. (1974) *Strindberg in Inferno*, trans. B. Jacobs, Cambridge, MA: Harvard University Press.

Carlson, H. (1996) *Out of Inferno: Strindberg's Reawakening as an Artist*, Seattle: University of Washington Press.

Chothia, J. (1991) *André Antoine*, Cambridge: Cambridge University Press.

Ekman, H. (2000) *Strindberg and the Five Senses: Studies in Strindberg's Chamber Plays*, New Brunswick, NJ: Athlone Press.

Malekin, T. (2010) *Strindberg and the Quest for Sacred Theatre*, Amsterdam: Rodopi.

Marker, F. and Marker, L. (2002) *Strindberg and Modern Theatre: Post-Inferno Drama on the Stage*, Cambridge: Cambridge University Press.

Robinson, M. (ed.) (2009) *The Cambridge Companion to August Strindberg*, New York: Cambridge University Press.

Sprinchorn, E. (1982) *Strindberg as Dramatist*, New Haven: Yale University Press.

Strindberg, A. (1955) *Six Plays of Strindberg*, trans. E. Sprigg, New York: Anchor Books. [Includes *Miss Julie* and *The Ghost Sonata*.]

Szalczer, E. (2011) *August Strindberg*, New York: Routledge.

Expressionism in the United States

In the 1920s, playwrights and directors in the U.S. embraced a more conservative version of Expressionism than in Germany and Scandinavia. Within the goal of combining "subjectivity" and "objectivity" on stage, it had always been possible for playwrights to organize their plots and characters so that some of their on-stage episodes recognized and emphasized external, objective realities, while other moments allowed them to explore the subjective psychology of their protagonists. This dramatic strategy would encourage spectators to validate their photographic sense of a visible, material world, while also permitting them to understand that world from the main character's subjective point of view. This was essentially the compromise that several U.S. playwrights and their directors arrived at in the 1920s. Although never a radical, avant-garde movement, Expressionism moved U.S. theatre away from traditional realism and established the foundation for a general style that later playwrights could build upon. Psychological realism, as that style came to be called in the 1940s, did not settle the larger question about the nature of reality, but it did speak to the needs of artists and audiences eager to explore what they understood as both the objective and subjective worlds of a play. As we will see in Chapter 12, several varieties of psychological realism flourished in the works of Tennessee Williams, Arthur Miller, and their contemporaries in the 1940s and 1950s.

The Provincetown Players (probably the closest before the 1950s that the U.S. theatre ever got to an actual avant-garde group) launched the careers of two of these Expressionist playwrights, Eugene O'Neill (1888–1953) and Susan Glaspell (1876–1948). The Province-towners started an artists' colony in New England during the Great War in 1916 and drew their energy from a mix of American pragmatism, the politics of anarchism, and the philosophy of Nietzsche. By 1922, when the group disbanded, they had produced nearly a hundred plays, a few of them by Glaspell and O'Neill. Glaspell wrote *The Verge* (1921) in an Expressionist style that merges feminism with a Nietzschean will to power in order to explore a female artist's attempts to push beyond convention to true innovation. Like the work of other U.S. Expressionists, *The Verge* places the protagonist in a recognizably objective social world, but also finds ways of exploring her subjective, psychological sides. By the 1920s, O'Neill had moved from the realism of his early one-acts to write two Expressionist plays, *The Emperor Jones* (1920) and *The Hairy Ape* (1921). The first is a peeling-away of the layers of civilization in the mind of a black man and the second focuses on a working-class loner struggling to find a group where he feels he "belongs." Both gained artistic and box office success in New York, where the Provincetowners had opened a commercial theatre.

U.S. Expressionism in the early 1920s was mostly a home-grown style. Before American artists and audiences had seen much of it from Germany, playwrights O'Neill and Elmer Rice (1892–1967) apparently used the term "expressionism" to point to similarities between their dramas and the expressive culture movement, a broad-based program in the U.S. that sought to counter anxieties about the modern world by drawing on the performing arts. Rice's best-known play, *The Adding Machine* (1923), depicts the recycling of an alienated office worker, Mr. Zero. In this Nietzschean grotesque comedy, Zero refuses possible freedom and floats from a pointless job adding up figures, through death and finally to eventual reincarnation as another cowardly office worker. The short scenes of the play tend to build cinematically, partly a result of Rice's earlier work as a screenwriter in Hollywood. Sophie Treadwell (1885–1970), another U.S. Expressionist, demonstrated the need for a middle-class woman to rebel against her robotic life in *Machinal* (1928). Treadwell's protagonist murders her husband, an act which eventually sends her to the electric chair.

Although O'Neill left Expressionism behind in the early 1920s, he continued to draw on the "subjective" side of the objective/subjective divide in the West for his themes and dramatic forms. In *Desire Under the Elms*, for example, he explores Freudian unconscious desire as the primary motivation for an adulterous affair between the young wife (Abbie) of an old man and her mature stepson (Eben) (Figure 10.7). The 1924 production shocked many proper theatregoers in the U.S. because the play effectively excuses the young couple's immoral behavior as inevitable. If "desire" is unconscious and powerful, as Freudian psychoanalysis seemed to suggest, how could society blame Abbie and Eben for their crime, which also included the murder of their newborn child? O'Neill's plot sends the couple to jail in the end, but the play's sympathies lie with them as victims of a force beyond their control. As we have noted, the new audiophonic media influenced Freud's understanding of the unconscious mind as well as subjectively oriented theatre. Psychoanalysis and its spinoffs in popular psychology would continue to shape the American theatre for the next 40 years.

Like many other Western playwrights, O'Neill continued to draw from both sides of the objective/subjective dichotomy. *The Great God Brown* (1926) emphasizes this division through the device of masks; the social masks worn by the actors depict the constrictions of "objective," external reality, while their unmasked monologues directed at the audience reveal their "subjective," psychological selves underneath. Like Strindberg, O'Neill vacillated between plays that affirmed an objective, positivist view of reality and others that explored subjective vision through such Symbolist and Expressionist devices. Although he concluded his career with *A Long Day's Journey Into Night* (written 1939–1941, produced 1957), a piece that emphasizes the "objective" side of psychological realism, O'Neill came no closer than Strindberg to resolving the subjective/objective problem of modern, print-based theatre.

Figure 10.7
Old Cabot (Walter Huston) looks down on Abbie, his young wife (Marry Morris), who is comforting Eben Cabot (Charles Ellis) in O'Neill's *Desire Under the Elms*. The Experimental Theatre, an outgrowth of the Provincetown Players, produced the drama in 1924.
© Museum of the City of New York.

Institutionalizing the avant-garde

A few directors involved in first-generation avant-garde groups, such as Antoine and Meyerhold, worked in both avant-garde and mainstream theatres. Others, like Stanislavsky, who produced several Symbolist as well as Naturalist works at the Moscow Art Theatre, temporarily embraced one or another of the avant-garde movements. Although most avant-garde artists had declared their independence from conventional theatre, this did not stop those directors committed to mainstream theatres from borrowing from the avant-garde to shape their own productions. These successful directors and their institutions helped to popularize first-generation avant-garde styles with a wider audience.

As we began to explore in the Strindberg case study, the German director Max Reinhardt was one of the most influential mediators between the early avant-garde movements and the bourgeoisie during the first third of the twentieth century. Believing that no single style suited all plays and theatrical occasions, Reinhardt directed Naturalist, Symbolist, and Expressionist plays in Germany and Austria in a variety of spaces, often to wide public acclaim. As we saw in the case study on Strindberg, Reinhardt honed his Expressionist style during and immediately after the Great War by directing several of Strindberg's post-inferno plays. He incorporated the innovations of Appia, Craig, and others in lighting and design and sought out new training techniques for his actors. Reinhardt was able to embrace such eclecticism because he worked closely with his collaborators while insisting on final artistic control. He also maintained a significant degree of stage realism in his productions; his actors generally used realist props and costumes and typically did not acknowledge the presence of the audience. Reinhardt's production of Frank Wedekind's *Spring's Awakening* in 1906, for example, featured frilly transparent curtains (of the kind that proper bourgeoisie used to dress their windows) over much of the stage opening and created innovative lighting effects, but kept his actors behind

Figure 10.8
Karl Walzer's rendering of his design for a scene from Reinhardt's production of
Wedekind's *Spring's Awakening* (1906). Wedekind's play about adolescent sexuality and
the repressiveness of German culture created a scandal when it was published.
Max Reinhardt Archive, State University of New York, Binghamton.

the proscenium frame (Figure 10.8). After the Great War, Reinhardt staged many of his
productions in churches and other non-theatre settings, such as public squares. Reinhardt's
success exerted an immense influence in German-speaking theatre between 1910 and 1925.

Several other pre-1930 directors followed Reinhardt's lead, adapting relevant avant-garde
techniques to their mainstream productions. As director of the Odéon in Paris, Firmin Gémier
(1869–1933), an early proponent of bringing theatre to all of the French people through tent
productions, produced and directed an eclectic mix of conventional and avant-garde styles in
the 1920s. In Germany, Leopold Jessner (1878–1945), director of the Berlin State Theatre from
1919 until 1933, incorporated several Expressionist design principles into many of his
productions. These often featured Appia-inspired flights of stairs, non-realist lighting, and
symbolic costuming. In the U.S., the Theatre Guild, which enjoyed a broad subscription base
of spectators, brought a few avant-garde productions to audiences from 1919 into the 1930s.
Phillip Moeller (1880–1958), who generally worked in a style of modified realism, was the
Guild's chief director. Through the influence of these directors and their institutions, plus the
adoption of similar innovative practices elsewhere, the early avant-garde gradually altered the
expectations of mainstream audiences throughout the West.

Like Reinhardt, however, these directors were generally careful not to push their mostly
middle-class spectators too far or too fast into the worlds of avant-garde theatre. In this

conservative approach to change, the directors were actually helped by the general orientation of all first-generation avant-garde movements to their artistry. Taking their cue from Wagner's commitment to a total work of art, the early avant-gardists sought to reconstitute theatrical representation on the basis of their own beliefs, but did not question theatrical representation itself. That is, they assumed that the theatre must attempt to create a separate world that was a truthful representation of the actual one. The Symbolists, for example, sought to immerse spectators in a sound-surround of mythic belief and fate, but their images generally remained behind the proscenium and their actors never violated the representational basis of characterization. Even the Expressionists understood the angst and ecstasy of their actors as representing the true inner feelings of real people. This generally shared acceptance of the representational nature of theatre, which many second-generation avant-gardists would dispute, created an unspoken common ground between much of the early avant-garde and the bourgeois theatres they were loudly rejecting. It also provided an aesthetic basis for Reinhardt and other directors to graft avant-garde innovations on to their own, more mainstream productions.

SUMMARY

This chapter concludes Parts II and III of our textbook, both of which focused on the causal relations among print culture, historical contexts, and the theatre. Looking back, it is clear that the objective/subjective divide that structured many of the conflicts in Western theatre by the 1920s was partly due to a division that emerged with periodical print culture around 1700 in the distinction between the public and private spheres. Newspapers, treatises, and many other public print media propagated "hard" facts and often partisan contention, while the private sphere of confessionals, novels, and most popular magazines thrived on "soft" psychological insights and domestic affairs. While the objective/subjective divide in the theatre that provided the focus of this chapter was not altogether new, it is clear that specific historical pressures from photographic and audiophonic media helped to intensify it and brought it to a kind of crisis in the 1920s.

As we have seen, that division resulted in two very different kinds of theatrical expression, perhaps best exemplified in the extreme contrast between European Naturalism and Symbolism in the 1890s. Instead of depending on the external, material realities of biological evolution and industrial capitalism to undergird their theatre, the Symbolists looked to the evanescence of sound and the inner promptings of religion and psychology to shape dramas that called forth universal yearnings wrapped in gauze and half-light and performed through poetic evocation and ritual chanting. The Aestheticists and Expressionists pushed this subjective faith in new directions – the former idealizing artistic experience as a realm apart from the workaday world and the latter exploring emotional extremes animated by generational hatreds, war-soaked fears, and revolutionary hopes. Despite their rejection of conventional society, first-generation avant-gardists helped to shift conventional Western theatre away from the constraints of stage realism and toward the possibilities of theatrical modernism. This was especially apparent in work of many mainstream directors, such as Reinhardt, who borrowed from the techniques and designs of the avant-garde theatres to shape productions that spoke more directly to the needs of their mostly bourgeois spectators.

In retrospect, however, the nineteenth century's photographic and audiophonic media probably did as much to extend the life of print-based theatre as to undermine it by demonstrating its internal conflicts. Most historical peoples have lived relatively untroubled for centuries with such inherent contradictions in their culture. When severe crises arrive, however, such divisions make it easier to abandon old ways of thinking and believing in the search for new meanings and solutions. This is what happened, over time, with the problem of "objectivity" and "subjectivity" in the theatre and culture of the West; what had seemed immensely important to many people between 1900 and about 1930 gradually faded in significance. The Great War and moving pictures fragmented many of the assumptions, beliefs, and procedures upon which Western culture had been based. We are still picking up the pieces from the after-effects of the Great War, and film was only the first of many media shocks to the system – shocks that would proliferate with increasing speed into the twenty-first century. Part IV of our book brings the story of media, history, and the theatre up to the present.

*

Part III: Works cited

Other consulted resources and additional readings for Part III are listed on the **Theatre Histories** *website.*

Audio-visual resources

German Expressionism

<http://Everything2.com/index.pl?node_id=166783> (2009), website (on German Expressionism, with many links to other sources).
German Expressionism Collection (2008), DVD-video (4-disc set, includes *Cabinet of Dr. Caligari* and other films).

Variety theatre

Vintage Variety Stage and Vaudeville Film Collection (2009), DVD, Bestsellers in Movies and TV.

Blackface minstrelsy

"Stephen Foster," American Experience Series (Public Broadcasting System, 2000) <http://www.pbs.org/wgbh/amex/foster/sfeature/sf_minstrelsy.html>.
"Blackface Minstrelsy, 1830–1852" <http://www.iath.virginia.edu/utc/minstrel/mihp.html >.
"The Legacy of Blackface: National Public Radio" <http://www.npr.org/templates/story/story.php?storyId=1919122> .

Japonisme

"Curator's Perspective: Vincent Van Gogh and Japan" – excellent illustrated lecture by art historian (1 hour, 2 minutes) <https://www.youtube.com/watch?v=-mnBo87-T80>

The Mikado

Excellent full production by D'Oyly Carte Opera, 1992 (2 hours, 22 minutes): <https://www.youtube.com/watch?v=f2TW90OEU-U>

Full-length feature film *Topsy-Turvy* by Mike Leigh detailing the partnership of Gilbert and Sullivan, specifically the creation of *The Mikado*. Includes many scenes replicating the original production, costuming, and rehearsals as well as other aspects of Victorian life and theatre: <https://www.youtube.com/watch?v=BxqTaIdpvCs>

Madama Butterfly

Filmed version, filmed realistically in Japan (not on stage) with English subtitles (2 hours, 14 minutes): <https://www.youtube.com/watch?v=dhGZMPMJuTg>

Books and articles

Anderson, B. (1991) *Imagined Communities*, 2nd edn, London: Verso.

Benedetti, J. (1999) *Stanislavski: His Life and Art*, 3rd edn, London: Methuen.

Berghaus, G. (2005) *Theatre, Performance, and the Historical Avant-garde*, New York: Palgrave Macmillan.

Buckley, M. (2006) *Tragedy Walks the Streets: The French Revolution in the Making of Modern Drama*, Baltimore: Johns Hopkins University Press.

Carlson, M. (1985) *The Italian Shakespearians: Performances by Ristori, Salvini, and Rossi in England and America*, Washington, DC: Folger Books.

Collier, J. (1974) "A Short View of the Immorality and Profaneness of the English Stage" (1698), in B.F. Dukore (ed.) *Dramatic Theory and Criticism*, New York: Holt, Rinehart and Winston.

Connon, D. (2012) "The Theatre of the Parisian Fairs and Reality," *Romance Studies* 30(3–4): 186–92.

Craig, E.G. (1911) *On the Art of the Theatre*, London: Heinemann.

Dukore, B.F. (ed.) (1974) *Dramatic Theory and Criticism*, New York: Holt, Rinehart and Winston.

Eagleton, T. (1983) *Literary Theory: An Introduction*, Minneapolis: University of Minnesota Press.

Fowler, W. (2008) *Latin America since 1780*, London: Hodder Education Press.

Fredrickson, G. (2002) *Racism: A Short History*, Princeton: Princeton University Press.

Gilmour, D. (2011) *The Pursuit of Italy: A History of a Land, its Regions and their Peoples*, London: Penguin.

Gold, A. and Fizdale, F. (1991) *Divine Sarah: A Life of Sarah Bernhardt*, New York: Vintage.

Habermas, J. (1989) *The structural transformation of the public sphere: an inquiry into a category of bourgeois society*, trans T. Burger, Cambridge, MA: MIT Press.

Hemmings, F.W.J. (1993) *The Theatre Industry in Nineteenth-Century France*, Cambridge: Cambridge University Press.

Hoffenberg, P.H. (2001) *An Empire on Display: English, Indian, and Australian Exhibitions from the Crystal Palace to the Great War*, Berkeley and Los Angeles: University of California Press.

Kramnick, I. (ed.) (1995) *The Portable Enlightenment Reader*, London: Penguin.

Lessing, G.E. (1962) *Hamburg Dramaturgy*, trans. H. Zimmerman, intro. V. Lange, New York: Dover.

Mackerras, C. (ed.) (1983) *Chinese Theatre from its Origins to the Present Day*, Honolulu: University of Hawaii Press.

Maeterlinck, M. (1897) "The Tragical in Everyday Life," in *The Works of Maurice Maeterlinck* (1913–1914), New York: Dodd, Mead.

Ockman, C. (2005) "Was She Magnificent? Sarah Bernhardt's Reach," in C. Ockman and K. Silver (eds) *Sarah Bernhardt, The Art of High Drama*, produced for the Bernhardt exhibit of the Jewish Museum, New York, 2005–2006, New Haven: Yale University Press.

Peters, J.S. (2000) *Theatre of the Book, 1480–1880: Print, Text, and Performance in Europe*, Oxford: Oxford University Press.

Roach, J.R. (1985; reprint 1993) *The Player's Passion: Studies in the Science of Acting*, Ann Arbor: University of Michigan Press.

Said, E. (1978) *Orientalism*, New York: Vintage.

Salmi, H. (1999) *Imagined Germany: Richard Wagner's National Utopia*, New York: Peter Lang.

Schumacher, C. (ed.) (1996) *Naturalism and Symbolism in European Theatre*, Cambridge: Cambridge University Press.

Sontag, S. (1977) *On Photography*, New York: Delta Books.

Sosulski, M.J. (2007) *Theater and Nation in Eighteenth Century Germany*, Williston, VT: Ashgate Publishing.

Vincent-Buffault, A. (1991) *The History of Tears: Sensibility and Sentimentality in France*, Houndmills, Basingstoke: Macmillan.

Wichmann, S. (1999) *Japonisme: The Japanese Influence on Western Art since 1858*. London: Thames and Hudson.

Williams, K. (2001) "Anti-Theatricality and the Limits of Naturalism," *Modern Drama* 44(3): 284–99.

Williams, R. (1966) *Modern Tragedy*, Stanford: Stanford University Press.

Williams, R. (1969) *Drama from Ibsen to Brecht*, New York: Oxford University Press.

Zola, É. (1881) "Naturalism in the Theatre," in E. Bentley (ed.) *The Theory of the Modern Stage*, London: Penguin, 1968.

Theatre and performance in electric and electronic communication culture

PART IV TIMELINE

DATE	THEATRE and PERFORMANCE	CULTURE and COMMUNICATION	POLITICS and ECONOMICS
1856–1950	George Bernard Shaw, playwright		
1858–1943	André Antoine, director		
1859		Charles Darwin, *On the Origin of Species*	
1860–1904	Anton Chekhov, playwright		
1861–1941	Rabindranath Tagore, playwright		
1863–1938	Konstantin Stanislavsky, director		
1867		Karl Marx, *Capital* vol. 1	
1867–1936	Luigi Pirandello, playwright		
1872–1946	Kawakami Sadayakko, actor		
1872–1966	Edward Gordon Craig, theatre theorist		
1876		Electric telephone	
1876–1948	Susan Glaspell, playwright		
1877		Phonograph	
1877–1927		Isadora Duncan, dancer	
1879		Electric light bulb	
c.1880–c.1900	Avant-garde theatre, first generation		
1880–1914			"Scramble for Africa": European powers divide Africa among themselves
1881–c.1914	Naturalist movement		
1881–1973		Pablo Picasso, artist	
1882–1971		Igor Stravinsky, composer	
1884–1885			First Sino–Japanese War
1885		Automobiles	
1887–1896	Théâtre Libre		
1888–1953	Eugene O'Neill, playwright		
1894–1961	Mei Lanfang, actor		
1894–1991		Martha Graham, dancer-choreographer	
1895		First public motion picture screening, France	
		Radio	
c.1895–c.1930	*Shimpa*		
1896–1948	Antonin Artaud, actor and theorist		
1898			Spanish–American War
1898–1948		Sergei Eisenstein, film director	
1898–1956	Bertolt Brecht, playwright		

PART IV TIMELINE

DATE	THEATRE and PERFORMANCE	CULTURE and COMMUNICATION	POLITICS and ECONOMICS
1898–	Moscow Art Theatre (various name changes after 1932)		
1900		Sigmund Freud, *The Interpretation of Dreams*	
c.1900–c.1970	Modernist stage design	Modernism in art and literature	
1903		First successful airplane	
1904		Vacuum tube: beginning of electronics	
		Sigmund Freud, *The Psychopathology of Everyday Life*	
1906–1989	Samuel Beckett, playwright		
1907–	*Huaju*		
1909–	*Shingeki*		
c.1910–c.1925		Cubism in art	
c.1910–c.1930	Avant-garde theatre, second generation		
1911–1983	Tennessee Williams, playwright		
1914–1918			Great War (aka First World War)
1914–	Takarazuka Revue		
c.1915–c.1930	Expressionist theatre in the U.S.		
c.1915–		Jazz	
1915–2005	Arthur Miller, playwright		
1917			Russian Revolution
c.1918–c.1935		Harlem Renaissance	
1918–2007		Ingmar Bergman, film and theatre director	
c.1920–	Musical theatre		
1922–1991			Soviet Union
1923		First public screening of sound film	
1925–1970	Mishima Yukio, playwright		
1926–	Dario Fo, performer-playwright		
1930–c.1940			Great Depression worldwide
1930–1965	Lorraine Hansberry, playwright		
1930–2008	Harold Pinter, playwright		
1930–	Stephen Sondheim, musical theatre composer-lyricist		
1931–2009	Augusto Boal, theatre creator and theorist		
1932–	Athol Fugard, playwright		

PART IV TIMELINE

DATE	THEATRE and PERFORMANCE	CULTURE and COMMUNICATION	POLITICS and ECONOMICS
1933–1945			Nazi concentration and labor camps in Germany and Eastern Europe
1933–1999	Jerzy Grotowski, director		
1934–2014	Amiri Baraka (aka LeRoi Jones), playwright		
1934–	Wole Soyinka, playwright		
1935–1939	Federal Theatre Project, U.S.		
1935–1983	Terayama Shūji, playwright and director		
1936		Television broadcasting	
1937–	Tom Stoppard, playwright		
1938–	Caryl Churchill, playwright		
1939–1945			Second World War
1939–	Suzuki Tadashi, director		
c.1940–c.1970	"Golden Age" of Broadway musical theatre		
1940–	Gao Xingjian, playwright		
	Luis Valdez, playwright-director		
1941–	Robert Wilson, director-designer		
1942		All-electronic computer	
1945			Nuclear bomb used on Hiroshima and Nagasaki, Japan
1945–2005	August Wilson, playwright		
1947		Transistor: basis of all modern electronic equipment	
1947–1991			Cold War: the U.S. and its allies vs. Soviet Union and its allies
1947–	Living Theatre, U.S.		
1949	Berliner Ensemble founded		People's Republic of China (Communist China) established
1950–1953			Korean War
1951–1980			African independence movements
c.1955		Television becomes an important medium	
1955–1975			Vietnam War
1956–	Tony Kushner, playwright		
1957			Sputnik 1 (Soviet satellite)
1957–	David Henry Hwang, playwright		
1959		Beginning of *butoh* dance	
1959–c.1990	Happenings		

PART IV TIMELINE

DATE	THEATRE and PERFORMANCE	CULTURE and COMMUNICATION	POLITICS and ECONOMICS
c.1960	Beginnings of civil rights era theatre movements		
c.1965–c.1975	Main period of political theatre		
c.1960–	Performance art		
c.1962–	*Angura*		
c.1962–		Rock music	
1963–	Suzan-Lori Parks, playwright		
1964		Communications satellites	
1964–1971			Worldwide protests against the Vietnam War
c.1965	Beginnings of feminist, Latino, gay, and lesbian theatre		
1966–1976			Chinese Cultural Revolution
c.1966–	*Yangbanxi* (Chinese revolutionary opera)		
1967		Jacques Derrida, *Of Grammatology*	
1967–			European Community (starting point of the European Union)
1968	U.K. ends theatre censorship		May 1968 events in France
			Martin Luther King assassinated, U.S.
1969		Moon landing	
		First network of computer networks (beginning of the Internet)	
c.1970–c.1980		Birth of Hip Hop and rap	
c.1970–c.1985	Nuevo Teatro Popular		
1974			U.S. President Richard Nixon resigns
1976		Satellite television	
		Michel Foucault, *The History of Sexuality*	
1977		Mass-market personal computers	
c.1980			AIDS crisis begins
1983		Commercially available mobile phones	
1989			Berlin Wall falls, Germany
			Tiananmen Square protests, China
c.1990		Commercially available digital cameras	

PART IV TIMELINE

DATE	THEATRE and PERFORMANCE	CULTURE and COMMUNICATION	POLITICS and ECONOMICS
1991		World Wide Web	Break-up of the Soviet Union
1993–			European Union
1994		Web-based social networking	
2000		Smartphones	
2001			September 11th attacks on the World Trade Center and Pentagon, U.S.
2001–2014			Wars in Afghanistan and Iraq
2003–2011			Iraq War
2007–?			Great Recession worldwide
2010–2012			Arab Spring

Introduction: Theatre and the unceasing communications revolutions

Tobin Nellhaus

The twentieth century was a period of upheaval and invention. There were two world wars, several genocides, a massive economic depression, plus several smaller versions of each. Some major countries had political revolutions; many more achieved independence from imperialist control, but sometimes only to plummet into dictatorships or civil wars. Liberalizations of cultural values and the creation of social support programs were followed by conservative reactions, and back again. Much like the 1600s, religious faith could reverse into a fanaticism that led people to repress and even kill others. Cars and planes transformed transportation, and rockets landed men on the moon. Globalization knotted national economies together, and enabled people around the world to talk with each other. Simultaneously, it highlighted the uniqueness of the local, although occasionally fragmenting societies.

One of the key forces behind those constant sea changes was the industrialization of electricity. One technology after another manipulated electricity with ever-greater sophistication; each day brought it further into people's lives, to the point that without a source of electrical power, nearly all devices and machines today would be no better than rocks. Communication media in particular were radically and repeatedly altered or invented. Political,

A transistor and a vacuum tube.
Fuse/Getty Images.

economic, and social events strongly affected theatrical developments, especially topically – but the unending innovations in communication played a fundamental role in changing the styles and methods of performance. These developments are the focus of Part IV.

Already in the nineteenth century, numerous new communication technologies had changed people's lives, including telegraphs, photography, typewriters, telephones, phonographs, radios, and silent films. Most of them utilized electricity as a source of power to move mechanical parts, but also – as electromagnetic radiation, namely light – as a catalyst for chemical reactions (which is how photography worked). In these ways, electricity became an element in the very production and transmission of words, sounds, and images – culture itself.

We described in Chapter 10 how some of these early electricity-based communication media influenced theatre in multiple and sometimes opposite ways, especially the contrast that emerged between Naturalism and Symbolism. By the close of the nineteenth century, theatre had divided into two major artistic branches: mainstream realism and the avant-garde. The contrast and even antagonism between them rapidly intensified. The avant-garde, already split from the mainstream aesthetically, began to produce plays that aimed to subvert bourgeois culture. At the same time, some Naturalist playwrights began to incorporate political critique within their plays. These varying approaches soon also appeared in theatre's rapidly growing relative, the movies.

The era covered by Part IV started with two developments that in different ways shook the world, as Chapter 11 explains. One was the Great War (aka the First World War, 1914–1918) and its aftermath, which accelerated theatrical movements against bourgeois society. Anti-capitalist playwrights increasingly joined the avant-garde in rejecting Naturalist styles, and a number of second-generation avant-gardists rejected capitalism. A third branch of theatrical performance also emerged: political theatre with a non-realistic style. Nevertheless, realism (whether or not political) and the apolitical avant-garde remained stronger than the political theatre. The impulses behind these two branches were conjoined in modernism, a form of theatre that utilized some avant-garde techniques, but aimed not to challenge bourgeois society, merely to transcend it through abstraction and idealism.

The other development was a technological innovation. In 1904, the vacuum tube was invented, which made it possible to control electricity in highly refined ways. It was the first electronic technology. By 1930, vacuum tubes had dramatically improved and commercialized radios and phonographs, and allowed images and sound to be synchronized on film. As Chapter 11 shows, radio and especially sound film (the "talkies") had major effects on the theatre of the time, sometimes to be used, sometimes to be resisted. However, the applications of vacuum tubes did not end there: they could manipulate light waves, and they could be combined into complex switches. The former led to television, and broadcasting to the public began in 1936. The latter resulted in the first wholly electronic computer, which was built in 1942. One generation later, these devices would upend the world.

The Second World War (1939–1945) involved nearly every country around the globe, and was even more devastating than its predecessor. As Chapter 12 observes, few of the second-generation avant-gardes survived the war; some had faded away even before then. Nevertheless, to varying extents in each country, theatre in the postwar era continued the three rough types from before: psychological or social realism, which sometimes adopted elements of avant-garde styles, and sometimes had a politically critical edge; avant-garde genres with varying relationships with bourgeois culture; and political non-realism. Theatre in the U.S. predominantly focused on psychological realism, sometimes within a naturalistic setting, sometimes in a more abstract style similar to modernism or Expressionism. Even plays critical of mainstream politics tended to employ psychological realism. Soviet state policy locked theatre into "socialist realism," which stylistically differed little from bourgeois realism. Political theatre became an important trend in South Asia, Africa, and Latin America. Europe and Japan contended with both the destruction left by the warfare, and the political and moral legacies of fascism, genocide, and the atomic bomb. Thus the war raised profoundly disturbing questions and disillusionment with Enlightenment ideas of truth, reason, and progress, which was often reflected in non-realist drama. However, in the midst of the recovering economy of the late 1950s, alternative forms of performance arose in the U.S., Europe, Japan, and elsewhere, some of them tied to protests against postwar conformism and political inequities, and some of them wholly unlike theatre itself.

One element in both the recovery and the emergence of non-conformism in the 1950s was yet another transformative technology: the invention of the transistor in 1947. Transistors did the same things vacuum tubes did, but they were more reliable, smaller – and soon, cheaper. They revolutionized all of the previous devices, found new applications, and enabled whole new technologies. The vacuum tube had introduced a few electronic devices to people's homes; the transistor made electronics utterly ubiquitous. In the mid-1950s, the transistor radio became the first mass-produced mobile device. We began to enter the era of electric and electronic communication culture.

Now largely transistorized, televisions started residing in most living rooms, reshaping culture and influencing politics. By the mid-1960s, about 94 percent of homes in the U.S. and Japan, 86 percent in the U.K., and the majority of households in other industrialized countries owned television sets – and millions of viewers saw the war in Vietnam. The protests against the war were part of a turning point in world history: throughout the late 1960s and early 1970s, a wide range of political and cultural clashes erupted worldwide, some of them in opposition to global politics, some of them in opposition to domestic authoritarianism and lack of political equality. Chapter 13 shows how theatre often participated in the activism of the last third of the twentieth century, whether directly in political theatre, or through challenges to theatre's traditional hierarchies, such as the authority of the dramatic text.

The 1960s launched the current era of accelerating globalization, in which national economies – driven by multinational corporations, international trade agreements, supranational organizations such as the World Trade Organization, worldwide transportation systems, and global telecommunications – have become deeply interdependent, to some extent making nationalism moot. But this has had complex effects. Globally, treaties unify world economies and legal frameworks, businesses in one continent decide what farmers should grow in another, and McDonald's and Hollywood cover the planet. Locally, many people find declining self-governance, the disappearance of regional culture, environmental damage caused by import and export, and other effects. Sometimes the local and global have blended, for instance in regional versions of rap music. In Chapter 14 we discuss how these forces and concerns have been manifested in theatre, in everything from musicals, to the preservation of indigenous performance genres, to borrowing from foreign traditions. Theatre for social change has also been affected by the combined pressures of the global and the local.

The past fifty years has also been marked by the rampant growth of consumer electronics. A staggering list of devices permeated life in the industrialized countries, and increasingly in the developing world as well, including music players, cameras, video recorders, mobile telephones, and most importantly, computers. Devices that fit on a desktop became portable, portable became hand-held, hand-held became pocket-sized – and the pocket-sized packed together an increasing array of unrelated devices, such as phones with cameras.

The most fundamental advance occurred during that same turning point. In 1969, two computers were linked by telephone. A few more were soon added, forming a network. In 1971, the first email was sent, heralding the coming expansion of computers from advanced calculators to a new communication medium. Meanwhile, other computer networks were created. The networks swelled and interconnected, and in the early 1980s, the **internet** was born. Then in 1990, a standardized way to link electronic documents via the internet was developed; it was named the World Wide Web. Internet usage grew spectacularly. As early as 1995, 0.5 percent or so of the world's population used the internet, facilitated by the Web. In 2000 it connected about 7 percent of the world, around 400 million people. By 2010, that figure had leapt to 2 billion, around 30 percent. Just five years later, the number surpassed 44 percent – over 3.2 billion people. Increasingly they connected through sophisticated and affordable smartphones, integrating a large number of electronic devices (including a telephone, camera, Web browser, multimedia players, and geographical positioning system) into one hand-held unit. These devices' core purpose is not calculation, but data transfer – that is, communication.

The internet established a mode of communication with several crucial differences from print and most previous electric/electronic communication technologies. Those largely conducted one-way communication to large numbers of people, whether through the dissemination of physical books, recordings and photographs, or through on-air broadcasts. For most people, only the telephone allowed person-to-person communication. The internet, however, combines two-way communication with broadcasted communication. In principle, any individual can get in touch with any other individual. But also, in principle anyone can present whatever thoughts, pictures, or videos they choose before the entire world – and in principle, anyone can respond back. And all of that happens instantly. Thus the internet not only networks computers, it networks people. In addition, digital media provide new textual, mechanical, and visual tools. Chapter 15 explores a number of these issues as they emerge in performance. It focuses first on changes in the performer, such as her representation through projections, augmentation by electronic equipment, replacement by robots, and re-embodiment by avatars. Next it looks at new types of performance spaces – not just virtual realities, but also textual realms such as Twitter, and uses of public spaces. The chapter concludes by considering how concepts and practices derived from the virtual world are manifested in real-world performance genres and methodologies.

Networked culture is generating social changes. What they will be in the long run, we don't know. In Part III we saw the pivotal role periodical print culture played in establishing the distinction between the public sphere and the private sphere within bourgeois society; in the overthrow of absolutism and the creation of nation-states, usually with some type of democracy; and in transforming the audience's emotional response to dramatic characters. It is becoming increasingly clear that as networked culture begins, it is likewise presenting threats and changes to the established political, economic, and cultural order, particularly due to its potential for expanded democratic practices. Potential, however, does not equal actuality. The governments of China, Iran, and elsewhere attempt to prevent or impede dangers to their power by censoring, restricting, or even shutting down their country's internet, and sometimes even its phone network; the U.S., U.K., and other governments had or have programs to collect data on the personal communications of everyone in the country. In fact, when it comes to information – both its content and its ownership – the very concepts of public and private are now the subject of fierce arguments and legal battles. Businesses, seeking sales, extensively mine personal data; they also aggressively protect their copyrights, sometimes even subverting the right to fair use. At the same time, private property is challenged by the view that books, music, and films are or should be publicly available for free and without permission – a view some people hold unconsciously, others take as permission for what is currently theft, and still others propose as a fundamental principle based on a recognition of the importance of information and culture in society.

Far less clear is how networked culture may alter two concepts: the nature of knowledge and personhood. Both concepts directly affect theatre and performance. As we observed at several points in this book, arguments about truth have been wielded as a weapon against theatre, whether to condemn it as a hotbed of falsity and sham, or dismiss it as an empty distraction from wiser pursuits. Such antitheatricality, we have noted, has even appeared within theatre. Late twentieth-century "experimental" theatre might be either the last gasp of the insistence that theatre justify its existence by becoming a kind of laboratory, or the opening round in a new struggle to make performance a fully legitimate part of global culture. It could be the forge of performance methods that will become the theatrical norm expressing a new consensus about knowledge and theatre's relation to it.

The concept of personhood, in turn, directly shapes the portrayal of dramatic character, which in turn influences the stories theatres are likely to tell. As we saw in Part II, psychological interiority was born with print, and in Part III we described how periodical print culture ripened that interiority as part of the public/private distinction. If that distinction is now an area of conflict and change, the idea that a character should reveal a private self must surely become dubious as well. Some forms of theatre described in Part IV – such as those which discard the traditional division between actor and audience in favor of the participant, or abandon linear plot development for episodes, pastiche, simultaneity, and/or associative connections – make one wonder if such explorations in personhood have already begun.

In an era of unceasing communications revolutions when our everyday choices about how to communicate can have unexpected long-term consequences, we can be sure that such explorations will be ongoing. As we have seen throughout this book, changes in communication practices affect theatre on fundamental levels; but those changes are seldom immediate, and often lead in directions no one could predict.

★

CHAPTER 11

New theatres for revolutionary times, 1910–1950

Bruce McConachie

This chapter begins with a focus on two major causes of change in the theatre of the early twentieth century: the Great War and the movies. Both fragmented Western bourgeois culture, animating some theatre artists to demand radical change and leaving others to search for new forms of aesthetic order. The war led to the Russian Revolution in 1917, which had been preceded by socialist theatre and avant-garde movements calling for opposition to the cultural status quo. Following the Revolution, new models of political theatre from the Soviet Union (which included most of the former Russian Empire) proliferated in Europe, the U.S., India, and China. Film destabilized conventional notions of the self and society and directly challenged mainstream theatrical practice in the West. Theatre artists who professed modernism, alarmed by both film culture and the war, sought to transcend the fragmentations of Western culture through the invocation of ancient myths and universalizing philosophies; some playwrights in Japan adopted modernism as well.

War and the movies

The Great War (1914–1918) was a catastrophe for mainstream Western culture. Most immediately, it wreaked unprecedented devastation on lives, wealth, and established political power. The war broke apart four major European empires – the German, Austro-Hungarian, Russian, and Ottoman empires – and left many new nations – including Finland and Poland in northern Europe and Hungary and Bulgaria further south – to struggle for independence and national coherence in the 1920s and 1930s (see Figure 11.1). The Great War was a direct cause of the Russian Revolution and civil war (1917–1921), which led to the first anti-capitalist regime in modern times. The upheavals of the Russian Revolution, especially when joined with earlier revolutions in China (1911–1912) and Mexico (1910–1921), animated widespread desire for radical change. Indirectly, the 1914–1918 war precipitated the decline of Western imperialism around the world, contributed to the rise of European fascism in the 1920s, and helped to

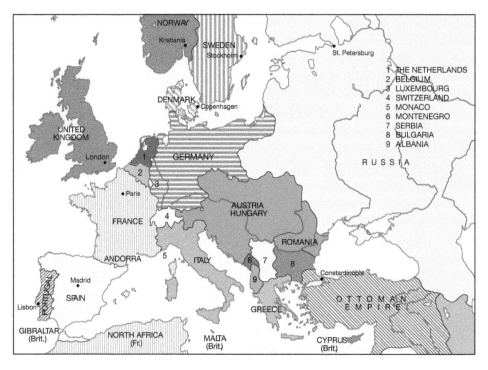

Figure 11.1
Political maps of Europe before (1914) and after (1922) the Great War.

cause the worldwide economic Depression of the 1930s. In these and other ways, the Great War fractured Western bourgeois culture and introduced new realities and possibilities undreamed of before 1914.

The war and its aftermath altered all of the major areas of theatrical activity in the West. In political theatre, the Russian Revolution undermined the deterministic side of Naturalism and sparked widespread theatrical activism. The initial success of the Revolution converted many avant-gardists in Russia, Germany, and elsewhere to communism and they began to experiment with a variety of forms and styles to move people to political action. Before 1914, all of the significant avant-garde movements had been international, with artists freely trading ideas and performances across borders. After the war, the international characteristics of the avant-garde gradually disappeared, as political differences splintered avant-garde networks. By the mid-1930s, with Europe preparing for another war, the avant-garde was dead.

The international popularity of silent films after the Great War radically altered popular entertainments at circuses, world fairs, and on variety stages – never more popular than in the decade before 1914 – and drove some out of business. All forms of live entertainment declined after 1918, a trend accelerated by the arrival of the "talkies" in 1927. The telephone and phonograph, much more widespread in the 1920s than before, increased their challenges to print culture and photography, which dominated theatrical representation before the war. In addition to these older audiophonic media, radio listening rapidly gained in popularity from the late 1920s through the 1930s, despite the Depression. Among all media, however, it was the movies that offered the most provocations to pre-1914 culture in the West. The cultural fragmentations caused by the war and the popularity of film animated radical theatre artists to question the older premises of theatrical representation and it gave rise to a conservative movement known as modernism, discussed in subsequent sections of this chapter.

Powering some of the optimism about possibilities for revolutionary change was electricity. Following inventions by Thomas Edison, Nikola Tesla, and others in the late nineteenth century, economic and political elites used electrical power to illuminate their businesses and public buildings and to run their factories and theatres by 1910. In Chapter 10, we noted that electric lights made possible more realistic effects and a more private viewing experience for theatrical audiences. But coal and gas continued to heat the homes and shops and to illuminate the dwellings and streets of most Westerners. After the war, the rapid electrification of cities in the West transformed the everyday lives of many citizens. In addition to illumination, electricity powered heating, hot water, and an increasing range of appliances, from vacuum cleaners and irons to refrigerators and toasters, in the homes of many urbanites by 1930. The power generated to run the new phonographs and movies (initially shot and projected by hand-cranking) was a part of the general electrification of Western culture.

Following France in 1895, the first public exhibition of a film in the U.S. occurred at a New York vaudeville house in 1896. Soon "nickelodeons" (so named because the entry fee was a nickel) sprang up in major urban centers in the U.S. By 1914, most variety theatres had integrated silent films into their entertainments, a trend that undermined the presentation of live acts and eventually doomed the vaudeville stage. Early French and U.S. film-makers borrowed extensively from the theatre, taking variety acts, scenic conventions, modes of storytelling, acting styles, and musical underscoring (played by musicians during the screening) from the popular stage. French film director George Méliès (1861–1938), for example, built a proscenium stage at his film studio, equipped with the machinery and two-dimensional scenery of a typical Parisian theatre, so that he could provide the kinds of illusionistic pleasures in his films, such as *A Trip to the Moon* (1902), that delighted popular theatrical audiences.

Director D.W. Griffith (1875–1948), who had largely failed as an actor and playwright, brought with him a strong taste for melodramatic stage scripts, conventional acting styles, and paternalistic control as a director when he switched from live theatre to the moving picture business in 1907. He based one of his most successful and notorious films, *The Birth of a Nation* (1915), on earlier stage performances of *The Clansmen* that celebrated the rise of the white-supremacist Ku Klux Klan in the American South after the Civil War. Until 1915, most theatre artists looked down on film as a lower-class entertainment of little artistic worth. By the end of the Great War, however, when better technology had led to a much wider range of shots, locations, and editing possibilities and when mass distribution was attracting the middle classes for feature-length films starring Charlie Chaplin (1889–1977) and other international stars, the balance had shifted. From the 1920s onward, film had more of an influence on the stage than the other way around.

As an extension of photography, film seemed to uphold an "objective," positivistic view of the world, even though the subject matter of most films was clearly imagined and "subjective." But shooting and editing for film also cut up the perceived world into various points of view; no moving picture could be reduced to a single photograph, "objective" or not. As well, the pieced-together nature of films, despite Hollywood editing techniques that suggested a seamless flow of images, underlined the fragmented nature of human perception. Sometimes, it seemed, people saw reality in close up, while at other times, they perceived the world in long perspective or even as a whirling nightmare; the movies heightened the suspicion that reality might be inherently unstable. Because film was able to take viewers from what appeared to be a clear-eyed view of the real in one moment and into a dreamy vision the next, it largely erased the objective/subjective dichotomy of photographic and audiophonic perceptions prevalent in late print culture, without, however, providing a synthesis of these different modes of understanding reality.

Nonetheless, by the mid-1920s, the largely unconscious effects of the movies were less important for many Westerners than the expectation that film offered a revolutionary potential for altering modern life. It was clear to all that the movies had vastly increased human agency in the age-old quest to effectively persuade others of important values and ideas. During the 1920s, revolutionary movements around the globe were using the new medium, along with the theatre, to challenge the political and ideological status quo.

One result of the ubiquity of film after the war was to popularize some of the innovations that avant-gardists had been pushing since the 1890s. Many of the Symbolists and Expressionists had explored a wide variety of locales in their productions, a fluid use of space impossible to achieve in realist and Naturalist productions. Film could easily take spectators into numerous places, and audiences began to expect the same kinds of flexibility while watching a play on stage. Appia, Craig, and others had anticipated filmic effects in their suggestions that lighting instruments could be used to heighten an actor's presence, gain design flexibility, and speed playing time. Many directors and designers in the 1920s, taking advantage of darkened house lights, effectively turned follow-spots into cameras. Before film scripts demonstrated the power of short scenes with little dialogue and heightened action, playwrights Strindberg, Kaiser, and Blok had already explored these possibilities.

Because film had aroused cultural awareness of a fragmented world, its perceived effects challenged playwrights and directors after 1920 either to explore the fragments or to present a vision that might unite them – or to attempt both. German Expressionism in the 1920s largely focused on the shattered bodies and psyches left by the war, although it also offered some believable utopian visions to heal them. Even as the theatrical side of the movement was in decline, however, the Expressionist films of Fritz Lang (1890–1976), especially *Dr. Mabuse* (1922) and *Metropolis* (1927), and of other film directors, kept Expressionist acting and design before the public. As we will see, most of the politically oriented theatre artists under discussion in this chapter struggled both to acknowledge the fragmented nature of society and to suggest a unifying vision that might unite humankind. Also influenced by filmic perceptions, the modernists adopted a different position. Turning their backs on politics, they sought to transcend a broken reality by invoking idealized truths and/or ancient myths. In the process, they championed the apparent stability of print-based insights against the fractured world suggested by film.

Revolutionary predecessors

As noted, three major revolutions rocked the bourgeois world of the 1910–1920 decade. In 1910, revolutionaries in Mexico ousted a corrupt dictator with ties to U.S. imperialists, established a constitution in 1917 in the midst of a civil war, and continued to fight for radical change into the 1920s. Revolution against European and Japanese imperialism began in China in 1911 and won some limited reforms in 1912; it would continue intermittently until the Communists were able to claim victory in 1949. Led initially by Sun Yat-sen (1866–1925), the Nationalist Party fought primarily against Western-backed warlords during the first decade of the revolution in an attempt to unify China under one government. Secretly transported back to Russia by the Germans during the Great War, Vladimir Lenin (1870–1924) helped to transform an uprising against tsarist rule in Russia into the Communist Revolution in 1917. By the early 1920s, Communists under Lenin and others had consolidated their power in most of the former Russian Empire and embarked on a campaign of political agitation and upheaval in much of Europe and Asia that would last for the next 30 years. As we will see, this revolutionary decade spawned worldwide theatrical developments.

Before 1910, however, there were already political and theatrical signs of the radical challenges that might lie ahead. Since the 1890s, many Europeans believing in socialism had warned that the increasing disparities in power and wealth between capitalists and workers could lead to revolution. Socialists pointed out that market forces caused frequent depressions and argued that unimpeded capitalism would lead to long-term misery for most of the population. By 1890, socialist political parties with a base in the working class were electing representatives in all industrial countries that had a modicum of democracy. Socialists throughout the world drew on Marx's arguments about the inherent class conflict between workers and capitalists, but often differed on the question of revolution. Most argued that political and economic reform might alter the capitalist system to produce more economic justice, while a minority believed that only violent revolution could truly transform the system.

As we noted in Chapter 9, before the Russian Revolution most socialist playwrights and audiences gravitated to Naturalism. (Lenin's wife later proclaimed Hauptmann's *The Weavers*, about a worker rebellion, one of her favorite plays.) For some socialists concerned to effect change, however, a major problem with Naturalism was its deterministic point of view. Naturalism could examine the brutalities of capitalism with photo-like acumen, but its basis in Social Darwinism and positivism suggested that the masses, once degraded by heredity and their social-economic environment, rarely roused themselves from their situation to take control of their lives. Or, if they started a revolt, the authorities would quickly intervene to restore order, as related by Hauptmann in his historically based play. Most socialists continued to write Naturalist dramas that exposed the problems of capitalism, but there was a tension between their pessimistic plays and their hopeful politics. Later socialists and communists, such as Vsevolod Meyerhold, Erwin Piscator, and Bertolt Brecht, would reject Naturalism for this reason.

George Bernard Shaw's (1856–1950) response to the deterministic tendencies of Naturalism made him the most outspoken socialist playwright of the 1890–1914 period. Shaw became a socialist in 1882 and soon after joined the Fabian Society, a group of British journalists, professionals, and others who campaigned to end capitalist oppression by gradualist, political means. Shaw's first plays in the 1890s carried Fabianism into the London theatre by attacking slum-landlordism, capitalist profits from prostitution, and the foolishness of armies and war.

In *Man and Superman* and *Major Barbara* (both performed in 1905), Shaw dramatized a political philosophy that joined socialism to vitalism, the belief in a "life force" that could make it possible for people to control evolution. With these plays, Shaw discarded the Social Darwinist side of Naturalism to emphasize that human agency could work through evolution to effect progressive change. In *Major Barbara*, Shaw's audience learned that social conscience without economic power is useless and, finally, unethical (Figure 11.2). Further, *Man and Superman* demonstrated that all the political power in the world cannot alter material reality unless it works in conjunction with evolution. Shaw's Fabian vitalism, his conjuring of a life force that could animate individuals to push humanity toward evolutionary progress, trumped the pessimistic conclusions that many Social Darwinists predicted for humankind. (Shaw's

Figure 11.2
Photograph from the 1905 production of Shaw's *Major Barbara* at the Royal Court Theatre, London. Louis Calvert played Undershaft and Granville Barker (with drum), who also directed, performed Cusins. The photograph appeared with others from this production in the *Illustrated Sporting and Dramatic News* (January 20, 1906), one of several news magazines in Europe and the U.S. after 1900 that regularly ran photographs of current events.

interest in vitalism and evolution also led him to embrace eugenics, the attempt to shape the future of humankind by manipulating the gene pool.) While Shaw's philosophy and the plays that embodied it may no longer seem politically relevant, Fabian vitalism did change political discourse in England before 1914. Shaw's efforts helped to lay the groundwork for the eventual political triumph of the Labour Party after the Second World War and its commitment to democratic socialism in Great Britain. His comedies from this period continue to startle playgoers with their combative debates and acute social analyses.

In addition to the socialists, several second-generation avant-garde movements also attacked bourgeois society, warned of possible chaos to come, and proposed utopian alternatives to conventional, middle-class life. As Peter Bürger (a celebrated theorist of the avant-garde) insists, avant-garde artists could not break their ties to the dominant culture until they attacked "the status of art in bourgeois society" (Bürger 1984: 49). Accordingly, second-generation avant-garde movements stopped treating "the arts" as a separate arena of practice within bourgeois society and began to reconfigure their artistic work as the genuine basis for a utopian society. Instead of producing individual works that might (or might not) have some limited effects on the dominant culture, as the Naturalists and Symbolists had done, avant-gardists started to use their own theatres to explore the possibilities of new modes of experience and social organization. We saw this change in some of the productions of the German Expressionists after the war. The Futurists and Dadaists took the first tentative steps toward realizing this challenge.

Most of these second-generation movements also undercut the representational basis of the theatre. As noted in Chapter 10, the shared assumption that the theatre should somehow imitate and represent "reality" (whatever that might be) had united many professional artists in mainstream theatre with the early avant-garde, allowing them to incorporate many avant-garde experiments into their commercial productions. As early as 1896, however, one avant-garde production had already attacked the mimetic basis of the stage – *Ubu Roi* (*King Ubu*), by Alfred Jarry. The play satirized a bourgeois anti-hero as a gross, ambitious, and murderous boob; Ubu simply slaughters others for pleasure and power. Jarry combined characters and situations from *Macbeth* with conventions from rural French puppet theatre (where he had worked), put them on the stage of the Théâtre de l'Oeuvre with deliberately crude and highly stylized scenery, and instructed his actors to perform mechanically, like marionettes (Figure 11.3). As this description suggests, *Ubu* did not fit within any of the representational commercial or avant-garde movements of the day; it mocked realism and Naturalism and avoided the principles and beliefs of Symbolism and Aestheticism. Instead of representing reality, the production of *Ubu* was forthrightly presentational; spectators always knew they were in a theatre watching actors present a (strange and disturbing) piece of fiction.

Despite the production's cancellation after only two performances, *Ubu* gained a kind of mythic notoriety for shocking the bourgeoisie and causing a riot that fed the imaginations of second-generation avant-gardists through the 1920s. The facts of its production, however, contradict the myth. According to the evidence, there were some calculated confrontations of support and opposition among the invited intelligentsia at the preview performance. Many of these spectators had read previously published excerpts of the play and planned to demonstrate, as had vocal claques at other Parisian performances throughout the century. But there was no riot among a scandalized bourgeoisie. Such theatregoers did attend the official opening on the second night and some may have been shocked, but the performance passed without incident.

Figure 11.3

Alfred Jarry's lithographed program for the 1896 Paris premiere of his play *Ubu Roi* (*King Ubu*), at the Theatre de l'Oeuvre, staged by Aurélien Lugné-Poe. It was published by the journal *La Critique*, with other programs for the theatre's season. The corrupt Ubu carries the "pshitt sword" he refers to in the play and a bag of money. The burning house probably depicts the home of one of Ubu's subjects who did not pay his taxes.

The Spencer Museum of Art, Museum purchase: Letha Churchill Walker Memorial Art Fund, 1990.0085.

Why the myth of scandal and riot? Part of it was apparently the result of Jarry's self-promotion, but its perpetuation also stems from the need for later avant-garde artists and their allies to create an us/them situation of persecuted Romantic artists vs. a foolish and angry bourgeoisie. (Unfortunately, most historical accounts of *Ubu* have continued to recount this myth.) More important in the production of *Ubu*, however, was its radical break with the representational basis of nearly all theatre in the 1890s.

Perhaps hoping for similar alleged shock effects, Filippo Marinetti (1876–1944) began **Futurism** in Italy with the publication of "The Founding and Manifesto of Futurism" in 1909. The manifesto damned the art of the past, including museums, concert halls, and conventional theatre, and, in a slap at Symbolism, called for artistic forms that would exalt the speed and dynamism of the machine age. Earlier than other avant-garde artists, Marinetti embraced the revolutionary potential of film to transform the theatre. More manifestos followed, and soon Marinetti was producing "Futurist evenings" in large auditoriums that included lectures, poetry readings, art displays, and theatrical skits. Some skits were little more than conventional variety sketches, but others explored themes and conflicts that were anti-positivist, alogical, and abstract, as well as occasionally thrilling and visionary. Marinetti also experimented with performer–spectator dynamics, usually in an attempt to outrage bourgeois audiences. As a presentational trickster, Marinetti never let his audience forget that they were watching a performance that rarely attempted to represent "reality." Because Marinetti glorified warfare as a necessary source of modern dynamism, Futurism declined in Italy with the mounting devastations of the Great War.

Nonetheless, the utopian possibilities of second-generation avant-gardism flourished after 1914. Interest in the potential of Futurism to inspire a machine-age heaven-on-earth blossomed in Russia, perhaps because the Russian Empire, one of the most backward areas of Europe, was in need of vast transformation. The Russian Futurists, like their Italian counterparts, scoffed at the idealizing mysticism of the Symbolists and looked to the machine and to film as engines for utopian change. Soon after the 1917 Revolution, Vladimir Mayakovsky (1893–1930), leader of Futurism in Russia, aligned the movement with communism and worked to create effective propaganda for the struggling regime. With Meyerhold, Mayakovsky co-directed his play *Mystery-Bouffe* (1918), which depicts the establishment of a futurist paradise. As we will see, this production helped to move Meyerhold away from Aestheticism and toward his eventual embrace of Constructivism, the major avant-garde movement to emerge from the Russian Revolution.

Artist-refugees, most of them French, initiated Dada in a cabaret in neutral Zurich in Switzerland during the Great War. The Dadaists (who apparently chose their name randomly by opening a dictionary) rejected the rationality that they believed had led to war. Partly inspired by the myth of *Ubu Roi*, as well as by Marinetti's Futurist experiments, the Dadaists played with satire and anarchy in their cabaret performances. Unlike the Futurists, however, the Dadaists leavened their oppositional anger against bourgeois art with greater experimentation and a wider range of playful visions. Several Dadaist musicians included a variety of everyday sounds in their compositions, for example. Moving beyond the Futurists, the Dadaists also questioned the causal connections between sensations and behaviors that provided the basis for representational theatre. During and after the war, some of the Zurich Dadaists attempted to live according to the notions of chance, fragmentation, and simultaneity that they were exploring in their art.

Theatricalizing the Russian Revolution

The victory of communism in Russia in 1921 sharply altered the dynamics of political theatre in the West. Only later would democratic socialists discover that the Russian Communist Party generally had little use for democracy and would soon institute many forms of political oppression. In the afterglow of the Revolution, however, the short-term sacrifice of some democratic rights seemed to many European socialists a small price to pay for the opportunity to transform an entire economy and society. Despite the setbacks caused by the Great War, eager socialists renewed revolutionary action in Eastern and Central Europe and nearly toppled some postwar liberal regimes, including the fragile German state opposed by some of the radical Expressionists. Although liberal governments were soon established in the nations of the former German and Austro-Hungarian empires, a new, revolutionary form of Russian theatre soon spread from the Soviet Union to socialists around the world.

To teach peasants and workers the basics of communism, the Communists organized Blue Blouse troupes, named for the color of workers' shirts, and fostered their establishment around the country. A collection of short skits legitimating the radical changes brought by the Revolution, many of these Blue Blouse revues were called "living newspapers"; through speech, music, gestures, and spectacle, their primary aim was to instruct the many Russians who could not read. In style and ideology, the Blue Blouse revues were anti-capitalist and anti-Naturalist. Through presentational skits that directly acknowledged the presence of the audience, they asserted that workers and peasants could take control of their lives and effect radical change. Many Russian vaudeville performers, mostly unemployed since the war and Revolution, joined the Communist Party to write sketches and participate in the Blue Blouse movement. By 1927, more than five thousand Blue Blouse troupes were active in the Soviet Union.

Inspiring some of the Blue Blouse innovations was the work of avant-garde artist Vsevolod Meyerhold. Meyerhold had journeyed from Naturalism to Symbolism and into Retrospectivism by 1907. From 1907 to 1917, Meyerhold had directed operas, plays, and entertainments at the Imperial Theatres in St. Petersburg, while also working under a pseudonym to stage more than twenty experimental pieces in little theatres, private apartments, and cabarets around the city. By 1917, he had also been teaching regularly and directing short films. Meyerhold welcomed the Revolution and led members from several factions of the Russian avant-garde into active collaboration with the Communists. While holding several leadership positions in the new government, Meyerhold also continued his theatrical experiments, which included a system of actor training known as biomechanics and the elaboration of Constructivism, the final avant-garde movement of his career.

Partly a synthesis of Retrospectivism and Futurism, Constructivism sought to energize audiences with actors and designs that demonstrated how human beings could use their bodies and machines to produce engaging art and a more productive life. Meyerhold collaborated with Lyubov Popova (1889–1924) on a Constructivist set for *The Magnificent Cuckold* (1922), for instance, that used platforms, ramps, slides, ladders, and three moving wheels to suggest a mill that had been transformed into a huge mechanical toy (Figure 11.4). As the actors performed, the wheels of the mill turned to complement their timing. In effect, the production fused the clowning of Retrospectivism with the mechanical rhythms of Futurism. During the 1920s, Meyerhold applied his presentational Constructivist style to several plays that advocated Communist propaganda, to Mayakovsky's grotesque Futurist dramas, and to a range of Russian classics. In one scene of his Constructivist production of Gogol's *The Inspector General* in 1926, 15 officials popped out of 15 doors around the stage to offer a bribe to the man they took for an inspector.

As these examples suggest, Meyerhold drew direct inspiration from filmic techniques. "Let us carry through the 'cinefication' of the theatre, let us equip the theatre with all the technical refinements of the cinema," he wrote in 1930 (Meyerhold 1969: 254). His work also influenced the great Russian film director Sergei Eisenstein (1898–1948), best known for his *Battleship Potemkin* (1925) and *Ivan the Terrible* (1944). Eisenstein, a student of Meyerhold's, claimed that he learned the filmic technique of montage from Meyerhold's inventive sequencing of stage actions for his productions.

Increasingly out of favor with Joseph Stalin (who ruled the Soviet Union from 1924 until his death in 1953) and tethered by the dictates of socialist realism, an official policy that required artists to celebrate the victories of the Communist state in a mode of heroic realism,

Figure 11.4

Lyubov Popova's Constructivist set for Meyerhold's 1922 production of *The Magnanimous Cuckold*, by Fernand Crommelynck. The ramps and machinery provided a practical playground for biomechanical acting.

© Society for Cooperation in Russian and Soviet Studies, London.

Meyerhold lost his theatre in 1938. In retrospect, it is clear that Lenin, Stalin, and other Communist leaders needed Meyerhold and the Russian avant-garde in the early 1920s to stabilize their regime internally and to give it credibility and influence outside Russia, especially since the initial foreign policy of the Soviets was to foment international revolution. After the mid-1920s, however, when hopes for worldwide revolution had dimmed, Stalin and his bureaucrats began tightening the funding and freedoms of the avant-garde. They squeezed out and eventually executed Meyerhold and others who would not conform to the narrow political and aesthetic constraints of socialist realism. After Stalin's death in 1953 and the 1956 "thaw" in the Cold War, however, the ideas and images of Meyerhold's Constructivist theatre and his biomechanical training for actors began to emerge. They influenced theatrical practice throughout the world, especially in England, Germany, and Eastern Europe.

CASE STUDY: Lenin's Taylorism and Meyerhold's biomechanics

Bruce McConachie

History abounds in ironies. One of the more fascinating is the fact that the Russian Communists, soon after attaining power in the early 1920s, borrowed extensively from the ideas of Frederick W. Taylor (1856–1915). Taylor, the American originator of "scientific management," had helped to make U.S. capitalism more efficient and profitable. Although the Communists despised capitalism, they also realized that they had to adopt systematic management techniques as well as new technologies if they were to pull the Soviet Union out of its traditional Russian backwardness and into the twentieth century. Lenin had read essays about Taylorism, as Taylor's principles had come to be called, and he was impressed by Russian engineers who had studied some of Taylor's publications, including *The Principles of Scientific Management* (1911). A few Communist engineers had also witnessed the wonders of Henry Ford's assembly-line manufacturing and believed, as did many Americans and Russians, that Ford and similar modern industrialists had simply translated Taylor's "time-and-motion" principles into industrial practice.

Soon after the Revolution, Lenin spoke publicly about the transformational possibilities of Taylorism. His 1918 address, one of several that invoked Taylorism as a light for the future, encapsulated several of the prominent features of "scientific management" that Meyerhold would soon adopt to train his actors. "The Taylor system," said Lenin,

> is a combination of the subtle brutality of bourgeois exploitation and a number of its greatest scientific achievements in the field of analyzing mechanical motions during work. The elimination of superfluous and awkward motions, the working out of correct methods of work, the introduction of the best system of accounting and control, etc. The Soviet Republic must at all costs adopt all that is valuable in the achievements of science and technology in this field. . . . We must organize in Russia the study and teaching of the Taylor system and systematically try it out and adapt it to our purposes.
>
> (Hughes 1989: 256)

Lenin correctly understood that Taylor had observed and tested the physical motions of workers in factories to discover how they might streamline their tasks, that Taylor believed there was one best way to perform all factory jobs and all workers should conform to that ideal, and, finally, that a top-down approach – from knowledgeable managers to compliant workers – was the correct way to increase efficient production. Lenin surely knew that Taylorism had also encountered stiff resistance from U.S. workers, but he apparently believed that the benefits to be gained for all Soviet citizens outweighed the problem of the loss of worker control on the factory floor.

Soon after Lenin's early death in 1924, Joseph Stalin celebrated the synthesis of American Taylorism and Russian energy as the primary legacy of their fallen leader: "American efficiency is that indomitable force which neither knows nor recognizes obstacles . . . and without which serious constructive work is inconceivable. . . . The combination of the Russian Revolutionary sweep with American efficiency is the essence of Leninism" (Hughes 1989: 251). Needless to say, such proclamations were an embarrassment to both the Russians and the Americans during the Cold War a few decades later, when neither side wanted to admit that it had accepted or given aid to its enemy. Although other efficiency experts in the U.S. were already improving on Taylor's principles by 1924, Taylorism would help to transform industrial production in the Soviet Union during the 1920s and 1930s.

Under Meyerhold's leadership, Taylorism would also help to transform a significant segment of post-revolutionary theatre in the new Communist nation. Soon after the October Revolution of 1917, Meyerhold had been the first major theatre artist to meet with the Communists to discuss the future of theatre and culture in the new nation; in contrast, most of his colleagues at the Imperial Theatres were horrified by the Revolution. Meyerhold severed his links with those artists, managed to mount significant productions during the difficult days of 1918, and staged theatricals for the Red Army in the midst of civil war. By 1920, when the regime summoned him from St. Petersburg to Moscow, Meyerhold was one of the most accomplished and politically radical theatre artists in the new Soviet Union. He was also ready to reimagine and rebuild Russian theatre practice in accordance with the revolutionary ideas of Lenin.

Whether Meyerhold fully shared Lenin's faith in the revolutionary possibilities of Taylorism for training actors cannot be known. But it is clear that he took Lenin's advice to "adapt" much of Taylor's system when he began workshops for his company in 1921. In addition to the kinds of exercises Meyerhold had used before to train young actors, he required all of his performers to participate in a one-hour activity called **biomechanics**. Although the term was new, the notion that actors should seek to fuse the biology of their bodies with the motions of machinery was straight out of Taylorism. The term "biomechanics" also included a nod to the psychology of Ivan Pavlov, who had discovered that animals could be trained to behave in certain ways through positive conditioning. Introducing his ideas to the public in 1922, Meyerhold directly compared biomechanics to the "scientific" principles of Taylor. He also stated:

> In the past the actor has always conformed to the society for which his art was intended. In future, the actor must go even further in relating his technique to the industrial situation. For he will be working in a society where labor is no longer regarded as a curse, but as a joyful vital necessity. In these conditions of ideal labor, art clearly requires a new foundation. . . . Art should be based on scientific principles; the entire creative act should be a conscious process. The art of the actor consists in organizing his material; that is, in his capacity to utilize correctly his body's means of expression.
>
> (Braun 1995: 172–3)

By invoking conformity, industry, the joy of labor, a new foundation, scientific principles, and a correct way of movement, Meyerhold knew he was speaking a Taylorist discourse that would please the new Soviet intelligentsia.

Several of Meyerhold's workshop exercises practiced the Taylorism that he preached. Underlying Meyerhold's concept of an "acting cycle," for example, was Taylor's notion of a "working cycle." Following Taylor's language, Meyerhold instructed his actors to think in terms of three "invariable stages" (Braun 1995: 174) when they performed a task on stage – intention, realization, and reaction. Meyerhold developed what he called "études" to give his actors practice in working through a complete acting cycle. In his "Shooting a Bow" étude, for example, the actor pantomimes a series of rhythmic movements that suggest running toward a quarry, shooting an imaginary arrow, and celebrating the kill. The exercise involves a thorough workout of the pursuit of an "intention," the various muscular tensions involved in its "realization," and the release (or "reaction") the actor feels when the task is complete. Central to this kind of work is the actor's ability to manipulate him/herself as a physical object, the same kind of control that Taylor required of workers under his supervision (see Figure 11.5). The études, like several other of Meyerhold's physical exercises, trained actors in the efficient use of their bodies.

Figure 11.5

The "meat mincer" setting, designed by Varvara Stepanova, for Meyerhold's 1922 production of *The Death of Tarelkin*, by Alexander Kobylin. Stepanova referred to her set pieces as "acting instruments," designed to enable vigorous biomechanical performance.
© University of Bristol Theatre Collection.

On the other hand, Meyerhold gave his actors much more freedom than Taylor allowed his factory workers. As a teacher and director, Meyerhold sometimes gave direct orders to students and actors, but he preferred to encourage their own decision-making. Knowing they had to make hundreds of choices to put together a performance, he praised the brains of his students and actors as well as their bodies. Meyerhold also understood that an actor's movements invariably triggered emotional states within the performer. In contrast, Taylor had neglected the emotional side of physical labor, a problem that sometimes led him to misunderstand worker complaints.

As Meyerhold developed biomechanics during the 1920s, he devoted more attention to the complex dynamics linking physical activity to emotional stimulus and response. In 1934, when asked about his training under Meyerhold, Russian actor Igor Ilinsky (1901–1987) emphasized the comprehensive nature of biomechanics:

> People think that essentially biomechanical acting is rather like acrobatics. . . . But not many realize that the biomechanical system of acting, starting from a series of devices designed to develop the ability to control one's body within the stage space in the most advantageous way, leads on to the most complex questions of acting technique. . . . The emotional state of the actor, his temperament, his excitability, the emotional sympathy between the actor as artist and the imaginative processes of the character he is performing – all these are fundamental elements in the complex system of biomechanics.
>
> (Braun 1995: 176–7)

By 1930, Meyerhold had expanded biomechanics to include more freedom for his actors and a firmer link to their emotional lives on stage.

Biomechanics had also proven its practical applicability. One of Meyerhold's first successes with his biomechanically trained actors was *The Magnanimous Cuckold* (1922). In Fernand Crommelynck's (1886–1970) tragi-farce, a village miller, Bruno, is infatuated with his lovely young wife, Stella, but so doubtful of his own sexual appeal that he believes Stella must have a lover. So he forces her to sleep with every man in the village to discover who the lover is. Maria Babanova (1900–1983), a small, energetic actor, played Stella as a series of related character types. According to one eyewitness report,

> [Babanova's] performance is based on rhythms, precise and economical like a construction .... The role develops, strengthens, matures without restraint – violently, yet according to plan. One moment, she is talking innocently to a little bird, the next she is a grown-up woman, delighting in the return of her husband; in her passion and devotions, she is tortured by his jealousy. And now she is being attacked by a mob of blue-clad men, furiously fending them off with a hurricane of resounding blows.
>
> (Braun 1995: 182)

Although this report is not precisely worded, it is clear that Babanova moved quickly among several character types, dropping one to embody another, often without transition. Igor Ilinsky, quoted above on biomechanics, also deployed several types to depict Bruno. He even undercut his most prominent characterization of the miller with clowning. As a fellow actor stated,

> Bruno ... stood before the audience, his face pale and motionless, and with unvarying intonation, a monotonous declamatory style, and identical sweeping gestures he uttered his grandiloquent monologues. But at the same time this Bruno was being ridiculed by the actor performing acrobatic stunts at the most impassioned moments of his speeches, belching, and comically rolling his eyes whilst enduring the most dramatic anguish.
>
> (Braun 1995: 183–4)

By all reports, the workers who enjoyed *The Magnanimous Cuckold* often burst into raucous laughter. Avoiding psychological characterization, Meyerhold's use of biomechanics with his actors helped them to induce a more direct and contagious response from his audience.

By training his actors to physicalize social types for the stage through biomechanics, Meyerhold wanted to call attention to the kinds of physical and social transformations necessary to build the new Soviet Union. From his other writings, it is clear that Meyerhold conceived of spectators as similar to a group of filmgoers whose physical responses to his productions would help to transform the new nation. For Meyerhold, these were not Hollywood consumers, as movie audiences would later become, but self-conscious viewers aware, like him, of the construction of a film and its potential meanings. Rather than creating an illusion on the stage, Meyerhold sought to invent a kind of carnival in the entire auditorium, and he often had his actors breaking the illusion of the fourth wall or even running through the playhouse to engage spectators directly. During the 1920s, Meyerhold believed that his theatre could help to move Russia toward a communist utopia by providing new social models trained and energized with physical efficiency. Ironically, he drew on the work of an American capitalist to do it.

Key references

Banta, M. (1993) *Narrative Productions in the Age of Taylor, Veblen, and Ford*, Chicago: University of Chicago Press.

Braun, E. (1995) *Meyerhold: A Revolution in Theatre*, Iowa City, IA: University of Iowa Press.

Hughes, T. (1989) *American Genesis: A Century of Invention and Technological Enthusiasm, 1870–1970*, New York: Viking.

Leach, R. (1989) *Vsevolod Meyerhold*, Cambridge: Cambridge University Press.

Meyerhold, V. (1969) *Meyerhold on Theatre*, trans. and ed. E. Braun, New York: Hill and Wang.

Revolutionary theatres West and East

As we have seen, the Russian Revolution transformed aspects of German Expressionism. The failure of postwar revolutionaries in Germany to establish a communist state, however, led to the rapid decline of theatrical Expressionism and to a counter-reaction. In the mid-1920s, German socialists began experimenting with more dispassionate means of inducing audiences to alter their society. When in 1927 a Russian Blue Blouse company visited Germany, German troupes had been performing the Russian-inspired revues for several years. At Berlin's Volksbühne (People's Theatre), director Erwin Piscator (1893–1966) expanded on the techniques of the Blue Blouse troupes to teach straightforward lessons about socialism that emphasized that the working class could exercise power. Piscator used situations of class conflict, film clips of historical scenes, and a panoply of on-stage technological devices to create presentational history lessons in socialism. Piscator termed his plays documentary "montages," in recognition of his debt to the artistry of film.

Dramatist and director Bertolt Brecht (1898–1956) also worked in film as well as the theatre. Influenced by his experience as a medical orderly in the Great War and by the failure of Expressionist utopianism in Germany, Brecht gained commercial success with his cynical *The Threepenny Opera* in 1927 and then turned his back on bourgeois theatre to embrace communist politics in 1928. Convinced that German communists needed to discipline themselves for the long fight against capitalism, Brecht wrote a series of presentational "learning plays" in the early 1930s before fleeing the rise of Nazi power in 1933. In exile in Scandinavia and the United States until 1947, Brecht expanded his vision of what he called his "epic theatre" to tell historical and allegorical tales that encouraged spectators to look at the present world of capitalism and **fascism** from the point of view of a future communist utopia. Aware firsthand of the persuasive charisma of politicians, the dangerous emotions of nationalism, and the callous manipulations of the economically powerful, Brecht sought to educate, entertain, and empower his audiences. Several of the plays he wrote while in exile – which often mixed representational scenes with presentational performance modes – have been celebrated as masterpieces of the twentieth-century stage, including *The Life of Galileo*, *Mother Courage and Her Children*, *The Good Person of Setzuan*, and *The Caucasian Chalk Circle* (all four written 1937–1945; first produced 1941–1948).

In addition to playwriting, Brecht's epic theatre forged several innovations in production and performance. To prepare his spectators to accept his Marxist understanding of the economic circumstances of the twentieth century, Brecht generally wanted them to view the actions of his main characters as odd and unusual. Brecht interrupted the story of *The Good Person of Setzuan*, for example, with songs and poetry to encourage his audience to perceive the strange circumstances of Shen Te, the good prostitute of the title, who is forced to invent an evil male cousin (Shui Ta) to save her from the consequences of her desire to love others and share her wealth. As the play points out in several ways, acts of goodness under capitalism can only lead good people into economic ruin. Brecht called his technique *Verfremdungseffekt* [fehr-FREHM-dungs-eh-fehkt], a term he coined to indicate his interest in arousing audience curiosity about his characters and their situations for the purpose of revolutionary change. Sometimes mistranslated as "alienation effect," *Verfremdungseffekt* is better understood as the effect of making something on stage "strange" or "distant," so that it arouses audience interest and curiosity. Brecht meant the term to stand as the German translation of a Russian word used by the aesthetician Victor Shklovsky to describe the Russian director's similar interest in making stage events "strange" to spark audience interest.

In addition to using music and poetry to comment on character actions in his plots, Brecht usually deployed metatheatricality (explored in Chapter 5) to keep his spectators aware of the inherent doubleness of all actor/characters on his stage. In *Good Person*, for instance, the audience always knows that Shen Te and Shui Ta are the same person, even though that insight is not available to the other characters in the drama. Brecht also instructed his actors to emphasize the social position rather than the inner psychology of their characters, so that spectators could better understand how economic circumstances shaped their actions. In keeping with this idea, he asked his actors to underline the difficult kinds of social and economic choices their characters must make, which he understood as a part of the actors' *gestus* [GHE-stoos], a term which refers both to the individual gestures made by an actor and to the general movement of all of the actors on stage that embody social attitudes and relationships. At one point in *Good Person*, Shen Te must decide whether to marry for love or to transform herself into her businessman cousin so that he can call off the wedding. Brecht has the actor playing Shen Te use gestures to weigh both possibilities; she finally adopts the mask of Shui Ta, the businessman, who abruptly cancels the wedding to avoid economic calamity. In his comments about how to stage *Good Person* and other of his plays, Brecht urged directors to pay close attention to the groupings of his actor/characters so that the audience could read the economic relations among them from the stage picture. Overall, Brecht sought to induce his audiences to respond rationally rather than emotionally to productions of his plays. Our second case study at the end of this section examines Brecht's understanding of empathy and emotions.

Other radical theatres flourished in France in the wake of the Russian Revolution. Russian Blue Blouse troupes traveled to France in the 1920s and helped to turn Surrealism, the last major European avant-garde movement of the interwar years, toward communism. André Breton (1896–1966) and other Parisians had been experimenting with "automatic writing," in the belief that chance, spontaneity, and the unconscious might lead a writer into a dreamlike state in which he or she could discover the source of aesthetic truth. For a short time, a group of French Dadaists returning from Zurich joined Breton and his circle, but in 1924 Breton issued a manifesto proclaiming his allegiance to "Surrealism," which isolated the Dada anarchists from the psychoanalytic aims of Breton's followers. Breton took the new name from Guillaume Apollinaire (1880–1918), who had subtitled his fanciful 1903 play, *The Breasts of Tiresias*, a "*drame surrealiste.*" Although the 1924 manifesto was heavily indebted to Freud and mostly apolitical, Breton's next manifesto in 1929 embraced communism. Suspicious of theatre and eager to make

Surrealism more militant, Breton denounced many former colleagues after this manifesto, including all of those who wished to use Surrealism on stage. Breton had appointed Antonin Artaud (1896–1949) his first director of research for Surrealism in 1924, but then kicked him out of his coterie two years later. In response, Artaud and others staged Surrealistic productions in a space they named the Théâtre Alfred Jarry. (Artaud had swallowed the myth of *Ubu* and hoped to outrage bourgeois spectators.) He wrote manifestos and struggled to start new theatres until psychiatrists institutionalized him for insanity in 1937.

Despite his mental problems, Artaud's manifestos, published in 1938 as *The Theatre and Its Double*, gained substantial influence among other theatre avant-gardists after his death in 1949. Writing in the tradition of Rousseau, who believed that civilization had corrupted humankind, Artaud argued for a theatre that would return modern humans to primitive mysteries through their bodies. He urged theatre artists to reject the dramatic masterpieces of the Western tradition – in fact, to throw out all text-based theatre – and embrace performances involving music, dance, and spectacle. Artaud conjured what he called a Theatre of Cruelty, a kind of production that could unite actors and audiences in a collective purgation of their rational restraints and individual freedoms. Critics have noted similarities between his Theatre of Cruelty and the fascist rallies that were occurring in France and the rest of Europe in the 1930s. Although *The Theatre and Its Double* had little influence on theatrical practice during Artaud's life, avant-garde theatre artists unfamiliar with Artaud's attraction to fascism would be inspired by his visions in the 1960s and 1970s, as we will see in Chapter 13.

Breton broke with Artaud over the theatre, but he embraced the revolutionary potential of film for Surrealism. Indeed, Surrealists Salvador Dali (1904–1989) and Luis Buñuel (1900–1983) had already made *Un chien andalou* (*An Andalusian Dog*) in 1928, on the eve of Breton's second manifesto. One unforgettable sequence early in this influential film juxtaposes the apparent slicing of a human eyeball by a razor together with the similar "slicing" of an image of a round moon by a cloud passing in front of it. Breton and his followers believed that such dream-like filmic experiences could help them to accomplish their psychoanalytic and social goals. By the mid-1930s, several French Surrealists were working again in the theatre as well as film. Socialist Jean Cocteau (1892–1963), for example, directed seven feature films in addition to his copious work as a playwright and director for the stage.

Socialism and communism gained many theatrical adherents among English-speaking artists and spectators as well. In Great Britain, Canada, Australia, and the U.S., amateur workers' theatre groups performed Blue Blouse-like revues in union halls and at factory strikes. Called agit-prop plays – short for agitation and propaganda – these short pieces generally involved stereotypical characters and a chorus of workers in class-conflict situations. Relying on bold gestures, mass chants, evocative tableaux, and emblematic props and costuming, agit-prop performances helped workers to organize politically and motivated their economic demands. Amateur agit-prop theatre proliferated during the early years of the Great Depression.

In addition to amateur theatre, international communism influenced many left-wing theatre artists and groups after 1920. In Ireland, Sean O'Casey (1880–1964) wrote socialist plays for production at the Abbey Theatre. His Dublin trilogy, *The Shadow of a Gunman, Juno and the Paycock*, and *The Plough and the Stars* (1923–1926), presents incidents in the Irish fight for independence from the anti-heroic view of people living in the Dublin slums. Even in the U.S., there were a few socialist plays, such as John Howard Lawson's (1895–1977) *Processional* (1925) and *Internationale* (1928), which departed from the generally conservative politics of the

Figure 11.6

Image from *Triple-A Plowed Under*, a 1936 "living newspaper" production by the U.S. Federal Theatre Project about the Agricultural Adjustment Act.

From Mordecai Gorelik, *New Theatres for Old,* (tenth printing, Samuel French, 1952).

country in the 1920s. Socialist hopes also shaped some of the many productions of the Federal Theatre Project (FTP) in the United States. Under President Franklin Delano Roosevelt's New Deal, the government organized and funded the FTP in 1935 to create jobs for out-of-work theatre professionals during the Depression. FTP "living newspapers," which derived from the Blue Blouse form and dramatized such social and economic problems as housing, agriculture, and electrical power through large-cast shows, were among the organization's most distinctive productions (Figure 11.6). However, the U.S. Congress, fearing the influence of communism in the nation, shut down the FTP in 1939.

Revolutionary theatres emerged in those Latin American countries that would allow them following the Mexican Revolution. Several leftist theatres and avant-garde groups began performing in Mexico City after the Constitution of 1917. Enthusiastic Mexican revolutionaries mounted huge outdoor performances, primarily colorful pantomimes with music, to celebrate the nation's Aztec roots and its new independence from U.S. and European imperialism. Mexicans modeled some of their later performances on *The Storming of the Winter Palace*, the dramatic re-creation of a crucial episode during the Russian Revolution enacted by nearly a thousand workers in St. Petersburg in 1920 to celebrate the triumph of the people. Many other festivals, however, fused Mexican festive traditions with leftist politics. Influenced by Piscator's work in Germany, Mexican dramatist Juan Bustillo Oro's (1904–1989) *Masses* put the audience in the midst of political rallies and strikes with film clips and loudspeakers to tell the story of a corrupt revolutionary leader's fall from power. In Argentina, different groups of theatre artists debated the merits of European-inspired political theatre in journal articles and stage productions during the 1930s. One theatre collective in Buenos Aires, the People's Theatre, produced and toured a range of productions to diverse audiences and engaged them in often heated post-performance discussions. Their most renowned dramatist was Roberto Arlt (1900–1942), whose 1930s plays critiqued contemporary fascism, brought to Argentina by Italian expatriates loyal to Benito Mussolini, the dictator of Italy during the decade.

Marxist *shingeki* (Western-style) dramas were also written in Japan. One of the best was *The Land of Volcanic Ash* (1938), by Kubo Sakae (1900–1958), also an important translator of German drama. In Kubo's celebrated play, an agricultural scientist tries to reclaim land polluted by volcanic ash on the island of Hokkaido. The six-hour, two-part play portrays the difficult lives of many social groups in this rural environment and also features the hero's inner conflict over his growing commitment to communism. Due to the play's Marxism and Kubo's communist beliefs, the Japanese government prohibited production of the play and sentenced Kubo to house arrest or jail for much of the war. Until its defeat in 1945, imperial Japan closed Marxist *shingeki* theatres, censored all theatrical productions, and even turned performances of traditional *nō* plays to patriotic purposes. Some leftist theatre artists such as the director Seki Sano (1905–1966), who had studied with Meyerhold, were forced into exile. Sano left Japan in 1930, eventually settling in Mexico in 1939, where he had a profound influence on a generation of Mexican theatre artists.

CASE STUDY: Brecht and the science of empathy

Bruce McConachie

> Bad as it may sound, I have to admit that I cannot get along as an artist without the use of one or two sciences.
>
> (Brecht 1964: 73)

The ideas of Bertolt Brecht continue to guide theatre artists and critics today, especially those committed to politically progressive theatre. Brecht read widely in many sciences, including psychology, during the 1920s and 1930s and believed that he was creating a theatre that could intervene to shape a more just society based on scientific Marxism. After Brecht's death in 1956, however, new psychological sciences emerged to study cognition and emotion, and some of their findings undermine the assumptions upon which Brecht based parts of his early theories. In particular, recent insights into empathy contradict the conclusions that Brecht reached before 1940 about audience response in the theatre.

If Brecht were alive today, would he turn his back on recent science because it undermined his old ideas about empathy? Or would he embrace the insights from cognitive psychology and use them to advance the goals of his revolutionary theatre? This case study is based on the assumption that Brecht would take the latter path. Science – indeed, Brecht's entire body of theatrical theory – was primarily a means to an end for him. After he turned to Marxism in the late 1920s, Brecht believed that the plays and essays he was writing could help to create a socialist utopia in Germany. Had Brecht carried his ideas about science and politics into the twenty-first century, there is little doubt that he would have used the best science available about empathy to move his spectators toward a Marxist revolution.

Brecht inherited his ideas about empathy, called *Einfühlung* [AHYN-few-lungk] in German, from the nineteenth-century German Romantics. The Romantics used the word and its cognates to mean the ability of individuals to project themselves into the soul of another person or into nature. They were trying to understand how a poet might temporarily merge his identity with a famous classical hero or how a painter could come to feel what it is like to be a blasted tree on a mountaintop. From the Romantics' perspective, this notion of identification and mystical merging involved conscious projection and the temporary loss of the self in another person or object. Philosophers of aesthetics continued to use the concept of *Einfühlung* in this way, while other Germans in the early twentieth century applied it more broadly to mean losing yourself in any reality outside of the self. As late as 1909, there was no English word for the German term. Although E.B. Tichener first translated *Einfühlung* as "empathy" in that year, the English meanings of "empathy" have never been stable.

Following the Great War, Brecht began writing, directing, and occasionally performing in Berlin during the height of postwar German Expressionism. From Brecht's point of view, Expressionist actors too easily lost themselves in the characters they performed and German audiences were immersing themselves in stories that allowed them to forget about social and economic realities. Although Brecht agreed with the radical political goals of some of the artists, he came to see Expressionism as *Einfühlung* run amok. After embracing Marxism, Brecht rejected Romantic identification and mystification for what he understood as Marxist science. From 1928 until 1933, when he left Germany following Hitler's election, Brecht sought to build his theatre on the basis of rational, rather than empathetic response. He feared that empathy would cause spectators to lose themselves in the point of view of the dramatic characters they were watching. Assuming a dualism between reasoned response and empathy, Brecht argued that *Einfühlung* "wears down the capacity for action" in the audience (Brecht 1964: 37). Also, under the spell of empathy, said Brecht, "nobody will learn any lessons" (26) about politics and the economy. Believing that the German Romantic understanding of *Einfühlung* was correct, Brecht assumed that spectators had the ability to choose or reject empathy as a mode of spectatorship and that they would turn away from *Einfühlung* if induced to enjoy performances in other ways.

Scientific approaches to empathy

If empathy were what Brecht believed it to be, his strategies to counter empathetic identification might have been effective. No current definition of empathy in **cognitive science**, however, assumes that audiences can control their responses in the way that Brecht proposed. Nor do most recent definitions of empathy suggest that it involves the loss of the self and its mystical merging with some other person or object. This is not to say that psychologists agree on a definition of the term, however. In a 2009 survey of contemporary

continued

understandings of empathy, C. Daniel Batson found eight related but distinct uses of the term. Some psychologists, recognizing the fraught history of "*Einfühlung*" and "empathy," have decided to abandon both words for a term that carries a more specific meaning. Most cognitive scientists, however, continue to use "empathy" to indicate, as Batson says, how one person tries to "know what another person is thinking and feeling" (Batson 2009: 3). Batson is clear that empathy is not the same as sympathy. Although empathy is often used in casual conversation as a synonym for sympathy ("I empathize with your pain"), most scientists distinguish between the two. From their point of view, empathy is a cognitive operation, not an emotion, that provides a means of "reading the minds" of other people. Emotional responses such as guilt, happiness, embarrassment, and sympathy may result from empathetic "mind reading," but it is important to keep the two distinct.

Citing several empirical studies, biologist Evan Thompson distinguishes among four different levels of empathy, the first two of which are foundational for audience response in the theatre. The first level, termed "sensorimotor coupling" (Thompson 2007: 393–5), is based on the recent discovery of mirror neuron systems in monkeys and humans. In brief, groups of neurons in the brain are equipped to "mirror" intentional motor activity produced by other humans. When one person watches another grasp a can of soda, for instance, the same group of neurons is activated in the observer as if the observer had grabbed the soda for him or herself. In this way, we can begin to know "intuitively" what that other person is experiencing. In a good theatrical production, too, spectators probably "mirror" the same groups of neurons and muscles as some of the actors, although this response has yet to be tested. For this reason, Vittorio Gallese, one of the first to investigate mirror neuron systems in monkeys, and his co-workers have identified the mirror system as "the basis of social cognition" (Gallese et al. 2004: 1–8). This makes sensorimotor coupling, Thompson's lowest level of empathy, the physiological basis for the other levels above it.

"The second type of empathy is the imaginary transposition of oneself to the other's place," states Thompson (2007: 395). This is akin to "putting yourself in another person's shoes." Imaginary transposition builds on sensorimotor coupling; using their memories of "resonating" with others, humans can recall what it was like to experience others' motoric responses. Then, through imagination, people can attempt to see the world through another's eyes, even when that other person is not present. Thompson emphasizes that this form of empathy can range from simple emotional agitation in the presence of another to a rich understanding of that other person's situation. Imaginary transposition, which develops in children at about nine to twelve months of age, requires more active and higher-level cognition than sensorimotor coupling. At both levels, however, empathy is natural, spontaneous, commonplace, and mostly unconscious. This does not mean, of course, that empathy always produces correct assumptions; people misunderstand the thoughts and feelings of others all the time. In the controlled situation of a play performance, however, the author, actors, and other theatre artists have usually tried to make the intentions and emotions of the characters and their situations transparent enough to allow spectators' attempts at imaginary transposition to work most of the time. Although empathy is not an emotion in itself, sensorimotor coupling and imaginary transposition often call forth various emotional responses.

None of the science about empathy was available to Brecht when he began working against the lures of *Einfühlung* for his spectators in the 1920s. Concerned that audiences might lose themselves in the actor/characters they were enjoying on stage, Brecht typically peopled his early plays with grotesque characters with whom spectator identification was difficult. The premiere of Brecht's *Baal* in Leipzig in 1923, for instance, created a scandal by confronting the audience with a poetic protagonist consumed by a voracious appetite for liquor and women and a disgust with normal social conventions – the intentional opposite of the idealistic poet type depicted in many Expressionist plays. *The Threepenny Opera* (1928), Brecht's most popular production in the 1920s, effectively dared spectators to identify with his main character, nicknamed Mack the Knife, a bank robber and murderer. The success of this cynical masterpiece with Berlin theatregoers, however, also convinced Brecht that simply placing grotesque characters in decadent situations was not enough to inhibit audience identification; too many spectators enjoyed the vicarious pleasures of putting themselves into the roles of pimps, gangsters, and prostitutes to attach much significance to the political critique that *Threepenny* also intended.

After his turn to Marxism, Brecht found additional ways of keeping his spectators distanced from his primary characters and their situations. Several of his "learning plays" of the early 1930s, for example, challenged spectators with metatheatricality and multiple casting in an attempt to induce them to grapple with his Marxist parables. In *The Measures Taken* (1930), for example, two dramatic stories intersect throughout – a present narrative involving the report of four Communist agitators to a Chorus of judges in Moscow and a past story acted out by the four agitators. The agitators use role-playing to demonstrate to the judges their reasons for killing a fifth agitator who accompanied them, a Young Comrade who bungled their attempt to incite revolution in China. Unfortunately, from the point of view of the four agitators and the judges, the Young Comrade showed too much sympathy for the Chinese peasants and this emotion got him involved in situations that endangered their overall mission in China. Through this use of metatheatricality, Brecht sharpened his attack on colonialism and heightened his call for Communist Party discipline. Through multiple casting and the creation of collective roles (the agitators and the Chorus of judges), *The Measures Taken* also invited the audience to watch each actor in several different roles, another way of inhibiting spectator identification with a specific actor/character. At the conclusion of the play, the Chorus of judges decides that the four agitators were right to kill the Young Comrade; the "measures taken" were necessary for the larger goal of communist revolution in China.

Another technique Brecht used in several plays to diffuse *Einfühlung* and spectator identification was to split his major characters in two. We have already discussed the Shen Te/Shui Ta split in *The Good Person of Setzuan*. In *The Causasian Chalk Circle*, as well, Brecht depicts Azdak, the judge who must make the most important decision of the play, as a liar and drunkard and also as an upstanding and moral citizen. Brecht reasoned that spectators would have difficulty identifying with someone who is so full of contradictions.

As he does in most of his other late plays, Brecht frequently breaks the conventions of realistic illusion to exploit presentational possibilities in *Good Person*. Narrators speak directly to the audience, a functional setting avoids realism to present only what is necessary for the action, and songs sung by individuals and groups of actors generalize the lessons of a particular scene. Brecht took ideas for staging his Marxist parables from several sources, including the Constructivism of Meyerhold, the presentational clowning of Charlie Chaplin, Piscator's socialist documentary theatre, and the efficient acting of Mei Lanfang, a Chinese actor he had applauded in Moscow in 1935. From the 1930s to his work at the Berliner Ensemble in the 1950s, Brecht employed direct address to the audience, documentary film footage, songs to put across a political point, agit-prop choric speaking, projections of statistical material, knock-about clowning, and simple political placards, as well as short realistic scenes to advance his plots. Instead of fusing these and other elements into an organic whole, in the mode of stage realism or musical comedy, Brecht separated these elements, so that each could be understood and appreciated for itself without the force of the whole dramatic illusion immersing the audience in an emotional bath. The sheer variety of these staging techniques and types of theatrical involvement invited spectators to connect many kinds of insights and construct larger meanings for themselves.

As a frequent director of his own plays, Brecht also worked to clarify his political intentions through arresting stage pictures and strong emotional reversals for his spectators. In the first scene of his play *Mother Courage and Her Children*, as he directed it in Berlin in 1949, Brecht kept the four actors playing the mother and her three adult children in a tight circle center

Figure 11.7

Helene Weigel singing as Mother Courage in the first scene of Brecht's staging of *Mother Courage and Her Children* in Berlin, 1949. From the Willy Seager Archive.

From the Willy Saweger Archive. © The Deutsches Theatermuseum, Munich.

stage near the wagon they had been pulling, as two army recruiters circled them, trying to lure one of the sons into joining the army (see Figure 11.7). Brecht set *Mother Courage* in the midst of the Thirty Years War (1618–1648) in Germany, partly as a means of providing some historical distance for his postwar Berlin audience as they struggled to come to terms with what they had done under Nazism. By selling supplies from her wagon to the troops on both sides of the Thirty Years' War, Mother Courage profits from the killing. To expose this contradiction, Brecht blocked the actors to show how capitalism and warfare could divide a family and lead to its eventual ruin. In his staging, one of the actor/recruiters moved actor/Mother Courage around to one side of the wagon to bargain with her over a belt buckle while the other actor/recruiter lured her strong son, actor/Eilif, away from the rest of the family to offer him a bonus for joining the army. At the end of the scene, Courage has sold a belt buckle, but the once tight-knit family has been divided and one of her sons has left (and is eventually killed). While Mother Courage haggles, the war takes her children – a motif that would be repeated several times during the play, until she is left with no children at all.

While in exile from Nazi Germany, Brecht began to modify his ideas about *Einfühlung*. Although he still believed that empathy could get in the way of learning, he also recognized that some strategic uses of *Einfühlung* might be useful in sparking sympathy as a means of advancing spectator understanding. And he wrote several scenes in his major, post-1937 plays that invited spectators to temporarily identify themselves with the situation of one of his

Figure 11.8
Katrin, Mother Courage's daughter, beats her drum to warn the townspeople in Scene 11 of the 1949 production of Brecht's *Mother Courage*.
© The Deutsches Theatermuseum, Munich.

characters. Mother Courage's loss of her third child, Katrin, involves such identification and is also placed at the emotional climax of the play. To warn the townspeople and save their children from an imminent, pre-dawn attack, Katrin climbs on to the roof of a peasant's house near the town and begins beating a drum (Figure 11.8). The attacking soldiers, who cannot reach her (she pulls the ladder up after her), try to bribe her to stop the noise. They even begin destroying her mother's supply wagon, left in Katrin's care, but she continues drumming to alert the town. Finally, the soldiers bring on a large musket, set it up on its forked holder, and shoot her. As Katrin is dying on the roof, the sound of cannon and alarm bells from the town indicate that she has succeeded and the children of the town will survive.

Brecht's use of rhythm and spatiality made this a powerful scene for his Berlin audience in the 1949 production. Actor/Katrin's intermittent, but progressively louder and longer drumming provided the scene's empathetic key for spectators, much as extended drumming in a musical concert will tend to draw most spectators into the drummer's rhythm. In Thompson's terms, the drumming established "sensorimotor coupling" between actor/Katrin's muscles and the muscles of the spectators, allowing them to resonate with her movements. Her drumming also encouraged spectators to involve themselves in Thompson's "imaginary transposition," temporarily putting themselves "in her shoes" so that they, too, could imagine themselves saving children through their heroic action. Brecht did not write about this scene in terms of evoking empathy, but in retrospect we can see that empathy led spectators to sympathy for Katrin.

The impact of the scene provided an emotional climax for spectators at the 1949 production of Brecht's anti-war, anti-capitalist play. In fact, according to contemporary reviewers and reports, the Berlin spectators were emotionally shattered by their experience of *Mother Courage*. There was audible sobbing throughout most performances and long, appreciative cheering at the curtain calls. Brecht's wife, Helene Weigel, performed the title role with grit and determination, but seemed utterly exhausted at the end, when, after burying her daughter, she was forced to pull her battered, near-empty wagon by herself to catch up with some departing troops in the hope of making a sale. (To make herself look even more gaunt and hollow-cheeked for the last scene, Weigel removed her false teeth.) The success of *Mother Courage* with the Berlin audience in 1949 led to the founding of the Berliner Ensemble under the leadership of Brecht and Weigel – a company that soon emerged as a leader in postwar European theatre.

Brecht understood that the emotional involvement of the audience had ensured the success of the production and even helped in the creation of the Ensemble. When asked about the drum scene in *Mother Courage*, he said, "Spectators are permitted to identify with Katrin in this scene. They may identify with this being and note with pleasure that they have such powers even within themselves" (Fuegi 1987: 125). In this statement, Brecht recognized that spectators often delight in imaginary transposition, even though he did not call it empathy. But the statement also indicates that Brecht, like most others at midcentury, continued to credit the German Romantic view of *Einfühlung* as good science. Engaging in empathy is not a matter of "permission," allowed by the self or by some other person, because empathy is not fully controlled by the will. At the level of sensorimotor coupling, empathy is almost entirely involuntary. And even imaginary transposition, which involves some initial choice, relies on a combination of emotion and reason. From a contemporary scientific perspective, Brecht's strict division between emotion and reason – a misperception he shared with most of the Western world in the middle of the last century – undermined his ability to alter his understanding of empathy.

On the other hand, Brecht's plays indicate that he had a clear, intuitive sense of the importance of what some scientists today would call empathetic identification. The plays invite audiences to resonate with what his actor/characters are doing on stage and many of them involve spectators in complex negotiations with regard to character identification. Most audience members, for example, will put themselves in the shoes of Mother Courage many times and this will lead them, alternately, to admire her in some scenes and despise her in others. And that spectator response, which tracks when Courage acts either as a mother or as a capitalist, fits very well with Brecht's political intentions for the play. Brecht was certainly right to worry that the German Romantic sense of *Einfühlung* would compromise his political goals. But if that notion of empathy is incorrect, we need to look again at the plays and productions to measure them by a different yardstick for empathy. Ironically, as the 1949 production of *Mother Courage* suggests, spectator sensorimotor coupling and imaginary transposition probably enabled rather than inhibited Brecht's Marxist goals throughout his career.

Key references

Batson, D. (2009) "These Things Called Empathy: Eight Related but Distinct Phenomena," in J. Decety and W. Ickes (eds) *The Social Neuroscience of Empathy*, Cambridge, MA: MIT Press, 3–16.

Brecht, B. (1964) *Brecht on Theatre: The Development of an Aesthetic*, ed. and trans. J. Willet, New York: Hill and Wang, 26–9, 33–42.

Brecht, B. (1972) *Mother Courage and Her Children*, in R. Manheim and J. Willett (eds) *Bertolt Brecht: Collected Plays*, vol 5, New York: Random House.

Fuegi, J. (1987) *Bertolt Brecht: Chaos, According to Plan*, Cambridge: Cambridge University Press.

Gallese, V. et al. (2004) "A Unifying View of the Basis of Social Cognition," *Trends in Cognitive Sciences* 8: 1–8.

Thompson, E. (2007) *Mind in Life: Biology, Phenomenology, and the Sciences of Mind*, Cambridge, MA: Harvard University Press.

Theatres of anti-imperialism, 1910–1950

In addition to its influence in the West, the Russian Revolution also speeded revolts against imperial domination. By 1914, the imperial powers – chiefly England, France, the Netherlands, Germany, the United States, and Japan – had occupied crucial islands in the Caribbean and Pacific, solidified their control in most of South Asia, extracted sizeable chunks from the Ottoman and Chinese empires, and carved up nearly all of Africa. Although rebellions against foreign capitalists had occurred before 1914, nationalistic movements in India, China, and elsewhere gained more leverage against the imperial powers during and shortly after the Great War, when the combatants in Europe needed their help. The war in Europe, however, emboldened Japanese imperialists, who saw the decline of European power in China and the Pacific as a chance to expand their hegemony. The triumph of the Communists in Russia inspired nationalists in the colonized countries, in part because they too identified imperialism with capitalism. If workers in one country had destroyed capitalism, nationalists might destroy imperialism in their own.

Many educated colonials also worked against imperialism after 1914 because they saw widening differences in standards of living, democratic rights, and literacy between the populations of their own countries and those in Japan and the West. In per capita income alone, the developed countries surpassed the rest by 2:1 in 1880. By 1914, the ratio was 3:1 and it rose to 5:1 by 1950. While most Westerners enjoyed some individual and political rights, slavery and various forms of serfdom persisted in many parts of the colonial world. Literacy increased rapidly among both sexes and all classes after 1850 in Europe, Japan, and North America, but remained a privilege of the social and economic elite in most areas of Africa, Asia, and Latin America. Although the imperial powers generally believed they were civilizing and improving their subjects, the realities of empire bred Orientalism, racism, exploitation, and degradation.

Revolution against the imperialists had begun in China in 1911 and continued through the 1920s. As noted, Sun Yat-sen's Nationalist Party fought to unify the nation. Sun's politics, like those of many anti-imperialists, mixed liberalism and socialism, but emphasized nationalism above both. For a few years during the 1920s, the Nationalists collaborated with Russian-based Communists to purge China of foreign imperialists, an alliance that was revived in 1937 when China refused further Japanese demands and declared war on Japan. The defeat of Japan in the Second World War finally ended a century of foreign domination. The Chinese Communists, who won the civil war against the Nationalists in 1949, benefited throughout this period from the perceived alliance between communism and anti-imperialism.

The development of Chinese theatre between 1914 and 1950 followed the political fortunes of the country. As in Japan, Western realist theatre had been introduced before the Great War and began to flourish in the 1920s with the founding of modern theatres, an increase in translations and performances of Western plays, the establishment of new training centers for actors, and the eventual casting of women in female roles. As noted in Chapter 9, *jingju* (Beijing Opera), however, remained the dominant genre throughout China. Several Communist troupes emerged in the 1930s to protest Japanese imperialism; their "living newspapers," modeled on the Soviet example, appealed to thousands in the countryside and in cities unoccupied by the Japanese. Following China's declaration of war in 1937, Chinese Nationalists and Communists used theatre to rally patriotic support against the Japanese.

Within Communist-controlled areas of the country, Chinese artists developed a new form of theatre called *yanggeju* [yahng guh ju] based on the fusion of folk songs, local theatre and *yangge*, traditional Spring Festival celebrations. Featuring 20 to 30 dancers accompanied by drums, flute, and other instruments, *yanggeju* formed part of the basis for the emergence of a new national drama called *geju* [guh ju], or song drama. *Geju* was designed as the Chinese equivalent of Western opera, based on Chinese music, folk songs and musical elements from traditional theatre. Originally developed in the 1920s, it flourished after the Communist victory in 1949. *Geju* typically involved disputes among villagers over abusive social practices and village ethics, performed in a question-and-response pattern. Hugely popular, *The White-Haired Girl* (1945) is considered a milestone, inspiring later *geju* glorifying communist heroism. By the 1960s, other types of state-sponsored performances featured thousands of professional and amateur performers and integrated the music and dance traditions of several minority groups within China. The performances both embodied and propagated the ideology of strength through collective effort put forward by Mao Zedong (1893–1976), the revolutionary leader and political dictator of China until 1976. More than a thousand performers staged *The East Is Red* in 1964, for example, a nationally famous spectacle.

In India, the introduction of Western-style, spoken drama had spawned two closely related theatrical movements in the nineteenth century. The first type was social drama, which criticized the inequalities of India's traditional socio-economic system and argued for liberal reform. By the late 1800s, some British and Indian writers were attacking traditions that relegated most Indians to low caste status, kept many peasants working in compulsory positions on huge landed estates, and trapped numerous young women in arranged marriages. Reformers in southern India began mounting protest plays in 1929 with the production of *From the Kitchen to the Stage*, by V.T. Bhattathiripad (1896–1982), which opposed polygamy and the marriage of high-caste old men to young girls. A later play, *Rental Arrears*, focused on the eviction of a tenant farmer from the land and its effects on his family. Some social dramas drew thousands of spectators in open-air, rural theatres during the 1930s and 1940s. Though aimed primarily at social and economic arrangements, these plays occasionally attacked the Raj (as British imperial rule in India was termed) for supporting traditional customs.

In contrast, anti-colonial drama directly resisted English culture and British authority. An 1872 production of *Indigo Mirror* (*Nil Darpan*), by Kolkata playwright Dinabendhu Mitra (1830–1873) began this movement; the play focused on the plight of peasant workers oppressed by British indigo planters. The British banned a later anti-imperialist play, *Sirajuddaula* by

Bengali playwright Girish Chandra Ghosh (1844–1912), in 1905 for inciting Indian nationalism. Anti-colonialism intensified in India after the Great War and the Russian Revolution and reached a peak during the Second World War. In 1943, the Communist Party of India founded the Indian People's Theatre Association (IPTA), which established regional centers throughout the country to produce anti-colonial plays. Perhaps its best-known production was Bijon Bhattacharya's (1917–1978) *New Harvest* in 1944, which incited anger against British failures to help the starving during a Bengali famine that killed more than three million people. The IPTA fragmented in 1947 following India and Pakistan's independence from Britain.

Internationally, the most famous playwright and theatre artist to emerge in India in the 1910–1950 period was Rabindranath Tagore (1861–1941). Tagore was acclaimed for his lyrical plays, mystical poetry, paintings, and songs and for his insightful short stories and essays on subjects ranging from educational reform to nationalism, which he denounced in favor of universal humanism. Tagore's poetry and prose won him the Nobel Prize in Literature in 1913; he was the first non-European so awarded. Although Tagore denounced the British Raj, he was best known as a social and educational reformer in Bengal, in northeastern India. Several of his many plays, including *Sacrifice* (1890) and *The Post Office* (1912), achieved Indian and international success. In *Sacrifice*, Tagore used historical events to pit a devout Maharaja against a fanatical head priest in order to denounce cruel and superstitious rites. The more mystical *Post Office* focuses on a sick boy who falls asleep (and probably dies), according to Tagore, to gain spiritual release from "the world of hoarded wealth and certified creeds" (Tagore 1961: 123–4). Contemporary Indian theatre artists continue to venerate Tagore for his imaginative fusion of traditional forms and modern ideas.

Theatrical modernism

In addition to animating Western and international political opposition to capitalism and imperialism, the cultural fragmentations caused by the Great War and the movies led other theatre artists to search for principles of cohesion and transcendence. Most critics and historians begin their definitions of theatrical modernism by noting that this twentieth-century orientation to the arts emphasized the vision of the dramatist as the primary carrier of meaning in the theatre. Modernism was not a movement, in the sense that avant-garde artists consciously organized themselves into exclusive groups, published manifestos, and adhered to a specific style. Indeed, modernist playwrights and others generally worked within the conventional arrangements of the commercial theatre. Perhaps the primary difference between the modernists and most avant-gardists was their interest in crafting productions that could provide an alternative to the excesses of the modern world. Instead of trying to alter or to create a utopian alternative to the status quo, the modernists looked to new modes of aesthetic order that could help people to transcend the fragmentation and chaos of modernity.

In their drive to constitute a formal aesthetic sphere, separate from commerce, politics, and other areas of practical life, the modernists revived the aesthetic ideas of Immanuel Kant. This Enlightenment philosopher had distinguished aesthetic experience and judgment from the realms of science and morality. Kant limited aesthetics to bodily feeling and further rarified it by insisting that feeling was subjective and private, with no connection to conceptual thought. With Kant, the modernists insisted that the activities of producing and responding to a work of art had to be understood on their own autonomous terms; like the avant-garde Aestheticists, the modernists believed in "art for art's sake." In judging art, including theatrical productions, the modernists instructed critics to look for those aspects in the work itself that gave it meaning and aesthetic unity. From this formalist point of view, questions about a production's relations to its audience or to its social context were mostly irrelevant. Politically, modernism was a conservative retreat from the challenges of twentieth-century revolutions.

Like the Symbolists and Aestheticists before them, the modernists aimed to induce readers and listeners to climb into their imaginations, but they did not adhere to the representational goals of those earlier avant-garde artists. That is, they did not want spectators to interpret the sounds and images on stage as depicting objective, subjective, or spiritual truth. The theatrical modernists relied on two major techniques to separate the imaginations of their spectators from the mundane realities of the stage: focus audience attention on voice and language and transport them to a unified aesthetic world. First, they resorted to metatheatricality, which (as discussed in Chapter 5) typically frames the fiction of the theatrical illusion within another fiction to create a play-within-a-play. By calling attention to the artificiality of the stage, metatheatricality interrupts the flow of a performance and temporarily undercuts its representational effects. Spectators frequently reminded of the fictive nature of a play cannot immerse themselves in a Wagnerian *Gesamtkunstwerk* or any other representational performance. Second, the modernists tried to get spectators to separate the actors' bodies from their characters' words. More interested in their written dialogue than in the usual fusion of actor and character in a theatrical representation, modernists attempted to minimize the physical presence of actors on the stage and to reduce the actors to their voices. Like metatheatricality, this attempt temporarily undermined representational believability and also troubled conventional modes of spectator identification with actors as characters.

Yeats, Pirandello, and the modernist legacy

Although the plays of Ibsen, Chekhov, and other realists are sometimes included in discussions of modernism, most early modernists rejected the photographic surfaces of realism to focus on transcendent values communicated primarily through language. Further, many modernist playwrights looked as much to publishing as to performance for the success of their writing. William Butler Yeats (1865–1939) mostly wrote poetry, Luigi Pirandello (1867–1936) turned to drama after a career as an Italian novelist and short-story writer, Paul Claudel (1868–1955) and Thornton Wilder (1897–1975) published in a variety of genres, and T.S. Eliot (1888–1965) made his primary reputation as a poet and critic. While these authors hoped that their plays would be staged and enjoyed by spectators, they also celebrated their encounter with the reading public. Modernists relied on the continuing prestige and power of print to shape their theatre. To a significant degree, they wanted to attract audiences in the theatre who would respond to their plays like readers.

To emphasize his imagistic poetry, Irish writer and theatre manager William Butler Yeats tried to alter the actor's embodiment of a character, the basis of theatrical representation. As a young man, Yeats saw several Symbolist productions at the Théâtre de l'Oeuvre and returned to Dublin convinced that Ireland needed a poetic stage. Intrigued by Craig's interest in substituting marionettes for actors, Yeats experimented with some of the actors at the Abbey Theatre to see if he could minimize their physical expressiveness and turn them into mouthpieces for his words. He wrote that actors "must not draw attention to themselves at wrong moments, for poetry and indeed all picturesque writing is perpetually making little pictures which draw the attention away for a second or two from the player" (Puchner 2002: 129). Yeats realized, in other words, that the physical presence of the actor would interfere with the "little pictures" that he hoped his poetry would spark in the heads of his audience members. Although his experiments to turn spectators into readers were initially unsuccessful, Yeats bragged that he had "been the advocate of poetry against the actor" and vowed to keep trying (2002: 129).

Yeats had more success with a Westernized version of Japanese *nō* drama (discussed in Chapter 2). In 1915, the poet Ezra Pound introduced Yeats to Itō Michio (1892–1961), a dancer from Japan who had studied eurhythmics and performed dances in a style that combined European and Japanese traditions. Yeats had been reading translations of some Asian plays, including Tagore's *The Post Office* and several *nō* dramas, and was eager to adopt *nō* as a partial model for his poetic theatre. With two other Japanese performers, Itō introduced an already Europeanized version of *nō* dancing to Yeats. Yeats revised the script of *At the Hawk's Well* (1914–1916) for Itō, who choreographed and performed a major role in the production in 1916. As described in Chapter 2, *nō* uses musical accompaniment behind a chorus of voices, sometimes speaking the words of the main character, to tell a story, while other performers dance the action. Likewise, *At the Hawk's Well* separates much of the spoken narrative from the embodied action. A chorus of three "musicians," as Yeats calls them, frames the entire performance by introducing the characters, narrating the action, and occasionally adding their own commentary. In addition, they set the scene by appealing to the imagination of each spectator. Instead of looking at actual scenery on the stage, the audience is encouraged by the narrator-musicians to envision "A well long choked up and dry / And boughs long stripped by the wind" in their imaginations (Yeats 1952: 399). Even after the actors enter playing specific characters, Yeats's musicians comment on their actions, effectively reducing them to marionettes who must pantomime exactly what the musicians report. Yeats wrote several more plays based, like *Hawk's Well*, on a mythic Irish past and evocative language. He recognized that his poetic theatre would never be popular, but hoped to inspire a coterie audience with his poetic visions.

Luigi Pirandello did not directly attack the representational link between actors and characters, but rather subverted the believability of the conventional theatre through metatheatricality. Although he had written a few plays during 20 years of publishing poetry, novels, and short stories, Pirandello turned more frequently to drama during the Great War, when Italy (though on the winning side) began to slide toward social and political disorder. The postwar period added wrenching economic problems and, like many Italians, Pirandello sought order in the midst of this apparent chaos. He found it in the philosophies of Hegel and Kant that he had studied as a student in Germany and that had anchored much of his previous writing. Pirandello believed that the ideal forms of art championed by Kant and others were more enduring and ennobling than the paltry, ever-changing lives of modern people. Attempting to dramatize this conflict between the reality of art and the illusory qualities of lived experience, Pirandello soon crystalized this insight in the play that would make him famous, *Six Characters in Search of an Author* (1921). Despite a scandalous opening, *Six Characters* succeeded in Milan in 1922, then Paris, and eventually throughout the world.

Six Characters contrasts the lives of actors – Pirandello's symbols of people with no firm identity – with those of fictitious characters whose identity has been written for them. Apparently abandoned by their author, however, the six characters cannot escape from their melodramatic conflicts, and they seek a resolution to their ongoing drama from the actors. The result is a play within a play, as the actors put aside the production they have been rehearsing and attempt to enact the roles and relationships of the six characters before them. By showing how the actors utterly fail to embody and perform the reality of these characters, Pirandello critiques the general failure of the stage to represent ideal reality. A larger point, though, is that authors writing literature can approach the enduring truths of idealized character types, but the attempt at truth on the stage will always be compromised by the imperfect and mortal bodies of the performers. Only an author can help the six characters, implies Pirandello; the stage will always fail them. To emphasize the unchanging truths of art, Pirandello instructed the actors playing the six characters to wear masks. Although the play seems to throw up its hands about the nature of truth and illusion, Pirandello does not endorse relativism; art is true and life is illusory.

Pirandello's search for order through art led him to explore the themes and techniques of *Six Characters* in several subsequent plays. These included *Naked* (1922), *Each in His Own Way* (1924), *Tonight We Improvise* (1930), and *Henry IV* (1922), in which Pirandello worked through the problem of time and art, touched on in *Six Characters*, through the situation of a man pretending to be insane. These plays, too, relied on metatheatricality to interrupt and undermine theatrical representation, challenging spectators to question their own illusions. Perhaps hoping that Mussolini could bring some of the order of art to the chaos of Italian life, Pirandello joined the Fascist Party in 1924 and remained a Fascist until his death in 1936.

Whereas Pirandello relied on German philosophy and Yeats invoked the pagan myths of an Irish past in their attempts to gain relief from the fragmentations of the modern world, other modernists turned to Christianity, the traditional road to transcendence in the West and another arena for Kantian aesthetics. Like Pirandello and Yeats, the Christian modernists looked back to the spirituality of the Symbolists and, before them, to nineteenth-century Romanticism. French diplomat, poet, and playwright Paul Claudel celebrated the mysteries and saving grace of Catholicism and the Catholic Church in several plays over a long career. His most famous work, *The Satin Slipper*, a seven-hour epic written between 1919 and 1924, is set in the Spanish Golden Age. In formal, elevated language, Claudel's stately pageant explores the religious fervor that drove the Spanish conquest of the New World and the need to sacrifice earthly passions for the sake of divine salvation. *The Satin Slipper* received an influential production at the Comédie Française in 1943, which led to a Claudel revival in the postwar period.

Although U.S. novelist and dramatist Thornton Wilder was less insistently religious than Claudel, his faith in a benign American Protestant God is evident in many of his plays. In *Our Town* (1938), a folksy, God-like Stage Manager calls forth actors who demonstrate that people are destined to repeat universal patterns designed by "the mind of God" without knowing that they are doing so. *Our Town* illustrated Wilder's belief that the theatre was uniquely suited, as he said, "to raise the exhibited individual action into the realm of idea and type and universal" (Bigsby 1982: 262).

T.S. Eliot generally attempted to bridge poetic and realist theatre, with mixed results. A convert to Catholicism, Eliot wrote *Murder in the Cathedral* (1935) in verse to engage his spectators in the experience of Thomas Becket's martyrdom in medieval Britain. Eliot relies on a chorus of women in the ritual-like tragedy to lead his audience toward an understanding of the design of God and return them to Catholic faith. Most of Eliot's later plays, such as *The Cocktail Party* (1949) and *The Confidential Clerk* (1953), continue to use verse to reach for Catholic and sometimes Buddhist universality, often by contrasting the shadow world of contemporary society with the spiritual substructure that informs what he took to be its true reality.

Many of Japan's theatre artists had embraced Western concepts such as Christianity and Hegelian idealism, and some became modernists. One of the most significant was Kishida Kunio (1890–1954), a member of the Tsukiji Little Theatre who studied in France with Jacques Copeau in 1921 and 1922. Like many European modernists, Kishida attempted to evoke humanistic idealism through his plays. Their apparent lack of political content protected Kishida during the Second World War, when more outspoken (often Marxist) playwrights, actors, and directors who criticized the militarist government were jailed. Kishida insisted that the playwright is the primary theatre artist, whereas traditional Japanese performance modes celebrated the actor and his movement, speech, and costuming. In contrast to the stylized, non-realistic (and sometimes incomprehensible) vocal delivery of *nō* or *kabuki*, Kishida insisted, "The theatre must depend on the words of the play. Surely the theatre will come to demonstrate the essential importance, not of 'plays for the eye,' but of 'plays for the ear.' A playwright, more than anything else, must now be a 'poet'" (Rimer 1974: 137–8).

Theatricalizing modernism

Many directors and designers also looked to the authority and language of dramatists as the basis of theatrical meaning and stability in a fractured world. Before 1910, a few scholars and artists in England had advocated a return to Elizabethan playing conventions for Shakespeare's plays, but Herbert Beerbohm Tree's (1852–1917) style of pictorial realism for the Bard held the commercial stage. Near the turn of the century, scholar-director William Poel (1852–1934) produced Shakespeare on an Elizabethan-like stage (placed behind a regular proscenium, however) and effected the continuous playing that Shakespeare had intended without the long pauses for the scene changes that were typical of the period. In a few productions before 1914, H. Granville Barker (1877–1946), who directed many of Shaw's plays, used suggestive scenic pieces, draped curtains, and metaphorical props and costumes to keep the Shakespearean action moving in performances that emphasized simplicity and poetry. Most critics scoffed at Poel and Barker, but their ideas undergirded many later reforms.

After the Great War, pictorial Shakespeare seemed cumbersome and unbelievable, mostly because of the movies. A succession of directors at London's "Old Vic" Theatre incorporated several modernist innovations that moved Shakespearean performance away from the clutter of realism. Chief among them was Tyrone Guthrie (1900–1971), artistic director of the Old Vic from 1937 to 1945. Guthrie deployed Appia-like settings of ramps and platforms, mostly realist props and costumes, rapid movement and speech by the actors, and quick lighting changes to lend Shakespearean production the speedier rhythms and heightened contrasts of the cinema (Figure 11.9).

Working with modernist directors, actors John Gielgud (1904–2000), Sybil Thorndike (1882–1976), Laurence Olivier (1907–1989), and others developed energetic playing styles that emphasized the psychology of their characters rather than their realist situations. Olivier's success in filming several Shakespearean plays – notably his *Henry V* (1944) and *Richard III* (1955) – confirmed the popularity of a more cinematic acting style for Shakespeare on the stage. For spectators attuned to the perceived effects of the movies, Guthrie's and Olivier's modernist staging and acting rejuvenated Shakespearean production in the 1930s and 1940s. Like other

Figure 11.9

The Old Vic production of Shakespeare's *The Tempest*, 1934, with Charles Laughton as Prospero and Elsa Lanchester as Ariel.

© V&A Images, Victoria and Albert Museum.

artists committed to the tenets of modernism, Guthrie and the others believed they were scraping away realist encrustations on the plays to reveal transcendent, Kantian truths embedded in the language. For these modernists, Shakespeare, rightly staged, could elevate spectators to appreciate and enjoy universal meanings.

The fragmentations of the modern world also troubled many theatrical modernists in France. In the 1930s and 1940s, several directors and playwrights drew on their heritage of Racinean tragedy and the comedy of Molière to fashion a distinctive theatre of lyric abstraction, which emphasized the lyricism of the French language in often minimalist and allegorical settings. Even before then, the work of Jacques Copeau (1879–1949) turned the French stage toward modernism. Like the Shakespearean modernists, Copeau, a critic turned producer-director, eliminated realist details to emphasize the work of his actors in the French classics. At his small theatre, the Vieux-Colombier, Copeau produced several plays before 1914 with minimal realism for audiences of only 400 people (Figure 11.10). He resumed productions at the Vieux-Colombier for a short time after the war and later directed at the Comédie Française, the prestigious national theatre, from 1936 until 1940. Copeau and his successors enlivened the character types and generalized themes of the French classics with a fresh, lyrical energy. He applied this style to Shakespearean productions and modern plays as well. Directors who modeled their artistry on Copeau's – a group that included Louis Jouvet (1887–1951) and Charles Dullin (1885–1949) – emphasized adherence to the language and rhythms of the script

Figure 11.10

Stage of the Vieux-Colombier, designed by Jacques Copeau, as adapted for Shakespeare's
Twelfth Night.

Redrawn from *Theatre Arts Magazine*, 1924.

and strove to invest their stylized costumes and minimalist scenery with symbolic significance.
After the Second World War, two of Dullin's students, directors Jean-Louis Barrault (1910–
1994) and Jean Vilar (1912–1971), continued to refine and extend this tradition.

French playwrights influenced by lyric abstraction tended to write allegories in which the
general problems of humanity predominated over historical or psychological concerns. The
first major playwright to work in this style was Jean Giraudoux (1882–1944), who collaborated
closely with Jouvet to stage his plays. These included *The Trojan War Shall Not Take Place* (1935)
and *The Madwoman of Chaillot* (1945), an amusing attack on the excesses of French capitalism.
Similarly, Jean Anouilh (1910–1987) wrote light comedies with fairy-tale-like resolutions,
such as *Thieves' Carnival* (1938), and dark allegories, the most famous of which was *Antigone*,
composed in 1943 during the German occupation of France. Anouilh's *Waltz of the Toreadors*
(1952) provides a ready example of the lyric abstraction that demonstrates its faith in universal
truths and its ties to French modernism. Like Molière, Anouilh uses the structure of farce to
explore a serious theme – the depredations of time on romantic love in the case of *Waltz*. The
play's chief representative of foolish old age is a French general still in love with a mistress who
returns, after many years, to discover that she would rather fall in love with the general's young
male secretary. The general is upset, but finally resigns himself to the triumph of fiery passion
over cooling embers. Emblematic characters, a universal theme, an appeal to an imagined past,
intimate staging, and an action that verges on allegory helped to mark this confection as a
product of modernism.

SUMMARY

The revolutionary decades between 1910 and 1950 spawned immense political and theatrical changes. The Great War and the Russian, Chinese, and Mexican revolutions shattered the old order and generated demands for radical political changes that played out in the theatres of Meyerhold, Brecht, and other revolutionary theatre artists and reshaped the theatres of many European and American countries, as well as generating anti-imperialist theatres in India and China. Filmic fragmentation – the recognition that the movies could take apart and reassemble reality in innumerable ways – ensured that most practitioners of the new political theatre would not return to the kinds of representational theatre offered by the realists, Naturalists, and Symbolists of the past. Instead, these radical artists forthrightly acknowledged the theatrical basis of their presentational work. Even the modernists, who rejected the political radicalism of the revolutionary artists in an attempt to return to Kantian universals, had lost faith in representational realism, primarily because it mandated the fusion of actors and characters, leaving little room for an author's voice. Nonetheless, as we will see in the next chapter, the comforts of bourgeois realism on the stage enjoyed a resurgence after the Second World War.

★

CHAPTER 12

The aftermath of the Second World War: Realism and its discontents in an increasingly shrinking world, 1940–1970

Carol Fisher Sorgenfrei
Contributor: Bruce McConachie

As we saw in Chapters 10 and 11, the shock of the Great War and the widespread use of radio and film deeply affected society and theatre. In this and the following chapter, we will consider similarly profound responses to the Second World War.

The origins of the Second World War lay in the end of the Great War. Germany had been forced to accept concessions and blame. In response, the fascist Nazi Party formed, attaining power in 1933; it then strived to dominate Europe. Meanwhile, Japan sought control over Asia, and its invasion of Manchuria (China) in 1937 foreshadowed the war. The League of Nations (a predecessor of the United Nations) lacked the force to counter these aggressions. Germany's 1939 invasion of Poland instigated the Second World War in Europe. Japan's attack on Pearl Harbor (Hawaii) in December, 1941 forced the United States to join the conflict.

Only 21 years separated the 1918 Armistice ending the Great War and the outbreak of the Second World War. Between them lay the worldwide Great Depression. Often soldiers who had fought and survived the Great War as 20-year olds were called back into service in their 40s – sometimes along with their own sons. By 1945, when the Second World War was ended by atomic bombs that devastated the Japanese cities of Hiroshima and Nagasaki, they had spent much of their lives in battle; civilians had suffered decades of destruction and deprivation; and around 11 million people had been murdered by the Nazis. Refugees from the war-ravaged lands sought new lives, but many could understand neither the language nor the culture of their newly adopted homes. In much of Europe, Asia, the Pacific, and Africa – where the brutal battles of the Second World War had been fought – cities were wrecked and food remained scarce. Rebuilding ruined lives and ruined cities was costly, time-consuming, and emotionally difficult. All these survivors (soldiers and civilians, the victors and the defeated) desired a world of calm.

Because the United States had escaped such physical devastation, it emerged from the war far richer than the rest of the world. This fact, combined with the desire to solidify its military and political position as the main opponent of communism, meant that the U.S. became the central purveyor of money and goods for rebuilding the postwar world.

With the end of the Second World War, hostility between two superpowers – the United States and the Soviet Union, former allies who had been victorious over the Nazis – hardened into an ideological struggle between "free market" capitalism and authoritarian communism. This conflict, which lasted over 40 years, was named the Cold War because it never broke out into direct combat: nuclear warfare would lead to mutually assured destruction. But other nations were pressured to align themselves with Russia or the U.S.; although a few like India remained neutral, most succumbed through military might, economic power, coups, and/or diplomatic leverage. China's rise as a major world power widened the scope of the Cold War. All three superpowers engaged in various "proxy wars," injecting their influence and sometimes their troops into regional and civil conflicts in countries such as Korea and Vietnam. By the 1960s, most politicians and much of the population of the superpowers viewed all international and even domestic conflicts – whether nationalist, anti-imperialist, ethnic, racial, or even gender-based – through the "us-versus-them" lens of the Cold War.

Nevertheless, anti-imperialist sentiment and nationalist political action (often including violent revolutions) grew in the colonized areas. As colonies became independent countries, the old empires began to crumble. Although decolonization had been encouraged by the League of Nations following the Great War, little actually took place until after the Second World War. When the Great War began in 1914, there were more than 120 colonized territories in the world; in contrast, by 2013, the United Nations listed only 17 non-self-governing territories. Africa exemplifies these rapid changes. As noted in Chapter 9, the Berlin Conference of 1894–1895 had divided Africa into numerous European colonies. By 1905, the only non-colonized areas in Africa were Liberia (founded by former African-American slaves) and Ethiopia (which had successfully resisted Italian colonization). By the start of the Second World War, a total of only five African nations were independent. However, between 1951 and 1960, 25 African nations gained independence. From 1961–1980, they were joined by 26 more, with another three following by 1993.

But conflict seemed both ubiquitous and unending. Not only were many decolonizing nations embroiled in rebellion and war as they fought for independence, but after winning independence, internal fighting for political power often ensued. As each proxy war was fought, another seemed always around the corner. The threat of nuclear annihilation loomed over battle. Thus, the end of the Second World War saw initial relief at international peace gradually shift to concerns over ongoing warfare throughout the world.

Conflict also grew within the industrialized world. With their common enemy, the Nazis, defeated, the victorious countries began to question their own value systems. Economic growth nourished desires for greater democracy, which were blocked by the conservative values of anti-communism. Although the focal point varied from country to country, around the world there were mounting efforts to achieve political, legal, social, cultural, and even economic equality.

During the 1950s, television became affordable for many. However, it brought not only entertainment into people's living rooms, but also news of distressing world events, many of them the direct result of Cold War politics. In the mid-1960s, students, minorities, and others throughout the world rebelled against the status quo, demanding an end to war, poverty, racism, sexism, colonialism, and authoritarian university policies. The dramatic changes and upheavals across the world led to a global crisis often marked by the year 1968.

This chapter is divided into three parts. We first consider the devastating impact of the Second World War on Europe and Japan, noting how a new postwar understanding of reality altered theatrical styles. We then turn to theatre during the Cold War. The World War had produced sharp differences between the U.S. and the rest of the world. The U.S. was relatively unscathed and became obsessed with communism and the Cold War. Most other countries, in contrast, were either still deeply disturbed by the meaning of the war or were attempting to extract themselves from imperialist power. As a result, theatre in the U.S. differed from theatre elsewhere. During this time, film and radio continued to influence approaches to theatre and drama. Finally, we take a first look at the alternative theatres that developed in the U.S. just before the turning point of 1968, as the anger simmering over the previous two decades, international awareness of social and political injustice, and anti-colonial movements created by the growing power of television, set the stage for the momentous transformations of the next era. Thus, this chapter traverses the tension between realism and its intensifying discontents.

The impact of the Second World War on the victors and the defeated

In Europe and Asia, where the war had devastated many cities and created massive civilian suffering, theatre artists turned increasingly to new philosophical or political systems in order to make sense of the world. For many, neither prewar modernism, revolutionary theatre, nor the old avant-gardes seemed adequate to express contemporary reality. New approaches appeared, including variations of Brecht's political theatre, revisions of the surrealist ideas of Artaud, a revised modernism, and plays that have been (somewhat questionably) called "Theatre of the Absurd."

Beckett and the end of high modernism

One of the key theatrical and literary voices in the early postwar period was Samuel Beckett (1906–1989). Although born in Ireland, Beckett lived in Paris from 1922 to 1930, intermittently from 1931–1937, and permanently from 1937 to his death in 1989. He wrote many of his plays in French. He felt that using his second language forced him to constantly be aware of the precise meaning of every word. Beckett's stage plays kept film's insistent realism at bay by a poetic minimalism that tightly controlled what his actors could do and what his audience experienced as reality. At the same time, he experimented with film, radio, and tape recording.

Beckett's plays may be seen as transitional, because they contain aspects of both prewar modernism and the sense of futility and lack of meaning that characterized many postwar plays. They also have elements that were later adapted by postmodernism. However, Beckett's modernism differs from that of his predecessors. Modernists from Ibsen to Eliot had built their theatrical "castles in the air" on the premise that there was another reality, idealist or religious (or both), that transcended the modern, material world. Beckett's theatre, in contrast, was more in line with Chekhov's strand of modernism. Like Chekhov's characters, Beckett's figures can find no relief in a spiritual realm from the mundane tedium of their very material lives. How to pass the time, a problem for many of Chekhov's characters, becomes an obsession for many of Beckett's. Time is a fundamental concern in the action of two of Beckett's early plays, *Waiting for Godot* (1952) and *Endgame* (1957) (Figures 12.1 and 12.2).

Beckett's theatrical ideas and practices extend and complicate techniques typical of high modernism. For example, his use of metatheatricality differs from that of his predecessors. In

Figure 12.1

Samuel Beckett's *Waiting for Godot* in a 1970 revival directed by Roger Blin (seated), setting by Mathias. Company Renaud-Barrault at the Théâtre Récamier. Actors, left to right: Marc Eyraud (Estragon), Michel Robin (Lucky), Lucien Raimbourg (Vladimir), and Armand Meffre (Pozzo).

Photo: Roger Pic © Bibliotheque Nationale, Departement des ASP.

performance, Beckett's plays find subtle ways of insisting that they are constructed artifices, while avoiding Pirandello's sometimes cumbersome metatheatrical structures. In *Endgame*, for example, when one character asks another what keeps him "here," a reference to the room that the two characters occupy, the other answers, "The dialogue" (Beckett 1958: 58); "here" has changed from a represented place in the drama to suggest the stage on which the two actors perform. Beckett's theatrical minimalism and precisely crafted action rarely allow spectators to forget that they are in a theatre. In *Ohio Impromptu* (1981), Beckett places two men, dressed identically, sitting across from one another at a table with their heads bowed, in a precise mirror image of each other. There is nothing else on stage to suggest a theatrical illusion; the two are surrounded by darkness. They sit nearly motionless for the 15 minutes of the play, while one reads the "sad tale" of the other's life from a book. At the end, Beckett's stage directions specify that the two "[s]imultaneously . . . lower their right hands to table, raise their heads and look at each other. Unblinking. Expressionless. Ten seconds. Fade out" (Beckett 1984: 288). Beckett gives us no illusion to get lost in. This performance style – like that of *Breath* (1969), a stage play with no actors, no dialogue, and no visual action – is nearly as far from an enveloping Wagnerian *Gesamtkunstwerk* as the theatre can take its spectators. In terms of philosophy, Beckett's theatre is a clear statement of the disillusionment and sense of helplessness felt by many people in the postwar era. Beckett emphasizes the concrete "here" and offers no religious or spiritual alternatives to the apparent meaninglessness of existence.

Like earlier high modernists, Beckett attacked the mimetic basis of acting. He severely restricted the freedom that actors usually have to interpret and embody their characters. As Beckett director Alan Schneider once noted, "Actors feel like impersonal or even disembodied puppets of his [Beckett's] will" (Puchner 2002: 159), a remark that recalls Craig's and Yeats's interest in substituting large puppets for live actors. Beckett placed actors in barrels (*Endgame*), encased them up to their necks in dirt (*Happy Days*, 1961) and entombed them in urns (*Play*, 1963). This practice not only restricts the actors' movements, but visually expresses the idea of the futility of action. Sometimes he reduced the actors to mouthpieces for his words, as in *Not I* (1972), where all of the words spoken during the minimal action of the play emanate from a female character named Mouth. The actor playing Mouth must stand on a platform behind a painted black wall or curtain with a small hole in it and place her head against a padded frame behind the hole so that only her lips can be seen by spectators as she speaks. In rehearsing *Not I*, the actor Billie Whitelaw (1932–2014) reported extreme "sensory

Figure 12.2

Clov (Jean Martin) pushes Hamm (Roger Blin) in his chair in the Paris premiere production of Samuel Beckett's *Endgame (Fin de partie)* in 1957 at the Studio Champs-Élysées. Beckett preferred the simpler costumes and staging of this production to the one in London earlier in the same year.

Photograph by J.-P. Mathevet, in Deirdre Bair, *Samuel Beckett, a Biography* (New York and London: Harcourt Brace Jovanovich, 1978, pp. 370–1.

deprivation." She said, "The very first time I did it, I went to pieces. I felt I had no body; I could not relate to where I was; and, going at that speed [in speaking Beckett's monologue], I was becoming very dizzy and felt like an astronaut tumbling into space" (Worthen 1992: 138). Critic W.B. Worthen compares the rigors of Beckettian acting to physical torture. Beckett insisted that other directors follow his printed scripts precisely – including all stage directions – and he actually sued the American Repertory Theatre over their 1984 production of *Endgame* because he objected to casting women in male roles and to setting the action in a realistic underground train station that was being used as a shelter following a nuclear war, rather than the abstract time and place that the printed script specified. Beckett's position was that as long as he was alive, directors should respect his scripts' words and stage directions. This point is crystalized in *Act Without Words I* (1956) and *Act Without Words II* (1956), stage plays totally lacking dialogue. The scripts consist entirely of stage directions that the actors and technicians must follow as precisely as choreography for a ballet.

Such power over actors and directors corresponds to Beckett's worldview, in which unknowable forces and seemingly arbitrary events control our lives. In *Waiting for Godot*, for example, strangers come in the black of night, kicking and beating the two tramps for no reason; a character who once had sight is inexplicably struck blind; and day after day, Godot keeps sending word that he is delayed.

Beckett was also intrigued by new modes of communication. He realized that electric and electronic media could control what the audience – and the characters – experience. In *Krapp's Last Tape* (1958), Krapp listens to his recorded voice from the past, almost as though it is a stranger's voice lacking meaning, and repeatedly fast-forwards just before a major revelation that the audience never hears. Beckett wrote several plays for radio, including *All That Fall* (for the BBC, 1956) and *Nacht und Traume* (for German radio, 1982). Unlike theatre or film, radio plays deprive the audience of vision, forcing them to use imagination. In contrast, *Film* (1965) is a silent movie starring Buster Keaton. By eliminating the sense of hearing, the audience must focus on the visuals. He also wrote several works for television, including *Eh, Joe* (1965) and *Quad I+II* (1981).

THINKING THROUGH THEATRE HISTORIES

Existentialism and the so-called "Theatre of the Absurd"

Historians in every field frequently debate the validity and application of commonly used terminology and periodization. For example, the usefulness and specific meanings of terms such as "the Renaissance," "the modern period," "the Elizabethan age" or even "the Sixties" (as discussed in Chapter 13) are hotly contested. Many historians now use terms such as "the long eighteenth century" (1688–1815 or 1660–1830, in reference to Britain), the "long nineteenth century" (1789–1914) or "the short twentieth century" (1914–1991). Because change is a gradual process, some artists and thinkers are said to be "ahead of their time" or "behind the times." Similarly, geographic boundaries are porous and changeable. Is Samuel Beckett an Irish writer or a French one? What is the precise definition and where are the boundaries of "Asia?" Style and genre can also become overly generalized. For example, is Beckett's *Waiting for Godot* a comedy, a tragedy, or something else entirely? One of the historian's problems is how to use commonly accepted but often misunderstood or deceptive terms. "Absurdism" offers an example.

Absurdism is frequently associated with existentialist philosophy. Søren Kierkegaard (1813–1855) is usually said to be the first existentialist philosopher, but Jean-Paul Sartre (1905–1980) and Albert Camus (1913–1960) are often viewed as its main exponents, although Camus denied being an existentialist.

Existentialism came into its own during and after the devastation and horrors of the Second World War, and was in many ways a response to that war. According to this philosophy, "existence precedes essence." Each individual is responsible for her own actions. Her own consciousness dictates who she is – her choices define her concrete "existence." There is no eternal "essence" outside the individual – no identity based on concepts such as the soul, truth, beauty, God, politics, race, gender, and so on. To become oneself, one must act "authentically," that is, according to a deep understanding of one's personal needs and desires, not according to some outwardly imposed code (such as religious or civil law). However, authentic action is not simply self-interest. Rather, it demands that each person

continued

respects the existential needs and realities of others, implying a kind of innate or natural morality.

Sartre's philosophical treatises are often dense, but he also wrote plays that he hoped would make his philosophy accessible to ordinary people. For example, in *No Exit* (1944) he uses a realistic dramatic style and structure to demonstrate the terrifying results of living an inauthentic life. In this play, the dead confront neither God nor the devil, but instead must live eternally with others in whose eyes they are defined. In the play's most famous line, they realize that "Hell is other people."

Such ideas conflict with many traditional worldviews. For example, Plato and his followers insisted that only abstract ideas exist, and that what we see and experience are merely imperfect reflections of the true reality. Most religions and many political ideologies share such ideas, offering hope of a better future in which justice prevails, with the good being rewarded and the evil punished.

In contrast, existentialism suggests that the universe is random and lacks purpose, as demonstrated by the horrors of both the Great War and Second World War. Only human actions and how we interpret those actions define and create meaning. Consequently, the cruelties and injustices of life appear absurd. In this sense, "absurd" does not mean comical but simply incomprehensible, arbitrary, and meaningless.

Albert Camus, who was born to a poor family in French Algeria, passionately advocated Algerian independence and an end to poverty. Like Sartre and Beckett, he was active in the French Resistance (an underground movement in the Second World War that fought against the Nazi Occupation of France). His philosophical essay "The Myth of Sisyphus" (1942) is often cited as the first clear depiction of "Absurdism." In this essay, Camus compares modern life to the Greek myth of Sisyphus, who was condemned to push the same rock eternally up a hill, despite the fact that each time he almost reaches his goal, the rock rolls back to the bottom of the hill. Camus maintained that contemporary humans, lacking religion or some other eternal truth, strive vainly to find logic in an apparently illogical universe. Rather than reacting with despair and suicide, however, Camus suggests that humans must rebel against this meaningless absurdity; for him, passionate opposition to absurdity and the freedom to rebel against it create meaning, even though the rebellion is doomed to failure.

The term "**Theatre of the Absurd**" was created in 1961 by the Hungarian-British critic Martin Esslin (1918–2002), whose book of that title noted certain philosophical and stylistic similarities in diverse postwar plays. It is a good example of how a commonly used term can foster historical misunderstanding. One objection to the term "Theatre of the Absurd" is that, unlike avant-garde artists prior to the Second World War, these playwrights did not intentionally create a new genre and they were not part of a conscious movement. Rather, each artist, working independently (and often unaware of the others), happened to develop plays with shared characteristics. They were responding in the only way they could to an incomprehensible reality. As critic David Pattie notes, "[T]o say that Absurdist Theatre was a coherent movement with clearly defined aims and goals, was to simplify what was in

continued

practice a rather disparate collection of plays and playwrights, unified (apparently) only by a common rejection of the world run on rational principles" (Pattie 2000: 114).

Unlike existentialism, the so-called "Theatre of the Absurd" is generally unconcerned with individual choice and authenticity; however, it shares with existentialism a focus on the meaninglessness of action, the cruelty or arbitrariness of fate, and an emphasis on the here-and-now. Playwrights usually considered "Absurdist" include Samuel Beckett (generally considered to be the most significant writer), Eugène Ionesco (1909–1994), Harold Pinter (1930–2008; early works only), Sławomir Mrożek (1930–2013), Abe Kōbō (1924–1993; also known as Kōbō Abe – Abe is his family name), Edward Albee (1928–; early works only), and many others. In addition to meaninglessness, arbitrariness, and inaction, their plays are often characterized by apparently nonsensical dialogue coupled with black comedy or an uncanny feeling of menace.

Despite the fact that these playwrights never defined themselves as "Absurdists," and that some, such as Albee, actually refused the label, various critics and historians have found the concept useful. For example, in his influential *Shakespeare Our Contemporary* (1964), Jan Kott (1914–2001) read Shakespeare from the perspectives of existentialism, Absurdism, and his own experiences as a Pole in war-ravaged Europe. Others have suggested that, because the dialogue and action are so often illogical or dreamlike, "Absurdist" plays are descended from Surrealism. Still others dispute such ideas or make different connections.

The authors of this book acknowledge that the term "Theatre of the Absurd" is a widely used but highly problematic designation. Because students will inevitably come across the term (or may have already encountered it), we feel that it is important to clarify the debates surrounding it. Understanding that common concepts and terms may be misleading – and that meanings can change over time – helps us to be more precise in our usage, and to avoid generalizations that may lead to confusion.

Transforming modernism in Europe

Ever since the first generation of modernism, modernists in the theatre had struggled against the constraints of photographic realism. As a moving "picture," film continued photography's ties to the literal, material world. Because the high modernists had privileged the representational validity of print, they had also regarded film (but not, usually, the radio) with suspicion. But film had been transforming the expectations of theatre audiences and artists since the 1920s. Postwar theatre would employ filmic techniques to create several new models of modernist theatre in the West during the 1940–1970 era.

Many playwrights after the Second World War had grown up watching the movies, and this affected their perception of reality and how it might be enacted on stage. Luckily for these later dramatists, an earlier generation of directors and designers had also been experimenting with filmic ways of streamlining their national classics, primarily Shakespeare and Molière, to keep them popular on the stage.

One such director in England is Peter Hall (1930–). Although well known for directing Shakespeare, in 1955 Hall mounted the first English-language production of Beckett's *Waiting for Godot* at his Arts Theatre in London. Even after becoming artistic director of the new Royal Shakespeare Company (previously called the Shakespeare Memorial Theatre) in 1961, he continued to alternate contemporary and classical productions. By the mid-1960s, Hall had developed a distinctive style for all of his projects, a heightened realism that mixed close attention to the language of the play, a generally spare but distinctive use of design elements, and carefully crafted, often forceful movement. It was a modernist style that worked as well for the plays of Harold Pinter as for those of William Shakespeare.

At first Pinter's darkly comic plays mystified but intrigued the British public with their strange oppressors, panic-stricken artists (*The Birthday Party*, 1958), and garrulous drifters (*The Caretaker*, 1960). When Hall directed a Royal Shakespeare cast in Pinter's *The Homecoming* in 1965, some British theatregoers and critics were outraged by the dramatist's send-up of conventional family values, but the play ran for 18 months. Initial appearances of the characters to the contrary, *The Homecoming* gradually reveals a working-class family as a group of animalistic thugs and pimps and shows the home-comers of the title – a seemingly abstracted academic and his attractive middle-class wife from America – to be as heartless and bestial as the rest of the family (Figure 12.3). The success of the U.S. production in 1967 (with most of the same cast) confirmed the play as a modernist classic.

The rhythms of Pinter's dialogue, including its many pauses, reveal an ear attuned to the bleak comedy of Beckett's early plays and also show the influence of radio, for which Pinter had written several one-acts. Like many of his plays, *The Homecoming* explores the dynamics of dominance, exploitation, and victimization, themes that Pinter first dramatized in personal and psychological terms and which he would later treat in more directly political ways. In his Nobel Prize acceptance address in 2005, Pinter spoke of the compulsive but never-completed search for truth in the language of the drama, and he then criticized the U.S. for its calculated language of deception in foreign policy since the Second World War. With that language and those policies, said Pinter, the U.S. engendered brutal dictatorships and created justifications for brutal wars and torture, notably in the war in Iraq.

The Polish playwright Sławomir Mrożek began as a newspaper humorist and cartoonist. His early one-acts set up ironic models of political power and undercut them through their own logic. *The Police* (1958), for example, depicts a perfect but radically dysfunctional police state. In *Out at Sea* (1961), three starving characters on a raft establish a socialist republic, then proceed to define justice and freedom in such a way that two of them are able to eat the third, who agrees with the logic of his sacrifice. Mrożek fled

Figure 12.3

Peter Hall's production of Pinter's *The Homecoming* for the Royal Shakespeare Company which opened at the Aldwych Theatre in London, 1965. From left to right: Michael Bryant (Teddy), Terence Rigby (Joey), and Ian Holm (Lenny).

Photo © Zoë Dominic.

Poland in 1963, but continued to write plays that barely skirted censorship and delighted Polish audiences. Critics Martin Esslin and Jan Kott placed Mrożek in the tradition of Polish political Surrealist dramatists Stanislaw Ignacy Witkiewicz (1885–1939) and Witold Gombrowicz (1904–1969). Like Pinter and Beckett, Mrożek was introduced to London audiences by Peter Hall. Mrożek's most important play, *Tango* (1965), was produced by Hall's Royal Shakespeare Company in 1966 at the Aldwych Theatre in London. *Tango* is a black comedy that satirically deploys the tired form of domestic family comedy to examine the failure of ex-radicals to stop Europe's slide into totalitarianism. In Mrożek's parable family, each of the three generations represents a different political view, from the 1920s to the 1960s. Perhaps the most foolish are the grandparents, who prattle on in the language of the Dadaists and Surrealists while raw power takes over the household. The irony is that the victory of the idealistic but conservative Hamlet-like son over his bohemian family results in stifling totalitarianism. *Tango* was one of the first works directed by Trevor Nunn (1940–), who later served as artistic director of both the Royal Shakespeare Company (1968–1986) and the National Theatre (1996–2003) in the U.K., and as stage director of numerous plays, including international mega-musical hits such as *Cats* (1981) and *Les Misérables* (1985). The translation of *Tango* by Nicholas Bethell was further polished by the then-unknown playwright Tom Stoppard (1937–), who gained fame the following year with the National Theatre production of his *Rosencrantz and Guildenstern are Dead* (which, like *Tango*, eerily reflects and reconsiders *Hamlet*).

Other playwrights from this era – especially those from Eastern Europe – also wrote politically inflected works. For example, Eugène Ionesco's *Rhinoceros* (1959) depicts a society where all the citizens, except one man, blindly rush to transform into wild beasts. The memory of wartime horror was seldom far from the surface in major plays of this period.

Postwar theatre in a defeated Germany

The advent of Nazism in 1933 closed left-wing and avant-garde theatres in Germany, silencing or exiling many of Germany's best theatre artists. After the war, the defeated nation was divided into two. The DDR (Deutsche Demokratische Republik, also called the German Democratic Republic or East Germany) became a communist nation aligned with the Soviet Bloc, while the BRD (Bundesrepublik Deutschland, also called the Federal Republic of Germany or West Germany) was a capitalist nation aligned with Western Europe and the U.S. The former capital city, Berlin, which was fully within the borders of East Germany, was itself divided into East Berlin (a part of East Germany) and West Berlin (which, despite its location, was legally a part of West Germany). Germany would not be reunited until 1990. In East and West Germany after 1945, local governments quickly rebuilt their playhouses as a matter of civic pride, but a national German theatre emerged more slowly.

Until the mid-1950s, the Berliner Ensemble (in East Berlin) was the only German theatre with an international reputation. Soon after Bertolt Brecht and his wife, actress Helene Weigel (1900–1971), established the Ensemble in 1949, it became the most influential socialist theatre of the postwar era. Working as both playwright and director, Brecht exposed the contradictions of capitalism and explored theatrical means of animating audiences to political action. (See Chapter 11 and its case study for further discussion of Brecht's theories and practice.)

In the 1960s, a new generation of German theatre artists also looked to the documentary tradition of the German stage to examine the Holocaust and the Nazi past. Several socialist playwrights, including Rolf Hochhuth (1931–) and Peter Weiss (1916–1982), used documentary devices to expose the extent to which thousands of ordinary Germans, not just the Nazis in command, had been responsible for the extermination of millions of Jews, Slavs, Romani, homosexuals, and other minorities. A firestorm of controversy swirled around Hochhuth's play, *The Deputy*, when it opened in 1963. The play drew on written evidence to suggest that many German Catholics and even the Pope himself had condoned the slaughter of European Jewry. In *The Investigation* (1965), Peter Weiss used dialogue taken directly from official transcripts of the investigations into the Auschwitz extermination camp. In their lack of spectacle, both *The Deputy* and *The Investigation* suggest that emotion-laden pictures of the Holocaust, whether photographs or films, would detract from the necessity of probing Germany's guilty past. The assumption was that understanding an event of such magnitude and preventing a recurrence of the attitudes that fostered it requires close attention to the logic and morality of its perpetrators. Other German documentary plays of the 1960s used similar minimalist methods to focus audience attention on British war crimes, European imperialism, the development of the hydrogen bomb in the U.S., and the U.S. war in Vietnam. This socialist "theatre of fact," as it was called, generally shunned complex media effects to rely on the theatre's oldest weapons, the actor's voice and the moral imagination of the audience.

Although some of the techniques of the "theatre of fact" departed from the general aesthetic approach of the Berliner Ensemble, Brechtian and documentary German theatre shared the same general moral and political point of view in the 1960s. Even though the Berliner Ensemble was located in East Berlin, many socialist artists in both East and West Germany looked to the Ensemble's productions as models for their work. In addition to Brecht's plays, the Berliner Ensemble regularly produced the dramas of Shakespeare and the German classics. Brecht's death in 1956 and the assumption of the Ensemble's leadership by Helene Weigel did not diminish the influence of Brechtian theatre (and may even have enhanced it). In East Germany, the work of playwright Heiner Müller (1929–1995) and director Peter Palitzsch (1918–2004) (who began with the Ensemble and later moved to West Germany) derived from, but went beyond, Brecht. Müller's later works, such as *Hamletmachine* (1977), have been crucial in defining postmodernism (considered in Chapter 13).

Brechtian theatre also crossed the Cold War divide. For example, West German playwright Tankred Dorst (1925–) and the Austrian Peter Handke (1942–) joined Hochhuth and Weiss in their embrace of Brechtian politics. Similarly, the Swiss Freidrich Dürrenmatt (1921–1990), who wrote in German, combined Brechtian techniques with other styles to critique both totalitarianism and capitalism in his best-known work, the macabre black comedy *The Visit* (1956).

Japanese theatrical responses to defeat in the Second World War

Like much of Europe, Japan's cities and infrastructure were in ruins by the end of the war. Japan surrendered only after Hiroshima and Nagasaki were destroyed by atomic bombs. The Japanese and the world gradually learned that these new, incomprehensibly powerful weapons could not only kill (and even evaporate) all living beings near the blast's epicenter, but that nuclear fallout could contaminate the land, cause cancer in survivors, and create genetic mutations in the unborn for generations to come. The Japanese people would also learn about the brutal war crimes inflicted by their own soldiers and military leaders on enemy combatants and women.

In the wake of such unspeakable horrors, how can art find an appropriate language? One solution is to abandon words completely. Turning to the body, some postwar Japanese choreographers created *butoh* [boo-toh] (also romanized as *butō*), a non-verbal performance genre that rejects both traditional Japanese and Western aesthetic concepts. Originally called *ankoku butoh* ("dance of darkness"), the first public performance took place in 1959. The creators of this movement offered divergent approaches. Hijikata Tatsumi (1928–1986) choreographed and performed intentionally crude, contorted movements that derived from his childhood memories of poverty in rural, northeastern Japan. In contrast, Ōno Kazuo (1906–2010) created gentle, nostalgic, often mystical works that emphasized the feminine. Many variations followed. *Butoh*'s extreme physical and mental rigor achieved international notoriety in 1985 when a dancer from the troupe Sankai Juku, performing hanging upside down outside a building in Seattle, fell to his death. Regardless of the specific style, *butoh* is generally characterized by dead-white, full-body makeup, grotesque or contorted physical gestures, extreme slowness, and a suggestion of the forbidden and taboo. Using various styles that sometimes fuse *butoh* with local popular culture, *butoh* troupes now exist throughout the world. The genre has powerfully impacted modern dance worldwide.

In contrast, only a few playwrights attempted to probe the meaning of the nuclear holocaust and of Japan's role in the war; until the 1960s, the majority seemed to want to forget the traumas of war and defeat by writing non-political plays in the traditions of prewar modernism or psychological realism.

After the war, the Japanese government was forcibly transformed by the imposition of Western-style institutions. From 1945 to 1952, the United States military essentially ruled Japan in what is called the Occupation. The goal of the Occupation was to turn a former enemy into a permanent ally by substituting American-style democracy for traditional Japanese values. However, long-held cultural practices and traditional beliefs were not eliminated.

To curb the possibility of rebellion and to encourage the growth of constitutional democracy in Japan, the Occupation practiced censorship. Because many *kabuki* plays celebrated the values of revenge, feudalism, emperor worship, and the subjugation of women, *kabuki* theatre in general was suppressed, while Western-derived, realist *shingeki* plays flourished. Thus, Japan's first postwar production – just four months after the surrender – was a revival of Chekhov's *The Cherry Orchard*. Many characters in *The Cherry Orchard* are nostalgic for a vanished past. They also fear a rapidly transforming present and a future they cannot comprehend. Such emotions resonated deeply with the audience in a devastated, postwar Japan.

Despite the Occupation's efforts to prevent the return of militarist ideology, one of the most popular *shingeki* playwrights of the postwar era was Mishima Yukio (1925–1970), also well known outside Japan as Yukio Mishima, the Western order of his name. Although Mishima was an ultranationalist who despised Westernization and longed for a return to samurai values, he preferred Western clothing, Western housing, and often wrote Western-style *shingeki* plays. He also adapted the stories of *nō* plays into *shingeki*, using modern settings and psychology, and was an important author of new *kabuki* plays, including one inspired by Racine's *Phèdre*. Japanese critics and audiences consistently name his all-female *Madame de Sade* (1965) the best Japanese postwar play. *Madame de Sade* has had several important English-language productions, including one at London's Donmar Warehouse in 2009, starring Judy Dench (1934–).

Another key *shingeki* playwright, Kinoshita Junji (1914–2006), sometimes moved beyond the constraints of realism. His *Twilight Crane* (1949), based on folklore, remains the most produced play in Japan. In this play, Kinoshita turned to his nation's mythic past to create a new artistic genre, reliant on a fresh vernacular dialect and a notion of "pure Japanese essence" uncontaminated by the West. In contrast, his realist *Between God and Man* (1970) is one of the few dramatic attempts to come to terms with Japanese war crimes.

Many younger Japanese artists came to believe that *shingeki's* realist, materialist conventions could not adequately explain their nation's defeat or the shock and devastation of Hiroshima and Nagasaki. Beginning primarily in the 1960s, *shingeki* split into various subgenres, several of which experimented with new ways to incorporate traditional Japanese performance.

Anti-*shingeki* artists began to appear around the time that Japanese radicals and workers staged mass protests in 1960 against the ratification of the United States–Japan Mutual Security Treaty. The treaty, still in effect in 2014, essentially places Japan under the military protection of the United States. The protestors were demanding a return to Japanese autonomy and an end to the use of Japan as a base for American soldiers and nuclear submarines. During the 1960s, some of these artists wrote and directed plays that fused traditional Japanese and international modernist elements. Betsuyaku Minoru's (1937–) *The Elephant* (1962), for instance, deals with the horrors of nuclear contamination in a style inspired by *kyōgen* and Beckett's *Waiting for Godot*. It is generally considered the first *angura* [ahn-goo-rah] play (from the Japanese pronunciation of "underground"). Akimoto Matsuyo (1911–2001), one of Japan's first modern female playwrights, wrote *Kaison, the Priest of Hitachi* (1965), which features a young man who escapes from his historical burden of war guilt into mythic time to become Kaison, a twelfth-century warrior. By the late 1960s new companies, such as Tenjō Sajiki, the Situation Theatre, and the Black Tent Theatre, were experimenting with forms of staging and actor–audience relationships that greatly diverged from the realist conventions of *shingeki*.

Postwar theatre and the Cold War

As we described in the introduction to this chapter, the Second World War had left massive destruction and dislocation in its wake, especially in Europe and Japan, profoundly affecting their view of the world. In the U.S., on the other hand, cities (except for Honolulu, site of Pearl Harbor) and most civilians had not experienced battles or bombardments. For those who had not served in the military, the horrors of the war remained distant. As the Cold War settled in, this difference strongly shaped the theatre.

Psychological realism in the United States

Although the United States remained physically intact, families had suffered and soldiers had been killed or maimed. Many women who had discovered their value as paid workers during the war found themselves replaced by returning male soldiers. They were forced into less satisfactory or lower-paying jobs or, more often, retreated to their prewar roles as wives and mothers. Similarly, minority soldiers – especially African-Americans, who were still subject to legal segregation, and Japanese-Americans, who had voluntarily joined the military to demonstrate patriotism in light of the forced internment of west-coast Americans of Japanese descent – returned to find that their service abroad had not changed their second-class status at home. Nevertheless, since disruptions had been far less drastic than in much of the rest of the world, it was easier for theatre artists and audiences in the United States to maintain a relatively unchanged view of life. In addition, American fears of communism stifled overtly political theatre and sent "un-American" war refugees such as Bertolt Brecht, who had settled in California, back to Europe. Consequently, theatre in the U.S. initially continued to emphasize positivist values and psychological realism.

Unlike modernism in Europe, modernist theatre in the U.S. did not begin with theatrical innovators eager to reinvigorate a hallowed national tradition. Political and economic pressures, a legacy of realist theatre, a self-flattering notion of popular psychology, plus the emphatically realistic quality of film and radio, had encouraged the adoption of psychological realism in the United States. Although the roots of this style date from the late nineteenth century and include many of the plays of Eugene O'Neill, the kind of theatre that O'Neill's plays hint at could not have flourished on the stage without the necessary acting, directing, and design practices to support it.

During the 1930s, Lee Strasberg (1901–1982) and other members of the Group Theatre in New York had applied what they took to be Stanislavsky's precepts about acting to their work on realist plays. Although their understanding of Stanislavsky was inaccurate, the actors and directors of the Group had forged various acting "systems" that helped actors to empathize deeply with their stage characters. After the war, Strasberg's version – usually called "the Method" – trained a generation of actors. Unlike Stanislavsky's System, Strasberg's Method emphasized the actor's memory of her personal experiences and emotions, in order to connect to the character. Stella Adler (1903–1992), also an original member of the Group, briefly studied with Stanislavsky himself. Her work with Stanislavsky convinced her that Strasberg's Method was flawed. Instead of the actor's personal emotions, she focused on "the given circumstances" of the drama as written – including historical period, location, culture, and so on. Thus Adler stressed what the character in the play (not the actor) experienced. She trained actors such as Marlon Brando (1924–2004). Other notable actors trained in some version of the Method or of Stanislavsky's System include Marilyn Monroe (1926–1962), Robert De Niro (1943–), and Johnny Depp (1963–). By the 1950s, Method Acting and its variations dominated theatrical performance in the U.S. This acting style, psychologically attuned directing, and fluid scenography had produced a theatre of psychological realism that became a distinctive national style.

While the influence of Appia and Craig on the New Stagecraft Movement during the decade of the Great War had moved some U.S. stage design away from the dictates of literal realism, most scenic and lighting designs for dramatic productions in the 1920s and 1930s continued to emphasize the massiveness of realist rooms and exteriors. However, Jo Mielziner (1901–1976) and a few other designers of Broadway productions drew on European ideas to discover more abstract solutions for staging realist plays. At the same time, the pressure from film to create quickly shifted scenic locales was also moving realism away from three-dimensional units toward more lightweight, lyrical designs. This led Mielziner, especially, toward a visual poetic realism with the use of color and soaring vertical lines in scene designs that left rooms without ceilings and substituted transparent walls made of painted scrim for the material solidity of regular stage flats.

Consequently, when Mielziner designed Tennessee Williams' *The Glass Menagerie* in 1945, he knew he could regulate the flow between the scenes of narration in the present and the scenes of memory in the past through the manipulation of scrim and lighting. When lit from the front, scrim can give the illusion of a solid wall. Illuminated from behind as well, the wall of scrim becomes transparent, allowing spectators to see objects and actors through a gauzy grain. Mielziner's painterly, soft-edged designs nicely complemented the psychological realism of Williams' plays. He designed seven modernist productions for Williams between 1945 and 1963, including *A Streetcar Named Desire* (1947) and *Cat on a Hot Tin Roof* (1955).

Although Mielziner's use of lighting and scrim to shift between locales or atmospheric effects permitted the kind of scenic transformation that film editing could accomplish, the lighting-and-scrim shift also borrowed from the sound transition that radio drama producers called a "segue." By the 1940s, many popular radio serials used a musical or vocal bridge that faded in and out to move from one scene to another. At times, the segue moved the listener inside the narrator's head, sharing intimate thoughts, daydreams, or flashbacks.

The principle of the radio segue shaped playwriting as well as design on the postwar American stage. "Inside of His Head" was Arthur Miller's initial title for *Death of a Salesman* (1949), which deploys several radio-drama techniques to tell the story of the dreams of material and capitalistic success that push salesman Willy Loman to suicide. Mielziner's design for *Salesman* used lighting-and-scrim shifts to move spectators inside Willy's head, where they could see the world from the perspective of Miller's Everyman character (Figure 12.4). Audiences familiar with the "voice-over" convention of radio drama – a narrator taking the listener directly to a new episode in the plot – had no difficulty following Willy's vocal transitions from present time and place into his daydreams located in the past. Many radio plays divided the internal psychology of the protagonist into different voices and sounds so that the split desires of the main character could be dramatized. Miller, who had written radio plays in the early 1940s, achieves a similar effect in *Salesman* by dividing the voices "inside of his [Willy's] head" among several characters. Directly shaped by the techniques and effects of radio drama, *Death of a Salesman* was a milestone in American psychological realism.

Figure 12.4
A rendering of Jo Mielziner's setting for Arthur Miller's *Death of a Salesman*, 1949.
Photo: Peter Juley & Son. © The Smithsonian Institution, Washington, D.C.

Salesman was directed by Elia Kazan (1909–2003), the premier director of psychological realism in the U.S. from the late 1940s through the 1950s. During those years, Kazan also enjoyed a successful career in Hollywood and brought several of the techniques of film directing to his work in New York. Kazan had been a member of the Group in the 1930s and, like several of his cohort, continued to use Method Acting and its variations with actors in stage productions such as Miller's *All My Sons* (1947) and Williams' *Sweet Bird of Youth* (1959), and in such films as *On the Waterfront* (1954) and *East of Eden* (1955). Kazan directed both the stage and film versions of Williams' *A Streetcar Named Desire* (1947, 1951). He carefully coached his actors and used their edgy, high-strung psychological rhythms to shape their stage movements and his camera shots. Kazan's success helped to ensure that psychological realism would unite the film screens and the theatrical stages of modern America. Given the widespread influence of film on the postwar imagination in the West and Japan (and the power of Hollywood's distribution system), it is not surprising that filmic images of psychological realism achieved international renown.

In the U.S., theatre artists generally thought of themselves as apolitical. Nevertheless, most productions supported capitalist notions of individual success, consumer choice, and corporate power, while accepting limits on democracy and on the ability of the government to change patterns of economic inequality and traditional racist behavior. These basic values were apparent in most musical comedies, especially those by Rodgers and Hammerstein, and in the intense psychological dramas that relied on Method Acting and its variations for their success.

A few mainstream playwrights dissented from the consensus. Lorraine Hansberry's (1930–1965) *A Raisin in the Sun* (1959) managed to offer a mostly white audience a realistic view of the daily lives of African-Americans and the problems they faced due to racial inequality, which the burgeoning civil rights movement had begun to contest. Hansberry was the first African-American woman playwright to have a Broadway production, and the play's director, Lloyd Richards (1919–2006), was Broadway's first African-American director. Tennessee Williams attacked homophobia and consumerist values in *Cat on a Hot Tin Roof* (1955) (Figure 12.5), while Arthur Miller's *The Crucible* (1953) equated U.S. anti-communist hysteria and blacklisting (specifically the activities of the Congressional hearings led by Senator Joseph McCarthy and the House Committee on Un-American Activities, also called HUAC) with the Salem witch trials of 1692–1693. HUAC forced many theatre and film artists to testify, asking them "Are you now or have you ever been a member of the Communist Party?" Those who refused to answer or who were merely named by others (even if they had only attended a single rally or meeting prior to the Second World War) were

Figure 12.5

Scene from the Broadway production of Tennessee Williams' *Cat on a Hot Tin Roof* in 1955, with Ben Gazzara as Brick and Burl Ives as Big Daddy.

Photo by Fred Fehl, courtesy of Gabriel Pinski. Supplied by New York Public Library Photographic Services.

subsequently "blacklisted," which meant that they were forbidden to work in the film industry. Many never recovered their careers. A few blacklisted screenwriters, however, were able to survive by secretly having their non-blacklisted friends take credit for scripts they had written. Others found that they could still work in New York theatre. Fear of communism fueled many Hollywood films, especially science fiction films which often presented the threat of alien invasion and mind control.

Despite the powerful anti-communism of this period, most plays – and most members of the audience – were not overtly political. Audiences tended to be more concerned with their personal lives and with improving their economic conditions. Our first case study examines audience reception of the initial Broadway production of *A Streetcar Named Desire*.

CASE STUDY: Cultural memories and audience response: *A Streetcar Named Desire* in the 1940s

Bruce McConachie

American writer Flannery O'Connor (1925–1964), complaining about Northern U.S. stereo-types of the South, noted that "[A]nything that comes out of the South is going to be called grotesque by the Northern Reader, unless it is grotesque, in which case it is going to be called realistic" (O'Connor 1961: 40). When *A Streetcar Named Desire* premiered on Broadway in 1947, most New York critics badly misinterpreted the play and its performers in the way that O'Connor feared. Today, critics and historians generally recognize Southern playwright Tennessee Williams' drama as a masterpiece and nearly all spectators sympathize with his protagonist, Blanche DuBois. Driven from her teaching position and family plantation in Mississippi, Blanche struggles to make a place for herself in New Orleans, where she goes to live with her sister Stella and brother-in-law, Stanley Kowalski. Sexual tensions soon erupt between Blanche and Stanley, however, and he rapes her near the end of the play, driving the already mentally unstable Blanche into insanity.

In a letter concerning the Hollywood film version of *Streetcar* (released in 1951), Williams recognized that Stanley would draw some sympathy from viewers but characterized his rape of Blanche as "the ravishment of the tender, the sensitive, the delicate, by the savage and brutal forces in modern society" (quoted in Cohan 1997: 318). In 1947, however, although the critics praised Williams' play, admired Elia Kazan's directing, and celebrated Marlon Brando's depiction of Stanley, a majority found Jessica Tandy's Blanche unsympathetic (Kolin 2000: 1–33). In fact, several newspaper critics branded Blanche as a drunk, a Southern decadent, a home-wrecker, and a neurotic nymphomaniac. Critic Howard Barnes, for example, identified Blanche as a "boozy prostitute," while Robert Coleman typed her as a "paranoic-nymphomaniac." Seven of the nine critics who wrote reviews also explained Blanche's actions in the play by referring negatively to her Southern heritage. According to Richard Watts, Blanche represented "a long line of decadent Southern aristocrats," while for Ward Morehouse, she was simply "the faded, shattered daughter of the South." Most reviewers also felt Blanche was delusional. John Chapman noted that Blanche "shuns the reality of what she is and takes gallant and desperate refuge in a magical life she has invented for herself." Louis Kronenberger flayed Blanche as "the most demonically driven kind of liar – the one who lies to the world because she must lie to herself." In sum, most of the reviewers in 1947 saw Blanche as a sexual predator or a lying tramp, whose Southern past had left her deluded and neurotic (*New York Theatre Critics Reviews* 1948: 249–52). Because *Streetcar* invites spectators to sympathize with both Blanche and Stanley at different times during most of the play, the critics invariably took sides between the two in their reviews. However, most spectator-journalists tilted sharply toward Stanley. While none of the reviewers applauded Stanley's rape of Blanche, most ignored it or used euphemisms to evade its implications; the word "rape" occurred in none of the New York reviews. For these critics, Blanche was predestined to end up in a mental institution even before Stanley laid a hand on her.

Why did these critics withdraw their sympathy from Blanche and avoid the implications of her rape by Stanley? Most of these critics had seen and reviewed thousands of plays; they were professionals, hired by some of the best papers in the theatrical capital of the nation, not cub reporters unaccustomed to challenging new plays. Although Elia Kazan had knowingly directed Jessica Tandy to create a shrill and nervous Blanche in the early scenes of the play, while coaching Brando to work for spectator interest, he expected audience sympathies to shift away from Stanley and toward Blanche midway through the play. For many reviewers, however, that shift never came (Kolin 2000: 10). Why did they misread Williams' play?

One way for the theatre historian to approach this problem is to focus on the mindset of the New York audience, including the critics, who brought certain cultural memories with them when they went to the theatre. While such collective memories are never monolithic, some may be widely shared and these invariably shape audience expectations and initial responses in all dramatic productions. This case study singles out five of these clusters that appear to have been important in 1947: the American South, female sexuality, heterosexual marriage, the moral status of male veterans, and female mental health.

From the perspective of postwar New Yorkers, the South of Blanche DuBois was a foreign country. The inheritor of plantation-era traditions and sensibilities, Blanche and her kind

THINKING THROUGH THEATRE HISTORIES

Cultural memories and audience response

Students of theatre often hear from professors and friends that they should go to see a new play with "an open mind." But of course our minds are never truly "open" and have not been since before we were born, because they are shaped by personal habits, family customs, acquired language, and cultural memories – nearly all of which operate unconsciously in our daily lives. Although education and "openness" can help us appreciate new experiences, we can also misinterpret significant theatrical events for which we are unprepared. Among the most important reasons for spectator misunderstandings are cultural memories, which can sway audience perceptions, holding even professional critics in their grip.

This case study demonstrates how Americans in 1947 translated their recent memories and experiences of the Second World War (both actual and those manufactured by Hollywood) and their long-held cultural assumptions about gender and the American South, into misinterpretations of a play that would become one of the great classics of psychological realism.

probably represented the faded gentility, aristocratic pretenses, and emotional extremes of the Old South that spectators associated with romantic novels and Hollywood films such as *Gone With the Wind* (1939). For Northerners, the most popular guide to such traditional character-types in the 1940s was W.J. Cash's *The Mind of the South* (1941), which presented the South as culturally distinctive, resistant to change, willfully individualistic, and extravagantly romantic (Reed 2003: 15–27). Most New Yorkers could define themselves as more cosmopolitan, more accepting of progress, more cooperative, and more rational than Blanche.

According to historian Elaine Tyler May, most Americans after the war, including women, believed that a woman's "normal" place was in the home. These memories and beliefs, says May, resulted in a domestic version of containment (the politics of keeping communism outside the U.S.) from the mid-1940s into the 1960s: "Within [the home], potentially dangerous social forces of the new age might be tamed. . . . More than merely a metaphor for the Cold War on the home front, containment aptly describes the way in which public policy, personal behavior, and even political values focused on the home" (May 1988: 14). The postwar consensus embraced heterosexual marriage and a happy home as the answers to containing the sexual desires of men and women.

Blanche's presence in the Kowalski household presents a direct threat to the norms of domestic containment. Most audience members would have seen Blanche as a potential home-wrecker and blamed her for the heightened tensions in the household. From this perspective, it is understandable that the male critics in 1947 could not bring themselves to call Stanley's attack on Blanche a rape. Her presence in the house, her flirting with Stanley, and her apparent sexual availability, from their point of view, had simply caused the poor boy to explode.

The image of Stanley as a heroic veteran also played a role in spectator response. The popular mythology surrounding "the good war" (a common term for the Second World War, since Nazism was seen as an evil that only America could destroy) tended to conflate "our boys" – all veterans were implicitly "boys" regardless of their age – with America itself. Hundreds of war films in the 1940s delivered characterizations of innocent, valiant soldier boys and none of these movies showed American soldiers raping local women. In Hollywood mythology, if a veteran sexually molested a woman, he must have been driven to it. Consequently, many New York spectators would have understood the sexual tensions between Stanley and Blanche and the eventual rape as a case of "she was asking for it" (McConachie 2003: 56–61).

Freudian psychiatry had long warned that women were more vulnerable to psychological problems than men. Further, postwar psychiatry preached that rebellion against normative social roles could lead women to psychological distress and neurosis; social conformity, in other words, was the key to personal mental health, as demonstrated in many Cold War Hollywood films. Blanche's presence, her past, and her demands that she had a right to find a place for herself were an affront to the norms of Cold War American life as they were emerging in 1947.

Such cultural ideas, images, and prejudices in the memories of New Yorkers helped to shape their perception of the drama. A brief discussion of the play's first four scenes will illustrate this point.

In scene 1, an exhausted Blanche, under extreme duress, drinks compulsively to quiet her nerves, careens between extremes of affection and combativeness in her interactions with her sister Stella, and sinks into depressed memories of death when she recalls the recent parade of funerals at the family plantation, now lost to creditors. While it is possible to sympathize with

Blanche because of what she has been through, spectators who already believed that the South housed neurotic women could also define Blanche as another grotesque victim of Southern tradition and female psychological weakness. Apparently, many of the critics chose the latter response.

The next scene begins with an argument between Stanley and Stella about demanding a share of the profits from the sale of the plantation (even though no profits exist) and leads to Stella's angry exit. Then Blanche emerges from the bathroom in a slip and red satin robe and begins to flirt with Stanley, presumably because she heard parts of their argument and seeks to win him over. Spectators who had stereotyped Blanche as a potentially neurotic and decadent Southerner in scene 1, however, might easily have understood Blanche's flirtation as an attempt to seduce Stanley. She then sends Stella off to the drugstore to buy her a coke so that she can speak to Stanley alone. Although Williams is clear later in the play that Blanche has often relied on playful flirtation to control her relations with men, at this point the audience could have believed that she had gotten rid of her sister in order to continue her seduction.

Convinced that there was something psychologically wrong with this faded Southern belle, audience members could begin to explain Blanche's behavior as an attempt to wreck her sister's marriage in order to steal Stanley. This interpretation weaves together many of Blanche's significant actions, grounds them in the actual circumstances of what the audience understood so far about her past and present, and tracks her life in terms of an overall goal – to get a husband – that would have seemed believable and even necessary to many 1947 spectators. The story also explains why so many spectators in 1947 attributed the trait of nymphomania to Blanche's personality.

In scene 3, Blanche finds a group of men playing poker in the Kowalski kitchen and singles out Mitch, an awkward bachelor, for flirtatious engagement. Spectators already alarmed at Blanche's sexuality would also note that she lies about her age and dims the bedroom light to shade her wrinkles. At this point, viewers might be divided on seeing her as a home-wrecker and nymphomaniac, or more charitably, as a lonely woman exploring the possibility of Mitch as a potential husband.

Scene 4, however, likely revived and validated the interpretation of Blanche as a home-wrecker. Repulsed by Stanley's attack on Stella at the climax of the poker party scene and by their subsequent lovemaking, Blanche urges Stella to run away with her. Blanche fantasizes about an old beau who could rescue them, tries to call Western Union to send him a telegram, and argues with Stella about the brutishness of her marriage – all actions that probably revived the stereotype of Blanche as a neurotic Southern belle and confirmed the suspicion that Blanche wanted to wreck the marriage of this potentially happy couple. At the end of scene 4, the final scene before the first intermission in 1947, Stanley enters and Stella embraces him fiercely, signaling her decision to stay with her husband. As the houselights came up in the theatre, many spectators must have wondered how this loving couple could ever manage to get rid of Stella's crazy, lying, and predatory sister.

Ironically, audience misunderstanding probably increased the financial success of *A Streetcar Named Desire* in the late 1940s. The Broadway production ran for over two years and a successful road show followed. Spectators evidently enjoyed what they took to be a play about grotesque Southerners, female neurosis, and decadent nymphomania. Cultural memory always shapes spectator response and sometimes produces ironic results.

Key references

Cohan, S. (1997) *Masked Men: Masculinity and the Movies in the Fifties*, Bloomington: Indiana University Press.

Kolin, P. (2000) *Williams: A Streetcar Named Desire*, Plays in Production, Cambridge: Cambridge University Press.

McConachie, B. (2003) *American Theater in the Culture of the Cold War: Producing and Contesting Containment*, Iowa City: University of Iowa Press.

McConachie, B. (2014) "All in the Timing: The Meanings of *Streetcar* in 1947 and 1951," in B. Murphy (ed.) *The Theatre of Tennessee Williams*, London: Bloomsbury Methuen Drama, 181–205.

May, E. (1988) *Homeward Bound: American Families in the Cold War Era*, New York: Basic Books.

New York Theatre Critics' Reviews (1948) Vol. 8, New York: Critics' Theatre Reviews, 249–52.

O'Connor, F. (1961) "Some Aspects of the Grotesque in Southern Fiction," in S. Fitzgerald and R. Fitzgerald (eds) *Mystery and Manners: Occasional Prose*, New York: Farrar, Strauss & Giroux.

Reed, J. (2003) *Minding the South*, Columbia, MO: University of Missouri Press.

A Streetcar Named Desire: The Original Director's Version (1993) DVD, Warner Brothers.

Williams, T. (1951, 1975) *A Streetcar Named Desire*, New York: Penguin Putnam.

The Cold War and theatre outside the U.S.

The situation was different elsewhere in the world. As we have observed, the frequently complacent realism that dominated theatre in the U.S. was contrasted by social and theatrical discontent in other countries. Brechtian theatre often provided a model. For example, following the influential European tour of the Berliner Ensemble in 1956, English playwrights John Arden (1930–2012) and Edward Bond (1934–), director Joan Littlewood (1914–2002), and others were inspired to use Brechtian style to improve the democratic socialism that had begun to flourish in the United Kingdom after the war. Italian Giorgio Strehler (1921–1997) also directed productions of Brecht's plays. For these and many other artists, Brechtian theatre emerged as an alternative response to conforming to the ideology of either superpower.

In Latin America, long dominated by U.S. interests, Brechtian theatre was especially influential during the 1960s. Argentinean playwright and director Osvaldo Dragún (1929–1999) modeled many of his short plays in the 1950s and 1960s on Brecht's dramas to point up the sacrifice in human dignity demanded by capitalist economics. Brechtian theatre influenced several Mexican playwrights and directors, such as Luisa Josefina Hernández (1928–). Her *Popul Vuh* (1966) dramatized the traditional sacred book of the Mayan people. In Colombia, Enrique Buenaventura (1925–2003) led the charge, staging Brechtian productions, writing plays with revolutionary messages, and helping to reorganize the university theatre movement in the country for radical purposes. Although the authorities suppressed the collective theatre movement Buenaventura had helped to begin, its legacy continued in Bogotá and other major cities, with radical street theatre and plays that dramatized Colombia's oppressive history. In São Paulo, Brazil, the Arena Theatre modified Brechtian techniques to search for a specifically Brazilian stage language for social criticism. International activist Augusto Boal (1931–2009) joined Arena in 1956, wrote and directed several politically radical plays, and began experimenting with participatory forms of theatre, which later found expression in his 1974 book *Theater of the Oppressed*, discussed in more detail in Chapter 14. Along with Buenaventura, Boal would have enormous influence in the New Popular Theatre (Nuevo Teatro Popular) movement in Latin America during the 1970s and 1980s (see Chapter 13).

More significant than Brecht for Mexican oppositional theatre was the legacy of Surrealism, which Mexican playwrights began to transform for their own uses soon after the Second World War. The leading dramatist of the postwar generation, Emilio Carballido (1925–2008), freely mixed reality and fantasy in a wide range of genres, from film scripts and children's theatre pieces to over 100 works written for the professional stage. A critic of traditional Mexican culture in his opposition to patriarchy, the divisions been rich and poor, and his focus on serious socio-political concerns (often under the mask of farce), Carballido also engaged the positive possibilities of Catholicism and celebrated some of Mexico's founding national myths.

His most famous play, *Yo tambien hablo de la rosa* (*I, Too, Speak of the Rose*) (1966), has been identified as a surreal allegory, a Brechtian parody, and a postmodern paradox, to note only a few of the critical tags it has evoked. Through popular storytelling and songs, send-ups of Freudian and Marxist rhetoric, news accounts and poetic metaphors, and even occasional snippets of dramatic realism, the play depicts multiple representations of the same train derailment, as well as several versions of the events that led up to it and the responses that followed. Even as this multi-layered pastiche invites several interpretations, it also makes fun of the act of interpretation itself. At the same time, a rough populist energy animates the play; marginal members of Mexican society pushed the powerful train off its tracks and proceeded to loot it when it was down. This oppositional and possibly revolutionary action remains a potent fact during the performance, despite the ridiculous attempts of others in Mexican society to explain what happened. Whatever else it is, *I, Too, Speak of the Rose* seemed to be a warning to those who controlled the public discourses of Mexican society that the poor will not be ignored.

Figure 12.6

Okhlopkov's production of *Hamlet* relied on a triptych-like design to suggest the prince's imprisonment in traditional culture. Produced at the Mayakovsky Theatre in Moscow in 1954, soon after the death of Stalin.

© The Society for Cooperation in Russian and Soviet Studies, London.

In contrast, the Soviet Union's ideology of socialist realism, plus censorship and control, kept most Soviet theatre within the boundaries of Cold War communism, even after the death of Stalin in 1953. A few directors, however, including Nikolai Okhlopkov (1900–1967), were permitted to experiment with new ideas and forms (Figure 12.6). While approving of Brecht's Marxism, the Soviets kept Brechtian theatre at arm's length; they recognized that its antimilitarism and democratic socialism subverted their authoritarian power.

Our second case study focuses on some of the ways that theatre and politics intersected in this period.

CASE STUDY: Social drama in Kerala, India: Staging the "revolution"

Phillip B. Zarrilli, with Carol Fisher Sorgenfrei

> There once was a time like this. A time when human lives burned in the "test fires" of social change.
>
> Tooppil Bhaasi, playwright and director, Kerala

Indian theatres of decolonization

Anti-colonial nationalism intensified in British-ruled India after the Great War and the Russian Revolution, reaching a peak during the Second World War. After Indian independence in 1947, many leftists joined with some of the liberal reformers to begin new theatre troupes in Indian cities. Among the most influential was the Group Theatre in Calcutta (now renamed Kolkata), which challenged the dominant, Western-style commercial theatre of the city. Where the old imperial theatres had featured British plays, occasional hybrid shows written by Indians, and the latest hits from London, the Group produced modernist European classics (Chekhov, Pirandello, and Ibsen, for example) and several politically radical plays by Brecht and others. By performing canonical Western plays in an Indian context, the Group hoped to cultivate an audience of serious theatregoers who would reject the frivolous entertainments of imperial times for politically engaged drama. Director Sombhu Mitra (1914–1997) worked briefly with the Group and then founded his own company, Bohurupee. Mitra directed a localized version of Ibsen's *A Doll House* for Bohurupee in 1958 and successfully adapted several plays by Rabindranath Tagore (1860–1941), one of the leading writers of the early twentieth century, whose plays had resisted modern modes of staging until that time. Mitra's modernist vision for his theatre led him to stage productions of *Oedipus the King* and Tagore's *Rājā* on consecutive nights in 1964.

Far to the south, in the state of Kerala, a very different form of grassroots, anti-colonialist theatre developed.

Tooppil Bhaasi and the Kerala People's Arts Club

Tooppil Bhaasi (1924–1992) was born in Vallikkunu, a typical agricultural village in south central Kerala, India. He received his lower school education in a Sanskrit school, and went on to pass his examination in traditional Indian medicine (*Ayurveda*). However, Bhaasi never

---

THINKING THROUGH THEATRE HISTORIES

Politics, ideology, history, and performance

Janelle Reinelt raises several important questions about writing histories of theatre when she asks, "what is the relationship of politics [and ideology] to culture? How does social change result in cultural change – or can various cultural practices initiate or precipitate change?" (Reinelt 1996: 1).

Throughout this book, we have attempted to locate various types of theatre within their specific historical, political, cultural, and ideological frameworks. We have emphasized how ideologies change over time, and how specific social or political realities are reflected in – or even brought about by – local theatre. In the current chapter, for example, we suggest that understanding various responses to the traumatic events of the Second World War and the subsequent Cold War can clarify the emergence of certain styles and genres of performance.

Cultural theorist Terry Eagleton maintains that "there is one place above all where . . . consciousness may be transformed almost literally overnight, and that is in active political struggle" (Eagleton 1991: 223–4)

This case study examines the interconnections between theatre and political struggle in the state of Kerala in a newly postcolonial India.

---

pursued a career in medicine. Rather, like many other young men receiving an education during this turbulent period, he became a student activist and leader, working in the student congress movement as part of the national drive toward independence from British colonial rule. He later joined the Communist movement. By Indian Independence Day (August 15, 1947), he was temporarily in the Allappuzha jail. He had been arrested for his activities of organizing low-caste agricultural workers, protesting against the hoarding of food grains and black-marketeering by wealthy landholders, for the cultivation of waste land, and for attempting to overturn the hierarchical caste system. The ultimate goal of this movement was to replace the old social and economic order with progressive social-democratic models that would gradually and peacefully move from capitalism toward socialism by creating extensive governmental support systems.

Between 1946 and 1952, the Communist Party of India was advocating active and some-times violent revolutionary struggle against the new Indian government. As a Communist, Bhaasi and other activists were forced to live in hiding because some of their activities were declared illegal. While in hiding, in 1952 he wrote his first play, *You Made Me a Communist*, and the Kerala People's Arts Club (KPAC) almost immediately produced it. Founded in 1950 by a group of student activists at the Law College in Ernakulam Town, KPAC began to produce dramas as one means of raising socio-political issues. The group first used shadow puppets and then staged the political drama *My Son is Right*. But it was their production of Bhaasi's *You Made Me a Communist* that launched KPAC on to the path toward becoming Kerala's most visible contemporary theatre company.

You Made Me a Communist enacts the struggles of agricultural laborers and poor peasants for a better life by focusing on how Paramu Pillai, a conservative farmer, makes the decision to become a Communist. The play focuses on his change in socio-political consciousness and calls for the revolutionary overthrow of landlordism. With its very loose structure, and with characters who burst into song at unexpected moments during the course of the story, *You Made Me a Communist* swept across the length and breadth of Kerala. Dr. Radhakrishnan of the Gandhi Centre, New Delhi, recalled his experience of it:

> Even though a child, I could sense the excitement! There were nights when KPAC had more than four performances. From one place, they went on moving for months on end. . . . KPAC became a very powerful social inspiration for people to fight against social injustice and for their rights. It gave them the feeling that anybody, irrespective of their low birth [could be] equal.
>
> (Radhakrishnan, personal communication)

There can be no doubt that attending a performance of *You Made Me a Communist* in 1952–1953 was a special event. It was not simply a dramatic representation of a fictionalized story and its characters, but part of an unfolding and evolving socio-political revolution as it was happening. Journalist, essayist, playwright, and activist Kaniyapuram Ramachandran explained both the timeliness and excitement generated by this interrelationship between stage and life in Bhaasi's early social dramas, and in *You Made Me a Communist* in particular:

> The fourth element of drama is the audience; and the audience is the fourth character. That dividing line between stage and audience was simply erased! What they saw there was their real lives! The workers, agricultural laborers, people coming on stage and speaking their own dialects and ordinary language – not literary language. The ultimate aim is to make the audience part of the experience. There is no detachment, but attachment. So with the social issues in the play – it was all so relevant. At the end of a performance the entire audience would come to its feet. So, *You Made Me a Communist* wasn't a drama at all! The social relevance of the play made people forget everything when they saw it. It was a drama for the people, by the people. It gave people what they wanted to see at the right time. It was a magic wand. The audience was like a mental vacuum that sucked up what was given. . . . In 1951 it was so apt! It was the medicine that the patient was waiting for. People were ready for that message of social change.
>
> Bhaasi always wanted the audience to first understand his plays. They should be clear and straight. He was speaking to the heart, and not the intellect. He used to talk to the emotions, and through the emotions, people would change their thinking.
>
> (Ramachandran 1993)

The impact of the production of this play on the Malayalis was remarkable. So important was it for the spread of the Communist point of view from 1952 to 1954 that some commentators have suggested that without it the emergence of the first democratically elected Communist government to the newly established state of Kerala in 1957 would never have happened.

Since 1952, *You Made Me a Communist* has been performed well over 2,000 times and continues to be part of KPAC's active repertory of social dramas. Bhaasi went on to become

Figure 12.7

In a 1993 production of *Memories in Hiding* by Tooppil Bhaasi, in Thiruvananthapuram, Kerala, the Landlord (right, with scarf) forces Teevan to yoke together his father, Ceenan, and Paramu Naayar to plough a paddy field.

Photo © Phillip B. Zarrilli.

one of Kerala's most important playwrights, providing KPAC with a series of highly popular social dramas, including *The Prodigal Son* (1956), in which a wayward, selfish rowdy is transformed into a champion of the low castes. His *Aswameetam* (1962) explores the social stigma of leprosy. His political satire, *Power House* (1990), focuses on the irresponsible behavior of a government institution – the Kerala State Electricity Board. *Memories in Hiding*, which won the Kerala Best Play Award in 1992, was his final play. In *Memories in Hiding*, a tenant-farmer, whose family has for generations devotedly served a landlord as virtual slaves, realizes that the landlord will not step forward to aid the tenant-farmer's falsely arrested son. The tenant-farmer then courageously declares his independence and walks out (Figures 12.7 and 12.8).

From its nineteenth-century realities as a hierarchically ordered, feudal social system ridden with caste and class conflicts, with high birth and infant mortality rates, Kerala was gradually transformed into a turn-of-the-twentieth-century social-democratic state with radical reductions in population growth and infant mortality rates. Illiteracy was virtually eradicated, many previously dispossessed peasants and communities were enfranchised, and there was extensive land reform, with the redistribution of considerable amounts of land to the landless. This transformation of Kerala in just over 100 years into a new model of social development has taken place peacefully within a democratic framework and without the outside assistance of global institutions such as the International Monetary Fund or the World Bank (Parayil 2000: 1–15).

Figure 12.8

In *Memories in Hiding*, the jailed Paramu Naayar shouts defiantly near the end: "Our voices will be heard even after we die. They are the voices of revolution."

Photo © Phillip B. Zarrilli.

Spoken drama and theatre, together with numerous modes of public performance, have clearly played an essential role in redefining individual, social, and political awareness in contemporary Kerala.

A more detailed version of this case study, including additional historical, political, and cultural background, can be found on our website.

Key references

Bhaasi, T. (1996) *Memories in Hiding*, trans. J. George and P.B. Zarrilli, Calcutta: Seagull.

Eagleton, T. (1991) *Ideology: An Introduction*, London: Verso.

Handelman, D. (1990) *Models and Mirrors: Towards an Anthropology of Public Events*, Cambridge: Cambridge University Press.

Namboodiripad, E.M.S. (1976) *How I Became a Communist*, Trivandrum: Chinta Publications.

Parayil, G. (ed.) (2000) *Kerala: The Development Experience*, London: Zed Books.

Ramachandran, K. (1993) Interview with the author.

Reinelt, J. (ed.) (1996) *Crucible of Crisis: Performing Social Change*, Ann Arbor: University of Michigan Press.

Happenings, protest, and the growth of alternative theatre in the U.S.

Some of the most radical political performance during the 1960s flourished on the margins of mainstream theatre in the United States. The agit-prop tradition, a significant part of working-class theatre in the U.S. during the 1930s, blossomed again in the mid-1960s, as small groups on college campuses and elsewhere sought to protest the war in Vietnam. Vietnam had become a pawn in the Cold War, and the U.S. gradually ramped up its military commitment to prevent what it feared would be a communist takeover of the country.

Theatre and other artists also practiced new tactics to destroy audience complacency. Allan Kaprow (1927–2006) was a painter and aesthetic theorist who popularized concepts such as performance art, environmental art (including theatre), and **Happenings**. A typical Happening might involve spectators at an art gallery who would encounter not only paintings and sculptures, but actors engaged in unrelated, random activities. Happenings could occur anywhere, sometimes without the audience realizing they would be involved. Participatory and interactive, Happenings aimed to destroy the fourth wall between actor and audience. Kaprow first used the term "Happening" in a 1958 essay; by the early 1960s, they had become significant in the art world.

Related to Happenings was an avant-garde movement called Fluxus, a loose international alliance of musicians and performers dedicated to continuing the experiments of composer John Cage (1912–1992) with chance events, mundane sounds, and the embodiment of everyday rituals in performance. Fluxus began in 1948 when Cage and dancer Merce Cunningham (1919–2009) worked together at Black Mountain College in North Carolina. Like the Futurists and Dadaists, Cage had been experimenting with everyday sounds and chance occurrences to expand the range of "music," while Cunningham explored modes of movement that might correspond with Cage's mix of unconventional sounds. Both objected to the modernist removal of aesthetics from everyday life and the utilitarian narrowness of Cold War American society. An untitled performance of theirs in 1952 included reading a Dadaist poem, showing a film on the ceiling, and pouring water from one bucket into another.

Cage's class in experimental music at the New School for Social Research in 1958 generated several Fluxus events, as did his international travels and collaborations in Europe and Japan during the 1960s. One event, *Snowstorm No. 1* (1965), put together by Czech Fluxus artist Milan Knížák (1940–), simply instructs the facilitators to distribute paper airplanes to the expectant audience and invite them to fly them around the auditorium. For Knížák, the point was to enjoy the beauty of the gliding paper and the fun of exchanging the planes with others. At a time when many real airplanes carried atomic bombs, however, some saw the Fluxus event as a demonstration for peace.

Cage also influenced the Living Theatre, a group begun by Julian Beck (1925–1985) and Judith Malina (1926–2015) in 1951. In 1960, they produced a theatre piece that played with his combinations of sounds, props, and actions. The year before, Beck and Malina had produced *The Connection*, a play by Jack Gelber (1932–2003) that purposefully invited audience confusion about whether the drug addicts and jazz players on stage were real people or fictional characters. Their Pirandellian experiments with reality and illusion soon combined with an interest in the ideas of Artaud after the initial publication in English of his *The Theatre and Its Double* in 1958. Following tours to Europe, the Living Theatre returned to the U.S. in 1968 with a group-created production entitled *Paradise Now* that called for the realization of utopia through Artaud's Theatre of Cruelty and a fusion of life and art. Artaud's influence on the Living Theatre and other groups after 1968 is discussed more fully in Chapter 13. Like several first-wave avant-gardists, the Living Theatre collective strove to live its artistic practices through its everyday life.

Less strident in its demands but no less utopian in its politics was the Bread and Puppet Theater, founded by Peter Schumann (1934–) in 1961. Schumann began aligning his puppet pageants and street shows with anti-war demonstrations in 1964. For the rest of the 1960s, the oversized puppet heads of his peasants, washerwomen, and workers, plus his bad guys like King Herod and Uncle Fatso (a capitalist-exploiter dressed like Uncle Sam), were marching against the war, homelessness, and nuclear arms. Schumann and his loose collective of puppet animators also mounted parable-like productions, such as *The Great Warrior* (1963) and *The Cry of the People for Meat* (1969), that explored mostly timeless problems of peace and justice through slow-moving puppets that were sometimes 30 feet tall.

The San Francisco Mime Troupe also used a traditional form, *commedia dell'arte*, to satirize the U.S. war in Vietnam and push for social justice. Begun in 1959 by actors interested in exploring the traditions of *commedia*, the group moved toward Marxist politics in the 1960s and formed itself into a collectively run theatre in 1970. The Mime Troupe denounced the war in their adaptation of a traditional *commedia* script by Carlo Goldoni, *L'Amant militaire* (1967). In later productions, the company used comic-book stereotypes and fast-action farce to demand women's rights and expose the lies of local politicians. Today, over half a century after being formed, the San Francisco Mime Troupe, the Living Theatre, and the Bread and Puppet Theater all continue to perform vital, provocative, political theatre.

Enraged by the slow pace of civil rights progress and continuing racism in the U.S., the Black Theatre Movement (BTM) called for revolutionary action in the 1960s. Scorning moderate black artists and religious leaders in the U.S., the BTM artists allied themselves with the Black Power movement of the late 1960s and called for the cultivation of black consciousness and the political overthrow of white regimes. In manifestos, plays, and performances, leaders Amiri Baraka (formerly LeRoi Jones, 1934–2014) and Ed Bullins (1935–) demanded the abolition of mainstream white culture and the immersion of black audiences in ritual-like experiences to enable them to gain a physical understanding of their past. In an article originally commissioned in December 1964 by *The New York Times*, but which that paper subsequently refused to publish, Baraka (still called LeRoi Jones) called for a "Revolutionary Theatre" that would

> force change . . . . The Revolutionary Theatre must EXPOSE! Show up the insides of these humans, look into black skulls. White men will cower before this theatre because it hates them. Because they themselves have been trained to hate. The Revolutionary Theatre must hate them for hating. For presuming with their technology to deny the supremacy of the Spirit. . . . It should stagger through our universe correcting, insulting, preaching, spitting craziness – but a craziness taught to us in our most rational moments. . . . The Revolutionary Theatre is shaped by the world, and moves to reshape the world. . . .
>
> (Jones 1965: 1–3)

One of Baraka's most compelling works is *Dutchman* (1964), a play about the birth of black consciousness in a mild-mannered subway rider killed by white vigilantes. Baraka started the

Figure 12.9

Photograph from a 1970 production of Amiri Baraka's *Slave Ship*, directed by Gilbert Moses at Theatre-in-the-Church, New York, NY. Photo: Bert Andrews. Permission given by Marsha Hudson, executrix of the estate of Bert Andrews.

Photo courtesy of the Billy Rose Theatre Collection, the NY Public Library for the Performing Arts, Astor, Lennox and Tilden Foundations.

Black Arts Repertory Theatre in Harlem in 1965 and premiered his ritualized historical pageant *Slave Ship* in 1967 at Spirit House in Newark, New Jersey (Figure 12.9). After 1970, Baraka devoted most of his energy to social action rather than theatre, and Bullins, who produced his plays with the New Lafayette Theatre Company in Harlem, came to prominence. Bullins used ritualistic, often jazz-inspired structures for his plays, such as *In the Wine Time* (1968), which explored the limitations and possibilities for black revolutionary action. Bullins's plays were sometimes criticized as languishing in despair. Other playwrights chose to focus on the quiet heroism of ordinary black people, rather than Baraka's active revolution or Bullins's victimhood and despair. For example, Alice Childress (1916–1994) wrote *Wedding Band: A Love/Hate Story in Black and White* (written 1962, premiere 1966), about a forbidden, interracial love affair. The play was considered so shocking that it was not produced in New York until 1972. When it was filmed for TV, some stations refused to air it.

SUMMARY

In this chapter, we explored the postwar conflict between psychological realism and rebellions against it. Because the U.S. had experienced far less damage than the rest of the world during the Second World War and had emerged as a wealthy superpower, theatre in the U.S. at first continued to rely on psychological realism. However, new developments in Europe reflected the devastation of the war. Such developments included the philosophy of existentialism and the so-called "Theatre of the Absurd." In the defeated nations of Germany and Japan, playwrights found various ways to come to terms with their nations' past and present. While some of the innovations and responses to the war did impact theatre in the United States, most mainstream U.S. theatre continued to reflect psychological realism. Nevertheless, the politics of the Cold War impacted U.S. theatre and theatre throughout the world, creating various tensions and discontent.

One of the forces driving discontent that soon would become so prominent was access to information. During the 1950s, television became more common. Events in distant areas became more significant, and protests against unpopular wars or social injustices occurred sooner, with more people becoming involved. Television also altered the way theatre was made. Especially in the U.K. and the U.S., television permitted more people to see great actors performing in important plays, broadcast live (not pre-recorded) from the studio. Although highly popular in its heyday, live theatre on commercial TV fell out of favor after the 1970s (although it began to reappear after 2000).

Arguably, the tipping point for television's rise to cultural dominance was around 1968. We will begin Chapter 13 with a brief discussion of the invasion of the living room, through television, by the momentous events of the mid- to late 1960s – including anti-war and civil rights protests, racial and political riots, police and military crackdowns, even the first man on the moon. These events, which previously would have been read about in newspapers, heard on the radio, or seen in movie newsreels days or weeks after they took place, were suddenly broadcast live or within hours of happening. Careful editing and censorship certainly occurred, but the events themselves often carried incredible shock value. How did audiences and theatre makers respond to this unprecedented assault on their senses and their intellects?

★

CHAPTER 13

Art, politics, or business? Theatre in search of identity, 1968–2000

Carol Fisher Sorgenfrei

Contributors: Gary Jay Williams, Tamara Underiner, and Bruce McConachie

The era called "The Sixties" established radically new ways of being, thinking, and performing – and reactions against them – that continue to this day. That period launched a series of upheavals in every area of life, particularly politics, economics, sexuality, culture, and of course the media. While many important theatre artists of the early twenty-first century began their careers in (or were deeply influenced by) the political/cultural upheavals of the 1960s, others rejected connections with the period. The 1980s–1990s saw a growing emphasis on theatre as part of a globalized, money-making entertainment industry, but there was also major growth in theatre having little or no profit motive. At the same time, some artists insisted that their goal was solely one of personal fulfillment or artistic transformation. For them, both political/cultural change and financial gain were beside the point.

To accommodate the discussion of all these transformations, this and the subsequent chapters have considerable chronological overlap. Here we will focus on the period from the 1960s to the 1990s, although we will occasionally go beyond because many of the issues, theatres, and people of the time are still quite active today. The next chapter is centered on the complex impact of globalization, including intercultural contact and a renewed exploration of the local. Chapter 15 closes the book by examining new types of performance associated with the rise of networked culture and its social effects.

We begin this chapter with a historical overview of the 1960s, and next consider some of the effects that changes in the media were having on theatre. Then we will address three major topics. First, escalating political tensions in the early 1960s led to an explosion of sometimes controversial theatre advocating or participating in political and cultural change. At the same time, as the subsequent section will show, many theatre artists were challenging the primacy of the text within performance. Last, we will consider the changing circumstances of subsidized national theatres and the development of non-profit theatres.

The 1960s: A historical crossroads

Historians sometimes define "The Sixties" as lasting from *c*.1958 to *c*.1974. Major cultural shifts occurred throughout the world. Focusing on Europe and the U.S., Arthur Marwick notes specific characteristics of this crucial period, including: criticism of established society; individualism; youth power; technological advances; public spectacles; international cultural exchange; improvements in material life; upheavals in race, class, and family relationships; sexual permissiveness; new modes of self-presentation; rock music as a universal language; original developments in elite thought and culture; growth of progressive ideology in institutions of authority; reactionary and violent responses by police and some religious bodies; increased concern for civil and personal rights; and awareness of multiculturalism. The concepts "counterculture" and "underground" defined developments in theatre and the arts (Marwick 1998: 16–20). To this list we must also add the widespread, increased use of illegal and psychedelic drugs.

Outside Europe and the U.S., the changes might be different but were no less significant. In the People's Republic of China (PRC), the Cultural Revolution (1966–1976) attempted to eliminate all vestiges of traditional Chinese culture and capitalist influence. Artists, physicians, academics, landowners, and other "elitists" were sent into the countryside and forbidden to practice their skills; Buddhist temples were shut down; Communist orthodoxy was rigorously enforced. The result was economic and political stagnation. The Cultural Revolution only ended when China's dictator Mao Zedong died and his major supporters (dubbed "The Gang of Four") were imprisoned.

In Africa, Latin America, and other areas, nations were breaking free of colonial subjugation or partition, resulting in political and economic instabilities that were often accompanied by wars, bloody coups, terrorism, mass killings, poverty, and starvation, all of which provoked migrations. The continuing Cold War between the U.S. and the Soviet Union exacerbated these problems.

The year 1968 is often chosen as the dividing line between the more complacent "Fifties" and the radically transforming "Sixties." A few key events of 1967–1969 will demonstrate the cataclysmic nature of the cultural shift, and the complex, ever-changing emotions of people throughout the world.

On January 14, 1967, the first "Human Be-In" took place in San Francisco's Golden Gate Park. This self-described "gathering of the tribes" was populated by "hippies," anti-establishment youth rejecting conformity, war, and materialism, and advocating communal sharing. The Human Be-In inspired *Hair: The American Tribal Love-Rock Musical* (1967; book and lyrics by James Rado and Gerome Ragni, music by Galt MacDermot). It was at the Human Be-In that Timothy Leary (1920–1996), a former Harvard professor who advocated the use of psychedelic drugs such as LSD, first urged the world's youth to "turn on, tune in, drop out." The Human Be-In gave rise to 1967's "Summer of Love," when about 100,000 "flower children" gathered peacefully in San Francisco's Haight-Ashbury district, openly taking psychedelic drugs, enjoying music, and engaging in uninhibited sex.

The imagined idyll of the Summer of Love was followed by the harsh brutalities of 1968. In France, Japan, Italy, the U.S., the U.K., Germany, Mexico, and elsewhere, protests by students and workers against the Vietnam War, authoritarian governments, social/racial inequality, and educational practices resulted in violent police and military responses. Historians often cite May 1968 in Paris as the defining moment. Following extensive student protests, the closure of universities, and violent military responses, over 11 million workers (more than one fifth of the population of France) went on strike (including spontaneous "wildcat" strikes) for two weeks, virtually shutting down the French economy and threatening to topple the government. Repercussions are still felt, nearly half a century later.

In Poland, strikes by university students and intellectuals were harshly suppressed by Russian-backed security forces. Soon after, an anti-Semitic campaign forced the mass emigration of Polish Jews. In what was then Czechoslovakia, a movement for political change ("the Prague Spring") was crushed by the invasion of Soviet and Eastern Bloc troops. Police brutality in Northern Ireland signaled the beginning of a long-lasting insurrection against British rule ("The Troubles"). In Japan, students and intellectuals had been protesting the government's policies, including support of the Vietnam War, since autumn 1967, resulting in brutality by the riot police. By early 1968, demonstrations and police actions were widespread and many universities had been shut down.

In the U.S., 1968 was traumatic as well. Both black civil rights leader Dr. Martin Luther King, Jr. and probable Democratic presidential nominee Robert F. Kennedy were assassinated; riots, looting, and arson erupted in 110 poor, black, urban ghettos, eliciting police and National Guard brutality. Partly because the government was drafting college-age males to fight, the war in Vietnam aroused massive protests on college and university campuses, especially between 1968 and 1971. The authorities responded violently to student demonstrations and strikes at the University of California at Berkeley, Columbia, and other universities, and to anti-Vietnam War demonstrations at the Democratic National Convention in Chicago. Agit-prop groups, calling themselves guerrilla theatre companies (after jungle-fighter revolutionaries in Latin America), staged cartoon-like skits at rallies and elsewhere to protest the war. For example, some anti-war protesters mocked society with guerrilla theatre, including nominating a pig (called Pigasus the Immortal) for U.S. president. By 1970, there were probably 400 student guerrilla troupes in the U.S. Students in Western European cities formed similar troupes to protest American militarism in Vietnam.

Despite the violence and despair, there were important advances in social welfare, civil rights for African-Americans, science, and technology. An estimated 530 million television viewers watched the U.S. astronauts land on the moon in July 1969, planting the nation's flag on its surface. As a technological triumph and landmark media event, it symbolized a new era, a new global consciousness and a U.S. public relations victory in the Cold War. A few years later, the U.S.'s National Aeronautics and Space Administration (NASA) released its famous "blue marble" color satellite photos, showing the planet earth floating in space. Circulating on global television, the images of a beautiful, fragile earth reinforced the hope that humankind might cease its destruction of itself and its home.

Between the 1950s and the 1990s, radio, film, television, satellite television, video cassettes, and compact discs, and finally the internet brought an increasing number of ordinary people into new cultural negotiations daily. The violent events of the 1960s were all broadcast globally on television. So too were international sports and cultural events such as the Olympics or the Oscars. The end of the Cold War in 1989 was viewed worldwide when television carried images of people tearing down the wall separating East and West Berlin and toppling statues of Lenin. Such dramatic gestures continue to be broadcast on television and the internet. For example, in early 2011, mobile cellphones and television cameras captured shocking images of Japan's devastating earthquake, tsunami, and resulting damage to a nuclear power plant, as well as the anti-government protests and armed rebellions throughout the Middle East that were dubbed "The Arab Spring." The immediacy of televised and internet news far surpassed the power of newspaper accounts. As we will see in the next chapter, the technology of computers and satellites that made the moon landing possible would stimulate the new processes of globalization, further challenging traditional boundaries.

Theatre and electronic media

Media technologies have had obvious impact on the forms, styles, and techniques of the theatre. As we saw in Chapter 12, Arthur Miller's *Death of a Salesman* had its roots in radio, and Jo Mielziner's setting offered a film-like fluidity. By the 1970s, verbal language no longer always occupied a central, dominating place, and less linear dramatic structures began to be more common. By the 1990s, digitized visual sequences allowed thematic or symbolic associations and multiple readings. Scenic spectacularism had become a star performer in big-budget American and British musicals, such as *The Phantom of the Opera* (1984). Musicals and some non-musical plays began to equip actors with wireless microphones and to digitally balance and distribute blends of singers and orchestras, creating soundscapes that differ greatly from traditional (non-amplified) live performance. Stage musicals were recycled into films, CD soundtracks, DVDs, and touring shows for international audiences. Large-scale musicals are further discussed in Chapter 14.

The borders between all media and genres were growing increasingly permeable. These shifts, plus increasing use of computers and video games, suggest a change in cultural sensibilities – more interest in non-verbal emotional expression, less confidence in the truth-value of verbal language or linear continuities, greater visual sophistication, and interest in alternative, interactive realities. One result was that many serious theatre and performance artists moved away from the dominance of the once-primary, sacrosanct verbal play text in search of a greater expressive range – a topic we will explore below.

Theatre, politics, and cultural change

During the turbulent 1960s, many people in theatre asked how theatre might be an advocate in political change and cultural controversies. The uprisings of 1968 had awakened a generation of theatre artists eager to help the oppressed. These radical artists recognized the power disparities caused by class, racial, gender, and/or regional differences and hoped to forge an alternative culture to help workers, peasants, and others to oppose capitalist power. They typically performed in parks, community centers, popular demonstrations, village squares, churches, and similar gathering places. As noted in Chapter 12, the U.S.'s Living Theatre, San Francisco Mime Troupe, and Bread and Puppet Theater appeared before 1968, and as of 2014, all are still flourishing.

In Provence, France, the Lo Teatre de la Carriera emphasized southern France's unique culture by using the Occitan dialect and by decrying the region's industrialization by Parisian "imperialists." In Berlin, the West German Grips Theater produced radical plays for children and youth. In Spain, despite rigorous censorship, several theatres opposed dictator Francisco Franco and his repressive regime during the early 1970s. These included Barcelona's Els Joglars, agitating for Catalan independence in northern Spain, and Madrid's Tabaño, which mocked Spanish consumerism, authoritarianism, and the Catholic Church.

In 1971, British playwright/theorist John McGrath (1935–2002) founded 7:84, a theatre company named for a statistic published in 1966 in *The Economist* stating that 7 percent of the population of Great Britain owned 84 percent of the capital wealth. His productions, using broad humor, catchy tunes, and identifiable locations, were performed in working-class halls and pubs throughout the 1970s. His *The Cheviot, the Stag, and the Black, Black Oil* (1973) demonstrated how capitalists' desire to profit from North Sea oil was simply one more episode in the long exploitation of the Scottish poor by the English rich.

In 1968, Italian playwright-performer Dario Fo (1926–) and his playwright-actor wife, Franca Rame (1929–2013), broke from the commercial theatre to establish a theatrical cooperative, which soon produced *Mistero Buffo* (1969), a one-person show (with Fo as court jester) that satirized Catholicism. *Accidental Death of an Anarchist* (1970) was a farcical attack on police corruption (Figure 13.1). During the 1970s and 1980s, Fo explored Italian folk drama, including *commedia dell'arte*, wrote several more plays, and expanded his repertoire of theatrical clowning. Rame wrote and performed feminist pieces, such as *All Bed, Board, and Church* (1977), which excoriated Italian patriarchy. Fo and Rame performed at many rallies for progressive causes and in culturally deprived zones, often donating the proceeds to radical political movements. These proceeds might be quite substantial; in the mid-1980s, Fo often attracted over 10,000 spectators per performance. In 1997, he was awarded the Nobel Prize for Literature.

Despite such successes, the radical theatre movement as a whole had little impact on Western society. Critics have suggested two reasons. One was that Cold War ideology, perpetuated by Western nation-states and the commercial media, limited options for change. It was one thing to cheer the radical socialist vision of the San Francisco Mime Troupe or 7:84 at a weekend performance, but quite another to act on those beliefs in the union hall or at the voting booth. Another reason was that with increasing globalization, workers and others began to define themselves primarily as consumers, undercutting their commitment to radical politics. Although many theatre troupes in the West clung to the utopian hopes of the late 1960s, their audiences were moving towards other values and identities.

In contrast, radical theatre in many parts of Africa, the Philippines, and Latin America found responsive audiences. Some theatre companies chose active opposition and helped their oppressed countrymen toward better lives and political liberation.

Social activism and theatre in postcolonial Africa

As previously noted, the end of colonialism in Africa often resulted in poverty, political instability, and ethnic wars. After independence, some indigenous theatre artists began

Figure 13.1

Poster for a production of Dario Fo's *Accidental Death of an Anarchist*, at Wyndhams Theatre, London, 1980.

© V&A Images, Victoria and Albert Museum.

to reclaim tribal myths and performance practices and, at the same time, develop new, often politically themed works that assessed the damage or critiqued the new regimes, sometimes leading to the artists' imprisonment. This section presents only a small sampling of work to suggest the breadth of postcolonial African performance.

Nigeria, which became independent from Britain in 1960, includes several distinct ethnicities and languages. This diverse culture offers a wide spectrum of theatrical styles and perspectives. Hubert Ogunde (1916–1990) founded the Ogunde Concert Party, Nigeria's first professional theatre company, in 1945. Both his anti-colonial plays before independence (many of which were banned) and his post-independence *Yoruba Awake!* (1964) drew on Yoruba myths. During Nigeria's civil war, Wole Soyinka (1934–), Nigeria's best-known playwright and winner of the 1986 Nobel Prize for Literature, was detained without trial and subsequently went into exile. His *Madmen and Specialists* (1971) is a bitter, enigmatic play inspired by those events. As noted in Chapter 1, Soyinka's *Death and the King's Horseman* (1975) uses the *Egúngún* masquerade to critique colonialism. After returning from exile, Soyinka staged *Opera Wonyosi* (1977), a Nigerian amalgam of *The Beggar's Opera* (1728) by John Gay (see Chapter 7) and Brecht's *Threepenny Opera* (1928). It satirizes a self-proclaimed African emperor and the Nigerian middle class. Fellow Nigerian Femi Osofisan (1946–), influenced by Marx and Brecht, looks unfavorably on Soyinka's sometimes abstruse metaphysics. Osofisan's plays reflect both his own aesthetic interests and his passionate advocacy of social justice. His *Once Upon Four Robbers* (1980) satirized the Nigerian military government, and his adaptation of Nikolai Gogol's *The Inspector General* (1836) mocks the ruling elite. Osofisan uses traditional dance, music, myth, and folklore to explore modern class polarities in *The Chattering and the Song* (1976). His *Tegonni: An African Antigone* (1999) deconstructs both colonial and patriarchal authority by juxtaposing the classical Greek character with a nineteenth-century Yoruba princess.

The choice of language is often a significant issue in postcolonial societies. In Sierra Leone, independent since 1957, Thomas Decker (1916–1978) promoted theatre in Krio, an urban, English-based Creole language that developed in the interchange among freed slaves in Freetown, their European colonial masters, and the indigenous people of the region. Krio theatre serves a wide cross-section of society and has inspired a number of playwrights, including the radical Yulisa Amadu Maddy (1936–2014). His play *Big Berrin* (1976) – the title means "big death" – is critical of the plight of the urban poor and resulted in his imprisonment.

South Africa became an independent state in 1934, but a legacy of Dutch and then British colonial practices remained. Part of this legacy was apartheid (a Dutch and Afrikaans word meaning "apartness"), a policy that relegated black people to separate, inferior living and working conditions. Despite being the minority, white descendants of the colonialists controlled the government. In 1948, they formally instituted apartheid as a legal system. After four decades of organized resistance, apartheid was abolished in 1990.

In the 1960s, resistance to apartheid by both black and white theatre artists fueled the creation of politically dangerous works. The anti-apartheid, multiracial Serpent Players (further discussed in the case study below) was founded in 1963 by initially untrained actors, primarily service and industrial workers, led by Norman Ntshinga (1933–2000). Its name derived from the locale of its first production: the snake pit at a former zoo in Port Elizabeth. The Serpent Players' productions included *Sizwe Bansi is Dead* (1972) and *The Island* (1973), collectively created through improvisation by Athol Fugard (1932–), John Kani (1943–), and Winston Ntshona (1941–). *Sizwe Bansi Is Dead* is about a man who obtained a "pass," a document

Figure 13.2

Percy Mtwa and Mbongeni Ngema in the "pink-nose" mimicry scene in *Woza Albert!*, by Percy Mtwa, Mbongeni Ngema, and Barney Simon, directed by Barney Simon, at the Market Theatre, Johannesburg, South Africa, 1982.

Photo © Ruphin Coudyzer, The Market Theatre.

necessary for black men to work in South Africa, by taking on the identity of a dead man. It had wide success in Africa, the U.S., and elsewhere. It inspired other collectively created works, including *Woza Albert!* (1980) by Barney Simon (1932–1995), Mbongeni Ngema (1955–), and Percy Mtwa (1954–). *Woza Albert!* is a political satire in which Jesus's return to Earth occurs in South Africa (Figure 13.2). Under the artistic direction of Barney Simon, Johannesburg's Market Theatre (founded 1976) came to be known as the "Theatre of the Struggle." By 2014, it had won 21 international and over 300 South African awards for excellence.

Our first case study explores how some South African theatre artists actively fought apartheid.

CASE STUDY: Athol Fugard: Theatre of witnessing in South Africa

Carol Fisher Sorgenfrei

Athol Fugard (1932–), a white South African playwright, actor, and director, spent the years prior to the end of apartheid in 1990 collaborating with black theatre artists in order to "bear witness" to, and protest, apartheid. Such collaborations were internationally applauded but semi-legal; at various times Fugard was placed under government surveillance or had his passport revoked, and he and his family endured threats and police raids. Many of the black actors he worked with were arrested. In 1962, he used his growing international fame to lead playwrights throughout the world in refusing to allow segregated theatres to produce their work. However, in 1968, he changed his mind and urged (unsuccessfully) that the boycott be lifted. Since the end of apartheid, he has continued to write internationally acclaimed plays, often of a more personal and sometimes autobiographical nature. A documentary about his struggles during apartheid was released in 2012.

Fugard's plays usually focus on a few individuals who are closely tied – by blood, love, or friendship – and the complex, private agonies they inflict upon each other. Several of his realist plays are well known outside South Africa, including *Boesman and Lena* (1969), and *Master Harold and the Boys* (1982), an autobiographical play about how a white boy destroys his relationship with his black fellow-worker due to biases the boy learned from apartheid. Although critic Loren Kruger suggests that Fugard's international success may have compromised his integrity, many others feel that his plays reveal the political evils and personal suffering caused by apartheid. By "bearing witness," the plays focus attention on how personal traumas are embedded in (and exacerbated by) political reality.

Life under apartheid

Apartheid classified people according to four racial groups – "black," "white," "colored" (mixed race), and "Indian" – with the last two having further subdivisions. Everyone had to carry identification cards specifying their race. It was illegal to marry or have sexual relations with a person of a different race, and the races had separate public facilities such as restrooms, swimming pools, restaurants, hospitals, theatres, and schools. The so-called tribal homelands had separate governing bodies. All political protest or opposition to the government and its policies was outlawed. Blacks were forcibly "resettled" in an attempt to create whites-only areas. Despite international protests, in 1955 at least 60,000 blacks were removed by armed soldiers from Sophiatown, an area in Johannesburg. Sophiatown was demolished and its former residents were forced to live in the newly created black suburb of Soweto, an acronym for South Western Townships. Where Sophiatown once stood, a new white town called Triomf (Triumph) was built. Although focused on blacks, forced resettlement was also practiced on other non-whites, such as Indians and Chinese. It has been estimated that over three and a half million people were forcibly removed.

In 1960, 69 peaceful protesters were massacred in Sharpeville (followed by the arrest of 18,000 people) and three years later the UN implemented an embargo on arms sales to South Africa. The year 1977 saw shocking police brutality against the people of Soweto. By the 1980s, there was virtual civil war in South Africa, and most of the world participated in political, economic, and cultural boycotts of the nation. In 1990, the ruling National Party renounced apartheid, and in 1994 Nelson Mandela (1918–2013), who had been a political prisoner from 1963 to 1990, was elected the nation's first black president. In 1995, the government established the Truth and Reconciliation Commission to permit victims of human rights violations to speak out and to consider amnesty for perpetrators.

Athol Fugard and theatre under apartheid

South African theatre is rich and varied. The experiences of apartheid, however, clearly molded the development of recent drama. As Dennis Walder perceptively notes:

If there is one common impulse, it has been the urge to tell a story; and not just to tell a story, but to bear witness. The idea of witness, with its overtones of truth and sacrifice, has particular power in the face of the darkest events of our times. It is an idea that suggests the potential of art to respond to such events, and to reach across the boundaries of class, race, gender and nation, without descending into facile universalism.

(Walder 2003: 1)

In 1958, Fugard joined the interracial Union of South African Artists, and soon after he helped create the African Theatre Workshop. Fugard's play *Blood Knot* (1961, originally titled *The Blood Knot*) was groundbreaking. It was written partly in response to the horrific Sharpeville massacre. Directed by the author, it starred himself and black actor Zakes Mokae (1934–2009) as brothers who had the same mother but different fathers. One appears white-skinned and the other appears black-skinned. Although they love each other, the realities of racial discrimination cause conflict. For example, the light-skinned brother could choose to live as a white man (although risking arrest if caught) whereas his dark-skinned brother will never have such a choice, and must always suffer. When the light-skinned brother dresses up "white" to meet a white woman, he begins to treat his brother as an inferior. In turn, the dark-skinned brother reveals submerged fury, even hatred. Eventually, they remain together as blacks, but the brothers clearly signal complex feelings for each other. When the play opened, a South African newspaper noted:

Theatre history was made in Johannesburg this week when a White man and a Black man acted together publicly in the same play. . . . Municipal by-laws purport to prohibit racially mixed performances, but . . . producer Leon Gluckman has taken a chance and "The Blood Knot" opened in the Y.M.C.A.'s intimate theatre on Wednesday night before a fashionable and wildly applauding (White) audience. . . . The authorities have taken no action (yet) to stop the performance, possibly because the legal aspect has been delicately avoided so far.

(Wertheim 2000: 18)

Productions in London and New York signaled the start of Fugard's international recognition, and helped prevent censorship at home. However, the day after *The Blood Knot* was broadcast on British television in 1967, Fugard's passport was taken away, supposedly for reasons of national security.

Collaborative creation and witnessing

In 1963, Fugard and a group of inexperienced black actors founded the Serpent Players. Their first productions were adaptations of works such as Georg Büchner's (1813–1837) *Woyzeck* and Brecht's *Caucasian Chalk Circle*, setting them in a South African township to emphasize their relevance to daily life. In late 1966, they presented their first collaborative, improvisationally developed work, Fugard's *The Coat*. Fugard was influenced by Jerzy Grotowski's concept of "poor theatre" that relies on actors' bodies and voices, not spectacle. (We will discuss Grotowski below.) Fugard has said that reading Grotowski helped him realize new ways to work. He sought

techniques for releasing the creative potential of the actor. . . . The basic device has been that of Challenge and Response. As a writer-director I have challenged, and the actors have responded, not intellectually or merely verbally but with a totality of Being that at the risk of sounding pretentious I can only liken to a form of Zen spontaneity.

(Fugard et al. 1974: xi–xii)

Fugard's collaborative works emphasize the actors' personal experiences. In a 1973 interview regarding the creation of *Sizwe Bansi is Dead*, he said, "[O]bviously, I did a hell of a lot of actual writing. But I've not been allowed inside a black township in South Africa for many years, so I am very dependent on the two actors for a basic image, a vitality, an assertion of life" (quoted in Wertheim 2000: 80).

The Serpent Players' productions – including *Sizwe Bansi is Dead* (1972), *The Island* (1973), and *Statements After an Arrest Under the Immorality Act* (1974) – were often performed in secure locations such as garages or private homes to evade the police, and the actors did not take home written scripts in order to avoid being arrested for keeping "subversive materials." Their collaborative process – blacks and whites together, regardless of the consequences – shows how "witnessing" can create art, encourage social justice and political change, and enable audiences to more fully understand the past and present.

A longer version of this case study may be found on the website.

Key references

Cima, G.A. (2009) "Resurrecting *Sizwe Banzi is Dead* (1972–2008): John Kani, Winston Ntshona, Athol Fugard and Postapartheid South Africa," *Theatre Survey* 50: 91–118.

Clark, N.L. and Worger, W.H. (2004) *South Africa: The Rise and Fall of Apartheid*, Harlow, UK: Pearson Education.

Davis, G. and Fuchs, A. (eds) (1996) *Theatre and Change in South Africa*, Amsterdam: Harwood.

Fugard, A. (1983) *Notebooks: 1960–1977*, ed. Mary Benson, Johannesburg: Ad. Donker.

Fugard, A. (1987) *Selected Plays*, Oxford: Oxford University Press.

Fugard, A. (1992) *Playland . . . and Other Words,* Johannesburg: Witwatersrand University Press.

Fugard, A., Kani, J., and Ntshona, W. (1974) *Statements: Three Plays*, Oxford: Oxford University Press.

Gray, S. (ed.) (1982) *Athol Fugard*, Johannesburg: McGraw-Hill.

Hauptfleish, T. (1997) *Theatre and Society in South Africa*, Pretoria: J.L. van Schaik.

Hutchinson, Y. and Breitinger, E. (eds) (2000) *History and Theatre in Africa*, Bayreuth: African Studies Series and South African Theatre Journal, Bayreuth University.

Kruger, L. (1999) *The Drama of South Africa: Plays, Pageants and Publics since 1910*, London: Routledge.

McDonald, M. (n.d.) "Space, Time, and Silence: The Craft of Athol Fugard," unpublished ms.

McDonald, M. (2006) "The Return of Myth: Athol Fugard and the Classics," *Arion* 14(2): 21–47.

McDonald, M. and Walton, J.M. (eds) (2002) *Amid Our Troubles: Irish Versions of Greek Tragedy*, London: Methuen.

Price, R.M., and Rosberg, C.G. (eds) (1980) *The Apartheid Regime: Political Power and Racial Domination*, Berkeley: University of California Press.

Walder, D. (1987) "Introduction," in A. Fugard, *Selected Plays*, Oxford: Oxford University Press.

Walder, D. (2003) *Athol Fugard*, Tavistock, Devon: Northcote House.

Wertheim, A. (2000) *The Dramatic Art of Athol Fugard: From South Africa to the World*, Bloomington and Indianapolis: University of Indiana Press.

Figure 13.3

The Philippine Educational Theatre Association's *1896*, performed in 1995 and 1996. Libretto by Charley de la Paz; music by Lucian Leteba; directed by Soxie Topacio.

Photo © PETA.

Theatre and resistance in the Philippines

Perhaps the most successful political theatre in the developing world has been the Philippine Educational Theater Association (PETA), a network of community-based theatres that opposed the dictatorship of Ferdinand Marcos from 1967 until its fall in 1986. During the 1970s, PETA members combined improvisational exercises, values from Catholic liberation theology, and the radical educational ideas of Brazilian Paolo Freire (1921–1997) to train themselves in theatrical skills and community organizing. Core groups of facilitator-organizers moved from Manila and other cities into the countryside, helping locals to create scripts analyzing their social, economic, and political conditions, and suggesting solutions. By 1986, nearly 300 local theatres, run by fishermen, peasants, students, industrial workers, and others, comprised the PETA network.

After 1986, PETA shifted its emphasis from socialism and anti-imperialism to examining and protesting the effects of local, national, and global policies on everyday lives. In addition to many touring shows, PETA mounts large productions in the courtyard of a former Spanish fort in downtown Manila. In 1995, PETA collaborated with the San Francisco Mime Troupe on a musical satire about elections in the Philippines. Its play *1896* was staged in 1996 to mark the centennial of the Filipino revolution against Spain (Figure 13.3). PETA's 2011 musical *Care Divas* portrayed Filipino transgender health-care providers working in Israel. Most of PETA's financing now comes from external NGOs (non-governmental organizations) and from local contributions and fees.

Theatre and resistance in Latin America

In the Americas, the Cold War between the Soviet Union and the United States played itself out in revolutions and rebellions (as in Cuba and Colombia) and in dictatorships and dirty wars seeking to quell all opposition (as in Brazil, Guatemala, Chile, Argentina, and Peru), often with the support of the superpowers interested in protecting both ideological and business interests.

Soon after the Cuban Revolution in 1959, leader Fidel Castro (1926–) and his deputies began to use a type of theatre for development (further discussed in Chapter 14) to transform Cuba. In 1969, they sent a professional theatre company into the Escambray region, where counter-revolutionary groups had been active in the early 1960s, to prepare the traditional small farmers and peasants for collectivization. Mixing revolutionary propaganda with participatory techniques and developmental strategies, Teatro Escambray became a model for Cuban revolutionary theatre by the mid-1970s.

The combination of radical political theatre and theatre for development exemplified by Teatro Escambray exerted wide influence in Latin America during the 1970s and 1980s. Some companies pushed for a Cuban-style revolution, but many more worked toward versions of democratic socialism. In Mexico, where over 200 theatres joined socialist politics to community development, this movement was called Nuevo Teatro Popular (New Popular Theatre), a term that can be applied to the movement as a whole.

Throughout Latin America, Nuevo Teatro was nearly as various as it was huge, embracing amateurs and professionals, performing in agit-prop and realistic styles, drawing urban intellectual and village peasant audiences, and ranging widely among aesthetic and political priorities. Nuevo Teatro helped to empower peasants and workers in Colombia, Peru, and Mexico, worked against repressive dictatorships in Brazil, Argentina, and Uruguay, and supported democratic socialist regimes in Chile and Nicaragua.

Although varying widely in style, radical Nuevo Teatro troupes drew from a common tradition of Brechtian theatre and politics. The troupes often shared actors, directors, and playwrights, sometimes because exile from one country would force a theatre artist to work in another. The major troupes met regularly in festivals and conferences to compare productions and to workshop new strategies. Not surprisingly, Cuba took the initiative, promoting significant hemispheric meetings of theatre artists and troupes in 1964 and 1967.

After 1990, with the end of the Cold War, the decline of Cuba, and the fall of most dictatorial governments in Latin America, the Nuevo Teatro movement lost momentum. Nevertheless, many troupes made a successful transition to the globalization era. The Yuyach-kani company in Peru, for example, began moving away from Marxist theatre in the 1980s in response to the mass killings of indigenous and rural mestizo populations by Maoist revolutionaries known as The Shining Path. In such pieces as *Contralviento* (1989) and *Adios Ayacucho* (1990), Yuyachkani — the name translates roughly as "I am remembering" in Quechua — memorialized the victims of these genocides and affirmed the need to understand their traumas.

Brazilian director Augusto Boal (see Chapter 12) was a key influence on the Nuevo Theatro movement. Boal recognized that theatre could oppose, from the ground up, the imposition of capitalist ideologies and the social inequities they produced. His methods continue to be utilized by grassroots movements throughout the world. After adapting international classics for the Arena Theatre in São Paulo, he began working with Brazilian playwrights. However, beginning in 1964, his cultural activism made him a target of Brazil's military dictatorship. He was kidnapped, tortured, and in 1971, he was exiled to Argentina. While in exile, he developed his influential "Theater of the Oppressed," described in Chapter 14.

Politics meets globalization: Theatre and media in China

Political theatre's goals need not be confined to overturning an oppressive regime. In mainland China, artists (often carefully controlled by the government) have used theatre to foster patriotism, encourage a revised ideology, and more recently, to support a limited embrace of capitalism. Thus, political theatre is not necessarily distinct from the business of theatre — the entertainment industry.

During the Cultural Revolution (1966–1976) in the People's Republic of China (PRC), traditional Chinese theatre, translations of Western plays, and Chinese-written spoken drama (*huaju*, which first appeared in 1907 and was heavily indebted to Western realism) were forbidden by Maoist extremists who considered them to be decadent and counter-revolutionary. Instead, they fostered a new form of musical theatre called *yangbanxi* [yahng bahn shih] "revolutionary model drama"). *Yangbanxi* combines *jingju* and Western performance traditions. Some are based on traditional plays, rewritten to eliminate "feudal" elements and to emphasize their version of Communist ideology. The first *yangbanxi* was *Taking Tiger Mountain by Strategy* (*Zhiqu Weihu Shan*, 1969), based on a novel inspired by an actual 1946 incident from the Chinese civil war. It is filled with patriotic fervor and revolutionary propaganda. In 2014, a Hong Kong studio released a 3D film with the same title, based on the original novel.

After the end of the Cultural Revolution, China began to gradually embrace capitalism and globalization. Many theatre artists experimented with non-illusionistic and Brechtian styles, often attempting to combine Chinese "tradition" and Western "modernity." They were led by theorist/director Huang Zuolin (1906–1994) who had introduced a version of Stanislavsky's acting method to China in 1938–1940. Beginning in the 1960s, he also advocated including acting styles derived from Brecht, Piscator, Meyerhold, and Chinese *kunqu* and *jingju* in actor training. Prominent playwrights and directors experimented with his ideas, but the government censored work satirizing or criticizing the Communist Party, including Sha Yexin's (1939–) *What If I Were Real* (*Jairu wo shi zhende*, 1979) and Gao Xingjian's (1940–) *Bus Stop* (*Chezhan*, 1983). (For more on Gao, see the case study in Chapter 14.)

Fearing rapid Westernization, in June 1989, the PRC government took military action against pro-democracy student demonstrators at Beijing's Tiananmen Square. The media and arts were severely censored. Censorship has lessened in recent years; nevertheless internet communications unfavorable to the Chinese government continue to be suppressed. Although the content of theatre and film is carefully monitored, stylistic experimentation in theatre is often encouraged.

Meng Jinghui (1966–) is an influential experimental stage director who often explores intersections among theatre, architecture, music, installation, and multimedia. He directed Shen Lin's (1958–) *Bootleg Faust* (*Daoban fushide*, 1999) which satirized Chinese popular consumer culture by intermingling elements from Goethe's *Faust* with Chinese slang, classical Chinese poetry, Greek mythology, and Chinese television.

Also encouraged are selected films for export. Hong Kong has long produced popular Chinese-language films that exploit international fascination with martial arts. *Crouching Tiger, Hidden Dragon* (2000), directed by Taiwanese Ang Lee (1954–), was a cooperative production involving China, Taiwan, Hong Kong, and the United States – a global enterprise. Despite content that many critics argue demeans women and exoticizes China, the film won more than 40 international awards and was at the time the highest grossing foreign language film in American history. In 2008, the internationally televised Beijing Olympics, with the epic-scale performances of its opening ceremonies, signaled China's status as an economic superpower.

Questioning the author(ity)

One of the most characteristic slogans of the 1960s was "Question authority." In literary criticism, the questioning turned toward the authority of authorship and texts themselves. For example, in 1967, literary theorist Roland Barthes (1915–1980) wrote an essay titled "The Death of the Author." Barthes argued that meaning arises only through the interaction between the reader and text, not through an author's intentions or personal/historical circumstances. Intellectual historian Michel Foucault's (1926–1984) article "What is an Author?" (1969) analyzed the author as an effect of society and language use – a kind of symbol. And in *Of Grammatology* (1967), philosopher Jacques Derrida (1930–2004) "deconstructed" texts to show the instability of their meaning and their self-contradictions. Doubts about the position – even meaningfulness – of writers and writing were very much in the air.

In theatre circles, the author was being similarly questioned. Scripts no longer seemed quite so central and unassailable; other aspects of theatrical performance were perhaps more important. To some, the key element was the performer, especially the performer's body and embodied encounter with the audience. To others, the director's vision was uppermost. The play text – or any text – could be used as mere raw material, to be manipulated or uprooted for performance. Possibly texts were unnecessary: observation, personal interactions, and staged imagery could constitute performance. In short, many theatre artists decided that the play was *not* the thing: performance was. Occasionally, displacing the text suggested powerful cultural or political critiques.

Performing in the flesh

One of the most urgent and influential theatre voices decrying the limits of conventional, text-bound theatre was that of Antonin Artaud. As discussed in Chapter 11, his *The Theatre and Its Double* posited a cleavage between spirit and body and between civilized culture and the mysterious, dangerous forces at the heart of existence. To restore unity, he claimed, the theatre must directly access these forces, without the obstacles of indirect representation, including written language. He called for a Theatre of Cruelty that would liberate audiences from linear storytelling, from keyhole realism with its character psychology, and from the masterpieces of the past (Artaud 1958: 7–13, 33–47, 84–92). The famous title of one chapter is "No More Masterpieces." Artaud envisioned a primal, non-verbal theatre affecting the whole organism, with performances enveloping the spectator using incantation, ancient musical instruments, rhythmical dance, symbolic gestures, masks, mannequins, and ritual-like costumes. Inspired by his brief experience with Balinese dance theatre, Artaud wrote mystically of the need for the actor to access a realm of passions through the body (1958: 89–100).

"We shall not act a written play," he wrote, but "make attempts at direct staging, around themes, facts, or known works" (1958: 98). He suggested, for example, performing an erotic tale by the Marquis de Sade, staging incidents about the conquest of Mexico, Elizabethan plays "stripped of their texts," and romantic melodramas – any material that would allow "a passionate and convulsive conception of life," and correspond to "the unrest characteristic of our epoch" (1958: 89–122).

Artaud's influence was modest until the 1960s, when his ideas suddenly caught fire. His mystical jeremiad against a text-based theatre opened a path for experiments seeking more sensuous performances and challenging the limits of illusionistic representation. His enthusiasts were probably unaware of his fascist leanings – most believed the Theatre of Cruelty was liberating and revolutionary. The Living Theatre's collectively created *Paradise Now* (1968) was probably the most Artaudian of their productions. The performance was structured around rituals, outcries against oppression, and calls for audience participation, including joining a nude quasi-orgy on stage. It concluded with a procession out to the streets. The goal was to break down the boundary between performers and audience as a step toward political freedom.

Similarly, *Dionysus in '69* (1968), a rendering of Euripides' *The Bacchae* by Richard Schechner (1934–) with his Performance Group (1967–1980), combined narrative and extra-textual, faux-ritual scenes. It pitted Dionysian sexual freedom against repression, but also hinted at the dangers of unrestrained freedom. Like *Paradise Now*, it was notorious for orgiastic nude scenes that included audience members; and like the Living Theatre, the Performance Group hoped to have a political effect – in this instance, to somehow influence the 1968 US presidential election. *Dionysus in '69* also demonstrated Schechner's ideas of "environmental theatre": no demarcation between actor and spectator space; multiple events competing with each other to diffuse any single focus; and actors interacting with audience members in character and personally (Aronson 2000: 97–102). Although Schechner is often credited with creating environmental theatre, it clearly derives from the ideas of Allan Kaprow (see Chapter 12).

The Polish director Jerzy Grotowski's (1934–1999) approach to performance was less ecstatic but similarly body-oriented. His "poor theatre" would be stripped of elaborate production elements typical of the commercial stage. Scripts would emphasize archetypal human dimensions and productions would be forged in collective collaborations. The "holy actor" would be an ascetic athlete of the soul, physicalizing the sufferings and ecstasies of the human spirit, uniting psychic and bodily powers to achieve "translumination" (Grotowski 1968: 15–59). The actor would become theatre's chief poet, creating "his own psychoanalytic language of sounds and gestures in the same way that a great poet creates his own language of words." The actor would sacrifice personal psychology and eliminate bodily resistance to full expression through a *via negativa*: a holy path of eradication of the self to expose primal truths.

Grotowski limited his audiences to 100 to assure immediacy and intimacy. His theoretical language was sometimes obscure and mystical, redolent of both his Polish Catholic background and existentialist despair. But clearly, performance itself was the authentic center, the object and subject of performance, rather than a realistic representation of another thing. Grotowski's sources included Stanislavsky's method of physical actions, Meyerhold's biomechanics, Indian *kathakali*, Chinese *jingju* (Beijing Opera), Japanese *nō*, and Carl Jung's theory of archetypes that activate the collective unconscious.

Grotowski's productions in his Laboratory Theatre in Wroclaw included *Akropolis* (1962), a free adaptation of a work by Polish playwright Stanislav Wyspiański (1869–1907). The original play was set in the Royal Palace at Krakow (a Polish version of the Athenian acropolis – the height of civilization), where figures from its tapestries come alive and are led by the resurrected Christ to redeem Europe. In Grotowski's dark, ironic conception, the acropolis was the Nazi extermination camp at Auschwitz (not far from Krakow). In this symbolic cemetery of Western civilization, Jewish prisoners labored to build cremation ovens and fantasized about love and happiness. In this production and *Apocalypse cum figuris* (1969), Grotowski's key actor, Ryszard Cieslak (1937–1990), reportedly achieved a trance-like state. His interpenetration of actor and role realized Grotowski's vision of externalizing inner suffering – the actor becoming both subject and object (Figure 13.4).

Figure 13.4
Ryszard Cieslak as Esau, one of the Jewish prisoners in Auschwitz, dreaming of the freedom of the life of a hunter, in Jerzy Grotowski's production of *Akropolis* at the Polish Laboratory Theatre, Wroclaw, 1962.

Photo © The Grotowski Centre, Wroclaw.

Grotowski's productions toured the world, and together with his writings and workshops, influenced many directors. In the late 1970s, he renounced this phase of his work, believing his ideas had been misunderstood, especially in America, and that he had not broken through theatre's division between actor and spectator.

The focus on the body was not limited to the West. Japanese director Suzuki Tadashi (1939–), sometimes known in the West as Tadashi Suzuki, developed a physical training method for actors (the Suzuki Method) now used internationally. The Suzuki Method posits a constant tension between the upper body (seen as the origin of the conceptual and the conscious) and the lower body (seen as the origin of the physical and the unconscious). His acting exercises, influenced by *nō*, *kabuki*, *kathakali*, and Japanese martial arts, help the actor create a powerful stage presence by using highly energized but restrained physical motions. These include slow movements, rhythmic foot stamping, crouching, and tension-informed stances, sometimes combined with vocalizations (Carruthers and Takahashi 2004: 70–97). The exercises have become expressive parts of his productions. In 1992, Suzuki and American director Ann Bogart (1951–) founded SITI (Saratoga International Theatre Institute) in New York state to train performers using both the Suzuki Method and Bogart's own method, called Viewpoints.

Performance art

In the mid-1960s, some artists in other fields were also questioning authority. However, rather than rebelling against the power of the author, they challenged the power of the usual modes of art production and of how and where art is displayed or performed. For example, some visual artists rebelled against traditional painting and sculpture, venues such as museums, and aesthetic norms. Like many innovative theatre artists, they often presented their works to unsuspecting audiences in unusual locales. In addition, they rejected the strict division of the arts into self-limiting categories, preferring instead to blur the boundaries between, for example, theatre and sculpture or dance and painting.

Contemporary **performance art** (sometimes called "live art" in the UK) clearly descended from Kaprow's Happenings. However, unlike spontaneous, intentionally disruptive Happenings, performance art is usually sponsored by an authorizing institution, such as an art gallery, museum, or university. Performance art – like Dada and other avant-garde movements of the early twentieth century – questions how art is classified, or framed, as art. It seldom uses a clear narrative line or linear script. Often, it aims to demystify high art and call attention to the social processes that "confirm" art as art. Whether solo work or large spectacle, performance art always seeks to destroy the boundaries between art and life.

Performance artists often use their own bodies as performance instruments and their own lives as subjects. They are interested in embodied expression, not written dramatic texts. They may use video, dance, sculpture, painting, or music, and often perform outside of theatres: on roofs, in shop windows, in airports, in lobbies, or on street corners. Early performance artists associated themselves with the visual arts, not theatre. A few performed works only once, creating a never-to-be-repeated experience between artist and spectator which could not be purchased or commodified. In contrast, most performance artists today repeat the event and charge admission, and sometimes perform in theatres. Well-known performance artists include Carolee Schneemann (1939–), Chris Burden (1946–2015), Marina Abramović (1946–), and Laurie Anderson (1947–). Each is unique in style, vision, and goal.

Some performance artists, like Guillermo Gómez-Peña (1955–), raise social issues in their work. Born in Mexico and coming to the United States in 1978, he calls himself

> a nomadic Mexican artist/writer in the process of Chicanization, which means I am slowly heading North. . . . I make art about the misunderstandings that take place at the border zone. But for me, the border is no longer located at any fixed geopolitical site. I carry the border with me, and I find new borders wherever I go.
>
> (Gómez-Peña 1996: 5)

Working solo or in collaboration with Coco Fusco (1960–) and Roberto Sifuentes (1967–), his works focus on the Latino experience in the United States to highlight how national and cultural identities are constructed. For example, he had an online "performance photo essay" that used an interactive test to demonstrate the dangers of ethnic profiling in the post-9/11 era.

In 1994–1996, Gómez-Peña and Sifuentes collaborated on the *Temple of Confessions*, in which they became exhibits in Plexiglas booths, like archaeological relics or scientific specimens. They were advertised as the last living saints from a "border region." Spectators were invited to confess their "intercultural fears and desires" to them. The "confessions" ranged from guilt to anger to sexual desire. Richard Schechner suggests the performance revealed people's "sense of resigned desperation" regarding the inevitability of globalization and their need for human interaction to counter its alienating and homogenizing effects (Schechner 2002: 261).

Performance art and similar alternative, anti-text-based performances form part of the experimental scene throughout the world. For example, in the People's Republic of China, the all-female, Shanghai-based Niao Collective performs multimedia dance-theatre pieces. *Tongue's Memory of Home* (2005) challenged traditional Confucian and patriarchal values, socialist ideology, and the dominance of spoken theatre. "[A] tongue, once stripped of language, has other ways of remembering – tasting, touching, feeling. Stripped of language, it is no longer a mouthpiece for ideology and is in fact more free than human beings themselves" (Borneoco n.d.). In China's recent past, such performances would have been highly provocative.

The director as auteur

"*Auteur*" is a French word meaning "author." An *auteur director* (a term borrowed from film criticism) sees herself – not the playwright or the actor – as the primary "author" of the performance. Many *auteur* directors, especially ones working in mainstream theatre, direct written plays, but they de-emphasize the text or subordinate it to their vision. In this way, they shift authority from the playwright to the director. *Auteur* directors produce their own interpretations by exerting total control of the *mise en scène* [meez on sehn] (a French term denoting all visual aspects of a production, from set design, costumes, makeup, and lighting to the placement and movement of actors and use of new technologies).

By the late 1960s, the idea of the director as the primary artist, or at least a coequal with the playwright, was emerging. It was becoming commonplace to speak not of Shakespeare's but Peter Brook's *A Midsummer Night's Dream* (1970), not of Molière's but Roger Planchon's *Tartuffe* (1962, 1973), not of Euripides' but Suzuki Tadashi's *The Trojan Women* (1974). We will look at these directors' work in turn.

British director Peter Brook (1925–) is perhaps the foremost *auteur* director in the English-speaking world. His wide array of theatrical experiments across 40 years have established him as one of the most innovative, sometimes controversial, directors in twentieth-century theatre. He brought Artaud, Brecht, and Beckett to bear on his 1962 *King Lear* with the then-new Royal Shakespeare Company. His production sought to emphasize an existential vision of a cruel, godless universe; he eliminated lines that countered that vision. When the elderly Gloucester's eyes are gouged out, Brook located the scene downstage close to the audience. He also brought up the house lights to strip away any comfort that theatrical illusion might have afforded.

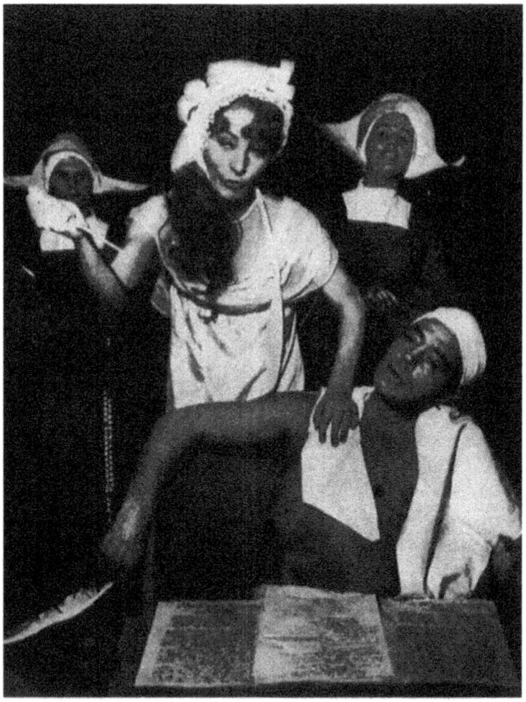

Brook conducted Theatre of Cruelty experiments in 1964, culminating with the Royal Shakespeare Company's production of *The Persecution and Assassination of Jean-Paul Marat as Performed by the Inmates of the Asylum of Charenton under the Direction of the Marquis de Sade* (usually called *Marat/Sade*) by German-born playwright Peter Weiss (1916–1982). Weiss's verse text, about the assassination of a leader of the French Revolution, rendered a morally chaotic world in grim corporeal imagery, graphically physicalizing the inmates' madness in a claustrophobic acting space where they perform their play within the play. Charlotte Corday's murder of Marat in his bath was performed in a ritualistic manner, visually echoing Jacques-Louis David's 1793 painting *The Death of Marat*. A courtier's speech filled with pompous but ironic platitudes about the glories of France and of Enlightenment rationalism agitated the inmates into a frenzied attempt to overtake the asylum. The play closes with an indictment of complacency towards poverty and political repression – an echo of Marat's own deepest concerns (see Figure 13.5).

In his manifesto *The Empty Space* (1968), Brook called for a "holy theatre" marked by sincerity and authenticity to replace the pre-packaged "deadly theatre" of a consumer society. His Royal Shakespeare Company production of *A Midsummer Night's Dream* (1970) used bright, contemporary

Figure 13.5
The premiere production of Weiss's *Marat/Sade*, at the Schiller Theatre in Berlin in 1964. Influenced by Brechtian theatre, this widely produced play about the political failure of the French Revolution was directed by Konrad Swinarski and designed by Weiss.

Photograph: Heinz Köster.

Figure 13.6
Oberon (Alan Howard) casts a spell on Titania (Sara Kestelman) in her "bower," assisted by Puck (John Kane), in Shakespeare's *A Midsummer Night's Dream*, directed by Peter Brook with the Royal Shakespeare Company, 1970. Setting by Sally Jacobs.
Photograph © Thomas F. Holte, courtesy Shakespeare Centre Library, Stratford-upon-Avon.

theatricality to replace the play's romantic stage traditions. With fairies on trapezes, non-illusionistic white box setting, flower-children young lovers, and playful eroticism, the production seemed to offer the promise of a new age of authentic young love born out of the youthful social revolution against an older order (see Figure 13.6). Although Brook did not tamper with Shakespeare's language, the performance itself became the ground of authenticity, coequal to the text.

Brook's *Dream* toured internationally for three years. Such mainstream visibility in an era of social upheaval made it a reference point for performance practice of Shakespeare and other classics by suggesting that productions of classical plays are transactions between past and present, bound to generate new meanings (Williams 1997: 213–33; Worthen 2003: 28–58). By the end of the century, this practice had reached mainstream film. Julie Taymor's film *Titus* (1999), based on Shakespeare's *Titus Andronicus*, and Baz Luhrmann's film *William Shakespeare's Romeo + Juliet* (1996) juxtaposed the plays' Elizabethan verse with a contemporary, fast-paced filmic language of images. Costumes and settings were literally layered with conflicting remnants of the historical past and bold swatches from the contemporary world. In all, performance and text critiqued one another.

French director Roger Planchon (1931–2009) viewed the director as equal to the author. Influenced by Artaud, Brecht, and Marx, Planchon's politically committed productions utilized what he called "scenic writing," that is, vivid stage images that conveyed his vision of a play (Bradby and Williams 1988: 51–6). For many years, he headed the Théâtre National Populaire (TNP) in Villeurbane (a suburb of Lyon), desiring to bring theatre to the working classes outside of Paris. Although clearly an *auteur* director, Planchon did not radically alter the written text.

For his 1962 staging of Molière's *Tartuffe*, Orgon's home was a kind of mini-Versailles palace. Orgon's devotion to the bogus cleric Tartuffe suggested unconscious homosexual yearning, adding sexual confusion to blind religious devotion. When Orgon is saved at the last instant, the staging evoked a chilling demonstration of Louis XIV's absolute power. Directing the same play in 1973, Planchon had Orgon's house dismantled room by room. Orgon and his family were herded into a dungeon beneath the stage floor before being released. There have been many interpretations of the original ending of Molière's play (see the case study in Chapter 6); Planchon apparently was suggesting that the bourgeois Orgon was being stripped of far more than his delusions about Tartuffe.

Suzuki Tadashi's radical adaptation of *The Trojan Women* in 1974 was the first time a Japanese director had not imitated Western staging conventions for a Greek classic. From its opening in Tokyo in 1974 through its final performance in Helsinki in 1989, *The Trojan Women* played in 34 cities around the world, and some compared its importance to Brecht's *Mother Courage* and Brook's *A Midsummer Night's Dream* (Carruthers and Takahashi 2004: 124). Suzuki's production combined a Japanese translation of Euripides' play with newly commissioned poetry. Resisting conventional ideas of a noble, classical world, Suzuki created images evoking war's brutality: memories of the nuclear annihilation of Hiroshima and Nagasaki combined with condemnations of military atrocity in general. In the premiere version, three main actors performed together in three distinct styles: *nō*, *shingeki*, and Suzuki Method. Major characters were presented in a *kabuki*-style dumb-show (*danmari* [dahm-mah-ree]). They were led on stage by Jizō, Buddhist guardian deity of children, who then watched impassively, unable to intervene in the horrors of war. The chorus women were homeless survivors of both Troy and Hiroshima/Nagasaki; the Greek soldiers were *kabuki*-like samurai who violently raped Andromache and dismembered her son (a doll) on stage. At one point, the chorus of Trojan women circled in a slow, rhythmic dance, defiantly stamping their feet, lifting their knees to their chests.

Over the years, Suzuki experimented with various endings that disrupted any easy consolations. In the premiere, a group of Japanese tourists (including a giant Japanese soldier) appeared on a guided tour of the battlefield at Troy. In the 1979 touring version, the cast exited, abandoning the old homeless woman who in her fantasy had become Hecuba. Watched over by the powerless Jizō, she sorted through her few belongings and tried to sleep, somewhat reminiscent of a character from Beckett (Carruthers and Takahashi 2004: 124–53). In all versions, Suzuki's *Trojan Women* presented a vision of Japan as both defeated victim and militaristic victimizer. It ultimately condemned all wars.

Suzuki is very clear about his role as an *auteur* director. Speaking of his freedom with Shakespeare's text in his *Tale of Lear* (1988), he said: "[T]he first responsibility of a director is to define what interests him the most, what resonates with his current concerns" (Mulryne 1998: 84).

Challenging an important premise of modernism, many *auteur* directors no longer viewed the classics as self-enclosed, timeless, and universal. Productions began to emphasize the contemporary encounter with classic texts, often insisting that the fissures between a play from

Figure 13.7
Dionysus (Michael König) on a hospital gurney in the opening scene of Euripides' *The Bacchae*, directed by Klaus-Michael Grüber, Schaubühne Theatre Company, Berlin, 1974.

Photograph © Helga Kneidel.

the past and the culture of the present be exposed. In this view, any performance will generate new meanings alongside the old; performance is seen as the theatre's authentic work. *Dionysus in '69*, discussed above, is an early example. A different kind of *auteur* production – also taking off from Euripides' original – is Klaus-Michael Grüber's 1974 production of *The Bacchae* at the Berlin Schaubühne. The production used Euripides' script but went beyond any attempt either to "recover" the ancient play or to reinvent Euripides as a postwar existentialist. Grüber's production instead critiqued such projects, staging a never-ending process of stitching and restitching ancient fragments together, with the result open to varying readings (Fischer-Lichte 1999: 16–17). The performance began with the weakened Dionysus, god of the theatre, being rolled out on a hospital gurney, barely able to speak his name in the opening line, "I am Dionysius, the son of Zeus" (Euripides 1959: 155) (see Figure 13.7).

THINKING THROUGH THEATRE HISTORIES

The impact of literary criticism

The new directorial approaches were sometimes congenial with, or even influenced by, developments in twentieth-century literary theory, as noted earlier in this chapter. Many theorists pointed out that human constructions, such as languages, literature, or gender, are embedded with particular ideologies – local value systems and social practices. The term "text" began to be used for any symbolic system a culture might construct, be it a religious ritual, clothing fashions, or the script of *Hamlet*.

One key theatrical development that dovetails with literary criticism is **postmodernism**. Grüber's production of *The Bacchae* may be described as *postmodern*. Postmodernism is a much-debated term that has had many applications and many theorists (we include references to many of them on the companion website). It can signal liberation from modernism as well as an apocalyptic collapse of all meaning. Philosopher Jean-François Lyotard suggests that postmodernism implies "a deep incredulity toward metanarratives" – that is, toward descriptions of human history presenting grand, all-encompassing truths (Lyotard 1984: xxiv). Many postmodern theatre productions feature non-linear narratives, pastiches or samplings of pre-existing but unrelated texts, and an ironic perspective toward those texts.

In contrast to traditional and modernist approaches to drama, which seemed to hold out a promise of eternal, redeeming truths lying behind the plays, postmodern performance offers only the "empty presence" of the here and now (Connor 1989: 140–1). It refuses to allow a singular, comfortable, stable meaning or value. Not all postmodern theatre is as radical as Grüber's *The Bacchae*, which foregrounded the process of performance to question what representation can accomplish. But generally postmodern performance aims to provoke the viewer/reader to be aware of, and to critique, the very strategies of representation.

Postmodern and other theoretically derived critiques help remove literary and theatrical works from their exclusive status as self-enclosed high art, instead viewing them as products of particular historical cultures. In addition, they offer opportunities to incorporate fresh ideas and practice derived from disparate fields of study (such as anthropology, neuroscience, or gender studies) into theatre practice. Nevertheless, some scholars have expressed concern that over-dependence on literary theory – or on theories derived from other non-theatrical disciplines – could undermine the legitimacy of theatre as a discrete area of academic inquiry. Such scholars warn that theatre must develop theoretical and critical practices of its own.

Creating "performance texts"

Not all directors were *auteurs*. Some actually went further down the Artaudian path by eliminating the traditional playwright and devoting themselves to collective creation, text collages, chance encounters, or visuality.

In Paris in 1968, Jean-Louis Barrault (1910–1994) staged a three-hour adaptation of writings by sixteenth-century French author François Rabelais, and Ariane Mnouchkine's (1939–) Théâtre du Soleil (founded 1964) assembled a collage of sketches on the French

Revolution titled *1789*. Both emphasized the relation of French history and culture to the then-current spectacle of student uprisings and the desire to free body and spirit from traditional restraints. *The Serpent* (1969), created by American director Joseph Chaikin (1935–2003) with his Open Theatre company, was a collage of material from the Bible and scenes from the recent assassinations of U.S. President John F. Kennedy and black civil rights leader Martin Luther King, Jr. Suzuki created several collages in his own hybrid style. He titled these *On the Dramatic Passions* (1969), and included scenes from the *bunraku/kabuki* classic *Kanadehon Chūshingura* (*The Treasury of Loyal Retainers*, 1748), the highly romantic French play *Cyrano de Bergerac* (1898) by Edmond Rostand (1868–1919), and the somewhat Beckettian *Zō* (*The Elephant*, 1961) by Japanese playwright Betsuyaku Minoru (1937–). Polish director Tadeusz Kantor's (1915–1990) *The Dead Class* (1975) combined his own writings and works by other Polish authors. The "text" of Peter Brook's *Orghast* (1971) was an arrangement of musical phonemes and fragments of ancient languages compiled by poet Ted Hughes, intoned by the actors along with ancient music. Performed in the ruins of Persepolis at the Shiraz Festival in Iran, it opened with the Prometheus myth. (Brook's 1985 epic *Mahabharata* is discussed in Chapter 14.)

Romanian director Andrei Serban (1943–) brought new rigor in the early 1970s to the American experimental scene at Ellen Stewart's (1919–2011) La Mama Experimental Theatre Club (founded 1961). Artaud's ideas inspired *Fragments of a Trilogy* (1974), composed of portions of Euripides' *Medea*, *Electra*, and *The Trojan Women*, which Serban developed over a three-year period. Serban had worked with Peter Brook on the non-verbal *Orghast* in Iran in 1970–1971. Like that project, the goal here was to create a non-verbal, aural score to communicate the power and passion of the Greek plays. Fragments of Senecan Latin, Greek, and English, were woven together with primitive vocalizations and Elizabeth Swados's (1951–) original score. *Trilogy* was staged throughout an empty, rectangular, galleried hall, and the audience moved to follow the action. The basic emotions of the plays – fear, love, hate – were communicated powerfully. The work achieved nearly legendary status and was revived in 1999.

The Wooster Group developed from Schechner's Performance Group beginning in 1975, taking its formal name in 1980. It continues to emphasize radical reworkings of canonical plays, developing its pieces in collective improvisations, from which director Elizabeth LeCompte (1944–) shapes the final collage product. Departing from the quest for communal authenticity that was characteristic of the 1960s, the Wooster Group performs deconstructive, skeptical critiques of the processes of meaning-making in a postmodern, mediatized culture. The Wooster Group frequently uses technology – videotaped segments, microphones, recorded music or voices – calling attention to how technologies affect meaning, and to the audience's processes of interpreting a performance. Such self-reflexive strategies short-circuit any continuities in Wooster works.

In the 1980s, the group deconstructed both *Our Town* (1938) by Thornton Wilder (1897–1975) and *The Crucible* (1953) by Arthur Miller. *Route 1 & 9* (1981) juxtaposed portions of *Our Town* with a re-creation of a routine called "The Party," recorded in 1965 by black artist Pigmeat Martin, and a sexually graphic film. The intent was to explode Wilder's picture of an all-white, small-town America as an embodiment of universal human experience. The routes in the title referred to the film's scenes of sexually explicit behavior during a van ride on highways running not through Wilder's Grover's Corners but through the industrial sites and oil refineries of urban New Jersey.

In *L.S.D. (. . . Just the High Points . . .)* (1984), the Wooster Group critiqued *The Crucible*, which, as noted in Chapter 12, draws parallels between the Salem witch trials and anti-communist hysteria. The four-part production used various devices to create a discontinuous collage of scenes. In "Part Two – Salem," portions of the dialogue were read at a table with microphones, seeming to evoke and query both the infamous televised McCarthy hearings and Miller's play itself as processes leading to truth (Figure 13.8). The women were dressed in historical costumes, suggesting their traditional, gendered position. The men, by contrast, wore contemporary clothes and, unlike the women, were given microphones, tools of authority. This and other devices pointed to the limits of Miller's play, which as Philip Auslander writes, seems "unable to represent the persecution of witches as the effort of a patriarchal society to suppress independent women" (Auslander 1992: 92). The formidable white actress Kate Valk played the black slave girl Tituba (Miller's invention), in minstrel-style blackface, with a fake "darky" accent. By invoking an American theatre tradition of racist representation in minstrel shows and Aunt Jemima figures (Rouse 1992: 148–51), the performance sought to probe the authority of Miller's representation of race in America.

More recently, the Wooster Group has used simultaneous video, film, and other uncon-ventional tactics to explore or challenge such canonical works as Eugene O'Neill's *The Emperor Jones* (1993 and 2006), *Hamlet* (2007 and 2012), Racine's *Phèdre* in *To You, The Birdie!* (staged as a tennis match, 2002), and Tennessee William's *Vieux Carré* (2011).

Figure 13.8
The *Crucible* sequence from the Wooster Group's *L.S.D. (. . . Just the High Points . . .)*,
directed by Elizabeth LeCompte. Left to right: Matthew Hansell, Ron Vawter, Nancy Reilly,
Peyton Smith, Elion Sacker, Kate Valk, and Anna Kohler.

Photograph © Nancy Campbell.

In Japan, the raw materials for theatre productions were less the classic texts than the performance traditions themselves. Among a new generation of Japanese theatre artists who sought to revitalize their theatre, especially important were the playwright/director Terayama Shūji (1935–1983) and directors Suzuki and Ninagawa Yukio (1935–). (Ninagawa's work is discussed in the case study on "Global Shakespeare" on the website.) All emerged during Japan's Little Theatre movement (*angura* – underground) in the 1960s in which many directors and playwrights rebelled – in various ways – against the Western-derived drama and theatre practices in Japan (*shingeki*). Many were also involved in radical anti-Vietnam War and anti-government demonstrations. Overall, their work reflects Japan's vexed negotiations with its own past and its cultural longings to be a modern presence on the global stage after its defeat in the Second World War. How would it remain connected with its own pre-Western traditions and still find, after the American occupation, its own new identity? As Carol Fisher Sorgenfrei has noted, Japan's theatrical innovators attempted variously to destroy, redefine, or reinvent the nation's traditional theatre forms such as *nō*, *kyōgen*, *bunraku*, and *kabuki*. "Some aligned themselves with, or set themselves against, the Western avant-garde; and some searched for totally new modes of expression and identity" (Sorgenfrei 2005a: 131).

Terayama Shūji, playwright, poet, director, film-maker, and essayist, led his experimental company, Tenjō Sajiki, from 1967 until his death at 47 in 1983. He created fresh, eclectic work that challenged theatrical conventions and left a reputation of legendary proportions. Early works written and directed by Terayama, such as *The Hunchback of Aomori* (*Aomori-ken no semushi otoko*, 1967), *The Dog God* (*Inugami*, 1967), and *Heretics* (*Jashūmon*, 1971), featured surreal evocations of Buddhist superstitions and old-time side-shows, coupled with psychedelic music and the discontent of postwar youth.

Some of Terayama's works might be characterized as metatheatre. All of his works suggest a desire to shake audiences out of complacency. Plays such as *Opium War* (*Ahen sensō*, 1972), *Blindman's Letter* (*Mōjin shokan*, 1973), and *A Journal of the Plague Year* (*Ekibyō ryūkōki*, 1975) were described by Terayama as "invisible theatre" that plunged audiences into terrifying total darkness or forcefully separated them into private, curtained rooms. The assault on the audience's senses sometimes led to claustrophobia, hysteria, violence, and even police intervention. In one case, a fire-breathing actor severely burned an audience member's face. German reviewers damned *Heretics* as "the madness of Faust combined with karate chops" and a "bad epidemic from Japan." One article was titled "Hitler Was Better" (Sorgenfrei 2005b: 18).

Theatres of observation and images

The furthest possible questioning of authorship is its complete elimination. In Chapter 12, we saw one example of this in Happenings. Another approach is to create theatre "in the moment" by observing chance events. Terayama provides a good example. From the early 1970s, he created outdoor "city dramas" that often involved unsuspecting citizens as audience or even as actors. For example, *Knock* (*Nokku*, 1975) consisted of sites and events spread across 27 locations throughout a district of Tokyo, to which spectators could journey over a 30-hour period. Critic Senda Akihiko wrote of following a map leading him to various sites, including a clock shop with an array of broken clocks lined up in front, a pile of broken toys in the window, and no one inside. Had it been so arranged for this event, or had it always looked that way? When Senda and others followed a married couple arguing their way loudly through the streets, what did bystanders make of the spectacle? Who were the actors? Who were spectators? What was Senda to make of the four people emerging from a manhole, swathed in bandages? Although the work may seem akin to Happenings, Terayama insisted that, unlike his "city dramas," Happenings lacked dramaturgical structure. He wrote, "Drama that is dragged into the streets will be instantly systematized, institutionalized, and placed in a museum unless it is based on a dramaturgical structure that sucks in and manipulates the continuum of time called everyday reality" (Sorgenfrei 2005b: 143–4). Terayama's "city dramas" aim to provoke a reassessment of how theatres and spectators construct meaning (Senda 1997: 56–60). Other unorthodox, subversive works written and staged by Terayama included the sado-masochistic *Directions to Servants* (*Nuhikun*, 1979) and *Lemmings* (*Remingu*, various versions 1979–1983). Some Terayama plays incorporated a series of visually striking scenes in which the walls around people imprisoned in private pursuits of individuality dissolved, exposing them to random, sometimes violent experiences.

In the 1970s, some theatre artists, dancers, and choreographers began to create multimedia performances using visual and aural landscapes that defied conventional concepts of artistic order, continuity, and time. These came to be known as "Theatre of Images." The term was first applied to the theatre productions of the American Robert Wilson (1944–). His works present surreal landscapes of discontinuous, dream-like images, encompassed by music and sound; often, the few spoken words are part of a trance-inducing aural score. Meticulously choreographed performers slowly move in and out of tableaux, often in front of giant projection screens on which may float clouds or everyday items in iconic size (such as a huge shoe).

Spectators of Wilson's productions are to make whatever associations they please, meditate among half-remembered archetypes, or perhaps reflect on their own perceptual processes. A refined visual aesthetic governs the formal, modernist images, working hand-in-glove with an earnest postmodern indeterminacy and irony. As Arnold Aronson notes, Wilson's spectacles demand "a new kind of watching" (Aronson 2000: 125).

Wilson's *Life and Times of Joseph Stalin* at the Brooklyn Academy of Music in 1973 was a 12-hour "opera" in seven acts, requiring 140 actors. *Einstein on the Beach* (1976), written with composer Philip Glass (1937–), presented Einstein as dreamer and scientist. Its repeated images of a train, a spaceship, and a trial seemed to raise issues about scientific progress. But it was the overall orchestration of images, trance-like music, and hypnotic movement that audiences found compelling (see Figure 13.9). Wilson's monumental *the CIVIL warS: a tree is best measured when it is down* (1984) was more thematic though no more linear. It dealt generally with human conflict at many levels through evocative images and icons, among them battlefield gunfire and a pageant of historical and fictional figures that included King Lear, Marx, Abraham Lincoln, and a Native American tribe.

In contrast, some of Wilson's more recent work is very accessible to general audiences. In 2004, he collaborated in the creation of *The Temptation of St Anthony* with Bernice Johnson Reagon (1942–), scholar, civil rights activist, and founder of Sweet Honey in the Rock, a widely admired all-female, African-American *a capella* group. They adapted Gustave Flaubert's 1874 French novel exploring Anthony's troubled journey to faith in a spectacular and musically rich production that combined African-American gospel and jazz with elegant scenic images by Wilson. In 2005, he collaborated with the Comédie Française, designing a wry, amusing staging of Jean de la Fontaine's *The Fables*. He frequently directs operas and has collaborated with performing artists as diverse as ballet dancer/actor Mikhail Baryshnikov

Figure 13.9
Performers in the "Spaceship" section of *Einstein on the Beach* (by Robert Wilson and Philip Glass) at the Brooklyn Academy of Music's Howard Gilman Opera House, Brooklyn, New York, December 8, 1984.
Photo by Jack Vartoogian/Getty Images.

(1948–) and pop singer Lady Gaga (1986–). Wilson now lives in Germany where state subsidies support his technologically advanced imaging and his meticulous lighting. Among his productions at the Berliner Ensemble are Brecht's *Threepenny Opera* (2007, continuing in repertory and on international tour) and *Shakespeare's Sonnets* (2009, continuing in repertory).

Théâtre de Complicité is a London-based company which began in 1983 as a collective of actors trained in the methods of Jacques Lecoq. It specializes in a Theatre of Images based on "extreme movement," mime, and clowning techniques. They achieved international acclaim with the 1992 *The Street of Crocodiles*, based on the life of Polish writer Bruno Schulz, in which the poetic and surreal aspects of Schulz's memoirs were theatricalized by the collective in music, image, rhythm, movement, and action.

Some works of Chinese-American director Ping Chong (1946–) might also be described stylistically as Theatre of Images. Chong's productions of the 1970s and 1980s were collaboratively developed, plotless, carefully choreographed, sometimes meditative works. They often involved themes of cultural and spiritual dislocation, deriving from Chong's own experiences as an outsider in America. In his amusing production *Noiresque: The Fallen Angel* (1989), an Asian-American girl, a modern Alice in Wonderland, boards a train bound for an Orwellian technocracy that is inhabited by dehumanized, mechanized residents. Chong's *A.M./A.M – the Articulated Man* (1982) took up the Frankenstein legend and featured a robot who, unable to become socialized, kills and flees into the city. In what seems to be a clear reference to the sense of spiritual dislocation of many Asian-Americans, Chong said of this production, "When human beings in a society fail to have a rich psychic life, then it's ripe for fascism" (Leiter 1994: 62). His *Nosferatu* (1985) alternated portions of F.W. Murnau's early vampire film with scenes from the lives of a soulless yuppie couple in Manhattan who confront a vampire.

The non-death of the author

Despite the radical questioning of the author, playwrights never disappeared. Some of the most important theatre after 1968 involved new plays. For example, *Angels in America* (1992), the two-play, Pulitzer Prize-winning epic by American playwright Tony Kushner (1956–), combined rich language with almost cinematic scenic collages to juxtapose scenes such as an angel bursting through the bedroom ceiling of a gay man suffering from AIDS, a political conservative's discovery of his homosexuality, a Cold Warrior's visitations by a ghost from his past, and an agoraphobic Mormon woman's hallucinatory friends (Figure 13.10).

Although psychological realism was still dominant, more and more mainstream playwrights and directors found ways to depart from it. Even in relatively realistic drama, playwrights such as Harold Pinter, Sam Shepard (1943–), and David Mamet (1947–) probed the emotionally volatile and destructive forces beneath the surfaces of language. For many, language no longer seemed to represent thought and feeling.

Documentary plays influenced by film and television also proliferated. African-American writer/actor Anna Deavere Smith's (1950–) one-person shows on urban unrest in the U.S., *Fires in the Mirror* (1992) and *Twilight: Los Angeles, 1992* (1994), focused on language but drew from film and video documentary techniques. Smith interviewed people involved in the events and performed their actual words and gestures, selecting the "shots" and editing the results.

Some playwrights defended the primacy of the text on legal grounds. The Wooster Group's production of *The Crucible* drew Miller's wrath. Insisting his copyright had been violated, Miller threatened legal action, which forced the closing of *L.S.D. (. . . Just the High Points . . .)* even after the Wooster Group had eliminated Miller's actual words. A similar argument against directorial meddling in 1984 resulted in the lawsuit filed by Samuel Beckett and Grove Press threatening legal action against the American Repertory Theatre at Harvard University over director Joanne Akalaitis's (1937–) production of *Endgame* (see Chapter 12). Especially after the early 2000s, the Dramatists' Guild of America (a professional association for U.S. playwrights, composers, lyricists, and librettists) energetically advocated legal action against directors and/or theatres that cut or changed scripts (including stage directions and casting requirements) without the playwright's approval. Although upheavals in communications were altering attitudes, print culture's concept of copyright was still very much alive.

The growth of non-commercial theatres

Starting in the 1960s, many countries developed extensive networks of theatre outside the commercial arena. Several new national (i.e., government-subsidized) theatres were created, while older ones occasionally found themselves in complex circumstances. Numerous small theatre companies arose, either to provide traditional theatre, produce "experimental" plays, or serve a particular "niche" audience. Once stabilized, those companies that did not aim to make profit often sought a special tax status allowing them to accept donations and operate without paying taxes. Here "profit" means earnings beyond those needed to pay reasonable salaries and expenses. (Not-for-profit is a U.S. federal tax category of organizations exempt from taxes; the U.K. equivalent is a registered charity.)

In the United Kingdom, the Royal National Theatre (known as "the National" or NT) and the Royal Shakespeare Company (RSC) vied for government funding. Both have relied on Shakespearean productions to promote the theatrical prestige of Great Britain at home and to the larger world, as does Shakespeare's Globe (opened 1997; see Chapter 14). The National

Figure 13.10
The appearance of the angel in the final scene of Tony Kushner's *Angels in America, Part One: Millennium Approaches* (1990). From the 1992 production of the Royal National Theatre, London, directed by Declan Donnellan, with Stephen Spinella as Prior Walter and Nancy Crane as the Angel.

Photograph: Lebrecht Music and Arts.

opened in 1963 under the artistic direction of Sir Laurence Olivier, with a production of *Hamlet* starring Peter O'Toole. In 1976, it moved to its current home, a three-theatre complex on the south bank of the Thames in London that cost over £17 million (GBP) ($28 million U.S.) to construct. The National continues to produce and simulcast its productions of plays by Shakespeare and other classics, as well as contemporary works. In 1982, the RSC, which makes Shakespearean production central to its mission and had been producing Shakespeare in Stratford-upon-Avon since 1961, added two performance spaces at London's Barbican, making it the world's largest theatrical institution. By the mid-1980s, both companies needed big budgets.

At stake in the success of both companies was the international theatrical prestige of the United Kingdom as well as financial gain from tourism. Both theatres strived to produce the best of classical and contemporary theatre and boasted world-class companies and artistic directors. Trevor Nunn (1940–) managed the RSC from 1968 until 1986, and Peter Hall, who had resigned from the RSC, replaced Laurence Olivier as director of the National in 1973 (Figure 13.11).

However, controversy surrounded the London operations of both theatres from their inceptions. Opponents, especially outside London, argued that the tax-generated sums spent on constructing the National should have been spread among many smaller groups. Hostility increased when the government revealed that a quarter of the Arts Council's drama budget in 1975–1976 had gone to the National, much of it for operating costs. Critics also attacked the poor design of the impenetrable Barbican Centre, used by the RSC for its London shows, especially its huge main stage and inadequate second space. This and other factors led the RSC to abandon the Barbican in 2002, returning in 2013. Both the RSC and the National struggled to meet their massive budgets, often by resorting to smaller shows, shorter seasons, and extensive touring and residencies. In addition to producing plays by Shakespeare and his contemporaries, the RSC mounted large money-makers, including *Nicholas Nickleby* (1980) and *Les Misérables* (1985). In the face of shrinking subsidies and smaller audiences, in 1999 the Arts Council for England required more educational initiatives and innovative productions. The National and the RSC were caught between national budgetary constraints and international expectations.

A somewhat similar conflict faced the major theatres of Berlin. During the Cold War – before German reunification in 1990 – East and West Germany lavished subsidies on several theatres in East and West Berlin. They became international showplaces for the two superpowers' rival cultures. In West Berlin, the Schiller Theater offered bourgeois classics and contemporary plays from Western Europe and the United States. The city hosted yearly festivals to display the best West German productions to the world. In East Berlin, the Berliner Ensemble, the Volksbühne, and the Deutsches Theater (once the center of Max Reinhardt's theatrical enterprises) flourished during the 1970s and 1980s.

But after reunification, Germany could no longer afford to support all these world-class theatres in Berlin, partly because state subsidies in Germany typically covered about 80 percent of all operating costs. The competition for spectators and subsidies, plus major reorganization in several companies, forced some, including the Schiller Theatre, to close. The Berliner Ensemble lessened its ties to the traditions of Brechtian production – offering a variety of plays, including those of Brecht, directed in a variety of styles. To enhance the reputation of Berlin as a center for global performances, Theatertreffen, the festival that showcases the year's best

Figure 13.11

Peter Hall's 1984 production of Shakespeare's *Coriolanus* at the National Theatre, starring Ian McKellen and Irene Worth. Hall resigned from the National in 1988 to found his own company.

Photograph John Haynes/Lebrecht Music and Arts

German-language productions, added a few international productions and now offers English supertitles for selected shows. Like London, Berlin remains a center of globalized theatre.

National theatres were created in many parts of the world. For example, the National Theatre of Japan opened in 1966, followed by the National Nō Theatre in 1983, and the National Bunraku Theatre in 1984. Mexico's National Theatre Company was founded in 1977. However, there is no national theatre in the United States.

In the "not-for-profit" world, markets are often defined in terms of values and purposes, but the practice of seeking a specific audience is essentially the same. In the United States, for example, regional not-for-profit theatres aim to attract upscale, educated, and "cultured" audiences in urban areas outside of New York, audiences whose season subscriptions would support them. Many were created starting in the early 1960s, first with support from private grant foundations, and later with the help of government grants. These theatres see themselves as non-commercial alternatives to the broadly popular entertainments of film and Broadway musicals and comedies.

Unlike commercial star-centered productions imported from "out of town," large and mid-size regional theatres catering to local audiences often use a combination of local actors supplemented by the occasional well-known star. A few smaller companies retain semi-permanent ensembles. Although regional theatres define themselves as artistically independent of Broadway, the transfer of a regionally developed production to Broadway has often been a source of pride.

Another development in the 1970s and 1980s was the construction of performing arts centers (containing both theatres and concert halls) in regional urban areas, modelled on venues such as New York City's Lincoln Center or London's South Bank Centre.

Most experimental theatre in the United States during this period originated in New York City. To distinguish their work from commercial performances typical of large theatres on or near Broadway, these new, smaller companies came to be known as "Off-Off-Broadway." Today, the term defines theatres that have 99 or fewer seats, or which employ non-Equity actors (Equity is the trade union to which professional actors belong). "Broadway" refers to large, mainstream theatres in a specific area of Manhattan. "Off-Broadway" theatres may or may not be in that same area, but they are designated "Off-Broadway" because they have 100–499 seats or, if fewer than 100, they employ Equity actors. Thus the designations refer more to the business of theatre (How large is the audience? How much money are the actors paid?) than to the content or style of production. Today, many newer, small, or experimental groups prefer the term "Fringe Theatre."

The Japanese Little Theatre movement (discussed above) is the equivalent of Fringe Theatre. Its origin dates from 1966 when director Suzuki, playwright Betsuyaku, and several actors founded the Waseda Shōgekijō (Waseda Little Theatre) in Tokyo. By 1970, Suzuki had become the sole director and was constructing collages of texts and performances that privileged no single author. From 1976 to 1999, much of Suzuki's work was done in the rural, mountain village of Toga, six hours from Tokyo, to which he moved seeking greater artistic freedom. With the help of government subsidies, Toga Art Park became a large complex of theatres and rehearsal halls, providing a laboratory for experimental collaborations with international visiting artists and a pilgrimage destination for the tourists who came to its festivals. Suzuki renamed his troupe the Suzuki Company of Toga (SCOT). From 1996–2007, he served as artistic director of the Shizuoka Performing Arts Center (SPAC), which is only an hour from Tokyo. The international theatre festival is now held at SPAC, while the theatres and laboratories at Toga are devoted primarily to training young theatre artists, especially directors. Suzuki's international focus is further represented by the creation of the BeSeTo (Beijing-Seoul-Tokyo) Festival, meant to foster cultural awareness and greater understanding between China, South Korea, and Japan. Suzuki's career demonstrates how an initially experimental, privately funded theatre company sometimes metamorphoses into a national or global phenomenon.

Targeted "niche" theatres

Many industries engage in niche marketing: the capitalistic, competitive process in which sellers identify and pursue potential consumers in a well-defined segment of the population identified by factors such as age, gender, family size, levels of income, education, ethnic or racial self-identification, uses of leisure time, and geographic location. It proliferated in media and theatre in the late twentieth century. Radio stations in the United States, for example, target specific audiences with rap, Latin American music, sports, commentary (both right- and left-wing), jazz, rock hits from the 1950s, classical music, religious programs, and so on. By the late 1990s, cable television offered hundreds of channels for every possible interest, including multiple languages. These offerings reflect increased cultural diversity within "national" boundaries.

From the mid-1960s onwards, theatres and theatre companies developed in many countries dedicated to audiences defined by their interests in issues of race, ethnicity, gender, or unorthodox political views. Some of these niche theatres provided the first homes for playwrights who later met with success on Broadway or in London's West End. Most not-for-profit (and some commercial) theatres today also attempt to reach diverse audiences through a combination of their own "brand" of plays and selected other works targeting non-traditional audiences. Professional resident theatres housed at universities often present difficult or experimental shows targeting niche audiences more tolerant of artistic risk.

As noted in Chapter 12, African-American theatres developed in the U.S. following the civil rights movement. Among the most notable were the Free Southern Theater (1963–1980), the Harlem-based New Lafayette Theatre (1967–1973), and the Negro Ensemble Company, founded in 1968. These helped pave the way for the wide critical interest in the works of black playwrights, both experimental and relatively traditional in form. Two who are especially notable are Suzan-Lori Parks (1963–), who writes in an often experimental style, and August Wilson (1945–2005), whose plays are largely in the form of modern American realism. As a young man, Wilson also started an African-American theatre. Parks' *Topdog/Underdog* won the Pulitzer Prize for drama in 2002. Wilson's *Fences* (1987) and *The Piano Lesson* (1990), both Pulitzer Prize winners, are parts of his ten-play cycle on the African-American experience. Both playwrights have been produced on Broadway and by major regional theatres.

Following the lead of African-American theatre, other theatres for specific U.S. audiences developed. El Teatro Campesino was founded in 1965 by Luis Valdez (1947–) to dramatize the exploitation of Mexican farm workers and has continued to nourish plays reflecting Mexican-American experiences. Latin American theatre groups representing intersections of U.S. cultures and Cuban, Chicano, and Puerto Rican cultures proliferated in the 1980s. Intar Theatre in New York, under the direction of Eduardo Machado (1950–), is devoted to producing new plays by Latino writers – many of them taught by Cuban-born María Irene Fornés (1930–). Her emotionally compressed works, including *Fefu and Her Friends* (1977) and *Conduct of Life* (1985), highlight the subjugation of women, appealing to both feminist and Latin American "niche" audiences. Fornés's *And What of the Night?* was a 1990 Pulitzer Prize finalist.

Plays on the Asian-American experience are the specialty of the East-West Players, founded in Los Angeles in 1965. In 1998, it moved from a 99-seat theatre to a newly built 240-seat Equity house in the Little Tokyo area of downtown Los Angeles. In Seattle, the Northwest Asian American Theatre grew out of earlier Theatrical Ensemble of Asians, founded in 1974 at the University of Washington. New York's Pan Asian Repertory Theatre emerged in 1978. Among Asian-American playwrights, the best known is David Henry Hwang (1957–), whose *M. Butterfly* (1988) was a Pulitzer Prize finalist. It investigates Orientalist perceptions by combining the opera *Madame Butterfly* (see the case study in Chapter 9) with a fictionalized account of a real love affair between a French diplomat and a *jingju* actor. All of Hwang's plays deal with some aspect of Asian-American identity, and their mainstream success is a matter of Asian-American pride. Los Angeles' East-West Players' main stage is now named the David Henry Hwang Theatre, and its program to develop Asian-American writers is the David Henry Hwang Writers' Institute.

Another major set of niche theatres is oriented on gender issues. The Ridiculous Theatre Company, founded in New York in 1967 by actor/playwright Charles Ludlam (1943–1987), created comic, campy, pastiche-gothic plays that had special appeal for the gay community. Split Britches, co-founded in 1980 in New York by performer/writers Peggy Shaw (1946–),

Lois Weaver (1951–), and Deb Margolin (1953–), uses a broadly satirical, gender-bending style to highlight lesbian and feminist issues. Founded in 1982, the Celebration Theatre in West Hollywood, California, offers a wide range of plays exploring gay, lesbian, bisexual, transgender, and queer issues.

The Lilith Theatre in San Francisco and the Women's Project of the American Place Theatre in New York promote the work of female writers and directors. Founded in 1976 as a feminist collective, the performance group Spiderwoman evolved into a company that primarily showcases the experiences of Native American women.

Similar patterns exist in other nations with multicultural populations. In the U.K., for example, immigrants (or their children) from former colonies in South Asia such as India, Pakistan, and Bangladesh created theatre companies to address their specific concerns and to help "mainstream" South Asian theatre artists. Key British South Asian theatre companies include Tara Arts (founded in 1977) and Tamasha (founded in 1989).

Britain's former colonies are often multicultural themselves. In Australia, the first work by an indigenous playwright to break into mainstream theatre was *The Cherry Pickers* (1968) by Kevin Gilbert (1933–1993), a member of the Wiradjuri and Kamilaroi nations. The Noongar playwright Jack Davis (1917–2000) combined traditional Aboriginal visual and performance culture with historical and contemporary stories in plays such as *The Dreamers* (1982). Canada's best-known First Nation playwright is probably Tomson Highway (1951–), a Cree. Among his works are the multiple award-winners *The Rez Sisters* (1986) and *Dry Lips Oughta Move to Kapuskasing* (1989). Singapore, a former British colony that is now a multicultural, multilingual nation, is home to both small and large theatre companies. Among them is TheatreWorks, founded in 1985 by the innovative director Ong Keng Sen (1963–). Singapore also hosts an international festival of the arts, which includes many theatre offerings. Local and international festivals are considered in greater detail in Chapter 14.

SUMMARY

The 1960s brought momentous political, social, cultural, and technological changes. People all over the world were suddenly able to witness historical events as they happened, transforming how they thought of themselves and the universe. The tensions that had started to emerge in the early 1960s erupted into demonstrations, riots, sometimes even revolutions, and decolonization movements. Theatre groups worldwide explored ways in which performance could contribute to social, political, and cultural change. At the same time, there was a significant shift from the primacy of the written script to that of the *auteur* director, and from the power of words to the power of images. No longer was there a clear distinction between live and mediatized genres. The institutional landscape was transfigured too, as non-commercial venues became commonplace, some producing mainstream drama, others producing theatre for particular communities. By the end of the twentieth century, a "new normal" had become established, in which the non-commercial and the commercial, the experimental and the mainstream, and the political and the staid all found opportunities to flow into each other. But these processes, as we will see next, were also entangled in larger worldly developments, as the local and the international increasingly crashed into each other through the forces of globalization.

★

CHAPTER 14

Theatres of local roots and global reach, 1970–present

Tamara Underiner

Contributors: Bruce McConachie, Carol Fisher Sorgenfrei, and Gary Jay Williams

In 1962, Canadian media theorist Marshall McLuhan suggested that "the new electronic interdependence recreates the world in the image of a global village" (1962: 31). Indeed, his prediction of a shrinking world has in many ways been realized. Migrations to urban centers have meant that the populations of the world's cities have become much more culturally and ethnically complex than they were half a century ago. International travel by the middle class of wealthier nations has become a major industry. In developed nations, international concert tours have become commonplace, as have educational exchanges. Above all, as McLuhan predicted, the electronic media – television, radio, video and audio recordings, and the internet – have become key factors in negotiations of cultural change, even though the effects, positive and negative, remain unevenly distributed.

As a result, it is common to speak of this time in history as the era of globalization: an age characterized by the interaction and integration of the world's peoples through processes driven largely by economic systems and aided by information technology, with effects on everything from individual wellbeing to the environment. The first trans-continental trade route or trans-oceanic crossing centuries ago may have initiated the process we now call globalization, but today the speed of information and its ability to connect peoples who otherwise might know nothing of each other distinguishes the current era of globalization from previous periods of global exploration and exploitation. Neither governments nor the corporate electronic media are wholly in control of the social, economic, and political relations that result.

The focus of this chapter is the effect of globalization on culture – particularly theatre culture – and in turn the way theatre culture might affect these processes. (We will return to communications technologies as a central focus of our final chapter.) Responses to globalization move in different and often opposed directions, as the title of this chapter suggests. They range from an embrace of the global reach of "world culture" in music, fashion, cuisine, and consumer products, to the promotion and assertion of resolutely local roots in resistance to the pressures of global conformity on local ways of living. Falling somewhere between these two extremes – of cultural homogenization on the one hand, and cultural differentiation on the other – is the phenomenon of cultural hybridity, or the fusion of material from two or more cultures. Some type of hybridity results any time cultures come into contact with each other and intermingle for any length of time. The recent coinage of the word "glocal," popularized by sociologist Roland Robertson, attempts to capture this sense of the push-pull between globalizing and localizing processes. (An example is how even McDonald's, perhaps *the* symbol of globalization, has begun to adapt its menus to local norms and customs, offering shrimp burgers in Japan and Singapore, "Vegemite McMuffins" in Australia, and "McAloo Tikki" vegetable burgers in India.) Now more than ever, individuals and societies take the stuff of culture – theirs and others' – and make of it something new.

The general themes and movements we have identified as being important for understanding "theatres of local roots and global reach" offer a kind of compass for pursuing four major directions taken by theatre after 1968. The first is *global theatre culture*, as exemplified in the increasing importance of international theatre festivals and the emergence of the mega-musical in the United Kingdom and North America. The next is *theatre of cultural differentiation*, which celebrates local heritage and national patrimony, often in touristic settings, and offers a site for the critique of globalization's more all-encompassing tendencies. Third, we explore theatre as a *zone of contact* within and between cultures, often resulting in hybrid or newly "glocal" forms. Finally, we will consider *theatre for social change*, a term given to theatre that has some kind of social aim at its heart, and is manifest in both local and global (and sometimes local-to-global) forms. Our case study considers in more detail how cross-cultural artistic experimentation in China helped to redefine nationalism, through Nobel Prize-winning Chinese-French playwright Gao Xingjian's play *The Wild Man*.

We open with an examination of Shakespeare's iconic status as an international presence, which offers a point of entry into discussing the four strains of globalization that we will focus on in this chapter – cultural homogenization, cultural differentiation, cultural hybridity, and theatre for social change. Our Shakespearean examples also demonstrate some of the tensions and overlaps among these categories.

Local roots, global reach, hybrid play, and social change in "Shakespeare"

Into the first quarter of the twenty-first century, William Shakespeare remains the most performed playwright on the planet. His plays have been translated into every major language, and many less widely spoken ones as well; they are produced in theatre venues all over the world; and many have been adapted into popular films for markets far away from his native England. As Gary Jay Williams points out in his online case study, "All of this could be claimed as evidence of Shakespeare's universality, of the ease with which his plays (ostensibly) leap all historical, linguistic, and cultural boundaries." However, as Williams also observes, Shakespeare's stature as an international writer has been the result not only of the power of his writing, but also of the economic and cultural power it might confer on those who produce it. Seen this way, writes Williams, "globalized Shakespeare has become a marketable prestige commodity, a *Shakespeare*™ ready to be packaged and distributed by global capitalism through all its technological platforms. Global Shakespeare is exemplary of a Western modernity to which developing nations aspire, a problematic byproduct of colonialism." When we put quotation marks around "Shakespeare," as we have in the heading to this section, it is to highlight his status as a global icon or industry.

At the same time, "even in the West, each age and nation has, to a considerable degree, reinvented the Shakespeare it needed," argues Williams. Thus, productions of Shakespeare's plays also function within the other paradigms we discuss in this chapter: as examples of cultural or nationalist differentiation (through heritage promotion); as examples of cultural hybridity, in which artists adapt Shakespeare's plays to local and contemporary norms and customs; and even as theatre for social change, as our final example of this section will show.

England's National Theatre and Royal Shakespeare Company (discussed in Chapter 13) are examples of theatre for nationalist differentiation. In 2012 the RSC sponsored the World Shakespeare Festival to coincide with the London Olympics, which both showcased England's national heritage and, through the presentation of international work, emphasized (as well as further constructed) the notion of Shakespeare's universality. The RSC's ambitious world touring schedule over the years, garnering regular reviews by the world's leading theatre critics, represents another point of intersection between the national and the international.

While both the National and (to a lesser degree) the RSC produce works outside the Shakespearean canon, the newer Shakespeare's Globe (which opened in 1997, see Figure 5.2) trades more overtly on a notion of authenticity related to Shakespeare's relationship as house playwright for the Globe Theatre.

The brainchild of American actor/director Sam Wanamaker (1919–1993), under the patronage of Prince Phillip, the new Globe was intended to be as scrupulous a replica as possible of the original "wooden O." It was built on the south bank of the River Thames, close to the site of the original Globe. Shakespeare's Globe considers itself to be a laboratory for the ongoing exploration of Shakespeare's plays in performance, pursued through the close approximation of architecture and stage conventions based on the company's meticulous research. Over the years it has broadened its agenda to include reconceptions of Shakespeare's plays and the commission of new work.

The new Globe's original attention to historical authenticity troubled some critics, for a variety of reasons. Some doubt the possibility of such a re-creation at all, given the scarcity of evidence available about the old Globe, gleaned from one sketchy drawing of another theatre of the time, some incomplete archaeological evidence, visitors' accounts, and whatever evidence the playtexts themselves might yield. As a result, scholars are still debating some of the decisions made. For example, some question the choice to feature permanent, highly decorated painted décor inside the new Globe, maintaining that the wood of the original interior had been left plain and temporary decorations hung for each play. Since the facts of the Globe's history will always be elusive, other critics are suspicious of the motives behind and effects of the desire for production authenticity. One concern is that, even if one could find all the necessary facts, a museum-quality attention to details may not speak across the ages and might stifle the drama. Another is that this desire serves to uncritically reinforce the idea of Shakespeare as the world's most important playwright. Still other critics have fretted that the attention to architectural and stage detail has come at the expense of the contributions of the actor's voice and body, and of the Shakespearean text itself. Despite these concerns, Shakespeare's Globe has thrived, drawing tourists from all over the world. In recent years it has expanded its focus on original practices to include new adaptations – such as *Henry VIII* as seen from the Spanish point of view – and premieres of new work. In 2013, a new indoor playhouse opened, allowing for year-round programming.

Thus, although the National, the RSC, and Shakespeare's Globe all began as national(ist) ventures to celebrate English theatre for English-speaking audiences, a combination of international tourism, global criticism, and high aesthetic expectations have put all in the world's limelight.

Across the pond in Canada, the annual Stratford Festival has come to represent a flashpoint in ongoing conflicts between national and international priorities over the figure of Shakespeare in the arena of cultural heritage. Begun in 1953 in a town named after Shakespeare's birthplace in the province of Ontario, the Stratford Festival is now the largest repertory company in North America and is heavily subsidized by the Canadian government.

In his *Shakespeare and Canada*, Canadian theatre historian Ric Knowles points out several ironies that have dogged the Stratford Festival since its beginnings. Many Canadians understood the initial success of the Festival as a marker of Canada's maturity as a nation-state, despite the fact that Stratford rested on the authority of a famous English playwright and borrowed most of its actors and its first artistic director (Tyrone Guthrie) from the country that had once ruled it as a colony. Thus, from the late 1960s through the 1970s, Stratford struggled to find a more "Canadian" identity; its board appointed a Canadian artistic director and more Canadian actors were hired. In the late 1970s the word "Shakespeare" was dropped from the official title of the festival in response to these pressures. During the 1980s and into the 1990s, many Canadian playwrights and directors targeted "Shakespeare" at Stratford for satiric attack and re-appropriated the Bard's plays for their own uses, which might be described as culturally hybrid approaches. Black Theatre Canada produced a "Caribbean" *A Midsummer Night's Dream* in 1983, for instance, while Skylight Theatre set *The Tempest* (1987) in aboriginal Canada, and Theatre Under the Bridge staged an urban *Romeo and Juliet* (1993), literally under a bridge in downtown Toronto.

By the 1990s, the Stratford Festival had begun to look to multinational corporate sponsors, international consumers, and global criticism for its legitimacy and prestige. Knowles examined Stratford during the 1993 season and concluded that globalization had triumphed over national priorities, with a full 14 pages of the souvenir program devoted to listing the individual and corporate donors for the season. The subsequent history of the Festival reveals ongoing ambivalences in the strategic use of "Shakespeare" for the Festival's purposes. In 2007, "Shakespeare" was returned to the title of the Festival as part of a new branding strategy for it. In 2012, facing a shortfall of $3.4 million (Canadian), and under new artistic direction, "Shakespeare" was removed once again from the Festival's name, his plays confined to a third of the 2013 season.

Whatever one's personal views of Shakespeare's plays and stature as an icon of prestige, it is difficult to deny the important role of that influence in contemporary theatre production. But it would be a mistake to think of "Shakespeare" as a theatrical juggernaut, absorbing all things unto itself in its global reach. Our next example shows how strategic adaptations of Shakespeare's plays can serve quite powerful local purposes, resulting in interesting hybrid versions.

In 1990, a company of Mexican indigenous performers based in the western state of Sinaloa, with a cast comprising actors whose original languages were Maya, Mayo, and Spanish, staged a tri-lingual production of *Romeo y Julieta* in New York's Central Park, as part of Joseph Papp's Festival Latino of the Public Theatre. Under the direction of Maria Alicia Martínez Medrano (1937–), El Laboratorio de Teatro Campesino e Indígena (Indigenous and Farmworker Theater Lab) set the story of two doomed lovers on a debt-slavery plantation on the Yucatán peninsula in the early twentieth century. This move allowed them to explore a combination of Mexican political history and interethnic conflict, in the process also redefining what "Shakespeare," "Mexican theatre," and "indigenous theatre" all might signify to New York audiences.

The Maya of southeastern Mexico and the Mayo of the northwest are two of more than 50 indigenous groups in Mexico. The Maya and Mayo do not share a bloodline, language, or customs, and would likely never have encountered much of each other had the latter group not actively opposed the Mexican government under Porfirio Díaz (1830–1915; in office 1876–1880 and 1884–1911). Díaz's policies against indigenous groups had led to rebellion and guerrilla warfare; his response in turn was to displace and deport large groups of insurgents within and outside of Mexico. Many Mayo were rounded up from the northwest and sent to work as slaves on the Yucatán plantations in southeastern Mexico. The local Maya, themselves working in serf-like conditions, did not welcome them. Martínez Medrano used this history to set the stage for a Mayo Romeo to fall in love with a Maya Julieta.

Of course, *Romeo and Juliet* seems meant for adaptations that explore interracial or intercultural conflict, and many theatre companies have done just that over the years. The LTCI production is unique, however, in its exploration of a little-known aspect of pre-Revolutionary Mexican history. More importantly, by situating the conflict between two indigenous groups within that history – and by casting indigenous actors, speaking "Shakespeare in tongues he surely never heard," as one *New York Times* critic put it – LTCI expanded the horizon for understanding Mexican theatre in general and its indigenous cultural history in particular. By incorporating indigenous languages, it suggested that that history is not over. By having those languages translate Shakespearean English, it subtly reminded audiences that indigenous cultures are not somehow removed from Western history either, but participant within it. Finally, the Mexican setting allowed audiences to reflect on the role the indigenous peoples have played within Mexican history and politics – and not always as a unified front.

"Shakespeare in tongues he surely never heard" appears all over the world, as the online case study shows. Interestingly, in those places where English is not the principal language, there is far more latitude of adaptation than we see where the English of Shakespeare may not be spoken, but is nevertheless revered.

His plays have also appeared in places he surely never would have imagined, as our final example illustrates. Since 1992, the "Shakespeare Behind Bars" program has worked with correctional facilities in Kentucky and Michigan to produce Shakespeare's plays with casts of incarcerated and post-incarcerated adults and youths. The program operates according to the belief that "[p]articipation in the Shakespeare Behind Bars program can effectively change our world for the better by influencing one person at a time, awakening him or her to the power and the passion of the goodness that lives within all of us" (Shakespeare Behind Bars 2014). Participants explore personal and social issues through their work on Shakespeare's plays, and build important life skills that help them in their return to society. While national re-arrest rates range between 60 and 75 percent, the rate for participants in Shakespeare Behind Bars is only 5.8 percent (Shakespeare Behind Bars 2014).

Taken together, these examples of "Shakespeare" the icon suggest that a global phenomenon can also catalyze local and "glocal" creativity. In the remaining sections of this chapter, we will look in turn at individual instances of these overlapping categories.

Global theatre culture

While the electronic media have contributed to the spread of knowledge about theatre in the world, two developments in global theatre culture still depend on live, real-time interaction between players and audiences: the growth of international festivals, and the increasing popularity of the mega-musical.

Our discussion of "Shakespeare," for example, shows that many local productions of such plays would not have been visible to the historical record if they had not been included in international theatre festivals, like Stratford in Canada or Papp's Festival Latino in New York City. We turn our attention now to such festivals, which represent another way some theatre has achieved a kind of global reach.

International festivals

Since the middle of the last century, the growth of transnational festivals – invited gatherings of several theatre companies in a limited area for a limited time – has become a key factor in theatrical globalization. Such festivals tend to internationalize aesthetic trends and provide an important showcase for directors with global reputations. For producers, festivals are a chance to re-mount their best shows, usually with low production costs and excellent publicity. Because many festivals invite small companies as well as large ones, some marginalized and experimental troupes can gain more international exposure. For theatregoers, festivals typically offer the opportunity to see a number of critically acclaimed productions in a few days.

Two notable festivals, both founded in 1947, have been the Avignon Festival, led by director Jean Vilar (1912–1971), and the Edinburgh Festival, directed by civic and cultural leaders. Both were established to bring high culture to the common people, featuring theatre as an instrument for international understanding, and both were eventually challenged by alternative ("**fringe**") festivals that have come to rival the originals in attendance. These fringe festivals also provide a chance for some troupes to emerge as globally known companies.

By 1963, Avignon was attracting over 50,000 spectators for French theatre. Vilar added new spaces and brought in younger directors. Although several of Vilar's productions and the ones he championed at Avignon had challenged the French status quo, the radical Living Theatre from the U.S. (see Chapters 12 and 13) led demonstrations in 1968 against what they called his "reactionary" leadership of Avignon and demanded that the Festival open its doors to all comers at no admission charge. The next year, several French-language troupes began offering fringe performances at Avignon, outside of the official program. These unofficial groups proliferated in the 1970s and 1980s – amateur and professional troupes performing everything from edgy minimalism to fully staged classics – and gradually created a second Festival, called "Avignoff."

In 1994, the official Festival began to internationalize its own offerings, although French-language productions still predominated. Avignon/Avignoff now boasts over 500 productions throughout the month of July, with most of them at the Avignoff. French subsidies and corporate sponsorship, however, have elevated the official Festival to the status of global culture. There, jet-set playgoers, the French elite, and international critics can enjoy high-priced theatrical fare at Avignon that some contend does little to challenge audience values. Although the fringe continues to dominate in sheer number of performances, by a ratio of about 10:1, few fringe productions are attended by these global players.

Most view the Avignon Festival as a success, but its two-track festival – the official Avignon for the international elite and the Avignoff for others – clearly was not what Vilar (or the Living Theatre) had in mind. A similar phenomenon emerged at the Edinburgh Festival in the U.K., whose Fringe is now the largest annual arts festival in the world. Its origins were humble: eight theatre companies organized their own separate event in the first year of the International Festival. The larger Festival officially recognized its fringe festival as a separate operation much sooner than did the organizers of the Avignon, and its openness to alternative selection criteria has resulted in an explosion of more than 25 parallel festivals, organized by different sponsors but understood as part of one big summer-long arts festival in the city, visited by hundreds of thousands of international visitors each year.

Using theatre for greater international understanding has been a key strategy of UNESCO – the United Nations Education, Scientific, and Cultural Organization, which formed in 1945 with the aim of promoting world peace and preventing another world war through a variety of initiatives, among them the preservation and promotion of cultural expressions. In 1948 UNESCO launched the International Theatre Institute, which in 1957 sponsored the first of many annual "Theatre of the Nations" festivals in Paris. The Festival showcased the theatre of 10 different countries, including *jingju* (Beijing Opera), *kabuki*, and dramatic work from the Moscow Arts Theatre and the Berliner Ensemble. Starting in 1972, the Festival began to be hosted by other participating cities, which helped to confer on them a certain status as international theatre capitals. Thus, according to Latin American theatre scholar Juan Villegas, 1993 marked an important moment in the internationalization of Chilean theatre, for that was the year the Theatre of the Nations Festival came to Santiago. Not only did this bring a large roster of international theatre companies to Chilean audiences, it also registered the power of theatre to function as an instrument of cultural and political legitimation in the country's return to democracy after the military dictatorship (1973–1990) ended. Chile has since then maintained an active international theatre presence, between 2005 and 2013 exporting more than 500 works to festivals around the world.

The notion of "exporting" suggests that the internationalization of theatre, whatever laudable nationalist purposes it may also serve on the stage of international visibility, runs the risk of becoming too much like a "product" in an international marketplace. Thus, Villegas and other theatre scholars have examined the costs to cultural specificity such commodification might exact, as the plays are selected (and perhaps developed) with audiences in mind who may otherwise know very little of local realities. Perhaps the biggest drawback of international festivals is the decontextualization of their performances. Most productions at festivals have originated in a different city and with a local audience, one that might not share the interests and concerns of the national and international spectators attending the festival. Many directors and companies get around this problem by mounting well-known plays for festival spectators – the plays of Shakespeare, Beckett, and Chekhov, for example. Perhaps that is why, when the DuMaurier World Stage festival in Toronto invited Brazil's Grupo Galpão, a street theatre troupe, to perform in 1998, the results were disorienting for most of the audience. Few Toronto spectators could understand the conventions of the neo-medieval biblical pageant that the Grupo Galpão had reshaped for their radical political purposes. The production, thrust out of

Figure 14.1

A touring production of *Romeu & Julieta* by Grupo Galpão in 2000, which met with more success among global spectators than some of their earlier work. Here the company is performing at Shakespeare's Globe Theatre in London.

Photograph by Sheila Burnett.

its normal context in the streets of Brazil, became mostly an exercise in exotic tourism (see below on theatre and tourism). Not all festival productions suffer this level of decontextualization, of course, but those that veer very far from the expectations of international audiences risk the most (Figure 14.1).

Despite such tensions between the local and the global, international festivals have increased. The Vienna Festival in Austria, begun soon after the Second World War like the Avignon and the Edinburgh, has long featured companies from Russia and Eastern Europe. Its popularity, coupled with the ongoing success of the Bayreuth music and opera festival and the Salzburg music and drama festival, both of which date from before the war, has helped to foment the international festival spirit in other German-speaking areas. The Bonn Biennale, for example, got underway in 1992, and the Ruhr Triennale began in 2002. Many other cities around the globe now sponsor one or more international festivals. As nation-states have lost power in the globalization process, large cities have gained it, and hosting an important festival boosts a city's international reputation. These cities include Montreal, Toronto, Los Angeles, Miami, Cádiz, Mexico City, Buenos Aires, Wellington (New Zealand), Sydney, Melbourne, Singapore, Hong Kong, Tokyo, Athens, Rome, Paris, London, and Dublin, to name some of the most prominent. In addition, large cities have been hosting the International Theatre Olympics, a festival lasting over two months, which has staged more than 150 productions between 1995 and 2010.

Mega-musicals

International theatre festivals are one way that theatre both reaches global audiences and runs the risk of assimilating to a homogenized, international aesthetic. The global mega-musical is another. Such musicals feature technologies of reproduction that not only extend their global reach but also make them the closest thing theatre has to being mass-industrialized (Rebellato 2009: 40). Producing musicals is now a global business. Composers, directors, and producers design musical spectaculars as franchise operations that several companies can run for years in all the major cities of the world, in English and in translation; an early and well-known example is Andrew Lloyd Webber's (1948–) *The Phantom of the Opera*.

Phantom and its offspring have been called mega-musicals for their spectacular visual and aural effects, enormous investments, high ticket prices, and potential for huge profits. They are sometimes disparagingly referred to as "McTheatre" because, as Dan Rebellato writes in *Theatre and Globalization,*

> There is something very distinctive and unusual about the way these shows have proliferated around the world. When you buy the rights to put on *Phantom of the Opera*, you're not given a score and a script and told to get on with it; you buy the original productions: sets, costumes, direction, lighting, the poster, and all the merchandise. This means that all productions of *The Phantom of the Opera* are, to a very significant extent, identical.
>
> (2009: 41)

This homogenization not only works on the level of individual play productions, but over time has come to represent a certain aesthetic dominated by lavish production values and songs that cross over into popular music. After two years in New York and with the "Broadway" label affixed to its price tag, a mega-musical can be exported to the international market; *The Lion King* has not stopped touring since 1998. With very few exceptions, its audiences go to see not the latest new conception of *The Lion King*, but the original production they've already heard so much about, without any risk that this particular production might be a flop. They attend in large numbers, paying high ticket prices, a quarter or more of which goes directly back to the financial investors (see "Anatomy of a Broadway ticket price," below).

In mega-musicals like *The Lion King*, the show itself is the star, rather than a particular celebrity. Investors prioritize its development (for example, through out-of-town tryouts) over its talent, so that, once a musical is up and running, operational expenses are relatively low. This helps to contribute to the musicals' seemingly infinite reproducibility.

In the past, producers typically formed short-term corporations. Today, global corporations, long-standing firms with investments in a range of products, are coming to take their place. The transition to risk sharing and corporate production for mega-musicals began in the 1980s. When London producer Cameron Mackintosh (1946–) teamed up with Lloyd Webber to produce *Cats* in 1981, the lush pop music and grand spectacle of this dance-based production outclassed most of the other musical offerings in London and New York. The show began an international run that lasted more than 20 years. Mackintosh followed with other musical hits in the 1980s – *Les Misérables* (1985), *Phantom of the Opera* (1986), and *Miss Saigon* (1989). Following his work with Mackintosh, Lloyd Webber formed a corporation, Really Useful

Group, to produce his subsequent musicals, which have included *Sunset Boulevard* (1993), *Bombay Dreams* (2002), and the sequel to *Phantom of the Opera*, *Love Never Dies* (2010).

More corporations entered the mega-musical business in the 1990s. In Toronto and New York, Livent produced two musical splashes, including *Ragtime* (1996, Toronto), before ending in bankruptcy. The Walt Disney Corporation began producing on Broadway in 1994 with *Beauty and the Beast*; it renovated a theatre on 42nd Street to house *The Lion King* (1998) and future productions (see Figure 14.2). In London's West End, Disney co-produced *Mary Poppins* with Mackintosh in 2004. Clear Channel Communications, a corporation with major investments in radio and television, also began developing mega-musicals (usually with other producers), but its major interest, in corporate lingo, was "feeding the road": creating musical products that supplied its road companies with profitable fare. To ensure these profits, both conglomerates primarily featured "family entertainment," such as *Rugrats – A Live Adventure* (1998).

As costs and investment time continue to rise, Disney and other producers have found ways to share their risks with non-commercial theatres in the U.S. When the non-profit regional theatre movement in the U.S. began in the late 1950s, companies in Chicago, Minneapolis, San Francisco, and elsewhere looked primarily to European theatres and classical plays for their models, not to commercial Broadway. Few even produced musicals on a regular basis until the 1980s. The success of *A Chorus Line* (1975) at the New York Public Theatre (**NYPT**) and its transfer to Broadway for a 15-year run, with the resulting infusion of millions of dollars to the

Figure 14.2
The cast of the musical *The Lion King* performs at the 62nd Annual Tony Awards in New York, Sunday, June 15, 2008.

Source: AP Photo/Jeff Christensen.

NYPT, however, permanently altered the non-profit landscape. The La Jolla Playhouse in San Diego has transferred several musicals to New York, including *The Who's Tommy* (1993) and many revivals. Disney opened an initial version of its *Aida* (1998) at the non-profit Alliance Theatre in Atlanta. Even the Guthrie Theatre in Minneapolis, the model of the classically oriented regional theatre, has played the mega-musical game: in 1999, Mackintosh took his production of *Martin Guerre* to the Guthrie to prepare it for a Broadway opening. Once indifferent to each other's fortunes, the non-profits and the commercial theatres of the U.S. are now cooperating in the hope of milking musical cash cows.

By the second decade of the twenty-first century, a mega-musical in New York cost about $10 million to produce and roughly half a million per week to run. With a possible weekly gross of around $800,000, most musicals must play for a year and a half before they break even. Ticket prices are therefore high; in 2013 the average was $101 a seat. The accompanying box shows where that money goes, using the hit musical *Mamma Mia!*, playing at the 1,500-seat Winter Garden, as an example, and rounding the ticket price down to $100.

Anatomy of a Broadway ticket price

- $1.25 Theater facility fee, not to be confused with
- $6.70 Theater rent (A Broadway house costs about $15,000 per week, plus 5 to 6 percent of the show's gross sales.)
- $11.20 Advertising/marketing
- $5.30 Salaries (cast)
- $6.90 Salaries (crew)
- $2.00 Salaries (musicians)
- $1.40 Salaries (other – press agents, ushers, box office)
- $4.10 Box-office commissions (paid to group sales and theater party ticket brokers)
- $4.50 Theater utilities and miscellaneous expenses
- $1.00 Insurance/accounting
- $4.10 Rentals (lighting, sound equipment, etc).
- $9.90 Union benefits/payroll taxes
- $1.20 Upkeep of costumes
- $15.70 Royalties
- $24.75 Return of capital to producers

Source: Jesse McKinley, *New York Times*, May 19, 2002

In 2003, the musical *Wicked* opened on Broadway, and became the top-grossing musical of the twenty-first century, earning upwards of $2 million per week ten years later. Based on the 1995 best-selling novel by Gregory Maguire, *Wicked* tells the story of how the Wicked Witch of the West came to be both wicked – or so she seems – and green. While in some ways it can be considered a mega-musical – for its spectacular effects, musical themes, and global marketing and distribution – musical theatre scholar Stacy Wolf argues that in other respects, it follows the more traditional conventions of the "integrated musicals" of the mid-twentieth century, with a few important twists. Whereas these other musicals tend to uphold white, heterosexual norms, *Wicked* emphasizes the bonds of female friendship between a green witch who is "wicked" and a white one who is "good" (or at least, "popular"), inter-species solidarity between humans and animals, and a love story that breaks with the usual happily-ever-after protocols of musical romances. For Wolf, *Wicked*'s distinction lies in "how it uses a very traditional musical theatre formula, but infuses the formula with newly gendered and queered content and relationships that are in large part responsible for its enormous theatrical and financial success" (Wolf 2008: 6).

Many of the stage musicals of the mid-twentieth century (e.g., *Oklahoma!*, *South Pacific*) were made into movie musicals, bringing something of the experience of seeing them within affordable reach. Following in this tradition, in 2012, *Les Misérables* became an Oscar-nominated film. In recent years, the relationship between stage musicals and film and other media has become increasingly intertwined. Of course, *The Lion King* and *Beauty and the Beast* were animated films before they were Broadway mega-musicals. *Spiderman: Turn Off the Dark* (2011) was based on the Marvel comic book series and film franchise. More and more film studios are becoming theatre producers on Times Square; in addition to Disney, the list includes Sony Pictures, MGM, and Warner Bros. And 20th Century Fox recently announced plans to develop at least nine of its film releases into stage musicals in a partnership that includes film, theatre, and entertainment executives. A relatively recent trend is the musical without original music. Examples are *Mamma Mia!* (1999), based on songs by ABBA, and *Jersey Boys* (2005), based on those of Frankie Valli and the Four Seasons. (For some background on how Broadway became the launching pad for mega-musicals and similar entertainments, see "The Vortex of Times Square," our online case study examining the history of Broadway and Times Square.)

Of course, Broadway wouldn't be Broadway today without the significant presence of international tourists, who descend upon Times Square not only to attend the theatre, but also to shop at the various emporia devoted to American mass culture that surround the Square. Tourists seeking different kinds of experiences from those they can find in their own countries help to fuel another aspect of theatrical globalization – cultural tourism, in which witnessing local performances is a key draw. Their desire to experience "other" cultures often intersects with a desire on the part of local performers and cultural authorities to assert local cultural expression in the face of globalization's homogenizing pressures. The next section looks at these strategies of cultural differentiation both as celebrations of local roots and as negotiations with international spectatorship.

Theatres of cultural differentiation

Home becomes "home" in a different way once a visitor walks through the door and starts looking around, inevitably making value judgments based on his or her own ideas of home. So too with cultural encounters represented by conquest or colonialism; by the imposition of foreign values exported via film and other media; or by the incursions of foreign tourists and their money.

In this section, we pursue the second direction of theatrical activity within globalization, exploring several examples in which theatre and performance are used to assert cultural differentiation. The examples cover three principal trends: (1) theatre for the preservation and articulation of local culture meant principally (but not only) for local audiences; (2) the emergence of theatre meant to restore and promote cultural heritage, also for both local and wider audiences; and (3) the increasing type and variety of performances aimed at satisfying tourist curiosity about local culture. In all three, the local and the global intersect; what distinguishes them from the more "glocal" performances described later on in this chapter is the degree to which cultural differentiation is held up as a key virtue. In its own way, each also illustrates that even the most local of celebrations and theatrical explorations of culture can enter into complicated and often contentious relationships with national and international interests.

Theatre for cultural assertion and preservation

Two examples from southern Mexico reveal how theatre has been used to assert local knowledge, even (and especially) under pressure of national and global processes of homogenization. In the middle of the last century, many cultural observers became concerned about the erosion of indigenous languages in Mexico in the wake of national programs of modernization and Spanish-language literacy. Teams of cultural and linguistic anthropologists thus traveled to the southern state of Chiapas in order to record as much as possible about Mayan languages and customs there, before they disappeared. For their part, a small group of their Mayan informants was concerned that this knowledge, heretofore passed down from generation to generation in the form of storytelling, would live on only in the dusty tomes of foreign libraries in works published by the visiting anthropologists in their own foreign languages, and therefore inaccessible to the Mayans about whom they wrote. The group's solution was to form a multi-lingual writers' collective in 1983, which published works in local Mayan and Spanish languages; by 1985 they added a puppet theatre company called Lo'il Maxil (Tzotzil Maya for "Monkey Business"). Eventually the troupe grew to incorporate live performances to supplement the collective's Mayan-language literacy workshops and publishing endeavors. Two members of the troupe – Isabel Juárez Espinosa and Petrona de la Cruz Cruz – went on in 1994 to form La Fomma (an acronym for the Spanish "Strength of the Mayan Woman"), a collective devoted to exploring and improving the lives of local Mayan women, also using theatre as part of their multilingual programming.

Both troupes began as attempts to preserve local culture and languages through the recuperation of local legends and the staging of local realities; both received significant Mexican and international support for cultural heritage preservation. In contrast to the *Rabinal Achi* in neighboring Guatemala, which is more a "performance of patrimony" of the sort described below, the new Mayan theatre in Mexico is also concerned with problems of pressing contemporary concern, exploring them through theatre techniques they have appropriated from other performance traditions, which they study through collaborations with visiting artists and participation in international theatre festivals.

For example, in 1994 Lo'il Maxil explored the roots of indigenous unrest that had led to the Zapatista uprising earlier the same year. This indigenous-led action took the name of a national hero of the earlier Mexican Revolution, Emiliano Zapata, invoking his legacy to take the Mexican government to task for its failure to consider indigenous perspectives in its rapidly globalizing economic policies. The play *De todos para todos* (*From All, For All*, 1994) examined the situation of a rural Mayan community robbed of its lands and banished to the jungle. Although the people take up arms to reclaim their heritage, the ending of the play recommends negotiation with the Mexican government, not the continuation of armed rebellion. La Fomma has also looked closely at national issues, with particular attention to their effects on women and children. In addition to producing plays aimed at assisting women with a variety of new social problems, their dramas target the economic policies that have forced the separation of Mayan family members. Other plays, such as *Échame la mano* (*Lend Me a Hand*) (2001), explore the dangers for women of participating in the international tourist trade.

Performances of patrimony

> With the dawn of the new millennium, we are witnessing the rise of a new paradigm: a veritable wave of "patrimonialization" is sweeping the entire world. The list of acts and displays declared to be cultural heritage over the past 10 years – the Argentine tango and the Mediterranean diet, Mongolian chants and human pyramids in Spain, the nō theater of Japan and the carnivals of Colombia, just to name a few – reads more like a poem by Borges than the official program of a supranational organization. It is, in sum, a politically correct and updated expansion of the Seven Wonders of the World.
>
> Paolo Vignolo (2012: 4)

There's a lot at work in Colombian performance studies scholar Paolo Vignolo's observation here. First, he suggests that the ephemera of culture – notably, performance culture – have now become monumentalized as cultural patrimony, testaments to the unique contributions of a given nation, ethnic group, or region to the larger world. Whereas at one time, natural and human-made structures were what made a place a destination, a "wonder of the world," now it is more likely some kind of performance tradition of song, dance, or theatre that merits special consideration. (The UNESCO proclamation in 2005 of the Guatemalan *Rabinal Achí* as a "Masterpiece of the Oral and Intangible Heritage of Humanity" is an example of this trend.) Second, he points to the contingent nature of this wave – that is, that there are no generally enforceable standards about what constitutes patrimony that some "supranational organization" (not even UNESCO, which is Vignolo's referent here) can impose, because culture is so heterogeneous. Finally, his reference to political correctness suggests a discomfort with the phenomenon in general. On the one hand, it may be laudable to move away from a classical, old-world sense of what is wondrous in the world to incorporate heretofore under-recognized "wonders." On the other hand, somebody (or some political body) will still be making decisions about what is included and what is excluded from a given people's "patrimony" – and such a process is never agenda-free.

Vignolo is concerned specifically with the particular Colombian carnival tradition of Barranquilla – claimed by Colombia's tourism bureau as "The Most Colorful Carnival in the World," second in scale only to that of Rio de Janeiro. For more than a century the Carnival was sponsored by political patrons seeking to gain the favor of the electorate; in 1991, it was privatized and is now owned by a company of local elites, who installed seats and stages, sold advertising space, and began to charge admissions and fees. Writes Vignolo, "In short, a collective festival was transformed into an economic engine for profit" (2012: 2). Ironically, in 2003 UNESCO designated the Carnival as a masterpiece of world heritage, precisely to reduce "cultural alienation produced by commercialization" (quoted in Vignolo 2012: 2). While the aim of most patrimonial policies is to preserve heritage and to strengthen cultural identities, the support of the state often makes them more attractive to economic interests as well. In the case of Barranquilla, what started out as a local celebration soon became an important

Figure 14.3

A scene from the Colombian Carnival of Barranquilla. Here, a local tradition begun in 1888 has come to draw thousands of international tourists, especially since its designation in 2003 by UNESCO as a Masterpiece of Oral and Intangible World Heritage.
Photo by Federico Rios.

international tourist attraction that, in order to perpetuate itself, must work harder at "preservation" than at presenting changing notions of identity – ethnic, gender, sexual, etc. – within Colombia (see Figure 14.3). As a result, some groups have begun to stage their own dissident parades a few streets over from the main parade route.

"Performing patrimony" can take place anywhere. For an extended discussion of a small Wisconsin town's annual staging of its own Swiss roots, see our online case study, "Backstage/frontstage: Ethnic tourist performances and identity in 'America's Little Switzerland,'" by Phillip B. Zarrilli.

Performances of (and against) "authenticity"

The desire to explore other lands and know other cultures is evident in the travel literature and travel pictures of many cultures over many centuries, which record pilgrimages to capital cities, religious shrines, and scenic natural wonders. By the end of the seventeenth century in Europe, the "grand tour" to sites of classical monuments and to museums and galleries became a regular rite in the education and maturation of the sons of aristocracy and gentry. Over the next two centuries the development of a middle class with increasing leisure time led to an increase in tourism. In turn, tourist destinations responded with improved presentation of sites and added attractions. Today, national and international tourism is a major industry, serving a large middle class in developed nations. Sites once remote have become more accessible through air travel and package tours.

Whether travelers are seeking historic sites or different cultures, they seek their own sensuous confirmation of the existence of the world they have imagined and anticipated. Further, as mediated experience comes increasingly to structure contemporary life, many tourists also travel in search of an experience of authenticity. Often, local performances of various kinds are an important part of their experience. As we have discussed, theatre festivals have become destinations for pilgrimage audiences, as has Shakespeare's Globe. Tourism companies and state agencies have also helped develop performances or exhibitions for travelers that draw on the music and dance traditions of local and indigenous cultures. In Seville, for example, tourists may cap a visit to the Museum of Flamenco with a Museum-sponsored flamenco dance exhibition, or choose another tourist package that features an evening of dinner and flamenco without the educational contextualization. *Kathakali* continues to draw tourists to Kerala, India, as does *jingju* in Beijing, and *kabuki* and *nō* in Japan. These examples illustrate that, while theatre that relies for its impact on verbal communication may find it harder to attract tourists who don't share the language, language difference is not always an obstacle.

In some parts of the world, everyday life itself has been theatricalized and consciously staged for tourist consumption, sometimes under the rubric of education and cultural exchange, sometimes as frankly commercial ventures. Such ventures allow local communities to participate in global trade, offering aspects of their cultural distinction as commodities for exchange in the international marketplace. These kinds of performances have in turn raised questions about the desire for and pursuit of authenticity as a function of privilege, unevenly distributed across the world, a question taken up by artists in performances that challenge this desire.

In India, for example, Jaipur's Rex Tours arranges for urbanized Rajasthanis and foreign visitors to observe "authentic" rural Indian life in a specially built village, where they watch craftsmen work and enjoy traditional food, dance, and music. The tour company brochure invites the traveler to "take a peek into the lives of rural folk, their abodes, social setup [*sic*], religious beliefs, and innovative cuisine" (quoted in Schechner 2002: 236). In Rio de Janeiro, Brazil, a company called "Be a Local Tours" (with the slogan, "Don't Be a Gringo, Be a Local!") offers insider tours of the city, including not only Rio's famous Carnival but also its infamous *favelas*, inviting tourists to "really experience what it means to be a Carioca" (bealocal.com). In Ireland, the Bunratty Folk Park functions as a "living reconstruction" of a nineteenth-century Irish village – complete with school, shops, post office, and pub, worked by costumed personnel who demonstrate their various occupations – located conveniently near Shannon Airport.

Another set of tourist performance examples comes from the relatively recent phenomenon of "dark tourism," where tourists visit sites of death, disaster, or tragedy. Theatre intersects with tourism in those cases where tourists take on the roles of the historical participants. Sometimes referred to as "immersive tourism," examples include simulated experiences of the Underground Railroad in the United States; illegal border crossing in Mexico; and "Escape from the U.S.S.R.," a simulated prison break in Latvia.

In those contexts where ethnic or economic "Others" are the principal attraction for tourists, such performances raise ethical questions. When are these performances meaningful examples of cultural exchange and sustainability, and when do they become demeaning exhibitions for the consuming gaze of tourists? At the same time as historical villages and heritage tours are creating jobs and keeping a local economy going, are they also an appealing "eternal past" that spectators can view with comfortable detachment, even nostalgia, a past unconnected to any problems in the past or in the present? Is the tourist seeking escape, or will she/he have any opportunity to be active rather than passive and to ask questions about such issues?

Some performance artists have devised presentations for tourist settings that confront tourists with the very issue of the touristic gaze. Mexican-American performance artist Guillermo Gómez-Peña (see Chapter 13), collaborating with the Cuban-American performance artist Coco Fusco (1960–), arranged such an event in 1992 in Madrid's Columbus Square on the 500th anniversary of Christopher Columbus's "discovery" of America. It was designed to help spectators recognize the ways in which "exotic peoples" have been exploited and conceptually colonized. The artists set up a 12-foot square golden cage in which they portrayed two recently discovered "primitive" native residents of the entirely fictive "Guatinaui" people, supposedly from an island in the Gulf of Mexico. The couple was dressed exotically, spoke gibberish, watched TV, and posed for photos (Figure 14.4). Ethnographic handouts described the "specimens" and their typical behavior. Over the next two years, the exhibit toured to art galleries and museums in the United States, and spectators' responses varied widely. Some believed they were seeing rare natives; some complained that the display was inhumane; some, especially patrons of elite art galleries, saw the performance as a performance (Schechner

Figure 14.4

A tourist photographs the performance work *Two Amerindians Visit*. Guillermo Gómez-Peña and Coco Fusco played fictive "Amerindians" as caged, exotic specimens in this performance piece, created in 1992 in Madrid's Columbus Square on the 500th anniversary of Christopher Columbus's "discovery" of America.

Source: Photo © Coco Fusco.

2002: 261). Whatever the interpretation and ethical ramifications (for example, some questioned the wisdom of allowing school-age children to interact with the "natives"), the notion of humans on display was not itself completely foreign to visitors to the installation. The 1993 documentary *Couple in the Cage*, produced by Fusco and Paula Heredia, captures the sense of these varying interpretations.

For the Vienna Festival in the summer of 2000, German director Christoph Schlingensief (1960–2010) created a performance work that scandalized Austria, the more so for being set up next to the Vienna State Opera, a prime site for the tourists it was designed to reach. Entitled

THINKING THROUGH THEATRE HISTORIES

Doing theatre history in a local/global world

Cross-cultural conversations are not new in theatre history. Japan was importing masked dance forms from Korea, China, and India between the sixth and eighth centuries CE. Roman drama and theatre architecture were the godchildren of Greek forms. When the Italian humanist academies of the sixteenth century attempted to resurrect Greek tragedy, it resulted in the fusion we know as opera. Some later Renaissance playwrights borrowed from the plays of ancient Rome. The *kathakali* dance-drama was woven from strands of several indigenous performance traditions, including the Sanskrit temple dance-drama, *kutiyattam*. Japan's *shingeki* (new theatre) movement in the late nineteenth century brought the influence of Western drama and acting to Japan. Irish playwright William Butler Yeats was influenced by Japanese *nō* drama. Bertolt Brecht's theories of acting were based in part on his observation of the Chinese actor Mei Lanfang. These could be considered early examples of "intercultural" theatre, latter-day examples of which we'll discuss more below.

Such historical perspective reminds us that cultures are never completely uniform nor unchanging, and it would be a mistake to suppose that traditional theatre genres (*kabuki*, for example) exist today in pure and unchanging form. Nor does culture tend to fit neatly within national borders. Some nations have, at least in theory, built their identities on the mixture of cultures and linguistic traditions they comprise. (Consider India, a nation in which there are 18 official languages and more than 1,500 different languages spoken.) Others are continuing to work out the relationships between aboriginals and European settler/colonizers. Uneven development even within nation-states has also contributed to internal migration from the countryside to the cities, changing the nature of urban culture as well as the lived experience of rural emigrants. The theatre that emerges from these realities is called **multicultural** theatre.

But when they appear before the word "cultural," prefixes like "inter" and "multi" almost force us to view cultures as rather stable, even when we know they are not. This can be a hindrance to tracking the movements of people and objects (including theatrical practices) in zones of contact, but it can also serve as an important caution. There are legitimate reasons both to celebrate the new forms that emerge when different cultures meet each other, and to be wary of cultural "borrowings" that are really (sometimes violent) appropriations; therefore, it is important to approach a given instance of inter- or multicultural theatre with careful attention to its historical and contemporary contextual pressures.

Please Love Austria, it employed a "residential container" in which 12 actual (though unnamed) refugees from different countries who were seeking asylum in Austria stayed awaiting their fate. They were guarded and their daily routines filmed and shown on television screens in the plaza. Over the container was a slogan representative of the extreme right-wing politics of Austria's Freedom Party and its leader, Jörg Haider (1950–2008), "*Ausländer raus*" ("Foreigners out"). Schlingensief shouted extreme right-wing slogans from a nearby rooftop and shocked tourists in the plaza below by welcoming them to Austria, "the Nazi factory." As Gitta Honegger explains, "The container installation was the simulation of a culture that had absorbed Haider's extremist rhetoric" (Honegger 2001: 5).

In this section we have examined touristic performance as a zone of contact between cultures. The theatre itself has always been such a zone, offering artists and audiences the opportunity to "visit" other times, places, and peoples. The next section explores some of the issues involved in these cross-cultural encounters.

Theatre as a zone of contact

Although they may to some degree engage both local and global influences and effects, the examples we have been discussing so far have tended to move in one or the other of our first two directions: either toward global theatre culture, or toward a more local theatre of cultural differentiation. In this section, we explore a third direction of theatre in globalization: theatre as a zone of cultural contact, where the local and the global influence each at a fundamental level. We focus here on three broad types of theatrical activity: multicultural, intercultural, and hybrid theatres, in several different contexts. Our case study discusses a multicultural Chinese play that also features intercultural and hybrid elements.

Multicultural theatre

Multicultural theatre combines performance modes from different cultural traditions or communities within nation-state boundaries, rather than across them (which we discuss below as "intercultural" theatre). *Jingju*, as discussed in Chapter 9, is an example because it draws on various performance traditions from within China. At its most ideal, such theatre has inclusion at the heart of its mission, staging both form and content understood to represent the variety of cultural contributions to the society in which the theatre finds itself. An early example of such a theatre is the San Francisco Mime Troupe, which began in 1959 as an avant-garde company devoted to exploring alternative theatrical forms, eventually becoming a multiracial collective exploring politically charged themes. Its roots as a touring company began in 1965 with *A Minstrel Show, or Civil Rights in a Cracker Barrel*, which used the exploitative form of nineteenth-century minstrelsy to stage a critique of twentieth-century racism.

Whereas for the San Francisco Mime troupe multiculturalism is a practice, for Mixed Blood Theatre in Minneapolis, Minnesota, it is the point. Founded in 1976 by artistic director Jack Reuler (1954–), Mixed Blood's mission is to promote "cultural pluralism and individual equality through artistic excellence, using theater to address artificial barriers that keep people from succeeding in American society" (Mixed Blood Theatre 2015). Mixed Blood's seasons thus typically explore a range of American lived experiences and social issues, both historical and contemporary, native and immigrant; nearly half of its more than 175 productions have been American or world premieres. Some of its plays are presented in both English and the relevant immigrant language. While most of its productions feature characters and themes reflecting the changing face of America, the company has also staged plays written by non-American playwrights about their local perspectives on global issues. (Its current website extends a "Welcome to Our Global Village.") Mixed Blood's commitment to inclusion and access extends beyond season selection: its program of "Radical Hospitality" donates half of its house, every night, to customers who cannot otherwise afford to pay the $20 ticket charge.

In the small city of Victoria in British Columbia, Canada, Chilean émigré Lina de Guevara (1933–) has developed another model of multicultural theatre. In 1988, she founded PUENTE Theatre; its name means "bridge" in Spanish, and its mission is to "build bridges between cultures." In the 1970s, many emigrants from Central and South America fled the violence and political strife of their countries, seeking new beginnings in Canada, with its open territory and similarly open immigration policies. In Canada, however, they met with a rhetoric of multicultural inclusion that didn't seem to play itself out in daily life. PUENTE was formed as a way for new Latina/o Canadians to come together to devise theatrical works based on their experiences and adjustments to their new Canadian realities. Their works, developed collectively, explored issues of racism, workplace discrimination, human rights abuses, sexual harassment, and other forms of oppression. Today, second and third generations of participants are exploring their mixed legacy, under the new artistic direction of Guevara's successor, Mercedes Bátiz-Benét (1977–).

In other contexts, "multicultural theatre" has not been so successful, and has been critiqued as a form of tokenism that keeps intact the privilege and prioritization of the dominant culture. This can be seen, for example, in attempts by some large non-profit theatres to "diversify the season" through the inclusion of one or two [name the minority] plays per cycle; or in the choice to "colorblind cast" canonical works rather than to stage lesser-known but deeper explorations of local experience, for fear of losing the subscriber base. Such considerations and constraints reveal the need for theatre to remain fluid and responsive to changing social contexts – not always an easy matter once it has become institutionalized. In India, for example, a major movement known as "theatre of roots" developed in the 1950s and extended into many cities. It sought to draw on rural Indian folk forms and performance styles for contemporary, cosmopolitan Indian theatre. Director K.N. Panikkar (1928–) of Kerala was a major figure in the movement. In recent years, it has declined, however, criticized for decontextualizing the traditions it has borrowed and reducing them to exotica. A similar phenomenon is considered in our case study, "Imagining contemporary China."

CASE STUDY: Imagining contemporary China

Carol Fisher Sorgenfrei

After the disastrous, anti-intellectual Cultural Revolution in mainland China (the People's Republic of China, or PRC), during which many people were brutalized or killed (1966–1976), China underwent rapid economic and social Westernization. Today, especially in major cities such as Beijing, Shanghai, and the Hong Kong Special Administrative Region, there is an active theatre scene, despite selective government repression and cautious self-censorship.

A number of recent dramas feature Western characters and deal with cross-cultural themes. For example, Sun Huizhu (William Sun, 1951–) and Fei Chunfang (Faye C. Fei, 1957–), who are both Chinese-born but now living both there and in the U.S., co-author plays interrogating Chinese identity. Their *China Dream* (*Zhongguo meng*, 1987) and *Swing* (*Qiuqian qingren*, 2002) chronicle the complex dilemmas, dreams, and memories plaguing Chinese women living in America, including what it might mean to marry a foreigner. Taiwanese playwright/director Lai Shengchuan (Stan Lai, 1954–) was born in Washington, D.C. and has spent his life shuttling between Taiwan and the West. His *Secret Love in Peach Blossom Land* (*Anlian Taohuayuan*, 1986; film, 1992) questions Taiwanese identity in relation to the PRC by showing two theatre companies – one *jingju*, one *huaju* – crossing paths when both are scheduled to rehearse plays at the same time and place. The stage play has been performed many times in both Taiwan and the PRC. In 2007, Lai directed his own English translation at Stanford University.

Such works demonstrate what Una Chaudhuri calls "geopathology," that is "the characterization of place as problem" and "negotiation with the power of place" (Chaudhuri 1995: 213). What does it mean to be Chinese if you no longer live in China? Or if the country you grew up in is fundamentally changed? This case study will consider these issues by focusing on the controversy sparked by the 2000 Nobel Prize for Literature, which was awarded to playwright/novelist/painter Gao Xingjian (1940–).

Gao left China in 1987 and has lived as a self-defined exile in Paris since 1988 (taking French citizenship in 1998). He is the first Chinese-language author to win the Nobel Prize for Literature. Rather than celebrating this achievement as a national victory, however, Chinese newspapers were reluctant to carry the news. Many Chinese officials and intellectuals assumed the award was politically motivated, noting that no play by Gao had been produced in China since 1986, when his *The Other Shore* was banned, and that Gao had abandoned China the following year. They suggested that authors still residing in China had been ignored. Their discomfort reflects two issues of "geopathology": what does it mean to be Chinese, and where exactly does China exist?

China(s), Chineseness, and Gao's theatre

As noted in previous chapters, by the mid-twentieth century, foreign colonization and imperialism had eroded Chinese domination and independence. Both the Nationalists (led by Chiang Kai-shek) and the Communists (led by Mao Zedong) supported reinventing "China" as a "modern nation" and both fought Japanese and European colonialists. However, they also fought each other for control of China. Eventually, the Nationalists retreated to the island of Taiwan, establishing the Republic of China. The mainland PRC (established in 1949 by the victorious Communists) sees Taiwan as a Chinese province. The issue is further complicated by divisions within Taiwan, where some residents want to form a separate nation unrelated to the mainland, and others seek reunification.

Both "Chinas" created national narratives to support legitimacy. For example, when the Nationalists fled to Taiwan, they took many priceless works of art. These are displayed in the National Museum in Taipei, the capital of Taiwan. To some, this act suggests the government's concern for protecting the ancient Chinese cultural heritage from wanton destruction; to others, it represents the act of a bandit regime that plundered national treasures. This issue continues to be highly sensitive on all sides.

As noted in Chapter 13, during the Cultural Revolution in the People's Republic of China, professional *jingju* and *huaju* actors, as well as doctors, intellectuals, teachers, and others, were beaten, imprisoned, or sent to the countryside to be "re-educated." Among these was Gao Xingjian, who spent six years in southwestern China after "volunteering" to destroy a suitcase filled with his early manuscripts.

Gao's forced sojourn in the provinces, where many minorities reside, exposed him to the multicultural nature of China. Despite Communism's official atheism, many rural peoples practiced the ancient *wu* religion – pre-Confucian shamanism featuring spirit possession, exorcism, and ritualized, theatrical performances using brightly painted wooden masks, dance, drama, and song (for more on shamanistic performance, see the online case study "Korean shamanism and the power of speech"). Such influences – as well as a deep concern for the welfare of the environment and a strong, nostalgic connection to a specific place – are evident in Gao's 1985 play *Wild Man (Yeren)*.

Wild Man is about an ecologist assigned to teach forest conservation to peasants in a remote river valley. Deforestation and the resulting severe flooding are consequences of China's rapid industrialization. The play features conflicts between ecological conservation and local economic/social realities, and between "factual" science and "superstitious" belief. The play has 41 characters, plus singers, musicians, and 12 separate groups of crowds. Each actor portrays many characters. Scenes flow into and are juxtaposed against each other; time is not chronological. Multiple scenes are performed simultaneously, and locales shift through creative use of sound, lighting, and other theatrical or cinematic effects. A traditional singer and his assistant "narrate" the action. Ancient *wu* rituals are performed, including the sacrifice of a live rooster, and local styles of ethnic minority performances alternate with psychologically motivated acting.

Prior to *Wild Man*, Gao's most famous work had been *Bus Stop* (*Che zhan*, 1983), inspired by Samuel Beckett's *Waiting for Godot*. Unlike Beckett's play, *Bus Stop* offered a social message, suggesting that people must actively take charge of their own lives, not passively wait for a savior. The play was criticized as being "too Western" and contributing to "spiritual pollution." Although the excesses of the Cultural Revolution were over, the government dictated (and continues to dictate) approved ways for theatre to represent the nation. Playwrights wishing to experiment were ordered to turn to Chinese – not Western – models. *Wild Man* combines Chinese minority performance genres with Chinese modifications of Brechtian devices, making it something of a hybrid of these influences.

Gao and others who have reinvented Brecht for use in China maintain that they have avoided Brecht's tendency to exoticize Asia by employing traditional Chinese performance styles. However, because most Chinese academics suggest that these traditional performance genres are dead (or nearly dead) "museum pieces" in need of preservation, it can be argued that plays incorporating such practices perpetuate the stereotype of ethnic minorities as "primitive," further marginalizing the rural population (Sorgenfrei 1991). Such concerns can be applied to *Wild Man*. At the same time, the play's use of a Chinese response to Brecht (who creatively appropriated what he mistakenly imagined to be Chinese tradition) and of minority performance genres means that we can analyze it as multicultural theatre, as an example of "geopathology," or as intercultural performance (further discussed in the next section).

Claiming Gao: Chinese or French? Political or non-political?

Even after Gao left China, events in China affected his work. Following the mid-1980s campaign against "spiritual pollution," a new period of political openness and artistic experimentation ensued. However, fears that this openness was excessive led to another government crackdown. On June 4, 1989, the Chinese government sent troops and tanks into Beijing's Tiananmen Square to clear students and intellectuals who were demanding greater democracy and artistic freedom. Public protests began in April and persisted until June 4, at times reaching numbers exceeding one million citizens. The events were watched on global television by millions. The concluding military attack resulted in an as-yet unspecified number of fatalities, though some estimates were in the thousands. Some dissidents fled the country, fearing a return of totalitarianism.

Gao had already emigrated to France, partly due to negative government reactions to his work. Nevertheless, some foreign advocates of human rights viewed him and other Chinese exiles as exemplars of the need for changes in the Chinese government. Gao's 1990 play *Escape* (*Taowang*, 1990) was a direct response to Chinese politics, specifically the events at Tiananmen Square, and it sealed the ban on Gao's works in China. However, since 1993, Gao's plays have not dealt with China or Chinese politics.

Let us, then, return to China's lukewarm reaction to Gao's Nobel Prize in 2000. The reason may well be that official China sees the award as a Western attempt to influence internal Chinese policies. Gao may be seen as having successfully manipulated Western intelligentsia for his own benefit. From this perspective, Gao's work fails to represent current Chinese concerns and even current artistic strategies. To those who hold this view, Gao Xingjian's plays (some of which were written in French) are no longer imagined as part of China's quest for a sense of nationhood in the contemporary world. Rather, they are seen as products of a primarily European imagination.

Gao's case brings up several questions of place and identity: what does it mean to be Chinese? What does it mean to be French? What is the meaning of home: is it where I was born, or where I currently reside? What does it mean to write in a foreign language? While there are no easy answers, such questions are crucial in the current world of globalization.

Key references

Audio-visual resources
Performance Workshop: http://www.pwshop.com/en/about_us/stan-lai-lai-sheng-chuan/. Many excellent articles and excerpts about Stan Lai, from the website of his Taipei-based Performance Workshop.

Books and articles

Anderson, B. (1983; rev. 1991) *Imagined Communities: Reflections on the Origin and Spread of Nationalism*, London and New York: Verso.

Chaudhuri, U. (1995) *Staging Place: The Geography of Modern Drama*, Ann Arbor: University of Michigan Press.

Chen, X. (2002) *Acting the Right Part: Political Theatre and Popular Drama in Contemporary China*, Honolulu: University of Hawaii Press.

Chen, X. (2003) *Reading the Right Text: An Anthology of Contemporary Chinese Drama*, Honolulu: University of Hawaii Press.

Cheung, M.P.Y. and Lai, J.C.C. (eds) (1997) *An Oxford Anthology of Contemporary Chinese Drama*, New York: Oxford University Press.

Conceison, C. (2004) *Significant Other: Staging the American in China*, Honolulu: University of Hawaii Press.

Fei, F.C. (1999) *Chinese Theories of Theatre and Performance from Confucius to the Present*, Ann Arbor: University of Michigan Press.

Feugi, J., Voris, R., Weber, C., and Silberman, M. (eds) (1989) *Brecht in Asia and Africa: The Brecht Yearbook XIV*, Hong Kong: The International Brecht Society, Department of Comparative Literature, University of Hong Kong.

Gao, X. (1990) "*Wild Man*: A Contemporary Chinese Spoken Drama," trans. B. Roubicek, *Asian Theatre Journal* 7: 184–249.

Kruger, L. (1992) *The National Stage: Theatre and Cultural Legitimation in England, France and America*, Chicago and London: University of Chicago Press.

Lilley, R. (1998) *Staging Hong Kong: Gender and Performance in Transition*, Honolulu: University of Hawaii Press.

Lovell, J. (2006) *The Politics of Cultural Capital: China's Quest for a Nobel Prize in Literature*, Honolulu: University of Hawaii Press.

McKerras, C. (ed.) (1983; paper, 1988) *Chinese Theatre from Its Origins to the Present Day*, Honolulu: University of Hawaii Press.

Phillips, H. (2009) "The Yellow Earth Becomes the Yellow Dragon: Eco-Consciousness in Chinese Theatre of the 1980s," *Asian Theatre Journal* 26(2): 135–47.

Sorgenfrei, C.F. (1991) "Orientalizing the Self: Theatre in China after Tiananmen Square," *The Drama Review* (Winter): 169–85.

Sun, W.H. and Fei, F.C. (1996) "*China Dream*: A Theatrical Dialogue between East and West," in P. Pavis (ed.) *The Intercultural Performance Reader*, London: Routledge.

Tian, M. (1997) "'Alienation-Effect' for Whom? Brecht's (Mis)interpretation of the Classical Chinese Theatre," *Asian Theatre Journal* 14: 200–22.

Tung, C. and McKerras, C. (eds) (1987) *Drama in the People's Republic of China*, New York: State University of New York Press.

Yan, H. (ed.) (1998) *Theatre and Society: An Anthology of Contemporary Chinese Drama*, Armonk, NY and London: M.E. Sharpe.

Yu, S. (trans. and ed.) (1996) *Chinese Drama after the Cultural Revolution, 1979–1989*, Lewiston, NY: Edwin Mellen Press.

Yu, S. (2009) "*Cry to Heaven*: A Play to Celebrate One Hundred Years of Chinese Spoken Drama by Nick Rongjun Yu," *Asian Theatre Journal* 26(1): 1–53.

Zhao, Z. (2009) *Prisoner of the State: The Secret Journal of Premier Zhou Ziyang*, trans. and ed. Bao Pu, Rene Chiang, and Adi Ignatius, New York: Simon and Schuster.

Intercultural theatre

Intercultural theatre may be defined as the practice in which theatre artists use the texts, acting styles, music, costumes, masks, dance, and/or scenic vocabularies of one culture and adapt and modify them for audiences of another culture, across national boundaries rather than within them. Since the 1970s, productions of this kind have developed in the context of globalization, with its imbalances of power and wealth, and against the backdrop of historical colonialism. Some productions have toured internationally, often to festival venues, their spectacle and music playing a large role in the endeavor to make them accessible to audiences of different cultures and languages. Many have been especially designed for such venues. Intercultural theatre is both filled with the promise of cultural exchange and fraught with the possibility of cultural appropriation, depending on the relationship between the source material and the production results and contexts. We consider four different combinations to illustrate the key issues involved in international theatre production.

Productions in which Western artists have borrowed (some have said "kidnapped") East and South Asian performance modes have been of keen interest and hotly debated. Two examples illustrate the contours of concern over such productions, and it may be useful to think about them in light of Chapter 9's "Thinking through theatre histories" discussion about Orientalism. The first involves the staging of a non-Western text, the Indian epic the *Mahabharata*, within a Western mode of theatrical production. The second considers the staging of four Greek tragedies using non-Western theatrical conventions. Do these examples represent latter-day "Orientalist" approaches that demonstrate the West's belief in its own superiority, or is something more complex at work?

British director Peter Brook (1925–) collaborated with French writer Jean-Claude Carrière to create a French-language adaptation of the *Mahabharata*, which premiered at the Avignon Festival in 1985. It was then adapted into English and toured to six countries in 1987–1988 (Figure 14.5). The production was monumental in scope, and generated much critical conversation.

Vijay Mishra's favorable review, for example, found the production added a new dimension to the *Mahabharata* texts that would "radically challenge (if not alter) the Indian regimes of reading" (D. Williams 1991: 204). Indian critic and director Rustom Bharucha (1988) was not

Figure 14.5

In Peter Brook's *The Mahabharata*, the archery tournament for the young cousins, in *Part I: The Game of Dice*, from the 1986 production at the Bouffes du Nord, Paris.

Source: Photo © Gilles Abegg.

convinced, however, arguing that the reworking of an Indian religious text for insertion into a secular Western theatre mode represented an insensitive use of the source material. Here, intercultural theatre may be said to mirror some of the problems and opportunities inherent in globalization: on the one hand, the forced encounter between powerful and less powerful cultures has the potential to overrun the cultural identities of the poorer cultures of the world as they are absorbed into more dominant forms; on the other hand, it also presents an opportunity to break down problematic Western attitudes of superiority to these cultures.

Our second example illustrates a different relationship between source text and theatrical modality: Ariane Mnouchkine's 1990–1993 staging of four Greek tragedies in Paris, presented in a non-traditional theatre space and relying extensively on Asian performance conventions. Reconstructing the glories of ancient Greece – the usual Western humanistic mode of production – was not the goal here. For Mnouchkine (1939–) and her Théâtre du Soleil company, the staging of the tragedies (under the collective title *Les Atrides – House of Atreus*) was an experiment in recovering them as works to be acted, danced, and sung, in this case using *kathakali* dance and Chinese costume influences. She hoped to liberate the Greek tragedies from text-oriented, literary scholarship and Western staging conventions, and additionally to introduce a feminist point of entry and reflection in the work (see Figures 14.6 and 14.7).

For *Les Atrides*, one entered the auditorium of the hangar-like building that houses the Théâtre du Soleil by crossing a bridge over a simulation of the site of a recent archaeological

Figure 14.6
Dancing chorus members in Euripides' *Iphigenia in Aulus*, in the *Les Atrides* cycle as staged by the Théâtre du Soleil, directed by Ariane Mnouchkine at the Cartoucherie, Paris, 1990.

Source: Photo © Martine Franck/Magnum Photos.

Figure 14.7

Orestes (Simon Akarian) dances around the dead bodies of Clytemnestra and Aegisthus in Aeschylus's *Agamemnon*, in the *Les Atrides* cycle of the Théâtre du Soleil, directed by Ariane Mnouchkine, Cartoucherie, Paris, 1990.

Source: Photo © Martine Franck/Magnum Photos.

dig in China. It had uncovered thousands of life-size Chinese soldiers in terracotta protecting the burial chambers of China's first emperor, Qin Shi Huangdi (247–210 BCE). The costumes of the principals in the Greek tragedies were influenced by those worn by the Chinese figures. Each production began with a long crescendo from a large tier of ancient percussion instruments located on a large platform above stage left. Drums propelled the chorus on stage and drove the plays forward thereafter. The chorus dances were derived mostly from Indian *kathakali* dance-drama, as were their costumes of black tunics and white skirts over pantaloons and elaborate headdresses. Their faces were whitened and their eyes dramatically highlighted. Individual chorus members hovered around the action, peering over the walls and around panels in front of the enclosing walls.

Mnouchkine's production was successful with audiences in France and on tour in Vienna, Montreal, and New York. It was less criticized than Brook's *Mahabharata*, perhaps because Mnouchkine had not reworked an Eastern text. For some, her production's exotic, fable-like milieu sometimes seemed a remote cultural fantasy; for others Mnouchkine's vision was transcultural and epic, offering a god-like view of the human condition. As with other intercultural productions, its global touring life – with its Asian visual vocabulary and its performances always in French – raises the question of what it meant, or could have meant, for its various audiences. In order to make themselves available to international audiences, intercultural theatre productions must rely on labor-intensive translations, or on the non-verbal languages of the theatre – scenic spectacle, music, and dance.

Intercultural productions have not been limited to those originating in Western cultural capitals, as numerous adaptations of Shakespeare attest (again, see our online case study about global Shakespeare). Two final examples illustrate this point. In New Delhi in 2004, director Amal Allana (1947–) staged *Eréndira*, an adaptation of a story by Colombian Gabriel García Márquez (1928–2014), who won the Nobel Prize for Literature in 1982. The New Delhi company adapted his early short novel *The Incredible and Sad Tale of Innocent Eréndira and Her Heartless Grandmother* into the Rajasthani dialect of Hindi. It is a tale which blurs the lines between fantasy and reality. A grandmother who was once a prostitute and who has pretensions to grandeur is served, hand and foot, by her granddaughter, Eréndira (Figure 14.8). Blaming Eréndira for a fire that destroys their home, the evil grandmother prostitutes her. She takes her, chained to her bed, on an epic journey lasting years, with men lining up for miles to enjoy the legendary Eréndira. The New Delhi company of six women and one man staged the journey in a sequence of striking visual images intended to correlate with Márquez's verbally rich narrative. They used music, dance, and masks, drawing on Indian and American sources, including Rajasthani folk music and Colombian carnivals. *Eréndira* toured in India and played in Singapore and London, always using supertitles in English.

Figure 14.8

The grandmother in *Eréndira*, an adaptation from Gabriel García Márquez's short novel, directed by Amal Allana, New Delhi, 2004. In this scene, several actresses play the granddaughter, Eréndira, bathing the grandmother.

Source: Photo © Kaushik Ramaswamy.

Whereas the example of *Eréndira* shows how local traditions can be used in dialogue with a foreign text, our final example shows how a foreign text can be more fully "transplanted" into local soil, this time to make a critique of globalization. Mexican playwright Sabina Berman (1955–) saw fascinating intercultural possibilities in the Irish playwright Marie Jones's 1999 play, *Stones in His Pockets,* which won the Olivier Award for Best Comedy in London and was subsequently produced throughout Europe and finally on Broadway. Berman is known internationally herself for her theatrical explorations of the seams and tears of gendered, cultural, and cross-cultural identifications; in 2003 she translated, produced, and directed Jones's play in Mexico City with the new title of *eXtras*, which enjoyed a run of several years there (Figure 14.9).

The original play features two characters – Jake Quinn and Charlie Conlon – who play extras in a Hollywood movie being filmed in their hometown in County Kerry, as well as extra roles in the play proper. The title refers to the fate of a young local whose dreams of stardom are crushed by the filmmakers; he fills his pockets with stones and drowns himself. In response to this tragedy, the villagers rise up against the foreign producers and the threat they represent to the erosion of local culture and values. In the end, the two principals, now playing themselves, decide to make their own film, casting the dead boy in the lead role and Hollywood stars as extras.

Jones intends their story to represent "the whole disintegration of rural Ireland" (quoted in Bixler 2004: 431). Given the similarity in economic conditions between rural Ireland and rural Mexico, Berman saw possibilities in a close adaptation. Jake and Charlie become José and Charlie, County Kerry becomes Chiconcuac, a poor pueblo in the state of Morelos, and the shoes that were used to represent character and identity changes become red bandannas, a familiar symbol of Mexican revolution from the original time of Zapata (a native of Morelos) to the more recent Zapatista movement. According to scholar Jacqueline Eyring Bixler,

> Berman recognized that the acts of adaptation and translation themselves convey what is perhaps the most important message of *Stones in His Pockets*, which is that U.S. culture – particularly that produced and marketed by Hollywood – has a pervasive and pernicious effect on the rural, impoverished, desperate, and brainwashed masses, not only in Ireland but throughout the world. In other words, the act of translating the play is itself a form of intercultural performance, or what [Marvin] Carlson calls "the weaving of complex patterns of contact with other cultures or other cultural performances."
>
> (2004: 432)

Figure 14.9

Cover image from playbill for *eXtras*, Mexico City, 2003, starring "two of the three Bichir brothers" – popular Mexican movie stars – on any given night. Part of the appeal of this production was metatheatrical, as the audience waited to see which two would star in the production as the extras heading to Hollywood, and which would actually be an extra in this production.

Source: Photo by Jacqueline Eyring Bixler in *Theatre Journal* 56(3) (October 2004): 438.

"Glocal" performance: Where the local and global influence each other

The performances described above are among the many manifestations of the cultural hybridity that has resulted from the movements of people, ideas, and art forms in the era of globalization, whereby different systems of beliefs, social practices, or aesthetics are merged together. The resulting fusions may represent disproportionate influence by the dominant power, as historically has happened in eras of colonialism, with its military conquests, religious evangelism, settlement, and commerce. They can also represent an integration or interpenetration by the less powerful; Roman Catholic masses are often celebrated with indigenous music. Music itself offers numerous examples of cultural fusion. In 1977, for example, the British rock group Queen (whose lead singer Freddie Mercury was of Iranian descent) recorded "We Will Rock You," known to millions as a thundering victory chant performed at athletic events worldwide. What may be less well known is that its beat was derived from the rhythms of a Muslim rite of self-flagellation practiced by Iranian males.

Hybridity of form and practice in theatrical performance is also quite common. The Japanese dance theatre form of *butoh*, introduced in Chapter 12, provides an example. Having declined in Japan, it experienced a resurgence outside that country beginning in the 1980s, when troupes began to tour. Perhaps the best known of those performances was by the group Sankai Juku, when they performed in Seattle, Washington in 1985. Their performance required troupe members to hang from ropes attached to tall buildings; one of them broke, and a dancer fell to his death in front of a live audience and video cameras, thus propelling *butoh* into a more international spotlight.

Since the 1980s, *butoh* has gained in global awareness not only as a form in and of itself, but also as a training technique for performers preparing for non-*butoh* work, incorporating aspects of it into other types of dance and theatrical performance. In fact, it is now better known abroad than it is in Japan. Many of these international performers are of Japanese descent, but many more are not. In Europe, Canada, and Africa new *butoh* or *butoh*-inspired troupes have emerged, their work ranging from the minimalist to the spectacular. In West Africa, Eseohe Arhebamen (1981–) combined *butoh* with elements of traditional Nigerian dance styles, mixing them with song, speech, gestures, sign language, spoken word poetry, and experimental vocalizations in a very hybrid new form. While in some cases the darkness of *butoh's* Japanese origins seems to be erased by its abstraction into pure style, others maintain its original intent to have the dancing body bear the enormous burden of history; the 2003 piece *Fagaala*, a collaboration between Yamazaki Kota (1959–) and Germaine Acogny (1944–) of the Senegalese company Jant-Bi, used *butoh* to explore the Rwandan genocide of the mid-1990s (Figure 14.10).

Figure 14.10

Butoh dancer Akaji Maro performs during the dance festival in honor of Kazuo Ohno in Yokohama.

Source: © Kim Kyung-Hoon/Reuters/Corbis.

Another example of glocal adaptation comes from Indonesia, and illustrates the interplay of influence between patrimonial assertion, globalization, and electronic media culture: the *wayang golek* [wah-YAHNG goh-lek], a centuries-old tradition of puppetry in West Java, which has in recent years adapted itself to the medium of television. An expanded discussion of this example appears on the website.

In *wayang golek*, three-dimensional, carved, and painted wooden puppets tell stories in the Sundanese language. (In contrast, the Indonesian shadow puppets of the *wayang kulit* [wah-YAHNG koo-lit] are two-dimensional silhouettes and transparencies. Both, however, draw on the Hindu epics of the *Mahabharata* and the *Ramayana*, and probably arrived in Indonesia with Hinduism and Buddhism during the first century CE. See Figure 14.11.) In its original form, *wayang golek* performances are extremely social occasions, drawing large crowds and lasting for hours. The puppets represent a metaphysical view of the human condition, and are manipulated by artists adept at improvising based on audience responses, as the old tales may take on some contemporary resonance. As Indonesia modernized and entered the global economy, *wayang golek* artists created hybrid forms that took advantage of the new communication technologies, beginning with audio cassettes in the 1970s and moving to national television in the 1980s. These new technologies resulted in changes to the form, as

Figure 14.11

Backstage of a *wayang kulit* shadow-theatre in the city of Yogyakarta, Indonesia, where a *dalang* (puppeteer) manipulates his puppets behind the screen, accompanied by musicians, in a performance of a play about the Pandava brothers derived from the *Mahabharata*.

Source: Photo by J. Highet/Lebrecht Music & Arts.

they had to fit a shorter time frame, and could take advantage of multiple camera perspectives. However, these studio productions lacked live audience responses – a factor which suited the Suharto government then in power (1967–1998).

This began to change in 1996, when one well-known puppeteer, Asep Sunandar Sunarya (1955–2014), developed a new *wayang golek* derivative for television, a hybrid comic form featuring the traditional puppet character Cepot. This simple, country bumpkin figure's earthy lifestyle served as a foil for the excesses and corruptions of the Suharto regime, then in its last years in power, in new versions of the old tales. *The Asep Show* thus harnessed contemporary media to a traditional puppet theatre form, in order to make targeted critiques of the contemporary national situation in Indonesia.

Such strategies illustrate the fluidity and adaptability of traditional theatre practices within globalization, and help to ensure their continuance without becoming exoticized museum pieces. As the global village becomes ever smaller through the electronic media, the unequal distribution of its resources becomes harder and harder to ignore. Our fourth route through theatre in globalization illustrates how local communities the world over are using theatre to address some of these issues.

The global reach of theatre for social change

"Theatre for social change" is an umbrella term that captures several related movements – among them, "Theater of the Oppressed," "theatre for development" and "community-based theatre" – that have as their aim the use of theatre to explore and solve pressing social problems. While all theatre has the possibility to affect and effect social change in any number of ways, and certain manifestations of what we describe below can be found in earlier periods, "theatre for social change" began to emerge as a distinct category of theatrical practice during the 1970s. It is a broad and generous category, encompassing a variety of forms, working methods, and performance settings. In general, "theatre for social change" is distinguished from commercial, for-profit theatre that occurs in a formal theatre building; its workers are professionals who perform with participants and audiences who are, in the main, non-theatre professionals; and, as its name suggests, it aims to address, if not solve, social problems of concern to its participants. In this section, we focus particularly on those kinds of theatre for social change in which the local and international intersect in some way.

Theater of the Oppressed

Many of these movements draw on the theories and techniques of Brazilian theatre director Augusto Boal's Theater of the Oppressed, mentioned in Chapters 12 and 13. Strongly influenced by the ideas of educational theorist Paulo Freire in his 1968 book, *Pedagogy of the Oppressed*, Boal developed a series of theatrical innovations and interventions designed to raise awareness of the causes of oppression, identify key problems facing a given community, seek collective solutions to them, and implement them not only on stage, but in societal and political venues. In later years, working in exile in countries where the forms of oppression were less overt than those exercised by dictators, Boal developed his ideas into what he called "The Rainbow of Desire," which helped participants to become aware of "the cop" in their own heads – in other words, the subtle ways oppressions can become internalized.

In such theatre, trained practitioners work with groups – usually communities coming together around a specific cause, within an identified system of oppression, or within zones of ethnic or intercultural conflict – to explore collectively solutions to that cause or conflict. Practitioners affiliate through such organizations as Pedagogy and Theater of the Oppressed, Inc., a global forum for "people whose work challenges oppressive systems by promoting critical thinking and social justice through liberatory theatre and popular education" (ptoweb.org).

Key characteristics of Theater of the Oppressed are the inclusion of a facilitator (or "difficultator") called "The Joker," and an understanding of the audience as "spect-actors" rather than "spectators," called upon to propose and enact the contours of and solutions to the problem being explored. Forms and techniques of Theater of the Oppressed include:

- Image theatre, where participants use their bodies to form wordless images of a situation under discussion;
- Forum theatre, whereby different solutions to a given problem are proposed by the spect-actors, who then test them by acting them out in improvised scenarios;
- Newspaper theatre, drawing on an early form of documentary theatre to offer techniques for groups wishing to explore contemporary issues in their world;
- Invisible theatre, where spect-actors trained in Theater of the Oppressed techniques publicly enact a scenario that calls attention to some form of social injustice, in the context where the injustice regularly occurs, without calling attention to itself as theatre;
- Legislative theatre, a type of forum theatre that takes place in town halls and houses of legislature, where a given law, policy, or statute is being debated.

Boal's ideas have become internationalized in a variety of movements that draw on his Theater of the Oppressed techniques to serve particular glocal purposes.

Theatre for development

The term "theatre for development" (TFD) originated in Botswana, Africa, in the mid-1970s to describe performances intended to help communities address their difficulties with health, agriculture, literacy, and similar problems. The basic model, as it emerged in a series of conferences and workshops, involved theatre activists researching a community problem, creating a play through debate and improvisation, presenting the piece to the community, and following the performance with discussion and community planning. Well-funded by non-governmental organizations (NGOs), themselves often based in powerful countries far away, this model spread throughout English-speaking Africa in the 1980s. Many theatre and community leaders, however, criticized the early phase of TFD for its crude modernization ideology, its failure to involve community participants, and its blindness to local customs and political power struggles.

Most present versions of TFD have taken these criticisms to heart and have remained an important strategy for activists seeking theatrical means to improve the lives of many Africans. The Nigerian Popular Theatre Alliance (NPTA), for example, through its Theatre for Development [training] Centre, works in the areas of adolescent health and education, democratic citizenship, economic empowerment, and conflict resolution, an important concern for many Nigerians because of the bitter history of civil war in that country. Affiliated with a local university, the Centre also educates future leaders in the problems and possibilities of TFD.

Figure 14.12
A SEKA performer in a large mask clowns for Zambian villagers.
Source: Photo © Miranda Guhrs of Seka. <www.seka-educational-theatre.com>

In Zambia, SEKA, the acronym for Sensitisation and Education through Kunda Arts, works through university teachers, community activists, and theatre artists to tackle many of the problems of village life in central southern Africa. Among these are child labor, rampaging elephants, and HIV/AIDS, particularly rife in rural Zambia. To involve the villagers in their programs, SEKA relies primarily on interactive theatre that uses stories and songs from local life to demystify problems and create collective solutions (Figure 14.12). Partly to fund their major programs, SEKA also creates customized productions for conferences and performs traditional Zambian culture for tourists. SEKA's stated goal is an appropriate summary of the aims of many TFDs: "We believe in changing circumstances by changing minds and changing minds through the arts – theatre and stories in particular."

Community-based theatre

Though not a coordinated movement, community-based theatre is something of a worldwide phenomenon. It overlaps with theatre for development initiatives in Africa and India, and is sometimes referred to as "theatre for community cultural development" in the U.S., "community theatre" and "community plays" in the U.K. and Canada, and *teatro comunitario* in Latin America. Not to be confused with that form of "community theatre" in the U.S. that restages mainstream theatre with non-professional actors, community-based theatre draws on the legacy of Theater of the Oppressed, Nuevo Teatro Popular (see Chapter 13), and other socially engaged work that mixes political agitation and developmental strategies. Community-based theatres also depend upon ongoing dialogue between artists and spectators, and explore ways of maximizing the agency of a local audience.

Unlike the radical theatre movements of the 1960s, however, the political beliefs of artists committed to community-based work are not necessarily oriented to revolutionary action or democratic socialism, but grow out of their commitment to a local community or social group. Although most espouse liberal political values, some are motivated by a conservative desire to preserve the past, or to pursue notions of community development that align with the global development initiatives that have also inspired theatre for development movements. Not surprisingly, these political differences often translate into competing definitions of the term "community," which can serve one or more groups identified by a sense of regional, ethnic, or social class belonging. Community-based theatre's commitment to a "community" has been both a strength and a weakness, energizing some groups for self-improvement and progressive change, and limiting the social, political, and aesthetic reach of others. For those communities caught up in problems related to globalization, community-based theatre has primarily led to smart tactics and long-term adjustment or resistance, but at times also to parochialism and nostalgia.

There are thousands of community-based theatres around the globe. In Western Europe and North America, community-based artists and facilitators have focused much of their attention on empowering marginalized groups, celebrating the useable past of a community, and helping people to energize communities that have been damaged or destroyed. For example, Stut Theater in Utrecht, the Netherlands, devised a production involving Dutch, Turkish, and Moroccan young people and their parents to recognize the needs of the two marginalized groups and encourage intercultural understanding. In England, playwright and facilitator Ann Jellicoe (1927–) has helped several communities to celebrate their histories. Swamp Gravy, located in a small town in Georgia in the U.S., draws on local tradition and African-American Christianity to bridge the racial divide in the American South. The LAPD (the Los Angeles Poverty Department, not an official agency of the city, but use of its initials draws ironic attention to the failures of the city's safety nets) seeks to generate a sense of community among the residents of Skid Row in Los Angeles.

Several companies work toward all of the goals noted above. In the United States, one of the more established such groups is Cornerstone Theater. Now based in Los Angeles, Cornerstone began in 1986 as a traveling ensemble working with rural communities in the United States to bring their stories to the stage, and including members of the communities in the productions. Since 1992 they have focused more on urban issues and collaborations. Their model of theatre utilizes community-based, peer-to-peer education methods, based on gathering stories from community members and creating plays inspired by those stories. These plays are organized around themes and staged in multi-year cycles; since 1992 they have included the Watts Cycle (building bridges between African-American and Latino residents of the Watts neighborhood of Los Angeles); the Faith-Based Cycle (exploring the city's communities of faith); the Justice Cycle (exploring the relationship of law to community); and the Hunger Cycle, around issues of food justice. Cornerstone has also partnered with the National Day Laborer Organizing Network to help launch the Teatro Jornalero Sin Fronteras (Day Laborer Theater Without Borders), an ensemble of day laborers who use Cornerstone methodologies to educate immigrant workers about their rights and to humanize the immigration debate for the larger community.

Community-based theatres sometimes combine theatre work with social and economic transformation. In Brazil, Nos do Morro (Us from the Hillside) produces theatre for the poor citizens who live in the hills above the wealthy beach areas of Rio de Janeiro. While the theatre space also serves as a local community center that provides participatory entertainment, the company members engage in various interventions to help the workers, street children, and dispossessed of the area. In the Philippines and the Marshall Islands, respectively, the Philippine Educational Theatre Association (discussed in Chapter 13) and Jodrikdrik ñan Jodrikdrik ilo Ejmour (Youth to Youth in Health) train squads of young people to lead outreach programs using theatrical techniques that help other youth adjust to the many problems that globalization is bringing to the islands, including AIDS, increasing alcoholism, and the disruption of traditional culture. In Kenya, the Kawuonda Woman's Group shows the continuing influence of theatre for development programs in a small village. When the women dramatize one of their stories for the village, they typically rehearse them in the midst of doing the laundry or picking coffee beans, and they perform their short scenes within a circle of dancers and singers to demonstrate their female solidarity.

Many of the artists involved with these community-based theatres have adopted strategies to moderate or resist some of the effects of globalization that are changing the lives of the populations they assist. Global media, especially from the U.S., now saturate the lives of young people around the globe and are fast replacing traditional cultures as a common point of reference in most societies. Jodrikdrik recognizes this fact and encourages their participants to mix island traditions with popular songs and media genres from the U.S. in their annual talent show, called, appropriately, *Showtime!* In Rio, Nos do Morro has found film and television work for several of the young actors who have performed on its stage. Other community-based theatres, including PETA, La Fomma, and Aguamarina, have helped their participants to organize collectives to maintain the economic viability of traditional crafts in competition with international corporations.

The pressures of globalization are also changing the organizational strategies of community-based work. Yuyachkani in Peru maintains its company identity, but also facilitates the work of individual members to pursue projects related to company goals. Ground Zero in Toronto has abandoned the notion of a theatre company altogether. Its founder, Don Bouzek, now works with temporary alliances of funders, clients, and artists to produce theatre pieces that will advance progressive causes and alliances in Canada. In the United States, Michael Rohd's Sojourn Theatre, based in Portland, Oregon, operates on a similar model. Two scholars of contemporary interventionist theatre, Alan Filewod and David Watt, argue that such "strategic ventures" involving like-minded artists and activists collaborating together on specific projects, provide the best strategy for transforming communities in the global future (Filewod and Watt 2001: *passim*).

SUMMARY

Theatre has always been a site for cultures to come into contact with each other, materially and imaginatively. With the advent of the "global village" since the middle of the last century, the possibilities for such contact have been both broadened and deepened.

In this chapter, we have seen how theatre culture in the era of globalization has taken a variety of forms, ranging from the rather homogenized aesthetic of the mega-musical to the radically local and culturally specific performances of everyday life offered for tourists. Many theatre artists, seeking to advance and reanimate their practice, have looked to other traditions for inspiration, or have found new ways to reach international audiences for their work. At the local level, many performance traditions like the *wayang golek* puppet theatre have proven themselves adaptable to new media, in the process achieving a new political life. The processes of globalization have prompted theatrical responses that both preserve patrimony and urgently question its contours in contexts of international spectatorship. Finally, we have discussed a variety of instances and types of theatre that have as their heartbeat an impulse to change the world, community by community.

The notion of theatre as a "zone of (inter)cultural contact" carries with it the full gamut of possible outcomes, ranging from embrace of the foreign to active resistance against its incursions. One result is that much theatre in the era of globalization operates under the new norms of formal and cultural hybridity. Like any other social institution, theatre operates within power relations that are often highly imbalanced. An important task of the critic and historian, therefore, is to pay careful attention to how that power, a matter of cultural as well as political and economic capital, is flowing.

★

CHAPTER 15

Theatre in networked culture, 1990–present

Tamara Underiner

"Give me four trestles, four boards, two actors and a passion," Lope de Vega reputedly said, "and I will give you a play." A favorite adage among theatre people, it calls attention to theatre's most basic elements and alludes to its infinite possibilities. As we have seen throughout this book, theatre artists have frequently experimented with these elements. We have also seen how developments in theatre history have always been in conversation with changes in the culture that surrounds them; new technologies, communications and otherwise, have both enabled innovation and, on occasion, spurred the desire to get "back to basics." Now is no different.

As brick-and-mortar theatre spaces continue to produce work for live audiences, with live actors performing scripted drama on three-dimensional sets, other movements are afoot. Today, the "four trestles and four boards" may be a smart stage, in which actors trigger sensors that in turn trigger lights and sounds, or a virtual stage altogether. Of the "two actors," one might be a robot, or appear on a screen to interact with the other actor. The "passion" or driving force behind a theatrical experience may not be the vision of a single playwright or director, but arise instead from the collective experiments of a theatre ensemble. And the "plays" that result from these new combinations produce new audience experiences, including live and virtual interaction, in which audience contributions influence the action.

In this chapter, we discuss the interaction between *networked culture* as a whole and performance practices on and off the formal stage. While in a fundamental sense human history is itself a history of networked culture, over the past two decades new media technologies have made it easier than ever for people to connect with each other, and to remain aware of personal and world developments in real time. In North America, Europe, and Australasia, internet usage has begun to challenge and in some cases has surpassed television viewing. These new technologies, so central to everyday life, are also becoming increasingly integral to performance on stage, going far beyond their potential as special effects. At the same time, off-stage, social media such as Facebook, Twitter, and YouTube create opportunities for people to "stage" themselves, whether they see themselves as performers or not.

But "networked culture" does not refer only to the computational technologies that make real-time connectivity possible. It also refers to the way these technologies have influenced the ways we are or can imagine being social together. In this culture "the network" is not merely a technologized byproduct *of* social relations, but is fast becoming the dominant organizational paradigm for society itself, extending deeply *into* social, cultural, and political conditions. The results reach down to the level of the individual him- or herself, who is now conceived, increasingly if not exclusively, as a node in a network composed of both humans and objects (the "internet of things"). The category of creative expression has similarly become more decentralized, as audiences for art have become more and more participatory in its creation. Increasingly, new works are being developed by appreciators of visual and performing arts, who adapt and mix together elements from other works, and post the results via open platforms like YouTube. This kind of borrowing, mixing, and adaptation in order to make something new has itself borrowed a term from the music industry – the remix – and has become the prevalent aesthetic of networked culture.

Therefore, while much theatre being produced today continues earlier practices, in this chapter we focus particularly on theatre that registers network culture's varied (but ever-changing) influences and interactions. To organize the fluid array of ideas and examples available, we divide our coverage into three broad sections, roughly reminiscent of Lope's adage. Our first section considers the performers, human and otherwise, whose work calls attention to new technologies of the self in networked culture. Our second section covers some of the changing platforms for their performances, both virtual and real-world (although those distinctions tend to blur in networked culture). Finally, we will consider how the new logic of the network has contributed to a variety of performance types and styles, produced or accelerated different models for the collaborative aspects of the theatre-making process, and led to experiments in form and structure of a new kind of theatre called "postdramatic." Our case study on online role-playing games considers what happens when the platform is a virtual one, the players manipulate avatars, and their passions might be invented or reflect what's going on in their offline lives – all in an ever-evolving plot. The case study on Hip Hop theatre considers how this art form, called by Daniel Banks the "theatre of now," nevertheless serves as a register of a centuries-old heritage of theatrical practices.

Since this chapter is also the culmination of this particular theatre histories textbook, we take this as an opportunity to look not only *at* "theatre in networked culture," but also *through* it to examine how theatre (perhaps the original "social medium") has changed over time as a forum for reflection about society. Along the way, we should keep in mind that some of the characteristics of "networked culture" represent differences in kind from earlier forms of culture, and some are better understood as differences of degree. Distinguishing between the two is not always a simple matter. Consider, for example, what the ancient Greek philosopher Aristotle considered to be the key to effective dramatic plotting: the careful selection and arrangement of incidents from stories already in circulation and well known to the culture for whom the classic Greek playwrights wrote. Were those playwrights early aggregators and remixers, or is there something essentially different about the ways today's artists are re-assembling the raw materials of story as circulated by the media and social networks?

Or consider the matter of time and space in dramatic action and theatrical performance. While the neoclassicists may have insisted on preserving the unities of time, place, and dramatic action, theatre artists in all other times and places have taken great liberties with all three aspects of drama, and audiences have managed to follow along. But until very recently in theatre history, the performance of most stage plays – no matter how long their action was presumed to take, in however many locales – has unfolded in real time before their audience, and in a shared physical space. Do today's technologies of connectivity, and the subsequent experiments they allow in performance, represent a new phase in an ongoing evolution of temporal and spatial experimentation on stage, or a radical departure into a philosophical examination of theatrical time and space itself? The examples we follow in this chapter are meant to raise and shed light on such questions, rather than to definitively answer them.

New players

As we've seen in previous chapters, the role of the actor in society – whether elevated as celebrity or denigrated as vagabond – derives from the power actors are believed to have in shaping human values. Their larger-than-life significance is due, in part, to the double reality they inhabit on stage, a reality that borders on the virtual. They transform and extend themselves through both external means (costume, makeup) and internal means (physical, psychological, and emotional training and preparation), all the while remaining present to their audiences both as themselves and as their characters. They are both real and unreal; or, as Richard Schechner has elaborated, they are both "not me," and "not not me" (1985: 112).

Until very recently, however, actors have always been co-present with their spectators, sharing physical proximity with them in real time. In fact, for many it is this property of "presence" that has distinguished theatre from other forms of narrative and representational media. However, we can and often do experience this sense of presence with and through media as well, as when we watch a "livestream" of a performance or communicate with an online chatbot (and we notice it keenly when our devices "die"). Understood this way, "presence" has moved away from being seen as inherent to the theatrical form, and has taken up residence in the audience's experience of the form, if not in the technology itself. And that form has increasingly come to entangle live and media "performers."

Experiments with live and virtual actors

Perhaps the earliest performance pairing a live actor with a virtual performer was in a 1914 vaudeville act by Winsor McCay, who interacted with a film animation of Gertie the dinosaur. Since then, experiments have grown in complexity and sophistication. In the early days of the internet, performance artists and theatre companies were quick to explore the question of live/virtual performance. In 1995, Guillermo Gómez-Peña and Roberto Sifuentes (see Chapter 13) collaborated with James Luna (1950–) on an installation/performance called *The Shame Man and El Mexican't Meet the CyberVato*. Over the course of five days at an art gallery at Rice University, Luna as Shame Man and Gómez-Peña as "El Mexican't" performed various incarnations of how "Native Americans" and "Mexicans" should look, behave, and perform in the 1990s, based on suggestions posted by visitors to the performance's website, which also appeared on monitors in the performance space. Meanwhile, the character CyberVato (Sifuentes), an exaggerated Chicano gang member decked out in techno-gadgetry, captured images of his collaborators' transformations and transmitted them daily to the Web via video teleconferencing. The intent was "to politicize the debates around digital technologies and to infect virtual space with Chicano humor and *linguas polutas* (such as Spanglish)" (Gómez–Peña 2003: 38).

The following year, the San Francisco-based troupe George Coates Performance Works premiered *Twisted Pairs*, whose characters were based on personality types making early appearances in online chatrooms and bulletin boards; its action was structured according to the associative logic of internet surfing. (The title refers to the way electrical wires are twisted together to cancel out electromagnetic interference from other sources, key to clarity in telecommunications.) The plot, similarly convoluted, revolved around an Amish farmgirl who discovered a laptop by accident, and went on to become an internet celebrity calling herself "Annette Diva." Other characters were developed out of recognizable online personas and the live actors interacted with video projections and telecasts. At the time, such technologies were new enough that a glossary of internet terms was necessary for audience members – many of whom were not sufficiently literate in internet lingo to get many of the jokes.

In 2000, Steve Dixon, Paul Murphy, and Wendy Reed of Chameleons Group developed *Chameleons 3: Net Congestion*, which experimented with combinations of live actors with remote audiences, and with recorded characters. Actors performing on three separate stages in a black box studio interacted with pre-recorded characters projected on screens behind them, while the audience – none of whom was there in the studios, but watching over the internet – typed in suggestions for the performers to use or play with. Dixon writes, "Whilst a 'high-tech' project, the stage configuration itself harked back to the pageant wagon staging of Medieval Mystery Plays" (Dixon n.d.).

While technology has allowed actors to connect with audiences across time and space, new advancements in medical and cyber-technology have prompted many theatre and performance artists to explore the limits of "the human" itself in their work.

Exploring and expanding the limits of the human

The theatrical stage has always been a site for magic, where the supernatural and the superhuman can appear to have tangible reality. Today, a performer can do more than amplify the sound of her voice with a wireless mike; she can also manipulate other elements of the theatrical environment that previously had been run by crews behind the scenes. For example, her costume can be a smart one, outfitted with movement sensors that trigger sound, music, lights, and so forth, at her command. In one sense, this is an extension of centuries of experimentation with theatrical illusion and special effects. In another sense, the new possibilities for extending human powers through technology have raised compelling questions about where the human ends and the machine begins. Human–machine interactions have produced new ideas about being human in this digital, mediatized – some say posthuman – age. Theatre scholar Jennifer Parker-Starbuck refers to a "cyborg theatre" (2011), which explores this merging of human and technology, both literally and figuratively, toward moving past traditional notions of biology-based humanity.

For example, some artists have undergone extreme modifications of their own bodies in work that calls the "givenness" of that body into serious question as they experiment with body type, gender stereotype, and even human/animal hybridity. (Many of these experiments have come through the work of individual performance artists; for more information on "performance art" itself, see the Box in Chapter 13). For example, the work of the Australian digital/live performance artist Stelarc (1946–) has included both cybernetic performance and body modification. In the 1990s Stelarc created a series of live/internet performances in which his body was remotely controlled through interfaces with remote viewers and with the

Figure 15.1
Australian performance artist Stelarc in his 1994 work, *Amplified Body*.
Photo: Jan Sprij.

internet itself, resulting in his body being, literally, jerked around by remote controllers. More recently, Stelarc has been experimenting with more extreme and permanent body modification. In 2006, for example, he began work on an ongoing project in which he is growing an ear on his left forearm; it has been fitted with a microphone and wireless transmitter that allows remote listeners to hear what his arm/ear is "hearing" (through its built-in microphone) in real time over the internet (see Figure 15.1.) As a result of his experiments and speculations, Stelarc has come to consider the body increasingly obsolete – at least in terms of its former physiological limitations.

Actors and robots, robots as actors

Still other artists have experimented with humanoid robots to question our confidence in how special we humans might really be. Japanese playwright Hirata Oriza (1962–) collaborates with robot designer Hiroshi Ishiguro at Osaka University to stage humans and android robots together. Their 2010 play *Sayonara* is about a young woman with a terminal disease whose parents hire an extremely human-looking android to care for her, so that they can then abandon her. The voice and gestures of the android, "Geminoid F," were created off stage by an actress in a soundproof chamber, fed to the android via camera and replicated on stage. In 2012 *Sayonara II* featured a defective robot reading poems to comfort a girl dying of radiation exposure from the damaged nuclear power plant at Fukushima after the 2011 earthquake. Another collaboration resulted in the 2011 *I, Worker*, which features two non-humanoid robot maids. All have at their center an exploration of what it is to be human, forced into stark relief by robots (a frequent theme of science fiction, not yet fully realizable on stage).

Not every experiment with robotic performances has profound philosophical questions as its inspiration. In 2006, the Les Frères Corbusier production of Elizabeth Meriwether's *Heddatron* also featured live actors sharing the stage with radio-controlled robots, their operators off stage (Figure 15.2). Designed by Cindy Jeffers and Meredith Finkelstein of Botmatrix, an art robotics collective, the robots in *Heddatron* entice an unhappy housewife from Ypsilanti, Michigan, to the jungles of Ecuador, where they force her to perform the title role of Ibsen's *Hedda Gabler* (1890). They in turn perform the supporting roles, and that of Ibsen himself – who is, like his heroine, portrayed as suffering within a stifling marriage. Originating in New York, *Heddatron* has been produced in several other theatres across the United States, to generally enthusiastic reviews. Interestingly, these reviews tended to focus as much on the show's premise and themes – the identification of a contemporary woman with a character written over a century before her birth, and the redemptive possibilities of theatre itself – as they did on the fact that more than half the cast were robots.

One reviewer called attention to the robots' perfect comic timing, which raises an interesting point for theatre history. Unlike fully human actors, robots are able to achieve exact repetition from performance to performance, a fact which recalls certain other moments in theatre history. On the one hand, live theatre's unrepeatability is, for some, what makes it uniquely attractive. On the other, theatre history has also been marked by frequent demands to deliver fidelity to the playwright's text, and consistent, if not identical, performances along the course of a show's run. In the Hellenistic age, for example, proscriptions against actor improvisations were common. Also recall our discussion in Chapter 7 of Denis Diderot's eighteenth-century *The Paradox of the Actor*, in which the French philosopher praised performers who could separate

Figure 15.2

Robots inhabit both the domestic and forest world in Les Frères Corbusier's *Heddatron*, with scenic design by Cameron Anderson.

Photo: Cameron Anderson.

their emotions from their actions, their minds from their bodies, so that they could present their character in exactly the same way at every performance. Diderot argued that, to effectively move an audience, the actor must remain him/herself unmoved. This idea was later expanded upon by Gordon Craig (see Chapter 10), who longed to replace actors entirely with large puppets, or *Übermarionettes*, because they would be easier to control than live human beings. Theatre artists who share Craig's aims might envision robots as the new "superactors" of the theatre.

The replacement of actors on stage by robots may be unlikely, but there is a growing area within networked culture in which virtual bodies take center stage – and the stage itself is also a virtual one. Our first case study takes a closer look at the phenomenon of online role-playing games as a new form of theatre.

CASE STUDY: Online role-playing games as theatre

Tobin Nellhaus

Digital culture has made games a regular part of many people's lives, and scholars have begun to recognize their cultural importance. Online role-playing is a game that is also a type of performance. Some of its features are very similar to theatre as traditionally understood; other aspects, however, are quite different. How should we understand this sort of performance – as a game with only a superficial resemblance to theatre, a performance genre with theatre-like elements but (like performance art) not actually theatre, or in fact a new type of theatre? Also, if online role-playing truly is a new type of theatre, do its differences from traditional theatre have any special social or cultural significance?

Online role-playing games and virtual worlds

Modern role-playing games arose in the 1970s. In tabletop games, such as *Dungeons & Dragons*, players simply talk through their characters' actions. In live action role-playing games, players play their roles in person, perhaps re-creating a historical battle or staging an event in an imagined medieval world. The first online role-playing games were conducted in text only, but in the 1980s they gained graphics and soon developed virtual worlds.

Virtual worlds can depict any place imaginable, from a historical location such as 1920s Chicago, to a fictive but naturalistic setting like a small town in a valley, to an interstellar battlefield, to a fantasy world with elves and orcs. Players interact in the virtual world through avatars, which can also take any form – a human, an animal, a machine, or a creature from a fantasy or alien universe. Most players write text to "speak" in character; voice, if used, is usually for team coordination or for commentary (although some people do use it for role-playing).

In virtual worlds such as *World of Warcraft* and *Lord of the Rings Online* – known as massively multiplayer online role-playing games (MMORPGs, or often simply MMOs) – the narrative, the setting, the possible avatars, their weapons and clothing, and all of the other elements are provided by the game company, although some companies allow or even encourage modifications. Many players in these games don't role-play; instead they pursue individual quests and battles with computer-generated opponents as they strive to build up points, weapons, and skills. Sometimes the MMO simply allocates a few regions for role-play.

Figure 15.3
The Realm of Mystara, a role-playing region in *Second Life*.
© Tobin Nellhaus

MMOs are primarily intended for gaming. There are also open-ended (or platform) virtual worlds such as *Second Life*, *Metropolis*, and *InWorldz* where people mainly socialize (and shop) without role-play. However, because everything in open-ended virtual worlds is user-created – the settings, avatars, clothing, accessories, and all else – some users create role-playing regions following their own tastes and interests, including the region's backstory, its natural and/or architectural environment, and the eligible avatar types. Some regions are inspired by a movie or TV show, such as *Avatar* or *Game of Thrones*, but most are original (see Figure 15.3). The players exercise considerable freedom in designing settings, avatar types, costumes, and equipment. Role-playing in open-ended virtual worlds can involve armed combat, like the MMOs, but often the focus is on character interaction and group activity, without scoring points or even using weapons: enjoyment lies in the role-playing itself.

Performance techniques in online role-playing

To determine online role-playing's performance genre, we should start by exploring its performance methods. At a very general level, obviously people play characters and use them to enact a storyline or narrative events. If there are large events such as battles, the location and overall direction is generally planned. But the specific encounters are devised on the fly, wherever the players happen to be. Broadly speaking, then, online role-playing is similar to improvisational theatre. However, unlike improvisational theatre, numerous scenes occur simultaneously in various locations within the role-playing region, usually with little or no connection with each other. Another difference from improvisational theatre is that players don't use their own body, but instead choose their appearance, social type, species, and gender from the options offered (or invented) within the virtual world.

There are also similarities with dramatic literature. For example, players often provide their character with an extensive backstory. Sometimes the backstory is quite particular, providing the character with a history, a set of motivations, attitudes, fears, desires, and other traits. In this way the character can become roughly as detailed and individual as most dramatic characters (similar to the way some stage actors envision a complex backstory for their character).

One of online role-playing's performance techniques is highly distinctive: role-play is generally conducted through writing – not voice or movement. To overcome the extreme limitations of avatars' actions and the lack of vocal tone, these elements are described in sentences called "emotes." Almost all social interactions use emotes. Players may combat each other using weapons, but they can also employ emotes, and in some regions that's the only possibility.

The following example, drawn from *Second Life*, shows how this works. Its setting is a city riddled with crime and corruption. Cassie Manga, an arsonist, has set fire to a building; Murk23 Oh is a cop. (Names have been changed; genders have not.) The emotes are italicized, and the character name at the beginning of each sentence shows who wrote it.

> *Murk23 Oh sighs,* "Now you pesky little firebug, what will we do with you?" *He begins to pat her down, searching for her lighter.*
> *Cassie Manga feels him pat her down and tries to kick him back off of her.* "Leave me alone ya ass, I didn't do nothing wrong."
> *Murk23 Oh gets a kick to the shin and growls,* "I saw you on the camera, now where's that lighter?" *He steps back a little.*
> *Cassie Manga smiles a bit.* "What lighter, I don't smoke, if ya need a light I smell smoke somewhere, go get a light off of that."
> *Murk23 Oh grumbles as he leans down and attempts to grab her guns.*
> *Cassie Manga feels him take her guns.* "Dammit, give them back, I paid good money for them ya ass, if ya want a set go get ya own."
> *Murk23 Oh smiles as he begins to move away from her with her guns in hand.* "See you soon!"

The exchange follows the "best practices" of online role-play. Two rules are foremost. First, emotes should be written from an onlooker's perspective: in the third person, without access to the character's thoughts or feelings. "*Cassie Manga smiles a bit, knowing Murk23 won't find anything*" would be a faulty emote, because an outside observer can't read Cassie's mind. We'll call this the *rule of objectivity*. In practice, casual players seldom take umbrage at "subjective" emotes, and sometimes they're necessary in order to convey the right tone to the other players, such as when a snarl is playful, not threatening. Even highly skilled players occasionally disregard the objectivity rule; "*searching for her lighter*" is borderline (and Cassie's player ignores it). Nevertheless, objective emotes are recommended.

In contrast, breaking the second rule can be a serious violation of role-play etiquette. Each player should allow the other players to decide the result of any particular action. Murk23 *attempts* to grab Cassie's guns, but his player leaves open whether he succeeds – Cassie's player decides that he did. "*Murk23 Oh grabs Cassie's guns*" would be objectionable because his player takes over the scene, not allowing Cassie to perhaps dodge and draw her weapons (which might have been what Murk23's player expected). Letting Cassie's player decide the outcome of

Murk23's grab makes the role-play much more interactive, surprising, and fun. We will call this the *rule of reciprocal player agency*. Together these two rules make the role-playing highly collaborative, requiring players to be both spectators and performers sharing a scene – eliminating the traditional division between actor and audience.

From one perspective, emotes look novelistic, not dramatic – especially when they're paragraph length. But several elements bring them much closer to theatre and drama. For one thing, the rule of objectivity, including its use of the present tense, makes emotes similar to stage directions or blocking notes. In addition, the rule of reciprocal player agency, which leaves outcomes open, is effectively equivalent to a technique in improvisational theatre. Keith Johnstone, author of an improvisation textbook, describes the technique as "offering and accepting": one performer establishes a situation or even the bare beginning of a situation (the offer), which the other performer accepts and builds upon through another offer; the first performer accepts this offer and in turn develops the scene further. Johnstone gives this example:

A: Augh!
B: Whatever is it, man?
A: It's my leg, Doctor.
B: This looks nasty. I shall have to amputate.
A: It's the one you amputated last time, Doctor. [. . .]
B: You mean you've got a pain in your wooden leg?
A: Yes, Doctor.
B: You know what this means?
A: Not wormwood, Doctor!
B: Yes. We'll have to remove it before it spreads to the rest of you.
    (A's chair collapses.)
B: My God! It's spreading to the furniture!

(Johnstone 1979: 96)

In most cases, online role-playing is already heavily structured by the virtual world's setting and available roles, as well as any relationships the players already established (e.g., boss and employee). As a result, unlike Johnstone's improvised scene, players seldom have to create a situation from whole cloth. Still, the principle of offering and accepting is the same. It is the foundation of collaborative performance.

Embodiment, presence, and agency

The differences between theatre and online role-playing need to be addressed next, because they point to many people's concept of theatrical performance. Two are closely related: presence and embodiment. Both are connected to how agency is exercised in online role-playing.

"Presence" – also called "immediacy," "aura," and sometimes "liveness" – is often viewed as theatre's most distinctive feature (albeit not by all scholars). It is usually understood as involving the actual proximity of living, breathing, embodied actors and spectators. But if so, then online role-playing simply isn't theatre: the players are usually physically isolated during play, sometimes by continents.

However, the concept of presence has numerous aspects, and nearness and human bodies aren't necessarily viable criteria. For example, large auditoriums place back-row spectators hundreds of feet from the stage, yet they may feel presence. Likewise, if performers must use their own bodies, then puppetry (such as *bunraku*) cannot be theatre. In fact, under the standard definition of presence, one might doubt that blind people can experience theatrical performance.

Another definition of presence escapes those shortcomings by focusing on how people share not so much a physical space, but rather a *meaningful* space (Mennecke et al. 2011). This interpretation suggests that online role-players do experience presence with other players, regardless of distance, because their avatars immerse the players within a meaningful space, meaningfully shared. This concept of presence focuses on its social character. Virtual worlds are highly social environments that create social presence, in a mediated form that can be as lively and electric as physical presence. In some ways the sense of virtual presence can be stronger than in traditional theatre, because players always interact with other players directly, whereas in most theatre the spectators' interaction with actors is indirect or vicarious.

The sense of presence in virtual worlds (as in the material world) involves not only an awareness of other people, but also a feeling of one's own presence within the virtual environment, mediated by a kind of body, an avatar – and players are usually quite particular about their avatar's appearance, which is an abstract form of embodiment. But "being present" through one's personalized avatar doesn't entail identifying with the character. Experienced players recommend keeping some psychological distance between oneself and one's character in most types of role-playing; otherwise, one might (for example) misunderstand insults aimed at one's character as intended for the player, which can ruin the game play. Players should, however, understand and feel their character enough that they can act appropriately. In a way, the avatar is a role-player's second body, and role-playing in a virtual world via an avatar is akin to the embodiment of a character that an actor performs in theatre using all the tools available, including costumes, mannerisms, speaking style, and makeup. One's sense of self-presence is not identification, but rather immersion as a virtual body within the virtual space shared with others.

Constructing a narrative within a shared virtual space requires players to be conscious of each other's presence and enable their participation. In online role-playing, "shared" means that when players enter a virtual space, they implicitly promise to collaborate with others. Disputes do occasionally arise, and usually someone has the authority to adjudicate between players, but overall, by promoting collaboration that eliminates the distinctions between actor, audience, playwright, and director, role-playing games foster an egalitarian performance process – all the more so because players can freely choose the "body" in which they perform. Such egalitarianism might even be described as democratization, because the online environment allows vastly more people to become performers. (Some role players' behavior is far from egalitarian, but that is distinct from the structure of role-playing itself.)

The rules described earlier define collaboration in online role-playing. The rule of reciprocal player agency protects other players' ability to participate. When players use emotes, the rule of objectivity helps to ensure that other players have material their characters can respond to, keeping the narrative in motion. Thus the players recognize that they and the other players are agents in the material world, and that their characters are agents in the virtual world. Both of these create presence in the sense of participation within a shared, meaningful space.

So far, then, online role-playing seems similar to theatre, because it too engages presence during the performance of characters.

Online role-playing and the structure of theatre

To say X is like Y is not the same as saying it's a *type* of Y. For example, although salamanders look like lizards, they are not actually lizards. So is online role-playing just highly similar to theatre, or is it in fact a type of theatre?

Another element of online role-playing exposes a further reason for viewing it as a type of theatre. As we saw in the arsonist/cop scene, the direction that a scene takes can be decided on the fly. Alternatively, players can discuss what will happen before launching their scene. In addition, sometimes players need to alert the other players about something happening in their material world, such as having to take a phone call, or they want to note some other non-scenic issue. In these situations, the player must communicate out of character, which they often do by surrounding text with double parentheses. Here are two examples from observed online role-playing (names have been changed):

> Meeroo Milan: mhmm, what he said
> Meeroo Milan: she★
> Meeroo Milan: ((sorry))

Meeroo's player corrects a typo (flagging the correct text with an asterisk), and writes out of character to apologize for any confusion or inadvertent insult. In the next excerpt, a player teasingly remarks on the fact that even though the characters are together in a virtual world, the players themselves are scattered about in the material world.

> Liz Bennett: Why someone gotta be shooting in the morning?
> Greg Samsa: ((It's afternoon here :)))

Out-of-character communication underscores the fact that the two realms of player activity – the material world and the virtual world – are not "worlds apart": they exist simultaneously and they continually interact, although they remain distinct.

Beyond their straightforward difference, however, is a similarity. In the case study "Early modern metatheatricality and the print revolution" (Chapter 5), we saw a definition of theatre that involves a parallel between the strata of society and the strata of theatre. Each possesses three levels: (1) structures, consisting of resources and conditions such as the space and the social system (including the presence or absence of an audience/actor division); (2) agents (people) in real-life activities, and fictional agents (characters) in dramatic action; and (3) discourses (words and images expressing ideas and values) that affect the agents' activities and responses. When we examine the two worlds of online role-playing, we find that they both have these three levels as well.

In online role-playing's material world, the first level consists of physical circumstances, resources, and real-world social relationships; these include the internet itself, the game company's business needs, the degree of player creativity they provide, player demographics, and so forth. These are the structural preconditions for online role-playing. The second level of the material reality encompasses the players as agents who decide to engage in role-playing, select which online role-playing game to use, bring certain skills, etc. and their actual activities (typing and moving images on a computer screen). The third level comprises the images, situations, and scenarios borrowed from movies and TV, improvised texts and other ideas that the players use to create characters and actions, and the attitudes players bring into their role-playing activities, all of which are discourses.

In the virtual world, in contrast, the first level consists of the actual activity of role-playing, including the states of being in character and out of character, and the players' relationships with each other (mutual awareness, teamwork, conflict, etc.). Second, there are the characters themselves, as imaginary persons, along with their relationships, alliances, and opponents and the fictional environment in which the activity is set. The third level covers the virtual world's overall narrative, themes (such as honor and criminality), powers, restrictions, and typical character-types.

Our closer look at online role-playing shows that its two realms – the material world and the virtual world – each have three levels in the same way theatre does. On this definition, then, online role-playing games aren't merely *like* theatre, they *are* theatre.

Conclusion

Online role-playing, despite involving players who are physically distant from one another and use avatars to serve as their bodies, involves presence and embodiment, just as theatre does. It is also structured the same way theatrical performance is. Thus online role-players' game-play is play-making, in a new, online form of theatre that makes every participant a performer.

Key references

Johnstone, K. (1979) *Impro: Improvisation and the Theatre*, New York: Theatre Arts Books.

Mennecke, B.E., Triplett, J.L., Hassall, L.M., Conde, Z.J., and Heer, R. (2011) "An Examination of a Theory of Embodied Social Presence in Virtual Worlds," *Decision Sciences* 42: 413–50.

I would like to thank the anonymous role-play gamers I interviewed, who were highly informative.

Changing platforms for theatre and performance

Online role-playing games are but one example of another change brought about by networked culture: an expansion of possible platforms for performance beyond the material "four trestles" and "four boards" once required of the formal stage. Sometimes the new platforms are digital, in full or in part: theatre increasingly houses digital sets and scenic elements, or is being presented on wholly virtual platforms. But theatre is also taking place off the formal stage and in the "real" world, in ways that are themselves enabled by social media, used to attract both live and remote spectators.

Digital platforms

Live theatre has utilized film and electronic media for decades; as long ago as 1898, playwright Lincoln J. Carter (1865–1926) designed filmed scenery as backdrop to his stage action. Performances have long used closed-circuit television, motion-controlled projections, or online streaming media to add characters or create a setting on stage. In 1996, for example, the University of Kansas's Institute for Exploration of Virtual Reality staged Arthur Kopit's *Wings* (1978), using a completely electronic set design, which audience members accessed through

Figure 15.4

An early experiment combining live and virtual performance elements, by the University of Kansas's Institute for Exploration of Virtual Reality, in 1996. This scene is from Arthur Kopit's *Wings*, about a woman recovering from a stroke. Audience members watched the play through head-mounted displays, which allowed them to see through the computer graphics and live video being projected on their devices to the production's live actors and digital projections. (Director Ronald A. Willis, Designer/Technologist Mark Reaney, and Video Director Lance Gharavi.)

Source: Photo: Mark Reaney.

virtual reality headsets. (The play, which explores the effects of stroke on the language and mental processes of its victim, was originally written as a radio play. See Figure 15.4.)

Today, projections are commonly employed both as virtual scenery and as interactive elements in stage plays. Online, whole plays have been performed within a virtual world (often designed for the event), with the actors' lines expressed through voice, typing, or even icons. For instance, in *Second Life* people are able to create custom animations to make avatars move in a programmed way (walk, dance, hug, etc.). This capability was used in a performance of Sophocles's *Oedipus Rex* staged by the Avatar Repertory Theater in 2010–2011. The audience's avatars sat on cushions while they watched the play. Then, when the performance reached the play's choral odes, the cushions triggered animations that made the spectators move and gesture, often in unison, so that they became part of the performance itself – a new way to break down the actor/audience division (see Figure 15.5). The Australian performance artist Stelarc, mentioned above, has created performances within *Second Life* as well.

Figure 15.5
Oedipus Rex as performed in *Second Life* by the Avatar Repertory Theater, 2010–2011.
The spectators' avatars move and gesture through animations programmed into the
cushions they sat on, and triggered by a member of the theatre company.
Photo courtesy of Mary Linn Crouse.

Downloadable podplays, the descendants of the radio plays of the mid-twentieth century,
now let listeners access a variety of plays, some meant to be experienced anywhere, some
custom written for specific places and experiences.

Other artists have experimented with simultaneous stage spaces via network technology.
For example, media artist Adriene Jenik's 2007 *Open_Borders: Improvisation Across Networks,
Distance, Time Zones,* used Skype technology to unite 41 artists from 12 countries in 11 time
zones, in a single performance. Jenik's work highlighted not only questions of how liveness
operates through technology, but also questions about how technology serves to collapse and
stretch both time and space.

Finally, no discussion of new digital platforms for theatrical presentation would be complete
without mentioning Twitter, the online social networking service that allows subscribers to post
messages limited to 140 characters per post. These "tweets" are available to anyone to read,
allowing for real-time updates on everything from personal conversations to political revolutions.
When it debuted in 2006, theatre companies were quick to see its potential for generating
interest in productions that could be instantly reviewed by Twitter users and artistic staff. Twitter's
impact on theatre extends beyond building an audience base and into theatrical production,
however, and has led to innovations in both staging and dramaturgy. Audience tweets in response
to a production can be projected on to screens on stage, a strategy perhaps most effective for
theatre in which full absorption into the characters' dramas is less a priority than audience
engagement with the issues at hand. Some companies have used audience tweets as prompts
for improvisation, or to develop the plot of the drama itself in participatory forms of theatre.

There have also been a number of experiments in playwriting, leading to a burgeoning
body of "Twitter plays." Theatre scholar John H. Muse has identified two broad categories

encompassing four types of twitter plays: short-form "nanodramas," plays consisting of a single tweet; and long-form plays tweeted as a series of updates among the characters over the course of several days or weeks. Within the longer form are three subgenres: original works, impersonations of famous people (historical or fictional), and adaptations, all of which are performed in real time but in virtual spaces, and which take advantage of the conventions of Twitter to provide additional insight into characters' motivations and emotions (Muse 2012).

Many nanodramas have been inspired by challenges posed by the New York Neo-Futurists, a collective devoted to staging non-illusionistic theatre that foregrounds an awareness and inclusion of the actual world; their work often appears on material stages but embraces electronic platforms as well. In 2009 they began issuing calls for single-tweet plays that had to contain or be constrained by certain elements – e.g., at least three characters, the use of a certain prop, or particular action such "a big kiss." Within two years, some 800 Twitter playwrights responded, with more than 4,000 plays.

The first long-form Twitter play was created by Jeremy Gable; his *140: A Twitter Performance* followed four fictional characters from Idaho, whose story unfolded over the course of some 300 updates during a two-month period in the summer of 2009. Two years later, the Reorbit Project was launched as an experiment in social media "[c]alling all writers to inhabit a historical or fictional character in real-time over Twitter" (Reorbit 2010). The principal criterion, apart from the 140-character limit, is fidelity to the original character's persona; hence, tweets from a teenaged "Samuel Beckett" such as this: "Writing this way, writing in bits, has an appeal, has a pleasing brevity, the momentary pause discovered between dry heave and stomach cramp" (quoted in Muse 2012: 47). The most popular long-form Twitter plays have been adaptations, a prominent example being *Such Tweet Sorrow*, a 2010 co-production of the Royal Shakespeare Company and the Evanston, Illinois-based Mudlark Theater. Set in modern-day London, this version of Shakespeare's *Romeo and Juliet* had the actors playing the six principal characters post updates about their characters' dilemmas over the course of five weeks.

For Muse, Twitter plays, with their combination of compression and concision, and their appearance (in the longer form) of transpiring over the course of real character time, offer an opportunity to reflect on the nature of theatre itself. Can a play really be expressed in 140 characters? Is Twitter drama a new form of closet drama (meant to be read, rather than staged)? Or does the fact that it is "performed" via text in real-time updates make a significant difference? Is it more similar to serialized radio drama, or does the fact that it is "seen" and not heard significant? Thinking back to the case study above, and to Chapter 13's discussion about how the primacy of the text and author have been questioned since the 1960s – does Twitter theatre, with its actor/improvisers and audience interaction, represent a new phase of this democratizing creative impulse, or perhaps its ultimate fulfillment, at least among those with access to social media? And what does the evolving nature of the # hashtag – originally a search mechanism, now increasingly used to make meta-commentary on the tweet itself – suggest about the way the tweeter performs him- or herself? "To examine the ways artists are enlisting Twitter for theatrical ends reveals not only that playwrights are colonizing Twitter," Muse writes, "but also the extent to which social media are making playwrights, performers, and spectators of us all" (2012: 43), a point well illustrated by online role-playing games as well.

Socio-spatial performance experiments in the material world

For many artists and activists, social media and online archiving has turned the world literally into a stage for their artistic and political agendas. Their work ranges from runs of full productions taking place in a designated extra-theatrical space, to "pop-up" performances that come and go very quickly. At both ends of the spectrum, the performance and the space in which it happens are in conversation with each other, and are enhanced, if not enabled, by social media.

In the days before the construction of purpose-built theatre spaces, theatre was performed in and arguably conditioned by the particulars of the spaces in which it had to appear, be they tennis courts or city streets. The York Cycle's pageant wagons, for example, provided a near backdrop for the plays, and the city's buildings a further one; the staging of the cycle plays turned the entire city into something of a holy site once a year. Today, theatre artists sometimes specifically choose sites outside of existing theatre structures, for particular purposes and to make particular points. An example from 2007 is *Girls Just Wanna Have Fund$*, commissioned by the arts arm of the World Financial Center in New York City. This was a series of six 10-minute plays, developed by writers and directors associated with the Women's Project Theater Lab, which were presented 13 times over the course of four days in various public areas of the World Financial Center. The plays explored different aspects of women's relationship (or lack of relationship) to wealth. No one could buy a ticket for the performances, but audiences grew over the course of the three weekdays and one Saturday as word spread through social media.

Free theatre offered in public spaces is not new; since the middle of the last century, such performances have usually been subsidized by theatre companies in partnership with arts granting organizations and municipalities. (A prominent example is the Public Theatre's Shakespeare in the Park, in New York City.) But networked culture is further democratizing the experience, changing our expectation of who might appear on these new platforms, and who might be invited to the "show." The flashmobs of the past decade or so are one illustration. Here, organizers count on social media as well as the power of a seemingly spontaneous performance to gather audiences in the moment – and to ensure the performance has a virtual life afterwards on platforms such as YouTube. One of the earliest and most frequently imitated such performances is based on Michael Jackson's 1982 song *Thriller*, which has not only motivated dozens of Halloween performances every year, but has also been used to make political statements. In 2011 hundreds of Chilean students, angered by the fees charged by their increasingly privatized school system, choreographed a performance of *Thriller* outside the presidential mansion to protest their plight. The videos taken on personal cellphones soon went viral, subverting the "official coverage" and censorship of the Chilean news corporations.

GPS technology has inspired new forms of theatricality in unexpected places. For example, in 2008, Pittsburgh artists Robin Hewlett and Ben Kinsley created "Street with a View," a simulated street scene including both actors and local residents, who staged scenes specifically for the moment when the Google Street View vehicle was passing through their Northside neighborhood in May of that year. Their scenes included a parade, a garage band practice, a cat being rescued by firemen, and even a swordfight in seventeenth-century costume. Thus, for a time, when Google Map users later sought street views of those locations, they were treated to specially staged dramatic tableaux.

New performance structures and processes

As these experiments and innovations suggest, social media and the logic of networked culture within globalization have inspired new forms of staging and more democratized relations of theatrical production. In this section we will expand the focus to examine how this logic, if not the technology itself, has worked its way into dramatic structure. We will also consider how these influences have affected how plays come to be, with a closer look at recent developments in postdramatic and devised theatre.

Cultural critics often point to data mining and aggregation as key characteristics of networked culture, features that distinguish its conventions of information organization from those of prior periods. Whereas in the past, information archiving depended upon some kind of ordering principle – even if only as simple as "keep" vs. "toss" – nowadays everything that can be turned into data is – and is storable as such. The organization of all of this information depends not on *a priori* selections, but on the search preferences of the end user. The vast amounts of information now instantly available to searchers have contributed to the prevailing aesthetic of the remix we identified in the introduction to this chapter.

In 2011, the New York City-based theatre ensemble Elevator Repair Service incorporated both the technology and the logic of data mining and remixing into their work *Shuffle*, produced in collaboration with installation artist Ben Rubin and UCLA statistician Mark Hansen. The company had been working with adaptations and inventively staged readings of the novels *The Great Gatsby* (F. Scott Fitzgerald, 1925), *The Sound and the Fury* (William Faulkner, 1929), and *The Sun Also Rises* (Ernest Hemingway, 1926). Taking these sources as both inspiration and data, in 2011 they did a mashup of all three in the New York Public Library. Scripts were generated by digital algorithms drawn from the novels' "data"; the performers from the past productions now improvised upon the new remixed scripts in this one. Audience members were free to wander among the performers, as though they themselves were browsers, while they improvised. The point was not to preserve original plot lines and intentions but to call attention to the ways data mining and creative data analysis can produce startling juxtapositions and new, far-from-intended, meanings.

Social media has also highlighted the pliable nature of time and space in globalization, with its tendency to increase speed and shrink distance. What is the human experience of time in such circumstances? One notable theatrical response to this question was Robert Lepage and Ex Machina's 2001 *Zulu Time*, a "techno-cabaret" collaboration with musician Peter Gabriel (see Figure 15.6). The title refers to what the military and civil aviation call Greenwich Mean Time (GMT), the central – if somewhat arbitrary – point of reference for setting time across the world. The piece was divided up into 26 sections, one for each letter of the alphabet used in aviation radio transmissions (from A for Alpha to Z for Zulu). Each section featured a setting where time seems suspended – in waiting areas, airport restaurants and bars, hotel rooms, terminal walkways, and so forth, most having to do with travel and the in-between state that travel produces (neither here/home nor there/away). The stage set design was multi-level and dynamic and included film and video projections; the acrobatic actors moved between levels and interacted with flying insect- and animal-like robots. Each vignette was distinct and not overtly connected to the others in terms of character, plot, or even dramatic tone. Theatre scholar Patrice Pavis describes the production this way:

Figure 15.6
A scene from Robert Lepage's *Zulu Time* (2001).
Source: Photo: Emmanuel Valette

Characters talk in different languages; a lounge singer croons and tells jokes in Spanish and German, which no one understands; a woman listens to her erotic messages in a hotel room; we watch a screen display of a pregnant woman's unborn baby as she undergoes a hospital scan. Though characters do meet (and even dance and make love) the vignettes are generally far more about isolation and disconnection. The flight attendants, terrorists, drug-traffickers, and other dazed, time-lagged travelers are misplaced, lonely, and predominantly alone.... [I]n the sleepy somnambulance of transatlantic flight, each abandons his or her body to become "a machine that defies time, catches up with it, or at least neutralizes it, a short moment of eternity"

(quoted in Dixon 2007: 521).

In *Zulu Time*, air travel becomes a symbol of globalization's ability to collapse time and space together, producing at once the opportunity for high-level connectedness and extreme isolation. One of the scenes was eerily prescient of an event that would itself indelibly mark a certain day as a watershed moment in recent world history: in the "K for Kilo" section, a "bearded, turban-wearing Arab finishes his prayers, wires up a bomb in his briefcase, and puts on a pilot's uniform. The stage area suddenly transforms to the inside of an aircraft, complete with flight attendants" (Dixon 2007: 519). This scene caused the cancellation of the show's North American premiere in New York City, scheduled for 10 days after September 11, 2001.

That date has indeed become a pivotal point in world history. There is now a new world, marked "post-9/11," and theatre has registered its effects.

THEATRE IN RESPONSE TO 9/11

The post-9/11 world has produced new challenges for performance, as theatre artists have grappled with the question of representing the enormity of such an event. Some, like Michael Simon Hall's multimedia performance *Pieces of Paper* (2010) have focused on the stories of rescue volunteers who worked in the rubble in the immediate aftermath of the collapse of the World Trade Center towers. The title refers to the many pieces of paper that have since become historical records of the events – handwritten signs seeking missing persons, notes volunteers posted for each other, inventory lists, and so forth.

Other plays, such as Sarah Tuft's *110 Stories* (2003), explore the experiences of others directly affected – first responders, nurses, journalists, homeless eyewitnesses. The title refers to the number of floors in the World Trade Center Towers 1 and 2, and has been used in other contexts – including an augmented reality app that allows the Twin Towers to be drawn into a smartphone photograph taken when the phone is oriented toward the Trade Center; photographers can then post their pictures and 50-word captions to a website that serves as a "global repository of memories."

The memories of those ostracized by narrow interpretations of the roots of 9/11– notably, Muslims and people mistaken for Muslims – have been the subject of other works. For example, Rohina Malik explored the female experience of this perspective in her one-woman show, *Unveiled* (2009), in which she played five Muslim women living in the West, post-9/11. And still other works, such as Sean Farrell's 2002 *Life Separates Us*, take up what happens to everyday people who try to live normal lives in a new high-security world.

This world has produced new audiences for theatre as well, including the kinds who are hidden behind surveillance cameras. There are artists who create performances especially *for* the security cameras now proliferating in street corners and city buildings, with the intention of motivating spectators and passers-by to contemplate and question the increasing role surveillance plays in their lives. One of the principal groups associated with this activity actually pre-dates 9/11: in 1996, the Surveillance Camera Players of New York City staged Alfred Jarry's *Ubu Roi* at the subway station at 14th Street and Union Square. Most of their work since then has been the performance of various plays, in silence, for surveillance cameras in places such as Rockefeller Center, Washington Square Park, and Times Square.

Immersive theatre

In the second decade of this century, immersive theatre has been a prevalent trend. In this theatre, audiences play some kind of a role in the action of the play in performance, whether as witness or as character. Often, as in the case of *Shuffle*, they are allowed to roam freely around the performance space, choosing the order of their experience much as surfers on the internet move from point to point on the web. At times they may be invited by the performers to take a more active role in the action.

Immersive theatre seems to be inspired by a number of factors in networked culture: the associative logic of browsing, the increasingly immersive environment of "choose your adventure" online and video games, and possibly a sense of wanting to get out and interact with live human beings, albeit in the kind of impersonal way conditioned by social media, which can produce a sense of isolation despite its being all about connectivity. At the time of writing, two of the better-known examples of immersive theatre are Punchdrunk's production of *Sleep No More* (2003), based on Shakespeare's *Macbeth*, and Third Rail Projects' *Then She Fell* (2012), inspired by Lewis Carroll's life and writings, including his *Alice in Wonderland*.

Originally developed in London in 2003, *Sleep No More* has been restaged in Boston and New York. In Boston the playing space was an old school building; in New York, three abandoned warehouses were converted for the purpose into the fictional "McKittrick Hotel," featuring nearly a hundred different playing spaces distributed among five floors. The rooms in this hotel (named after the hotel in Alfred Hitchcock's 1958 film, *Vertigo*), are not typical hotel rooms; rather, they range from indoor spaces such as shops, padded cells, and doctor's offices to outdoor spaces such as a cemetery. After entering the first-floor lounge, audience members are given masks to wear, then move on to other floors and rooms, where they witness the actions that take place within them – all silent, all inspired in some way by the Shakespearean original, but in style not historically accurate, as the unmasked performers wear makeup and costume evocative of the style of *film noir*. Audience members are free to follow the actor/action of their choice, or to move around from place to place, in groups or alone, or to explore the other areas of the "hotel," for up to three hours, and are also free to leave whenever they wish. (Figure 15.7).

Figure 15.7
Masked audience members surround a silent actor performing alone in a room/scene of *Sleep No More*, New York production.
Source: Sleep No More/Yaniv Schulman.

A number of factors make the experience of *Sleep No More* something like a live version of a video or online role-playing game. The masks worn by the audience members protect their anonymity, also enjoyed by players in such games. As in immersive online environments like *Second Life* or *World of Warcraft*, they are free to explore the space as they wish, and to follow their curiosity where it may lead them – or not. Because there is no spoken language or prescribed order to the scenes a given audience member might experience, it is up to individual audience members to create for themselves any narrative throughline. Far from having any kind of "unified action," *Sleep No More* gathers audience members at the beginning of the night in the lounge and then sends them off to different floors, and doesn't bring them back together until the very end of the performance when everyone watches the banquet scene. And yet, the choices are not infinite and completely open-ended, and neither are audience members meant to do more than witness the action; they do not influence it or direct it in any way.

Although there are some similarities to *Sleep No More*, Third Rail's *Then She Fell* is a very different type of immersive theatre. Like *Sleep No More*, it is based on other work – in this case, the life and work of Lewis Carroll, familiarity with which helps to situate the spectator in its otherwise dreamlike landscape. Audience members are encouraged to rummage through the cabinets, trunks, and drawers containing Carroll's writings and other items. It too is staged in a found space, this time the Greenpoint Hospital in Brooklyn, New York, with rooms set up as individual performance spaces that audience members move into and out of. But *Then She Fell* allows only 15 (unmasked) audience members at a time to participate, breaking them up into increasingly smaller groups as they travel through the spaces, their routes controlled by company members. They may end up alone with one actor by the end of the evening. As a result, *Then She Fell* makes for a more intimate experience than *Sleep No More*.

As social networking technology can lead to both expansive socializing and increased isolation, so can immersive live theatre work in both directions. The actors may interact more with the audience members, but only as their characters or personae. *Sleep No More* audience members stay safely behind their masks, while individual *Then She Fell* audience members grow increasingly separated from the other 14 members. In this sense, is immersive theatre radically different from theatre that has come before? To some degree, theatre has also always produced this tension, functioning both as a social space that can generate dialogue, and as an event experienced differently from audience member to audience member, each of whom arrives with individual sets of desires and expectations, and leaves with independent personal reflections.

Postdramatic theatre

The work of Punchdrunk and Third Rail Projects, which is developed collectively and compels audiences to be more active than traditional spectators, calls attention to another hallmark of networked culture: interaction and collaboration. Such work often relies more on the pleasures of the immersion and discovery within the performance event, than on absorptions into ordered plots and character dramas. Theatre that emphasizes experience over narrative, plot, or character has been coined "postdramatic theatre" by German performance scholar Hans-Thies Lehmann (1999). Lehmann includes a variety of performance forms in his study, ranging from visual and performance art to stage plays and from single-authored works to collective creations. What characterizes this work is another kind of immersiveness, in which the dramatic text – if there

Figure 15.8
British playwright Sarah Kane's *4:48 Psychosis*, an exploration of depression, features no character attribution or stage directions, and is one example of a postdramatic theatre. Shown here in the U.S. premiere are, from left, Jo McInnes, Marin Ireland, and Jason Hughes.
Source: © Sara Krulwich/New York Times/Redux/eyevine.

is one – is subsumed to the other meaning-making elements of the production, including the acting, design, direction, and audience (see Figure 15.8).

Experiments with form and against narrative in drama were certainly taking place in the various avant-garde periods of theatre history described earlier in this book. Lehmann argues that recent postdramatic theatre marks a paradigm shift away from the centrality of dramatic action, and toward a more interactive experience both among the elements of production and between the production and audience. For Lehmann, the point of such theatre is expressly not to communicate something; rather, it is about proximity of and to the various elements involved in the theatre experience – in other words, a privileging of presence and aggregation over ultimate communicative effect. While multiple factors in theatre history have contributed to the emergence of postdramatic theatre, some aspects may seem familiar to students of networked culture, with its decentered, non-hierarchical approach to meaning-making, and the freedom it allows users to make their own connections and conclusions.

Collaborative theatre devisement

Throughout much of theatre history, hierarchies have tended to prevail, with companies and productions centering themselves on a playwright, a playtext, a star performer, or more recently, a director held to be the key person responsible for the overall experience. But since the 1960s there has been a trend toward collaborative theatrical devising by an ensemble or theatre collective. (Some historians trace the devising impulse back to *commedia dell'arte* – see Chapter 4.) An early commercial example was the dark musical comedy *Oh, What a Lovely War!* (1963), developed by the Theatre Workshop under Joan Littlewood's direction. Drawing on the tradition of the English music hall, the piece was meant to expose in an ironic mode the horrors and vulgarity of war. It was performed by actors in Pierrot costumes, wearing First World War helmets and singing tunes originally meant to glorify the war. Much of the work in theatre for social change discussed in Chapter 14 has considered the democratic process of devisement to be as important as the end results, when that process adopts a consciously egalitarian approach. Networked culture has accelerated this trend.

Increasingly, work is being brought to the stage that has not been authored by a single playwright but rather devised by a group of actors, sometimes with, sometimes without a director. While collective creation does not necessarily result in non-linear plot structures, much devised theatre of recent years does tend to resemble scenic variations on a theme – which are often developed through ensemble improvisation – than a straightforward development of plot, navigated by recognizable characters portrayed by actors trained in psychological realism or Method Acting.

Devised theatre today often starts with an idea or an inspiration, which the group explores together to bring to the stage. For example, in 2012 Washington DC's Impossible Theater Company began a project simply with the idea of "missed connections." The company

Figure 15.9
Roommates Penny (Heather Carter) and Dawn (Ava Jackson) prepare for the end of the world in Impossible Theater's *[missed connections]*, conceived and directed by Nick Jonczak and devised by members of the company.
Source: Impossible Theater/Paul B. Jones.

members' widely varying ideas were discussed, debated, and improvised upon over the course of six months before being condensed into an 80-minute piece called *[missed connections]* (Figure 15.9), which revolved around the question: "If you had one chance to be the person you always wanted to be, what would you do?" (Desaulniers 2012).

The company's six-month rehearsal schedule would be a luxury for most commercially oriented theatre. Devised theatre does not fit easily into existing producing structures, and for Equity houses especially such theatre would be extremely expensive. Still, Vanessa Garcia of the Florida-based ensemble touring troupe The Krane considers how "going mainstream" for devising companies might benefit theatre in general:

> Technology, which so often aids and abets devised theater, is trying to obliterate surface, after all. Our computers are getting thinner and thinner, inching towards a kind of space where there will be no surface, only a digital projection in air. And so, how do we make art in a world that seems obsessed with surface – a surface that is, technologically, and, ironically, about to disappear? The answer for theater, I believe, lies in devised theater – an art form that plays upon multiple surfaces in flux (the human body for one), and multimedia – all in order to reinstate a kind of underground. In a world in which surface is fetishized, devised theater tells the viewer, now you see surface, now you don't, playing with the appearance and disappearance of said surface and echoing back, always, towards something deeper.
>
> (Garcia 2013)

Our final case study considers a particular form of theatre in which the interplay between surface and depth – not to mention modern and ancient, technological and human, aesthetic and political, and local and global – all feature prominently: Hip Hop theatre.

CASE STUDY: Hip Hop theatre

Tamara Underiner

In 2004, Regina Taylor's *Drowning Crow* premiered on Broadway, three years after its world premiere at the Goodman Theatre in Chicago. An adaptation of Chekhov's *The Seagull*, it was set in the present-day Gullah Islands of South Carolina, with an African-American cast. Like the original, it featured a main character suffering from unrequited love, and struggling with his desire to forge a new form of theatre, one that would depart from the tired, "sold-out" traditions of the stage to capture the sensibility of a new age. In Chekhov's play, the new form was Russian symbolism. In Taylor's, it was Hip Hop theatre.

For many in the theatre world, Hip Hop theatre indeed represents a contemporary and necessary break from a mainstream theatre culture perceived as elitist and entrenched in outmoded themes and means of production. For others, it is mainstream theatre's best hope for the future. Practitioners understand that Hip Hop theatre emerges from within a larger international culture of the same name, one with its own worldview, ethics, and aesthetics, and that this culture has ancient roots. Born of political struggle and creative urgency, this culture represents not only a rupture with mainstream culture – which often works to commercialize and absorb it – but also a continuity with African-derived performance traditions that are themselves thousands of years old.

In this case study, we examine Hip Hop theatre both as an emergent performance form and as a historiographic practice in itself – that is, as a way of telling history. We cover its own history, aesthetics, worldview, and relationship to culture – both ancient and contemporary – paying particular attention to its innovative use of communication technologies. For every form of communication is present in Hip Hop theatre: from oral and written expression through highly mediated production and distribution technologies, with stylized vocabularies of movement and gesture added to the mix.

Hip Hop history, worldview, and aesthetics

Most narratives of Hip Hop culture situate its origins in the economic collapse of New York City in the early 1970s, particularly in the Bronx, but similar expressions arose in other urban centers as well at the same time. As white flight to the suburbs left behind unsaleable properties in the urban cores, absentee landlords found it more profitable to burn their holdings to the ground and collect the insurance money than to convert them to affordable housing; meanwhile, municipalities created policies of "planned shrinkage" that resulted in dispossession, unemployment, reduced social services, and increased poverty. Many responses to this situation were violent, as rival gangs fought over shrinking territory. The first artistic responses were made by visual artists, using inexpensive materials like aerosol paint, sprayed on available surfaces like building walls and subway train cars – these were the precursors to the aerosol art form known as Hip Hop *writing*. Of course these artistic expressions were not seen as such by building owners and transit authorities, but that was part of the artists' point: to assert a creative presence in the face of forced displacement, marginalization, and accelerated urban "decay."

With ever-decreasing opportunities to gather together, some young people with good record collections and the right equipment – among them Cindy Campbell and her brother Kool Herc, Grandmaster Flash, Grand Wizard Theodore, and Afrika Bambaataa – began playing recorded music in public parks and basketball courts (*DJ'ing*). Before long they had developed a particular technique of playing records on more than one turntable, enhancing and combining them with digital synthesizers (*sampling* and *remixing*), and incorporating spoken word, rhythmically delivered (*rapping*, *MC'ing*). The gathered young people soon developed new dance styles in response to the sampled and repeated *breakbeat* manipulated by the DJs' techniques, including *breakdancing*, *locking* (and eventually on the West Coast, *popping*). Soon, *B-boys* and *B-girls* began to engage in competitions of dance moves or improvisational spoken wordplay – *battling*, where two contestants face each other from within a circle formed by their communities of supporters (the Hip Hop *cipher*). These forms came before the advent of Hip Hop culture and then were integrated and innovated within it (see Figure 15.10).

The content of these performances is both explicit and coded. Many spoken word performances and rap songs call specific attention to the histories of oppression, police brutality, and economic exploitation that have produced the pervasive disenfranchisement of economically and culturally marginalized young people in some urban areas. They do so through recourse to a new vocabulary that has worked its way into mainstream culture, a vocabulary of word, movement, fashion, and gesture that calls members into a growing, global community. This community is networked through Hip Hop academies, workshops, and theatre festivals now appearing in many world capitals. Cultural historian Jeff Chang calls Hip Hop

Figure 15.10

B-boys breakdancing in San Francisco, 2008. As Hip Hop has become more popular, the cipher has expanded to include tourists and passers-by.

"one of the big ideas of this generation, a grand expression of our collective creative powers" (2006: x). As such, this "big idea" encompasses a worldview that extends beyond the form's aesthetic elements, even as those elements have come to influence virtually every genre and form of artistic expression.

Hip Hop has generally followed two different (but sometimes overlapping) trajectories over the past three decades. One path encompasses the commercialization of "urban black culture" in music and fashion that is sold, in large measure, to white consumers; rap music's excesses of strong language, provocative sexuality, and (hetero)sexist perspectives have been widely decried by both sides of the conservative/liberal spectrum. The other path is a more grassroots movement that connects practitioners globally from the ground up, and understands itself as both a culture and an art form that proclaims unity, peaceful resolution of conflict, democratic participation, and targeted social analysis and critique, and can serve as an "effective organizing tool for reaching youth and disenfranchised populations" (Uno 2006: 300).

Hip Hop theatre: Roots, functions, structures, and themes

To understand Hip Hop theatre's emergence and importance, it is important to keep the distinction between the two trajectories in mind, focusing less on the commercial lifestyle and more on the deep traditions upon which the more grassroots movement draws. According to Danny Hoch, founder of the New York Hip-Hop Theater Festival, the aesthetics that inform

Hip Hop theatre have as much to do with New York's demographics as they do with the socio-economic circumstances that produced so much urban blight and bleakness:

> Southern blacks living alongside Puerto Ricans, Dominicans, Jamaicans and a handful of working-poor whites, all of whom drew upon both inherited and appropriated cultures in the face of urban decay and accelerated technology – created a legacy of art forms and language that would wind up being inherited by various races, colors and classes around the world.
>
> (Hoch 2004)

Like the indigenous and diasporic African and American cultures from which it draws, Hip Hop theatre has shown itself to be a capacious form that can absorb many influences and in turn influence many other forms. The "inherited cultures" include those of the African and Caribbean continuum of storytelling and art, manifest in the "polycultural traditions of immigrants and migrants" (Hoch 2004). The "appropriated cultures" include European traditions, amplified through Japanese audio-visual technologies.

In its insistence on the power of the live, spoken word, artists and scholars see parallels between the MC and the storytelling traditions of Africa – specifically, the griot or griotte storyteller of West Africa (described in Chapter 1), and the *djeli* of Mande, the person who carries culture in stories, song, dances, riddles, and proverbs, oral traditions from which Hip Hop derives its status as a "method of sustenance and sustainability" (Banks 2011: 12). While in its rhythmic wordplay there are parallels with a variety of other performance traditions and types, including Djelyi, *kabuki* theatre, R&B, opera recitative, and the patter songs of Gilbert and Sullivan, in most cases the content of Hip Hop theatre is of urgent social, community, or spiritual concern. Poet/playwright/head Marc Bamuthi Joseph has spoken of the DJ's function as a community historiographer, telling the stories from the perspective of the people s/he represents, particularly young people.

> Like Hip Hop, spoken word reflects American diversity and engenders a community of young artists who reach across demographic boundaries toward self-exploration and growth, providing a platform where conflicts are resolved on the page or the stage, rather than on the street.
>
> (Joseph 2006: 17).

Among others, scholar/Hip Hop theatre artist Daniel Banks has argued that Hip Hop theatre exits on a historico-cultural continuum that includes epic poetry and the classic tragedy of ancient Greece: "Within a Hip Hop Theatre audience, there is a spectrum of trauma, oppression, and marginalization, and Hip Hop Theatre, perhaps like Athenian tragedy, is a safe space in which to express concerns, rehearse empowerment, and imagine solutions" (Banks 2010: 242). As Banks points out, there are some distinct theatrical predecessors as well – among them, the non-linear poetic and political drama of the Black Arts Movement of the 1960s and 1970s, and later work that incorporated text, music, and movement, often in a non-linear plotline, specifically to tell the stories of the disenfranchised. Some appeared on Broadway; many more in communities far from its "Great White Way" – such as through the work of Junebug Productions in New Orleans and Cultural Odyssey in San Francisco.

From these diverse yet intertwined roots, Hip Hop theatre emerged in the early 1990s. Multidisciplinary performance and visual artist Holly Bass was the first to use the term "hip-hop theatre" in print, in 1999, in reference to its status as a special category of performance in the National Black Theatre Festival that year in Winston-Salem, North Carolina. Jeff Chang situates its debut on stage seven years earlier with GhettOriginal Production Dance Company's 1992 production of *So What Happens Now?* at PS 122 in New York City, about the rise and fall of 1980s-style B-boying. This production inspired Hoch, Clyde Valentin, Kamilah Forbes, and others to establish the first Hip-Hop Theater Festival in New York City in 2000.

Playwright/poet Eisa Davis, who is credited with popularizing the term among practitioners, speaks to this theatre's capacity for both specificity and inclusion:

> I like the name "hip-hop theatre," because when it's ascriptive, voluntary and utilized by a self-described hip-hop generation that speaks through theatre, we are *found* in translation. Finally, a form that describes and comprises our multi-ness. When U.K.-based artist Benji Reid dances his monologues, it's new, and it's the best kind of new – the kind that plays with conventions and serves up their permutations. And we've got all kinds of historical precedents. Art forms progress when they mimic other art forms, whether it's Langston Hughes writing the blues on the page or Aaron Copland building symphonies from folk tunes or Lee Strasberg bringing the therapist's couch into acting. The purists shriek, the open-minded are jazzed, and the culture follows.
>
> (Davis 2004)

Further, Hip Hop theatre allies political urgency to ritual function, which as we've seen, has long been associated with theatre in many times and places:

> Like any culture's ritual theater, Hip Hop Theater is where members from within the culture come for reassurance, to find the values of the culture reiterated, to hear the history retold, and to locate ourselves inside of our own cultural frame. It is not just about information. Equally important is the cultural mind-set and logic. In terms of form, a Hip Hop head will, most likely, feel at home in a poetic, nonlinear, fragmented narrative with multiple ethnicities represented on the stage and multiple languages spoken. And the storytelling would almost certainly need to be interdisciplinary.
>
> (Banks 2011: 11)

The theatrical expression of this mindset and logic has manifested itself in a wide variety of original works and classical adaptations. Banks's comments appear in the introduction to his edited anthology of Hip Hop plays, *Say Word! Voices from Hip Hop Theater* (2011), which organizes its nine plays according to the formal categories "Spoken Word Theater," which focuses on heightened, poetic language; "Hip Hop Theater Plays," which both reference and include specific elements of Hip Hop culture; and "Solo Performance," which Banks argues manifest the links to a long tradition of oral culture and storytelling. A haunting example of the first category is Rickerby Hinds's *Dreamscape*, based on a true story of a 19-year-old African-American woman who was shot to death by a policeman while she was sleeping in her car. As the DJ/coroner attempts to categorize each of the 12 bullet wounds that led to her death, the young woman dances scenes of her childhood and more recent past. By the end of the play, her line, "You know me," challenges the audience to move past viewing her as yet another unfortunate statistic. "Hip Hop Theater Plays" feature characters in plotlines aimed at recovering Hip Hop history, dealing with contemporary issues of self-expression in what is often viewed as an illicit art form, or, as in the case of Zakkiyah Alexander's *Blurring Shine*, provide a blistering critique of the larger cultural industries that exploit young men in Hip Hop culture. The section on solo performances includes the link to a storyboard and script of a beatbox theatre piece, *From Tel Aviv to Ramallah*, by Rachel Havrelock with Yuri Lane and Sharif Ezzat, which tells the story of two young men living on either side of the border between Israel and Palestine. This piece illustrates the scope of Hip Hop's reach and speaks to its "ethic of inclusion" (Banks 2011: 1).

This scope and ethic is also manifest in dramaturg Kim Euell and playwright Robert Alexander's 2009 anthology, *Playz from the Boom Box Galaxy*, whose ten works are organized according to their content rather than their form. The plays collected under the theme "ruminations on identity" focus on the playwrights' search for individual self-formation within and against institutional archetypes and stereotypes of race, class, and gender. Whereas these plays tend to focus on personal and internal struggles, those in the next section, "cautionary tales," target the institutions themselves and the ways that capitalism intersects with racism and

Figure 15.11
Aya de León's *Thieves in the Temple: The Reclaiming of Hip-Hop* (2003) is a one-woman show that critiques sexism in Hip Hop. Among other characters, she plays a DJ with a form of Tourette's syndrome that forces him to reveal his sensitive side, and a blonde sex object on the verge of a nervous breakdown.

sexism to produce many forms of social violence. The plays in the final section, "trans-formationals," deepen the relationships and tensions between self and society, marshaling spirituality and creativity as key conditions for cultural survival.

Many writers refer to Hip Hop theatre as a "genre," which suggests a similarity of form, style, structure, or subject matter across its productions. What makes Hip Hop theatre recognizably "Hip Hop," however, is not so easy to pin down. To be sure, most plays explore some aspect of contemporary Hip Hop culture in their subject matter, even as they may draw on sources deep in African history, and most feature language drawn from well inside Hip Hop culture. Most also include one or more of Hip Hop's four principal elements (DJ'ing, MC'ing, breaking, and writing graffiti), but that is not required. For example, Ben Snyder's 2001 *In Case You Forget* is about a young graffiti writer's awakening to both love and political commitment; but its form is straightforward realism, no music or dancing is called for, and its action unfolds over two tightly structured acts covering the days before the main character will be sentenced to serve time. In general, however, Hip Hop theatre favors other styles over straight realism. Many plays follow a more epic, Brechtian structure, in which the action is episodic and inter-spersed with song and dance numbers or parodic interludes, and the fourth wall is broken (if it is even there to begin with) by DJs and MCs and choruses, which function much as they did in ancient Greece.

While many Hip Hop plays deal with tragic events and their aftermath, others have employed rollicking comedy. Kristoffer Diaz's 2002 *Welcome to Arroyo's*, for example, uses the DJ/rapper duo of Trip Goldstein and Nelson Cardenal (aka the "Tripnel Cartel") to narrate, interrupt, comment on, and sometimes even rewind and replay the action developing over the play's 39 short scenes. These scenes combine two love stories with a mystery about a Latina DJ, and point to Latina contributions to early Hip Hop culture.

Whereas some Hip Hop plays experiment with dramatic structure (e.g., *Dreamscape*), others are distinguished for their experiments with character and language. Chadwick Boseman's 2005 *Deep Azure* includes the allegorical character of "Street Knowledge," described as a "Duo angelic chorus" comprising Twin Lovers: Street Knowledge of Good (SK Good) and "Street Knowledge of Evil" (SK Evil), who transform into other characters in a play exploring the aftermath of a wrongful death by police – a common Hip Hop thematic (Banks 2011: 93). *Deep Azure* is written almost completely in verse that sounds both like spoken word and like Shakespeare. In the following passage, SK Evil ponders the truth behind the killing ("prince" refers to the victim, Bloods and Crip to rival gangs who wear red and blue, respectively):

SK EVIL: To what set and name falls the blame of this heinous deed?
          Witnesses saw no Bloods, 'cept blood the prince did bleed
          And though that boy was of blue, he showed no signs of Crip
          But hear this lie, more true than truth from my very lips.
          T'was an officer of "peace" that waged war on our warrior of light
          How this brutality came to a fatality one night, that is the question.
          What had he done? Possession?
          No gun. No boat. No bud. No crack. No transgression.

The poetic rhythms here invoke two cultures – Hip Hop and Elizabethan – and, for Banks, serve to decenter Shakespeare's place in the history of dramatic storytelling, placing him on a continuum between oral culture and Hip Hop. Perhaps this shift is also registered in the fact that Hip Hop theatre and spoken-word open mikes have begun to appear in a number of Shakespeare festivals around the world. While clearly there is an audience-development component to this phenomenon, it is also worth pointing out the growing scholarship on the similarities between spoken word and Shakespeare, which notes affinities of lyrical and rhythmic complexity, and in the demands on the listener made by both. A 2014 study by designer/coder/data analyst Matt Daniels determined that some rap music artists' vocabularies and new word coinages are, in fact, larger than Shakespeare's over a similar body of work.

Hip Hop theatre is also known for its "remixes" of the classics, as suggested in the example of *Drowning Crow* above, with Greek tragedy and Shakespeare as frequent sources. While Hip Hop has the potential to create vibrant new interpretations of classic texts, Hoch and others are concerned that such remixings will be taken simply as bids for legitimacy, casting Hip Hop elements as adornment rather than serious artistry, or sacrificing opportunities to stage stories emerging from Hip Hop culture itself. (All of these are possible interpretations of *Drowning Crow*, an adaptation of one of Chekhov's most open-to-interpretation plays.)

Thus, content and intent matter as much as form and structure. For Hoch, what makes a Hip Hop play a Hip Hop play is not that it includes all or even any of Hip Hop's four principal elements of DJ'ing, MC'ing, breaking, or writing graffiti. It is instead that it must be "*by, about and for* the Hip Hop generation, participants in Hip Hop culture or both" (Hoch 2004, original emphasis). Finally, Hip Hop playwright Will Power argues for a "fifth element" of Hip Hop culture as important as the first four: collective knowledge production. Seen this way, Hip Hop theatre serves for today's performers and audiences much the same function discussed in Part I: as a key preserver of social memory for a culture not content to allow larger narratives to constrain or co-opt it.

Theatre historians and critics play a role in documenting and preserving this form of social memory as well, but have some catching up to do. As Roberta Uno, founder of the New World Theater in Amherst, reminds us,

> Hip-hop artists state that critics lack a genre exposure. . . . They may like what they see without knowing breaking from B'boying; popping from locking; or toprocking from uprocking – the point is that even when hip-hop forms are noticed, they are not understood or critiqued from within the discipline vocabulary. This type of technical knowledge is as important as historical, cultural and self-knowledge. At the end of the day, it is this fifth element, glaringly absent from the marketplace, that may provide the space where art can flourish.
>
> (Uno 2006: 305)

The immensely popular Broadway production of *Hamilton* (2015) illustrates Uno's point. Lin-Manuel Miranda's (1980–) musical prominently features elements of Hip Hop music and dance in an otherwise period piece, set in the quarter century following the American revolution of 1776. Widely acclaimed by audiences and critics, it has been praised for its deft homage to, and reimagining of, America's past, through the lens of a multi-racial present. But not every reviewer acknowledges Hip Hop's contributions, because they have not been trained to recognize or critique it in the same way they would other elements of theatrical production. *Hamilton's* popularity may be the incentive for critics to "get real."

Daniel Banks calls Hip Hop theatre the "theater of now" (2011: 20). It will be interesting to see if future historians, with their penchant for assigning labels that characterize an era, will look back at this period of theatre history and call it something like the "age of Hip Hop." Or, considering the success of *Hamilton* as evidence of Hip Hop's capacity to absorb and influence other forms, perhaps it will always be known as the "theatre of now."

Key references

Banks, D. (2010) "From Homer to Hip Hop: Orature and Griots, Ancient and Present," *Classical World* 103(2) (Winter): 238–45.

Banks, D. (ed.) (2011) *Say Word! Voices from Hip Hop Theater*, Ann Arbor: University of Michigan Press.

Bass, H. (1999) "Blowin' Up the Set," *American Theater* 16(9) (November): 18–20.

Chang, J. (ed.) (2006) *Total Chaos: The Art and Aesthetics of Hip-Hop*, New York: Basic Civitas Books.

Davis, E. (2004) "Found in Translation: Hip-Hop Theatre Fuses the Thought and the Word, the Rhythm and the Rhyme, the Old and the New," https://www.tcg.org/publications/at/JulyAugust04/translation.cfm (Accessed May 31, 2014).

Euell, K. and R. Alexander (2009) *Playz from the Boom Box Galaxy*, New York: Theatre Communications Group Books.

George, N. (1993) "Hip-Hop's Founding Fathers Speak the Truth," *The Source* (November): 44–50.

George, N. (2005) *Hip Hop America*, New York: Penguin Books.

Hoch, D. (2004) "Here We Go, Yo . . . A Manifesto for a New Hip-Hop Arts Movement," http://www.tcg.org/publications/at/dec04/go.cfm (Accessed May 31, 2014).

Joseph, M.B. (2006) "(Yet Another) Letter to a Young Poet," in J. Chang (ed.) *Total Chaos: The Art and Aesthetics of Hip-Hop*, New York: Basic Civitas Books, 11–17.

Uno, R. (2006) "Theatres Crossing the Divide: A Baby Boomer's Defense of Hip-Hop Aesthetics," in J. Chang (ed.) *Total Chaos: The Art and Aesthetics of Hip-Hop*, New York: Basic Civitas Books, 300–5.

A special shout-out to Daniel Banks for his insights in the development of this case study.

SUMMARY: THINKING THROUGH THEATRE HISTORIES

In this chapter, we have considered how theatre has registered the influence of networked culture on the most basic elements of performer, stage, and performance type. More than ever, the experience of a play has come to depend not on the meanings "held" in a pre-written script authored by a single playwright, but in the complex interplay among a variety of factors, including collective devising and audience participation, that are manifest both on stage and online. We have seen how theatre's manipulation of new social media and other technologies has called attention to received notions of time, space, bodies, and theatre itself. The adage that opened this chapter situated theatre as a special event which takes place on "four trestles and four boards" established for the purpose – but networked culture has come increasingly to blur the lines between theatre and everyday life, taking advantage of other platforms originally designed for other purposes.

Some of this is new, to be sure, and some an extension of theatre's historic adaptability and responsiveness. Throughout this chapter and this text, we have considered how communication practices shape social structures and cultural dynamics, and how these cultural dynamics in turn shape theatrical activity. Thinking through this centuries-old interaction, we might ask ourselves the following questions:

- Throughout this book, we have seen theatre play a variety of roles in society: as a way to convey religious knowledge and values, especially in Chapter 3; as an instrument of state or political control such as in chapters 2 and 6; as a form of political activism in chapters 11 and 13; and of course in all periods, as a form of entertainment. How and why does theatre change its social role, and how does that affect its meaning and impact?

- In Chapter 5, we discussed the way print culture fostered a sense of personal interiority, and ultimately, individualism. How do communication practices alter our understanding of selfhood and the way we engage with the world?

- We saw in Chapter 7 that periodicals were crucial to the development of the public and private spheres and the concept of the nation-state. The larger question we can ask, then, is how do communication practices affect the way we interact with each other, and thereby influence the way we imagine and shape society?

- Chapter 9 considered photography's role in the rise of positivist philosophy, which portrays the world as wholly understandable through sense perception and objective facts. In what ways do communication practices shape our understanding of reality and truth?

- And how, finally, are such transformations manifested in performer/audience relation-ships, acting styles, stage design, character qualities, plot construction, and other aspects of theatrical performance?

The sky has been declared to have fallen on theatre many times over the period covered in Part IV, as communication technologies have proliferated the possibilities for storytelling by other means. Yet the sky remains above, where it now might share cloud space with Twitter plays, and theatre continues to transform in response to these evolving technologies. Some theatre artists have incorporated them into the formal performance space, be it stage, gallery, or street; others have engaged with it at the very level of its logic, exploring at a fundamental level what theatre might be, do, and become in an increasingly networked age. As it always has, theatre in this age continues to offer us a distinctive glimpse of who we are, where we've come from, and what we might become.

*

Part IV: Works cited

Other consulted resources and additional readings for Part IV are listed on the **Theatre Histories** *website.*

Audio-visual resources

Second-generation avant-gardes

"Futurism" website, including Marinetti's manifesto and other documents: http://www. unknown.nu/futurism/.

"MoMA Dada": http://www.moma.org/learn/moma_learning/themes/dada.

"Russian American Dramatic Arts Theatre: Meyerhold's Production of The Fairground Booth": https://sites.google.com/site/arttheatrestudio/meyerhold-s-production-of-the-fairground-booth. This site has information about the production, a few pictures, and a YouTube video at the bottom of the page about Meyerhold, theatre, and the Russian avant-garde.

"Surrealism" websites include http://surrealism-plays.com/ and the British Research Centre for the Study of Surrealism and its Legacies site: http://www.surrealismcentre.ac.uk.

"UbuWeb: Historical," a resource for the historical documents and manifestos on Dadaism, Surrealism, and Futurism, is at http://www.ubu.com/historical/.

"Federal Theatre Project Collection," website (Library of Congress), http://memory.loc.gov/ammem/fedtp/.

Chinese theatre

Secret Love in Peach Blossom Land. Film version of the play: https://www.youtube.com/watch?v=iyvXeQCQpCU (without subtitles). For a 2-minute video with English voiceover about the 2015 Oregon Shakespeare production, see https://www.youtube.com/watch?v=6hmQvd-radI.

The White-Haired Girl (1950), website with film: http://archive.org/details/the_white_haired_girl.

Yang Ban Xi: The Eight Model Works (2006) can be watched on Vimeo: https://vimeo.com/114648184.

Postwar theatre

The Samuel Beckett On-Line Resources and Links Pages (http://samuel-beckett.net/) contains an impressive number of links to reviews of Beckett plays, audio recordings of performances, links to articles from the Journal of Beckett Studies, biographical information, listings of video and audio recordings, critical essays, interviews, and more.

Jerzy Grotowski: A recording of *Akropolis* is availbale through Arthur Cantor Films in New York. The film *Training at Grotowski's "Laboratorium" in Wrocław in 1972* can be purchased from http://www.artfilms.co.uk. In addition, search YouTube for "Grotowski" for clips of performances and training sessions.

The Living Theatre: Some clips of *Paradise Now* can be viewed on YouTube at: https://www.youtube.com/watch?v=8ef51VmIWf8. There is also a montage of excerpts from major productions: "A Video Retrospective: The Living Theatre": https://www.youtube.com/watch?v=KVeuNhmaTEQ.

Suzuki Tadashi: A film of his *The Trojan Women (Toroia no Onna)* is in vol. 2 of *The Theater Goer's Collection, The Classics of Contemporary Japanese Theater*, DVDs published by Kazumo Co., Ltd., Tokyo, Japan. In addition, search YouTube for "Suzuki training" for clips of training sessions.

Robert Wilson: There are numerous excerpts of his work on YouTube, plus a two-part documentary called *Einstein on the Beach: the changing face of opera*.

Globalized, localized, and political performance

Augusto Boal and Theater of the Oppressed: YouTube has several videos demonstrating exercises and applications of Boal's methods, and a short 2-part interview from 2007.

Bread and Puppet Theater: A three-part documentary called *Ah! The Hopeful Pageantry of Bread and Puppet* can be found at https://archive.org/. Excerpts of shows are available on YouTube.

Mahabharata: Peter Brook's production has been made into a film and TV mini-series; visit IMDB. Excerpts also appear on YouTube.

Guillermo Gómez-Peña: A 30-minute documentary called *Two Amerindians Visit* is available from Data Bank in Chicago. See also the documentary "Couple in a Cage": http://vimeo.com/79363320.

The Hemispheric Institute (http://hemisphericinstitute.org/hemi/en/hidvl) has an extensive collection of online performance videos including:

- Latin American theatre such as Yuyachkani and FOMMA
- Social-group focused theatre such as Split Britches and El Teatro Campesino
- Performance artists like Guillermo Gómez-Peña
- Hip Hop performers such as Danny Hoch

Mega-musicals: There are many YouTube videos offering flavors of (and in some case full) productions of mega-musicals such as *Phantom of the Opera* and *Hamilton*.

Theatre in networked culture

Chilean Students "Thriller" Protest: see <http://www.huffingtonpost.com/2011/06/25/chilethriller-protest-students-michaeljackson-dance_n_884531.html>.

Gertie the Dinosaur and Winsor McCay: https://www.youtube.com/watch?v=lmVra1m W7LU.

George Coates Performance Works: http://stevemobia.com/WriteSubPages/George_Coates. htm.

Hirata Ozira interview: http://performingarts.jp/E/art_interview/0703/1.html.

Stelarc: A clip of "Amplified Body" is at http://v2.nl/events/amplified-body. He explains "Ear on Arm" at http://stelarc.org/?catID=20242.

Street with a View: http://benkinsley.com/street-with-a-view/.

Books, articles, and websites

Aronson, A. (2000) *American Avant-garde Theatre: A History*, London and New York: Routledge.

Artaud, A. (1958) *The Theatre and Its Double*, trans. M.C. Richards, New York: Grove Press. (Originally published in French in 1938.)

Auslander, P. (1992) *Presence and Resistance: Postmodernism and Cultural Politics in Contemporary American Performance*, Ann Arbor: University of Michigan Press.

Beckett, S. (1958) *Endgame*, New York: Grove Press.

Beckett, S. (1984) *The Collected Shorter Plays*, New York: Grove Press.

Bharucha, R. (1988) "Peter Brook's *Mahabharata*: A View from India," *Economic and Political Weekly* 23(32): 1642–7.

Bharucha, R. (2000) *The Politics of Cultural Practice: Thinking Through Theatre in an Age of Globalization*, Hanover and London: Wesleyan University Press.

Bigsby, C.W.E. (1982) *A Critical Introduction to Twentieth-Century American Drama*, Vol. 1, Cambridge: Cambridge University Press.

Bixler, J.E. (1997) *Convention and Transgression: The Theatre of Emilio Carballido*, Lewisburg: Bucknell University Press.

Bixler, J.E. (2004) "Performing Culture(s): Extras and Extra-Texts in Sabina Berman's *eXtras*," *Theatre Journal* 56(3): 429–44.

Borneoco (n.d.) "Zuhe Niao Performances" <http://www.borneoco.nl/zuhe-niao-performances.php>.

Bradby, D. and Williams, D. (1988) *Directors' Theatre*, London: Macmillan.

Bürger, P. (1984) *Theory of the Avant Garde*, trans. M. Shaw, Minneapolis: University of Minnesota Press.

Carruthers, I. and Takahashi, Y. (2004) *The Theatre of Suzuki Tadashi*, Cambridge: Cambridge University Press.

Connor, S. (1989) *Postmodernist Culture: An Introduction to Theories of the Contemporary*, Oxford and New York: Basil Blackwell.

Desaulniers, A. (2012) "Devised Theatre: The Art of the Impossible" <http://theatrewashington.org/content/devised-theatre-art-impossible>.

Dixon, S. (n.d.) "Practice: Chameleons 3: Net Congestion," *Absent Fields* <http://www.robat.scl.net/content/PaiPres/presencesite/html/dixchamel.html>.

Dixon, S. (2007) *Digital Performance: A History of New Media in Theater, Dance, Performance Art, and Installation*, Cambridge, MA: Massachusetts Institute of Technology Press.

Euripides (1959) *The Bacchae*, trans. William Arrowsmith, in D. Grene and R. Lattimore (eds) *Euripides V, The Complete Greek Tragedies*, Chicago: University of Chicago Press.

Filewod, A. and Watt, D. (2001) *Workers' Playtime: Theatre and the Labour Movement since 1970*, Sydney: Currency Press.

Fischer-Lichte, E. (1999) "Between Text and Cultural Performance: Staging Greek Tragedies in Germany," *Theatre Survey* 40(1): 1–29.

Garcia, V. (2013) "The Paradox of Devised Theater on the Twenty–First Century Stage," *howlround* July 21. <http://howlround.com/the-paradox-of-devised-theater-on-the-twenty-first-century-stage> (accessed Sept. 21, 2015).

Goodman, D. (trans.) (1986) *After Apocalypse: Four Japanese Plays of Hiroshima and Nagasaki*, New York: Columbia University Press.

Gómez-Peña, G. (1996) *The New World Border*, San Francisco: City Lights Books.

Gómez-Peña, G. (2003) *Dangerous Border Crossers*, London and New York: Routledge.

Grotowski, J. (1968) *Towards a Poor Theatre*, ed. E. Barba, New York: Simon and Schuster.

Honegger, G. (2001) "Austria: School for Scandal," *Western European Stages* 13:5–12.

Jones, L. (1965) "The Revolutionary Theatre," in *The Liberator* <http://nationalhumanitiescenter.org/pds/maai3/protest/text12/barakatheatre.pdf>.

Lehmann, H.T. (1999/2006) *Postdramatic Theatre*, London and New York: Routledge.

Leiter, S. (1994) *The Great Stage Directors*, New York: Facts on File.

Lyotard, J.-F. (1984) *The Postmodern Condition, A Report on Knowledge*, trans. G. Bennington and B. Massumi, foreword by F. Jameson, Minneapolis: University of Minneapolis Press.

McKinley, J. (2002) "And the Stub Is All Yours," *New York Times*. <http://www.nytimes.com/2002/05/19/arts/theater/19TICKET.html>.

McLuhan, M. (1962) *The Gutenberg Galaxy: The Making of Typographic Man*, Toronto: University of Toronto Press.

Marwick, A. (1998) *The Sixties*, Oxford: Oxford University Press.

May, E. (1988) *Homeward Bound: American Families in the Cold War Era*, New York: Basic Books.

Meyerhold, V. (1969) *Meyerhold on Theatre*, trans. and ed. E. Braun, New York: Hill and Wang.

Mixed Blood Theatre (2015) "Our Mission" <http://www.mixedblood.com/mission> (Accessed September 28, 2015).

Mulryne, J.R. (1998) "The Perils and Profits of Interculturalism and the Theatre Art of Tadashi Suzuki," in T. Sasayama, J.R. Mulryne, and M. Shewring (eds) *Shakespeare and the Japanese Stage*, Cambridge: Cambridge University Press.

Muse, J.H. (2012) "140 Characters in Search of a Theater: Twitter Plays," *Theater* 42(2): 42–63.

Parker-Starbuck, J. (2011) *Cyborg Theater: Corporeal/Technological Intersections in Multimedia Performance*, London: Palgrave Macmillan.

Pattie, D. (2000) *The Complete Critical Guide to Samuel Beckett*, London: Routledge.

Pocha Nostra (n.d.). "Ethno-cyborgs" <http://www.pochanostra.com/antes/jazz_pocha2/mainpages/ethno.htm>.

Puchner, M. (2002) *Stage Fright: Modernism, Anti-Theatricality, and Drama*, Baltimore and London: Johns Hopkins University Press.

Rebellato, D. (2009) *Theatre and Globalization*, Basingstoke: Palgrave Macmillan.

Reorbit (2010) <https://twitter.com/reorbitproject>.

Rimer, J.T. (1974) *Toward a Modern Japanese Theatre: Kishida Kunio*, Princeton: Princeton University Press.

Rolf, R. and Gillespie, J.K. (eds) (1992) *Alternative Japanese Drama: Ten Plays*. Honolulu: University of Hawaii Press.

Rouse, J. (1992) "Textuality and Authority in Theater and Drama: Some Contemporary Possibilities," in J.G. Reinelt and J.R. Roach (eds) *Critical Theory and Performance*, Ann Arbor: University of Michigan Press.

Schechner, R. (1985, rpt. 2011) *Between Theater and Anthropology*, Philadelphia: University of Pennsylvania Press.

Schechner, R. (2002) *Performance Studies: An Introduction*, London and New York: Routledge.

Senda, A. (1997) *The Voyage of Contemporary Japanese Theatre*, trans. T. Rimer, Honolulu: University of Hawaii Press.

Shakespeare Behind Bars (SBB) (2014) "About SBB: Mission & Vision" <http://www.shakespearebehind bars.org/about/mission/> (Accessed September 28, 2015).

Simon, J. (1975) "Grotowski's Grotesqueries," in J. Simon, *Singularities*, New York: Random House.

Sorgenfrei, C.F. (2005a) "Remembering and Forgetting: Greek Tragedy as National History in Postwar Japan," in K. Gounaridou (ed.) *Staging Nationalism*, Jefferson, NY: McFarland and Co.

Sorgenfrei, C.F. (2005b) *Unspeakable Acts: The Avant-Garde Theatre of Terayama Shūji and Postwar Japan*, Honolulu: University of Hawaii Press.

Tagore, R. (1961) *A Tagore Reader*, ed. A. Chakravarty, Boston: Beacon Press.

Vignolo, P. (2012) "Cultural Heritage as the Ultimate Utopia: Disputes around the Origins of the Carnival of Barranquilla," speech presented at the David Rockefeller Center for Latin American Studies at Harvard University, Cambridge, MA.

Williams, D. (ed.) (1991) *Peter Brook and* The Mahabharata: *Critical Perspectives,* London and New York: Routledge.

Williams, G.J. (1997) *Our Moonlight Revels:* A Midsummer Night's Dream *in the Theatre*, Iowa City: University of Iowa Press.

Wolf, S. (2008) "'Defying Gravity': Queer Conventions in the Musical *Wicked*," *Theatre Journal* 60(1): 1–21.

Worthen, W.B. (1992) *Modern Drama and the Rhetoric of Theater*, Berkeley: University of California Press.

Worthen, W.B. (2003) *Shakespeare and the Force of Modern Performance*, Cambridge: Cambridge University Press.

Yeats, W.B. (1952) *The Collected Plays*, New York: Macmillan.

Pronunciation guide

Pronunciations use common English spellings to approximate foreign sounds; compare with the online pronunciations. "Gh" represents the hard G as in *get*. Capitalized syllables are stressed. Japanese is unstressed, but to avoid mispronunciations you may lightly stress the first syllable. French normally stresses the last syllable, although in some contexts the first syllable sounds stressed.

TERM	PRONUNCIATION
Angura	ahn-goo-rah
Aragoto	ah-rah-goh-toh
Auteur	OH-tu(r)
Auto sacramental	OW-toh sahk-rah-men-TAHL
Bhava	PHAH-vuh
Bunraku	boon-rah-koo
Butoh	boo-toh
Capa y espada	KAH-pa ee es-PAH-thah
Castrato, -ti	kahs-TRAH-toh, -tee
Catharsis	kah-THAHR-sis
Comedia	koh-MEY-dee-ah
Comédie larmoyante	koh-meh-dee LAHR-mwah-yawnt
Commedia dell'arte	kohm-MAY-dee-ah dehl-AHR-tey
Commedia erudita	kohm-MAY-dee-ah eh-roo-DEE-tah
Corral	kohr-RAHL

TERM	PRONUNCIATION
Costumbrismo	kos-toom-BREES-mo
Danmari	dahm-mah-ree
Dengaku	dehn-gah-koo
Deus ex machina	deh-oos ex MAH-khee-nah
Dithyramb	DIH-thih-ram
Egúngún	EH-goon-goon
Einfühlung	AHYN-few-lungk
Geisha	gheh-sha
Geju	guh ju
Gesamtkunstwerk	ghe-ZAHMT-koonst-vehrk
Gestus	GHE-stoos
Hanamichi	hah-nah-mee-chee
Hashigakari	hah-shee-gah-kah-ree
Innamorato, -ta, -ti	in-nah-moh-RAH-toh, -tah, -tee
Jingju	jing ju
Kabuki	kah-boo-kee
Kathakali	kah-TAHK-ah-lee
Kōken	koh-kehn
Kunqu	kwin chu
Kutiyattam	KOO-tee-ah-TAHM
Kyōgen	kyoh-ghen
Landjuweelen	LAWHNT-yu-vay-lehn
Lazzi	LAH-dzee
Locus	LAW-koos
Ludi	LOO-dee
Mie	mee-eh
Mise en scène	meez on sehn
Monomane	moh-noh-mah-neh
Natyasastra	NAH-tyah-SHAS-tr
Naumachia	naw-MAH-khee-ah
Nō	noh
Onnagata	ohn-nah-gah-tah
Opera buffa	OH-peh-rah BOOF-fah
Opera seria	OH-peh-rah SEH-ree-ah

TERM	PRONUNCIATION
Parterre	PAH(r)-tehr
Philosophe	fee-loh-zohf
Platea	plah-TEH-ah
Polis	POH-lis
Purim shpil	POO-rehm shpihl
Rabinal Achi	drah-vee-NAHL ah-CHEE
Ramlila	rahm-lee-lah
Rasa	RAH-seh
Sarugaku	sah-roo-gah-koo
Scena per angolo	SHAY-nah pehr AHN-goh-loh
Shimpa	sheem-pah
Shingeki	sheen-gheh-kee
Shite	sh-teh
Shpil (plural, *shpiln*)	shpihl
Ta'ziyeh	TAH' zee-YEH
Theatron	THAY-ah-trohn
Tsure	tsoo-reh
Übermarionette	EW-behr-marionette
Vecchi	VEHK-kee
Verfremdungseffekt	fehr-FREHM-dungs-eh-fehkt
Volksgeist	FOYLKS-gahyst
Wagoto	wah-goh-toh
Waki	wah-kee
Wayang golek	wah-YAHNG goh-lek
Wayang kulit	wah-YAHNG koo-lit
Yangbanxi	yahng bahn shih
Yanggeju	yahng guh ju
Yūgen	yoo-ghehn
Zaju	zah ju
Zanni	ZAHN-nee

Glossary

Absolutism. The concentration of all political authority and state power in the person of the monarch. It is primarily associated with seventeenth-century France and Spain, although historical monarchies in China and Japan had features of absolutist rule. In drama it is associated with **neoclassicism**.

Absurd, Theatre of the. See **Theatre of the Absurd**.

Actor-managers. Actors, often ones playing lead roles, who also owned and managed an entire theatre company. They emerged in Europe during the 1550s, as potential for producing commercial theatre expanded during the Renaissance. One of the first actor-managers was Lope de Rueda of Spain.

Aestheticism. An **avant-garde** movement between 1890 and 1910 whose followers attempted to stage productions that encouraged spectators to escape the workaday world and revel in heightened aesthetic sensations. Believing in "art for art's sake," Aestheticists often chose contents and styles from the theatrical past to inspire new emotional responses.

Agit-prop theatre. Shortened from "agitation-propaganda," this term specifies a type of didactic theatre that originated in the Soviet Union. As performed by touring ensembles such as the Blue Blouse troupes, these were anti-naturalistic revues designed to instruct illiterate peasants and workers in the basic ideas of communism. The term "agit-prop" is also employed more broadly to identify (often pejoratively) overtly ideological types of performance.

Angura. The Japanese pronunciation of "underground," this experimental genre developed in the 1960s as a reaction to both realistic *shingeki* and to political and cultural turmoil.

Antiquarianism. The practice of staging plays with (ostensibly) historically accurate scenery and costumes. It is primarily associated with nineteenth-century British productions of Shakespeare by Charles Kemble, William Macready, and Charles Kean, who attempted to immerse spectators in the spirit of the English national past. Antiquarian staging practices also informed Orientalist melodramas set in the Middle East and other exotic locations of the British Empire after the 1880s. See Orientalism.

Antitheatricality. Opposition to theatrical performance. It can take many forms, such as religious expulsion of actors, or their vilification as liars, corruptors, or sexual deviants, and the use of theatre terms to denigrate someone or something. Antitheatricality is most common in the Western world. Although theatre everywhere has occasionally been banned or prohibited, the reasons have usually been to prevent social unrest or intermingling between social classes. In contrast, the antitheatricality one finds in the West involves fear or contempt for performance itself.

Aragoto. The "rough-house" style of kabuki acting typical of Edo (current Tokyo). These actors often wear striking, non-realistic make-up and greatly exaggerated costumes while also employing powerful gestures, such as the mie. Compare with wagoto.

Audiophonic media. Any media of communication that predominately features sound rather than one of the other sensory modes. In the modern era, these media include the telephone, the phonograph, and the radio.

Auteur director. A figure who takes author-like control of all the elements of stage or film production.

Auto sacramental. A sixteenth- or seventeenth-century Spanish one-act play on a religious topic. Many are about biblical events; others are allegorical, like morality plays.

Avant-garde. Borrowing a French military term referring to the forward line of soldiers in battle, various groups of artists since the 1880s have likewise thought of themselves as marching in the front ranks of artistic progress, fighting the propriety of the bourgeoisie, and inventing new aesthetic strategies in the service of utopian change. Examples of avant-garde movements are Symbolism, Futurism, Dadaism, Expressionism, and Surrealism.

Ballet. A dance with musical accompaniment characterized by precision of movement and an elaborate formal technique conventionally used to convey a story. In the 1500s and 1600s, European aristocrats performed in lavish ballet spectacles at royal courts. See also masques.

Baroque aesthetics. A late seventeenth-century orientation, especially popular in the Catholic courts of Europe, that celebrated allegory, grandeur, metamorphosis, sensuality, playfulness, and emotional extremes. In contrast with neoclassicism, it reasserted the centrality of visual and oral culture.

Beijing Opera. See jingju.

Bhava. The actor's embodiment of a character's state of mind/being/doing. A key element of Indian aesthetic theory. See rasa.

Biomechanics. A mode of training actors originated by the Russian director Vsevolod Meyerhold (1874–1940) designed to produce performers who could combine the arts of characterization, singing, dancing, and acrobatics with precise physical and vocal expression.

Blackface. A long tradition of Western performance in which masks, cosmetics, or other forms of makeup are used to give white performers the appearance of being street rowdies, circus clowns, and, in nineteenth-century American minstrel shows, African-Americans. Although often racist in intent, blackface has also served a variety of other purposes. See also yellowface.

Bourgeoisie. A socio-economic class consisting of property owners, merchants, bankers, shopkeepers, entrepreneurs, professionals, and similar figures. In Western Europe, during the eighteenth and nineteenth centuries, the bourgeoisie gained political power, supplanting the rule of royalty and landed aristocrats. Industrialists, merchants and commodity brokers, and financiers are the most powerful portion of the bourgeoisie and as a group are called capitalists. See also capitalism.

Box set. A stage setting that consists of the interior of a single room, usually under a proscenium arch, with an imaginary fourth wall facing the audience through which the audience watches the action.

Box. A private, enclosed seating area either adjacent or facing the stage.

Bunraku. Also known as *ningyō jōruri*, this is the traditional puppet theatre of Japan. In its current form, it is distinguished by the use of dolls that are expertly manipulated by a trio of visible puppeteers and voiced by a single chanter, accompanied by the *shaminsen* (a three-stringed instrument).

Burlesque. A form of variety theatre, particularly in the United States, that featured male comics, comic sketches, dance acts, musical pieces, plus scantily clad females in all of the numbers. It achieved the peak of its popularity in the early twentieth century.

Butoh. A genre of Japanese dance-drama that first appeared in between the late 1950s and the early 1960s, and which has had a major impact on modern dance worldwide. It typically employs grotesque gestures, slow movement, facial distortion, all-white body makeup, and extreme or even painful physicality. There are many varieties. Also spelled *butō*.

Capitalism. A complex system of economic organization based on the private ownership of property and other assets, the production of commodities for profit, and the loose regulation of supply and demand by market forces. Capitalists are part of the bourgeoisie. Capitalism also functions as an ideology (which may be believed by people who aren't capitalists) that is usually hostile to socialism and communism.

Carnival. In medieval Europe, a festival preceding the Catholic season of Lent. Lent is a pre-Easter period of self-denial and deprivation, whereas Carnival celebrates excess, pleasure, and humor. See carnivalesque.

Carnivalesque. As theorized by Mikhail Bakhtin, a type of humor that originated in the European Carnival tradition and similar cultural performances. Its chief characteristic is concern with the material base of reality, such as daily labor or the functions of the body. It also often involves reversals in social status.

Castrati. Male singers whose testicles have been removed to preserve the boyish pitch and purity of their voices. A few of them flourished as operatic stars during the eighteenth century.

Chariot-and-pole system. Stage machinery for quickly changing scenic "flats" riding on substage trolleys, invented by Giacomo Torelli in the 1640s.

Chorus. An organized group of performers who may either sing, dance, and/or speak dialogue. Examples of choric performance are those of ancient Greece (the **dithyramb**, **tragedy**, and **Old Comedy**) and the Japanese *nō* theatre.

Cognitive science. The sciences that study how the mind/brain consciously and unconsciously processes perceptions, engages emotionally with the world, and makes meaning from these experiences.

Comedia. A term originating in the Spanish Golden Age to describe the predominant form of secular drama in the sixteenth and seventeenth centuries: a three-act play combining serious and comic elements, in complex plots involving love, intrigue, and honor. Most often associated with the playwrights Félix Lope de Vega (1562–1635) and Pedro Calderón de la Barca (1600–1681).

Comédie larmoyante. Literally, "tearful comedy." The French version of sentimental comedy. See **sentimentalism**.

Comedy. A term covering an extremely wide variety of humorous plays. The earliest extant written comedies were written in ancient Greece during the fifth century BCE, and usually involved topical satire (see **Old Comedy**). Later comedies focused on domestic matters such as love (see **New Comedy**). Many other comedic genres exist.

Commedia dell'arte. A form of street theatre that originated in Italy during the 1540s. Professional troupes of between eight and twelve actors specialized in performing stock characters (indicated by grotesque half-masks and specific dialects), pre-arranged comic business (*lazzi*), and improvisations based on scenarios primarily drawn from the plays of Plautus and Terence.

Commedia erudita. Sixteenth-century European academic comedies for aristocratic patrons based on the texts of Plautus and Terence.

Commemorative drama. An umbrella term given to performances which have as their focus the memorialization of religious or civic events in a community's history. They can include a mixture of pious and **carnivalesque** elements.

Communism. A radical form of **socialism** initially developed by Karl Marx (1818–1883) that advocates the overthrow of **capitalism** in order to create a classless society. With the success of the Russian Revolution (1917), the political and economic theory of communism was soon conflated with the policies of the Communist Party (by both its supporters and opponents). Historically, governments controlled by a Communist Party have eschewed democracy in favor of single-party rule and state control over all social spheres, from the economy to the arts.

Community-based theatre (in the U.K. and elsewhere, called community theatre). Theatres dependent upon ongoing dialogue between artists and spectators, usually for the purpose of exploring ways in which the social agency of a local audience can be maximized.

Constructivism. The artistic synthesis of **Retrospectivism** and **Futurism** achieved by Russian director Vsevolod Meyerhold in the 1920s. It incorporated his acting experiments with biomechanics, and is best represented by Lyubov Popova's set designs consisting of elaborate ramps, slides, ladders, and moving wheels that allowed actors to demonstrate how human beings could use their emotions and machines to produce engaging art and a more productive life. Stalin censored these techniques during the 1930s in favor of promoting socialist realism.

Copyright. A legal protection extended to authors giving them control over the publication and performance of their work. The first comprehensive copyright law was enacted by France in 1790.

Corpus Christi cycle. See cycle play.

Corral. An enclosed, open-air theatre in Spain during the sixteenth and seventeenth centuries, originally the courtyard of an inn and later purpose-built.

Counter-Reformation. The years 1545–1648 in which the Catholic Church sought to suppress the Protestant Reformation through various reforms, new religious orders, and spiritual movements. It included the encouragement of Baroque art.

Cultural hybridity. A term used to describe the results of intercultural encounter, in which elements of each original culture combine to create something new, which nevertheless bears traces of the original separate contributions.

Cycle play. A series of short plays dramatizing key episodes from the Old and New Testaments, performed in medieval England during the Feast of Corpus Christi. The plays were produced and performed by trade guilds.

Dada. An avant-garde movement initiated in Switzerland during the First World War that employed cabaret sketches to experiment with the chance ordering of sounds, simultaneous poetry, and movements that mocked the absurdity of Western notions of logic and harmony.

Decorum. The precept of neoclassicism that plays should uphold the standards of taste and morality, and that there are behaviors appropriate for different social classes.

Devised theatre. Theatre or drama developed collectively by a group, usually of actors, starting from improvisations.

Dithyrambs. Choral songs and dances in honor of Dionysus performed at Athens' major theatre festival (the City Dionysia) and elsewhere in ancient Greece.

Drame. French domestic tragedy, comparable to sentimental drama. See sentimentalism.

Electric and electronic culture. A culture which utilizes electromagnetism (in forms such as electricity, radio waves, and visible light) for communication media. Electrical media include telegraphs, film projectors, photography (using photochemical reactions), and early telephones, phonographs, and radios. With the invention of the vacuum tube and later the transistor, media such as television, computers, mobile phones, and digital cameras became not only practical, but widespread and increasingly portable. When distant computers were connected, the internet was born, providing the foundation for networked culture, a subtype of electronic culture. Because of electronic media's usage level, it has already begun to have cognitive effects.

Elizabethan era. The period when Queen Elizabeth I reigned in England (1558–1603). It is often considered the high point of the English Renaissance. It was followed by the Jacobean era.

Empathy. A cognitive operation that has been defined in various ways. As we use the term, empathy is a relationship to another person that involves an attempt to take the perspective of and understand the emotions of that other.

Empiricism. The theory that knowledge is only or mainly derived from individual sense experience, such as the direct observation of natural phenomena and scientific experiments.

Enlightenment. An eighteenth-century European intellectual movement that asserted that human progress could only be achieved on the basis of political liberty, individual freedoms, and the rights of private property. See empiricism and rationalism.

Environmental theatre. See immersive theatre.

Evolution. The theory established by Charles Darwin and others that plants and animals flourish, mutate, or become extinct over time based solely on the process of natural selection, that is, their success within their environment based on the species' variations.

Exorcism. A ritual performance, common to many cultures, that addresses and expels demonic forces in order to heal an individual or a community.

Expressionism. An avant-garde movement that flourished in Germany after the First World War (1914–1918). Expressionist plays called for such anti-realist techniques as grotesquely painted scenery, exaggerated acting, and "telegraphic" dialogue. They frequently invited spectators to view the distorted dramatic action through the fevered eyes of the protagonist.

Farce. A type of comedy focusing on ridiculous and unlikely situations rather than character development. Often it includes confusion, slapstick, and absurdities.

Fascism. An extreme form of nationalism that emerged in Europe after the First World War (1914–1918). This ideology rejected Enlightenment universalism and liberal democracy in favor of racial purity and violent authoritarian rule.

Fourth wall. The realist convention of an imaginary "wall" across the proscenium opening enclosing an interior room in a box set. The spectators observe the action through this imaginary wall, and the actors perform as if they were unaware of the audience's presence.

Fringe theatre. Often small and experimental troupes that perform in the same cities hosting major international theatre events, but are not on the official program. The most famous sites for fringe theatre are the Edinburgh and Avignon festivals.

Futurism. An avant-garde movement that was launched in Italy in 1909 with the publication of a manifesto by F.T. Marinetti (1876–1944) damning the art of the past and advocating new forms exalting the dynamism of the machine age. Russian Futurists, led by Vladimir Mayakovsky (1893–1930), attempted to align this movement with the Soviet revolution until the onset of Stalinist persecution. See Constructivism.

Gallery. A balcony seating area. A theatre often has several levels of galleries.

Gesamtkunstwerk. Richard Wagner's (1813–83) influential term for a total, synthesized art work in which all elements of a theatrical production are controlled by the vision of a single master-artist. See *auteur director.*

Gestus. Bertolt Brecht's term for the expressive means an actor can employ – such as a way of standing, or moving, or a pattern of behavior – that indicates to the audience the social position or condition of the character that the actor is playing. See *Verfremdungseffekt*.

Globalization. The ongoing and accelerating process of widespread transnational engagement, driven largely by economic systems and aided by information technology, in which interaction among cultures has become commonplace.

Glocal. A term combining "global" and "local" to describe the ways global culture influences local culture, and vice versa.

Guilds. Medieval European associations of artisans or merchants that regulated wages and trade, trained apprentices, and undertook charitable projects such as the sponsorship of cycle plays.

Happenings. Performance events designed to blur the boundaries between the experience of art and commonplace experiences that were first created in New York and elsewhere in the 1960s.

High modernism. An orientation to the European stage prominent between 1910 and 1940 that emphasized written dialogue and frequently employed metatheatricality and the minimization of the actor's physical presence to create a theatre that would move people to transcend the material realities of the modern world. Exemplary figures were William Butler Yeats (1865–1939) and Luigi Pirandello (1867–1936). See modernism.

Historiography. The theories, methodologies, techniques, and narrative strategies involved in writing history. Also used to refer to the products of historical research, such as books and websites.

Huaju. Chinese spoken drama, originally based on Western models of realism. The first play in this style was written in 1907.

Humanism. Central to Western thought since the Renaissance, humanism arose during the fourteenth century as the study and emulation of classical Roman (and later, Greek) writings in order to return to the cultural heights of antiquity. It became a core of education throughout Europe, and its methodologies underlie what is now called "the humanities." In the sixteenth century humanism began to mean an emphasis on human experience and potential, rather than Christian faith. Today humanism is fundamentally the assumption that all people everywhere, in all times, share a common essence.

Iconology. The interpretive analysis of images to understand the cultural work the image was doing in its time. Among other things, such analysis considers visual vocabularies and conventions, inherited or innovative, and the cultural forces surrounding the artwork.

Ideology. The implicit and explicit ideas, theories, and assumptions about the social and natural world that inform people's interpretation of their individual and collective condition. An ideology often validates the status quo, in support of the interests of the most powerful social group(s).

Immersive theatre (a recent expansion of "environmental theatre"). Staging in which there is no demarcation between actor and spectator space, multiple events compete with each other to diffuse any single focus, and actors interact with audience members both in character and personally.

Imperialism. The ideology and action of creating and maintaining empires. Imperialism can be political, economic, military, religious, cultural, or a combination. Imperialist countries typically take control over conquered peoples and land by establishing colonies – subordinate political entities that are often subjected to ruthless exploitation. Imperialist countries usually justified this by claiming that "civilized" nations have the right (and moral obligation) to rule over "inferior" cultures (see **Orientalism**). Modern imperialism often consists of economic dominance over other countries, without direct political control.

Industrial Revolution. The late eighteenth- and nineteenth-century process of rapidly expanding **capitalism**, urbanization, and technological breakthroughs, particularly in the areas of manufacturing, transportation, and communications.

Inquisition. Institutions within the Roman Catholic Church which combated heresy through censorship, forced conversions, torture, execution, and other means, starting in the twelfth century and in most areas ending in the early nineteenth century. It was particularly aggressive in Spain, Portugal, and Mexico.

Interculturalism. The practice in which theatre artists use the texts, acting styles, music, costumes, masks, dance, or scenic vocabularies from more than one culture in a single production. Although intercultural artworks have always developed whenever one culture encounters another, consciously intercultural productions have proliferated during the past three decades in the context of **globalization**.

Internet. A system interconnecting many computer networks into one extremely large global network, in principle allowing any computer or similar digital device to communicate with any other via established protocols. One portion of the internet is the World Wide Web ("Web" for short), which features content that has been specially encoded to allow users easy access, interaction, and navigation of material on the Web.

Jacobean era. The period when King James I reigned in England and Scotland (1603–1625). It is considered the final part of the English **Renaissance**.

Jingju. The Chinese term for what is known elsewhere as "Beijing Opera." Created in 1790, it is a form of musical theatre that relates historical, romantic, and melodramatic stories through a mix of song, stylized speech, spectacular dance, pantomimed action, acrobatics, and orchestral music consisting of stringed and percussive instruments. Also known as *jingxi.*

Kabuki. A still-popular form of traditional Japanese theatre noted for its lavish use of scenic display, costumes, and makeup; the physical and emotional style of its actors; and its repertoire of plays, often involving painful complications between duty and emotion. It originated around 1600 as a mode of dance-drama that reflected an outrageous disdain for acceptable social behavior. Various restrictions eventually resulted in *kabuki* troupes being composed only of adult males. See **onnagata**, **aragoto**, and **wagoto**.

Kathakali. Literally "story" (*katha*), "dance" or "play," this form of south Indian dance-drama is distinguished by a highly physicalized style of performance based on traditional martial arts and its complex use of both gesture and expression to communicate the emotions/actions of a character.

Kōken. In both the Japanese *nō* and *kabuki* theatres, these are stage assistants who visibly, but unobtrusively, handle props, straighten costumes, and prompt actors. When dressed all in black, they are called *kurogo*.

Kunqu. A type of Chinese musical drama favored by elite Confucian audiences during the Ming dynasty (1368–1644).

Kusemai. Secular entertainments mainly performed by women dressed in male clothing that were popular in fourteenth-century Japan. Also the main dance in *nō*.

Kutiyattam. A style of staging late-Sanskrit drama that originated in the Indian state of Kerala, that employs Sanskrit and Pakrit as well as the local language, and takes place within a specific type of temple architecture.

Kyōgen. Short, often farcical interludes or entire short comedies performed with Japanese *nō* plays.

Lazzi. Comic, often physical stage actions performed in *commedia dell'arte*.

Liberalism. As political orientation, belief in the right of individuals to pursue their own interests as equals, unrestrained by aristocratic privileges or state constraints. As an economic orientation, support for individuals' pursuit of "free market" capitalism under minimal government regulation. Classical liberalism is also meritocratic, emphasizing the necessity of individuals to earn their social and economic security through their own efforts.

Literate culture. A culture in which the dominant means for verbal communication is writing. By itself, the presence of writing in a society doesn't necessarily make it a literate culture: cf. oral culture. Instead, writing must be dominant. This does not refer to the percentage of the population who can read and write, which can in fact be a small minority. Writing is dominant when it is considered more authoritative than speech or memory for political, legal, and cultural purposes, and has had significant cognitive effects upon those who use it. There are four main types of literate culture: manuscript culture, print culture, periodical print culture, and electric and electronic culture.

Locus. Latin for "place." In medieval theatre, a single stage, often an elevated platform or a pageant wagon, which is partly or totally surrounded by an open space (see *platea*). It is used to represent a specific location, such as a manger or a house. The dramatic location may be identified only by language, or the stage may have a setting or special effects scenery. See also mansions.

Ludi. "Games" to mark the observance of Roman public holidays as well as great funerals, military victories, and other state occasions. These eclectic festivities presented chariot racing, boxing, and gladiatorial contests as well as dramatic performances. The most important of these events were the *Ludi Romani* in honor of the god Jupiter.

Mansions. From a Latin term for "station" or "house." Elevated platforms representing different scene locations in medieval Christian dramas, and spectators generally move from one mansion to the next (see simultaneous staging). Arranged around an open space within a cathedral (see *platea*), or perhaps outdoors in ancient earthen rounds, mansions offered allegorical, rather than illusionistic, depictions of places within the Christian imagination, such as Eden and Hell. See also *locus*.

Manuscript culture. A type of literate culture in which writing can only be accomplished by hand. This includes inscriptions on wood, wax, stones, pottery, etc. Although writing has a significant place in manuscript cultures (in some of them, anchored by one or more sacred texts), the oral culture continues to be vibrant throughout the society, including among the literate elite.

Masques. Lavish court spectacles, often employing perspective scenery, which celebrated the nobility of seventeenth-century England, France, and Spain as powerful mythological figures. These expensive entertainments allegorically supported the prerogatives of absolutism.

Melodrama. A form of theatre that dramatizes social morality: it names "good guys" and "bad guys," helping audiences to negotiate such problems as political power, economic justice, and racial inequality.

Metatheatricality. Theatrical self-reference. Metatheatrical techniques include plays-within-plays (e.g., Pirandello's *Six Characters in Search of an Author*), production techniques and characters' comments pointing out that the current activity is a play performance (the former occurs in Brechtian productions, the latter in Beckett's *Waiting for Godot*), characters' discussions of plays and performance (like Hamlet's advice to the itinerant players), plays about actors or playwrights (such as a play about Molière), and more. The purpose of metatheatricality can vary. Metatheatrical plays are sometimes called "metatheatre" or "metadrama."

Method acting. A twentieth-century style of American acting that marries the personality of the actor to the character she or he is playing through psychological techniques of extreme empathy. It is often part of psychological realism.

Mie. A fierce pose struck by a *kabuki* actor. At climactic moments of a play, he may toss his head, raise his leg and stamp his foot, pose with open, outreached hand, grunt, and freeze his face in a cross-eyed grimace. See *aragoto*.

Mimesis. Aristotle's term in the *Poetics* (*c.*380 BCE) for the imitation or representation of action and characters.

Minstrel show. A form of racist blackface performance popular in the United States from the 1840s until the rise of vaudeville in the 1880s. A form of variety show, minstrel acts consisted of white male performers imitating slave festivities in the South, musical numbers, and parody.

Mise en scène. A French term denoting all visual aspects of a production, including set design, costumes, makeup, lighting, and the placement and movement of actors.

Modernism. A general orientation to the stage that emphasized the written texts of the playwright, questioned the representational basis of the theatre (often through the use of metatheatricality), and often posited the existence of an ideal realm that could transcend the anguish of material conditions, such as the perceived chaos of the modern city. In Europe and the U.S., modernism in the theatre lasted from 1920 to about 1975.

Monomane. A key aspect of Zeami's aesthetic theory, it refers to the *nō* actor's revelation of the fictional character's "invisible body" or essence. Sometimes translated as "imitation."

Morality plays. Late medieval Christian allegories usually focused on an "everyman" figure faced with a choice between good and bad behavior.

Moros y cristianos. A Spanish play of the fifteenth or sixteenth century pitting "Moors" (Muslims) against Christians.

Multiculturalism. A term describing works combining performance modes drawn from different cultural traditions within nation-state boundaries, rather than across them. Often critiqued for a tendency toward tokenism of minority cultures within a larger dominant one.

Mummers plays. Christianized versions of pagan rituals designed to ensure the return of spring, often featuring a white knight combating a blackened Turk.

Music hall. Although an English Victorian term, it may be used to designate any type of variety theatre that features a series of unconnected entertainments on an indoor stage.

Mystery cycle. See cycle play.

Nationalism. A political ideology based in the belief that a nation – a group loosely united by territory, language, and/or culture – has an inherent right to live and flourish within its own geographical and political state. Nationalism began in Europe in the seventeenth century and has taken several historical forms. *Liberal nationalism* involves a commitment to the Enlightenment ideals of individual liberty and constitutionalism. *Cultural nationalism* centers on a belief in the uniqueness and greatness of one's language-based culture. *Racial nationalism* mixes notions of racial superiority with cultural nationalism to produce the belief that a nation's superiority is based on racial purity.

Naturalism. An avant-garde movement, which flourished between 1880 and 1914, that portrayed heredity and environmental factors as the primary causes of human behavior through the accurate rendition of external realities.

Natyasastra. An encyclopaedic work on all aspects of drama attributed to the sage Bharata, authored or collected between 200 BCE and 200 CE. See Sanskrit drama.

Naumachiae. Sea battle re-enactments based upon episodes from Greek history that were staged as lavish public spectacles in ancient Rome.

Neoclassicism. A development in the Renaissance recovery of classical ideals and practices in art and literature and the rationalist elaboration of them, especially in the service of the absolutist monarchy in France in the mid- to late seventeenth century, when verisimilitude, decorum, and poetic justice were emphasized. See the rules.

Networked culture. A culture in which the internet is a major mode of communication, which people access using personal computers and mobile devices. Although it can be considered a type of literate culture because to some extent it uses text, it is also similar to oral culture because the same medium can be used both for communication between individuals, and for communication to a very large audience that includes the possibility of responses back.

New Comedy. A form of ancient Greek comedy, focusing on domestic (rather than political) issues. Its period is typically considered to be 323–260 BCE. The only extant plays are by Menander. Adapted by the Romans Plautus and Terence as *fabula palliata*, it became the model for Western comedy up to the present. Compare with Old Comedy.

Nō. A traditional form of Japanese theatre that was developed in the fourteenth century with multiple origins including Shinto ritual, Buddhist philosophy, and *kusemai* dance. Among its distinctive features are its stage architecture, finely wrought masks, delicate movement and dance, onstage musicians, and the use of a seated chorus who vocalize narration and dialogue. The dramatic texts of its greatest playwright, Zeami (*c.*1363–1443), often borrow plots from historical epics or novels and usually feature ghosts or characters of supernatural origin. Also spelled *noh.*

Old Comedy. Satirical commentaries on socio-political problems, sometimes employing bawdy humor and costumes, that were performed in ancient Athens. The only surviving examples are the comedies of Aristophanes (*c.*448–*c.*387 BCE). Compare with New Comedy.

Onnagata. A male *kabuki* actor who specializes in female roles.

Opera. A form of dramatic musical theatre in which the performers sing all their lines in the script. Opera began in Europe in 1607 and remains popular in the West today. Following the reign of Baroque opera in the seventeenth century, European opera split into two primary strands. *Opera buffa* (comic opera) drew much of its energy, many of its plots, and most of its stock characters from *commedia dell'arte*. In contrast, *opera seria* (serious opera) dealt with serious subjects and became an arena for the performance of castrati singers.

Opéra-comique. Eighteenth-century French comic opera in which the audience sang lyrics printed on a placard and set to a popular tune.

Operetta. Light operatic entertainments that emerged in the nineteenth century in Vienna, Paris, and London to amuse mostly bourgeois spectators.

Oral culture. A culture in which the dominant means for verbal communication is speech. Oral cultures may have writing, but it plays a relatively minor and subordinate cultural role and has few if any cognitive effects. Cf. literate culture.

Orientalism. Edward Said's term for the way Western countries represented the East, a vast territory that was imagined to stretch from the modern Middle East to Japan, and which was largely subjected to European imperialism in the nineteenth century. "Orientals" were depicted as weak, cunning, inscrutable, culturally backward, feminine, dangerous, and, above all, exotic. Today, the term is widely understood to refer to any culture that is seen as incomprehensibly "Other."

Pageant wagons. Mobile stages that were used in processional routes and sometimes gathered in fixed arrangements in a playing area for the performance of medieval cycle plays. A wagon usually provides the *locus* for a play, and the street around it is the *platea*.

Pantomime. A genre that developed in ancient Rome, consisting of solo performances to musical accompaniment that silently enacted all of the characters of a drama using a series of costumes and masks. A form of it re-emerged in eighteenth-century England, which became enormously popular and long-lived.

Passion play. Dramas depicting Jesus's sufferings that originated in medieval Europe and, in some places, remain in production, such as the *Oberammergau Passion Play*.

Patent. A license granting a company or an individual the privilege to pursue an activity that is otherwise subjected to restriction. Historically, governments, such as that of the English King Charles II (1630–1685), have made theatrical performances subject to a patenting process as a form of censorship.

Patrimonialization. The socio-political process by which certain traditions are turned into treasures of cultural, national, or international heritage.

Patronage. Support extended by a powerful individual or an elite to an arts-producing entity. Examples include legal permission to perform, financial subsidy, and protection from competing social groups. See patent.

Performance art. A contemporary expression of the avant-garde consisting of either solo works or larger spectacles that always seek to break through the separation of art and life. Often taking up social and political concerns, performance artists typically use their own lives as subjects and their own bodies as instruments.

Periodical print culture. A type of print culture is which periodicals – publications that appear on a recurrent cycle (often annually, monthly, weekly, or daily) and are distributed across a region (ranging from a city to the world) – play a significant social role. The transportation systems that enabled regular mail delivery were crucial to making periodical publication feasible. Periodicals provided a major practical basis for the public sphere.

Periodization. In writing historical narratives, the strategy of organizing human events and practices into shared categories of time, or "periods."

Perspective scenery. Scenery that depicts a landscape, urban location, or large building in a realistic manner by using the principle of perspective, in which objects appear to recede into the distance in a mathematically accurate manner.

Pit. The ground level of an English Renaissance theatre, usually below the stage, where spectators stood to watch the play. In France it was called the *parterre*; in Spain, the *patio*.

Platea. Latin for "plaza" or "broad street." In the staging of medieval European drama, an open space such as the nave of a cathedral or a city street, used as a neutral, unlocalized playing area that could be whatever location the text required at a given moment. See mansions and *locus*.

Poetic justice. A precept in neoclassicism, and a common plot device in general, that evil characters should be punished and good ones rewarded. Often poetic justice occurs through an ironic twist.

Poor theatre. Jerzy Grotowski's (1934–1999) conception of a theatre stripped of elaborate production elements and dedicated to the performance of "holy actors" athletically embodying the sufferings and ecstasies of the human spirit.

Positivism. The philosophy that scientific knowledge derives solely from measurable sensory experience, allowing for the detection of invariant general laws of both nature and society.

Postdramatic theatre. A term coined in 1999 by theatre scholar Hans-Thies Lehmann, to describe experimental or avant-garde theatre appearing after the 1960s in which the dramatic text and/or dramatic action are subordinated to a ruling idea, or sometimes eliminated entirely, with the aim of producing an effect upon the audience that is not dependent upon text or plot.

Postmodernism. A much-debated concept that was prevalent during the late twentieth century. Within philosophy, it is generally associated with a critique of the possibility of establishing and/or communicating stable meanings, e.g., the idea that binary oppositions can be clearly maintained, and often raises the connection between knowledge and power. Postmodern theatre and performance artists tend to emphasize a deep skepticism toward modernism's desire to wrap experience in a single, unified, pleasingly cohesive vision, and often take an ironic view of society and culture.

Print culture. A type of literate culture in which texts can be reproduced quickly, precisely, and in large quantities by mechanical means. The earliest form of printing used woodblocks on which were carved whole pages, but the production scale was small enough that the societies remained manuscript cultures. Machines that composed pages using small pieces for each word or letter were invented separately in China (c.1040), Korea (1234), and Europe (c.1440), but their use became far more widespread in Europe. Thus China and Korea continued to be manuscript cultures, but in Europe printing gained dominance over manuscript. In print cultures, oral culture takes a subordinate position, strongest in religion and the arts, but weak in most other realms. Handwriting assumes an even narrower role. Print culture began with books, but eventually periodical print culture became feasible.

Private sphere. The facet of social life consisting of personal matters, such as family, the home, friendship, religious feelings, and emotions. For many years, women were confined to activities in the private sphere. It is contrasted with the public sphere.

Proscenium arch. First created in the Renaissance, a visible and often highly ornate frame around the stage that is a permanent architectural element of some theatres.

Protestant Reformation. The schism in Western Europe in which Christianity split into Roman Catholicism and various types of Protestantism. It is often dated 1517–1648, although some scholars place the end either in 1555 or around 1750.

Psychological realism. An orientation to playwriting and staging that strives to present characters' thoughts, feelings, and psychological development in a realistic manner. Its hallmarks are psychologically attuned directing and (particularly in the U.S.) variations on Method Acting. Scenography can be somewhat flexible, rather than wholly realist. It effectively became the national style of the United States during the 1950s.

Public sphere. The facet of social life in which people discuss politics, economics, laws, and similar matters which (in theory) are open to debate by all people. It is contrasted with the private sphere. Although the terms "public sphere" and "private sphere" were developed in the twentieth century, the distinction itself dates from the eighteenth century with the political rise of the bourgeoisie and the formation of periodical print culture.

Purim shpil. A humorous, often satirical, play presenting the events commemorated in the Jewish holiday of Purim. The play is accompanied by enthusiastic audience involvement, such as hissing and noise-making.

Ramlila. An Indian commemorative drama that allows its participants immediate access to an encounter with the Hindu god Ram (sometimes called Rama). It is celebrated as a pluralistic, open-air event that features re-enactments of episodes from Ram's life. "*Lila*," in the word *Ramlila*, is the Hindu concept of "divine play" or joyful intervention of the gods into the human sphere.

Rasa. An ideal aesthetic experience in Sanskrit drama, compared to the various "tastes" savored at a meal. The concept, along with *bhava*, is central to Indian aesthetic theory.

Rationalism. A philosophy deriving from the ideas of René Descartes (1596–1650) that proposed that reason alone, independent of experience, is the source of truth. It seeks absolute, mathematical certainty in knowledge. See Enlightenment.

Realism. In theatre, a stage orientation that originated partly in response to the emerging technology of photography. It is also referred to as "stage realism." Its hallmark was the presentation of scrupulously observed material realities, and typically used historically accurate costumes, the fourth wall, and box sets. Initially employed in the commercial theatre by producer-directors who appealed to the public's desire for antiquarianism and melodrama, this style was later adapted for use by the Naturalists. It is still the dominant style in the West. See also psychological realism.

Remix. A term originally applied to a musical work that combines audio elements from other recordings, recently expanded to refer to any work of art or media that creates something new by adding, removing, or changing elements of one or more other works. Some use it to describe the dominant aesthetic of networked culture.

Renaissance. Literally "rebirth," this is a traditional category of periodization for European history from, roughly, the fourteenth century to the seventeenth century, but the period varies from country to country. The word reflects the growing interest taken by European elites in the "classical" cultures of the ancient world, such as Greek and Roman drama. This period also produced the ideologies of humanism and absolutism.

Restoration. The period in English national history (after the Civil War) that began in 1660 with the restoration of King Charles II to the throne. Most historians date the end of the Restoration period at 1688. The Meiji Restoration in Japan refers to the downfall of the Tokugawa shogunate in 1868 and the supposed return of authority to the emperor.

Retrospectivism. A stage orientation that arose in pre-revolutionary Russia that incorporated many of the elements of Symbolism. Retrospectivists like Nikolai Evreinov (1879–1953) aimed to recover older forms of theatre as a means of injecting their playful energy into contemporary life.

Rituals. Performances (often ceremonies) that occur on special occasions that form and re-form self and social identity, and are viewed as efficacious, i.e., their participants conceptualize these events as having real consequences, such as curing a disease or maintaining cosmological balance. Masking, costuming, impersonation, dance, music, narrative, and humor are all recurrent features of ritual performance.

Romanticism. A European aesthetic movement (1790–1840) that prized the subjectivity of genius, looked to nature for inspiration, elevated strong emotions above reasonable restraint, and often sought to embody universal conflicts within individual figures.

Rules, the. A set of requirements that, according to neoclassicism, plays must meet in order to be considered good drama. They include the unities, decorum, poetic justice, and verisimilitude.

Saint plays. Medieval European plays about Christian saints.

Sanskrit drama. An umbrella term for a rich variety of Sanskrit- and Prakrit-language theatre practices that date back at least to 300 BCE in what is modern-day India. See *Natyasastra*.

Satyr plays. Farcical renditions of Greek myth performed at ancient Athens' major theatre festival after a day's program of tragedies.

Sentimentalism. During the eighteenth century, this was a positive term for a social philosophy in which the intellect, emotions, and morality were harmoniously integrated. Sentimentalism emphasized virtuous decision-making and tearful reconciliations in drama, and shared many of the moral ideas of rationalism. Not to be confused with "sentimentality," which involves indulgent or mawkish emotions.

Shaman. The Siberian Tungus word for "one who is excited, moved, raised." The term can be applied broadly to a range of traditional specialists in rituals. Shamans are usually attributed with possessing specific powers (curing illness, counteracting misfortune) and they are typically able to access the spirit world after entering a trance.

Sharing system. The business model upon which many Elizabethan and European theatre companies were run in the sixteenth century. In this system, actor-managers, leading actors, financiers, and sometimes playwrights shared in the profits of a given run or theatrical season.

Shimpa. Literally "new style," the term refers to the late nineteenth- and early twentieth-century fashion of adapting Western dramatic forms, such as the "well-made play," to Japanese tastes. It is sometimes seen as a transitional form between *kabuki* and *shingeki*. Both actresses and *onnagata* sometimes portray female roles in the same play.

Shingeki. Western-style Japanese theatre, originated in 1909. At first referred only to spoken plays, but now includes musicals as well. After the Second World War, young theatre artists rebelled against *shingeki* and created alternative and experimental genres, such as angura.

Simultaneous staging. A medieval theatre convention in which the various scenes of a play were set on individual fixed stages (*mansions*) that were all visible at the same time. The actors (and spectators) progressed from set to set as the scenes changed and the dramatic action proceeded.

Social Darwinism. The discredited assumption that cultures, like species, have evolved, and can be viewed hierarchically from the "primitive" cultures on the bottom to the "great civilizations" at the top.

Socialism. A political and economic orientation that arose in the early nineteenth century that aims to have social needs and benefits prioritized over profits by establishing public or collective ownership of industry and public services. The socialist economist and philosopher Karl Marx (1818–1883) argued that there is an inherent class conflict between workers and capitalists. Unlike communism (and Marx), socialists have historically sought to promote economic justice through reform rather than violent revolution.

Socialist realism. The official aesthetic policy of the Soviet Union from 1930 to 1953, instituted by Joseph Stalin, which favored idealistic and heroic images of and plays about workers and Communist leaders to advance the aims of the state. This art was "realistic" only in so far as it was not abstract. The dictates of socialist realism were used against Communist artists such as Meyerhold who practiced other styles and forms.

Surrealism. A 1920s avant-garde movement that emphasized spontaneity, shock effects, and psychological imagery based in dreams.

Symbolism. An avant-garde movement flourishing in the 1890s that rejected Naturalism in order to concretize the unseen spiritual realities that the artists believed shaped human fate.

Ta'ziyeh. An Islamic/Persian commemorative mourning drama dedicated to Hussein ibn Ali, who was martyred at the Battle of Karbala (680 CE). *Ta'ziyeh* plays chronicle each episode of the event over the course of ten days.

Theatre of the Absurd. An expression coined by the critic Martin Esslin in 1961 to categorize plays by Arthur Adamov, Samuel Beckett, Eugene Ionesco, and Jean Genet. Relating them all to the existentialist philosophy of Albert Camus (1913–1960), Esslin presented these playwrights as unified in their portrayal of the human condition as meaningless. Once influential, this interpretation of certain post-Second World War drama is in declining usage.

Theatre of Cruelty. Antonin Artaud's (1896–1948) title for a theatre that would "break through language" to access the mysteries and darker forces of life left untouched by literary masterpieces.

Theatre for development. A kind of theatre used in the so-called "developing world" as a tool for community problem-solving and empowerment.

Theater of the Oppressed. A type of theatre developed by Brazilian director Augusto Boal, based on the pedagogical theories of Paulo Freire, which aims to raise awareness of the roots of oppression and rehearse responses to it.

Theatre for social change. An umbrella term for a variety of theatre activities aiming for improvements in political, economic, cultural, medical, or other conditions. Three major types are theatre for development, Theater of the Oppressed, and community-based theatre.

Tragedy. Originally, a form of drama created in ancient Athens, Greece, performed by three actors and a chorus of 12–15 men. An early form had been developed by 534 BCE. Greek tragedy was serious and sometimes involved misfortunes and terrible mistakes, but plays could also end on a positive note. When ancient Roman authors emulated Greek tragedy, it became more focused on awful and even horrific events. In modern times the term generally refers to drama with an unhappy ending in which the protagonist(s) suffers a major personal loss or even death.

Tropes. Bits of dialogue sung by the choir during parts of the medieval Mass, especially during the Easter observance, where they dramatized the story of the visitors to Christ's tomb. Some argue for the tropes as an early form of Church drama.

Übermarionette. Large puppets that, according to Edward Gordon Craig (1872–1966), should replace live performers because they would be easier to control than actors and more effective in evoking spiritual realities. Also see *Gesamtskunstwerk*.

Unities. According to neoclassicism, drama must meet the three "unities" of time, place, and action. The unity of time demanded that the dramatic action take place within one day. The unity of place required plays to be set in only one location. The unity of action prohibited multiple plots.

Variety theatre. A major form of popular performance that proliferated after 1850 that consisted of light entertainments unconnected by any overriding theme, story, or major star. See Vaudeville.

Vaudeville. A form of variety theatre that gradually replaced (and absorbed) the minstrel show in the United States during the 1880s. Representative acts included skits, comics who specialized in ethnic humor, trained animals, singers, dancers, and acrobats. Vaudeville declined during the 1920s as many of its performers began working in the new media of radio and film.

Verfremdungseffekt. Bertolt Brecht's term for the process of providing spectators of his productions with some distance and insight by rendering their past and present worlds strange and unusual for them, thus preparing them to accept his own vision of events. The term is sometimes mistranslated as "alienation effect."

Verisimilitude. The quality of appearing true, realistic, or probable which neoclassicism held to be a prime requirement of drama. In order to achieve verisimilitude, plays needed to obey the three unities of time, place, and action. See the rules, decorum.

Virtual. A term generally meaning "in effect, but not actually," by the end of the twentieth century it frequently referred to a computerized, non-physical environment or an item or activity within it. Although initially "virtual worlds" were wholly textual, today the term usually means a visual, onscreen depiction of a three-dimensional location, often the setting for a game; people are represented in this environment through avatars. Sometimes "virtual world" is misapplied to communication platforms such as Facebook and Twitter.

Volksgeist. Literally meaning the "spirit of the nation." The German historian Johann Gottfried von Herder (1744–1803) employed this Romantic belief to affirm that all nations possess highly distinct identities to counter Enlightenment notions of the potential universality of historical interpretation. Herder's ideas about history shaped most discussions about cultural nationalism during the nineteenth century.

Wagoto. A style of *kabuki* acting with more-or-less realistic voice, gestures, and costumes. Compare with *aragoto*.

Wayang golek. The Sudanese-language puppet theatre of West Java. Since the 1970s, a hybrid comic form of it has been regularly performed on Indonesian television.

Wayang Kulit. The traditional shadow puppet theatre of Java.

Well-made play. A form of drama pioneered by French playwright Eugene Scribe (1791–1861) that cleverly manipulates plot to reveal a secret whose disclosure in an "obligatory scene" is key to resolving the play's central conflict.

Wing-and-groove system. The British counterpart to the continental "chariot-and-pole" system for rapidly changing perspective scenery during the early eighteenth century, it operated by using flats that slid in grooves built on the stage floor and in supporting tracks behind the borders above.

World fairs. Urban carnivals that became potent entertainments to legitimate the capitalist-industrial (and often imperialist) order in the pre-1914 era, particularly in the United Kingdom and the United States. The first world fair was the Crystal Palace Exhibition in London in 1851.

Yangbanxi. "Model revolutionary opera," a genre of Chinese performance created during the Cultural Revolution, that combines aspects of *jingju* and Western performance.

Yellowface. The practice of using makeup and/or facial prosthetics to mimic Asian features (such as shape of eyes or skin color) by an actor who is not of Asian descent. It is the equivalent of **blackface**.

Yūgen. A deep, quiet, mysterious beauty tinged with sadness produced by *nō* dramas. A crucial aspect of Zeami's aesthetic theory.

Zaju. A Chinese variety theatre consisting of song, dance, monologues, and farce popular during the Ming dynasty (1368–1644).

Zanni. Servants in *commedia dell'arte*. They are usually smart and wily, and often try to fool their masters.

Index

E-Business and
E-Commerce Management